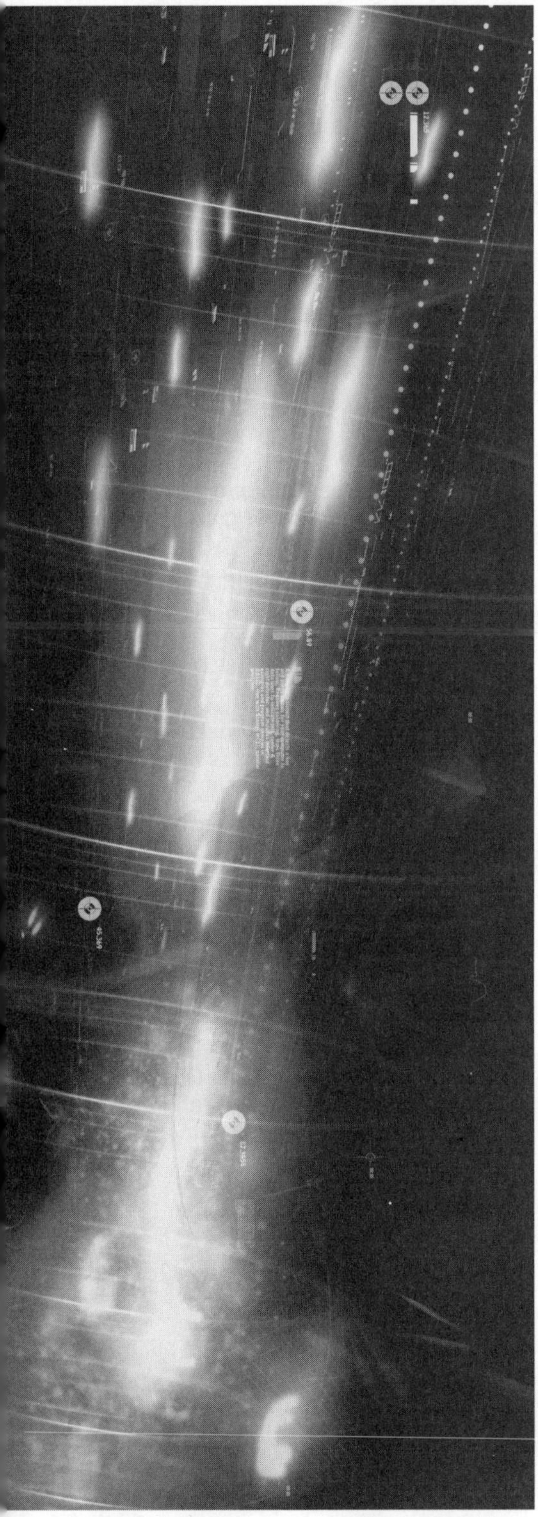

INFORMATION TECHNOLOGY AUDITING and ASSURANCE

James A. Hall
Lehigh University

Tommie Singleton
University of Alabama at Birmingham

2nd Edition

THOMSON
SOUTH-WESTERN

Australia · Canada · Mexico · Singapore · Spain · United Kingdom · United States

THOMSON
SOUTH-WESTERN

Information Technology Auditing and Assurance, 2e
James A. Hall and Tommie Singleton

VP/Editorial Director:
Jack W. Calhoun

VP/Editor-in-Chief:
George Werthman

Acquisitions Editor:
Sharon Oblinger

Developmental Editor:
Craig Avery

Marketing Manager:
Chris Kislack

Production Editor:
Stephanie Blydenburgh

Manager of Technology, Editorial:
Vicky True

Technology Project Editor:
Amy Wilson

Manufacturing Coordinator:
Doug Wilke

Production House/Compositor:
DPS Associates, Inc.

Printer:
West Group
Eagan, MN

Art Director:
Michelle Kunkler

Cover and Internal Designer:
Jennifer Lambert/Jen2Design
Cincinnati, OH

Cover Images:
© Digital Vision, Inc

Printed in the United States of America
1 2 3 4 5 07 06 05 04

ISBN: 0-324-19198-7

Library of Congress Control Number:
2004105684

For more information contact South-Western,
5191 Natorp Boulevard,
Mason, Ohio 45040.
Or you can visit our Internet site at:
http://www.swlearning.com

ACL™ Desktop Edition (full educational version) ©2004 ACL Services Ltd. Distributed by South-Western, a division of Thomson Learning, Inc.

Brief Table of Contents

TABLE OF CONTENTS

PREFACE

The second edition of the text contains key improvements and changes that continue to provide instructors and students with the best and most integrated auditing, assurance, and information technology and systems text available. Increased coverage and integration of ACL generalized audit software, new ACL tutorials and cases, a new fraud chapter with expanded, two-chapter fraud coverage, new and revised end-of-chapter material, a complete updating, and a new coauthor with a new perspective are some of the changes that continue to make this book unique in the changing IT auditing environment.

DISTINGUISHING FEATURES

- A **risk analysis approach.** This text focuses on identifying key threats and describes the audit tests and procedures in the following areas: Operating Systems (mainframes and PCs), Data Management, Systems Development, Electronic Commerce (including networks, EDI and Internet risks), Organizational Structure, Computer Center, ERP systems, and Computer Applications (Revenue and Expenditure cycle).
- **CAATTs.** Computer Aided Audit Tools and Techniques (CAATTs) are used in today's most cutting edge, modern organizations. These are discussed and illustrated in an easy-to-understand manner for the student.
- **ACL™ software.** ACL™ is the leading data extraction CAATT software. An instructional version is included with each NEW copy of the book, and the text integrates ACL into relevant text discussions and end-of-chapter problems. Text data files to support expanded integration of ACL cases and tutorials are also included on the book's Web site.
- **Computer control issues** and their impact on both operational efficiency and the auditor's attest responsibility are dealt with thoroughly in this edition. The book has been updated to address important control issues and responsibilities explicit and implicit in Sarbanes-Oxley legislation.

NEW FEATURES

- **Completely updated.** The second edition has been rigorously updated to include SAS 94, SAS 99, and the COSO standards.
- **NEW ERP systems chapter.** Chapter 6 now provides extensive coverage of enterprise resource planning (ERP) systems. This new chapter examines a number of audit issues related to the implementation and audit of ERP.
- **EXPANDED fraud coverage.** Chapters 11 and 12 are devoted to the topic of fraud. These chapters cover current emerging issues and fraud detection and prevention in more depth than did the previous edition.
- **NEW ACL tutorials.** Written by the authors, these 'how to' tutorials on the product Web site make it easier for students to understand how to use the software and what capabilities ACL software has so they can get up and running with ACL fast!

- **NEW ACL fraud and auditing case.** Due to popular demand for increased integration of ACL software into the text, we've added a NEW integrated ACL case called Bradmark that spans chapters 9, 10, and 12. This case will enable students to apply many concepts presented in the book using the ACL software.
- **NEW chapter-ending projects.** Selected chapters now conclude with projects and cases on disaster recovery, fraud, internal controls, emerging technologies, ERP, and XBRL; so that students can apply these current concepts covered in the text.
- **NEW coauthor.** Tommie Singleton (University of Alabama at Birmingham) brings expertise in both IT auditing and accounting information systems at the undergraduate and MBA levels.
- **NEW PowerPoint slides.** These downloadable slides, prepared by Tommie Singleton, are tightly integrated to the text and contain text page references, exhibits, lecture points, and topic summaries.

Risk Assessment Approach: A Framework

The first chapter presents **a risk assessment model** that identifies key areas of potential computer risk. These include operations, data management, systems development, systems maintenance, electronic commerce, and computer applications. This model provides a framework for the remainder of the text. The issues most relevant to the auditor's assurance responsibilities in each of these risk areas are developed in subsequent chapters. For clarity and comparability, the chapters are structured along similar lines. They begin with a discussion of the operational features and technologies employed in the area. Then they explain the nature of the risks and the controls that can be implemented to mitigate these risks. Finally, the chapters define specific audit objectives and present suggested audit procedures to achieve those objectives.

Organization and Content

Chapter 1, "Auditing, Assurance, and Internal Control"

Chapter 1 draws an important distinction between the auditor's traditional attestation function and the field of assurance services. While the material outlined in this chapter relates to tasks conducted by auditors providing attest and assurance services, the emphasis is placed on auditors' new attest responsibilities following from authoritative pronouncements, including the Sarbanes-Oxley Act. The chapter examines what constitutes an audit, who performs audits, and how audits are structured. It reviews the internal control concerns that underlie SAS 78, and presents the risk assessment model, which forms the basis for the rest of the book.

Chapter 2, "Computer Operations"

Chapter 2 examines the assurance issues related to computer operations. The chapter opens with a review of the advantages and potential risks associated with both centralized and distributed information technology (IT) structures. Next, it examines auditor concerns pertinent to the computer center, and discusses the key elements of a disaster recovery plan. It then examines the risks, controls, and audit issues pertaining to multi-user operating systems employed by networks and mainframes. The chapter concludes with a review of audit concerns unique to the personal computer (PC) environment.

Chapter 3, "Data Management Systems"

Chapter 3 deals with assurance issues pertaining to **data management systems**. This material is approached from the perspective of two commonly used models: the *flat-file* model and the *database* model. Private ownership of data, which characterizes the flat-file model, is the root cause of several problems that inhibit entity-wide data integration. On the other hand, data sharing and centralized control of data are the heart of the database philosophy. The philosophies and technologies underlying both approaches create special audit issues, which are examined at length in the chapter.

Chapter 4, "Systems Development and Maintenance Activities"

Chapter 4 explores the key activities that constitute the **systems development life cycle** (SDLC). It discusses the risks, controls, and audit issues related to systems planning, systems analysis, conceptual design, system selection, detailed design, systems implementation, and system maintenance.

Chapter 5, "Networks, Internet, and E-Commerce"

Chapter 5 has been completely revised to deal with the ever-evolving topic of **electronic commerce** (EC). Electronic commerce encompasses diverse business activities, including electronic trading of goods and services, online delivery of digital products, electronic funds transfer (EFT), electronic trading of stocks, and direct consumer marketing. To properly evaluate the potential exposures and risks in this environment, the modern accountant must be familiar with the technologies and techniques that underlay electronic commerce. Hardware failures, software errors, and unauthorized access from remote locations can expose the organization's accounting system to unique threats. This chapter considers three aspects of electronic commerce: (1) the intra-organizational use of networks to support distributed data processing; (2) business-to-business transactions conducted via EDI systems; and (3) Internet-based commerce, including business-to-consumer and business-to-business relationships. The appendix to this chapter presents a number of **emerging issues** that are of increasing interest and concern to auditors. These include privacy violations, audit implications of XBRL, continuous auditing, authentication, certification authority licensing, and the changing legal environment.

NEW: Chapter 6, "Enterprise Resource Planning Systems"

This new chapter presents a number of issues related to the **implementation and audit of enterprise resource planning** (ERP) **systems**. It is comprised of five major sections.

- The first section outlines the key features of a **generic ERP system** by comparing the function and data storage techniques of a traditional flat-file or database system to that of an ERP.
- The second section describes various ERP configurations related to **servers, databases, and bolt-on software**.
- Data warehousing is the topic of the third section. A **data warehouse** is a relational or multidimensional database that supports online analytical processing (OLAP). A number of issues are discussed, including data modeling, data

extraction from operational databases, data cleansing, data transformation, and loading data into the warehouse.

- The fourth section examines **risks associated with ERP implementation**. These include "big bang" issues, opposition to change within the organization, choosing the wrong ERP model, choosing the wrong consultant, cost overrun issues, and disruptions to operations.
- The fifth section reviews **control and auditing issues related to ERPs**. The discussion follows the SAS 78 framework.

The chapter appendix provides a review of the leading ERP software products including SAP, Oracle, PeopleSoft, J. D. Edwards, and BAAN.

Chapter 7, "Computer-Assisted Audit Tools and Techniques"

Chapter 7 presents the use of Computer Assisted Audit Tools and Techniques (CAATTs) for performing tests of application controls. The chapter begins with an extensive description of application controls organized into three classes: input controls, process controls, and output controls. It examines both the *black box* (audit around) and *white box* (audit through) approaches to testing application controls. The latter approach requires a detailed understanding of the application's logic. The chapter discusses five CAATT approaches used for testing application logic. These are the *test data method, base case system evaluation, tracing, integrated test facility,* and *parallel simulation.*

Chapter 8, "CAATTs for Data Extraction and Analysis"

Chapter 8 examines the uses of CAATTs for data extractions and analysis. Auditors make extensive use of these tools in gathering accounting data for testing application controls and in performing substantive tests. In an IT environment, the records needed to perform such tests are stored in computer files and databases. Understanding how data are organized and accessed is central to using data extraction tools. For this reason, a thorough review of common flat-file and database structures is provided. Data extraction software falls into two general categories: *embedded audit modules* (EAM) and *general audit software* (GAS). The chapter describes the features, advantages, and disadvantages of both. The chapter closes with a review of the **key features of ACL**, the leading GAS product on the market.

Chapters 9 and 10, "Auditing the Revenue Cycle" and "Auditing the Expenditure Cycle"

Auditing procedures associated with the revenue and expenditure cycles are examined in Chapters 9 and 10, respectively. Each chapter begins with a review of alternative technologies employed in legacy systems and modern computer systems. This review is followed by the audit objectives, controls, and tests of controls that an auditor would normally perform to gather the evidence needed to limit the scope, timing, and extent of substantive tests. Finally, the substantive tests related to audit objectives are explained and illustrated using ACL software. End-of-chapter material contains several ACL assignments including a comprehensive assignment, which spans chapters 9, 10, and 12.

EXPANDED COVERAGE: Chapters 11 and 12, "Introduction to Business Ethics and Fraud" and "Fraud Schemes and Fraud Detection"

Perhaps no aspect of the independent auditor's role has caused more public and professional concern than the external auditor's responsibility for detecting fraud during an audit. For this reason, **our treatment of fraud has been expanded in the second edition**. Chapter 11 examines the broader issues of fraud in business. It examines two closely related topics of ethics and fraud. The chapter begins with a survey of ethical issues that highlight the organization's conflicting responsibilities to its employees, shareholders, customers, and the general public. Management, employees, and auditors need to recognize the implications of new information technologies for such traditional issues as working conditions, the right to privacy, and the potential for fraud.

The chapter then considers basic fraud issues beginning with a definition of fraud. The chapter examines the nature and meaning of fraud, differentiates between employee fraud and management fraud, explains fraud-motivating forces, and reviews common fraud techniques. The chapter outlines the key features of SAS 99, "Consideration of Fraud in a Financial Statement Audit," and presents the results of a fraud research project conducted by the Association of Certified Fraud Examiners (ACFE).

Chapter 12 presents a number of specific fraud schemes and fraud detection techniques that are used in practice. The discussion follows the fraud classification format derived by the Association of Certified Fraud Examiners. It defines three broad categories of fraud schemes: financial fraud, corruption, and asset misappropriation. The chapter presents several ACL tests that auditors can perform to help them detect fraud. The end-of-chapter material contains a number of ACL fraud exercises as well as an integrated fraud case. The fraud assignments and their associated data may be downloaded from this book's Web site.

SUPPLEMENTS

The second edition contains enhanced learning and teaching aids: a new and improved version of ACL, new PowerPoint slides, and increased integration of ACL in our online resources.

ACL

ACL™ Desktop Edition (full educational version) CD, is bundled with each NEW copy of the text. ACL is the preferred software tool of audit and financial professionals for data extraction, data analysis, fraud detection, and continuous monitoring. Robust yet easy-to-use, ACL™ Desktop Edition, Version 8 software expands the depth and breadth of your analysis, increases your personal productivity, and gives you confidence in your findings.

With ACL you can:

- Perform analysis more quickly and efficiently
- Produce easy-to-understand reports—easily design, preview, and modify your results on-screen with drag & drop formatting
- Identify trends, pinpoint exceptions, and highlight potential areas of concern

- Locate errors and potential fraud by comparing and analyzing files according to end-user criteria
- Identify control issues and ensure compliance with standards

NEW PowerPoint™ slides, prepared by Tommie Singleton, provide invaluable lecture and study aids, charts, lists, definitions, and summaries directly correlated with the text.

The **Solutions Manual**, written by the authors, contains answers to all of the end-of-chapter problem material in the text.

The **Product Web site** contains a **NEW** ACL tutorials, **NEW** ACL cases, and data files along with instructor solutions. These exercises and cases are tied to chapters in the text.

Acknowledgments

We wish to thank the following reviewers for their useful and perceptive comments:

Faye Borthick
(Georgia State University)

John Coulter
(Western New England College)

Lori Fuller
(Widener University)

Jongsoo Han
(Rutgers University)

Sharon Huxley
(Teikyo Post University)

Louis Jacoby
(Saginaw Valley State University)

Orlando Katter
(Winthrop University)

Jim Kurtenbach
(Iowa State University)

Nick McGaughey
(San Jose State University)

Rebecca Rosner
(Long Island University—
CW Post Campus)

Hema Rao
(SUNY-Oswego)

Chuck Stanley
(Baylor University)

Tommie Singleton
(University of Alabama at Birmingham)

Brad Tuttle
(University of South Carolina)

Douglas Ziegenfuss
(Old Dominion)

Thanks also go to Louis R. Jacoby (Saginaw Valley State University) for his verification of the solutions manual.

We wish to thank ACL Services, Ltd. for its cooperation in the development of the second edition, for its permission to reprint screens from the software in the text, and for granting use of an educational version of the software to accompany our text.

Finally, we are grateful to the publishing team at Thomson South-Western for all their work: Sharon Oblinger, executive editor; Craig Avery, senior developmental editor; Chip Kislack, marketing manager; Stephanie Blydenburgh, production editor; Amy Wilson, technology project editor; and Doug Wilke, manufacturing coordinator.

Dedication

To my mother and the memory of my father. — James Hall

To the love of my life, and the pillar of support that enabled me to work on this book—my wife Rebecca. — Tommie Singleton

About the Authors

James A. Hall is associate professor of accounting and information systems at Lehigh University. After his discharge from the U.S. Army, he entered the University of Tulsa in 1970 and received a BSBA in 1974 and an MBA in 1976. He earned his Ph.D. from Oklahoma State University in 1979. Professor Hall has worked in industry in the fields of systems analysis and computer auditing and has served as consultant in these areas to numerous organizations.

Professor Hall has published articles in the *Journal of Accounting, Auditing & Finance, Management Accounting, Journal of Computer Information Systems, The Journal of Accounting Education, The Review of Accounting Information Systems,* and other professional journals. He is the author of *Accounting Information Systems*, Fourth Edition (Thomson South-Western).

Tommie Singleton is the Marshall IS Scholar and assistant professor of information systems at the University of Alabama at Birmingham. After his discharge from the U.S. Navy, he completed his BS in Accounting in 1977, and an MBA in 1979, both at the University of North Alabama. Professor Singleton received his doctorate from the University of Mississippi in 1995, after spending 11 years as president of a small software company. His career is a mix of accounting and information systems (IS) and includes consulting and providing continuing education to professionals regarding auditing and IS. He earned certifications as CPA, CMA, CISA, and CITP. In 1999, the Alabama Society of CPAs awarded him the "Innovative User of Technology Award" for 1998-1999.

Professor Singleton has published articles in the *Information Systems Control Journal, EDPACS, Journal of Cooperative Accounting, Journal of Corporate Accounting and Finance, Managerial Auditing Journal,* and others. He also coauthored the third edition of *Managing the Audit Function* with Michael Cangemi, released in 2003.

INFORMATION TECHNOLOGY AUDITING AND ASSURANCE

second edition

CHAPTER

1 Auditing, Assurance, and Internal Control

LEARNING OBJECTIVES

After studying this chapter, you should:

- Know the difference between attest services and assurance services and be able to explain the relationship between these two types of auditing.
- Understand the structure of an audit and have a firm grasp of the conceptual elements of the audit process.
- Understand internal control objectives promulgated by SAS 78.
- Understand how the unique features of the computer environment must be taken into account to achieve the control objectives specified in SAS 78.
- Be familiar with the key areas of risk in the IT environment.

Recent developments in **information technology (IT)** have had a tremendous impact on the field of **auditing**. IT has inspired the reengineering of traditional business processes to promote more efficient operations and to improve communications within the entity and between the entity and its customers and suppliers. These advances, however, have introduced new risks that require unique internal controls. They have engendered the need for new techniques for evaluating controls and for assuring the security and accuracy of corporate data and the information systems that produce it.

This chapter presents an overview of computer auditing. It begins with a general discussion of alternative audit approaches. It then reviews the internal control concerns that underlie SAS 78. Finally it then examines a framework for risk assessment that identifies seven areas of computer risk. The remainder of the text is based on this framework.

Different Types of Audits

The discussion of audits should begin with a definition of auditing.

> Auditing is a systematic process of objectively obtaining and evaluating evidence regarding assertions about economic actions and events to ascertain the degree of correspondence between those assertions and establishing criteria and communicating the results to interested users.[1]

The auditing profession is made up of several types of audits, each with its own perspective, objectives, and supporting professional organizations. Although all follow common and basic processes, guidelines, and standards, each is different in some ways. For example, the above definition generally would apply to any of the different types of audits. The following is a brief overview of these major types of audits.

Internal Audits

The Institute of Internal Auditors (IIA) defines **internal auditing** as an independent appraisal function established within an organization to examine and evaluate its activities as a service to the organization.[2] Internal auditors perform a wide range of activities on behalf of the organization, including conducting financial audits, examining an operation's compliance with organizational policies, reviewing the organization's compliance with legal obligations, evaluating operational efficiency, detecting and pursuing fraud within the firm, and conducting IT audits.

An internal audit is associated with auditors who work for the organization. These auditors are often certified as Certified Internal Auditor (CIA) or Certified Information Systems Auditor (CISA). Auditors self-impose independence in order to perform their duties effectively. They represent the interests of the organization, and generally answer to executive management of the organization (and/or usually the audit committee, if one exists). The standards, guidance, and certification of internal audits are governed mostly by the Institute of Internal Auditors (IIA) and, to a lesser degree, by the Information Systems Audit and Control Association (ISACA).

Information Technology Audits

An IT audit is associated with auditors who use technical skills and knowledge to audit through the computer system, or provide audit services where processes or data, or both, are embedded in technologies. These auditors are usually certified as Certified Information Systems Auditor (CISA). The IT auditor, if certified, is subject to ethics and guidelines that impose professionalism in his/her duties; e.g., independence, skepticism, and due diligence. The services provided by IT auditors are always associated with assurance regarding IT in some fashion. IT auditors work in internal audit departments, in external audit teams, and even in fraud audits. The standards, guidance, and certification of IT audits are governed primarily by the Information Systems Audit and Control Association (ISACA).

IT audits are risk-based audits, much like internal and external audits. The scope of IT audits has been increasing to include more depth of systems (e.g., systems

---

1 AAA Committee on Basic Auditing Concepts, "A Statement of Basic Auditing Concepts," *Accounting Review*, supplement to vol. 47, 1972.

2 Institute of Internal Auditors, *Standards of Professional Practice of Internal Auditing* (Orlando, FL.: Institute of Internal Auditors, 1978).

development procedures audit), and width (e.g., more systems and technologies). IT audits are characterized by the use of Computer-Assisted Audit Tools (CAATs), or the modern and inclusive term of Computer-Assisted Audit Tools and Techniques (CAATTs). CAATTs allow auditors to audit through the database and computer. For example, CAATTs allow auditors to view whatever audit trail exists in electronic form, typically invisible to people, and thus to analyze transactions, events, and account balances *through* the system. Another developing concept in IT audit is the emergence of IT governance as a subset of corporate governance.

Fraud Audits

A fraud audit is the newest area of auditing, arising out of both rampant employee theft of assets and major financial frauds (e.g., Enron, WorldCom, etc.). These auditors are hired by agreed-upon procedures, if external auditors, or by contract, if an independent fraud audit unit, or by charge to the internal audit function. The objective of a fraud audit is different from the others in that materiality has no meaning, and the goal is not assurance but rather an investigation of anomalies—the gathering of evidence of fraud, and the legal goal of a conviction (if sufficient evidence exists—i.e., "predication").[3] These auditors most often have earned the Certified Fraud Examiner (CFE) certification. Sometimes fraud audits are initiated by management looking into employee fraud. At other times, an outside entity will engage fraud auditors to look into fraud associated with executive management, be it theft of assets or financial fraud. A fraud audit, therefore, is very different from any of the other audits. The fraud auditor is much like a detective or forensic scientist engaged in a "whodonit" in search of evidence of fraud and a conviction of the fraudster. The standards, guidance, and certification of fraud audits are governed chiefly by the Association of Certified Fraud Examiners (ACFE).

External/Financial Audits

An external audit (i.e., financial audit) is associated with auditors who work outside, or independent of, the organization being audited. The audit objective is always associated with the presentation of financial statements—in particular, that in all material respects, the statements are fairly presented. These audits, therefore, are often referred to as *financial audits*. The external auditor is an independent auditor, and is certified as Certified Public Accountant (CPA). The Securities and Exchange Commission (SEC) requires all publicly traded companies be subject to a financial audit annually by an independent auditor (i.e., a CPA). The CPA represents the interests of outsiders: stockholders, creditors, government agencies, and the "public"; and is of necessity "independent" of the entity that employs the auditors. The certification of external auditors is governed by the American Institute of Certified Public Accountants (AICPA).

The external auditor must follow strict rules in conducting financial audits. These authoritative rules have been defined by federal law (Sarbanes-Oxley Act of 2002), the SEC, the Financial Accounting Standards Board (FASB), and the AICPA. Until recently, the SEC has delegated most of that authority to the AICPA and FASB; the majority of whose members are CPAs. But the Sarbanes-Oxley Act of 2002 established a different board to oversee much of the guidelines and standards of financial auditing (known as the Public Company Accounting Oversight Board—PCAOB—where CPAs are a minority of members), which potentially could replace the function served by the FASB, and some of the functions the AICPA once enjoyed (e.g., reprimands and

3 See Chapter 11 (Introduction to Business Ethics and Fraud) for more about predication and other fraud concepts.

penalties for CPAs who are convicted of certain crimes or guilty of certain infractions). Regardless, the SEC has final authority for financial auditing, by federal law!

External Versus Internal Audits

The characteristic that conceptually distinguishes external auditors from internal auditors is their respective constituencies: while external auditors represent outsiders, internal auditors represent the interests of the organization. Nevertheless, in this capacity, internal auditors often cooperate with and assist external auditors in performing financial audits. This cooperation is done to achieve audit efficiency and reduce audit fees. For example, a team of internal auditors can perform tests of computer controls under the supervision of a single external auditor.

The independence and competence of the internal audit staff determine the extent to which external auditors may cooperate with and rely on work performed by internal auditors. Some internal audit departments report directly to the controller. Under this arrangement, the internal auditor's independence is compromised, and the external auditor is prohibited by professional standards from relying on evidence provided by the internal auditors. In contrast, external auditors can rely in part on evidence gathered by internal audit departments that are organizationally independent and that report to the board of directors' audit committee. A truly independent internal audit staff adds value to the audit process. Internal auditors can gather audit evidence throughout a fiscal period, which external auditors can then use at year end to conduct more efficient, less disruptive, and less costly audits of the organization's financial statements.

What Is a Financial Audit?

A financial audit is an independent attestation performed by an expert—the auditor—who expresses an opinion regarding the presentation of financial statements. The auditor's role is similar in concept to a judge who collects and evaluates evidence and renders an opinion. A key concept in this process is *independence*. The judge must remain independent in his or her deliberations. The judge cannot be an advocate of either party in the trial, but must apply the law impartially based on the evidence presented. Likewise, the independent auditor collects and evaluates evidence and renders an opinion based on the evidence. Throughout the audit process, the auditor must maintain independence from the client organization. Public confidence in the reliability of the company's internally produced financial statements rests directly on an evaluation of them by an independent expert auditor.

The public expression of the auditor's opinion is the culmination of a systematic audit process that involves three conceptual phases: (1) familiarization with the organization's business, (2) evaluating and testing internal controls, and (3) assessing the reliability of financial data. Later in this section, the specific elements of the audit process will be examined.

Attest Services Versus Assurance Services

An important point about a financial audit is the distinction between the auditor's traditional attestation function and the emerging field of assurance services. The **attest service** is defined as

> . . . an engagement in which a practitioner is engaged to issue, or does issue, a written communication that expresses a conclusion about the reliability of a written assertion that is the responsibility of another party. (SSAE No. 1, AT Sec. 100.01)

The following requirements apply to attestation services:

- Attestation services require written assertions and a practitioner's written report.
- Attestation services require the formal establishment of measurement criteria or their description in the presentation.
- The levels of service in attestation engagements are limited to examination, review, and application of agreed-upon procedures.

Assurance services constitute a broader concept that encompasses, but is not limited to, attestation. The relationship between these services is illustrated in Figure 1-1.

Assurance services are professional services that are designed to improve the quality of information, both financial and nonfinancial, used by decision makers. The domain of assurance services is intentionally unbounded so that it does not inhibit the growth of future services that are currently unforeseen. For example, assurance services may be contracted to provide information about the quality or marketability of a product. Alternatively, a client may need information about the efficiency of a production process or the effectiveness of its network security system. Assurance services are intended to help people make better decisions by improving information. This information may come as a by-product of the attest function, or it may ensue from an independently motivated review.

The evolution of the accounting profession is expected to follow the assurance services model. All of the "Big Four" professional services firms have now renamed their traditional audit functions *assurance services*. The organizational unit responsible for conducting IT audits is usually named *IT Risk Management, Information Systems Risk Management*, or *Operational Systems Risk Management (OSRM)* and typically is a division of assurance services.

The material outlined in this chapter relates to tasks normally conducted by OSRM professionals while performing an IT audit. In the pages that follow, the material will examine what constitutes an audit, who performs the audits, and how audits are structured. Keep in mind, however, that in many cases the purpose of the audit task, rather than the task itself, defines the service being rendered. Therefore, the issues and procedures described in this text apply to the broader context of assurance

FIGURE 1-1

Relationship Between Assurance Services and Attest Services

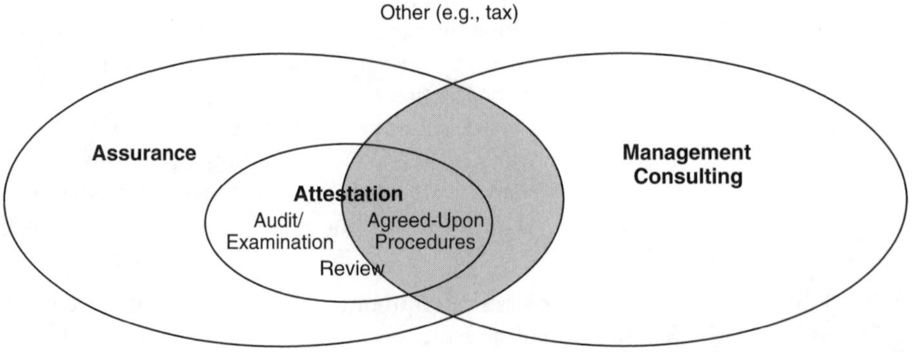

SOURCE: Based on the AICPA *Special Committee Report on Assurance Services.*

services, which include, but are not limited to, attest services. They also relate directly to the internal audit function.

Auditing Standards

The product of the attestation function is a formal written report that expresses an opinion about the reliability of the assertions contained in the financial statements. The auditor's report expresses an opinion as to whether the financial statements are in conformity with *generally accepted accounting principles (GAAP)*. External users of financial statements are presumed to rely on the auditor's opinion about the reliability of financial statements in making decisions. To do so, users must be able to place their trust in the auditor's competence, professionalism, integrity, and independence. Auditors are guided in their professional responsibility by the ten *generally accepted auditing standards (GAAS)* presented in Table 1-1.

Auditing standards are divided into three classes: general qualification standards, field work standards, and reporting standards. GAAS establishes a framework for prescribing auditor performance, but it is not sufficiently detailed to provide meaningful guidance in specific circumstances. To provide specific guidance, the American Institute of Certified Public Accountants (AICPA) issues *Statements on Auditing Standards (SASs)* as authoritative interpretations of GAAS. SASs are often referred to as *auditing standards*, or *GAAS*, although they are not the ten generally accepted auditing standards.

The first SAS (SAS 1) was issued by the AICPA in 1972. Since then, many SASs have been issued to provide auditors with guidance on a spectrum of topics, including methods of investigating new clients, procedures for collecting information from attorneys regarding contingent liability claims against clients, and techniques for obtaining background information on the client's industry.

TABLE 1-1

Generally Accepted Auditing Standards

General Standards	Standards of Field Work	Reporting Standards
1. The auditor must have adequate technical training and proficiency.	1. Audit work must be adequately planned.	1. The auditor must state in the report whether financial statements were prepared in accordance with generally accepted accounting principles.
2. The auditor must have independence of mental attitude.	2. The auditor must gain a sufficient understanding of the internal control structure.	2. The report must identify those circumstances in which generally accepted accounting principles were not applied.
3. The auditor must exercise due professional care in the performance of the audit and the preparation of the report.	3. The auditor must obtain sufficient, competent evidence.	3. The report must identify any items that do not have adequate informative disclosures.
		4. The report shall contain an expression of the auditor's opinion on the financial statements as a whole.

Statements on Auditing Standards are regarded as authoritative pronouncements because every member of the profession must follow their recommendations or be able to show why an SAS does not apply in a given situation. The burden of justifying departures from the SASs falls upon the individual auditor.

A Systematic Process

Conducting an audit is a systematic and logical process that applies to all forms of information systems. While important in all audit settings, a systematic approach is particularly important in the IT environment. The lack of physical procedures that can be visually verified and evaluated injects a high degree of complexity into the IT audit (e.g., the audit trail may be purely electronic, digital form, and thus invisible to those attempting to verify it). Therefore, a logical framework for conducting an audit in the IT environment is critical to help the auditor identify all-important processes and data files

Management Assertions and Audit Objectives

The organization's financial statements reflect a set of **management assertions** about the financial health of the entity. The task of the auditor is to determine whether the financial statements are fairly presented. To accomplish this goal, the auditor establishes **audit objectives**, designs procedures, and gathers evidence that corroborate or refute management's assertions. These assertions fall into five general categories:

1. The **existence or occurrence** assertion affirms that all assets and equities contained in the balance sheet exist and that all transactions in the income statement actually occurred.
2. The **completeness** assertion declares that no material assets, equities, or transactions have been omitted from the financial statements.
3. The **rights and obligations** assertion maintains that assets appearing on the balance sheet are owned by the entity and that the liabilities reported are obligations.
4. The **valuation or allocation** assertion states that assets and equities are valued in accordance with GAAP and that allocated amounts such as depreciation expense are calculated on a systematic and rational basis.
5. The **presentation and disclosure** assertion alleges that financial statement items are correctly classified (e.g., long-term liabilities will not mature within one year) and that footnote disclosures are adequate to avoid misleading the users of financial statements.

Generally, auditors develop their audit objectives and design audit **procedures** based on the preceding assertions. The example in Table 1-2 outlines these procedures.

Audit objectives may be classified into two general categories. Those in Table 1-2 relate to transactions and account balances that directly impact financial reporting. The second category pertains to the information system itself. This category includes the audit objectives for assessing controls over manual operations and computer technologies used in transaction processing. In the chapters that follow, we consider both categories of audit objectives and the associated audit procedures.

Obtaining Evidence

Auditors seek evidential matter that corroborates management assertions. In the IT environment, this process involves gathering evidence relating to the reliability of computer controls as well as the contents of databases that have been processed by computer programs. Evidence is collected by performing tests of controls, which

TABLE 1-2 Audit Objectives and Audit Procedures Based on Management Assertions

Management Assertion	Audit Objective	Audit Procedure
Existence of Occurrence	Inventories listed on the balance sheet exist.	Observe the counting of physical inventory.
Completeness	Accounts payable include all obligations to vendors for the period.	Compare receiving reports, supplier invoices, purchase orders, and journal entries for the period and the beginning of the next period.
Rights and Obligations	Plant and equipment listed in the balance sheet are owned by the entity.	Review purchase agreements, insurance policies, and related documents.
Valuation or Allocation	Accounts receivable are stated at net realizable value.	Review entity's aging of accounts and evaluate the adequacy of the allowance for uncorrectable accounts.
Presentation and Disclosure	Contingencies not reported in financial accounts are properly disclosed in footnotes.	Obtain information from entity lawyers about the status of litigation and estimates of potential loss

establish whether internal controls are functioning properly, and substantive tests, which determine whether accounting databases fairly reflect the organization's transactions and account balances.

Ascertaining the Degree of Correspondence with Established Criteria

The auditor must determine whether weaknesses in internal controls and misstatements found in transactions and account balances are material. In all audit environments, assessing materiality is an auditor judgment. In an IT environment, however, this decision is complicated further by technology and a sophisticated internal control structure.

Communicating Results

Auditors must communicate the results of their tests to interested users. An independent auditor renders a report to the audit committee of the board of directors or stockholders of a company. The audit report contains, among other things, an audit opinion. This opinion is distributed along with the financial report to interested parties both internal and external to the organization. IT auditors often communicate their findings to internal and external auditors, who can then integrate these findings with the non-IT aspects of the audit.

Audit Risk

Audit risk is the probability that the auditor will render an unqualified (clean) opinion on financial statements that are, in fact, materially misstated. Material misstatements may be caused by errors or irregularities or both. Errors are unintentional mistakes. Irregularities are intentional misrepresentations to perpetrate a fraud or to mislead the users of financial statements. In financial audits, the auditor's objective is to minimize audit risk by performing tests of controls and substantive tests.

Audit Risk Components

The three components of audit risk are inherent risk, control risk, and detection risk.

Inherent Risk

Inherent risk is associated with the unique characteristics of the business or industry of the client.[4] Firms in declining industries have greater inherent risk than firms in stable or thriving industries. Likewise, industries that have a heavy volume of cash transactions have a higher level of inherent risk than those that do not. Auditors cannot reduce the level of inherent risk. Even in a system protected by excellent controls, financial data and, consequently, financial statements can be materially misstated.

To illustrate inherent risk, let's assume that the audit client's financial statements show an accounts receivable balance of $10 million. Unknown to the auditor and the client, several customers with accounts receivable totaling $2 million are about to go out of business. These accounts, which are a material component of the total accounts receivable balance of $10 million, are not likely to be collected. To represent these accounts as an asset in the financial statements would be a material misstatement of the firm's economic position.

Control Risk

Control risk is the likelihood that the control structure is flawed because controls are either absent or inadequate to prevent or detect errors in the accounts.[5] To illustrate control risk, consider the following partial customer sales record, which is processed by the sales order system.

Quantity	Unit Price	Total
10 Units	$20	$2,000

Assuming the Quantity and Unit Price fields in the record are correctly presented, the extended amount (Total) value of $2,000 is in error. Elsewhere in the chapter we see that an accounting information system (AIS) with adequate controls should prevent or detect such an error. If, however, controls are lacking and the value of Total in each record is not validated before processing, then the risk of undetected errors entering the data files increases.

Auditors reduce the level of control risk by performing tests of internal controls. In the preceding example, the auditor could create test transactions, including some with incorrect Total values, which are processed by the application in a test run. The results of the test will indicate that price extension errors are not detected and are being incorrectly posted to the accounts receivable file.

---

4 Auditing Standards Board, *AICPA Professional Stanqards* (New York: AICPA, 1994), AU Sec. 312.20.

5 Ibid.

Detection Risk

Detection risk is the risk that auditors are willing to take that errors not detected or prevented by the control structure will also not be detected by the auditor.[6] Auditors set an acceptable level of detection risk (planned detection risk) that influences the level of substantive tests that they perform. For example, more substantive testing would be required when the planned detection risk is 1 percent than when it is 5 percent.

Audit Risk Formula/Model

Financial auditors use these components in a formula to assess the levels of risk in each area in order to determine the scope, nature, and timing of substantive tests. The audit risk formula/model is

$$AR = IR \times CR \times DR$$

Assume audit risk is assessed at a value of 5 percent, consistent with the 95 percent confidence interval associated with statistics. By illustration, assume IR is assessed at 40 percent, and CR is assessed at 60 percent. What would DR be?

$$5\% = 40\% \times 60\% \times DR$$
$$DR = 4.8\%$$

The Relationship Between Tests of Controls and Substantive Tests

Tests of controls and substantive tests are auditing techniques used for reducing total audit risk. The relationship between tests of controls and substantive tests varies according to the auditor's risk assessment of the organization. The stronger the internal control structure, the lower the control risk and the less substantive testing the auditor must do. This relationship is true because the likelihood of errors in the accounting records is reduced. In other words, when controls are strong, the auditor may limit substantive testing. However, the weaker the internal control structure, the greater the control risk and the more substantive testing the auditor must perform to reduce total audit risk. Evidence of weak controls forces the auditor to extend substantive testing to search for misstatements in financial data caused by control errors or weaknesses as well as business problems inherent to the organization.

To illustrate, assume last year's audit included risk assessments of 40 percent for IR and 60 percent for CR. Based on those figures, DR would be 4.8 percent (see above). Now, assume this year, controls are more reliable and reduces the CR factor to 40 percent. Thus, DR would be reduced as follows:

$$5\% = 40\% \times 40\% \times DR$$
$$DR = 3.2\%$$

Therefore, the more reliable the internal controls, the lower the CR probability. That leads to a lower DR, which will lead to fewer substantive tests being required. Because substantive tests are labor intensive and time consuming, they are expensive. Increased substantive testing translates into longer and more disruptive audits and higher audit costs. Thus, management's best interests are served by having a strong internal control structure.

What Is the Role of the Audit Committee?

The board of directors for large, publicly traded companies form a subcommittee known as the audit committee that has special responsibilities regarding audits. This committee is usually made up of three people, and should be outsiders (not associated with the families of executive management nor former officers, etc.). With the advent of the Sarbanes-Oxley Act, at least one of them must be a "financial expert." Frauds in the past have some commonalities related to audit committees: lack of independence of audit committee members, absence of audit committee or inactive one, and lack of experience by board members (per COSO landmark study of SEC violations).

Firms need an audit committee for several reasons, but the main one is the fiduciary responsibility it has to the shareholders. Management should also expect the audit committee to assist them in ensuring the integrity of financial reports and in deterring fraud. The public expects no surprises in the financial health of the company, and it expects to be able to trust the financial reports. Audit committees should be able to serve as guardians of the public interest. The audit committee serves as an independent "check and balance" for the internal audit function and liaison with external auditors. They interact with both these groups with the objective of ensuring data integrity in financial statements and the avoidance of fraud or illegal activities.

They also look for ways to identify deleterious events—that is, risk! For instance, they might serve as a sounding board for employees who find suspicious behaviors or outright fraudulent activities. The group should have a willingness to challenge the internal auditors (or the entity performing the function) as well as management when necessary. For those entities that employ outside auditors, the audit committee should be best positioned to determine whether the provision of any particular service by the audit firm is inappropriate. In fact, they are responsible for deciding which external auditor to hire (requirement of S-OX). In general, they become an independent source of protection of the entity's assets from a variety of risks, in whatever fashion is appropriate.

What Is an IT Audit?

An IT audit focuses on the computer-based aspects of an organization's information system. This audit includes assessing the proper implementation, operation, and control of computer resources. Because most modern information systems employ information technology, the IT audit is typically a significant component of all external (financial) and internal audits.

The IT Environment

There has always been a need for an effective internal control system to protect the integrity of the accounting processes and data. The design and oversight of that system has typically been the responsibility of accountants, especially auditors. The IT environment, however, complicates the design of effective internal controls for computer-based systems versus paper-based systems.

First, there is the concentration of data on the information system. Combined with the number of access connections, remote access, and linkages to other systems or computers, the modern IT environment exacerbates the design of effective controls. For example, all users are connected to the same system where the database is located, which holds all data, and is thus a risk for unauthorized access, theft, or destruction. In effect, there are thousands of control points with multiple controls needed. Contrast that with a paper-based system, or even the old legacy computer systems of the 1960s, which would involve fewer control points because of the centralized nature of the system's control points. Next, there has been an increase in the malicious activities initiated against systems, data, and assets. Finally, it is easy for management to override internal controls, and that can lead to financial fraud. Crimes in an IT environment include financial frauds (e.g., Equity Funding, Waste Management, Adelphia, Enron, WorldCom), employee theft of assets, and corruption. Other enterprise computer problems include disasters, whether natural or man-made, and system malfunctions.

The Structure of an IT Audit

The IT audit is generally divided into three phases: audit planning, tests of controls, and substantive testing. Figure 1-2 illustrates the steps involved in these phases.

Audit Planning

The first step in the IT audit is **audit planning**. Before the auditor can determine the nature and extent of the tests to perform, he or she must gain a thorough understanding of the client's business. A major part of this phase of the audit is the analysis of audit risk (discussed later). The auditor's objective is to obtain sufficient information about the firm to plan the other phases of the audit. The risk analysis incorporates an overview of the organization's internal controls. During the review of controls, the auditor attempts to understand the organization's policies, practices, and structure. In this phase of the audit, the auditor also identifies the financially significant applications and attempts to understand the controls over the primary transactions that are processed by these applications.

The techniques for gathering evidence at this phase include conducting questionnaires, interviewing management, reviewing systems documentation, and observing activities. During this process, the IT auditor must identify the principal exposures and the controls that attempt to reduce these exposures. Having done so, the auditor proceeds to the next phase, where he or she tests the controls for compliance with pre-established standards.

Tests of Controls

The objective of the **tests of controls** phase is to determine whether adequate internal controls are in place and functioning properly. To accomplish this, the auditor performs

FIGURE 1-2

Phases of an IT Audit

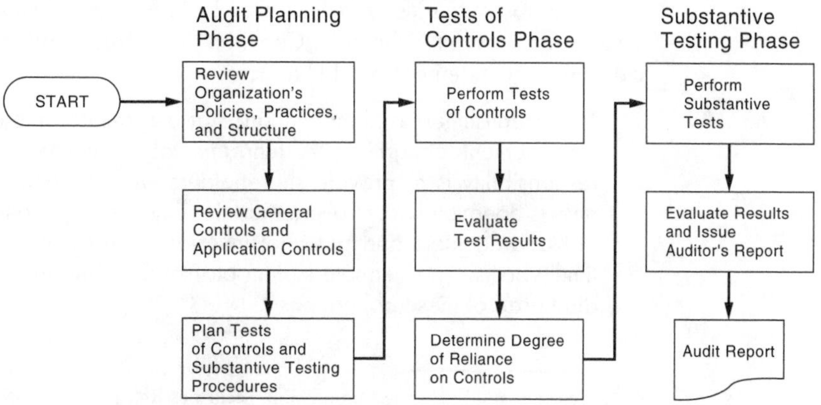

various tests of controls. The evidence-gathering techniques used in this phase may include both manual techniques and specialized computer audit techniques. These techniques use the system-based approach to IT audit, which focuses on controls and the system as a whole. We shall examine several such methods later in this text.

At the conclusion of the tests-of-controls phase, the auditor must assess the quality of the internal controls. The degree of reliance the auditor can ascribe to internal controls affects the nature and extent of substantive testing that needs to be performed. The relationship between tests of controls and substantive tests is discussed later.

Substantive Testing

The third phase of the audit process focuses on financial data. This phase involves a detailed investigation of specific account balances and transactions through what are called **substantive tests.** For example, a customer confirmation is a substantive test sometimes used to verify account balances. The auditor selects a sample of accounts receivable balances and traces these back to their source—the customers—to determine if the amount stated is in fact owed by a bona fide customer. By so doing, the auditor can verify the accuracy of each account in the sample. Based on such sample findings, the auditor is able to draw conclusions about the fair value of the entire accounts receivable asset.

Some substantive tests are physical, labor-intensive activities such as counting cash, counting inventories in the warehouse, and verifying the existence of stock certificates in a safe. In an IT environment, the information needed to perform substantive tests (such as account balances and names and addresses of individual customers) is contained in data files that often must be extracted using **Computer-Assisted Audit Tools and Techniques (CAATTs)** software. The database approach to IT audits uses CAATTs and substantive testing to investigate the integrity of the data. In other words, IT auditors use CAATTs to get the data to tell them about the data's integrity and reliability. Later in this text, we will examine the role of CAATTs in performing traditional substantive tests and other data analysis and reporting tasks.

INTERNAL CONTROL

Organization management is required by law to establish and maintain an adequate system of internal control. Consider the following Securities and Exchange Commission statement on this matter:

> The establishment and maintenance of a system of internal control is an important management obligation. A fundamental aspect of management's stewardship responsibility is to provide shareholders with reasonable assurance that the business is adequately controlled. Additionally, management has a responsibility to furnish shareholders and potential investors with reliable financial information on a timely basis. An adequate system of internal control is necessary to management's discharge of these obligations.[6]

6 Securities and Exchange Commission, Securities Release 34-13185 (19 January 1977).

The **internal control system** comprises policies, practices, and procedures employed by the organization to achieve four broad objectives:

1. To safeguard assets of the firm.
2. To ensure the accuracy and reliability of accounting records and information.
3. To promote efficiency in the firm's operations.
4. To measure compliance with management's prescribed policies and procedures.[7]

Brief History of Internal Control

Since much of the internal control system relates directly to transaction processing, accountants are key participants in ensuring control adequacy. This section deals first with a brief history of internal controls, and then an overview of internal control at a conceptual level. Lastly, it presents the authoritative control framework defined by SAS 78.

SEC Acts of 1933 and 1934

Following the stock market crash of 1929, and a worldwide financial fraud by Ivar Kruegar, the U.S. legislature passed two acts to restore confidence in the capital market. The first was the Securities Act of 1933, which had two main objectives: (1) require that investors receive financial and other significant information condering securities being offered for public sale, and (2) prohibit deceit, misrepresentations, and other fraud in the sale of securities. The second act, the Securities Exchange Act, 1934, created the Securities and Exchange Commission (SEC) and empowered it with broad authority over all aspects of the securities industry, which included authority regarding auditing standards. The SEC acts also required publicly traded companies to be audited by an independent auditor (i.e., CPA). But is also required all companies that report to the SEC to maintain a system of internal control that is evaluated as part of the annual external audit. That portion of the Act has been enforced on rare occasions. That leniency changed with the passage of Sarbanes-Oxley Act in July 2002.

Copyright Law–1976

This law, which has had multiple revisions, added software and other intellectual properties into the existing copyright protection laws. It is of concern to IT auditors because management is held personally liable for violations (e.g., software piracy) if "raided" by the software police (a U.S. marshal accompanied by software vendors' association representatives), and sufficient evidence of impropriety is found.

Foreign Corrupt Practices Act (FCPA) of 1977

Corporate management has not always lived up to its internal control responsibility. With the discovery that U.S. business executives were using their organizations' funds to bribe foreign officials, internal control issues, formerly of little interest to stockholders, quickly became a matter of public concern. From this issue came the passage of the **Foreign Corrupt Practices Act of 1977 (FCPA)**. Among its provisions, the FCPA requires companies registered with the SEC to do the following:

7 American Institute of Certified Public Accountants, *AICPA Professional Standards*, vol. 1 (New York: AICPA, 1987) AU Sec. 320.30-35.

1. Keep records that fairly and reasonably reflect the transactions of the firm and its financial position.
2. Maintain a system of internal control that provides reasonable assurance that the organization's objectives are met.

The FCPA has had a significant impact on organization management. With the knowledge that violation of the FCPA could lead to heavy fines and imprisonment, managers have developed a deeper concern for control adequacy.

Committee of Sponsoring Organizations–1992

Following the series of S&L scandals of the 1980s, a committee was formed to address the frauds. Originally, the committee took the name of its chair, Treadway, but eventually the project became known as COSO, based on the acronym of Committee of Sponsoring Organizations. The organizations that sponsored, and do sponsor, this entity include Financial Executives International (FEI), the Institute of Management Accountants (IMA), the American Accounting Association (AAA), AICPA, and the IIA. The Committee spent several years promulgating a response. Because it was determined early on that the best deterrent to fraud was strong internal controls, the committee decided to focus on an effective model for internal controls from a management perspective. The result was the COSO Model. The AICPA adopted the model into auditing standard with the adoption of SAS No. 78—*Consideration of Internal Control in a Financial Statement Audit*. This model will be explained in detail later in this chapter.

Sarbanes-Oxley Act of 2002

As a result of several large financial frauds (e.g., Enron, Worldcom, Adelphia, etc.) and the resulting losses suffered by stockholders, pressures were brought by the U.S. Congress to protect the public from such events. This pressure led to the passage of the Sarbanes-Oxley Act on July 30, 2002. In general, the law supports efforts to increase public confidence in capital markets by seeking to improve corporate governance, internal controls, and audit quality. The act likely will help management refocus on financial versus operational controls, internal audit to be a more critical resource for management, IT auditors to extend their work, a major overhaul to be undertaken in corporate governance (especially audit committees), and a major shift in providers of non-audit services that had been outsourced to external auditors.

Perhaps the greatest concern to auditors, especially internal auditors and IT auditors, is Section 404—Management Assessment of Internal Controls. Affected companies are required to do the following:

- State the responsibility of management for establishing and maintaining an adequate internal control structure and procedures for financial reporting.
- Maintain an assessment, as of the end of the issuer's fiscal year, of the effectiveness of the internal control structure and procedures of the issuer for financial reporting.

Additionally, Section 302—Corporate Responsibility for Incident Reports—of S-OX requires senior financial executives to disclose deficiencies in internal controls and fraud—whether it is material or not—for employees who have a significant role in internal control (almost a certainty when any fraud occurs). This required reporting will have an impact on internal and IT auditors because they most likely will complete the work, evaluate, assess and report on internal controls for management's report required by S-OX. The ISACA has established "IS Auditing Standards and Guidelines," which provide guidance for IT auditors to support the tenets of S-OX. Compared to other legislative events in history, S-OX will probably have the greatest impact on internal controls.

MODIFYING ASSUMPTIONS

Inherent in the control objectives are four modifying assumptions that guide designers and auditors of internal control systems.[8]

Management Responsibility

This concept holds that the establishment and maintenance of a system of internal control is a **management responsibility**. The FCPA supports this postulate. S-OX, however, makes it law!

Reasonable Assurance

The internal control system should provide **reasonable assurance** that the four broad objectives of internal control are met. This reasonableness means that no system of internal control is perfect and the cost of achieving improved control should not outweigh its benefits.

Methods of Data Processing

The internal control system should achieve the four broad objectives regardless of the **data processing** method used (e.g., paper-based, computer-based, Web-based). However, the specific techniques used to achieve these objectives will vary with different types of technology.

Limitations

Every system of internal control has **limitations** on its effectiveness. These include (1) the possibility of error—no system is perfect, (2) circumvention—personnel may circumvent the system through collusion or other means, (3) management override—management is in a position to override control procedures by personally distorting transactions or by directing a subordinate to do so, and (4) changing conditions—conditions may change over time so that existing effective controls may become ineffectual.

EXPOSURES AND RISK

Figure 1-3 portrays the internal control system as a shield that protects the firm's assets from numerous undesirable events that bombard the organization. These include attempts at unauthorized access to the firm's assets (including information); fraud perpetrated by persons both in and outside the firm; errors due to employee incompetence, faulty computer programs, and corrupted input data; and mischievous

8 American Institute of Certified Public Accountants, Committee on Auditing Procedure, Internal Control—Elements of a Coordinated System and Its Importance to Management and the Independent Public Accountant, *Statement on Auditing Standards No. 1*, Sec. 320 (New York: AICPA, 1973).

FIGURE 1-3

Internal Control Shield

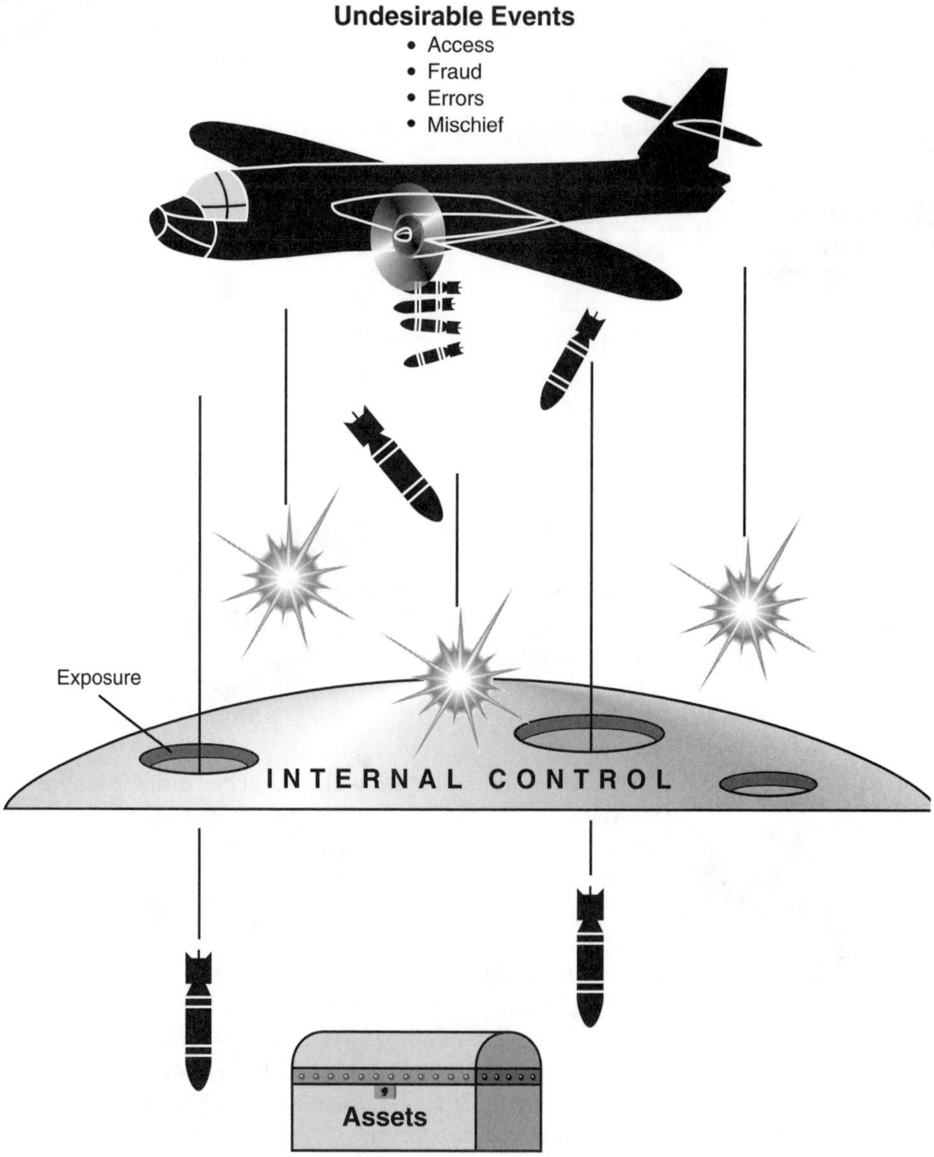

acts, such as unauthorized access by computer hackers and threats from computer viruses that destroy programs and databases.

A **risk** is the potential threat to compromise use or value of organizational assets. The absence or weakness of a control is called an **exposure**. Exposures, which are illustrated as holes in the control shield in Figure 1-3, increase the firm's risk to financial loss or injury from undesirable events. A weakness in internal control may expose the firm to one or more of the following types of risks:

1. Destruction of assets (both physical assets and information).
2. Theft of assets.

3. Corruption of information or the information system.
4. Disruption of the information system.

The PDC Model

Figure 1-4 illustrates that the internal control shield consists of three levels of control: preventive controls, detective controls, and corrective controls. This approach is called the **PDC control model**.

Preventive Controls

Prevention is the first line of defense in the control structure. **Preventive controls** are passive techniques designed to reduce the frequency of occurrence of undesirable events. Preventive controls force compliance with prescribed or desired actions and thus screen out aberrant events. When designing internal control systems, an ounce of prevention is most certainly worth a pound of cure. Preventing errors and fraud is far more cost-effective than detecting and correcting problems after they occur. The vast majority of undesirable events can be blocked at this first level. For example, a well-designed data entry screen is an example of a preventive control. The logical layout of the screen into zones that permit only specific types of data, such as customer name, address, items sold, and quantity, forces the data entry clerk to enter the required data and prevents necessary data from being omitted. Another example is effective access controls for remote access that prevent unauthorized access (e.g., crackers and hackers) to the organization's systems. However, not all problems can be anticipated and prevented. Some will elude the most comprehensive network of preventive controls.

FIGURE 1-4

Preventive, Detective, and Corrective Controls

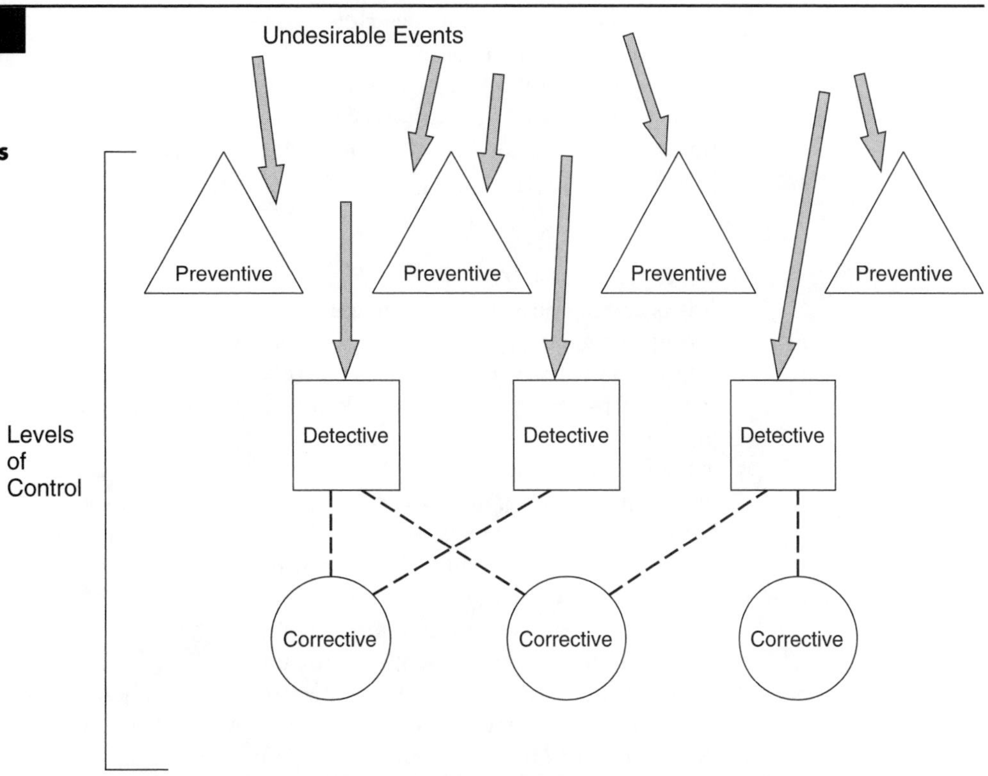

Detective Controls

Detection of problems is the second line of defense. **Detective controls** are devices, techniques, and procedures designed to identify and expose undesirable events that elude preventive controls. Detective controls reveal specific types of errors by comparing actual occurrences to preestablished standards. When the detective control identifies a departure from standard, it sounds an alarm to attract attention to the problem. For example, assume that because of a data entry error, a customer sales order record contains the following data:

Quantity	Unit Price	Total
10	$10	$1,000

Before processing this transaction and posting to the accounts, a detective control should recalculate the total value using the price and quantity. Thus, this error above would be detected.

Corrective Controls

Corrective actions must be taken to reverse the effects of detected errors. There is an important distinction between detective controls and corrective controls. Detective controls identify undesirable events and draw attention to the problem; **corrective controls** actually fix the problem. For any detected error, there may be more than one feasible corrective action, but the best course of action may not always be obvious. For example, in viewing the preceding error, your first inclination may have been to change the total value from $1,000 to $100 to correct the problem. This presumes that the quantity and price values in the record are correct; they may not be. At this point, we cannot determine the real cause of the problem; we know only that one exists.

Linking a corrective action to a detected error, as an automatic response, may result in an incorrect action that causes a worse problem than the original error. For this reason, error correction should be viewed as a separate control step that should be taken cautiously.

Predictive Controls

It is becoming possible with emerging technologies for IT auditors to actually predict certain malicious events. Two examples are artificial neural networks (ANN) and Internet Storm Center *(http://isc.incidents.org)*. ANN have the ability to "learn" or recognize patterns in transactions that contain error or irregularities (fraud) by exposing the system to actual instances from the past. Then, by using the ANN as an embedded audit module (EAM), the system could filter transactions looking for suspicious transactions, and alert the appropriate party as soon as it is entered. While it is true that this process is detective in nature, the fact it happens almost instantly to the entry makes it also predictive in nature. The second example is related to Internet security. The Internet Storm Center (ISC) combines logs from numerous Internet hosts to track activities on certain Internet ports. Then by tracking the level of activity, ISC has the ability to spot "anomalies" or unusual activities. This process has led to an early warning system that alerts interested parties about emerging viruses, worms, denial of service attacks, and other malicious activities. By becoming a subscriber to ISC, an organization can employ a predictive tool regarding Internet systems.

The PDC control framework is a conceptual model that offers little practical guidance for designing control systems. For this, we need a more precise set of objectives. The current authoritative document for specifying internal control objectives and techniques is the *Statement on Auditing Standards No. 78*.[9] We now discuss the key elements of this document.

Statement on Auditing Standards No. 78

Statement on Auditing Standards No. 78 (SAS 78) conforms to the recommendations of the Committee of Sponsoring Organizations of the Treadway Commission (COSO). Internal control as defined in SAS 78 consists of five components: the control environment, risk assessment, information and communication, monitoring, and control activities.

The Control Environment

The **control environment** is the foundation for the other four control components. The control environment sets the tone for the organization and influences the control awareness of its management and employees. It has several important elements:

- The integrity and ethical values of management
- The structure of the organization
- The participation of the organization's board of directors and the audit committee, if one exists
- Management's philosophy and operating style
- The procedures for delegating responsibility and authority
- Management's methods for assessing performance
- External influences, such as examinations by regulatory agencies
- The organization's policies and practices for managing its human resources

SAS 78 requires that auditors obtain sufficient knowledge to assess the attitude and awareness of the organization's management, board of directors, and owners regarding internal control. The following paragraphs provide examples of techniques that may be used to obtain an understanding of the control environment:

1. *Auditors should assess the integrity of the organization's management and may use investigative agencies to report on the backgrounds of key managers.* Some of the Big Four public accounting firms employ former FBI agents whose primary responsibility is to perform background checks on existing and prospective clients. If cause for serious reservations comes to light about the integrity of the client, the auditor should withdraw from the audit. The reputation and integrity of management are critical factors in determining the organization's auditability. Auditors cannot function properly in an environment in which client management is deemed to be unethical and corrupt.
2. *Auditors should be aware of conditions that would predispose the management of an organization to commit fraud.* Some of the obvious conditions may be lack of sufficient working capital, adverse industry conditions, bad credit ratings, and the existence of extremely restrictive conditions in bank or indenture

9 American Institute of Certified Public Accountants, SAS No. 78—Consideration of Internal Control in a Financial Statement Audit: An Amendment to *SAS No. 55* (New York: AICPA, 1995).

agreements. If auditors encounter any such conditions, their examination should give due consideration to the possibility of fraudulent financial reporting. Appropriate measures should be taken, and every attempt should be made to uncover any fraud.

3. *Auditors should understand a client's business and industry and should be aware of conditions peculiar to the industry that may affect the audit.* Auditors should read industry-related literature and familiarize themselves with the risks that are inherent in the business.
4. *Auditors should determine if the organization's board of directors is actively involved in establishing business policy and if it monitors management and organization operations.* An independent internal audit function that reports to the audit committee of the board of directors is an excellent environmental control.
5. *From organizational charts and job descriptions, auditors can assess whether segregation between organizational functions is adequate.* In particular, auditors are concerned with the segregation of duties within and between the accounting function and other functional areas.

Risk Assessment

Organizations must perform a **risk assessment** to identify, analyze, and manage risks relevant to financial reporting. Risks can arise out of changes in circumstances, such as the following:

- Changes in the operating environment that impose new competitive pressures on the firm
- New personnel who possess a different or inadequate understanding of internal control
- New or reengineered information systems that affect transaction processing
- Significant and rapid growth that strains existing internal controls
- The implementation of new technology into the production process or information system that impacts transaction processing
- The introduction of new product lines or activities with which the organization has little experience
- Organizational restructuring resulting in the reduction and/or reallocation of personnel such that business operations and transaction processing are affected
- Entering into foreign markets that may impact operations (i.e., the risks associated with foreign currency transactions)
- Adoption of a new accounting principle that impacts the preparation of financial statements

SAS 78 requires that auditors obtain sufficient knowledge of the organization's risk assessment procedures to understand how management identifies, prioritizes, and manages the risks related to financial reporting.

Information and Communication

The accounting information system consists of the records and methods used to initiate, identify, analyze, classify, and record the organization's transactions and to account for the related assets and liabilities. The quality of information generated by the AIS impacts management's ability to take actions and make decisions in connection with the organization's operations and to prepare reliable financial statements. An effective accounting information system will do the following:

- Identify and record all valid financial transactions
- Provide timely information about transactions in sufficient detail to permit proper classification and financial reporting
- Accurately measure the financial value of transactions so their effects can be recorded in financial statements
- Accurately record transactions in the time period in which they occurred

SAS 78 requires that auditors obtain sufficient knowledge of the organization's information system to understand these aspects:

- The classes of transactions that are material to the financial statements and how those transactions are initiated
- The accounting records and accounts that are used in the processing of material transactions
- The transaction processing steps involved from the initiation of an economic event to its inclusion in the financial statements
- The financial reporting process used to prepare financial statements, disclosures, and accounting estimates

Monitoring

Management must determine that internal controls are functioning as intended. **Monitoring** is the process by which the quality of internal control design and operation can be assessed. This assessment may be accomplished by separate procedures or by ongoing activities.

An organization's internal auditors may monitor the entity's activities in separate procedures. They gather evidence of control adequacy by testing controls, then communicate control strengths and weaknesses to management. As part of this process, internal auditors make specific recommendations for improvement to controls.

Ongoing monitoring may be achieved by integrating special computer modules into the information system that capture key data and/or permit tests of controls to be conducted as part of routine operations. Such embedded audit modules (EAMs) allow management and auditors to maintain constant surveillance over the functioning of internal controls and integrity of transaction data.

Another technique for achieving ongoing monitoring is the judicious use of management reports. Timely reports allow managers in functional areas such as sales, purchasing, production, and cash disbursements to oversee and control their operations. By summarizing activities, highlighting trends, and identifying exceptions from normal performance, well-designed management reports provide evidence of internal control function or malfunction. In Chapter 9, we review the Management Reporting System and examine the characteristics of effective management reports.

Control Activities

Control activities are the policies and procedures used to ensure that appropriate actions are taken to deal with the organization's identified risks. Control activities can be grouped into two distinct categories: *computer controls* and *physical controls*. Figure 1-5 illustrates the control activities in their respective categories.

FIGURE 1-5

Categories of Control Activities

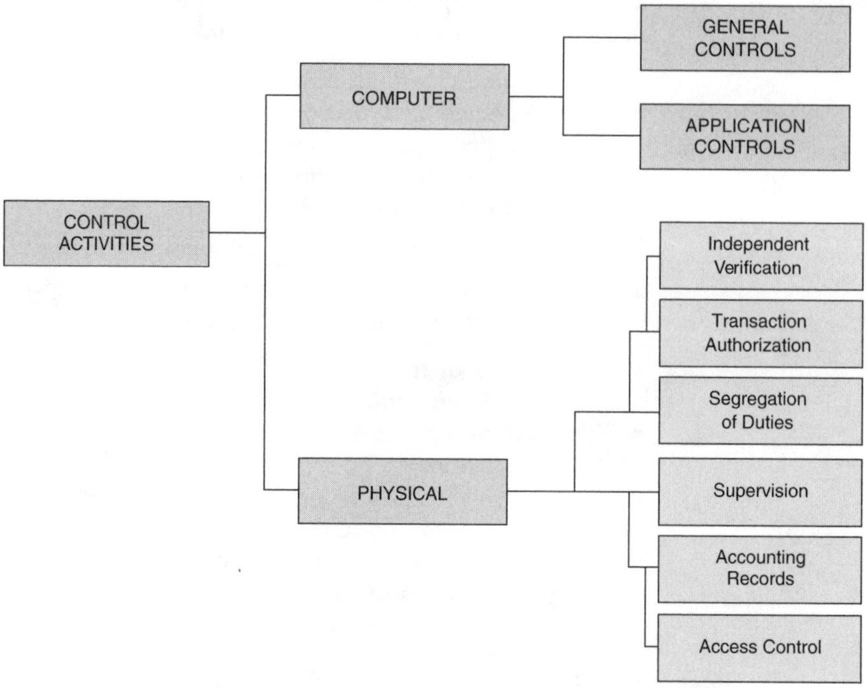

Computer controls constitute a body of material that is of primary concern to us. These controls, which relate specifically to the IT environment and IT auditing, fall into two broad groups: **general controls** and **application controls**. General controls pertain to entity-wide concerns such as controls over the data center, organization databases, system access, systems development, and program maintenance. Application controls ensure the integrity of specific systems such as sales order processing, accounts payable, and payroll applications. Later in the chapter we examine a framework for viewing general and application controls and the risks to which they relate. Subsequent chapters expand upon this framework to explore these issues in detail. However, before pursuing this material further, we need to review more fundamental, but important, physical control issues.

Physical controls relate primarily to traditional accounting systems that employ manual procedures. However, an understanding of these control concepts also gives insight to the risks and control concerns associated with the IT environment. Our discussion will address the issues pertaining to six traditional categories of physical control activities: transaction authorization, segregation of duties, supervision, accounting records, access control, and independent verification. For each control category, the IT implications will also be reviewed.

Transaction Authorization. The purpose of **transaction authorization** is to ensure that all material transactions processed by the information system are valid and in accordance with management's objectives. Authorizations may be general or specific. General authority is granted to operations personnel to perform day-to-day operations. An example of general authorization is the procedure to authorize the purchase of inventories from a designated vendor only when inventory levels fall to their predetermined reorder points. This procedure is called a *programmed* *procedure* (not necessarily in the computer sense of the word). The decision rules are specified in advance, and no additional approvals are required. By contrast, specific authorizations deal with case-by-case decisions associated with nonroutine transactions. An example of this situation is the decision to extend a particular customer's credit limit beyond the normal amount. Specific authority is usually a management responsibility.

In an IT environment, transaction authorization may consist of coded rules embedded within computer programs. For example, a program module in a purchases system will determine when, how much, and from which vendor inventory items are ordered. Such transactions may be initiated automatically and without human involvement. Within this setting, it may be difficult for auditors to assess whether these transactions are in compliance with management's objectives. For instance, is the organization buying inventory only when it is needed? Are correct quantities being purchased only from approved vendors? Because automated authorization procedures are unobserved by management, control failure may go unnoticed until the firm experiences some adverse symptoms. In the case of purchases authorization, symptoms of a problem may take the form of an inventory stockout or an excessive buildup of inventory. Controls may also be circumvented to perpetrate fraud. Unfortunately, by the time the problem is recognized, the firm may have incurred substantial financial losses.

In an IT environment, the responsibility for achieving the control objectives of transaction authorization rests directly on the accuracy and consistency (integrity) of the computer programs that perform these tasks. Later in the text, we explore several control techniques that promote computer program integrity. As we shall see, program integrity bears directly on many control issues.

Segregation of Duties. One of the most important control activities is segregation of employee duties to minimize incompatible functions. **Segregation of duties** can take many forms, depending upon the specific duties to be controlled. However, the following three objectives provide general guidelines applicable to most organizations. These objectives are illustrated in Figure 1-6.

FIGURE 1-6

Segregation of Duties Objectives

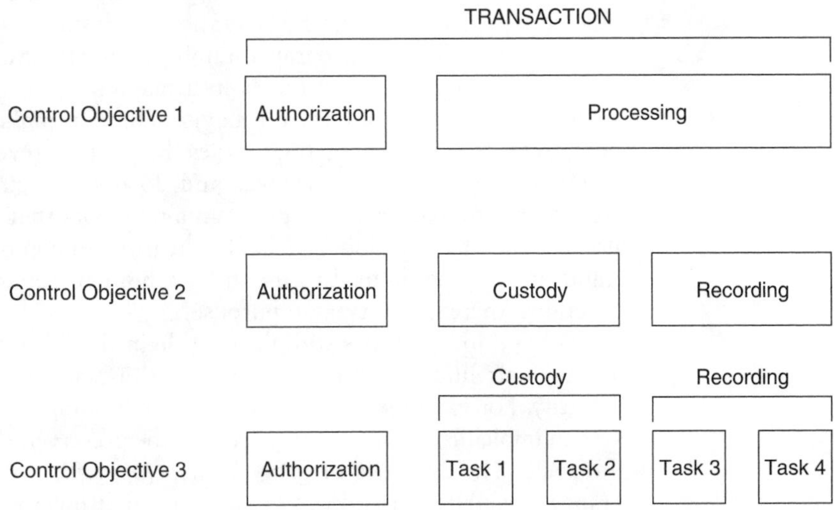

1. *The segregation of duties should be such that the authorization for a transaction is separate from the processing of the transaction.* For example, purchases should not be initiated by the purchasing department until authorized by the inventory control department. This separation of tasks is a control to prevent the purchase of unnecessary inventory by individuals.
2. *Responsibility for the custody of assets should be separate from the recordkeeping responsibility.* For example, the department that has physical custody of finished goods inventory (the warehouse) should not keep the official inventory records. Accounting for finished goods inventory is performed by inventory control, an accounting function. When a single individual or department has responsibility for both asset custody and recordkeeping, the potential for fraud exists. Assets can be stolen or lost, and the accounting records falsified to hide the event.
3. *The organization should be structured so that a successful fraud requires collusion between two or more individuals with incompatible responsibilities.* In other words, no single individual should have sufficient access to assets and supporting records to perpetrate a fraud. For most people, the thought of approaching another employee with the proposal to collude in a fraud presents an insurmountable psychological barrier. The fear of rejection and subsequent disciplinary action discourages solicitations of this sort. However, when employees with incompatible responsibilities work together daily in close quarters, the resulting familiarity will tend to erode this barrier. For this reason, the segregation of incompatible tasks should be physical as well as organizational. Indeed, concern about personal familiarity on the job is the justification for establishing rules prohibiting nepotism.

In an IT environment, segregation of duties is not identical to that of the manual environment. Computer programs typically perform tasks that are deemed incompatible in a manual system. For example, a program may be solely responsible for authorizing a purchase, processing the purchase order, and recording the account payable. When the supplier's invoice arrives, the computer will also determine the timing and amount of the payment to be made.

These are several reasons why duties that are separated in a manual system need not be separated in an IT environment. It would be inefficient, contrary to the objectives of automation, and operationally futile to separate incompatible tasks among several different programs simply to emulate traditional manual procedures. The reason for segregating duties in a manual environment is to control against some negative aspect of human behavior. Humans make mistakes and occasionally perpetrate frauds. Segregating duties helps to prevent and detect such acts. Computers do not make mistakes and do not perpetrate frauds. Most so-called computer errors are actually programming errors that are, in fact, human errors. Because they possess unimpeachable integrity, no computer has ever perpetrated a fraud unless programmed to do so by a human. Separating computer processing functions, therefore, serves no purpose.

Segregation of duties still plays a role in the IT environment. However, the IT auditor's attention must be redirected to those activities that threaten application integrity. For example, once the proper functioning of a program is established at system implementation, its integrity must be preserved throughout the application's life cycle. The activities of *program development*, *program operations*, and *program maintenance* are critical IT functions that must be adequately separated.

Supervision. Implementing adequate segregation of duties requires that a firm employ a sufficiently large number of employees. Achieving adequate segregation of duties often presents difficulties for small organizations. Obviously, it is impossible to separate five incompatible tasks among three employees. Therefore, in small organizations or in functional areas that lack sufficient personnel, management must compensate for the absence of segregation controls with close **supervision**. For this reason, supervision is often called a *compensating control*. The supervision can be in the form of physical supervision, reports, or other means.

An underlying assumption of supervision control is that the firm employs competent and trustworthy personnel. Obviously, no company could function for long on the alternative assumption that its employees are incompetent and dishonest. The "competent and trustworthy employee" assumption promotes supervisory efficiency. Firms can thus establish a managerial span of control whereby a single manager supervises several employees. In manual systems, maintaining a span of control tends to be straightforward because both manager and employees are at the same physical location.

In an IT environment, supervisory control must be more elaborate than in manual systems for three reasons. The first relates to the problem of attracting competent employees. The technology of data processing creates an exceedingly complex environment that demands a unique class of employees. Those who design, program, maintain, and operate the firm's computer system must possess highly specialized skills. These individuals operate in a dynamic setting characterized by a high rate of staff turnover. The task of restaffing is complicated further by rapid changes in technology, which tend to frustrate management's ability to assess the competence of prospective employees.

The second reason reflects management's concern over the trustworthiness of data processing personnel in high-risk areas. Some systems professionals serve in positions of authority that permit direct and unrestricted access to the organization's programs and data. The combination of technical skill and opportunity in the hands of an individual who may be mischievous or corrupt, represents a significant risk to the organization.

The third reason is management's inability to adequately observe employees in an IT environment. The activities of employees engaged in data processing are frequently hidden from management's direct observation. For example, data processing personnel may be distributed throughout areas and perform their functions remotely via telecommunications links. Supervisory controls must, therefore, be designed into the computer system to compensate for the lack of direct supervision.

Accounting Records. The traditional **accounting records** of an organization consist of source documents, journals, and ledgers. These records capture the economic essence of transactions and provide an audit trail of economic events. The audit trail enables the auditor to trace any transaction through all phases of its processing from the initiation of the event to the financial statements. Organizations must maintain audit trails for two reasons. First, this information is needed for conducting day-to-day operations. The audit trail helps employees respond to customer inquiries by showing the current status of transactions in process. Second, the audit trail plays an essential role in the financial audit of the firm. It enables external (and internal) auditors to verify selected transactions by tracing them from the financial statements, to the ledger accounts, to the journals, to the source documents, and back to their original source. For reasons of both practical expedience and legal obligation, business organizations must maintain sufficient accounting records to preserve their audit trails.

The obligation to maintain an audit trail exists in an IT environment just as it does in a manual setting. However, automated accounting records and audit trails are very different from those in manual systems. Some computer systems maintain no physical source documents. Journals and ledgers often do not exist in the traditional sense. Instead, records of transactions and other economic events are fragmented across several normalized database tables. Audit trails may take the form of pointers, hashing techniques, indexes, or embedded keys that link record fragments between and among the database tables. To meet their responsibilities, auditors must understand the operational principles of the database management systems in use and the effects on accounting records and audit trails of alternative file structures.

In the IT environment, part or all of the audit trail is in digital form. Because it resides on computers in files, if at all, it is basically invisible to auditors. Therefore, it is imperative in the IT environment that programmers and analysts understand the importance of logs, and how to capture a sufficient amount of data for audit trail purposes. For example, in file maintenance programs, the programmer should capture the values and data prior to the changes, and the new values after the changes, a reason for the changes (keyed by the operator), the operator's identification (user id, IP address, etc.), and a date-time stamp. Such information builds an effective audit trail that with a CAAT or query can be printed for the benefit of the IT auditors.

Access Controls. The purpose of **access controls** is to ensure that only authorized personnel have access to the firm's assets. Unauthorized access exposes assets to misappropriation, damage, and theft. Therefore, access controls play an important part in safeguarding assets. Access to assets can be direct or indirect. Physical security devices, such as locks, safes, fences, and electronic and infrared alarm systems, control against direct access. Indirect access to assets is achieved by gaining access to the records and documents that control their use, ownership, and disposition. For example, an individual with access to all the relevant accounting records can destroy the audit trail that describes a particular sales transaction. Thus, by removing the records of the transaction, including the account receivable balance, the sale may never be billed and the firm will never receive payment for the items sold. The access controls needed to protect accounting records will depend upon the technological characteristics of the accounting system. In a manual system, accounting records are physical and tend to be distributed among several locations. Indirect access control is accomplished by controlling the use of documents and records and by segregating the duties of those who must access and process these records.

In the IT environment, accounting records are often concentrated within the data processing center on mass storage devices. Data consolidation exposes the organization to two forms of threat: (1) computer fraud and (2) losses from disasters.

- *Fraud.* An individual with the proper skills and unrestricted access to accounting records is in a prime position to perpetrate a fraud. With all the necessary records in one location, the successful perpetrator does not need to gain access to several different places and is thus more likely to achieve his or her objective without detection.

- *Disasters.* Disasters such as fires in Los Angeles caused by civil unrest, earthquakes in southern California, floods in the Midwest, hurricanes in Florida, terrorists' attacks such as the bombing of the World Trade Center, and less spectacular events such as computer hardware failures all can destroy an organization's accounting records. A firm unable to recover its essential records may well be unable to continue in business. For example, if the firm's accounts receivable file is destroyed, it may be unable to determine what its customers owe for goods and services previously provided. Access control in the IT environment includes provisions for the physical security of the computer facilities. With all of its eggs in one basket, the firm must protect the basket well.

Another problem unique to the IT environment is controlling access to computer programs. During the development phase, computer applications come under a great deal of scrutiny and testing intended to expose logic errors. However, concern for application integrity should not cease when systems are implemented. Errors and fraud exposures are more likely to occur after implementation in the operational period of the system's life cycle, called the *maintenance phase.* During this period, which may last for years, a typical application may be modified dozens of times. These modifications present an opportunity for errors to be inserted unintentionally in the application and for the computer criminal to perpetrate a fraud by making an illegal program change.

Access control in an IT environment covers many levels of risk. Controls that address these risks include techniques designed to limit personnel access authority, restrict access to computer programs, provide physical security for the data processing center, ensure adequate backup for data files, and provide disaster recovery capability. Some access controls are technological procedures and devices, while others are physical barriers implemented through organizational segregation of duties. But underlying all access control techniques is the fundamental principle of "need to know." Individuals should be granted access to data, programs, and restricted areas only when a need in connection with their assigned tasks has been demonstrated. This principle should never be violated.

Independent Verification. **Verification procedures** are independent checks of the accounting system to identify errors and misrepresentations. Verification differs from supervision because it takes place after the fact, by an individual who is not directly involved with the transaction or task being verified. Supervision takes place while the activity is being performed by a supervisor with direct responsibility for the task. Through independent verification procedures, management can assess (1) the performance of individuals, (2) the integrity of the transaction processing system, and (3) the correctness of data contained in accounting records. Examples of independent verifications include:

- Reconciling batch totals at points during transaction processing
- Comparing physical assets with accounting records
- Reconciling subsidiary accounts with control accounts
- Reviewing management reports (both computer and manually generated) that summarize business activity

The timing of verification depends on the technology employed in the accounting system and the task under review. Some verifications occur several times an hour; some are done several times a day; and others are performed daily, weekly, monthly, and annually.

Independent verification control is needed in the manual environment because employees sometimes make mistakes or forget to perform necessary tasks. In an IT environment, computer programs perform many routine tasks. Once again, most of our concerns rest with application integrity. For example, after data have been entered into the system, check programs can be run to look for anomalies such as blank fields, values out of range, or missing foreign keys. The report from this check program can therefore be used to verify data integrity after keypunching (i.e., after the application has run). In the IT environment, IT auditors perform an independent verification function by evaluating controls over systems development and maintenance activities and occasionally by reviewing the internal logic of programs.

The Importance of the Internal Controls

The five components of internal control—the control environment, risk assessment, information and communication, monitoring, and control activities—provide the auditor with important information about the risks of material misrepresentation in financial statements and fraud. Auditors are therefore required to obtain a sufficient knowledge of the internal controls to plan their audits. For example, the internal controls in place affect how the auditor will assess whether an organization has reported all of its liabilities. The auditor must understand how purchases are initiated, processed, and recorded. The internal control structure provides this information and guides the auditor in the planning of specific tests to determine the likelihood and extent of financial statement misrepresentation.

General Framework for Viewing IT Risks and Controls

Figure 1-7 presents a framework for viewing areas of IT risks and controls. The areas of greatest potential risk are indicated by the circled numbers, which correspond to the following six topics.

1. Operations
2. Data management systems
3. New systems development
4. Systems maintenance
5. Electronic commerce
6. Computer applications

As stated earlier, IT internal controls are divided into the two broad categories of *general controls* and *application controls*.[10] General controls apply to a wide range of risks that systematically threaten the integrity of all applications processed within the IT environment. General controls are topics numbered 1 through 5. Chapters 2 through 8 examine the technologies, the control objectives, and the audit techniques related to each of these areas.

Application controls are narrowly focused on risks associated with specific systems, such as payroll, accounts receivable, and purchases. Tests of application controls relate to specific audit objects such as verifying the *completeness* of accounts payable. Chapters 9 and 10 deal with the audit objectives, tests of controls, and substantive tests related to revenue and expenditure cycle applications. The issue of computer fraud is examined in Chapters 11 and 12.

---

10 The Committee of Sponsoring Organizations of the Treadway Commission (New York: 1991), p. 115.

FIGURE 1-7 **Framework for Viewing IT Risks**

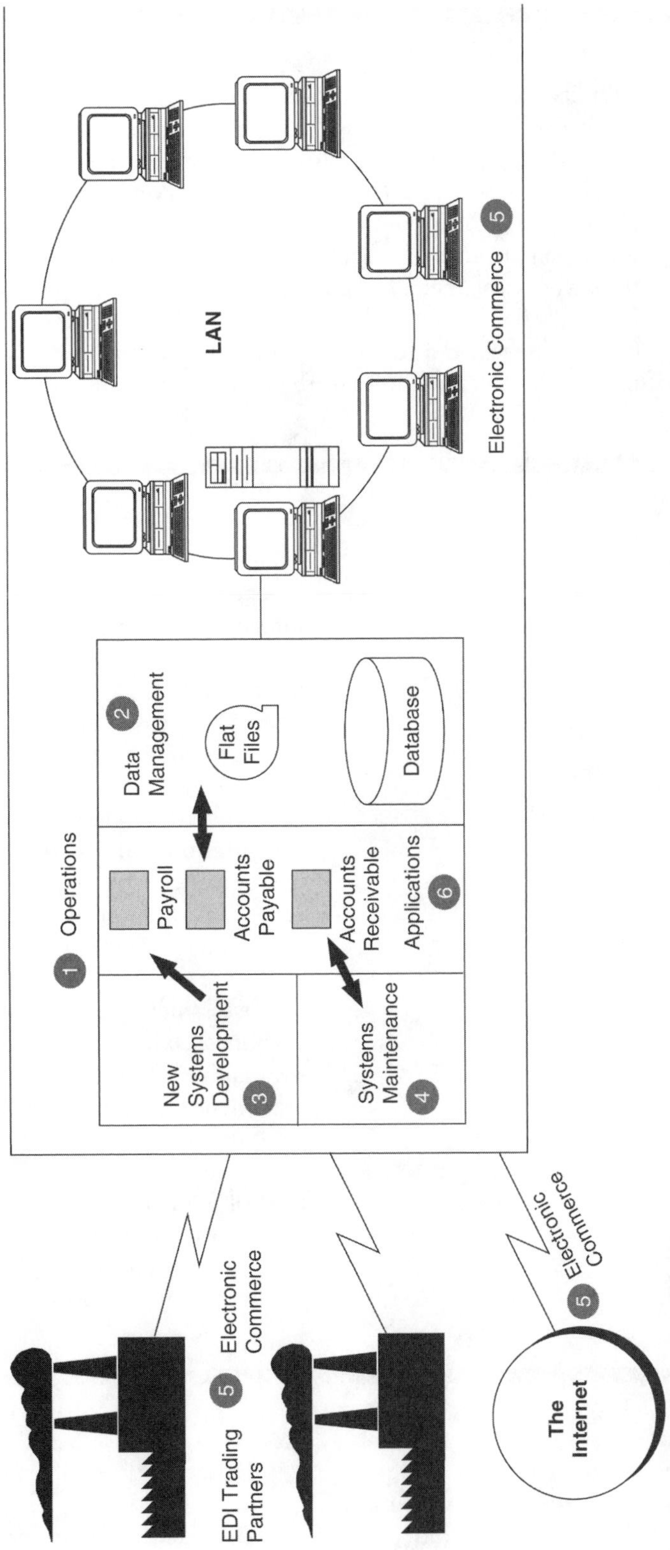

Summary

This chapter outlined the impact of information technology on the field of auditing. We began by distinguishing between the various types of audits, and within financial audits, the auditor's traditional attestation responsibility and the emerging field of assurance services. The chapter focused on issues that pertain primarily to attest services but which could also apply to assurance services. The structure of an IT audit, management assertions, audit objectives, tests of controls, and substantive tests were explained. The chapter outlined the key points of SAS 78, which defines internal controls in both manual and IT environments. The final section of the chapter presented a framework for risk assessment that identifies six areas of computer risk. The remainder of the text is based upon this framework.

Key Terms

access controls
accounting records
application controls
assurance services
attest service
audit objectives
audit opinion
audit planning
audit procedure
audit risk
auditing
completeness
Computer-Assisted Audit Tools and Techniques (CAATTs)
control activities
control environment
control risk
Copyright Law 1976
corrective controls
detection risk
detective controls
existence or occurrence
exposure
Foreign Corrupt Practices Act of 1977 (FCPA)
general controls
independence
information technology (IT)
inherent risk
internal auditing
internal control system
management assertions
monitoring
PDC control model
presentation and disclosure
preventive controls
reasonable assurance
rights and obligations
risk
risk assessment
Sarbones-Oxley Act 2002
segregation of duties
Statement on Auditing Standards No. 78 (SAS 78)
substantive tests
supervision
tests of controls
transaction authorization
valuation or allocation
verification procedures

Review Questions

1. What is the purpose of an IT audit?
2. Discuss the concept of independence within the context of a financial audit. How is independence different for internal auditors?
3. What are the conceptual phases of an audit? How do they differ between general auditing and IT auditing?
4. Distinguish between internal and external auditors.
5. What are the four primary elements described in the definition of auditing?

6. Explain the concept of materiality.
7. How does the Sarbanes-Oxley Act of 2002 affect management's responsibility for internal controls?
8. What are the four broad objectives of internal control?
9. What are the four modifying assumptions that guide designers and auditors of internal control systems?
10. Give an example of a preventive control.
11. Give an example of a detective control.
12. Give an example of a corrective control.
13. What is the objective of SAS No. 78?
14. What are the five internal control components described in the *Statement on Auditing Standards No. 78*?
15. What are the four broad classes of control activities defined by SAS No. 78?
16. How do automated authorization procedures differ from manual authorization procedures?
17. Explain why certain duties that are deemed incompatible in a manual system may be combined in an IT environment. Give an example.
18. Explain how the audit trail differs between a manual system and a computer system.
19. What risks do data consolidation in an IT environment pose?
20. Give some examples of independent verifications in an IT environment.
21. Differentiate between general and application controls. Give two examples of each.
22. Distinguish between tests of controls and substantive testing.
23. Define audit risk.
24. Distinguish between errors and irregularities. Which do you think concern auditors the most?
25. Distinguish between inherent risk and control risk. How do internal controls affect inherent risk and control risk, if at all? What is the role of detection risk?
26. What is the relationship between tests of controls and substantive tests?

Discussion Questions

1. Discuss the differences between the attest function and assurance services.
2. A CPA firm has many clients. For some of its clients, it relies very heavily on the work of the internal auditors, while for others it does not. The amount of reliance affects the fees charged. How can the CPA firm justify the apparent inconsistency of fees charged in a competitive marketplace?
3. Accounting firms are very concerned that their employees have excellent communication skills, both oral and written. Explain why this requirement is so important by giving examples of where these skills would be necessary in each of the three phases of an audit.
4. Discuss how the process of obtaining IT audit evidence is inherently different than it is in a manual system.
5. Explain the audit objectives of existence or occurrence, completeness, rights and obligations, valuation or allocation, and presentation and disclosure.
6. How has the Foreign Corrupt Practices Act of 1977 had a significant impact on organization management?
7. Discuss the concept of exposure and explain why firms may tolerate some exposure.
8. If detective controls signal errors, why shouldn't they automatically make a correction to the identified error? Why are separate corrective controls necessary?
9. Most accounting firms allow married employees to work for the firm. However, they do not allow an employee to remain working for them if he or she marries an employee of one of their auditing clients. Why do you think this policy exists?
10. Discuss whether a firm with fewer employees than there are incompatible tasks should rely more heavily on general authority than specific authority.
11. An organization's internal audit department is usually considered to be an effective control mechanism for evaluating the organization's internal control structure. The Birch Company's internal auditing function reports directly to the controller. Comment on the effectiveness of this organizational structure.
12. According to SAS No. 78, the proper segregation of functions is an effective internal control procedure. Comment on the exposure (if any) caused by combining the tasks of paycheck preparation and distribution to employees.

13. Explain whether authorizations are necessary in a computer environment.
14. Explain how an IT environment affects the segregation of functions.
15. Explain how an IT environment affects supervision.
16. Explain how an IT environment affects the firm's obligation to maintain adequate accounting records.
17. Explain how an IT environment affects access control.
18. Explain how an IT environment affects independent verification.
19. How has the Sarbanes-Oxley Act affected internal controls?

PROBLEMS

1. Audit Committee

CMA 6898 3-3

Micro Dynamics, a developer of database software packages, is a publicly held company whose stock is traded over the counter. The company recently received an enforcement release proceeding through an SEC administrative law judge that cited the company for inadequate internal controls. In response, Micro Dynamics has agreed to establish an internal audit function and strengthen its audit committee.

A manager of the internal audit department has been hired as a result of the SEC enforcement action to establish an internal audit function. In addition, the composition of the audit committee has been changed to include all outside directors. Micro Dynamics has held its initial planning meeting to discuss the roles of the various participants in the internal control and financial reporting process. Participants at the meeting included the company president, the chief financial officer, a member of the audit committee, a partner from Micro Dynamics' external audit firm, and the newly appointed manager of the internal audit department. Comments by the various meeting participants are presented below.

President: "We want to ensure that Micro Dynamics complies with the SEC's enforcement release and that we don't find ourselves in this position again. The internal audit department should help to strengthen our internal control system by correcting the problems. I would like your thoughts on the proper reporting relationship for the manager of the internal audit department."

CFO: "I think the manager of the internal audit department should report to me since much of the department's work is related to financial issues. The audit committee should have oversight responsibilities."

Audit committee member: "I believe we should think through our roles more carefully. The Treadway Commission has recommended that the audit committee play a more important role in the financial reporting process; the duties of today's audit committee have expanded beyond mere rubber-stamp approval. We need to have greater assurance that controls are in place and being followed."

External audit firm partner: "We need a close working relationship among all of our roles. The internal audit department can play a significant role in monitoring the control systems on a continuing basis and should have strong ties to your external audit firm."

Internal audit department manager: "The internal audit department should be more involved in operational auditing, but it also should play a significant monitoring role in the financial reporting area."

Required:

a. Describe the role of each of the following in the establishment, maintenance, and evaluation of Micro Dynamics' system of internal control.
   i. Management
   ii. Audit committee
   iii. External auditor
   iv. Internal audit department
b. Describe the responsibilities that Micro Dynamics' audit committee has in the financial reporting process.

2. Role of Internal Auditor

CMA 1290 4-Y8

Leigh Industries has an internal audit department consisting of a director and four staff auditors. The director of internal audit, Diane Bauer, reports to the corporate controller, who receives copies of all internal audit reports. In addition, copies of all internal audit reports are sent to the audit committee of the board of directors and the individual responsible for the area of activity being audited.

In the past, the company's external auditors have relied on the work of the internal audit department to a substantial degree. However, in recent months, Bauer has become concerned that the objectivity of the internal audit function is being affected by the nonaudit work being performed by the department. This possible loss of objectivity could result in more extensive testing and analysis by the external auditors. The percentage of nonaudit work performed by the internal auditors has steadily increased to about 25 percent of the total hours worked. A sample of five recent nonaudit activities follows.

- One of the internal auditors assisted in the preparation of policy statements on internal control. These statements included such things as policies regarding sensitive payments and the safeguarding of assets.
- Reconciling the bank statements of the corporation each month is a regular assignment of one of the internal auditors. The corporate controller believes this strengthens the internal control function because the internal auditor is not involved in either the receipt or the disbursement of cash.
- The internal auditors are asked to review the annual budget each year for relevance and reasonableness before the budget is approved. At the end of each month, the corporate controller's staff analyzes the variances from budget and prepares explanations of these variances. These variances and explanations are then reviewed by the internal audit staff.
- One of the internal auditors has been involved in the design, installation, and initial operation of a new computerized inventory system. The auditor was primarily concerned with the design and implementation of internal accounting controls and conducted the evaluation of these controls during the test runs.
- The internal auditors are sometimes asked to make the accounting entries for complex transactions as the employees in the accounting department are not adequately trained to handle such transactions. The corporate controller believes this gives an added measure of assurance to the accurate recording of these transactions.

Required:

a. Define objectivity as it relates to the internal audit function.
b. For each of the five nonaudit activities presented, explain whether the objectivity of Leigh Industries' internal audit department has been materially impaired. Consider each situation independently.
c. The director of internal audit reports directly to the corporate controller. Does this reporting relationship affect the objectivity of the internal audit department? Explain your answer.
d. Would your evaluation of the five situations in Question b change if the director of internal audit reported to the audit committee of the board of directors? Explain your answer.

3. Segregation of Function

CMA 1288 3-22

An effective system of internal control includes the segregation of incompatible duties. Some of the examples presented represent incompatible duties. Comment on the specific risks (if any) that are caused by the combination of tasks.

a. The treasurer has the authority to sign checks but gives the signature block to the assistant treasurer to run the check-signing machine.
b. The warehouse clerk, who has custodial responsibility over inventory in the warehouse, may authorize disposal of damaged goods.
c. The sales manager, who works on commission based on gross sales, approves credit and has the authority to write off uncollectible accounts.
d. The shop foreman submits time cards and distributes paychecks to employees.
e. The accounting clerk posts to individual account receivable subsidiary accounts and

performs the reconciliation of the subsidiary ledger and the general ledger control account.

4. **Segregation of Duties**
CMA 1288 3-23
Explain why each of the following combinations of tasks should, or should not, be separated to achieve adequate internal control.
   a. Approval of bad debt write-offs and the reconciliation of accounts payable subsidiary ledger and the general ledger control account.
   b. Distribution of payroll checks to employees and approval of sales returns for credit.
   c. Posting of amounts from both the cash receipts and the cash disbursements journals to the general ledger.
   d. Distribution of payroll checks to employees and recording cash receipts in the journal.
   e. Recording cash receipts in the journal and preparing the bank reconciliation.

5. **Internal Control**
CMA Adapted 1289 3-4
Oakdale, Inc., is a subsidiary of Solomon Publishing and specializes in the publication and distribution of reference books. Oakdale's sales for the past year exceeded $18 million, and the company employed an average of 65 employees. Solomon periodically sends a member of its internal audit department to audit the operations of each of its subsidiaries, and Katherine Ford, Oakdale's treasurer, is currently working with Ralph Johnson of Solomon's internal audit staff. Johnson has just completed a review of Oakdale's investment cycle and prepared the following report.

General

Throughout the year, Oakdale has made both short-term and long-term investments in securities; all securities are registered in the company's name. According to Oakdale's bylaws, long-term investment activity must be approved by its board of directors, while short-term investment activity may be approved by either the president or the treasurer.

Transactions

Oakdale has a computer link with its broker; thus, all buy and sale orders are transmitted electronically. Only individuals with authorized passwords may initiate certain types of transactions. All purchases and sales of short-term securities in the year were made by the treasurer. In addition, two purchases and one sale of long-term securities were executed by the treasurer. The long-term security purchases were approved by the Board. The president, having online authorization access to all transactions, was able to approve a sale of a long-term security. The president is given access to authorize all transactions engaged in by the firm. Because the treasurer is listed with the broker as the company's contact, all revenue from these investments is received by this individual, who then forwards the checks to accounting for processing.

Documentation

Purchase and sales authorizations, along with brokers' advice, are maintained in an electronic file with authorized access by the treasurer. Brokers' advice is received verbally on the phone, and this advice is noted on a broker advice form. This form is filed by the treasurer. The certificates for all long-term investments are kept in a safe deposit box at the local bank; only the president of Oakdale has access to this box. An inventory of this box was made, and all certificates were accounted for. Certificates for short-term investments are kept in a locked metal box in the accounting office. Other documents, such as long-term contracts and legal agreements, are also kept in this box. There are three keys to the box, held by the president, treasurer, and the accounting manager. The accounting manager's key is available to all accounting personnel, should they require documents kept in this box. Certificates of investments may take up to four weeks to receive after the purchase of the investment. An electronic inventory list is kept perpetually. The data are keyed in by accounting personnel who receive a buy/sale transaction sheet from the treasurer. The president, treasurer, and accounting manager all have passwords to access and update this inventory list. The accounting manager's password is known by two of the accounting supervisors in case the inventory list needs to be updated when the accounting manager is not available. Documentation for two of the current short-term investments could not be located in this box; the accounting manager explained that some of the investments are for such short periods of time that formal documentation is not always provided by the broker.

Accounting Records

Deposits of checks for interest and dividends earned on investments are recorded by the accounting department, but these checks could not be traced to the cash receipts journal maintained by the individual who normally opens, stamps, and logs incoming checks. These amounts are journalized monthly to an account for investment revenue. Electronic payments for investment purchases are authorized by the treasurer. If the amount is in excess of $15,000, an authorization code given by the treasurer or president is necessary.

Each month, the accounting manager and the treasurer prepare the journal entries required to adjust the short-term investment account. There was insufficient backup documentation attached to the journal entries reviewed to trace all transactions; however, the balance in the account at the end of last month closely approximates the amount shown on the statement received from the broker. The amount in the long-term investment account is correct, and the transactions can be clearly traced through the documentation attached to the journal entries. No attempts are made to adjust either account to the lower of aggregate cost or market.

Required:

To achieve Solomon Publishing's objective of sound internal control, the company believes the following four controls are basic for an effective system of accounting control.

- Authorization of transactions
- Complete and accurate record keeping
- Physical control
- Internal verification

a. Describe the purpose of each of the four controls listed above.

b. Identify an area in Oakdale's investment procedures that violates each of the four controls listed above.

c. For each of the violations identified, describe how Oakdale can correct it.

6. Internal Control

CMA 1290 4-2

Arlington Industries manufactures and sells component engine parts for large industrial equipment. The company employs over 1,000 workers for three shifts, and most employees work overtime when necessary. Arlington has had major growth in its production and has purchased a mainframe computer to handle order processing, inventory management, production planning, distribution operations, and accounting applications. Michael Cromley, president of Arlington, suspects that there may be internal control weaknesses due to the quick implementation of the computer system. Cromley recently hired Kathleen Luddy as the internal control accountant.

Cromley asked Luddy to review the payroll processing system first. Luddy has reviewed the payroll process, interviewed the individuals involved, and compiled the flowchart shown on the next page. The following additional information concerns payroll processing:

- The personnel department determines the wage rate of all employees at Arlington. Personnel starts the process by sending an authorization form for adding an employee to the payroll to Marjorie Adams, the payroll coordinator. After Adams inputs this information into the system, the computer automatically determines the overtime and shift differential rates for the individual, updating the payroll master files.
- Arlington uses an external service to provide monthly payroll tax updates. The company receives a magnetic tape every month, which the data processing department installs to update the payroll master file for tax calculations.

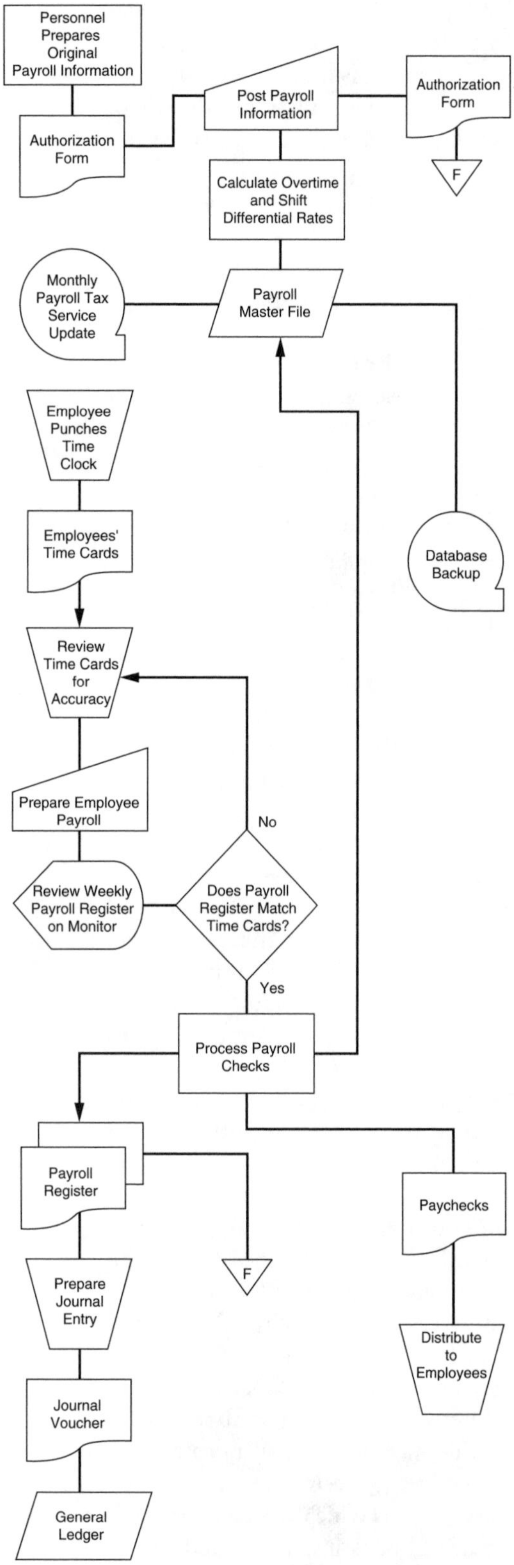

- Employees at Arlington use a time clock to record the hours worked. Every Monday morning, Adams collects the previous week's time cards and begins the computerized processing of payroll information to produce paychecks the following Friday. Adams reviews the time cards to ensure that the hours worked are correctly totaled; the system will determine whether overtime has been worked or a shift differential is required.
- All the other processes displayed on the flowchart are performed by Adams. The system automatically assigns a sequential number to each payroll check produced. The checks are stored in a box next to the computer printer to provide immediate access. After the checks are printed, Adams uses an automatic check-signing machine to sign the checks with an authorized signature plate that Adams keeps locked in a safe.
- After the check processing is completed, Adams distributes the checks to the employees, leaving the checks for the second- and third-shift employees with the appropriate shift supervisor. Adams then notifies the data processing department that she is finished with her weekly processing, and data processing makes a backup of the payroll master file to magnetic tape for storage on the tape shelves in the computer room.

Required:

By referring to the information in Problem 6 and the *flowchart*, identify and describe:

a. Five different areas in Arlington's payroll processing system where the system controls are inadequate.

b. Two different areas in Arlington's payroll processing system where the system controls are satisfactory.

PROJECTS

1. **Visit a Web site for one of the audit professional organizations. Find the answers to the following questions:**
   a. What relevant certification(s) is(are) supported by the organization? What is the cost to take the certification exam?
   b. What requirements does the organization have for continuing education requirements?
   c. How does the organization support IT auditors? Be specific.
   d. What publications are provided by the organization? How does the publication relate to IT audits?
   e. What services are provided by the organization to its members?
   f. Where is the closest chapter?
   g. Does a student membership program exist for the organization? If so, what is the cost for student members?

   TIPS: AICPA, ISACA, IIA, and ACFE

2. **Financial frauds such as Enron, WorldCom, and Adelphia led to the passage of the Sarbanes-Oxley Act of 2002. Using the Internet, find answers to the following questions about changes being made regarding audit committees in S-OX:**
   a. Describe a requirement for audit committees in S-OX.
   b. Describe a requirement for internal controls in S-OX.
   c. How do these changes affect IT auditors?
   d. How do these changes affect internal auditors?
   e. How do these changes affect financial auditors?

Description	URL – Web Site
Full text of S-OX ((H.R. 6763)—(PL 107-204))	http://www.riahome.com/newlaw/fulltext.pdf
S-OX's own Web Site	http://www.sarbanes-oxley.com/
SEC FAQ on S-OX	http://www.sec.gov/divisions/corpfin/faqs/soxact2002.htm
SEC implementation rule making for S-OX	http://www.sec.gov/news/press/2002-128.htm
More on rule making for S-OX	http://www.hinshawlaw.com/alerts/default.cfm?cat=cgov
Reaction of lawyers (American Bar Association) to S-OX	http://www.itaa.org/software/finance/tthabstract.cfm?ID=2168
AICPA S-OX Web Sites	http://www.aicpa.org/info/sarbanes_oxley_summary.htm http://www.aicpa.org/sarbanes/index.asp
PWC's take on S-OX	http://www.pwcglobal.com/
Implications for management	http://finance.pro2net.com/x35568.xml
S-OX or "Full-Employment Act for Lawyers, Accountants, and Insurance Executives"?	http://www.business2.com (Free registration required)
ISACA's Standard related to S-OX	http://www.isaca.org/
PCAOB	http://www.pcaob.com

CHAPTER

2 Computer Operations

LEARNING OBJECTIVES

After studying this chapter, you should:

- Understand the control and audit issues related to both the centralized and DDP approaches to structuring the IT function.
- Be familiar with computer center controls and the procedures used to test them.
- Understand the importance and basic elements of an effective disaster recovery plan, and the control and audit issues related to it.
- Understand the role that operating systems play in an organization's internal control structure and be familiar with the risks that threaten operating system security.
- Be familiar with the control techniques used to provide operating system security.
- Understand the audit objectives and audit procedures applicable to an operating system audit.
- Understand the risks unique to the PC environment and the controls that help to reduce them.

This chapter explores several audit issues related to computer operations. The topics covered are divided into the following categories: structuring of the information technology (IT) function, controlling computer center operations, the computer operating system and systemwide controls, and the personal computer environment. The chapter opens by reviewing the advantages and potential risks associated with both centralized and distributed IT structures. Control techniques, audit objectives, and audit procedures are examined. Next, computer center risks and controls are considered. The key elements of a disaster recovery plan and fault tolerance are presented. The chapter then presents an overview of multi-user operating system features common to networks and mainframes. Fundamental operating system objectives and the risks that threaten system security are reviewed. This material is followed by a discussion of operating system controls and audit techniques. The section presents a review of controls and audit issues associated with the enterprise system as a whole. The chapter concludes with a review of the features that characterize the personal computer environment. The primary risks, controls, and audit issues are discussed.

Structuring the Information Technology Function

The organization of the information technology (IT) function has implications for the nature of internal controls, which, in turn, has implications for the audit. In this section, some important control issues related to IT structure are examined. The chapter begins by reviewing basic processes and then examines two extreme organizational models—the centralized approach and the distributed approach. The risks, controls, and audit issues related to each model are then discussed. The reader should recognize that most organizational structures fall somewhere between these extremes and embody elements of both.

Centralized Data Processing

Under the **centralized data processing** model, all data processing is performed by one or more large computers housed at a central site that serve users throughout the organization. Figure 2-1 illustrates this approach, in which computer services activities are consolidated and managed as a shared organization resource. End users compete for these resources on the basis of need. The computer services function is usually treated as a cost center whose operating costs are charged back to the end users. Figure 2-2 illustrates a centralized computer services structure and shows its primary service areas: database administration, data processing, and systems development and maintenance. A description of the key functions of each of these areas follows.

Database Administration

Centrally organized companies maintain their data resources in a central location that is shared by all end users. In this shared data arrangement, an independent

FIGURE 2-1

Centralized Data Processing Approach

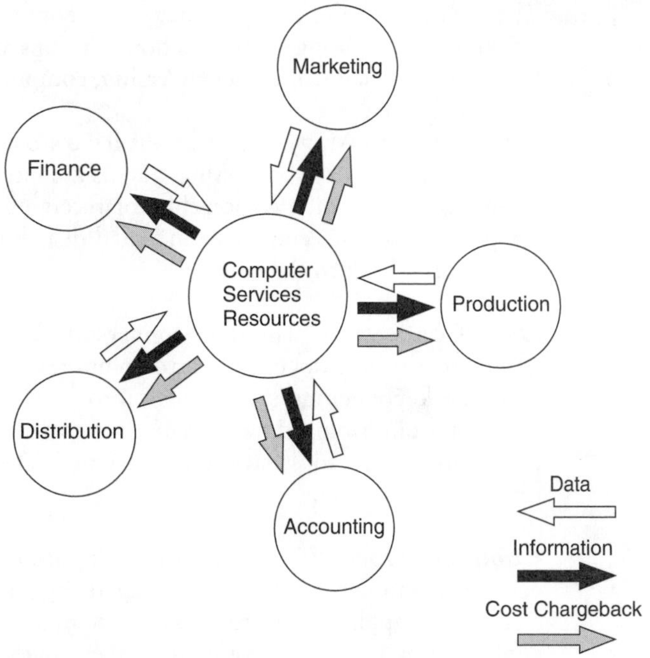

FIGURE 2-2 **Organizational Chart of a Centralized Computer Services Function**

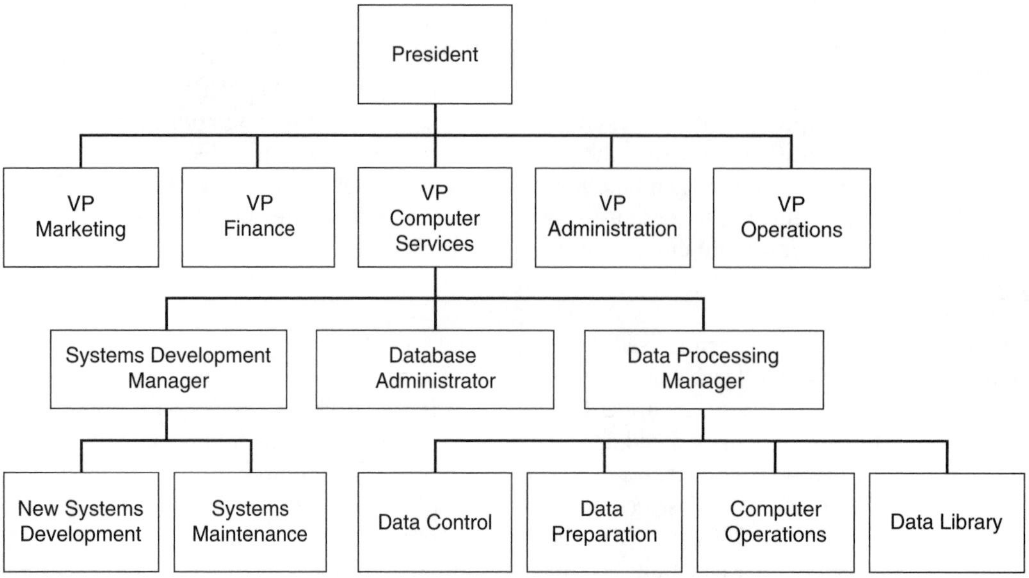

group—**database administration (DBA)**—headed by the database administrator is responsible for the security and integrity of the database.

Data Processing

The data processing group manages the computer resources used to perform the day-to-day processing of transactions. It consists of the following organizational functions: **data control, data conversion, computer operations**, and the **data library**.

Data Control. Many organizations have a **data control** group as liaison between the end user and data processing, and as a control function for computerized operations. Data control is responsible for receiving batches of transaction documents for processing from end users and then distributing computer output (documents and reports) back to the users.

Data Conversion. The data conversion function transcribes transaction data from paper source documents into computer input. For example, data conversion could be keypunching sales orders into a sale order application in modern systems, or transcribing data into magnetic media (tape or disk) suitable for computer processing in legacy type systems. The original source documents are returned to the user.

Computer Operations. The electronic files produced are later processed by the central computer, which is managed by the **computer operations** groups. Accounting applications are usually executed according to a strict schedule that is controlled by the central computer's operating system.

Data Library. The **data library** is a room adjacent to the computer center that provides safe storage for the off-line data files. Those files could be backups or current data files. For instance, the data library could be used to store backups on DVDs, CD-ROMs, tapes, or other storage devices. It could also be used to store live, current, data files on magnetic tapes and removable disk packs. In addition, the data library could be used to store the original copies of commercial software and their licenses for safekeeping. A data librarian, who is responsible for the receipt, storage, retrieval, and custody of data files, controls access to the library. The librarian issues data files to computer operators in accordance with program requests and takes custody of files when processing or backups are completed. The trend in recent years toward real-time processing and the increased use of direct-access files has reduced or even eliminated the role of the data librarian in many organizations. However, it still can be an effective control for commercial applications, licenses, and on-site backups.

Systems Development and Maintenance

The information systems needs of users are met by two related functions: system development and systems maintenance. The former group is responsible for analyzing user needs and for designing new systems to satisfy those needs. The participants in system development activities include systems professionals, end users, and stakeholders.

Systems professionals include systems analysts, database designers, and programmers who design and build the system. Systems professionals gather facts about the user's problem, analyze the facts, and formulate a solution. The product of their efforts is a new information system. One critical success factor to a successful system is the participation and input from end users.

End users are those for whom the system is built. They are the managers who receive reports from the system and the operations personnel who work directly with the system as part of their daily responsibilities.

Stakeholders are individuals inside or outside the firm who have an interest in the system, but are not end users. They include accountants, internal auditors, external auditors, and others who oversee systems development. However, the internal and external auditors need to be careful to not violate independence as defined in professional guidelines, or Sarbanes-Oxley requirements for the SEC with their involvement.

Once a new system has been designed and implemented, the systems maintenance group assumes responsibility for keeping it current with user needs. Over the course of the system's life (often several years), as much as 80 or 90 percent of its total cost will be incurred due to maintenance activities.

Segregation of Incompatible IT Functions

Segregating incompatible functions is no less important in the IT environment than it is in the manual environment. While the tasks are different, the underlying theory is the same. The following three fundamental objectives of segregation of duties were discussed in Chapter 1:

1. Segregate the task of transaction authorization from transaction processing.
2. Segregate record-keeping from asset custody.
3. Divide transaction processing tasks among individuals so that the perpetration of a fraud will require collusion between two or more individuals.

In the IT environment, a single application may authorize, process, and record all aspects of a transaction. Thus, the focus of segregation control shifts from the operational level (transaction processing tasks now performed by computer programs) to higher-level organizational relationships within the computer services function. Using the organizational chart in Figure 2-2 as a reference, these interrelationships among systems development, systems maintenance, database administration, and computer operations activities will be examined.

Separating Systems Development from Computer Operations

The segregation of systems development (both new systems development and maintenance) and operations activities is of the greatest importance. The relationship between these groups should be extremely formal, and their responsibilities should not be commingled. Systems development and maintenance professionals should create (and maintain) systems for users, and should have no involvement in entering data, or running applications (i.e., computer operations). Operations staff should run these systems and have no involvement in their design. These functions are inherently incompatible, and consolidating them invites errors and fraud. With detailed knowledge of the application's logic and control parameters and access to the computer's operating system and utilities, a privileged individual could make unauthorized changes to the application during its execution. Such changes may be temporary ("on the fly") and will disappear without a trace when the application terminates.

For instance, it is much easier for programmers to cheat the system than operators because they know the code. They know how to get around some, or most, of the embedded controls. Better yet, some programmers deliberately program code that gets them around controls and allows them to commit fraud.

Separating Database Administration from Other Functions

Another important organizational control is the segregation of the database administration (DBA) from other computer center functions. The DBA function is responsible for a number of critical tasks pertaining to database security, including creating the database schema and user views, assigning database access authority to users, monitoring database usage, and planning for future expansion. Delegating these responsibilities to others that perform incompatible tasks threatens database integrity. Thus, we see from Figure 2-2 how the DBA function is organizationally independent of operations, development, and maintenance.

Separating New Systems Development from Maintenance

Some companies organize their in-house systems development function into two groups: systems analysis and programming (see Figure 2-3). The systems analysis group works with the users to produce detailed designs of the new systems. The programming group codes the programs according to these design specifications. Under this approach, the programmer who codes the original programs also maintains the system during the maintenance phase of the systems development life cycle (discussed in Chapter 4). Although a popular arrangement, this approach is associated with two types of control problems: **inadequate documentation** and the potential for **program fraud**.

FIGURE 2-3

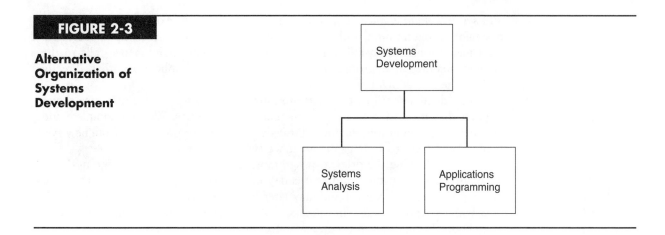

Alternative Organization of Systems Development

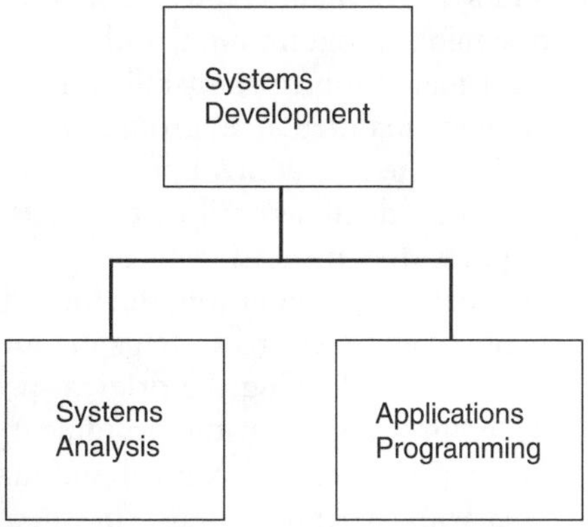

Improves Documentation. Poor systems documentation is a chronic problem for many firms. This is particularly true in companies that do not use computer-assisted software engineering (CASE) tools with automatic documentation features. There are at least two explanations for this phenomenon. First, documenting a system is not as interesting as designing, testing, and implementing it. Systems professionals much prefer to move on to an exciting new project rather than document one that is finished. Pressure from users demanding new systems makes the decision to prematurely move on to something else even easier.

The second reason for inadequate documentation is job security. When a system is poorly documented, it is difficult to interpret, test, and debug. Therefore, the programmer who understands the system (the one who coded it) is in a position of power and becomes relatively indispensable. However, when she or he leaves the firm, a new programmer must maintain the system. The new programmer may need to devote a great deal of time studying the detailed code of the application to glean an understanding of its logic. Depending on the complexity of the system, the transition period can be quite costly.

Deters Fraud. When the original programmer of a system also has maintenance responsibility, the potential for fraud is increased. Program fraud involves making unauthorized changes to program modules for the purpose of committing an illegal act. The original programmer may successfully conceal the fraudulent code among the thousands of lines of legitimate code and the hundreds of modules that constitute a system. However, for the fraud to work successfully, the programmer must have continued and unrestricted access to these programs. To control the situation, the programmer must protect the fraudulent code from accidental detection by another programmer (during maintenance) or by the auditor. Therefore, being vested with sole responsibility for maintenance is an important element in the duplicitous programmer's scheme. Through this maintenance authority, the programmer may freely access the system, disabling fraudulent code during audits and then restoring the code when the coast is clear. Frauds of this sort may go on for years without detection.

An Alternative Structure for Systems Development

Figure 2-2 presents a superior organizational structure in which the systems development function is separated into two different groups: *new systems development* and *systems maintenance*. The new systems development group is responsible for designing, programming, and implementing new systems projects. Upon successful implementation, responsibility for the system's ongoing maintenance falls to the systems maintenance group. This restructuring has implications that directly address the two control problems just described.

First, documentation standards are improved because the maintenance group requires documentation to perform its maintenance duties. Without complete and adequate documentation, the formal transfer of system responsibility from new systems development to systems maintenance simply cannot occur.

Second, denying the original programmer future access to the program deters program fraud. That the fraudulent code, once concealed within the system, is out of the programmer's control and may later be discovered increases the risk associated with program fraud. The success of this control depends on the existence of other controls that limit, prevent, and detect unauthorized access to programs (such as source program library controls). Organizational separations alone cannot prevent such unauthorized access. However, they are critical to creating the environment in which unauthorized access can be prevented.

Separating the Data Library from Operations

The data library is usually a room adjacent to the computer center that provides safe storage for the off-line data files, such as magnetic tapes and removable disk packs in legacy-type systems. A data librarian who is responsible for the receipt, storage, retrieval, and custody of data files should control access to the library. The librarian must keep a detailed log of each file, including file name, serial number, contents, creation date, and retention dates. The librarian issues scratch tapes (expired tapes that are going to be overwritten) to computer operators in accordance with system requests. When the program run is complete, the operator returns the file(s) to the librarian for storage. The separation of the librarian from operations is important for the physical security of off-line data files.

However, modern systems have changed the role or need for the data library function. For many organizations using legacy systems, the volume of tape file usage is insufficient to justify a full-time librarian. The trend in recent years toward real-time, online, and direct access systems has reduced the need for sequential tape storage. Thus, firms with modest tape usage—which still may represent several hundred tape volumes—often assign librarian functions to selected operators who perform these tasks on an ad hoc basis in addition to their usual operator functions. Yet there are other roles the data library could serve in modern systems. They include custody of on-site data backups and custody of commercial software and licenses.

Operators who are assigned library tasks must understand the control importance of this apparently mundane responsibility. Management should maintain strict control over who performs library functions to ensure that these responsibilities are not assumed by other operators during busy periods. This apparently innocuous transgression creates an environment of shared responsibility that inevitably deteriorates into one of no responsibility. In such an environment, data security suffers. The potential exposure can be illustrated through the following three scenarios.

1. *Computer centers become very busy at times.* Rushed operators, hurrying to start the next job, may forget to return to the library the tapes used by the program that has just completed processing. Lacking a librarian with the formal

responsibility to account for the disposition of all tapes, these tapes may remain in a corner of the computer room for days, exposed to physical damage, loss, theft, or corruption.

2. *Inexperienced individuals filling in as librarian during busy periods may return a tape to the wrong storage location in the library.* When it is needed again, the librarian may not be able to find it. This situation is analogous to placing an important book in a randomly selected shelf space in a library. How does one go about relocating it?
3. *The librarian is directly responsible for implementing the firm's scratch tape policy.* The librarian issues expired tapes to operators as scratch tapes for other systems. Inexperienced librarians have been known to issue current tapes, thinking they were scratch tapes. Such an error could result in the destruction of the organization's general ledger or other important accounting files.

Audit Objectives

- Conduct a risk assessment regarding systems development, maintenance, and operations.
- Verify that individuals in incompatible areas are segregated in accordance with the level of potential risk.
- Verify that segregation is done in a manner that promotes a working environment in which formal, rather than casual, relationships exist between incompatible tasks.

Audit Procedures

- Obtain and review the corporate policy on computer security. Verify that the security policy is communicated to responsible employees and supervisors.
- Review relevant documentation, including the current organizational chart, mission statement, and job descriptions for key functions, to determine if individuals or groups are performing incompatible functions.
- Review systems documentation and maintenance records for a sample of applications. Verify that maintenance programmers assigned to specific projects are not also the original design programmers.
- Through observation, determine that segregation policy is being followed in practice. Review operations room access logs to determine whether programmers enter the facility for reasons other than system failures.
- Review user rights and privileges to verify that programmers have access privileges consistent with their job description. User rights and privileges are discussed later in the chapter.

The Distributed Model

For many years, economies of scale favored large, powerful computers and centralized processing. However, recent developments in small, powerful, and inexpensive systems have changed this picture dramatically. An alternative to the centralized model is the concept of **distributed data processing (DDP)**. The topic of DDP is quite broad, touching upon such related topics as end-user computing, commercial software, networking, and office automation. Simply stated, DDP involves reorganizing the computer services function into small IT units that are placed under the control of end users. The IT units may be distributed according to business function, geographic location, or both. All or any of the computer services activities represented in Figure 2-2 may be distributed. The degree to which IT activities are distributed will vary depending upon the philosophy and objectives of the organization's management. Figure 2-4 presents two alternative DDP approaches.

Alternative A is actually a variant of the centralized model; the difference is that terminals (or microcomputers) are distributed to end users for handling input and output. This eliminates the need for the centralized data control and data conversion groups, since the user now performs these tasks. However, systems development, computer operations, and database administration remain centralized.

Alternative B is a radical departure from the centralized model. This alternative distributes all computer services to the end users, where they operate as standalone units. The result is the elimination of the central computer services function from the organizational structure. Notice the interconnections between the distributed units in Figure 2-4. These connections represent a *networking* arrangement that permits communication and data transfers between the units. Figure 2-5 shows a possible organizational structure following the distribution of all traditional data processing tasks to the end-user areas.

The client-server network (C/S) architecture has some features of both alternatives. It provides for the centralization of a database or software on a server, while also providing the functionality and independence of standalone microcomputers. It is this versatility that makes C/S networks attractive.

FIGURE 2-4

Two Distributed Data Processing Approaches

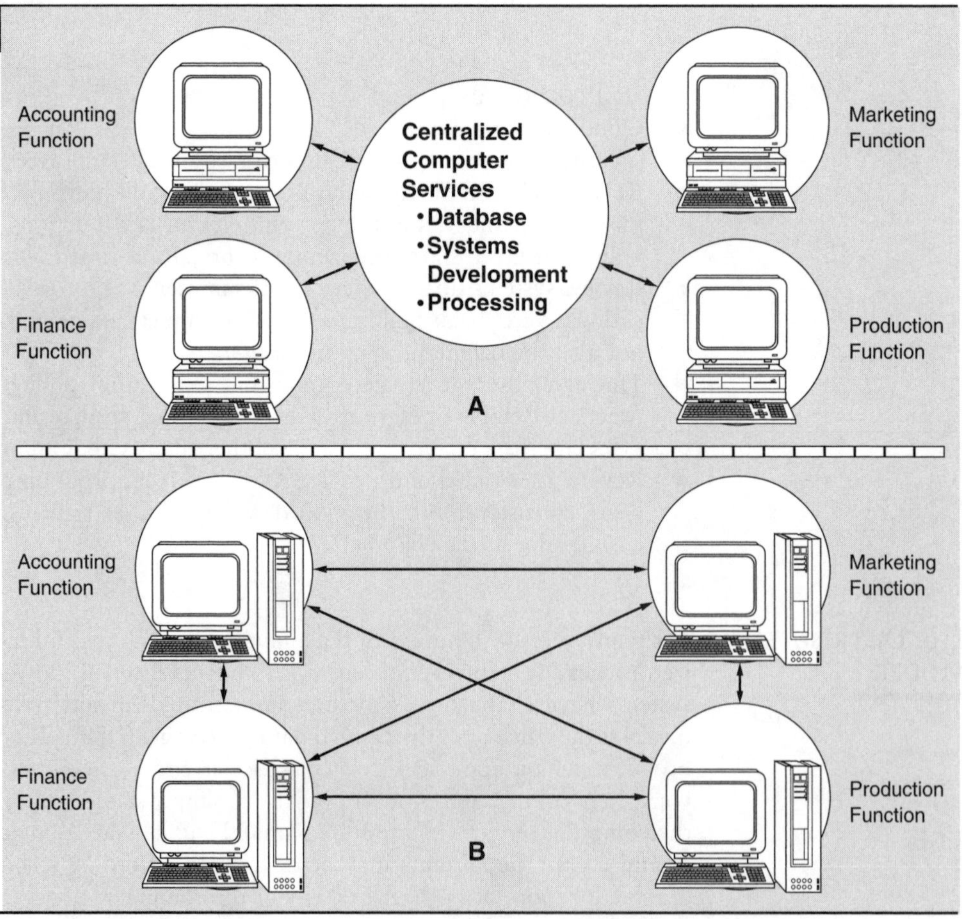

FIGURE 2-5

Distributed Organization with Corporate Computer Services Function

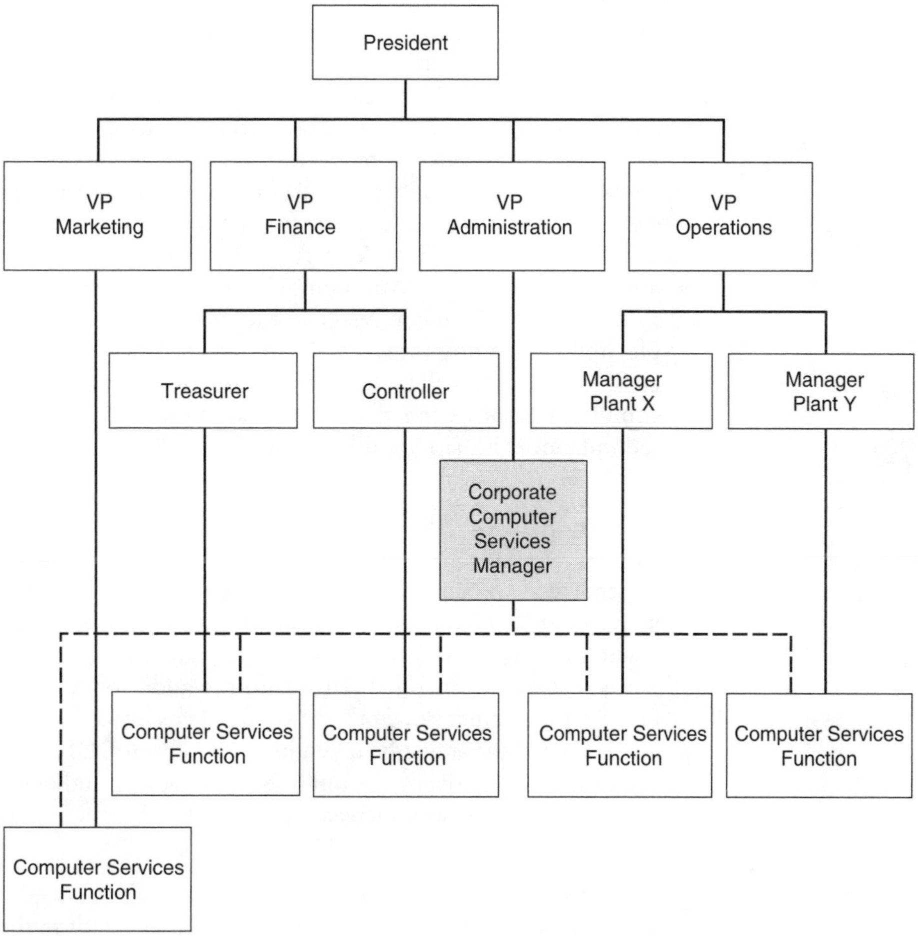

Risks Associated with DDP

This section discusses the organizational risks that need to be considered when implementing DDP. The discussion focuses on important issues that carry control implications that auditors should recognize. Potential problems include the inefficient use of resources, the destruction of audit trails, inadequate segregation of duties, an increased potential for programming errors and systems failures, and the lack of standards.

Inefficient Use of Resources. There are several risks associated with inefficient use of organizational resources in the DDP environment.

First, there is the risk of mismanagement of organization-wide resources, particularly by end users. Some argue that when organization-wide resources exceed a threshold amount, say 5 percent of the total operations budget, they should be controlled and monitored centrally. IT services (such as computer operations, programming, data conversion, and database management) represent a significant expenditure that needs careful management for many organizations. Those opposed to DDP argue that distributing responsibility for these resources will inevitably lead to their mismanagement and suboptimal utilization, by end users in particular.

Second, there is the risk of hardware and software incompatibility, again primarily by end users. Distributing the responsibility for hardware and software purchases to end users may result in uncoordinated and poorly conceived decisions. For example, decision makers in different organizational units working independently may settle on dissimilar and incompatible operating systems, technology platforms, spreadsheets, word processors, and database packages. Hardware and software incompatibilities can degrade and disrupt the connectivity between units, causing the loss of transactions and the destruction of audit trails.

Third, there is the risk of redundant tasks associated with end-user activities and responsibilities. Autonomous systems development initiative distributed throughout the firm can result in each user area reinventing the wheel. For example, application programs created by one user, which could be used with little or no change by others, will be redesigned from scratch rather than shared. Likewise, data common to many users may be recreated for each, resulting in a high level of data redundancy. This situation has implications for data accuracy and consistency.

Destruction of Audit Trail

The use of DDP can adversely affect the audit trail. Because audit trails in modern systems tend to be electronic, it is not unusual for the electronic audit trail to exist in part, or in whole, on end-user computers. Should the end user inadvertently delete the audit trail, it could be lost and unrecoverable. Or if an end user inadvertently inserts uncontrolled errors into the audit log, the audit trail could effectively be destroyed. Numerous other risks are associated, including care of the hardware itself. Special care must be taken in the design of DDP to protect the audit trail. For example, keeping the audit trail files on the server and never placing them on clients or end-user PCs would increase the security of the audit trail electronic files.

Inadequate Segregation of Duties

The distribution of the IT services to users may result in the creation of many small units that do not permit the necessary separation of incompatible functions. For example, within a single unit the same person may write application programs, perform program maintenance, enter transaction data into the computer, and operate the computer equipment. This condition would be a fundamental violation of internal control. However, achieving an adequate segregation of duties may not be possible in some distributed environments.

Hiring Qualified Professionals. End-user managers may lack the knowledge to evaluate the technical credentials and relevant experience of candidates applying for a position as a computer professional. Also, if the organizational unit into which a new employee is entering is small, the opportunity for personal growth, continuing education, and promotion may be limited. For these reasons, managers may experience difficulty attracting highly qualified personnel. The risk of programming errors and system failures increases directly with the level of employee incompetence. This problem spills over into the domain of accountants and auditors, who need requisite technical skills in order to properly audit accounting information systems embedded in computer technologies.

Lack of Standards. Because of the distribution of responsibility in the DDP environment, standards for developing and documenting systems, choosing programming languages, acquiring hardware and software, and evaluating performance may be unevenly applied or even nonexistent. Opponents of DDP argue that the risks associated with the design and operation of a data processing system are made tolerable only if such standards are consistently applied. This status requires that standards be imposed centrally.

Advantages of DDP

This section considers potential advantages of DDP, including cost reductions, improved cost control, improved user satisfaction, and backup.

Cost Reductions. For many years, achieving economies of scale was the principal justification for the centralized approach. The economics of data processing favored large, expensive, powerful computers. The wide variety of needs that centralized systems must satisfy calls for a computer that is highly generalized and employs a complex operating system. However, the sheer overhead associated with running such a system can diminish the advantages of its raw processing power. Thus, for many users, large, centralized systems represent expensive overkill that they must escape.

Powerful and inexpensive microcomputers and minicomputers that can perform specialized functions have changed the economics of data processing dramatically. In addition, the unit cost of data storage, which was once the justification for consolidating data in a central location, is no longer the prime consideration. Moreover, the move to DDP can reduce costs in two other areas: (1) data can be entered and edited at the user area, thus eliminating the centralized tasks of data preparation and data control; and (2) application complexity can be reduced, which in turn reduces development and maintenance costs.

Improved Cost Control Responsibility. End-user managers carry the responsibility for the financial success of their operations. This responsibility requires that they be properly empowered with the authority to make decisions about resources that influence their overall success. When managers are precluded from making the decisions necessary to achieve their goals, their performance can be negatively influenced. A less aggressive and less effective management may evolve.

If IT capability is critical to the success of a business operation, then management must be given control over these resources. This argument counters the earlier discussion favoring the centralization of organization-wide resources. Proponents of DDP argue that the benefits of improved management attitudes more than outweigh any additional costs incurred from distributing these resources.

Improved User Satisfaction. Perhaps the most often cited benefit of DDP is improved user satisfaction. This result derives from three areas of need that too often go unsatisfied in the centralized approach: (1) as previously stated, users desire to control the resources that influence their profitability; (2) users want systems professionals (analysts, programmers, and computer operators) who are responsive to their specific situation; and (3) users want to become more actively involved in developing and implementing their own systems. Proponents of DDP argue that providing more customized support (feasible only in a distributed environment) has direct benefits for user morale and productivity.

Backup Flexibility. The final argument in favor of DDP is the ability to back up computing facilities to protect against potential disasters such as fires, floods, sabotage, and earthquakes. The only way to back up a central computer site against such disasters is to provide a second computer facility. Later in the chapter we examine disaster recovery planning for such contingencies. The distributed model offers organizational flexibility for providing backup. Each geographically separate IT unit can be designed with excess capacity. If a disaster destroys a single site, the other sites can use their excess capacity to process the transactions of the destroyed site. This setup requires close coordination between the end-user managers to ensure that they do not implement incompatible hardware and software.

Controlling the DDP Environment

Careful planning and implementation of controls can mitigate the risks just discussed. This section reviews the controls and audit issues relevant to DDP.

Need for Careful Analysis

DDP carries a certain leading-edge prestige value that, during an analysis of its pros and cons, may overwhelm important considerations of economic benefit and operational feasibility. Some organizations have made the move to DDP without considering fully whether the distributed organizational structure will better achieve their business objectives. Many DDP initiatives have proven to be ineffective, and even counterproductive, because decision makers saw in these systems virtues that were more symbolic than real. Before taking an irreversible step, decision makers must assess the true merits of DDP for their organization. Auditors have an opportunity and an obligation to play an important role in this analysis.

Implement a Corporate IT Function

The completely centralized model and the distributed model represent extreme positions on a continuum of structural alternatives. The needs of most firms fall somewhere between these end points. For most firms, the control problems we have described can be addressed by implementing a *corporate IT function* such as that illustrated in Figure 2-5.

This function is greatly reduced in size and status from that of the centralized model shown in Figure 2-2. The corporate IT group provides systems development and database management for entity-wide systems in addition to technical advice and expertise to the distributed IT community. This advisory role is represented by the dotted lines in Figure 2-5. Some of the services provided are described next.

Central Testing of Commercial Software and Hardware. The corporate IT group is better able to evaluate the merits of competing vendor software and hardware. A central, technically astute group such as this can evaluate systems features, controls, and compatibility with industry and organizational standards most efficiently. Test results can then be distributed to user areas as standards for guiding acquisition decisions. Therefore, the organization should centralize the acquisition, testing, and implementation of software and hardware at the corporate IT function.

User Services. A valuable feature of the corporate group is its user services function. This activity provides technical help to users during the installation of new software and in troubleshooting hardware and software problems. The creation of an electronic bulletin board for users is an excellent way to distribute information about common problems and allows the sharing of user-developed programs with others within the organization. Some other modern forum should provide the same benefits; for example, a chat room, threaded discussions, or FAQs and intranet support. The organization could provide a help desk, where users can call and get a quick response to questions and problems. The user services staff in many organizations teaches technical courses for end users and their computer services staff; this raises the level of user awareness and promotes the continued education of technical personnel.

Standard-Setting Body. The relatively poor control environment imposed by the DDP model can be improved by establishing some central guidance. The corporate group can contribute to this goal by establishing and distributing to user areas appropriate standards for systems development, programming, and documentation.

Personnel Review. The corporate group is probably better equipped than users to evaluate the technical credentials of prospective systems professionals. Although the systems professional will actually be part of the user group, the involvement of the corporate group in employment decisions can render a valuable service to the organization.

Audit Objectives

- Conduct a Risk Assessment of DDP IT functions
- Verify that distributed IT units employ entity-wide standards of performance that promote compatibility among hardware, software applications, and data.

Audit Procedures

- Verify that corporate policies and standards for systems design, documentation, and hardware and software acquisition are published and sent out to distributed IT units.
- Review the current organizational chart, mission statement, and job descriptions for key functions to determine if individuals or groups are performing incompatible duties.
- Verify that compensating controls such as supervision and management monitoring are employed when segregation of incompatible duties is economically infeasible.
- Review systems documentation to verify that applications, procedures, and databases are designed and functioning in accordance with corporate standards.
- Verify that individuals are granted system access privileges to programs and data in a manner consistent with their job descriptions. User rights and privileges for distributed systems and PC environments are discussed later in the chapter.

The Computer Center

The objective of this section is to present computer center controls that help create a secure environment. The discussion will begin with a look at controls designed to prevent and detect threats to the computer center. However, no matter how much is invested in control, some disasters or major disruptions to systems availability simply cannot be anticipated and prevented. What does a company do to prepare itself for such an event? How will it recover? These questions are at the heart of the organization's disaster recovery plan. The second half of this section deals with issues pertaining to the development of a disaster recovery plan.

Computer Center Controls

Accountants routinely examine the physical environment of the computer center as part of their annual audit. Exposures in these areas have a great potential impact on information, accounting records, transaction processing, and the effectiveness of other more conventional, internal controls. The following are some of the control features that contribute directly to the security of the computer center environment.

Physical Location

The physical location of the computer center directly affects the risk of disaster and unavailability. To the extent possible, the computer center should be away from human-made and natural hazards, such as processing plants, gas and water mains, airports, high-crime areas, flood plains, and geological faults. The location should be away from normal traffic flows as much as possible, such as the top floor of a building, or a separate, self-contained building. Be aware that locating the computer center in the basement of a building might create an exposure to disaster risk such as floods. The Chicago Board of Trade computer center's systems were located in the basement of a multi-storied office building in Chicago. When the century-old water pipelines burst, the building flooded part of the first floor, and all of the basement. Trade was suspended on futures for several days until system functionality could be restored, causing the loss of millions of dollars. This disaster would not have affected Chicago Trade's computer center and information systems if they had simply been located on the top floor—still away from normal traffic flows, but also away from the risk of flood.

Construction

Ideally, a computer center should be located in a single-story building of solid construction with controlled access (discussed shortly). Utility (power and telephone) and communications lines should be underground. The building windows should not open. An air filtration system should be in place that is capable of excluding pollens, dust, and dust mites. If the computer center must be located in a multi-storied building, it should be located on the top floor, if possible.

Access

Access to the computer center should be limited to the operators and other employees who work there. Physical controls, such as locked doors, should be employed to limit access to the center. The main entrance to the computer center should be through a single locked door (accessible only by use of a keypad or swipe card, preferably), though fire exits with alarms are necessary. To achieve a higher level of security, access should be monitored by closed-circuit cameras and video recording systems. Computer centers should also use sign-in logs for programmers and analysts who need access to correct program errors. The computer center should maintain accurate records of all such traffic by those who do not work full-time in the computer center to verify access control.

Air Conditioning

Computers function best in an air-conditioned environment. For mainframe computers, providing adequate air conditioning is often a requirement of the vendor's warranty. Computers operate best in a temperature range of 70 to 75 degrees Fahrenheit and a relative humidity of 50 percent. Logic errors can occur in computer hardware when temperatures depart significantly from this optimal range. Also, the risk of circuit damage from static electricity is increased when humidity drops. High humidity, by contrast, can cause molds to grow and paper products (such as source documents) to swell and jam equipment. Even a group of PCs will generate a lot of heat, and thus rooms filled with PCs need special air conditioning as well.

Fire Suppression

The most common natural disaster-type threat to a firm's computer equipment is from fire. Half of companies that suffer fires go out of business because of the loss of critical records, such as accounts receivable. The implementation of an effective fire suppression system requires consultation with specialists. However, some of the major features of such a system include the following:

1. Automatic and manual alarms should be placed in strategic locations around the installation. These alarms should be connected to permanently staffed fire-fighting stations.
2. There must be an automatic fire extinguishing system that dispenses the appropriate type of suppressant for the location.[1] For example, spraying water and certain chemicals on a computer can do as much damage as the fire.
3. Manual fire extinguishers should be placed at strategic locations.
4. The building should be of sound construction to withstand water damage caused by fire suppression equipment.
5. Fire exits should be clearly marked and illuminated during a fire.

Power Supply

Commercially provided electrical power presents several problems that can disrupt the computer center operations, including total power failures, brownouts, power fluctuations, and frequency variations. The equipment used to control these problems includes voltage regulators, surge protectors, generators, and batteries. The extent and configuration of control equipment needed will depend on the firm's ability to withstand such disruptions and the power company's record for providing reliable service. Voltage regulators and surge protectors provide regulated electricity, related to the level of electricity (frequency), and "clean" electricity related to spikes and other potential hazards associated with electricity. Power outages and brownouts can generally be controlled with a battery backup (known as uninterruptible power

1 Some fire-fighting gases, such as halon, have been outlawed by the federal government. Make sure any gas used does not violate federal law.

supply). The decision regarding power controls can be an expensive one, and usually requires the advice and analysis of experts.

Audit Objectives

The overall objective regarding computer center controls is to evaluate those controls governing computer center security. Specifically, the auditor should verify that

- Physical security controls are adequate to reasonably protect the organization from physical exposures
- Insurance coverage on equipment is adequate to compensate the organization for the destruction of, or damage to, its computer center
- Operator documentation is adequate to deal with system failures

Audit Procedures

The following are tests of physical security controls.

Tests of Physical Construction. The auditor should determine that the computer center is solidly built of fireproof material. There should be adequate drainage under the raised floor to allow water to flow away in the event of water damage from a fire in an upper floor or from some other source. In addition, the auditor should evaluate the physical location of the computer center. The facility should be located in an area that minimizes its exposure from fire, civil unrest, and other hazards.

Tests of the Fire Detection System. The auditor should establish that fire detection and suppression equipment, both manual and automatic, are in place and are tested regularly. The fire detection system should detect smoke, heat, and combustible fumes. The adequacy of these devices can be determined by reviewing official fire marshal records of tests that are stored at the computer center.

Tests of Access Control. The auditor must establish that routine access to the computer center is restricted to authorized employees. Details about visitor access (by programmers and others), such as arrival and departure times, purpose, and frequency of access, can be obtained by reviewing the access log. To establish the veracity of this document, the auditor may covertly observe the process by which access is permitted, or review videotapes from cameras at the access point, if they are being used.

Tests of the Backup Power Supply. The computer center should perform periodic tests of the backup power supply to ensure that it has sufficient capacity to run the computer and air conditioning. These are extremely important tests, and their results should be formally recorded. As a firm's computer systems develop, and its dependency increases, its backup power needs are likely to grow proportionally. Indeed, without such tests, an organization may be unaware that it has outgrown its backup capacity until it is too late.

Tests for Insurance Coverage. The auditor should annually review the organization's insurance coverage on its computer hardware, software, and physical facility. New acquisitions should be listed on the policy and obsolete equipment and software should be deleted. The extent of coverage should reflect management's needs and objectives. For example, the firm may wish to be partially self-insured.

Tests of Operator Documentation Controls. The auditor should verify that systems documentation, such as systems flowcharts, logic flowcharts, and program code listings, are not part of the operation documentation. Operators should not have access to the operational details of a system's internal logic. However, the auditor should determine that adequate user documentation is available, or an adequate help desk function is in place, to reduce the number of errors in operating systems.

In legacy systems, computer operators use a *run manual* to perform certain functions. For example, large batch systems may require special attention from operators. During the course of the day, computer operators may execute dozens of computer programs, each of which processes multiple files and produces multiple reports. To achieve effective data processing operations, the run manual must be sufficiently detailed to guide operators in their tasks. The auditor should review the run manual for completeness and accuracy. Typical contents of a run manual include the following:

- The name of the system, such as Purchases System
- The run schedule (daily, weekly, time of day)
- Required hardware devices (tapes, disks, printers, or special hardware)
- File requirements specifying all the transaction (input) files, master files, and output files used in the system
- Run-time instructions describing the error messages that may appear, actions to be taken, and the name and telephone number of the programmer on call, should the system fail.
- A list of users who receive the output from the run

Disaster Recovery Planning

Figure 2-6 depicts three types of events that can disrupt or destroy the organization's computer center and information system(s). They are natural disasters, human-made disasters, and system failure (see Figure 2-6).

The results of natural disasters, such as fires, floods, wind, and earthquakes, are usually catastrophic to the computer center and information systems, even though the probability of such an occurrence is remote. Sometimes disastrous events cannot be prevented or evaded. Examples include hurricanes in Florida, widespread flooding in the Midwest, earthquakes in California, and the bombing of public buildings. The survival of a firm affected by such disasters depends on how well and how quickly it reacts. With careful contingency planning, the full impact of a disaster can be absorbed and the organization can still recover. Human-made disasters, such as sabotage or error, can be just as destructive. System failures, such as power outages or a hard-drive failure, are generally more limited in scope, but are the most likely disaster-type event to occur.

All of these disasters can deprive an organization of its data processing facilities, halt those business functions that are performed or aided by computers, and impair the organization's ability to deliver its products or services; that is, the company loses its ability to do business. The disaster could also result in the loss of investment in technologies and systems. The more a company is dependent on technology, systems, and the computer center, the more important disaster recovery planning is to that firm.

For many companies, such as Amazon.com or eBay.com, even the loss of a few hours of computer processing capabilities can spell disaster. To survive such an event, companies develop recovery procedures and formalize them into a business

FIGURE 2-6

Types of Disasters

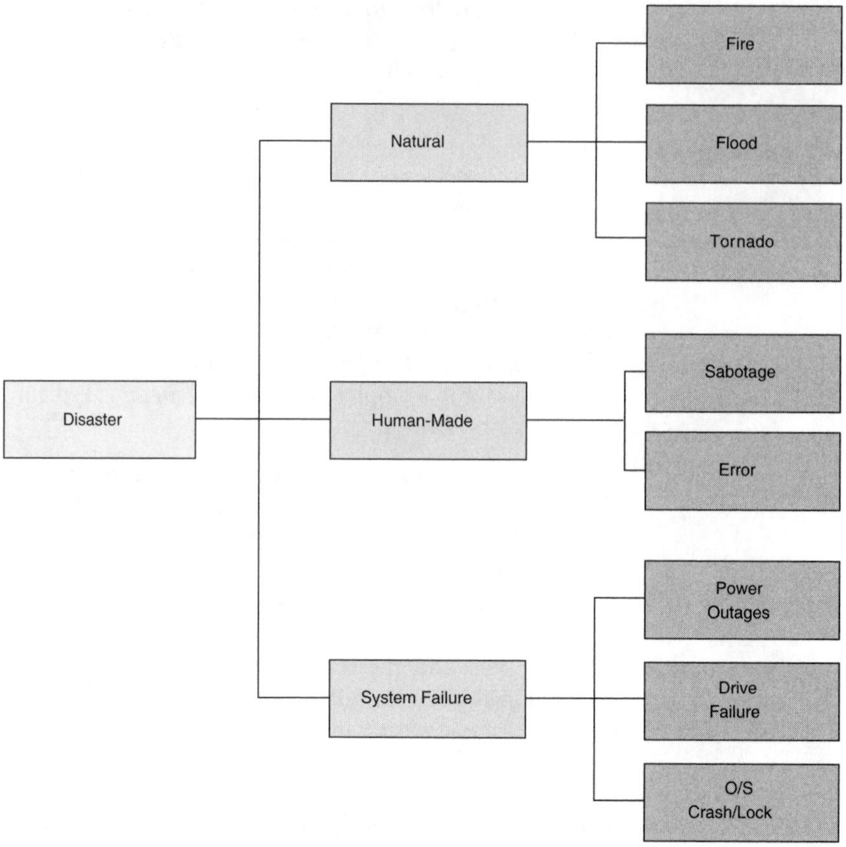

continuity plan, disaster recovery plan, or business recovery plan.[2] A **Disaster Recovery Plan (DRP)** is a comprehensive statement of all actions to be taken before, during and after any type of disaster, along with documented, tested procedures that will ensure the continuity of operations. For system failures, fault tolerance controls can help prevent a disaster, or minimize the deleterious results of a specific failure (see the section on "Fault Tolerance" for more information). Although the details of each plan are unique to the needs of the organization, all workable plans possess three common features:

1. Identifying critical applications
2. Creating a disaster recovery team
3. Providing site backup

The remainder of this section is devoted to a discussion of the essential elements of an effective DRP.

Identifying Critical Applications

The first essential element of a DRP is to identify the firm's critical applications and associated data files. Recovery efforts must concentrate on restoring those applications

2 These terms are all used to identify similar formal plans, but this book will use only disaster recovery plan.

that are critical to the short-run survival of the organization. Obviously, over the long term, all applications must be restored to pre-disaster business activity levels. However, the DRP should not attempt to restore the organization's entire data processing facility to full capacity. Rather, the plan should focus on short-run survival. In any disaster scenario, it is the firm's short-run survivability that is at risk.

For most organizations, short-term survival requires the restoration of those functions that generate cash flows sufficient to satisfy short-term obligations. For example, assume that the following items affect the cash flow position of a particular firm:

- Customer sales and service
- Fulfillment of legal obligations
- Accounts receivable maintenance and collection
- Production and distribution decisions
- Purchasing functions
- Communications between branches or agencies
- Public relations

The computer applications that support these items directly are critical. Hence, these applications should be so identified and prioritized in the restoration plan.

Application priorities may change over time, and these decisions must be reassessed regularly. Systems are constantly revised and expanded to reflect changes in user requirements. Similarly, the DRP must be updated to reflect new developments and identify critical applications. Up-to-date priorities are important, because they affect other aspects of the strategic plan. For example, changes in application priorities may cause changes in the nature and extent of second-site backup requirements and specific backup procedures.

The task of identifying critical items and prioritizing applications requires the active participation of user departments, accountants, and auditors. Too often, this task is incorrectly viewed as a technical computer issue and therefore delegated to systems professionals. Although the technical assistance of a systems professional will be required, this task is a business decision and should be made by those best equipped to understand the problem.

Creating a Disaster Recovery Team

Recovering from a disaster depends on timely corrective action. Failure to perform essential tasks (such as obtaining backup files for critical applications) prolongs the recovery period and diminishes the prospects for a successful recovery. To avoid serious omissions or duplication of effort during implementation of the contingency plan, task responsibility must be clearly defined and communicated to the personnel involved.

Figure 2-7 presents an organizational chart depicting the composition of a disaster recovery team. The team members should be experts in their areas and have assigned tasks. Following a disaster, team members will delegate subtasks to their subordinates. It should be noted that traditional control concerns do not apply in this setting. The environment created by the disaster may make it necessary to violate control techniques, such as segregation of duties, access controls, and supervision.

Providing Site Backup

A necessary ingredient in a DRP is that it provide for duplicate data processing facilities following a disaster. Among the options available are hot site (Recovery

FIGURE 2-7

Disaster Recovery Team

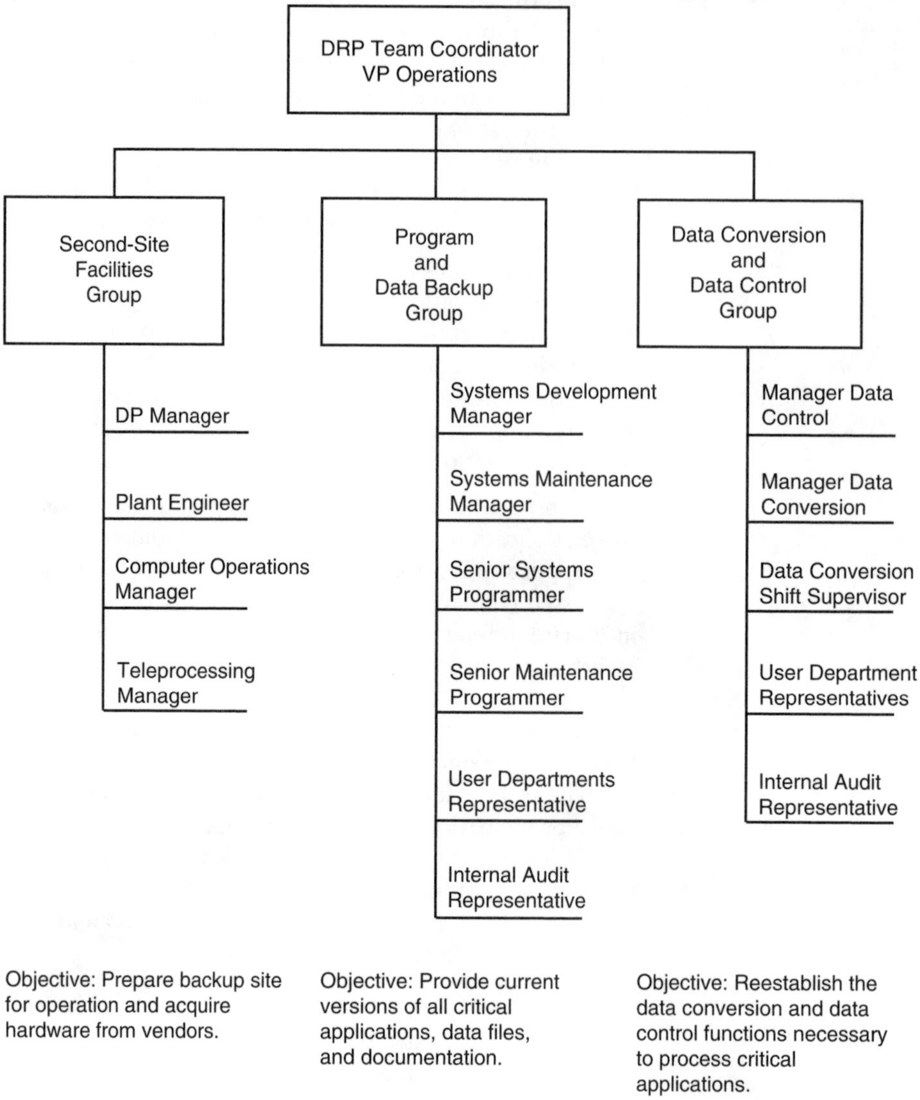

Operations Center), cold site (empty shell), mutual aid pact, internally provided backup, and others.

Hot Site/Recovery Operations Center. One approach to contracting for a backup site is the completely equipped *Hot Site* or *Recovery Operations Center (ROC)*. Because of the heavy investment involved, hot sites are typically shared among many companies. These firms either buy shares in or become subscribers to the hot site, paying a monthly fee for rights to its use. That situation does provide some risk in this approach for the simple reason that a widespread natural disaster will affect numerous entities in the same general geographic area. If multiple entities share the same ROC, some firm or firms will end up queued in a waiting line.

Hot sites may be tailor-equipped to serve the needs of their members, or they may be designed to accommodate a wide range of computer systems. The advantage of the hot site option over the cold site option is a vastly reduced initial recovery period. Hot sites have facilities, furniture, equipment (hardware) and even operating systems available. It can even be arranged for the system to be on and running all the time. That is, hot site facilities are ready for use. In the event of a major disruption, a subscriber can occupy the premises and, within a few hours, resume processing critical applications.

Cold Site/Empty Shell. A variation on the hot site approach is the cold site, or empty shell, option. Growing in popularity, this arrangement usually involves two or more user organizations that buy or lease a building and remodel it into a computer site, but without the computer and peripheral equipment. For example, shells are normally equipped with raised floors and air conditioning. In the event of a disaster, the shell is available and ready to receive whatever hardware the temporary user requires to run its essential data processing systems.

Although an improvement over the mutual aid pact, the empty shell approach has two major problems. First, recovery depends on the timely availability of the necessary computer hardware to restore the data processing function. Management must obtain assurances from hardware vendors that the vendor will give priority to meeting the organization's needs in the event of a disaster. An unanticipated hardware supply problem at this critical juncture could be a fatal blow.

The second problem with this approach is the potential for competition among users for the shell resources, the same as for a hot site. For example, a widespread natural disaster, such as a flood or earthquake, may destroy the data-processing capabilities of several shell members located in the same geographic area. Those affected by the disaster would be faced with a second major problem: how to allocate the limited facilities of the shell among them. The situation is analogous to a sinking ship that has an inadequate number of lifeboats. What equitable criteria should be used for assigning lifeboat seats?

The period of confusion following a disaster is not an ideal time to negotiate such property rights. Therefore, before entering into an arrangement to share the cost of shell facilities, management, accountants, and auditors should consider the potential problems of overcrowding and geographic clustering of members. Quotas limiting the number of members by size of firm and geographic location should provide effective control.

Mutual Aid Pact. A mutual aid pact is an agreement between two or more organizations (with compatible computer facilities) to aid each other with their data processing needs in the event of a disaster. In such an event, the host company must disrupt its processing schedule to process the critical applications of the disaster-stricken company. In effect, the host company itself must go into an emergency operation mode (and cut back on the processing of its lower-priority applications) to accommodate the sudden increase in demand for its IT resources.

Reciprocal agreements of this sort are a popular option. This fact is partly because they are relatively cost-free (as long as no disaster occurs) and provide some degree of psychological comfort. In fact, plans of this sort tend to work better in theory than in practice. To rely on such an arrangement for substantive relief during a disaster requires a level of faith and untested trust that is uncharacteristic of sophisticated management and its auditors.

Internally Provided Backup. Larger organizations with multiple data processing centers may prefer self-reliance provided by creating internal excess capacity. This option permits firms to develop standardized hardware and software configurations, which ensure functional compatibility among their data processing centers and minimize cut over problems in the event of a disaster. Basically, internally provided backup is similar to a mutual aid pact between branches of the same entity.

Hardware Backup. If the entity is using the cold site method of providing a backup site, then the entity must secure some assurance that equipment in the form of computer hardware will be readily available in case of an emergency.

Software Backup: Operating System. If the company uses a cold site or other method of backup site that does not include a compatible operating system (O/S), then the DRP must include a procedure to make a copy of the entity's operating system readily accessible in case of a disaster. This objective could be accomplished by keeping a valid, current copy of the O/S at or near the backup site. The data librarian, if one exists, would be a key person to involve in meeting this procedure, and the applications and data backups that follow.

Software Backup: Applications. Based on the critical applications step, the DRP should include a procedure to provide copies of the critical applications' software. Again, this procedure could be accomplished by providing adequate copies of the critical applications at or near the backup site.

Backup Data Files. Databases should be copied daily to high-capacity, high-speed media, such as tape or CDs/DVDs, and secured off-site. In the event of a disruption, reconstruction of the database is achieved by updating the most current backed-up version with subsequent transaction data. Likewise, master files and transaction files should be protected. Techniques for data backup were discussed earlier. Once again, this resource could be stored close to or at the backup site. In fact, keeping copies of the data backup in the DRP off-site could be integrated with the enterprise backup procedures.

Backup Documentation. The system documentation for critical applications should be backed up and stored off-site in much the same manner as data files. The large volumes of material involved and constant application revisions complicate the task. The process can be made more efficient through the use of CASE documentation tools. The DRP should also include a provision for copies of user manuals to be readily available.

Backup Supplies and Source Documents. The firm should provide backup inventories of supplies and source documents used in critical applications. Examples of critical supplies are check stocks, invoices, purchase orders, and any other special-purpose forms that cannot be obtained immediately. The DRP should specify the types and quantities needed of these special items. Because they are such an integral part of the daily operations, these items are often overlooked by disaster contingency planners. At this point, it is worth noting that a copy of the current DRP document should also be stored off-site at a secure location.

Testing the DRP. The most neglected aspect of contingency planning is testing the plans. Nevertheless, DRP tests are important and should be performed periodically.

Tests measure the preparedness of personnel and identify omissions or bottlenecks in the plan.

A test is most useful when the simulation of a disruption is a surprise. When the mock disaster is announced, the status of all processing affected by it should be documented. This approach provides a benchmark for subsequent performance assessments. The plan should be carried through as far as is economically feasible. Ideally, that would include the use of backup facilities and supplies.

The progress of the plan should be noted at key points throughout the test period. At the conclusion of the test, the results can then be analyzed and a DRP performance report prepared. The degree of performance achieved provides input for decisions to modify the DRP or schedule additional tests. The organization's management should seek measures of performance in each of the following areas: (1) the effectiveness of DRP team personnel and their knowledge levels, (2) the degree of conversion success (i.e., the number of lost records), (3) an estimate of financial loss due to lost records or facilities, and (4) the effectiveness of program, data, and documentation backup and recovery procedures.

Audit Objective. Verify that the organization's disaster recovery plan (DRP) is adequate to meet the needs of the organization and that implementation is feasible and practical.

Audit Procedures. Verify that management's DRP is a realistic solution for dealing with a catastrophe that could deprive the organization of its computer resources. The following tests focus on areas of greatest concern.

Site Backup. The auditor should evaluate the adequacy of the backup site arrangement. System incompatibility and human nature can both greatly reduce the effectiveness of the mutual aid pact. Auditors should be skeptical of such arrangements for two reasons. First, the sophistication of the computer system can make it difficult to find a potential partner with an identical or even a compatible configuration. Second, most firms do not have the necessary excess capacity to support a disaster-stricken partner while also processing their own work. When it comes to the crunch, the management of the firm untouched by disaster may have little appetite for the sacrifices that must be made to honor the agreement.

More viable but expensive alternatives to the mutual aid pact are the empty shell and the hot site or recovery operation center. These too must be examined carefully. The auditor should be concerned about the number of members in these arrangements and their geographic dispersion. A widespread disaster may create a demand that cannot be satisfied by the backup facility.

Critical Application List. The auditor should review the list of critical applications to ensure that it is complete. Missing applications can result in failure to recover. However, the same is true for restoring unnecessary applications. To include applications on the critical list that are not needed to achieve short-term survival can misdirect resources and distract attention from the primary objective during the recovery period.

Software Backup—Applications. The auditor should verify that copies of critical programs are stored off-site. In the event of a disaster or system failure, the production applications can then be reconstructed from the backup versions.

Data Backup. The auditor should verify that critical data files are backed up in accordance with the DRP. Data backup procedures were discussed in the examination of data resource controls.

Backup Supplies, Documents, and Documentation. The system documentation, supplies, and source documents that are needed to restore and run critical applications should be backed up and stored off-site. The auditor should verify that the types and quantities of items specified in the DRP exist in a secure location. Examples of critical supplies are check stock, invoices, purchase orders, and any other special-purpose forms that cannot be obtained immediately.

Disaster Recovery Team. The DRP should clearly list the names, addresses, and emergency telephone numbers of the disaster recovery team members. The auditor should verify that members of the team are current employees and are aware of their assigned responsibilities. On one occasion, while reviewing a firm's DRP, the author discovered that a team leader listed in the plan had been deceased for nine months.

Fault Tolerance Controls

Fault tolerance is the ability of the system to continue operation when part of the system fails due to hardware failure, application program error, or operator error. According to one of the Big Four accounting firms, 44 percent of the time a system is down is due to system failure—a far greater percentage than natural disaster or human disaster. Various levels of fault tolerance can be achieved by implementing redundant system components:

1. *Redundant arrays of inexpensive (or independent) disks (RAID).* There are several types of RAID configurations. Essentially, each method involves the use of parallel disks that contain redundant elements of data and applications. If one disk fails, the lost data are automatically reconstructed from the redundant components stored on the other disks.
2. *Uninterruptible power supplies.* In the event of a power outage, short-term battery backup power is provided to allow the system to shut down in a controlled manner. This process will prevent data loss and corruption that would otherwise result from an uncontrolled system crash.
3. *Multiprocessing.* The simultaneous use of two or more processors improves throughput under normal operation. During a processor failure, the redundant processors balance the workload and provide complete backup.

Implementing fault tolerance control ensures that there is no single point of potential system failure. Total failure can occur only in the event of the failure of multiple components.

Audit Objective

- Ensure that the organization is employing an appropriate level of fault tolerance.

Audit Procedures

- Most systems that employ RAID provide a graphical mapping of their redundant disk storage. From this mapping, the auditor should determine if the level of RAID in place is adequate for the organization, given the level of business risk associated with disk failure.

- If the organization is not employing RAID, the potential for a single point of system failure exists. The auditor should review with the system administrator alternative procedures for recovering from a disk failure.
- Determine that copies of boot disks have been made for each server on the network in the event of a boot sector failure. Since boot disks can be used to bypass the normal boot process, they should be secured and access to them restricted to the system administrator.

Operating Systems and System-Wide Controls

The **operating system** is the computer's control program. It allows users and their applications to share and access common computer resources, such as processors, main memory, databases, and printers. The modern accountant needs to recognize the operating system's role in the overall control picture to properly assess the risks that threaten the accounting system.

If operating system integrity is compromised, controls within individual accounting applications may also be circumvented or neutralized. Because the operating system is common to all users, the larger the computer facility, the greater the scale of potential damage. Thus, with more and more computer resources being shared by an ever-expanding user community, operating system security becomes an important control issue.

The operating system performs three main tasks. First, it translates high-level languages, such as COBOL, BASIC, C languages, and SQL, into the machine-level language that the computer can execute. The language translator modules of the operating system are called **compilers** and **interpreters**. The control implications of language translators are examined later in the chapter.

Second, the operating system allocates computer resources to users, workgroups, and applications. This task includes assigning memory workspace (partitions) to applications and authorizing access to terminals, telecommunications links, databases, and printers.

Third, the operating system manages the tasks of job scheduling and multiprogramming. At any point in time, numerous user applications (jobs) are seeking access to the computer resources under the control of the operating system. Jobs are submitted to the system in three ways: (1) directly by the system operator, (2) from various batch-job queues, and (3) through telecommunications links from remote workstations. To achieve efficient and effective use of finite computer resources, the operating system must schedule job processing according to established priorities and balance the use of resources among the competing applications.

To perform these tasks consistently and reliably, the operating system must achieve five fundamental control objectives:[3]

1. *The operating system must protect itself from users.* User applications must not be able to gain control of, or damage in any way, the operating system, thus causing it to cease running or destroy data.

---

3 F.M. Stepczyk, "Requirements for Secure Operating Systems," *Data Security and Data Processing*, vol. 5; Study Results: TRW Systems, Inc., (New York: IBM Corporation, 1974), pp. 25–73.

2. *The operating system must protect users from each other.* One user must not be able to access, destroy, or corrupt the data or programs of another user.
3. *The operating system must protect users from themselves.* A user's application may consist of several modules stored in separate memory locations, each with its own data. One module must not be allowed to destroy or corrupt another module.
4. *The operating system must be protected from itself.* The operating system is also made up of individual modules. No module should be allowed to destroy or corrupt another module.
5. *The operating system must be protected from its environment.* In the event of a power failure or other disaster, the operating system should be able to achieve a controlled termination of activities from which it can later recover.

Operating System Security

Operating system security involves policy, procedures, and controls that determine who can access the operating system, which resources (files, programs, printers) they can access, and what actions they can take. The following security components are found in secure operating systems: logon procedure, access tokens, access control list, and discretionary access control.

Logon Procedure

A formal **logon procedure** is the operating system's first line of defense against unauthorized access. When the user initiates the process, he or she is presented with a dialog box requesting the user's ID and password. The system compares the ID and password to a database of valid users. If the system finds a match, then the logon attempt is authenticated. If, however, the password or ID is entered incorrectly, the logon attempt fails and a message is returned to the user. The message should not reveal whether the password or the ID caused the failure. The system should allow the user to reenter the logon information. After a specified number of attempts (usually no more than five), the system should lock out the user from the system.

Access Token

If the logon attempt is successful, the operating system creates an access token that contains key information about the user, including user ID, password, user group, and privileges granted to the user. The information in the access token is used to approve all actions attempted by the user during the session.

Access Control List

Access to system resources such as directories, files, programs, and printers is controlled by an **access control list** assigned to each resource. These lists contain information that define the access privileges for all valid users of the resource. When a user attempts to access a resource, the system compares his or her ID and privileges contained in the access token with those contained in the access control list. If there is a match, the user is granted access.

Discretionary Access Control

The central system administrator usually determines who is granted access to specific resources and maintains the access control list. In distributed systems, however, resources may be controlled (owned) by end users. Resource owners in this setting may be granted **discretionary access control**, which allows them to grant access privileges to other users. For example, the controller, who is the owner of the general ledger, grants read-only privileges to a manager in the budgeting department. The accounts payable manager, however, is granted both read and write permission to the ledger. Any attempt by the budgeting manager to add, delete, or change the general ledger will be denied. The use of discretionary access control needs to be closely supervised to prevent security breaches due to its liberal use.

Threats to Operating System Integrity

Operating system control objectives are sometimes not achieved because of flaws in the operating system that are exploited either accidentally or intentionally. Accidental threats include hardware failures that cause the operating system to crash. Operating system failures are also caused by errors in user application programs that the operating system cannot interpret. Accidental system failures may cause whole segments of memory to be "dumped" to disks and printers, resulting in the unintentional disclosure of confidential information.

Intentional threats to the operating system are most commonly attempts to illegally access data or violate user privacy for financial gain. However, a growing form of threat is from destructive programs that create no apparent gain. These exposures come from three sources:

1. *Privileged personnel who abuse their authority.* Systems administrators and systems programmers require unlimited access to the operating system to perform maintenance and to recover from system failures. Such individuals may use this authority to access users' programs and data files.
2. *Individuals who browse the operating system to identify and exploit security flaws.* They can be either internal and external to the organization.
3. *An individual who inserts a computer virus or other form of destructive program into the operating system.* Sometimes this is accidental (e.g., bringing in a disk from home that contains a virus or downloading an infected game from the Internet). Other times it is intentional, and the virus is deliberately introduced to the operating system.

System-Wide Controls

The remainder of this section describes a variety of system-wide threats and control issues. The audit ramifications associated with them are discussed.

Controlling Access Privileges

User access privileges are assigned to individuals and to entire workgroups authorized to use the system. Privileges determine which directories, files, applications, and other resources an individual or group may access. They also determine the types of actions that can be taken. Recall that the system administrator or the owner of the resource may assign privileges. Management should be concerned that individuals are not granted privileges that are incompatible with their assigned duties. Consider, for example, a cash receipts clerk who is granted the right to access and make changes to the accounts receivable file.

Overall system security is influenced by the way access privileges are assigned. Privileges should, therefore, be carefully administered and closely monitored for compliance with organizational policy and principles of internal control.

Audit Objective

- Verify that access privileges are granted in a manner that is consistent with the need to separate incompatible functions and is in accordance with organizational policy.

Audit Procedures

- Review the organization's policies for separating incompatible functions and ensure that they promote reasonable security.
- Review the privileges of a selection of user groups and individuals to determine if their access rights are appropriate for their job descriptions and positions. The auditor should verify that individuals are granted access to data and programs based on their need to know.
- Review personnel records to determine whether privileged employees undergo an adequately intensive security clearance check in compliance with company policy.
- Review employee records to determine whether users have formally acknowledged their responsibility to maintain the confidentiality of company data.
- Review the users' permitted logon times. Permission should be commensurate with the tasks being performed.

Password Controls

A **password** is a secret code entered by the user to gain access to systems, applications, data files, or a network server. If the user cannot provide the correct password, the operating system will deny access. The foundation of access control and logon procedures is the effective use of a password system of controls. Access control is something you know (a password), something you have (e.g., a smartcard), or something you are (a biometric). But just having a password is not necessarily effective. The choice of the actual password content is important, as is the management of passwords and the processes used in the access control system.

While passwords can provide a degree of security, when imposed on nonsecurity-minded users, password procedures can result in end-user behavior that actually circumvents security. The most common forms of contra-security behavior include:

- Forgetting passwords and being locked out of the system.
- Failing to change passwords on a frequent basis.
- The post-it syndrome, whereby passwords are written down and displayed for others to see.
- Simplistic passwords that are easily anticipated by a computer criminal.

It is very costly to change passwords. According to Mandylion Research Labs, resetting a password security system of a company with 100 workers would cost $3,850 per year. If the company has 1,000 authorized personnel, the same process would cost up to $38,500 per year! A Post-It note with a password written on it is obviously a high-risk behavior. It is becoming more and more important to strengthen the actual password content as hacker tools are readily available to guess passwords. For example, hacker tools can be used to try every word in the dictionary in a matter of minutes in an attempt to gain unauthorized access. Therefore, if a password is a word or name in the dictionary, it is easily "hacked."

Reusable Passwords

The most common method of password control is the reusable password. The user defines the password to the system once and then reuses it to gain future access. Most operating systems set only basic standards for password acceptability. The quality of the security provided by a reusable password depends on the quality of the password itself. If the password pertains to something personal about the user, such as a child's name, pet's name, birthdate, or hair color, it can be deduced by a computer criminal. Even if the password is derived from nonpersonal data, such as a string of keystrokes (such as A-S-D-F) or the same letter used multiple times, the computer criminal can use a frequency table to run through the most common passwords very quickly. Reusable passwords that contain random letters and digits are more difficult to crack, but are also more difficult for the user to remember.

To improve access control, management should discourage the use of weak passwords. Inexpensive software is available that automatically scans password files and notifies the security administrator when weak passwords are detected, thus assuring that only smart passwords are used on the network. An alternative to the standard reusable password is the one-time password.

One-Time Password

The one-time password was designed to overcome the problems just discussed. Under this approach, the user's network password constantly changes. To access the network, the user must provide both a secret reusable personal identification number (PIN) and the current one-time only password for that point in time. The problem, of course, is how to advise the valid user of the current password?

One technology employs a credit-card-sized device (smart card) that contains a microprocessor programmed with an algorithm that generates, and electronically displays, a new and unique password every 60 seconds. The card works in conjunction with special authentication software located on the server. Each user's card is synchronized to the authentication software, so that at any point in time both the smart card and the network software are generating the same password for the same user.

To access the network, the user enters the PIN followed by the current password displayed on the card. The password can be used one time only. If, for example, a computer hacker intercepts the password and PIN during transmission and attempts to use them within the one-minute time frame, access will be denied. Also, if the smart card should fall into the hands of a computer criminal, access cannot be achieved without the PIN.

Password Policy

Executive management and IS management should devise an effective password policy based on these risks and potential controls. A suggested policy is found in

Table 2-1. This policy starts with communication. Management needs a means to make sure all employees and users are aware of the password policy. That means could be accomplished in the employee orientation program, if the entity has one. The password length should also be stipulated. The longer the content of the password, the more difficult it is to break (if it is not a word in the dictionary). Strong passwords, by definition, require numbers and special characters in addition to letters, and a minimum length of eight characters, and no word found in the dictionary contained in the password. Adding other devices or processes in the access control reduces risk of unauthorized or unauthenticated use of the entity's systems. For instance, smart cards, biometrics, and short-lived PIN numbers are options to consider. So is the usage of multilevel passwords as the user goes through different areas of the system. Users should be required to change their password regularly; 90 days is probably the most common time limit. The policy should prohibit the sharing of passwords, deliberate or inadvertent. And IT should be required to delete passwords immediately when an employee is terminated, and especially if the employee is disgruntled.

Audit Objectives

- Ensure that the organization has an adequate and effective password policy for controlling access to the operating system.

Audit Procedures

- Verify that all users are required to have passwords.
- Verify that new users are instructed in the use of passwords and the importance of password control.

TABLE 2-1

Password Policy

Proper Dissemination: Promote it, use it during employee training or orientation, and find ways to continue to raise awareness within the organization.

Proper Length: Use at least eight characters. The more characters, the more difficult to guess or crack. Eight characters is an effective length to prevent guessing, if combined with below.

Proper Strength: Use alphabet (letters), numbers (at least 1), and special characters (at least 1). The more non-alpha, the harder to guess or crack. Make them case sensitive and mix upper and lower case. A "strong" password for any critical access or key user. Password CANNOT contain a real word in the content.

Proper Access Levels or Complexity: Use multiple levels of access requiring multiple passwords. Use a password matrix of data to grant read-only, read/write, or no access per data field per user. Use biometrics (such as fingerprints, voice prints). Use supplemental access devices, such as smart cards, or beeper passwords in conjunction with remote logins. Use user-defined procedures.

Proper Timely Changes: At regular intervals, make employees change their passwords.

Proper Protection: Prohibit the sharing of passwords or Post-Its with passwords located near one's computer.

Proper Deletion: Require the immediate deletion of accounts for terminated employees, to prevent an employee who becomes disgruntled from being able to perpetrate adverse activities.

SOURCE: Derived from Cangemi, M. & T. Singleton, *Managing the Audit Function*, 3e, 2003, John Wiley & Sons: NY.

- Determine that procedures are in place to identify weak passwords. This may involve the use of software for scanning password files on a regular basis.
- Assess the adequacy of password standards such as length and expiration interval.
- Review the account lockout policy and procedures. Most operating systems allow the system administrator to define the action to be taken after a certain number of failed logon attempts. The auditor should determine how many failed-logon attempts are allowed before the account is locked. The duration of the lockout also needs to be determined. This could range from a few minutes to a permanent lockout that requires formal reactivation of the account.

Controlling Against Malicious Objects and E-Mail Risks

Controlling Against E-Mail Risks

Electronic mail (e-mail) is the most popular Internet function, and millions of messages circulate the globe each day. Most organizations receive e-mail, even if they do not have their own e-mail servers. But e-mail presents risks inherent in its use that the auditor must consider. A significant risk to the enterprise system is an infection from an emerging virus or worm. Viruses are spread most commonly via attachments to e-mail. The author hides the intent carefully, and more often than not, will use the address book of victims to send messages to his/her contacts as if from the victim, and thus deceiving the second series of recipients. This process makes the e-mail attachment look legitimate, and even has a legitimate and familiar return e-mail address.

Viruses are responsible for millions of dollars of corporate losses annually. There have been occasions where a single virus cost millions of dollars by itself. The losses are measured in terms of data corruption and destruction, degraded computer performance, hardware destruction, violations of privacy, and the personnel time devoted to repairing the damage. The discussion that follows outlines some of the more common types of malicious programs and other e-mail related concerns.

Virus

A **virus** is a program (usually destructive) that attaches itself to a legitimate program to penetrate the operating system. The virus destroys application programs, data files, and operating systems in a number of ways. One common technique is for the virus to simply replicate itself over and over within the main memory, thus destroying whatever data or programs are resident. One of the most insidious aspects of a virus is its ability to spread throughout the system and to other systems before perpetrating its destructive acts. Typically, a virus will have a built-in counter that will inhibit its destructive role until the virus has copied itself a specified number of times to other programs and systems. The virus thus grows geometrically, which makes tracing its origin extremely difficult.

Microcomputers are a major source of virus penetration. When connected in a network or a mainframe, an infected microcomputer can upload the virus to the host computer. Once in the host, the virus can spread throughout the operating system and to other users.

Due to the heavy dependency on connectivity, the proliferation of microcomputers, and the need for extensive application programming, it may be impossible to eliminate the threat of viruses from the modern business environment. Sometimes, viruses are created internally by disgruntled employees in positions of power. At other times, they are created outside the organization and are brought inside by unsuspecting users with legitimate access privileges to the system. Understanding how viruses work and how they are passed between systems is critical to their effective control.

Virus programs usually attach themselves to the following types of files:

1. An .EXE or .COM program file
2. An .OVL (overlay) program file
3. The boot sector of a disk
4. A device driver program
5. An operating system file (e.g., DLL)

When a virus-infected program is executed, the virus searches the system for uninfected programs and copies itself into these programs. The virus may thus spread to the applications of other users or to the operating system itself.

Personal computers are the most common source of virus infestation. Their proliferation in business and society, combined with their relatively unsophisticated operating systems, has created a fertile environment in which viruses can grow and spread. A contributing factor to the spread of viruses is the sharing of programs among users. The downloading of public-domain programs from network bulletin boards and the exchange of illegal 'bootleg' software are methods of virus transfer. Because of the lack of control features in microcomputer operating systems, microcomputers connected to mainframes pose a serious threat to the mainframe environment as well. For example, an application programmer may develop and test programs on a microcomputer and then upload the finished system to the mainframe. If a virus is in the microcomputer on which the program is developed, it can spread to the mainframe via the new application. When this program is executed, the virus can then spread to other applications on the mainframe.

Worm

The term **worm** is used interchangeably with virus. A worm is a software program that burrows into the computer's memory and replicates itself into areas of idle memory. The worm systematically occupies idle memory until the memory is exhausted and the system fails. Worms differ from viruses in that the replicated worm modules remain in contact with the original worm that controls their growth. The replicated virus modules, by contrast, grow independently of the initial virus.

Logic Bomb

A **logic bomb** is a destructive program, such as a virus, that is triggered by some predetermined event. Quite often a date (such as Friday the 13th, April Fool's Day, or a birthday) will be the logic bomb's trigger. The famous Michelangelo virus (triggered by his birth date) is an example of a logic bomb. Logic bombs have also been triggered by events of less public prominence, such as the dismissal of an employee. For example, during the customary two-week severance period, a terminated programmer may embed a logic bomb in the system that will activate six months after his or her departure from the firm.

Back Door

A back door (also called a *trap door*) is a software program that allows unauthorized access to a system without going through the normal (front door) logon procedure.

Programmers who want to provide themselves with unrestricted access to the programs that they are developing for users create a logon procedure that will accept both the user's private password and their own secret password, thus creating a back door to the system. The purpose of the back door may be to provide easy access to perform program maintenance, or it may be to perpetrate a fraud or insert a virus into the system.

Trojan Horse

A **Trojan horse** is a program whose purpose is to capture IDs and passwords from unsuspecting users. The program is designed to mimic the normal logon procedures of the operating system. When the user enters his or her ID and password, the Trojan horse stores a copy of them in a secret file. At some later date, the author of the Trojan horse uses these IDs and passwords to access the system and masquerade as an authorized user.

Threats from destructive programs can be substantially reduced through a combination of technology controls and administrative procedures. The following examples are relevant to most operating systems.

- Purchase software only from reputable vendors and accept only those products that are in their original, factory-sealed packages.
- Issue an entity-wide policy pertaining to the use of unauthorized software or illegal (bootleg) copies of copyrighted software.
- Examine all upgrades to vendor software for viruses before they are implemented.
- Inspect all public-domain software for virus infection before using.
- Establish entity-wide procedures for making changes to production programs. (This topic is examined in-depth in Chapter 4.)
- Establish an educational program to raise user awareness regarding threats from viruses and malicious programs.
- Install all new applications on a standalone computer and thoroughly test them with antiviral software prior to implementing them on the mainframe or LAN server.
- Routinely make backup copies of key files stored on mainframes, servers, and workstations.
- Wherever possible, limit users to read and execute rights only. This policy allows users to extract data and run authorized applications, but denies them the ability to write directly to mainframe and server directories.
- Require protocols that explicitly invoke the operating system's logon procedures in order to bypass Trojan horses. A typical scenario is one in which a user sits down to a terminal that is already displaying the logon screen and proceeds to enter his or her ID and password. This, however, may be a Trojan horse rather than the legitimate procedure. Some operating systems allow the user to directly invoke the operating system logon procedure by entering a key sequence such as CTRL + ALT + DEL. The user then knows that the logon procedure on the screen is legitimate.
- At regular intervals, scan systems. This scan uses antiviral software (also called vaccines) to examine application and operating system programs for the presence of a virus and removes them from the affected program. Antiviral programs are used to safeguard mainframes, network servers, and personal computers. Most antiviral programs run in the background on the host computer and automatically test all files that are uploaded to the host. However,

the software works only on known viruses. If a virus has been modified slightly (mutated), there is no guarantee that the vaccine will work. It is therefore important to maintain the current version of the vaccine.

Spoofing

Spoofing involves trickery that makes a message appear as if it came from an authorized individual or firm when it did not. Messages do not contain actual signatures nor are they on actual stationery. Thus it is not easy for the average person to ascertain the veracity of the sender. The intent is to fool the recipient into taking some action believing it is a legitimate request from the name at the bottom of the message. For example, a message could be broadcast to all employees using the chief executive officer's name typed at the bottom that proclaims a holiday for all employees when in reality, it was sent by someone other than the CEO. An appropriate control would be training of all employees on the signs of spoofing.

Spamming

Probably everyone who has used e-mail has received unwanted or unrequested mail. *Spam* is defined generally as any unsolicited e-mail. But spam also is associated with con-artist type requests. Such a message might offer to sell the original set of blueprints to the atomic bomb that was dropped on Hiroshima, or any other outlandish proposal. Spamming is of a concern because of the volume of messages that can fill the e-mail server and boxes, and thus clog the system with unnecessary files. It also takes time for employees to delete the messages. Anti-spam software is available to filter spam, with varying degrees of success, before the entity's e-mail server receives it.

Chain Letters

Another useless type of message is the chain letter. This type of message is usually associated with some emotional appeal to the recipient. For example, one such chain letter stated that Bill Gates would give money to deserving children based on the number of times the message was sent. Others promise discounts at Gap or other "too good to be true" stories. The objective of the author is to see how many copies of the message will circulate the globe, or how long it will take to get back to the sender. The letter always ends with a strong appeal to send the letter to all of one's friends. Chain letters, like spam, fill up e-mail boxes. Again, training or filtering of incoming e-mail could serve as controls.

Urban Legends

These stories have been around for centuries. For example, you probably heard the one about the conversation between a ship's captain and what he supposed was another ship's captain on a collision course. Each argued the other should change course. Finally, the second person informed the ship's captain that he was not also a ship's captain but rather the caretaker of a lighthouse. The stories are generally entertaining, and the last line in the message encourages the recipient to forward it on to his/her friends.

Hoax Virus Warnings

Another form of trickery is to send out hoax virus warnings. Such warnings describe the serious consequences of some non-existent virus, and end the message making an appeal to notify all your friends before they get infected. The truth is, the last statement is the author's objective: to see his message circulate the globe.

Notice that this problem and the last two have the same objective: multiplication. That last line is actually a red flag that helps to identify these three negative, and mildly malicious, types of e-mail.

Flaming

Human behavior on the Internet does not have the physical constraints of face-to-face human interaction. Therefore, many will do or say (write) things they would not do in public. *Flaming* is a message in which the writer attacks another participant in overly harsh and often personal terms. That includes making derogatory remarks about others or the organization. The risk from flaming is more serious because of federal laws regarding issues such as sexual harassment. Controls would include training and a policy prohibiting flaming with consequences if caught.

Audit Objective

- Verify that effective management policies and procedures are in place to prevent the introduction and spread of destructive objects.

Audit Procedures

- Through interviews with operations personnel, determine that they have been educated about computer viruses and are aware of the risky computing practices that can introduce and spread viruses and other malicious programs.
- Review operations procedures to determine if disks or CDs that could contain viruses are routinely used to transfer data between workgroups.
- Verify that system administrators routinely scan workstations, file servers, and e-mail servers for viruses.
- Verify that new software is tested on standalone workstations prior to being implemented on the host or network server.
- Verify that antivirus software is updated at regular intervals and downloaded to individual workstations.

Controlling Electronic Audit Trails

Audit trails are logs that can be designed to record activity at the system, application, and user level. When properly implemented, audit trails provide an important detective control to help accomplish security policy objectives. Many operating systems allow organization management to select the level of auditing to be provided by the system. This determines which events will be recorded in the log. An effective audit policy will capture all significant events without cluttering the log with trivial activity. Each organization needs to decide where the threshold between information and irrelevant facts lies. Audit trails typically consist of two types of audit logs: (1) detailed logs of individual keystrokes and (2) event-oriented logs.

Keystroke Monitoring

Keystroke monitoring involves recording both the user's keystrokes and the system's responses. This form of log may be used after the fact to reconstruct the details of an event or as a real-time control to monitor or prevent unauthorized intrusion. Keystroke monitoring is the computer equivalent of a telephone wiretap. Some situations may justify this level of surveillance. In some circumstances, however, keystroke monitoring may be regarded as a violation of privacy. Before implementing this type of control, management and auditors should consider the possible legal, ethical, and behavioral implications.

Event Monitoring

Event monitoring summarizes key activities related to users, applications, and system resources. Event logs typically record the IDs of all users accessing the system; the time and duration of a user's session; programs that were executed during a session; and the files, databases, printers, and other resources accessed.

Audit Trail Objectives

Audit trails can be used to support security objectives in three ways: (1) detecting unauthorized access to the system, (2) facilitating the reconstruction of events, and (3) promoting personal accountability.

1. *Detecting unauthorized access.* Detecting unauthorized access can occur in real time or after the fact. The primary objective of real-time detection is to protect the system from outsiders who are attempting to breach system controls. A real-time audit trail can also be used to report on changes in system performance that may indicate infestation by a virus or worm. Depending upon how much activity is being logged and reviewed, real-time detection can impose a significant overhead on the operating system, which can degrade operational performance. After-the-fact detection logs can be stored electronically and reviewed periodically or as needed. When properly designed, they can be used to determine if unauthorized access was accomplished, or attempted and failed.
2. *Reconstructing events.* Audit analysis can be used to reconstruct the steps that led to events such as system failures, security violations by individuals, or application processing errors. Knowledge of the conditions that existed at the time of a system failure can be used to assign responsibility and to avoid similar situations in the future. Audit trail analysis also plays an important role in accounting control. For example, by maintaining a record of all changes to account balances, the audit trail can be used to reconstruct accounting data files that were corrupted by a system failure.
3. *Promoting personal accountability.* Audit trails can be used to monitor user activity at the lowest level of detail. This capability is a preventive control that can be used to influence behavior. Individuals are less likely to violate an organization's security policy if they know that their actions are recorded in an audit log.

   An audit log can also serve as a detective control to assign personal accountability for actions taken that are violations of security policy. Serious errors and the abuse of authority are of particular concern. It may be easier to prevent unauthorized intruders from accessing a system than to ensure that authorized users act only in accordance with their assigned authority. For example, an accounts receivable clerk is authorized to access customer records. The audit log may disclose that the clerk has been printing an inordinate number of records, which could indicate that the clerk is selling customer information.

Implementing an Audit Trail

The information contained in audit logs is useful to accountants in measuring the potential damage and financial loss associated with application errors, abuse of authority, or unauthorized access by outside intruders. Logs also provide valuable evidence for assessing both the adequacy of controls in place and the need for additional controls. Audit logs, however, can generate data in overwhelming detail. Important information can easily get lost among the superfluous details of daily operation. Thus, poorly designed logs can actually be dysfunctional. Protecting exposures with the potential for material financial loss should drive management's decision as to which users, applications, or operations to monitor, and how much detail to log. As with all controls, the benefits of audit logs must be balanced against the costs of implementing them.

Audit Objective

- Ensure that the auditing of users and events is adequate for preventing and detecting abuses, reconstructing key events that preceded systems failures, and planning resource allocation.

Audit Procedures

Most operating systems provide some form of audit manager function to specify the events that are to be audited. The auditor should verify that the event audit trail has been activated according to organizational policy.

- Many operating systems provide an audit log viewer that allows the auditor to scan the log for unusual activity. These can be reviewed on screen or by archiving the file for subsequent review.

    The auditor can use general-purpose data extraction tools such as ACL for accessing archived log files to search for defined conditions such as:

    ✓ Unauthorized or terminated user
    ✓ Periods of inactivity
    ✓ Activity by user, workgroup, or department
    ✓ Logon and logoff times
    ✓ Failed logon attempts
    ✓ Access to specific files or applications
- The organization's security group has the responsibility to monitor and report on security violations. The auditor should select a sample of security violation cases and evaluate their disposition to assess the effectiveness of the security group.

Personal Computer Systems

This section of the chapter examines risks, controls, and audit issues related to the personal computing environment. The PC environment possesses significant features that characterize and distinguish it from the mainframe and client-server environments. The most important of these features are listed below:

- PC systems are relatively simple to operate and program and do not require extensive professional training to use.
- They frequently are controlled and operated by the end users rather than by systems administrators.
- PCs employ interactive data processing rather than batch processing.
- They typically run commercial software applications designed to minimize effort. Usually, data are entered by end users and may be uploaded to a mainframe or network server for further processing.
- Mainframe and client-server systems work behind the scenes. PCs download data from these machines for local processing.
- Users are able to develop their own software and maintain data (on spreadsheets and databases).

PC Operating Systems

The operating system is booted and resides in the computer's primary memory as long as it is turned on. The operating system has several functions. It controls the CPU, accesses RAM, executes programs, receives input from the keyboard or other input device, retrieves and saves data to and from secondary storage devices, displays data on the monitor, controls the printer, and performs other functions that control the hardware system.

The operating system contains two types of instructions. *System-resident commands* are active in primary memory at all times to coordinate input/output requests and execute programs. *Disk-resident commands* reside on a secondary storage device until a request is made to execute these special-purpose utility programs.

At one time, the most popular operating system for the IBM-compatible computer (also known as the PC[4]) was *DOS (Disk Operating System)*. Microsoft Corporation sold this product under the name MS-DOS (Microsoft Disk Operating System). An enormous number of microcomputers ran versions of DOS; as a result, there is an abundance of application software for DOS computers. Later, Microsoft modified its operating system to accommodate *multitasking* (which allows more than one task to be executed at a time in a single-user computer), multiple users (networking), and larger memory, and the new operating system became the Windows family of operating environments. This operating system takes advantage of the newer more powerful microprocessor chips, such as the Intel Pentium, which address more memory and run faster than the older microprocessors.

The computer's operating system defines the family of software that the computer can use. *Application software* is written for a particular operating system. For example, the user of an IBM-compatible microcomputer with the Windows operating system must select programs from the available software written for that operating system, and even perhaps the version of it (e.g., most applications written for earlier versions of Windows ['98 and prior] will not run on the latest version). The user of an IBM-compatible microcomputer with a different operating system, such as OS/2 or Linux, usually must select from a different set of software.

---

4 The first microcomputer from IBM was named "Personal Computer," and nicknamed "PC." The brand name became the generic nickname for all compatible microcomputers, and it has stuck.

PC Systems Risks and Controls

For mainframe and microcomputer environments, computer operating systems are an important element of the internal control structure. Mainframes, being multiuser systems, are designed to maintain a separation between end users and permit only authorized users to access data and programs. Unauthorized attempts to access data or programs can be thwarted by the security system. But PCs are a different situation. There are many new and different risks associated with PCs.

Risk Assessment

One of the most important functions of auditors today, be they internal or external, is the task of risk assessment. Internal auditing standards require auditors to begin their audit plans by conducting a risk assessment. Financial audits have always been associated with risk, as was discussed in Chapter 1, but Sarbanes-Oxley makes it imperative that external auditors do a thorough analysis of risk associated with audits. PCs introduce a lot of additional risks, or different risks, not associated with legacy systems and mainframes. Therefore, auditors must analyze all aspects of PCs to ascertain the specific risks for which the organization is subject, due to PCs. In some cases, the risk associated with the PC environment will remain an exposure, because nothing cost effective can be done about the risk.

Inherent Weaknesses

In contrast to mainframe systems, PCs provide only minimal security over data files and programs. This control weakness is inherent in the philosophy behind the design of PC operating systems. Intended primarily as single-user systems, they are designed to make computer use easy and to facilitate access, not restrict it. This philosophy, while necessary to promote end-user computing, is sometimes at odds with internal control objectives. The data stored on microcomputers that are shared by multiple users are exposed to unauthorized access, manipulation, and destruction. Once a computer criminal gains access to the user's microcomputer, there may be little or nothing in the way of control to prevent him or her from stealing or manipulating the data stored on the internal hard drive.

The advanced technology and power of modern PC systems stand in sharp contrast to the relatively unsophisticated operational environment in which they exist. Controlling this environment rests heavily on physical controls. Some of the more significant risks and possible control techniques are outlined on the following pages.

Weak Access Control

Security software that provides logon procedures is available for PCs. Most of these programs, however, become active only when the computer is booted from the hard drive. A computer criminal attempting to circumvent the logon procedure may do so by forcing the computer to boot from the A: drive, or the CD-ROM drive, whereby an uncontrolled operating system can be loaded into the computer's memory. Having bypassed the computer's stored operating system and security package, the criminal has unrestricted access to data and programs on the hard disk drive.

Inadequate Segregation of Duties

In PC environments, particularly those of small companies, an employee may have access to multiple applications that process incompatible transactions. For example, a single individual may be responsible for entering all transaction data, including sales orders, cash receipts, invoices, and disbursements. Typically, the general ledger and subsidiary accounts are updated automatically from these input sources. This degree of authority would be similar, in a manual system, to assigning accounts receivable, accounts payable, cash receipts, cash disbursement, and general ledger responsibility to the same person. The exposure is compounded when the operator is also responsible for the development (programming) of the applications that he or she runs. In small-company operations, there may be little that can be done to eliminate these inherent conflicts of duties. However, multilevel password control can reduce the risks.

Multilevel Password Control

Multilevel password control is used to restrict employees who are sharing the same computers to specific directories, programs, and data files. The employee is required to use another password at different appropriate levels of the system in order to gain access. This technique uses stored authorization tables to further limit an individual's access to read-only, data input, data modification, and data deletion capability. Although not a substitute for traditional control techniques such as employee supervision and management reports that detail all transactions and their effects on account balances, multilevel password control can greatly enhance the small organization's control environment.

A similar approach to multilevel password control is **multifaceted access control**. That is, the access control system employs more than one type of access control rather than more than one level of password control. For example, in addition to a password, the system may require biometric information. Biometrics, which is discussed in a future chapter, adds something physical to the access control system, such as a fingerprint, scan, or even keystroke peculiarities. Such features uniquely identify a person physically and thus limit "spoofing" by an authorized user.

Risk of Physical Loss

Because of their size, PCs are objects of theft. This is not the case for mainframes and minicomputers. The portability of laptops places them at highest risk. Procedures should be in place to hold users accountable for returning laptops. Other measures, such as locks, may be helpful for desktops. At a minimum, the entity should keep a log of PCs in service. The log should contain the PC's serial numbers, its business location, and responsible party.

Risk of Data Loss

In today's computer systems, data have become more and more valuable intrinsically. If data were destroyed, there is a definite cost (value) associated with recovering the data. Then there are those who use the data as a strategic tool, and for these entities, data has the highest value of any of these scenarios. Therefore, there is a risk of losing data to system failure, sabotage, hackers/crackers, and so on. Care should be taken to protect data as an asset, just as auditors do for any other valuable asset.

End-User Risks. Another risk to data is the users themselves. End users connected to the network systems have opportunities to deliberately erase hard drives, corrupt or sabotage data values, steal data, and otherwise cause serious harm to the enterprise's data in the PC environment. Care should be taken to limit this risk by controls such as training and creating an effective policy on computer usage, including stated penalties for stealing or destroying data.

Inadequate Backup Procedures Risk. To preserve the integrity of mission-critical data and programs, organizations need formal backup procedures. Adequate backup of critical files is actually more difficult to achieve in simple environments than it is in sophisticated environments. In mainframe and network environments, backup is controlled automatically by the operating system, using specialized software and hardware. The responsibility of providing backup in the PC environment falls to the user. Often, because of lack of computer experience and training, users fail to appreciate the importance of backup procedures until it is too late.

Computer failure, usually disk failure, is the primary cause of significant data loss in the PC environment. If the hard drive of the microcomputer fails, it may be impossible to recover the data stored on the disk. Formal procedures for making backup copies of critical data (and program) files can reduce this threat considerably. There are a number of options available for dealing with this problem.

- *Local backups on appropriate media.* Various media can be used to back up data files at the local PC. Media include floppy disks (although growing less and less practical), CD-R/CD-RW (compact disks), DVDs, and Zip disks. Files should be backed up locally from PCs to the appropriate media as part of a regular routine. These data disks can then be stored away from the computer. In the event of a microcomputer failure, the data file can be reconstructed from the backup disks. This process requires a conscious effort on the part of the user. Failure to back up data even one time can result in its loss.
- *Dual internal hard drives.* Microcomputers can be configured with two physical internal hard disks. One disk can be used to store production data while the other stores the backup files. A batch program or special software program which is run prior to or immediately after each data processing session, can copy data files to the backup device. Thus, backup is almost transparent to the user and involves a minimum of effort. This is a useful technique for the backup of large files that cannot be stored effectively on floppy disks. If one of the internal hard drives fails, the data files can be retrieved from the remaining hard drive.
- *External hard drive.* A popular backup option is the external hard drive with removable disk cartridge, which can store gigabytes of data per medium. Medium devices include CD, DVD, and Zip disks. When a disk device is filled, the user can remove it and insert a new one. Removable drives offer the advantages of unlimited storage capacity, portability, and physical security. This technology does not materially degrade computer performance. External hard drives compare favorably with internal hard drives in terms of access speed.

External hard drives can be used as an effective and simple backup technique. Dual external drives can be used to store both production and backup files. By using two separate drives, backup can be performed automatically before, during, or after the data processing session. Hence, the user does not need to physically switch cartridges and consciously perform the backup procedures, and the chance for human error is reduced. Also, with both versions of the data file residing on external drives, access control is improved. Both the backup and the original can be removed and stored in separate locations away from the microcomputer.

Risk Associated with Virus Infection

One of the most serious threats to PC integrity and system availability is virus infection. Strict adherence to organizational policies and procedures that guard against virus infection is critical to effective virus control. The auditor should verify that such policies and procedures exist and that they are being followed. But policy alone will not deter a resolute perpetrator. The organization must therefore resort to additional technical controls in the form of antivirus software.

The auditor can obtain corroborating evidence of virus control adequacy by performing the following tests:

1. The auditor should verify that the organization follows a policy of purchasing software from reputable vendors only.
2. The auditor should review the organization's policy for using antiviral software. This policy may include the following points:
   - Antiviral software should be installed on all microcomputers and invoked as part of the startup procedure when the computers are turned on. This will ensure that all key sectors of the hard disk are examined before any data are transferred through the network.
   - All upgrades to vendor software should be checked for viruses before they are implemented.
   - All public-domain software should be examined for virus infection before it is used.
   - Current versions of antiviral software should be available to all users. Verify that the most current virus data files are being downloaded regularly, and that the antivirus program is indeed running in the PC's background continuously, and thus able to scan all incoming documents. Corporate versions generally include a "push" update where the software automatically checks the home web site of the anti-virus vendor for new updates each time it is connected to the Internet and the PC is booted.
3. The auditor should verify that only authorized software is loaded on personal computers. This step is not only important regarding viruses, but also important because of the risk of pirated software.

Risk of Improper Systems Development and Maintenance Procedures

In Chapter 4, we examine control issues surrounding the development and maintenance of computer applications. The microcomputer environment lacks both the operating system features and the segregation of duties necessary to provide the necessary control. Management must thus compensate for these inherent exposures with other, more conventional control techniques.

To the extent possible, users should acquire commercial software from reputable vendors for their PC accounting applications. Many of the hundreds of packages on the market are general-purpose accounting systems. Others are special-purpose systems designed to meet the unique needs of specific industries. Commercial software purchased from a reputable vendor will normally be thoroughly tested and highly reliable.

Even small firms should employ formal software selection procedures that include the following steps:

1. Conduct a formal analysis of the problem and user needs.
2. Solicit bids from several vendors.

3. Evaluate the competing products in terms of their ability to meet the identified needs. (At this point, it is often wise to seek the help of a professional consultant.)
4. Contact current users of prospective commercial packages to get their opinions about the product.
5. Make a selection. (The firm should keep in mind the degree of support it will need and be sure that the vendor is willing and able to provide that support.)

Audit Objectives

- Verify that controls are in place to protect data, programs, and computers from unauthorized access, manipulation, destruction, and theft.
- Verify that adequate supervision and operating procedures exist to compensate for lack of segregation between the duties of users, programmers, and operators.
- Verify that backup procedures are in place to prevent data and program loss due to system failures, errors, and so on.
- Verify that systems selection and acquisition procedures produce applications that are high quality, and protected from unauthorized changes.
- Verify that the system is free from viruses and adequately protected to minimize the risk of becoming infected with a virus or similar object.

Audit Procedures

- The auditor should verify that microcomputers and their files are physically controlled. Desktop computers should be anchored to reduce the opportunity to remove them. Locks should be in place to disable input from the keyboard and the A: drive.
- The auditor should verify from organizational charts, job descriptions, and observation that the programmers of applications performing financially significant functions do not also operate those systems. In smaller organizational units where functional segregation is impractical, the auditor should verify that there is adequate supervision over these tasks.
- The auditor should confirm that reports of processed transactions, listings of updated accounts, and control totals are prepared, distributed, and reconciled by appropriate management at regular and timely intervals.
- Where appropriate, the auditor should determine that multilevel password control is used to limit access to data and applications.
- If removable hard drives are used, the auditor should verify that the drives are removed and stored in a secure location when not in use.
- By selecting a sample of backup files, the auditor can verify that backup procedures are being followed. By comparing data values and dates on the backup disks to production files, the auditor can assess the frequency and adequacy of backup procedures.
- The auditor should verify that application source code is physically secured (such as in a locked safe) and that only the compiled version is stored on the microcomputer.
- By reviewing systems selection and acquisition controls, the auditor should verify that commercial software packages employed on microcomputers were purchased from reputable vendors. The auditor should review the selection and acquisition procedures to ensure that user needs were fully considered and that the purchased software satisfies those needs.
- The auditor should review virus control techniques.

SUMMARY

This chapter explored operations control and audit issues related to the structure of the IT function, control of computer center operations, the computer operating system, and the personal computer environment. It opened by examining the potential risks and controls associated with the centralized and distributed approaches to IT organization. Audit objectives and suggested audit procedures were presented. Computer center risks and controls were then considered. The key elements of a disaster recovery plan and the advantages and disadvantages of various options were examined. The operating system and its role in the overall control structure were presented next. The operating system allows users and their applications to share and access common computer resources, such as processors, main memory, databases, and printers. Operating system integrity impacts all programs that run on the system. If operating system integrity is compromised, controls within individual accounting applications may be neutralized. The operating system discussion began with an overview of multiuser operating system features common to both networks and mainframes. Operating system objectives and the risks that threaten system security were examined. This was followed by a review of operating system controls and audit techniques. The chapter concluded with an analysis of the risks, controls, and audit issues pertinent to the personal computer environment.

KEY TERMS

access control list
audit trails
back door
centralized data processing
computer operations
database administration (DBA)
data library
disaster recovery plan (DRP)
distributed data processing (DDP)
empty shell
event monitoring
fault tolerance
keystroke monitoring
logic bomb
multifaceted access control
multilevel password control
mutual aid pact
one-time password
operating system
password
recovery operations center (ROC)
redundant arrays of inexpensive disks (RAID)
reusable password
Trojan horse
virus
worm

REVIEW QUESTIONS

1. What is distributed data processing?
2. What are the advantages and disadvantages of distributed data processing?
3. What types of tasks become redundant in a distributed data processing system?
4. What are the five control objectives of an operating system?
5. What are the three main tasks performed by the operating system?
6. What are the four techniques that a virus could use to infect a system?
7. What is the purpose of an access control list?
8. What is a vaccine, and what are its limitations?

9. What are the primary reasons for separating operational tasks?
10. What problems may occur as a result of combining applications programming and maintenance tasks in one position?
11. What is the role of a data librarian? Why is this role so important?
12. Why is poor systems documentation a prevalent problem?
13. Why is it important to separate the data library from operations?
14. What is the role of a corporate computer services department? How does this differ from other configurations?
15. What are the five control implications of distributed data processing?
16. List the control features that directly contribute to the security of the computer center environment.
17. What techniques are available in the microcomputer environment to reduce access exposure?
18. What is a mitigating control to inadequate segregation of duties in microcomputer environments?
19. What is data conversion?
20. What may be contained in the data library?
21. What is the client/server architecture?
22. What is spoofing?
23. What is spam?
24. List the types of files to which virus programs typically attach themselves.
25. What is an ROC?
26. What is a cold site?
27. What is fault tolerance?

Discussion Questions

1. What types of incompatible activities are prone to becoming consolidated in a distributed data processing system? How can this be prevented?
2. Why would an operational manager be willing to take on more work in the form of supervising an information system?
3. How can data be centralized in a distributed data processing system?
4. Should standards be centralized in a distributed data processing environment? Explain.
5. How can human behavior be considered one of the biggest potential threats to operating system integrity?
6. A bank in California has 13 branches spread throughout northern California, each with its own minicomputer where its data are stored. Another bank has 10 branches spread throughout California, with the data being stored on a mainframe in San Francisco. Which system do you think is more vulnerable to unauthorized access? Excessive losses from disaster?
7. Why would a systems programmer create a back door if he or she has access to the program in his or her day-to-day tasks?
8. Explain how a Trojan horse may help to penetrate a security system.
9. Many authorities believe that 90 percent of all computer fraud acts are not prosecuted by the employer. What do you think accounts for this lack of prosecution? Discuss the importance of the establishment of a formal policy for taking disciplinary (or legal) action against security violations.
10. End-user computing has become extremely popular in distributed data processing organizations. The end users like it because they feel they can more readily design and implement their own applications. Does this type of environment always foster more efficient development of applications? Explain your answer.
11. Compare and contrast the following disaster recovery options: mutual aid pact, empty shell, recovery operations center, and internally provided backup. Rank them from most risky to least risky, as well as from most costly to least costly.
12. Who should determine and prioritize the critical applications? How is this done? How frequently is it done?
13. What types of output would be considered extremely sensitive in a university setting? Give three examples and explain why the information would be considered sensitive. Discuss who should and should not have access to each type of information.
14. Why is it easier for programmers to cheat the system than operators?
15. Why should an organization centralize the acquisition, testing, and implementation of software and hardware within the corporate IT function?

16. Organizations sometimes locate their computer centers in the basement of their buildings to avoid normal traffic flows. Comment on this practice.
17. The 2003 blackout that affected the U.S. northeast caused numerous computer failures. What can an organization do to protect itself from such uncontrollable power failures?
18. Discuss the most important changes that have occurred to PC operating systems.
19. Discuss the most common forms of contra-security behavior pertaining to password control.
20. Discuss a potential problem with ROCs.
21. Discuss two potential problems associated with a cold site.
22. Discuss three techniques used to achieve fault tolerance.

MULTIPLE-CHOICE QUESTIONS

1. CMA 1289 5-6
   A system with several computers that are connected for communication and data transmission purposes but that permits each computer to process its own data is a
   a. distributed data processing network.
   b. centralized network.
   c. decentralized network.
   d. multidrop network.
   e. hybrid system.
2. CMA (Adapted) 687 5-15
   A major disadvantage of distributed data processing is
   a. the increased time between job request and job completion.
   b. the potential for hardware and software incompatibility among users.
   c. the disruption caused when the mainframe goes down.
   d. that users are not likely to be involved.
   e. that data processing professionals may not be properly involved.
3. Which of the following is NOT a control implication of distributed data processing?
   a. redundancy
   b. user satisfaction
   c. incompatibility
   d. lack of standards
4. Which of the following disaster recovery techniques may be least optimal in the case of a widespread natural disaster?
   a. empty shell
   b. mutual aid pact
   c. internally provided backup
   d. they are all equally beneficial
5. A user's application may consist of several modules stored in separate memory locations, each with its own data. One module must not be allowed to destroy or corrupt another module. This is an objective of
   a. operating system controls.
   b. data resource controls.
   c. computer center and security controls.
   d. application controls.
6. A program that attaches to another legitimate program but does not replicate itself is called a
   a. virus.
   b. worm.
   c. Trojan horse.
   d. logic bomb.
7. The identification of users who have permission to access the accounts receivable file is found in the
   a. operating system.
   b. systems manual.
   c. database schema.
   d. database file definition.
   e. access control list.
8. CMA 686 5-4
   An integrated group of programs that supervises and supports the operations of a computer system as it executes users' application programs is called a(n)
   a. operating system.
   b. RAID.
   c. utility program.
   d. language processor.
   e. object program.
9. Which of the following is NOT a feature of fault tolerance control?
   a. uninterruptible power supplies
   b. redundant arrays of inexpensive disks (RAID)
   c. multiprocessing
   d. multiprogramming

Problems

1. Internal Control

In reviewing the processes, procedures, and internal controls of one of your audit clients, Steeplechase Enterprises, you notice the following practices in place. Steeplechase has recently installed a new EDP system that affects the accounts receivable, billing, and shipping records. A specifically identified computer operator has been permanently assigned to each of the functions of accounts receivable, billing, and shipping. Each of these computer operators is assigned the responsibility of running the program for transaction processing, making program changes, and reconciling the computer log. In order to prevent any one operator from having exclusive access to the tapes and documentation, these three computer operators randomly rotate the custody and control tasks every two weeks over the magnetic tapes and the system documentation. Access controls to the computer room consist of magnetic cards and a digital code for each operator. Access to the computer room is not allowed to either the systems analyst or the computer operations supervisor.

The documentation for the EDP system consists of the following: record layouts, program listings, logs, and error listings.

Once goods are shipped from one of Steeplechase's three warehouses, warehouse personnel forward shipping notices to the accounting department. The billing clerk receives the shipping notice and accounts for the manual sequence of the shipping notices. Any missing notices are investigated. The billing clerk also manually enters the price of the item, and prepares daily totals (supported by adding machine tapes) of the units shipped and the amount of sales. The shipping notices and adding machine tapes are sent to the computer department for data entry.

The computer output generated consists of a two-copy invoice and remittance advice and a daily sales register. The invoices and remittance advice are forwarded to the billing clerk, who mails one copy of the invoice and remittance advice to the customer and files the other copy in an open invoice file, which serves as an accounts receivable document. The daily sales register contains the total of units shipped and sales amounts. The computer operator compares the computer-generated totals to the adding machine tapes.

Required:

Identify the control weaknesses present and make a specific recommendation for correcting each of them.

2. Internal Control

Gustave, CPA, during its preliminary review of the financial statements of Comet, Inc., found a lack of proper segregation of duties between the programming and operating functions. Comet owns its own computing facilities. Gustave, CPA, diligently intensified the internal control study and assessment tasks relating to the computer facilities. Gustave concluded in its final report that sufficient compensating general controls provided reasonable assurance that the internal control objectives were being met.

Required:

What compensating controls are most likely in place?

3. Operating System Exposures and Controls

Listed below are some scenarios. For each scenario, discuss the potential consequences and give a prevention technique.

a. The systems operator opened up a bag of burned microwave popcorn directly under a smoke detector in the computing room where two mainframes, three high-speed printers, and approximately 40 tapes were housed. The extremely sensitive smoke detector triggered the sprinkler system. Three minutes passed before the sprinklers could be turned off.
b. A system programmer intentionally placed an error into a program that caused the operating system to fail and dump certain confidential information to disks and printers.
c. Jane, a secretary, was laid off. Her employer gave her three weeks to find another job. After two weeks, Jane realized that finding another

job was going to be very tough, and she became bitter. Her son told her about a virus that had infected the computers at school. He had a disk infected with the virus. Jane took the disk to work and copied the disk onto the network server, which is connected to the company's mainframe. One month later, the company realized that some data and application programs had been destroyed.

d. Robert discovered a new sensitivity analysis public-domain program on the Internet. He downloaded the software to his microcomputer at home, then took the application to work and placed it onto his networked personal computer. The program had a virus on it that eventually spread to the company's mainframe.

e. Murray, a trusted employee and a systems engineer, had access to both the computer resource authority table and user passwords. He was recently hired away by the firm's competitor for twice his old salary. After leaving, Murray continued to browse through his old employer's data, such as price lists, customer lists, bids on jobs, and so on. He passed this information on to his new employer.

4. Disaster Recovery Plans

CMA 689 5-Y5

The headquarters of Gleicken Corporation, a private company with $3.5 million in annual sales, is located in California. Gleicken provides for its 150 clients an online legal software service that includes data storage and administrative activities for law offices. The company has grown rapidly since its inception three years ago, and its data processing department has expanded to accommodate this growth. Because Gleicken's president and sales personnel spend a great deal of time out of the office soliciting new clients, the planning of the EDP facilities has been left to the data processing professionals.

Gleicken recently moved its headquarters into a remodeled warehouse on the outskirts of the city. While remodeling the warehouse, the architects retained much of the original structure, including the wooden-shingled exterior and exposed wooden beams throughout the interior. The minicomputer distributive processing hardware is situated in a large open area with high ceilings and skylights. The openness makes the data processing area accessible to the rest of the staff and encourages a team approach to problem solving. Before Gleicken occupied the new facility, city inspectors declared the building safe; that is, it had adequate fire extinguishers, sufficient exits, and so on.

In an effort to provide further protection for its large database of client information, Gleicken has instituted a tape backup procedure that automatically backs up the database every Sunday evening, avoiding interruption in the daily operations and procedures. All tapes are then labeled and carefully stored on shelves reserved for this purpose in the data processing department. The departmental operator's manual has instructions on how to use these tapes to restore the database, should the need arise. A list of home phone numbers of the individuals in the data processing department is available in case of an emergency. Gleicken has recently increased its liability insurance for data loss from $50,000 to $100,000.

This past Saturday, the Gleicken headquarters building was completely ruined by fire, and the company must now inform its clients that all of their information has been destroyed.

Required:

a. Describe the computer security weaknesses present at Gleicken Corporation that made it possible for a disastrous data loss to occur.

b. List the components that should have been included in the disaster recovery plan at Gleicken Corporation to ensure computer recovery within 72 hours.

c. What factors, other than those included in the plan itself, should a company consider when formulating a disaster recovery plan?

5. Separation of Duties

Arcadia Plastics follows the philosophy of transferring employees from job to job within the company. Management believes that job rotation deters employees from feeling that they are stagnating in their jobs and promotes a better understanding of the company. A computer services employee typically works for six months as a data librarian, one year as a systems developer, six months as a database administrator, and one year in systems maintenance. At that point, he or she is assigned to a permanent position.

Required:

Discuss the importance of separation of duties within the information systems department. How can Arcadia Plastics have both job rotation and well-separated duties?

6. DDP Risks

Write an essay discussing the primary risks associated with the distributed processing environment.

7. Virus Risks

One of the most serious threats to PC integrity and system availability is infection with viruses and other malware. Write a brief essay outlining the procedures an auditor should employ to obtain corroborating evidence of virus control adequacy.

8. End-User Computing

CMA 1287 5-3

The internal audit department of Hastone Manufacturing Company recently concluded a routine examination of the company's computer facilities. The auditor's report identified as a weakness the fact that there had been no coordination by the data processing services department in the purchase of microcomputer systems for the individual departments of Hastone. Among the 12 microcomputers in the organization, there are three different hardware manufacturers. In addition, there are four to five different software vendors for spreadsheets, word processing, and database applications, along with some networking applications for clusters of microcomputers.

Microcomputers were acquired in the operating departments to allow employees in each department to conduct special analyses. Many of the departments also wanted the capability to download data from the mainframe. Therefore, each operating department had requested guidance and assistance from the data processing services department. Data processing, however, responded that it was understaffed and must devote full effort to its main priority, the mainframe computer system.

In response to the internal audit report, the director of data processing services, Stan Marten, has issued the following memorandum.

TO: All Employees
FROM: Stan Marten, Director
REFERENCE: Microcomputer Standardization

Policies must be instituted immediately to standardize the acquisition of microcomputers and applications software. The first step is to specify the spreadsheet software that should be used by all personnel. From now on, everyone will use Micromate. All microcomputer hardware should be MS-DOS compatible. During the next month, we will also select the standard software for word processing and database applications. You will use only the user packages that are prescribed by the data processing services department. In the future, any new purchases of microcomputers, hardware, or software must be approved by the director of data processing services.

Several managers of other operating departments have complained about Marten's memorandum. Apparently, before issuing this memorandum, Marten had not consulted with any of the microcomputer users regarding their current and future software needs.

Required:

a. When acquiring microcomputers for various departments in an organization, describe the factors related to:
   i. computer hardware that needs to be considered during the initial design and set-up phase of the microcomputer environment.
   ii. operating procedures and system controls that need to be considered.
b. Discuss the benefits of having standardized hardware and software for microcomputers in an organization.
c. Discuss the concerns that the memorandum is likely to create for the microcomputer users at Hastone Manufacturing.

9. End-User Computing

CMA Adapted 688 5-Y6

List the problems inherent in the use, by others, of spreadsheet models developed by users who are not trained in the procedural controls of system design and development.

10. Internal Control and Fraud

Stephanie Baskill, an unemployed accounting clerk, lives one block from the Cleaver Manufacturing Company. While walking her dog last year, she noticed some material resource planning manuals in the dumpsters. Curious, she took the manuals home with her. She found that the documentation in the manuals was dated two months ago, so she thought that the information must be fairly current. Over the next month, Stephanie continued to collect all types of manuals from the dumpster during her dog-walking excursions. Cleaver Manufacturing Company was apparently updating all of its documentation manuals and placing them online. Eventually, Stephanie found manuals about critical inventory reorder formulas, the billing system, the sales order system, the payable system, and the operating system. Stephanie went to the local library and read as much as she could about this particular operating system.

To gain access to the organization, she took a low-profile position with Cleaver as a cleaning woman. By snooping through offices and guessing at passwords, watching people who were working late type in their passwords, and ultimately printing out lists of user IDs and passwords using a Trojan horse virus, Stephanie was able to obtain all the necessary passwords she needed to set herself up as a supplier, customer, systems operator, and systems librarian. Further, as a cleaning woman, she had access to all areas in the building.

As a customer, she was able to order enough goods so that the inventory procurement system would automatically trigger a need for a purchase of raw materials. Then, as a supplier, Stephanie would stand ready to deliver the goods at the specified price. She then covered her tracks by adjusting the transaction logs once the bills were paid. Stephanie was able to embezzle, on average, $125,000 a month. About 16 months after she began working at Cleaver, the controller saw her arrive at a very expensive French restaurant one evening, driving a Jaguar. Further, she spoke very good French when she ordered her meal. He told the internal auditors to keep a close watch on her, and they were able to catch her in the act.

Required:

a. What weaknesses in the organization's control structure must have existed to permit this type of embezzlement?

b. What specific control techniques and procedures could have helped prevent or detect this fraud?

11. Internal Control and End-User Computing

CMA 1290 4-3

The National Commercial Bank has 15 branches and maintains a mainframe computer system at its corporate headquarters. National has recently undergone an examination by the state banking examiners, and the examiners have some concerns about National's computer operations.

During the last few years, each branch has purchased a number of microcomputers to communicate with the mainframe in the emulation mode. Emulation occurs when a microcomputer attaches to a mainframe computer and, with the use of the appropriate software, can act as if it is one of the mainframe terminals. The branch also uses these microcomputers to download information from the mainframe and, in the local mode, manipulate customer data to make banking decisions at the branch level. Each microcomputer is initially supplied with a word processing application package to formulate correspondence to the customers, a spreadsheet package to perform credit and financial loan analyses beyond the basic credit analysis package on the mainframe, and a database management package to formulate customer market and sensitivity information. National's centralized data processing department is responsible only for mainframe operations; microcomputer security is the responsibility of each branch.

Because the bank examiners believe National is at risk, they have advised the bank to review the recommendations suggested in a letter issued by banking regulatory agencies in 1988. This letter emphasizes the risks associated with end-user operations and encourages banking management to establish sound control policies. More specifically, microcomputer end-user operations have outpaced the implementation of adequate controls and have taken processing control out of the centralized environment, introducing vulnerability in new areas of the bank.

The letter also emphasizes that the responsibility for corporate policies identifying management control practices for all areas of information processing activities resides with the board of directors. The existence and adequacy of compliance with these policies and practices will be part of the regular banking examiners' review. The three required control groups for adequate information system security as they relate to National are (1) processing controls, (2) physical and environmental controls, and (3) spreadsheet program development controls.

Required:

For each of the three control groups listed

a. identify three types of controls for microcomputer end-user operations where National Commercial Bank might be at risk, and
b. recommend a specific control procedure that National should implement for each type of control you identified. Use the following format for your answer.

Control Types	Recommended Procedures

Destructive Programs

12. Types of destructive programs

Required:

Write a report outlining the key features of the following types of destructive programs: virus, worm, logic bomb, back door, and Trojan horse.

13. Controlling risk from destructive programs

Required:

Write an essay discussing the common technology controls and administrative procedures used to reduce threats from destructive programs.

14. Audit Trail Objectives

Required:

Write an essay outlining the following audit trail objectives: (a) detecting unauthorized access to the system, (b) facilitating the reconstruction of events, and (c) promoting personal accountability.

CHAPTER

3 Data Management Systems

Learning Objectives

After studying this chapter, you should:

- Understand the operational problems inherent in the flat-file approach to data management that gave rise to the database approach.
- Understand the relationships among the fundamental components of the database concept.
- Recognize the defining characteristics of three database models: hierarchical, network, and relational.
- Understand the operational features and associated risks of deploying centralized, partitioned, and replicated database models in the DDP environment.
- Be familiar with the audit objectives and procedures used to test data management controls.

This chapter deals with auditing the systems that manage and control the organization's data resource. Data management can be divided into two general approaches: the **flat-file model** and the **database model**. The chapter opens with a description of flat-file data management, which is used in many older (legacy) systems that are still in operation today. Private ownership of data, which characterizes this model, is the root cause of several problems that inhibit data integration. The section then presents a conceptual overview of the database model and illustrates how problems associated with the flat-file model are resolved under this approach. The notions of entitywide data sharing and centralized control of data lie at the heart of the database philosophy.

The second section describes the key functions and defining features of three common database models: the *hierarchical*, the *network*, and the *relational* models. The three models are presented from the perspective of a centralized IT function. The hierarchical and network models are called *navigational databases* because of their structure and inflexibility. Seen as a marked improvement over flat files, navigational databases were used in the design of many late-era legacy systems. Newer accounting information systems, however, make extensive use of the relational model. This flexible approach presents data in a two-dimensional format that is conceptually more pleasing to end users than complex navigational structures. When properly implemented, the relational model effectively supports entitywide data integration.

The third section examines the role of database technology in the distributed environment. Distributed data processing (DDP) empowers end users with ownership and control of IT resources, including databases. Since data ownership is contrary to traditional database philosophy, DDP presents an operational dilemma of sorts. This section presents techniques for achieving the goals of DDP while maintaining the principles of data sharing and integration. Three alternative configurations are examined: centralized, replicated, and partitioned databases.

The chapter concludes with a discussion of the control and audit issues related to data management. The risks, audit objectives, and audit procedures relevant to flat files, centralized databases, and distributed databases are presented.

DATA MANAGEMENT APPROACHES

There are two general approaches to data management: the flat-file model and the database model. The differences between the two approaches are both technical and philosophical. The defining features of each are presented below.

THE FLAT-FILE APPROACH

The flat-file approach is most often associated with so-called **legacy systems.** These are large mainframe systems that were implemented in the late 1960s through the 1980s. Organizations today still make extensive use of these systems. Eventually, they will be replaced by modern database management systems, but in the meantime, auditors must continue to deal with legacy-system technologies.

The flat-file model describes an environment in which individual data files are not related to other files. End users in this environment *own* their data files rather than *share* them with other users. Data processing is thus performed by standalone applications rather than integrated systems.

When multiple users need the same data for different purposes, they must obtain separate data sets structured to their specific needs. Figure 3-1 illustrates how customer sales data might be presented to three different users in a durable goods retailing organization. The accounting function needs customer sales data organized by account number and structured to show outstanding balances. This is used for customer billing, account receivable maintenance, and financial statement preparation. Marketing needs customer sales history data organized by demographic keys for use in targeting new product promotions and for selling product upgrades. The Product Service group needs customer sales data organized by products and structured to show scheduled service dates. Such information is used for making after-sales contacts with customers to schedule preventive maintenance and to solicit sales of service agreements.

The data redundancy demonstrated in this example contributes to three significant problems in the flat-file environment: **data storage**, **data updating**, and **currency of information.**

Data Storage

An efficient information system captures and stores data only once and makes this single source available to all users who need it. In the flat-file environment,

FIGURE 3-1 Flat-File Model

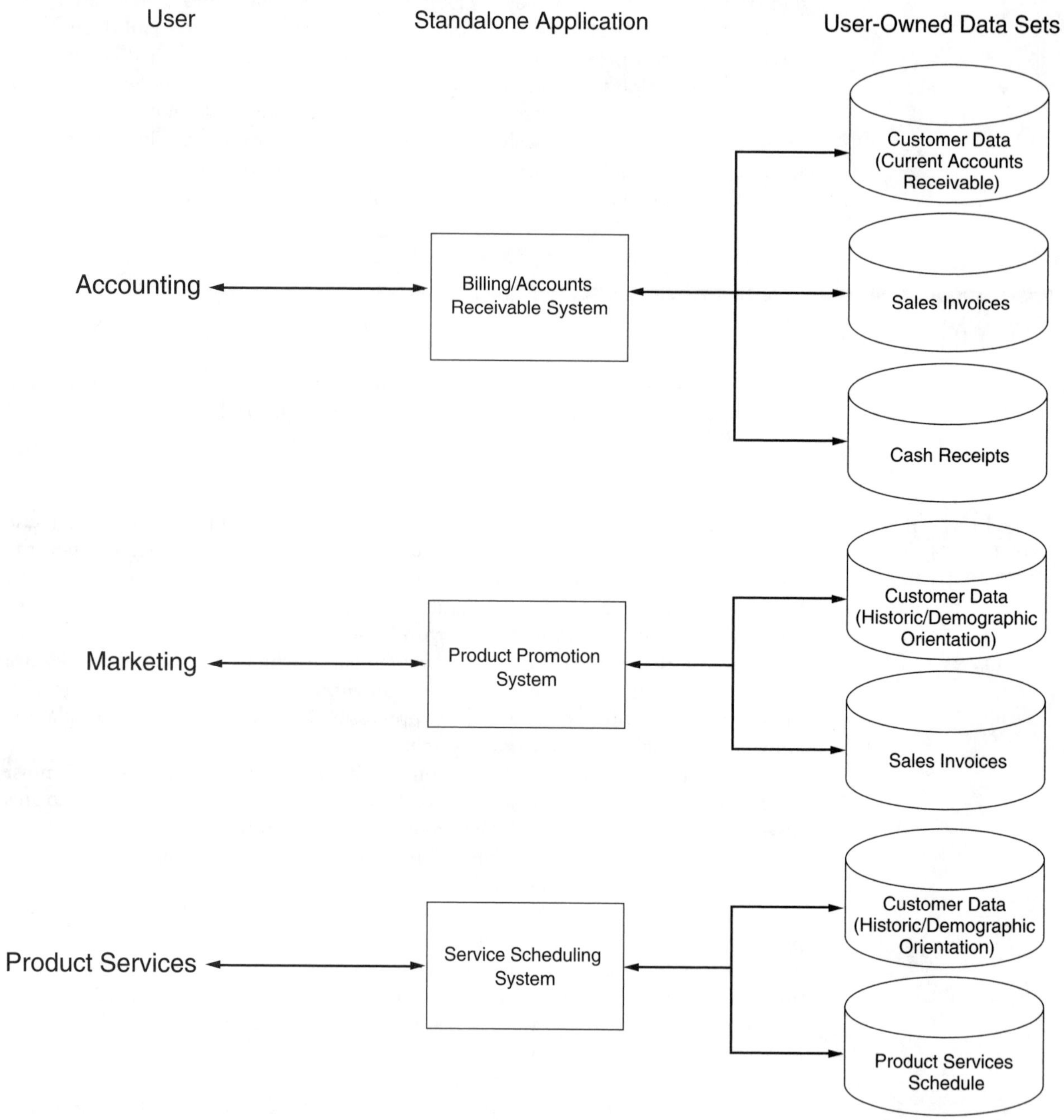

this is not possible. To meet the private data needs of users, organizations must incur the costs of both multiple collection and multiple storage procedures. Some commonly used data may be duplicated dozens, hundreds, or even thousands of times.

Data Updating

Organizations store a great deal of data on master files and reference files that require periodic updating to reflect changes. For example, a change to a customer's name or address must be reflected in the appropriate master files. When users keep separate files, all changes must be made separately for each user. This adds significantly to the task burden and the cost of data management.

Currency of Information

In contrast to the problem of performing multiple updates is the problem of failing to update all the user files affected by a change in status. If update information is not properly disseminated, the change will not be reflected in some users' data, resulting in decisions based on outdated information.

Task-Data Dependency (Limited Access)

Another problem with the flat-file approach is the user's inability to obtain additional information as his or her needs change, a problem known as **task-data dependency**. The user's information set is constrained by the data that he or she possesses and controls. Users act independently; they do not interact as members of a user community. In this environment, it is very difficult to establish a mechanism for the formal sharing of data. Therefore, new information needs tend to be satisfied by procuring new data files. This takes time, inhibits performance, adds to data redundancy, and drives data management costs even higher. The resulting limited access also inhibits the effective sharing of data among the entity's users.

Flat Files Limit Data Integration (Limited Inclusion)

The flat-file approach is a single-view model. Files are structured, formatted, and arranged to suit the specific needs of the *owner* or primary user of the data. Such structuring, however, may exclude data attributes that are useful to other users, thus preventing successful integration of data across the organization. For example, since the Accounting function is the primary user of accounting data, these data are often captured, formatted, and stored to accommodate financial reporting and GAAP. This structure, however, may be useless to the organization's other (non-accounting) users of accounting data, such as the marketing, finance, production, and engineering functions. These users are presented with three options:

1. do not use accounting data to support decisions
2. manipulate and massage the existing data structure to suit their unique needs or
3. obtain additional private sets of the data and incur the costs and operational problems associated with data redundancy.

The Database Approach

An organization can overcome the problems associated with flat files by implementing the database approach to data management.

Access to the data resource is controlled by a **database management system (DBMS)**. The DBMS is a special software system that is programmed to know which data elements each user is authorized to access. The user's program sends requests for data to the DBMS, which validates and authorizes access to the database in accordance with the user's level of authority. If the user requests data that he or she is not authorized to access, the request is denied. Clearly, the organization's procedures for assigning user authority are an important control issue for auditors to consider. Figure 3-2 provides an overview of the database environment.

This approach centralizes the organization's data into a common database that is *shared* by other users. With the enterprise's data in a central location, all users have access to the data they need to achieve their respective objectives. Through data sharing, the traditional problems associated with the flat-file approach *may* be overcome.

Elimination of Data Storage Problem

Each data element is stored only once, thereby eliminating data redundancy and reducing data collection and storage costs. For example, customer data exist only once, but data are shared by accounting, marketing, and product services users.

Elimination of Data Update Problem

Because each data element exists in only one place, it requires only a single update procedure. This reduces the time and cost of keeping the database current.

Elimination of Currency Problem

A single change to a database attribute is automatically made available to all users of the attribute. For example, a customer address change entered by the billing clerk is immediately reflected in the marketing and product services views.

Elimination of Task-Data Dependency Problem

The most striking difference between the database model and the flat-file model is the pooling of data into a common database that is shared by all organizational users. With access to the full domain of entity data, changes in user information

FIGURE 3-2 **Database Model**

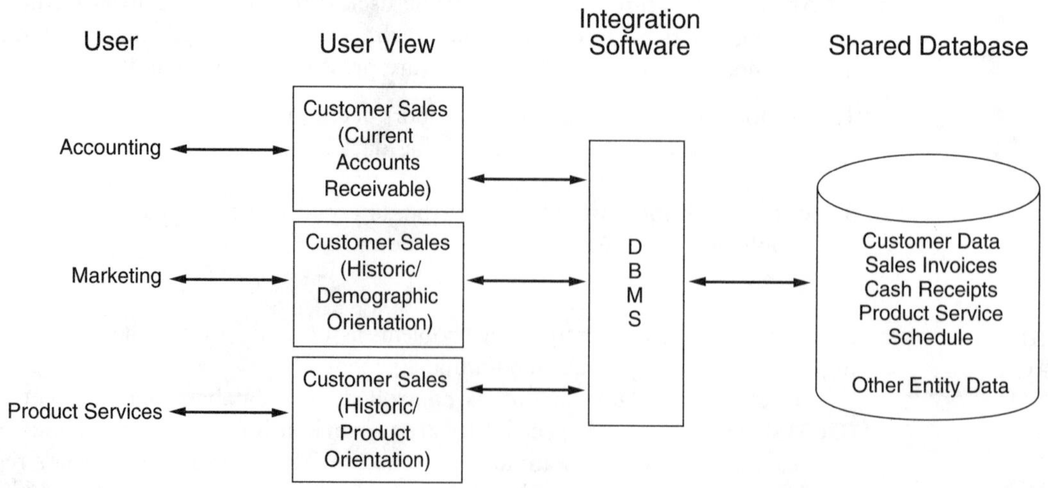

needs can be satisfied without obtaining additional private data sets. Users are constrained only by the limitations of the data available to the entity and the legitimacy of their need to access them. Therefore the database method eliminates the limited access that flat files, by their nature, dictate to users.

Elimination of Data Integration Problem

Since the data are in a common and globally accessible location, the data are able to be fully integrated into all applications for all users. Generally speaking, no one unit or group owns the data. If the design is done correctly, the data structures are not designed in such a way as to limit their usefulness to a broad set of users. Thus the database method can alleviate the data integration problem common to flat files.

Centralized Database Systems

Figure 3-3 presents a breakdown of the database environment into four primary elements: the DBMS, users, the database administrator, and the physical database. Each element is examined separately next.

Database Management System

Typical Features

The central element of the database approach depicted in Figure 3-3 is the database management system. The DBMS provides a controlled environment to assist (or prevent) access to the database and to efficiently manage the data resource. Each DBMS is unique in the way it accomplishes these objectives, but some typical features include:

1. *Program development.* The DBMS contains **application development software.** Both programmers and end users may employ this feature to create applications to access the database.
2. *Backup and recovery.* During processing, the DBMS periodically makes backup copies of the physical database. In the event of a disaster (disk failure, program error, or malicious act) that renders the database unusable, the DBMS can recover to an earlier version that is known to be correct. Although some data loss may occur, without the backup and recovery feature the database would be vulnerable to total destruction.
3. *Database usage reporting.* This feature captures statistics on what data are being used, when they are used, and who uses them. This information is used by the database administrator (DBA) to help assign user authorization and maintain the database. We discuss the role of the DBA later in this section.
4. *Database access.* The most important feature of a DBMS is to permit authorized user access, both formal and informal, to the database. Figure 3-3 shows the three software modules that facilitate this task. These are the data definition language, the data manipulation language, and the query language.

Data Definition Language

Data definition language (DDL) is a programming language used to define the database to the DBMS. The DDL identifies the names and the relationship of all

FIGURE 3-3 **Elements of the Database Concept**

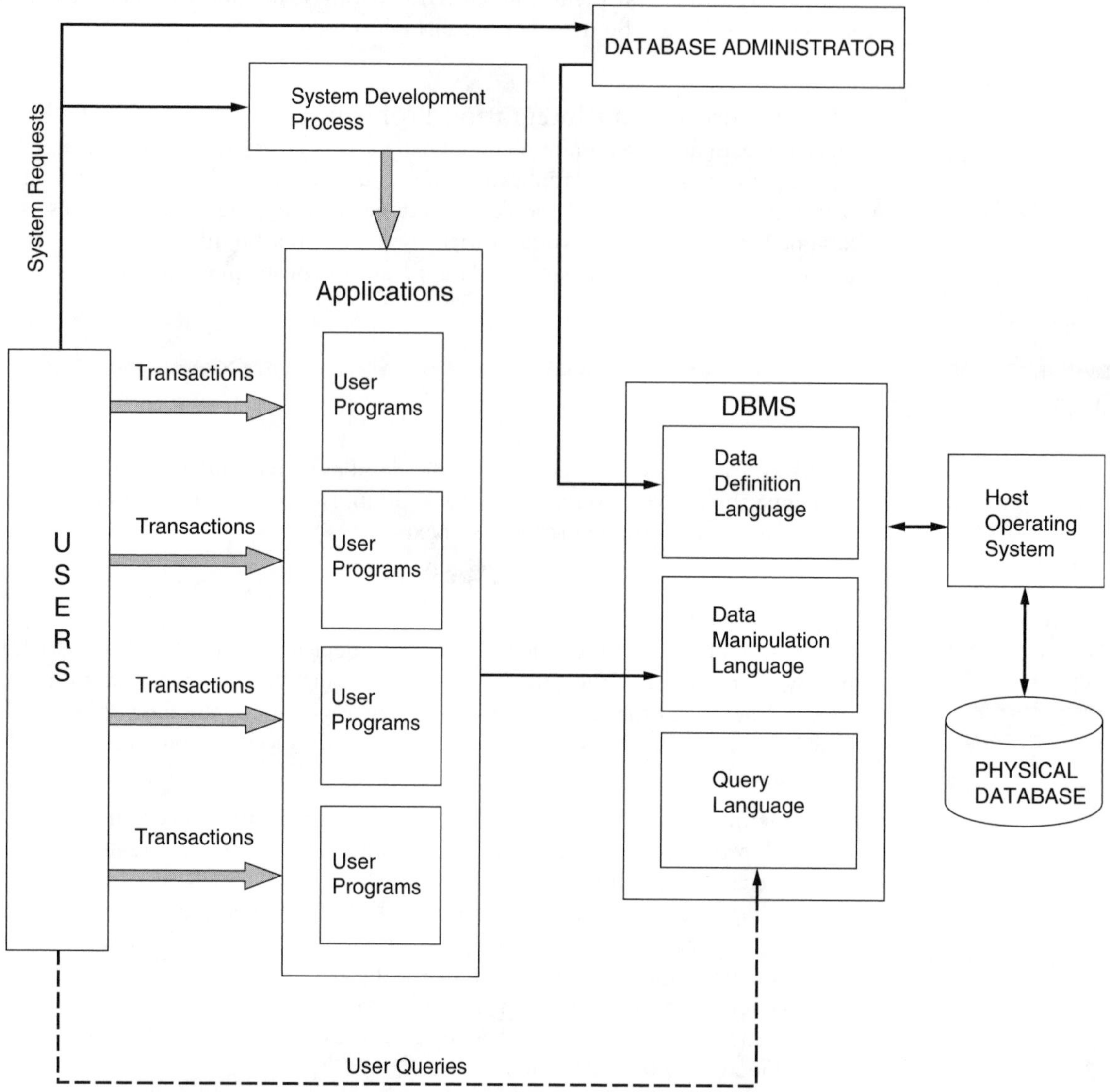

data elements, records, and files that constitute the database. There are three levels, called *views*, in this definition: the physical internal view, the conceptual view (schema), and the user view (subschema). Figure 3-4 shows the relationship between these views.

Database "Views" (Schemas)

Internal View/Physical View. The physical arrangement of records in the database is presented through the **internal view**. This is the lowest level of representation, which is one step removed from the physical database. This internal view describes the structures of data records, the linkages between files, and the physical arrangement and sequence of records in a file. There is only one internal view for the database.

Conceptual View/Logical View (Schema). The **conceptual view or schema** describes the entire database. This view represents the database logically and abstractly, rather than the way it is physically stored. There is only one conceptual view for a database.

External View/User View (Subschema). The **subschema** or **user view,** defines the user's section of the database—the portion that an individual user is authorized to access. To a particular user, the user view is the database. Unlike the internal and conceptual views, there may be many distinct user views. For example, a user in the personnel department may view the database as a collection of employee records and is unaware of the supplier and inventory records seen by the users in the inventory control department.

FIGURE 3-4 **Overview of DBMS Operation**

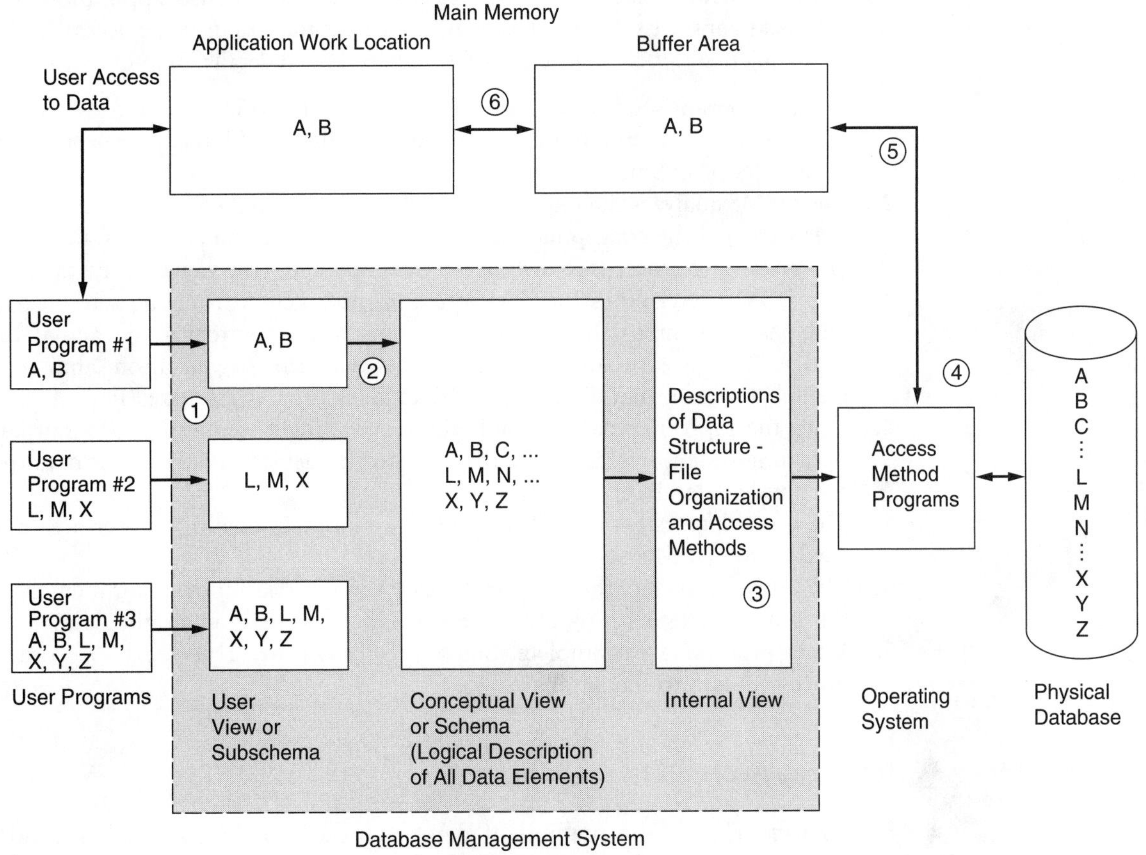

USERS

Formal Access: Application Interfaces

Figure 3-3 shows how users access the database in two ways. First, access is possible by the formal application interfaces. User programs, prepared by systems professionals, send data access requests (calls) to the DBMS, which validates the requests and retrieves the data for processing. Under this mode of access, the presence of the DBMS is transparent to the users. Data processing procedures (both batch and real-time) for transactions such as sales, cash receipts, and purchases are essentially the same as they would be in the flat-file environment.

Data Manipulation Language. **Data manipulation language (DML)** is the proprietary programming language that a particular DBMS uses to retrieve, process, and store data. Entire user programs may be written in the DML or, alternatively, selected DML commands can be inserted into programs that are written in universal languages, such as PL/1, COBOL, and FORTRAN. Inserting DML commands enables standard programs, which were originally written for the flat-file environment, to be easily converted to work in a database environment. The use of standard language programs also provides the organization with a degree of independence from the DBMS vendor. If the organization decides to switch vendors to one that uses a different DML, it will not need to rewrite all the user programs. By replacing the old DML commands with the new commands, user programs can be modified to function in the new environment.

DBMS Operation. Figure 3-4 illustrates how the DBMS and user applications work together. Let's consider the typical sequence of events that occur while accessing data. The following description is generic and certain technical details are omitted.

1. A user program sends a request for data to the DBMS. The requests are written in a special data manipulation language (discussed later) that is embedded in the user program.
2. The DBMS analyzes the request by matching the called data elements against the user view and the conceptual view. If the data request matches, it is authorized, and processing proceeds to Step 3. If it does not match the views, access is denied.
3. The DBMS determines the data structure parameters from the internal view and passes them to the operating system, which performs the actual data retrieval. Data structure parameters describe the organization and access method for retrieving the requested data. This topic is discussed later.
4. Using the appropriate access method (an operating system utility program), the operating system interacts with the disk storage device to retrieve the data from the physical database.
5. The operating system then stores the data in a main memory buffer area managed by the DBMS.
6. The DBMS transfers the data to the user's work location in main memory. At this point, the user's program is free to access and manipulate the data.
7. When processing is complete, Steps 4, 5, and 6 are reversed to restore the processed data to the database.

Informal Access: Query Language

Definition. The second method of database access is the informal method of queries. *Query* is an ad hoc access methodology that uses English-like commands to build lists or other basic information from a database. Users can access data via a direct query, which requires no formal user programs. The DBMS has a built-in query facility that allows authorized users to process data independent of professional programmers. The query facility provides a "friendly" environment for integrating and retrieving data to produce ad hoc management reports.

SQL. The query capability of the DBMS permits end users and professional programmers to access data in the database directly without the need for conventional programs. IBM's **Structured Query Language** (SQL, often pronounced *sequel* or S-Q-L) has emerged as the standard query language for both mainframe and microcomputer DBMSs. SQL is a fourth-generation, nonprocedural language (English-like commands) with many commands that allow users to input, retrieve, and modify data easily. The SELECT command is a powerful tool for retrieving data. The example in Figure 3-5 illustrates the use of the SELECT command to produce a user report from a database called *Inventory*.

As you can see from this example, SQL is a very efficient data processing tool. Although not a natural English language, SQL requires far less training in computer

FIGURE 3-5 **Example of SELECT Command Used to Query an Inventory Database**

Selected Attributes

Inventory

Item	Desc	On-Hand	W-House-Loc	Unit-Cost	Ven-Num
1567	Bolt 3/8	300	Chicago	1.34	1251
1568	Nut 1/4	500	Chicago	.85	1195
1569	Flange	65	Denver	56.75	1251
1570	Disc	1000	Tulsa	22.00	1893
1571	End Pipe	93	Denver	7.35	7621
1572	In-Pipe	93	Denver	18.20	1251
1573	Pump	603	Chicago	85.00	1195

Selected Records

SQL Command

```
SELECT  Item, Desc, On-Hand,
        W-House-Loc, Ven-Num

FROM    Inventory

WHERE   On-Hand > 300
```

Item	Desc	On-Hand	W-House-Loc	Ven-Num
1568	Nut 1/4	500	Chicago	1195
1570	Disc	1000	Tulsa	1893
1573	Pump	603	Chicago	1195

Report Produced

concepts and fewer programming skills than third-generation languages. In fact, the latest generation of query features require no SQL knowledge at all. Users select data visually by "pointing and clicking" at the desired attributes. This visual user interface then generates the necessary SQL commands automatically. The great advantage of the query feature is that it places ad hoc reporting and data processing capability in the hands of the user/manager. By reducing reliance on professional programmers, the manager's ability to deal with problems that pop up is greatly improved.

QBE. Another feature of modern queries is **query by example** (QBE). In GUI systems, the user can simply "drag and drop" objects to build a query, and see what the end-result query will look like while designing it. This method makes it easier for end users to develop working queries than by learning SQL.

This query feature is a most attractive incentive for users to adopt the database approach. The query feature is also an important control issue. Management must ensure that it is not used to achieve unauthorized access to the database.

THE DATABASE ADMINISTRATOR

Refer to Figure 3-3 and note the administrative position of **database administrator (DBA)**. This position does not exist in the flat-file environment. The DBA is responsible for managing the database resource. The sharing of a common database by multiple users requires organization, coordination, rules, and guidelines to protect the integrity of the database.

In large organizations, the DBA function may consist of an entire department of technical personnel under the database administrator. In smaller organizations, DBA responsibility may be assumed by someone within the computer services group. The duties of the DBA fall into the following areas:[1] database planning; database design; database implementation, operation, and maintenance; and database growth and change. Table 3-1 presents a breakdown of specific tasks within these broad areas.

TABLE 3-1

Functions of the Database Administrator

Database Planning:	**Implementation:**
Develop organization's database strategy Define database environment Define data requirements Develop data dictionary	Determine access policy Implement security controls Specify tests procedures Establish programming standards
Design:	**Operation and Maintenance:**
Logical database (schema) External users' views (subschemas) Internal view of databases Database controls	Evaluate database performance Reorganize database as user needs demand Review standards and procedures
	Change and Growth:
	Plan for change and growth Evaluate new technology

1 Adapted from F. R. McFadden and J. A. Hoffer, *Database Management*, 3d ed. (Redwood City, CA: Benjamin/Cummings Publishing, 1991), p. 343.

The Data Dictionary

Another important function of the DBA is the creation and maintenance of the **data dictionary**. The data dictionary describes every data element in the database. This enables all users (and programmers) to share a common view of the data resource, thus greatly facilitating the analysis of user needs. The data dictionary may be in both paper form and online. Most DBMSs employ special software for managing the data dictionary.

Organizational Interactions of the DBA

Figure 3-6 shows some of the organizational interfaces of the DBA. Of particular importance is the relationship among the DBA, the end users, and the systems professionals of the organization. Refer again to Figure 3-3 during our examination of this relationship.

As information needs arise, users send formal requests for computer applications to the systems professionals (programmers) of the organization. The requests are handled through formal systems development procedures; if they have merit, they result in programmed applications. Figure 3-3 shows this relationship as the line from the user block to the systems development block. The user requests also go to the DBA, who evaluates these to determine the user's database needs. Once this is established, the DBA grants the user access authority by programming the user's view (subschema). We see this relationship as the lines between the user and the DBA and between the DBA and DDL module in the DBMS. By keeping access authority separate from systems development (application programming), the organization is better able to control and protect the database. Intentional and unintentional attempts at unauthorized access are more likely to be discovered when these two groups work independently.

FIGURE 3-6

Organizational Interactions of the Database Administrator

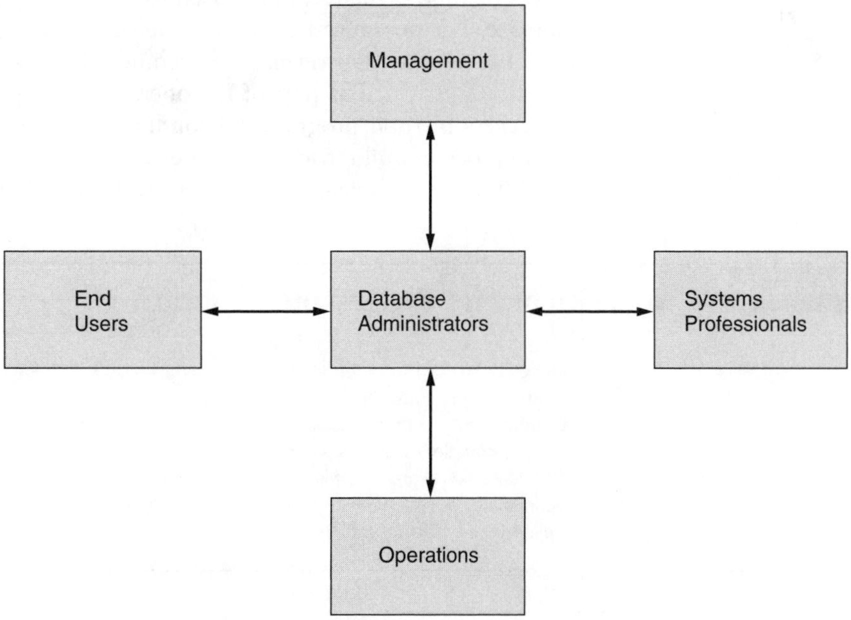

The Physical Database

The fourth major element of the database approach as presented in Figure 3-3 is the **physical database.** This is the lowest level of the database and the only level that exists in physical form. The physical database consists of magnetic spots on magnetic disks. The other levels of the database (the user view, conceptual view, and internal view) are abstract representations of the physical level.

At the physical level, the database forms a logical collection of records and files that constitute the firm's data resource. This section deals with the data structures used in the physical database. Table 3-2 contains a list of file processing operations that data structures must support.[2] The efficiency with which the DBMS performs these tasks is a major determinant of its overall success, and depends in great part on how a particular file is structured.

Data Structures

Data structures are the bricks and mortar of the database. The data structure allows records to be located, stored, and retrieved, and enables movement from one record to another. Data structures have two fundamental components: organization and access method.

Data Organization

The **organization** of a file refers to the way records are physically arranged on the secondary storage device. This may be either *sequential* or *random.* The records in sequential files are stored in contiguous locations that occupy a specified area of disk space. Records in random files are stored without regard for their physical relationship to other records of the same file. Random files may have records distributed throughout a disk.

Data Access Methods

The **access method** is the technique used to locate records and to navigate through the database. For our purposes, it is sufficient to deal with access methods at the conceptual level only. However, at a technical level, they exist as computer programs that are provided as part of the operating system. During database processing, the access method program, responding to requests for data from the user's application, locates and retrieves or stores the records. The tasks carried out by the access method are completely transparent to the user's application.

TABLE 3-2

Typical File Processing Operations

1. Retrieve a record from the file based on its primary key value.
2. Insert a record into a file.
3. Update a record in the file.
4. Read a complete file of records.
5. Find the next record in a file.
6. Scan a file for records with common secondary keys.
7. Delete a record from a file.

2 *Ibid.*, p. 287.

No single structure is best for all processing tasks. Selecting one, therefore, involves a trade-off between desirable features. The criteria that influence the selection of the data structure include

1. Rapid file access and data retrieval
2. Efficient use of disk storage space
3. High throughput for transaction processing
4. Protection from data loss
5. Ease of recovery from system failure
6. Accommodation of file growth

In Chapter 7, we introduce data extraction software for performing substantive tests of details. At that time, we examine a number of data structures used in both flat-file and database environments.

Data Hierarchy

Before introducing these models formally, we need to review some important database terms and concepts:

Data Attribute/Field. A **data attribute** or **field** is a single item of data, such as customer's name, account balance, or address.

Record. A **record** is a group of closely related fields that describe the relevant characteristics of an instance of the entity being tracked. A record can be visualized as something similar to a row in a table of data.

When we group together data attributes that logically pertain to an entity, they form a **record type**. For example, the data attributes describing the *sales* event could form the *sales order* record type. A record type is a multiple occurrence (one or more) of a particular type of record. This approximates a file in conventional terminology. A single occurrence of a record type is equivalent to a record.

Record types exist in relation to other record types. This is called a **record association**. There are three basic record associations: one-to-one, one-to-many, and many-to-many.

- *One-to-one association.* Figure 3-7(A) shows the **one-to-one (1:1) association.** This means that for every occurrence in Record Type X, there is zero or one occurrence in Record Type Y. For example, for every occurrence (employee) in the employee record type, there is only one (or zero for new employees) occurrence in the year-to-date earnings record type. Note the direction of the arrowhead on the line between the record types. This shows the nature (a single arrowhead is a 1:1 association) and the direction of the association.
- *One-to-many association.* Figure 3-7(B) shows the **one-to-many (1:M) association.** For every occurrence in Record Type X, there are zero, one, or many occurrences in Record Type Y. To illustrate, for every occurrence (customer) in the customer record type, there are zero, one, or many sales orders in the sales order record type. Note the double arrowhead notation representing a 1:M association and the direction of the association.
- *Many-to-many association.* Figure 3-7(C) illustrates a **many-to-many (M:M) association**, which is a two-way relationship. For each occurrence of Record Types X and Y, there are zero, one, or many occurrences of Record Types Y and

FIGURE 3-7 **Record Associations**

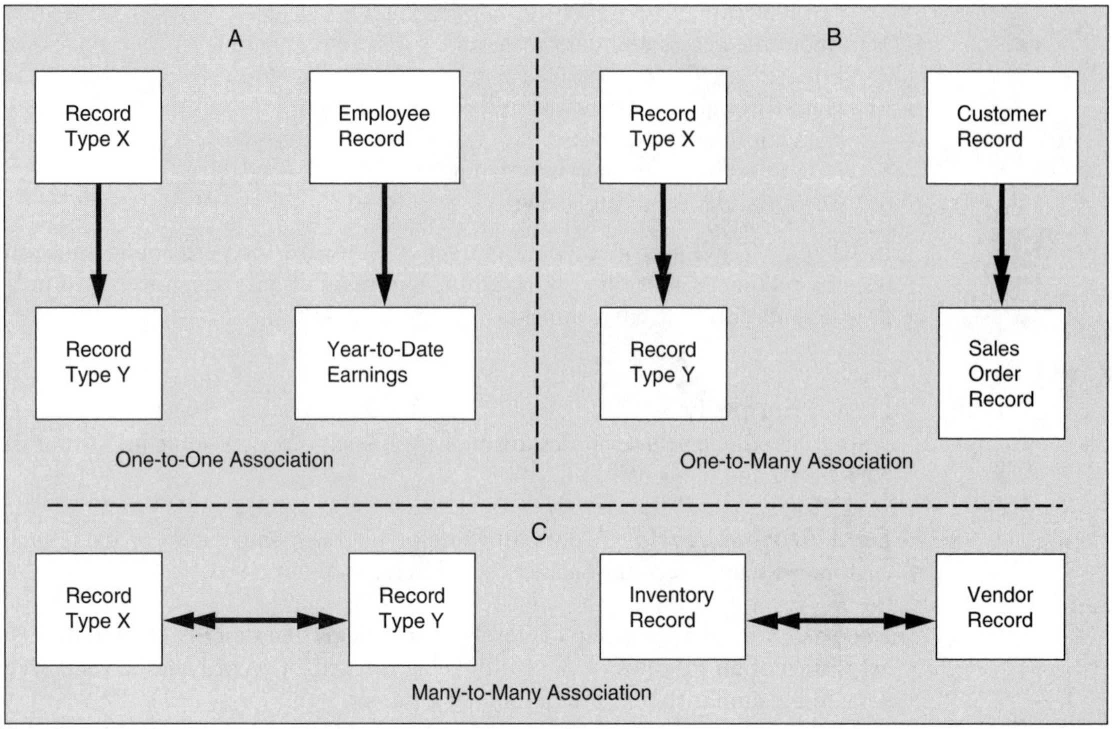

X, respectively. An M:M association often exists between a firm's inventory records and its vendor records. One or more vendors may supply a particular inventory item. At the same time, one vendor may supply more than one item class of inventory.

File/Entity. An **entity** is an individual resource, event, or agent about which we choose to collect data. Examples of entities are inventories, sales activities, customers, and employees.

Database. A **database** is closely related set of tables or files that together make an application capable of serving the needs of the user regarding a particular business process or function. For instance, a payroll database would include the relevant data pertaining to all of the entities necessary to properly execute the payroll processes needed by the organization.

Enterprise Database. An **enterprise database** is common set of data files or tables for the entire organization, or enterprise. The most recent application development systems, such as Oracle's latest package, or Microsoft's dot-net, focus on the ability to use an enterprise database as the foundation for applications that interface across the entire enterprise. The Enterprise Resource Planning (ERP) software so popular in the 1990s is also based on the principle of an enterprise database.

Three DBMS Models

A data model is an abstract representation of the data about entities, including resources (assets), events (transactions), and agents (personnel or customers, etc.) and their relationships in an organization. The purpose of a data model is to represent entity attributes in a way that is understandable to users.

Each DBMS is based on a particular conceptual model. Three common models are the hierarchical, the network, and the relational models. Because of certain conceptual similarities, we shall examine the hierarchical and network models first. These are termed **navigational models** because of explicit links or paths among their data elements. We shall then review the defining features of the relational model, which is based on implicit linkages between data elements.

The Hierarchical Model

The earliest database management systems were based on the **hierarchical data model**. This was a popular method of data representation because it reflected, more or less faithfully, many aspects of an organization that are hierarchical in relationship. Figure 3-8 presents a data structure diagram showing a portion of a hierarchical database. The hierarchical model is constructed of sets that describe the relationship between two linked files. Each set contains a *parent* and a *child*. Notice that File B, at the second level, is both the child in one set and the parent in another

FIGURE 3-8 Hierarchical Data Model

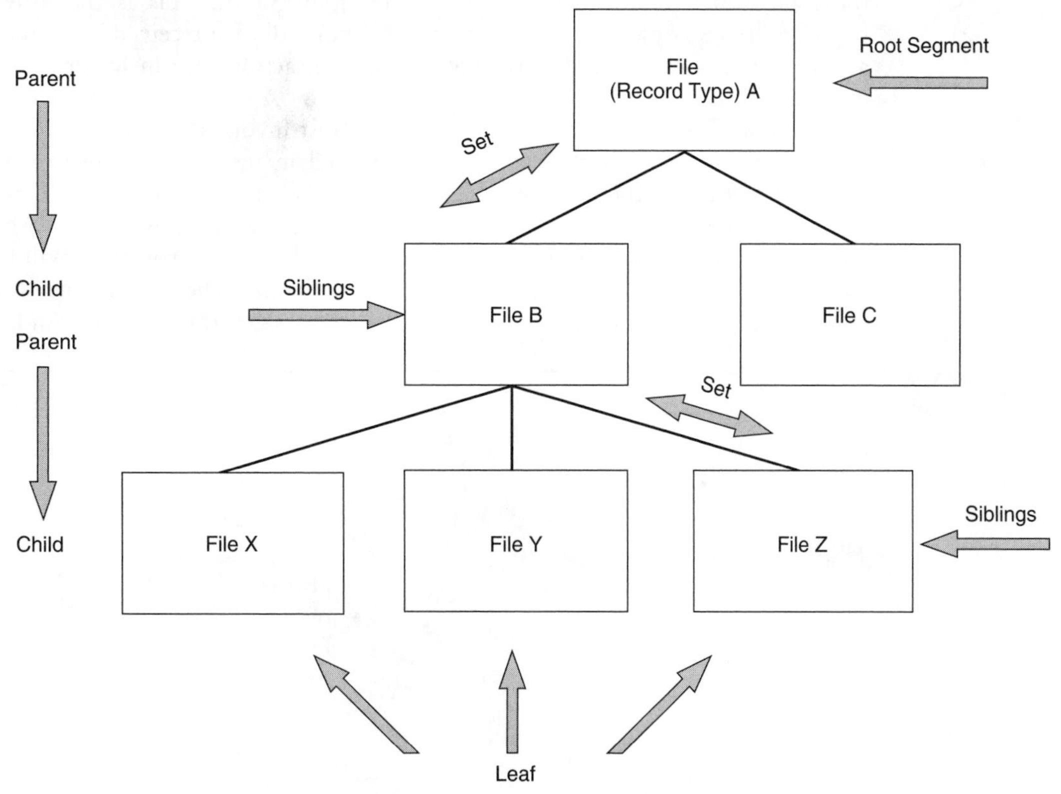

set. Files at the same level with the same parent are called *siblings*. This structure is also called a *tree structure*. The highest level in the tree is the *root* segment, and the lowest file in a particular branch is called a *leaf*.

Navigational Databases. The hierarchical data model is called a *navigational database* because traversing the files requires following a predefined path. This is established through explicit linkages (pointers) between related records. The only way to access data at lower levels in the tree is from the root and via the pointers down the navigational path to the desired records. For example, consider the partial database in Figure 3-9. To retrieve an invoice line item record, the DBMS must first access the customer record (the root). That record contains a pointer to the sales invoice record, which points to the invoice line item record. We examine the steps in this process in more detail later.

Data Integration in the Hierarchical Model. Figure 3-10 shows the detailed file structures for the partial database in Figure 3-9. Since the purpose of this example is to illustrate the navigational nature of the model, the data content of the records has been simplified.

Assume that a user wishes to retrieve, for inquiry purposes, data pertinent to a particular sales invoice (Number 1921) for a customer John Smith (Account Number 1875). The user provides the query application with the primary key (Cust# 1875), which searches the *customer* file for a corresponding key value. Upon matching the key, it directly accesses John Smith's record. Notice the customer record contains only summary information. The current balance figure represents the total dollar amount owed ($1,820) by John Smith. This is the difference between the sum of all sales to this customer minus all cash received in payment on account. The supporting details about these transactions are in lower-level sales invoice and cash receipts records.

From a menu, the user selects the option "List Invoices." From this input, the query application reads the pointer value stored in the customer record, which directs it to the specific location (the address) where the first invoice for customer John Smith resides. These invoice records are arranged as a linked-list, with each record containing a pointer to the next one in the list. The application will follow each of the pointers and retrieve each record in the list. The sales invoice records contain only summary information pertaining to sales transactions. Additional

FIGURE 3-9

Portion of a Hierarchical Database

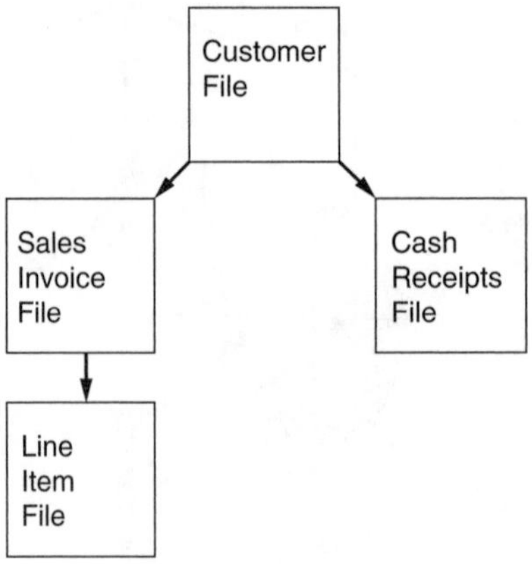

FIGURE 3-10 Data Integration in a Hierarchical Database

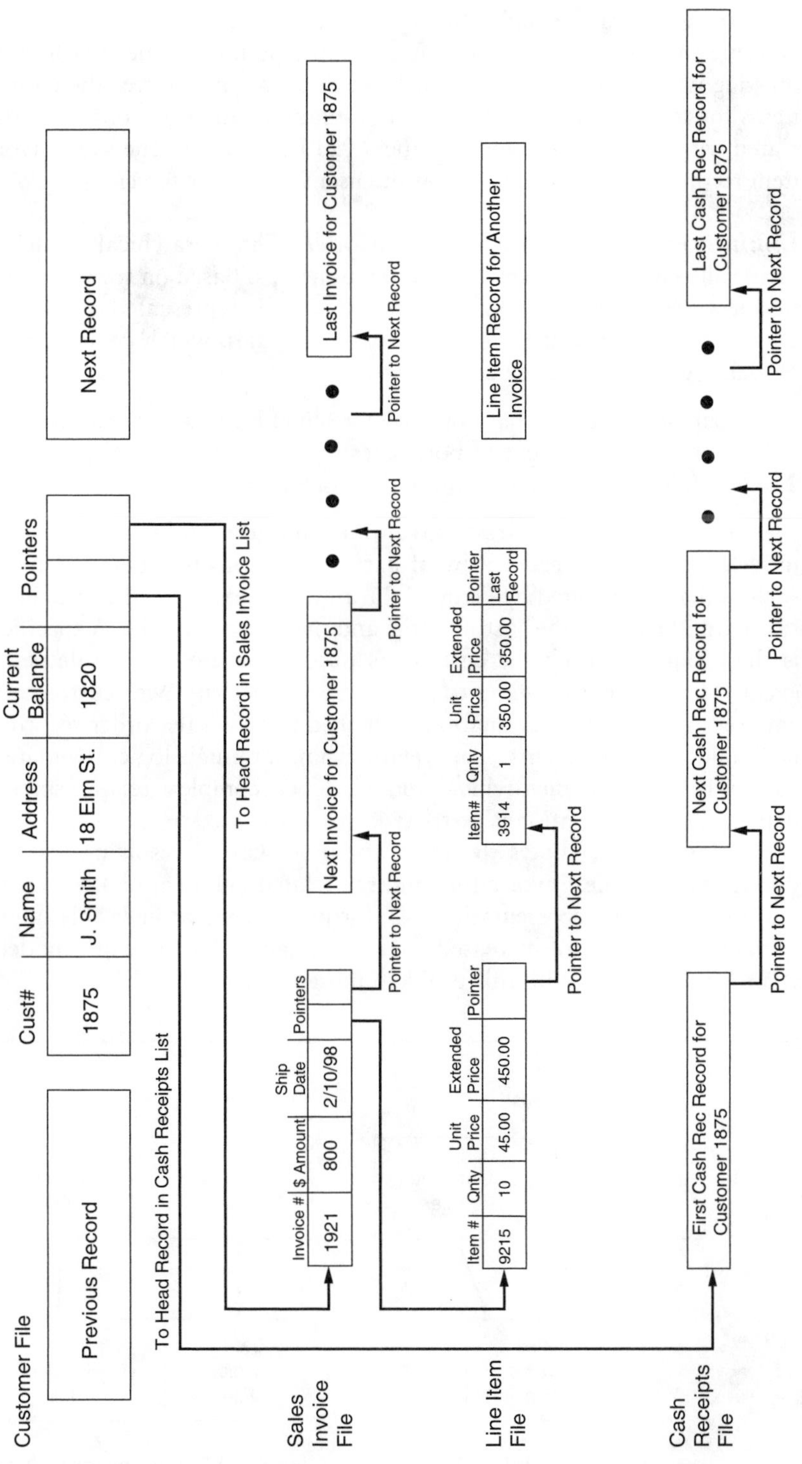

pointers in these records show the locations of supporting detail records (the specific items sold) in the invoice *line item* file. The application then prompts the user to enter the key value sought (Invoice Number 1921) or select it from a menu. Upon entering this input, the application reads the pointer to the first line item record. Starting with the head (first) record, the application retrieves the entire list of line items for Invoice Number 1921. In this example, there are only two records associated with the invoice—item numbers 9215 and 3914. The sales invoice and line item records are then displayed on the user's computer screen.

Limitations of the Hierarchical Model. The hierarchical model presents an artificially constrained view of data relationships. Based on the proposition that all business relationships are hierarchical (or can be represented as such), this model does not always reflect reality. The following rules, which govern the hierarchical model, reveal its operating constraints:

1. A parent record may have one or more child records. For example, in Figure 3-9, customer is the parent of both sales invoice and cash receipts.
2. No child record can have more than one parent.

The second rule is often restrictive and limits the usefulness of the hierarchical model. Many firms need a view of data associations that permit multiple parents, such as that represented by Figure 3-11(a). In this example, the sales invoice file has two natural parents: the customer file and the salesperson file. A specific sales order is the product of both the customer's purchase event and a salesperson's selling event. Management, wishing to integrate sales activity with customer service and employee performance evaluation, will need to view sales order records as the logical child of both parents. This relationship, although logical, violates the single parent rule of the hierarchical model. Since complex relationships cannot be depicted, data integration is restricted.

Figure 3-11(b) shows the most common way of resolving this problem. By duplicating the sales invoice file (and the related line item file), we create two separate hierarchical representations. Unfortunately, we achieve this improved functionality at the cost of increased data redundancy. The network model, which we examine next, deals with this problem more efficiently.

FIGURE 3-11

Multiple Parent Association

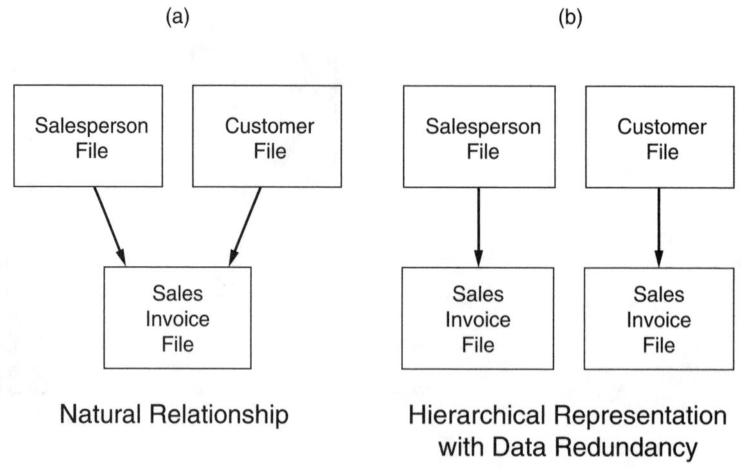

The Network Model

Like the hierarchical model, the **network model** is a navigational database with explicit linkages between records and files. The distinction is that the network model permits a child record to have multiple parents. For example, referring to Figure 3-12, Invoice Number 1 is the child of Salesperson Number 1 and Customer Number 5. Pointer fields in both parent records explicitly define the path to the invoice (child) record. This invoice record has two links to related (sibling) records. The first is a salesperson (SP) link to Invoice Number 2. This record resulted from a sale by Salesperson Number 1 to Customer Number 6. The second pointer is the customer (C) link to Invoice Number 3. This represents the second sale to Customer Number 5, which was processed this time by Salesperson Number 2. Under this data structure, management can track and report sales information pertaining to customers and sales staff.

The structure can be accessed at either of the root level records (salesperson or customer) by entering the appropriate primary key data (SP # or Cust #). Beyond this, the access process is similar to that described for the hierarchical model.

The Relational Model

E. F. Codd originally proposed the principles of the **relational model** in the late 1960s.[3] The formal model has its foundations in relational algebra and set theory, which provide the theoretical basis for most of the data manipulation operations used. The most apparent difference between the relational model and the navigational

FIGURE 3-12 **Linkages in a Network Database**

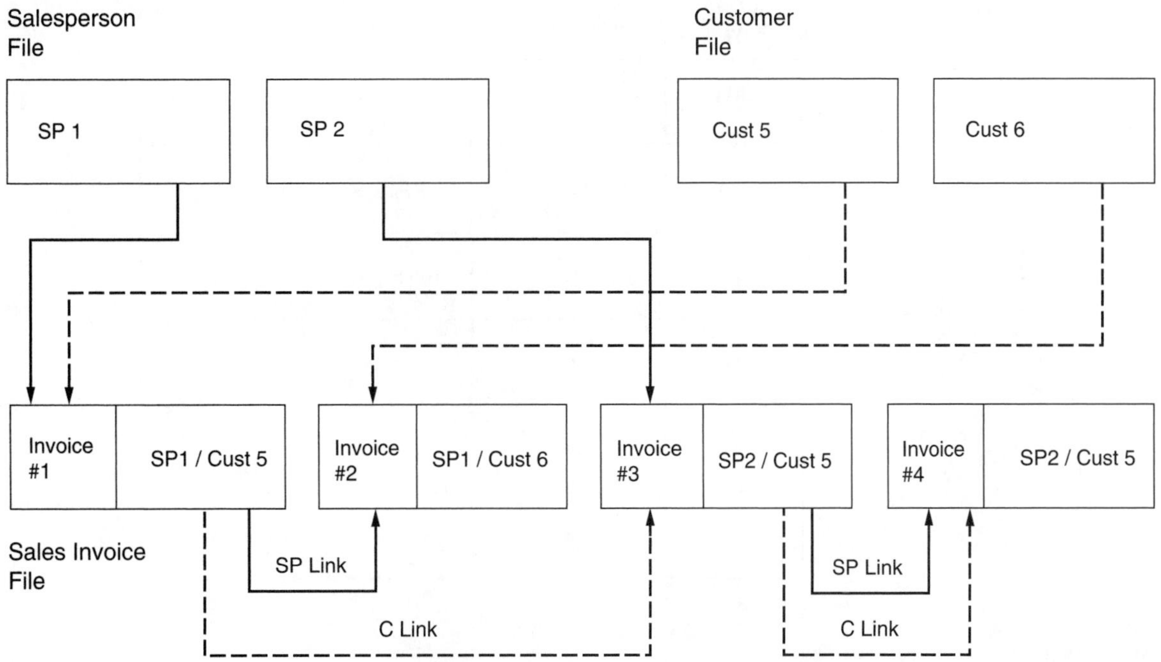

3 C. J. Date, *An Introduction to Database Systems*, vol. 1, 4th ed. (Reading, MS: Addison-Wesley, 1986), p. 99.

models is the way in which data associations are represented to the user. The relational model portrays data in the form of two-dimensional tables. Figure 3-13 presents an example of a database table called Customer.

Across the top of the table are **attributes** (data fields) forming columns. Intersecting the columns to form rows in the table are **tuples**. A tuple is a normalized array of data that is similar, but not precisely equivalent, to a record in a flat-file system. Properly designed tables possess the following four characteristics:

1. All occurrences at the intersection of a row and a column are a single value. No multiple values (repeating groups) are allowed.
2. The attribute values in any column must all be of the same class.
3. Each column in a given table must be uniquely named. However, different tables may contain columns with the same name.
4. Each row in the table must be unique in at least one attribute. This attribute is the primary key.

The table should be normalized. Each attribute in the row should be dependent on (uniquely defined by) the primary key and independent of the other attributes.

FIGURE 3-13 **A Relational Table Called Customer**

Attributes

Table Name = Customer

Tuples (Records)

Cust # (Key)	Name	Address	Current Balance
1875	J. Smith	18 Elm St.	1820.00
1876	G. Adams	21 First St.	2400.00
1943	J. Hobbs	165 High St.	549.87
2345	Y. Martin	321 Barclay	5256.76
•	•	•	•
•	•	•	•
•	•	•	•
5678	T. Stem	432 Main St.	643.67

In the previous section, we saw how navigational databases use explicit linkages (pointers) between records to establish relationships. The linkages in the relational model are implicit. To illustrate this distinction, compare the file structures of the relational tables in Figure 3-14 with those of the hierarchical example in Figure 3-10. The conceptual relationship between files is the same, but note the absence of explicit pointers in the relational tables.

Relations are formed by an attribute that is common to both tables in the relation. For example, the primary key of the Customer table (Cust #) is also an embedded foreign key in both the Sales Invoice and Cash Receipts tables. Similarly, the primary key in the Sales Invoice table (Invoice #) is a foreign key in the Line Item table. Note that the Line Item table uses a composite primary key comprising two fields—Invoice # and Item #. Both fields are needed to identify each record in the table uniquely, but only the invoice number portion of the key provides the logical link to the Sales Invoice table.

FIGURE 3-14 **Data Integration in the Relational Model**

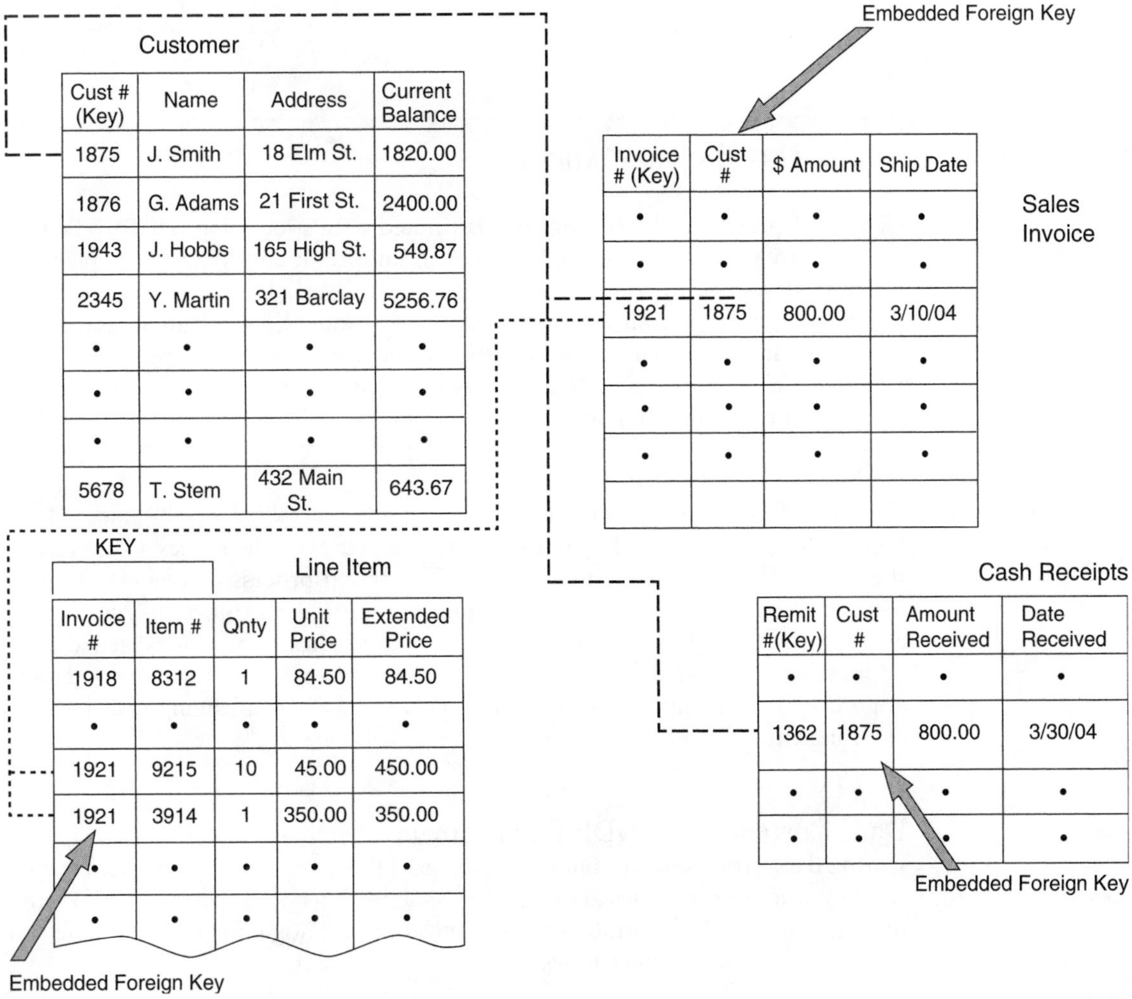

Customer

Cust # (Key)	Name	Address	Current Balance
1875	J. Smith	18 Elm St.	1820.00
1876	G. Adams	21 First St.	2400.00
1943	J. Hobbs	165 High St.	549.87
2345	Y. Martin	321 Barclay	5256.76
•	•	•	•
•	•	•	•
•	•	•	•
5678	T. Stem	432 Main St.	643.67

Sales Invoice

Invoice # (Key)	Cust #	$ Amount	Ship Date
•	•	•	•
•	•	•	•
1921	1875	800.00	3/10/04
•	•	•	•
•	•	•	•
•	•	•	•

Line Item

Invoice #	Item #	Qnty	Unit Price	Extended Price
1918	8312	1	84.50	84.50
•	•	•	•	•
1921	9215	10	45.00	450.00
1921	3914	1	350.00	350.00
•	•	•	•	•
•	•	•	•	•

Cash Receipts

Remit #(Key)	Cust #	Amount Received	Date Received
•	•	•	•
1362	1875	800.00	3/30/04
•	•	•	•
•	•	•	•

Linkages between records in related tables are established through logical operations of the DBMS rather than via explicit addressees that are structured into the database. For example, if a user wants to view all the invoices for Customer 1875, the system would search the Sales Invoice table for records with a foreign key value of 1875. We see from Figure 3-14 that there is only one—Invoice 1921. To obtain the line item details for this invoice, a search is made of the Line Item table for records with a foreign key value of 1921. Two records are retrieved.

The nature of the association between two tables determines the method used for assigning foreign keys. Where the association is one-to-one, it does not matter which table's primary key is embedded in the other as a foreign key. In one-to-many associations, the primary key on the "one" side is embedded as the foreign key on the "many" side. For example, one customer may have many invoice and cash receipts records. Therefore, Cust # is embedded in the records of the Sales Invoice and Cash Receipts tables. Similarly, there is a one-to-many association between the Sales Invoice and Line Item tables. Many-to-many associations between tables do not use embedded foreign keys. Instead, a separate link table containing keys for the related tables needs to be created. In Chapter 7, we examine the design of relational tables in more detail.

Databases in a Distributed Environment

Chapter 2 presented the concept of distributed data processing (DDP). The physical structure of the organization's data is an important consideration in planning a distributed system. In addressing this issue, the planner has two basic options: the databases can be centralized or they can be distributed. Distributed databases fall into two categories: partitioned databases and replicated databases. This section examines issues, features, and trade-offs that need to be evaluated in deciding the disposition of the database.

Centralized Databases

The first approach involves retaining the data in a central location. Remote IT units send requests for data to the central site, which processes the requests and transmits the data back to the requesting IT unit. The actual processing of the data is performed at the remote IT unit. The central site performs the functions of a file manager that services the data needs of the remote sites. The centralized database approach is illustrated in Figure 3-15. A fundamental objective of the database approach is to maintain data currency. This can be a challenging task in a DDP environment.

Data Currency in a DDP Environment

During data processing, account balances pass through a state of **temporary inconsistency** where their values are incorrectly stated. This occurs during the execution of a transaction. To illustrate, consider the computer logic for recording the credit sale of $2,000 to customer Jones.

FIGURE 3-15 **Centralized Database**

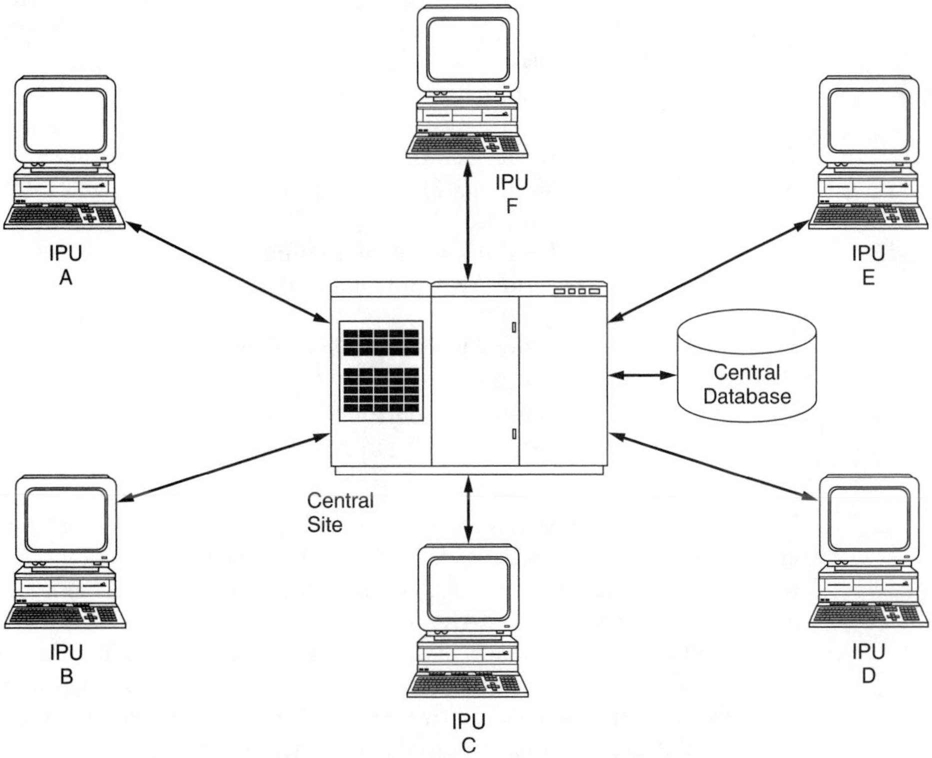

INSTRUCTION		DATABASE VALUES AR-Jones	AR-Control
	START		
1	Read AR-SUB account (Jones)	1500	
2	Read AR-Control account		10000
3	Write AR-SUB account (Jones) + $2000	3500	
4	Write AR-Control account + $2000		12000
	END		

Immediately after the execution of Instruction Number 3, and before the execution of Instruction Number 4, the AR-Control account value is temporarily inconsistent by the sum of $2,000. Only after the completion of the entire transaction is this inconsistency resolved. In a DDP environment, such temporary inconsistencies can result in the corruption of data. To illustrate the potential for damage, let's look at a slightly more complicated example. Using the same computer logic as before, consider the processing of two separate transactions from two remote IT units: Transaction 1 (T1) is the sale of $2,000 on account to customer Jones from IT unit at Site A; Transaction 2 (T2) is the sale of $1,000 on account to customer Smith from IT unit at Site B. The following logic shows the possible interweaving of the two processing tasks and the potential effect on data currency.

INSTRUCTION			DATABASE VALUES		
			Central Site		
IT UNIT A	IT UNIT B		AR-Jones	AR-Smith	AR-Control
T1	T2	START			
1		Read AR-SUB account (Jones)	1500		
	1	Read AR-SUB account (Smith)		3000	
2		Read AR-Control account			10000
3		Write AR-SUB account (Jones) + $2000	3500		
	2	**Read AR-Control account**			10000
4		Write AR-Control account + $2000			12000
	3	Write AR-SUB account (Smith) + $1000		4000	
	4	Write AR-Control account + $1000			11000
	END				

Notice that IT unit B seized the AR-Control data value of $10,000 when it was in an inconsistent state. By using this value to process its transaction, IT unit B effectively erased Transaction T1, which had been processed by IT unit A. Therefore, instead of $13,000, the new AR-Control balance is misstated at $11,000.

To achieve data currency, simultaneous access to individual data elements by multiple IT units must be prevented. The solution to this problem is to employ a **database lockout**, which is a software control (usually a function of the DBMS) that prevents multiple simultaneous accesses to data. The previous example can be used to illustrate this technique. Immediately upon receiving the access request from IT unit A for AR-Control (T1, Instruction Number 2), the central site DBMS should place a lock on AR-Control to prevent access from other IT units until Transaction T1 is complete. When IT unit B requests AR-Control (T2, Instruction Number 2), it is placed on "wait" status until the lock is removed. When site A's transaction has been posted, IT unit B is granted access to AR-Control and can then complete Transaction T2.

Distributed Databases

Distributed databases can be either partitioned or replicated. We examine both approaches in the following pages.

Partitioned Databases

The **partitioned database approach** splits the central database into segments or partitions that are distributed to their primary users. The advantages of this approach follow:

- Having data stored at local sites increases users' control.
- Transaction processing response time is improved by permitting local access to data and reducing the volume of data that must be transmitted between IT units.
- Partitioned databases can reduce the potential effects of a disaster. By locating data at several sites, the loss of a single IT unit cannot terminate all data processing by the organization.

The partitioned approach, which is illustrated in Figure 3-16, works best for organizations that require minimal data sharing among their IT units. The primary user manages data requests from other sites. To minimize data access from remote users, the organization needs to carefully select the host location. Identifying the optimum host requires an in-depth analysis of user data needs.

The Deadlock Phenomenon. In a distributed environment, it is possible for multiple sites to lock out each other from the database, thus preventing each from processing its transactions. For example, Figure 3-17 illustrates three IT units and their mutual data needs. Notice that Site 1 has requested (and locked) Data A and is waiting for the removal of the lock on Data C to complete its transaction. Site 2 has a lock on C and is waiting for E. Finally, Site 3 has a lock on E and is waiting for A. A **deadlock** occurs here because there is mutual exclusion to the data resource, and the transactions are in a "wait" state until the locks are removed. This can result in transactions being incompletely processed and the database being corrupted. A deadlock is a permanent condition that must be resolved by special software that analyzes each deadlock condition to determine the best solution. Because of the implication for transaction processing, accountants should be aware of the issues pertaining to deadlock resolutions.

Deadlock Resolution. Resolving a deadlock usually involves terminating one or more transactions to complete processing of the other transactions in the deadlock. The preempted transactions must then be reinitiated. In preempting transactions, the deadlock resolution software attempts to minimize the total cost of breaking the deadlock. Some of the factors that are considered in this decision follow:

- *The resources currently invested in the transaction.* This may be measured by the number of updates that the transaction has already performed and that must be repeated if the transaction is terminated.

FIGURE 3-16

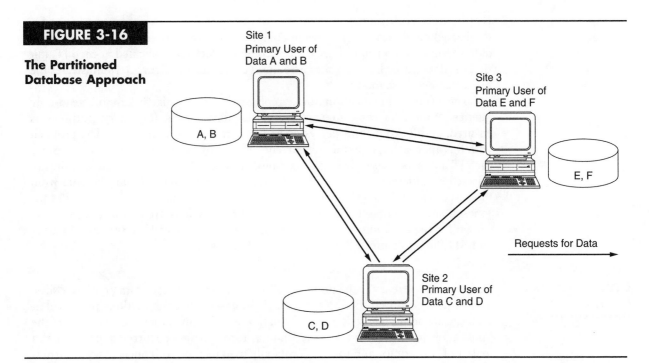

The Partitioned Database Approach

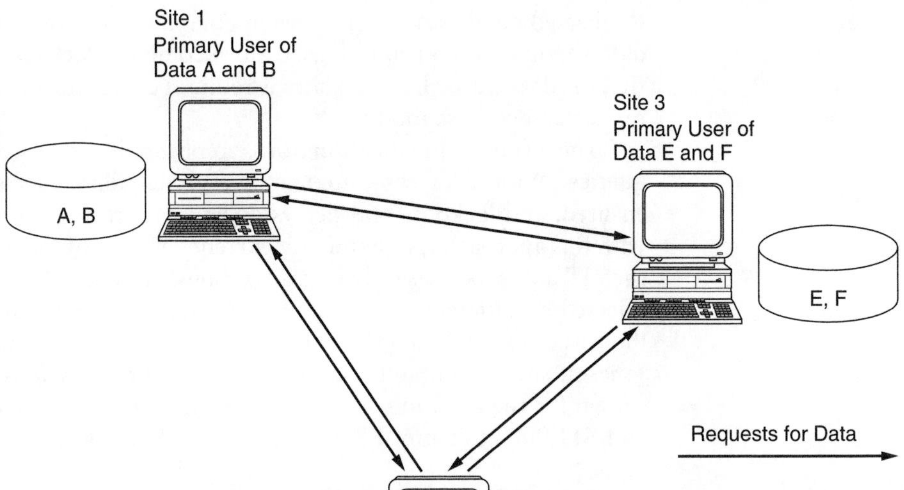

FIGURE 3-17

The Deadlock Condition

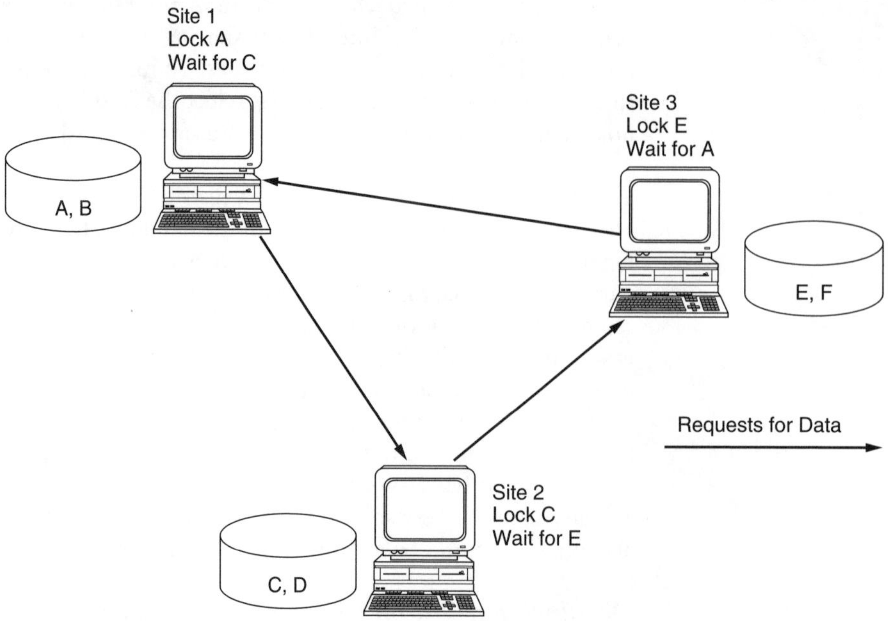

- *The transaction's stage of completion.* In general, deadlock resolution software will avoid terminating transactions that are close to completion.
- *The number of deadlocks associated with the transaction.* Because terminating the transaction breaks all deadlock involvement, the software should attempt to terminate transactions that are part of more than one deadlock.

Replicated Databases

Replicated databases are effective in companies where there exists a high degree of data sharing but no primary user. Since common data are replicated at each IT unit site, the data traffic between sites is reduced considerably. Figure 3-18 illustrates the replicated database model.

The primary justification for a replicated database is to support read-only queries. With data replicated at every site, data access for query purposes is ensured, and lockouts and delays due to data traffic are minimized. The problem with this approach is maintaining current versions of the database at each site. Since each IT unit processes only its transactions, common data replicated at each site are affected by different transactions and reflect different values. Using the data from the earlier example, Figure 3-19 illustrates the effect of processing credit sales for Jones at site A and Smith at site B. After the transactions are processed, the value shown for the common AR-Control account is inconsistent ($12,000 at IT unit A and $11,000 at IT unit B) and incorrect at both sites.

Concurrency Control

Database concurrency is the presence of complete and accurate data at all user sites. System designers need to employ methods to ensure that transactions processed at each site are accurately reflected in the databases of all the other sites. Because of the implication for the accuracy of accounting records, the concurrency problem is a matter of concern for auditors. A commonly used method for **concurrency control** is

FIGURE 3-18

Replicated Database Approach

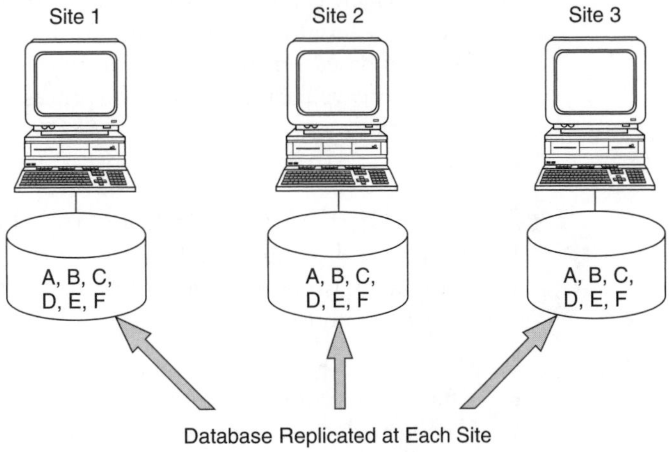

to serialize transactions by time-stamping. This method involves labeling each transaction by two criteria.

First, special software groups transactions into classes to identify potential conflicts. For example, read-only (query) transactions do not conflict with other classes of transactions. Similarly, accounts payable and accounts receivable transactions are not likely to use the same data and do not conflict. However, multiple sales order transactions involving both read and write operations will potentially conflict.

The second part of the control process is to time-stamp each transaction. A system-wide clock is used to keep all sites, some of which may be in different time zones, on the same logical time. Each time stamp is made unique by incorporating the site's ID number. When transactions are received at each IT unit site, they are

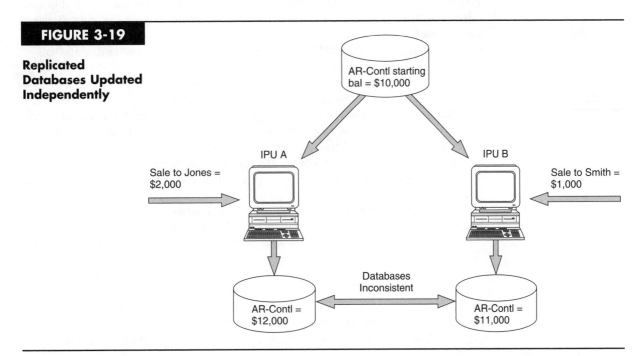

FIGURE 3-19

Replicated Databases Updated Independently

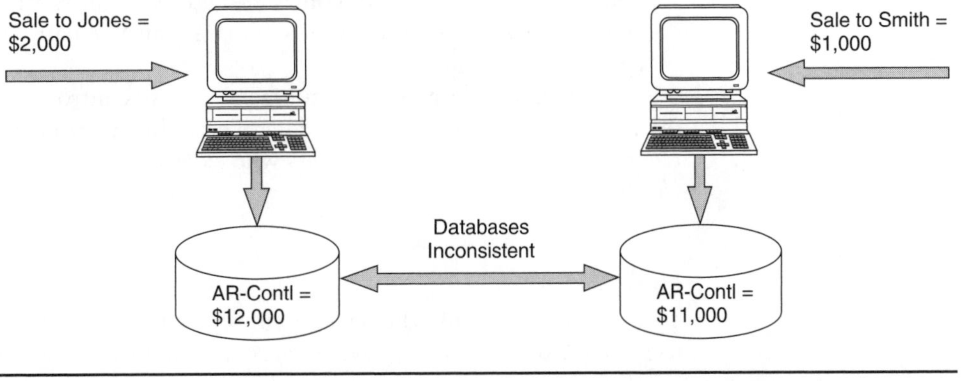

examined first by class for potential conflicts. If conflicts exist, the transactions are entered into a serialization schedule. An algorithm is used to schedule updates to the database based on the transaction time stamp and class. This method permits multiple interleaved transactions to be processed at each site with the effect of being executed serially.

Database Distribution Methods and the Accountant

The decision to distribute databases is one that should be entered into thoughtfully. There are many issues and trade-offs to consider. Here are some of the most basic questions to be addressed:

- Should the organization's data be centralized or distributed?
- If data distribution is desirable, should the databases be replicated or partitioned?
- If replicated, should the databases be totally replicated or partially replicated?
- If the database is to be partitioned, how should the data segments be allocated among the sites?

The choices involved in each of these questions impact the organization's ability to maintain data integrity. The preservation of audit trails and the accuracy of accounting records are key concerns. Clearly, these are decisions that the modern auditor should understand and influence intelligently.

Controlling and Auditing Data Management Systems

Controls over data management systems fall into two general categories: access controls and backup controls. **Access controls** are designed to prevent unauthorized individuals from viewing, retrieving, corrupting, or destroying the entity's data. **Backup controls** ensure that in the event of data loss due to unauthorized access, equipment failure, or physical disaster the organization can recover its database.

Access Controls

Users of flat files maintain exclusive ownership of their data. In spite of the data integration problems associated with this model, it creates an environment in which unauthorized access to data can be effectively controlled. When not in use by the owner, a flat file is closed to other users and may be taken off-line and physically secured in the data library. In contrast, the need to integrate and share data in the database environment means that databases must remain on-line and open to all potential users.

In the shared database environment, access control risks include corruption, theft, misuse, and destruction of data. These threats originate from both unauthorized intruders and authorized users who exceed their access privileges. Several control features are now reviewed.

User Views

The *user view* or subschema is a subset of the total database that defines the user's data domain and provides access to the database. Figure 3-20 illustrates the role of the user view. In a centralized database environment, the database administrator (DBA) has primary responsibility for user view design but works closely with users and systems designers in this task. Access privileges to the database, as defined in their views, should be commensurate with the users' legitimate needs.

Although user views can restrict user access to a limited set of data, they do not define task privileges such as read, delete, or write. Often, several users may share a single user view but have different authority levels. For example, users Smith, Jones, and Adams in Figure 3-20 all may have access to the same set of data: account number, customer name, account balance, and credit limit. Let's assume that all have read authority, but only Jones has authority to modify and delete the data. Effective access control requires more additional security measures, discussed next.

Database Authorization Table

The **database authorization table** contains rules that limit the actions a user can take. This technique is similar to the access control list used in the operating system. Each user is granted certain privileges that are coded in the authority table, which is used to verify the user's action requests. For example, Figure 3-20(a) shows that Jones, Smith, and Adams have access to the same data attributes via a common user view, but the authorization table in Table 3-3 shows that only Jones has the authority to modify and delete the data. Each row in the authority table indicates the level of action (read, insert, modify, or delete) that individuals can take based on their entering the correct password.

FIGURE 3-20

Subschema Restricting Access to Database

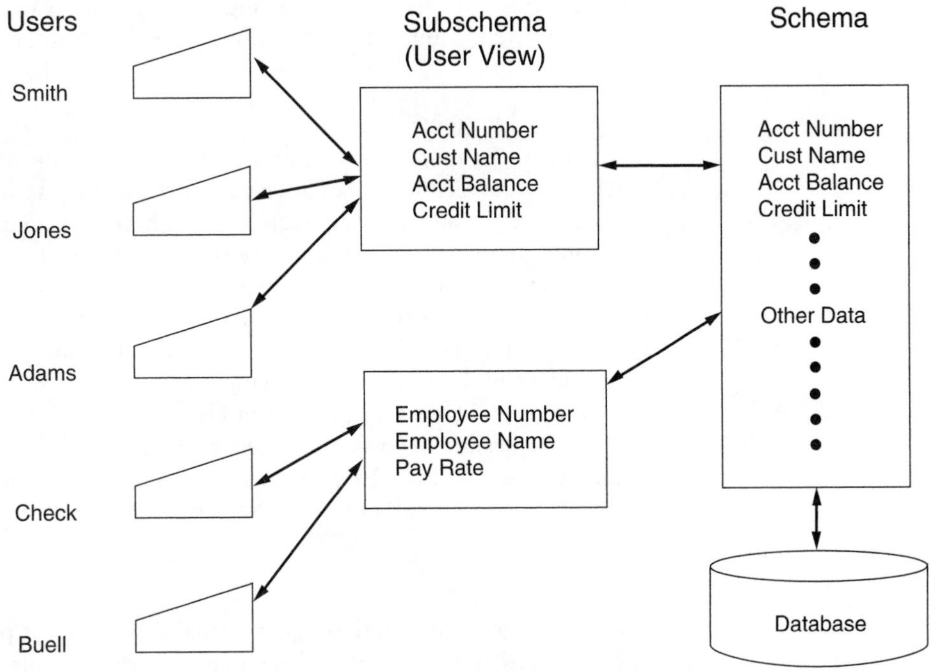

TABLE 3-3

Database Authorization Table

Dept	Accounts Rec			Billings	
User	Jones	Smith	Adams	Check	Buell
Password	Bugs	Dog	Katie	Lucky	Star
Authority:					
Read	Y	Y	Y	Y	Y
Insert	Y	N	Y	Y	N
Modify	Y	N	N	Y	N
Delete	Y	N	N	N	N

User-Defined Procedures

A **user-defined procedure** allows the user to create a personal security program or routine to provide more positive user identification than a single password. Thus, in addition to a password, the security procedure asks a series of personal questions (such as the user's mother's maiden name), which only the legitimate user should know.

Data Encryption

Many database systems use encryption procedures to protect highly sensitive data, such as product formulas, personnel pay rates, password files, and certain financial data. **Data encryption** uses an algorithm to scramble selected data, thus making it unreadable to an intruder "browsing" the database. In addition to protecting stored data, encryption is used for protecting data that are transmitted over communications lines. We examine encryption more fully in Chapter 5.

Biometric Devices

The ultimate in user authentication procedures is the use of **biometric devices,** which measure various personal characteristics, such as fingerprints, voice prints, retina prints, or signature characteristics. These user characteristics are digitized and stored permanently in a database security file or on an identification card that the user carries. When an individual attempts to access the database, a special scanning device captures his or her biometric characteristics, which it compares with the profile data stored on file or the ID card. If the data do not match, access is denied. Biometric technology is currently being used to secure ATM cards and credit cards. Because of the distributed nature of modern systems, the degree of remote access to systems, the decline in costs of biometric systems, and the increased effectiveness of biometric systems, biometric devices have a great potential to serve as effective means of access control, especially from remote locations.

Inference Controls

One advantage of the database query capability is that it provides users with summary and statistical data for decision making. For example, managers might ask the following questions:

- What is the total value for inventory items with monthly turnover less than three?
- What is the average charge to patients with hospital stays greater than eight days?
- What is the total cost of Class II payroll for department XYZ?

Answers to these types of questions are needed routinely for resource management, facility planning, and operations control decisions. Legitimate queries sometimes involve access to confidential data. Thus, individual users may be granted summary and statistical query access to confidential data to which they normally are denied direct access.

To preserve the confidentiality and integrity of the database, **inference controls** should be in place to prevent users from inferring, through query features, specific data values that they otherwise are unauthorized to access. Inference controls attempt to prevent three types of compromises to the database.[4]

1. *Positive compromise*—the user determines the specific value of a data item.
2. *Negative compromise*—the user determines that a data item does not have a specific value.
3. *Approximate compromise*—the user is unable to determine the exact value of an item but is able to estimate it with sufficient accuracy to violate the confidentiality of the data.

Let's use the payroll database table presented in Table 3-4 to illustrate how inference techniques are used to compromise a database. The salary field in the table is the confidential data being sought. Assuming that no inference controls are in place, a user wanting to determine the salary of Mary Swindle, a staff lawyer, could make the following queries:

Q. How many lawyers are female?
A. One.
Q. What is the average salary of all who are female and lawyers?
A. $65,000.

Since she is the only female lawyer, Mary Swindle's salary is explicitly provided by the query system through this statistical feature. This sort of compromise may be prevented by implementing the following inference control rule that places restrictions on the size of the query set to which the system will respond:

> The system will not respond to queries where fewer than two records satisfy the query.

However, a determined and creative user may easily circumvent this control with the following queries:

Q. What is the total salary for the payroll database?
A. $555,000.
Q. What is the total salary for all not lawyers and not female?
A. $490,000.

Swindle's salary can be calculated in this example by subtracting $490,000 from $555,000. Preventing this compromise requires further restrictions on the query set size. This may be accomplished with the following additional inference control rule:

---

4 R. Weber, *EDP Auditing Conceptual Foundations and Practice*, 2d ed. (New York: McGraw-Hill, 1988), p. 564.

TABLE 3-4

Payroll Database Containing Confidential Data

Payroll Database

Empl#	Name	Job Title	Salary	Sex	Other Data
5439	Jim Jones	Consultant	50,000	Male	• •
9887	Sam Smith	Lawyer	60,000	Male	• •
8765	Mary Swindle	Lawyer	65,000	Female	• •
4462	Bob Haub	Manager	60,000	Male	• •
7742	Joan Hess	Consultant	50,000	Female	• •
5532	Ben Huber	Lawyer	62,000	Male	• •
8332	John Enis	Lawyer	63,000	Male	• •
9662	Jim Hobbs	Consultant	70,000	Male	• •
3391	Joe Riley	Manager	75,000	Male	• •

> The system will not respond to queries where greater than $(n - 2)$ records satisfy the query (where n is the number of records in the database).

Under this rule, neither query would have been satisfied.

Audit Objective

- Verify that database access authority and privileges are granted to users in accordance with their legitimate needs.

Audit Procedures

Responsibility for Authority Tables and Subschemas. The auditor should verify that database administration (DBA) personnel retain exclusive responsibility for creating authority tables and designing user views. Evidence may come from three sources: (1) by reviewing company policy and job descriptions, which specify these technical responsibilities; (2) by examining programmer authority tables for access privileges to data definition language (DDL) commands; and (3) through personal interviews with programmers and DBA personnel.

Appropriate Access Authority. The auditor can select a sample of users and verify that their access privileges stored in the authority table are consistent with their organizational functions.

Biometric Controls. The auditor should evaluate the costs and benefits of biometric controls. Generally, these would be most appropriate where highly sensitive data are accessed by a very limited number of users.

Inference Controls. The auditor should verify that database query controls exist to prevent unauthorized access via inference. The auditor can test controls by simulating access by a sample of users and attempting to retrieve unauthorized data via inference queries.

Encryption Controls. The auditor should verify that sensitive data, such as passwords, are properly encrypted. Printing the file contents to hard copy can do this.

Backup Controls

Data can be corrupted and destroyed by malicious acts from external hackers, disgruntled employees, disk failure, program errors, fires, floods, and earthquakes. To recover from such disasters, organizations must implement policies, procedures, and techniques that systematically and routinely provide backup copies of critical files.

Backup Controls in the Flat-File Environment

The backup technique employed will depend on the media and the file structure. Sequential files (both tape and disk) use a backup technique called grandparent–parent–child (GPC). This backup technique is an integral part of the master file update process. Direct access files, by contrast, need a separate backup procedure. Both methods are outlined below.

GPC Backup Technique. Figure 3-21 illustrates the **grandparent–parent–child (GPC)** backup technique that is used in sequential file batch systems. The backup procedure begins when the current master file (the parent) is processed against the transaction file to produce a new updated master file (the child). With the next batch of transactions, the child becomes the current master file (the parent), and the original parent becomes the backup (grandparent) file. The new master file that emerges from the update process is the child. This procedure is continued with each new batch of transactions, creating generations of backup files. When the desired number of backup copies is reached, the oldest backup file is erased (scratched). If the current master file is destroyed or corrupted, processing the most current backup file against the corresponding transaction file can reproduce it.

The systems designer determines the number of backup master files needed for each application. Two factors influence this decision: (1) the financial significance of the system and (2) the degree of file activity. For example, a master file that is updated several times a day may require 30 or 40 generations of backup,

FIGURE 3-21

Grandparent–Parent–Child–Approach

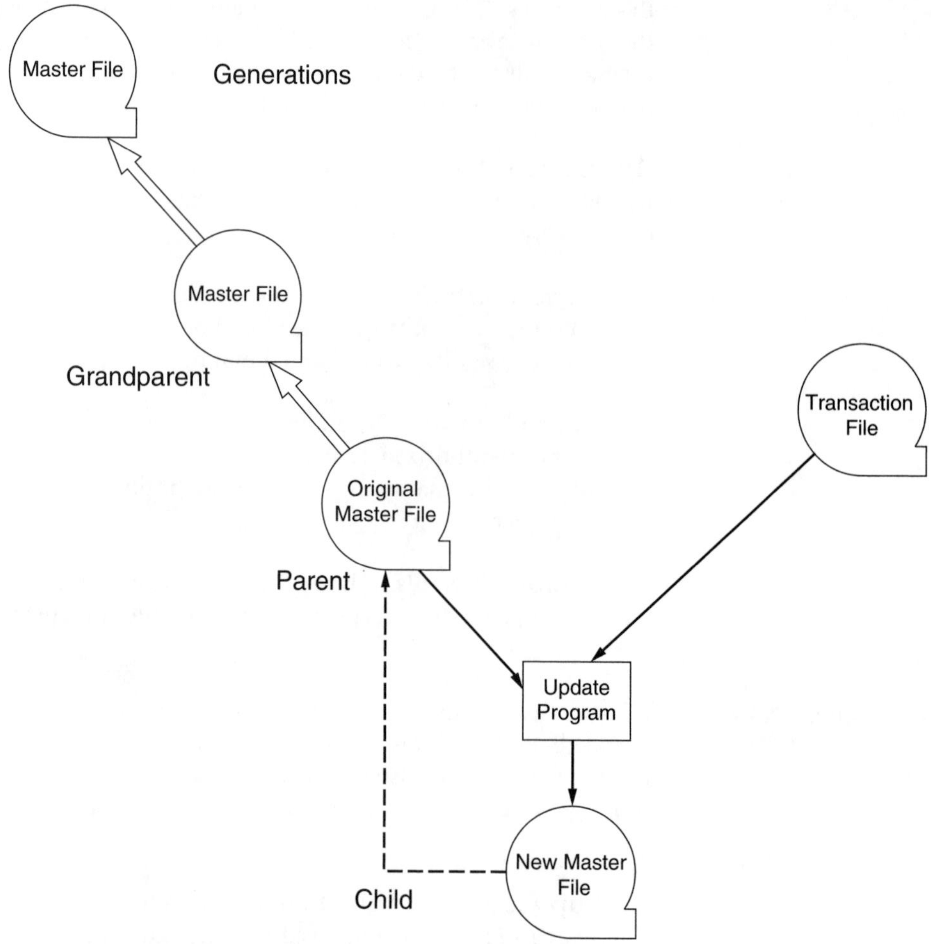

while a file that is updated only once each month may need only four or five backup versions. This decision is important, because certain types of system failures can result in the destruction of large numbers of backup versions within the same family of files.

The author was witness to one system failure that destroyed, through accidental erasure, more than 150 master files in only a few hours. The destruction began when the most current master file (parent) in each application being processed was erased. Then, one by one, the older generations were systematically scratched. Some systems lost as many as 20 backup copies. In fact, the accounts payable system had only one backup version left when the error was finally detected and stopped. Reconstruction of files after such a disaster requires locating the most current remaining backup version and methodically reprocessing the batches of past transactions until the current version of the master file is reproduced. This will also recreate all the intermediate generations of the master file. When using the GPC approach for financial systems, management and auditors should be involved in determining the needed number of backup files. Insufficient backup can result in the total destruction of accounting records. Most operating systems permit the creation of up to 256 generations for each application.

Direct Access File Backup. Data values in direct access files are changed in place through a process called *destructive replacement.* Therefore, once a data value is changed, the original value is destroyed, leaving only one version (the current version) of the file. To provide backup, direct access files must be copied before being updated. Figure 3-22 illustrates this process.

The timing of the **direct access backup** procedures will depend on the processing method being used. Backup of files in batch systems is usually scheduled prior to the update process. Real-time systems pose a more difficult problem. Since transactions are being processed continuously, the backup procedure takes place at specified intervals throughout the day (for example, every 15 minutes).

If the current version of the master file is destroyed through a disk failure or corrupted by a program error, it can be reconstructed with a special recovery program from the most current backup file. In the case of real-time systems, transactions processed since the last backup and prior to the failure will be lost and will need to be reprocessed to restore the master file to current status.

Off-Site Storage. As an added safeguard, backup files created under both the GPC and direct access approaches should be stored off-site in a secure location. **Off-site storage** was discussed in Chapter 2 in the section dealing with disaster recovery planning.

Audit Objective.

- Verify that backup controls in place are effective in protecting data files from physical damage, loss, accidental erasure, and data corruption through system failures and program errors.

Audit Procedures.

- *Sequential File (GPC) Backup.* The auditor should select a sample of systems and determine from the system documentation that the number of GPC backup files specified for each system is adequate. If insufficient backup versions exist, recovery from some types of failure may be impossible.
- *Backup Transaction Files.* The auditor should verify through physical observation that transaction files used to reconstruct the master files are also retained. Without corresponding transaction files, reconstruction is impossible.
- *Direct Access File Backup.* The auditor should select a sample of applications and identify the direct access files being updated in each system. From system documentation and through observation, the auditor can verify that each of them was copied to tape or disk before being updated.
- *Off-Site Storage.* The auditor should verify the existence and adequacy of off-site storage. This audit procedure may be performed as part of the review of the disaster recovery plan or computer center operations controls.

Backup Controls in the Database Environment

Since data sharing is a fundamental objective of the database approach, this environment is particularly vulnerable to damage from individual users. One unauthorized procedure, one malicious act, or one program error can deprive an entire user community of its information resource. Also, because of data centralization, even minor disasters such as a disk failure can affect many or all users.

FIGURE 3-22

Backup of Direct Access Files

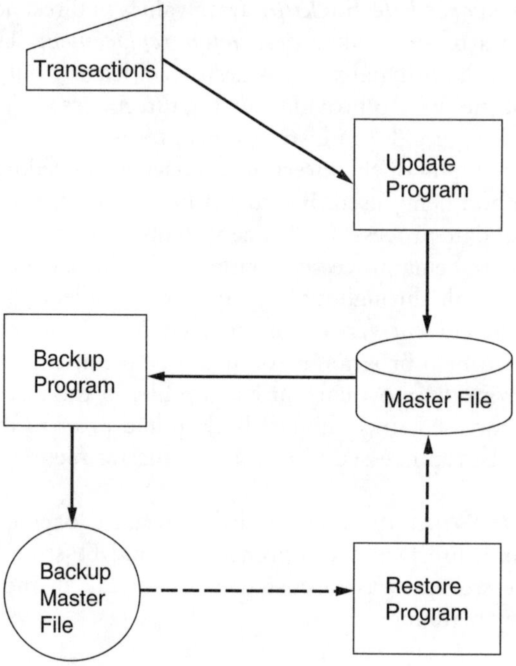

Real-Time Processing System

Real-time systems use timed backup. Transactions processed between backup runs will have to be reprocessed after restoration of the master file.

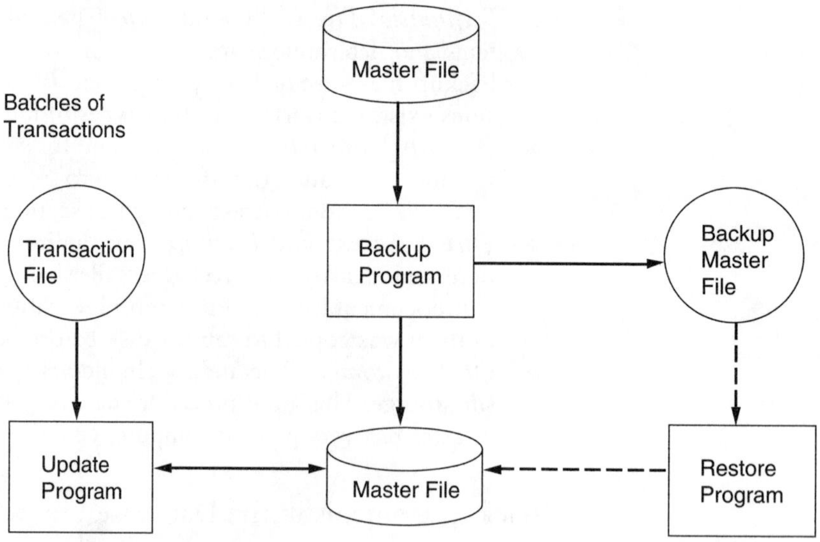

Batch Processing System

In a batch processing system using direct access files, the master file is backed up before the update run.

When such events occur, the organization needs to reconstruct the database to pre-failure status. This can be done only if the database was properly backed up in the first place. Most mainframe DBMSs have a backup and recovery system similar to the one illustrated in Figure 3-23. This system provides four backup and recovery features: database backup, a transaction log, checkpoints, and a recovery module:

Backup. The backup feature makes a periodic backup of the entire database. This is an automatic procedure that should be performed at least once a day. The backup copy should then be stored in a secure remote area.

Transaction Log (Journal). The **transaction log** feature provides an audit trail of all processed transactions. It lists transactions in a transaction log file and records the resulting changes to the database in a separate database change log.

Checkpoint Feature. The **checkpoint** facility suspends all data processing while the system reconciles the transaction log and the database change log against the database. At this point, the system is in a *quiet state*. Checkpoints occur automatically several times an hour. If a failure occurs, it is usually possible to restart the processing from the last checkpoint. Thus, only a few minutes of transaction processing must be repeated.

Recovery Module. The **recovery module** uses the logs and backup files to restart the system after a failure.

FIGURE 3-23

Database Backup and Recovery

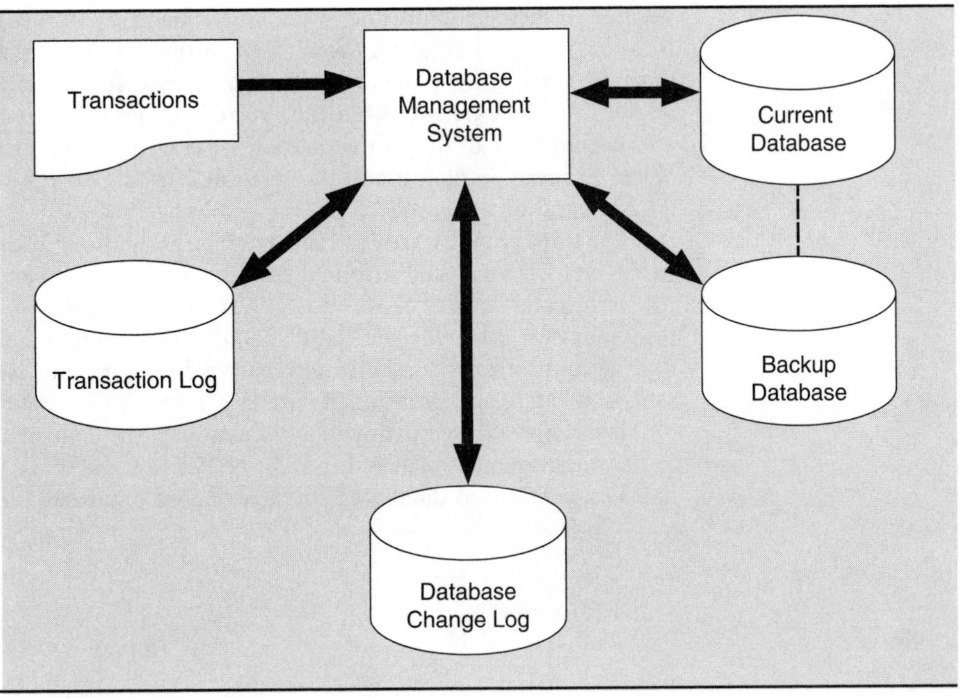

Audit Objective.

- Verify that controls over the data resource are sufficient to preserve the integrity and physical security of the database.

Audit Procedure.

The auditor should verify that backup is performed routinely and frequently to facilitate the recovery of lost, destroyed, or corrupted data without excessive reprocessing. Production databases should be copied at regular intervals (perhaps several times an hour). A balance must be sought between the inconvenience of frequent backup activities and the business disruption caused by excessive reprocessing that is needed to restore the database after a failure. The auditor should verify that automatic backup procedures are in place and functioning, and that copies of the database are stored off-site for further security.

SUMMARY

Data management can be divided into two general approaches: the flat-file model and the database model. The chapter began with a description of flat-file data management, which is used in many older (legacy) systems. Private ownership of data characterizes this model and is the cause of several problems that inhibit data integration. A conceptual overview of the database model was used to illustrate how the problems associated with the flat-file model can be resolved through data sharing and centralized control of data.

The second section described the key functions and defining features of three common database models: the hierarchical, the network, and the relational models. The hierarchical and network models are called navigational databases because of their structure and inflexibility. Seen as a marked improvement over flat files, navigational databases were used in the design of many late-era legacy systems that are still in operation today. Newer accounting information systems, however, make extensive use of the relational model. This model presents data in a two-dimensional format that is easy for end users to understand and work with. When properly implemented, the relational model effectively supports entitywide data integration.

The third section examined the database technology and applications in the distributed environment. Distributed data processing (DDP) empowers end users with ownership and control of IT resources, including databases. This section presented techniques for achieving the goals of DDP while maintaining the principles of data sharing and integration. Three alternative configurations were examined: centralized, replicated, and partitioned databases.

The chapter concluded with a discussion of the control and audit issues related to data management. The risks, audit objectives, and audit procedures relevant to flat files, centralized databases, and distributed databases were presented.

Key Terms

access controls
access method
application development software
attributes
backup controls
biometric devices
checkpoint
concurrency control
currency of information
data attribute (field)
data definition language (DDL)
data dictionary
data hierarchy
data encryption
data manipulation language (DML)
data storage
data structures
data updating
database administrator (DBA)
database authorization table
database lockout
database management system (DBMS)
database model
deadlock
direct access backup
enterprise database
entity
flat-file model
grandparent-parent-child (GPC)
hierarchical data model
inference controls
internal view
legacy systems
many-to-many (M:M) association
navigational models
network model
off-site storage
one-to-many (1:M) association
one-to-one (1:1) association
organization
partitioned database approach
physical database
record association
record type
recovery module
relational model
replicated databases
schema (conceptual view)
Structured Query Language (SQL)
subschema (user view)
task-data dependency
temporary inconsistency
transaction log
tuples
user views
user-defined procedure
users

Review Questions

1. What is a legacy system?
2. What is the flat-file model?
3. What are the four primary elements of the database approach?
4. What types of problems does data redundancy cause?
5. What flat-file data management problems are solved as a result of using the database concept?
6. What are four ways in which database management systems provide a controlled environment to manage user access and the data resources?
7. Explain the relationship between the three levels of the data definition language. As a user, which level would you be most interested in?
8. What is the internal view of a database?
9. What is SQL?
10. What is QBE?
11. What is a data dictionary, and what purpose does it serve?
12. What are the two fundamental components of data structures?
13. What are the criteria that influence the selection of the data structure?
14. What is a data attribute (or field)?
15. Define a data record.
16. What is a record association?
17. What is a database?
18. What is an enterprise database?

19. Discuss and give an example of one-to-one, one-to-many, and many-to-many record associations.
20. Why is a hierarchical database model considered to be a navigational database? What are some limitations of the hierarchical database model?
21. What is a partitioned database, and what are its advantages? Specify any disadvantages.
22. What is a replicated database, and why is concurrency control difficult to manage in this setting?
23. What is time-stamping, and why is it useful?
24. Explain the grandparent–parent–child backup technique. Is it used for sequential files or direct access techniques? Why? How many generations can be backed up?
25. Distinguish between data access and access privileges. Give an example by designing and explaining a database authorization table.
26. What are inference controls? Why are they needed?
27. What are the four basic backup and recovery features necessary in a DBMS? Briefly explain each.
28. What is data encryption?
29. What are biometric devices?
30. What is a user-defined procedure?

Discussion Questions

1. In the flat-file data management environment, users are said to own their data files. What is meant by this "ownership" concept?
2. Discuss the potential aggravations you might face as a student as a result of your university using a traditional data management environment—that is, different databases for the registrar, library, parking permits, and so on.
3. Discuss why control procedures over access to the database become more crucial under the database concept than in the flat-file data management environment. What role does the DBMS play in helping to control the database environment?
4. What is the relationship between a schema and a subschema?
5. Discuss the two ways in which users can access the database in a database environment.
6. How are special database commands inserted into conventional application programs? Why is this necessary?
7. Why might it be advantageous for an organization to use DML commands written in COBOL versus a proprietary programming language?
8. SQL has been said to place power in the hands of the user. What is meant by this statement?
9. Discuss the importance of the role of the database administrator. Why wasn't such a role necessary in the traditional data management environment? What tasks are performed by the DBA?
10. As users determine new computer application needs, requests must be sent to both the system programmers and the DBA. Why is it important that these two groups perform separate functions, and what are these functions?
11. How can data be centralized in a distributed data processing system?
12. In a distributed data processing system, why can temporary inconsistencies result in permanent damage to accounting records? Explain with an example.
13. Explain the deadlock phenomenon. Discuss how it could occur with a phone-in mail order system that locks the inventory records until the order is complete.
14. Which database method would be most appropriate for ticket sales at 30 different outlets to an assigned seating concert? Why?
15. Why is it risky to allow programmers to create user subschemas and assign access authority to users? What unethical technique do programmers sometimes use when they are not allowed to assign access authority to users?
16. Is access control of greater concern in the flat-file or database file environment?
17. How can passwords actually circumvent security? What actions can be taken to minimize this?
18. Describe the characteristics of properly designed relational tables.

19. In a database environment, individual users may be granted summary and statistical query access to confidential data to which they normally are denied direct access. Describe how security can be preserved through inference controls.
20. Describe the backup and recovery features of centralized DBMSs.

MULTIPLE-CHOICE QUESTIONS

1. CMA 1289 5-7
   The database approach to systems and the resulting concept of database management systems have several unique characteristics not found in traditional (flat-file) systems, specifically file-oriented systems. Which one of the following statements does not apply to database-oriented systems?
   a. Database systems have data independence; that is, the data and the programs are maintained separately, except during processing.
   b. Database systems contain a data definition language that helps describe each schema and subschema.
   c. The database administrator is the part of the software package that instructs the operating aspects of the program when data are retrieved.
   d. A primary goal of database systems is to minimize data redundancy.
   e. Database systems increase user interface with the system through increased accessibility and flexibility.
2. CMA 685 5-30
   One of the first steps in the creation of a database is to
   a. define common variables and fields used throughout the firm.
   b. increase the secondary storage capacity.
   c. obtain software that will facilitate data retrieval.
   d. integrate the accounting system into the database.
   e. study the need for a larger central processing unit.
3. CMA 685 5-33
   If a database has integrity, the
   a. software was implemented after extensive acceptance testing.
   b. database has only consistent data.
   c. database is secure from accidental entry.
   d. database and the system have been reviewed by an external auditor.
   e. incidence of failure for the database is within statistically acceptable limits.
4. CMA 687 5-14
   The installation of a database management system is not likely to have any direct impact on
   a. data redundancy within files.
   b. sharing of common data.
   c. inconsistencies within common data fields.
   d. the logic needed to solve a problem in an application program.
   e. the internal control of data accuracy and access.
5. CMA 1287 5-3
   The increased use of database processing systems makes managing data and information a major information service function. Because the databases of an organization are used for many different applications, they are coordinated and controlled by a database administrator. The functions of a database administrator are
   a. data input preparation, database design, and database operations.
   b. database design, database operation, and database security.
   c. database design, database operation, and equipment operations.
   d. database design, software support, and database security.
   e. database operations, hardware support, and software support.
6. CMA 689 5-8
   A disk storage unit may be preferred over a magnetic tape drive system because the disk storage unit
   a. is a cheaper medium for data storage.
   b. offers random access to data files.
   c. offers sequential access to data files.

d. can be measured in bytes per inch.
e. has nine tracks.

7. CIA 1186 III-33
In an inventory system on a database management system, one stored record contains part number, part name, part color, and part weight. These individual items are called
a. fields.
b. stored files.
c. bytes.
d. occurrences.

8. CIA 1187 III-28
Which of the following is a characteristic of a database system?
a. Data within the system exist separately from programs.
b. Database processing is inherently simple.
c. A database system is relatively inexpensive to purchase or develop.
d. Database processing was developed to meet microcomputer requirements.

9. CMA 1289 5-6
A system with several computers that are connected for communication and data transmission purposes but that permits each computer to process its own data is a
a. distributed data processing network.
b. centralized network.
c. decentralized network.
d. multidrop network.
e. hybrid system.

10. For those instances where individual users may be granted summary and statistical query access to confidential data to which they normally are denied access, which type of control is *most* suitable?
a. user-defined procedures
b. data encryption
c. inference controls
d. biometric devices

11. CMA 685 5-31
The identification of users who have permission to access data elements in a database is found in the
a. operating system.
b. systems manual.
c. database schema.
d. database authority table.
e. application programs.

12. A checkpoint or restart procedure is primarily designed to recover from
a. programming errors.
b. data input errors.
c. computer operator errors.
d. hardware failures.
e. All of the above.

PROBLEMS

1. DBMS versus Flat-File Processing
The Werner Manufacturing Corporation has a flat-file processing system. The information processing facility is very large. Different applications, such as order processing, production planning, inventory management, accounting systems, payroll, and marketing systems, use separate tape and disk files. The corporation has recently hired a consulting firm to investigate the possibility of switching to a database management system. Prepare a memo to the top management team at Werner explaining the advantages of a DBMS. Also, discuss the necessity of a database administrator and the job functions this person would perform.

2. Database Design
Design a relational database system for a large costume rental store. The store has approximately 3,200 customers each year. It is stocked with over 500 costumes in various sizes. The rental costumes and other items that may be purchased by the customer (e.g., make-up and teeth) are purchased from approximately 35 different suppliers. Design the necessary database files. Make sure they are in third normal form, and indicate the necessary linkages.

3. Database Design
Sears Roebuck, the most well-known and oldest mail-order retailer in the country, discontinued its

mail-order operations a few years ago. Other mail-order marketers use information systems to trim printing and postage costs of their catalogs. They also want to more effectively target their customers. Explain how an appropriately designed coding system for inventory items incorporated in a database management system with SQL capabilities could allow more cost-efficient and effective mail-order operations. Sketch the necessary database files.

4. **Database Deadlock**
How is a lockout different from a deadlock? Give an accounting example to illustrate why a database lockout is necessary and how a deadlock can occur. Use actual table names in your example.

5. **System Configuration**
First State Bank provides full banking services to its customers through
   a. automatic teller machines.
   b. checking and saving accounts.
   c. certificates of deposit.
   d. loans.
   e. electronic payroll.
   f. electronic payment of customers' bills.

The bank has 11 branch offices that cover a 30-mile radius. The main office maintains a mainframe computer that serves the branch offices. The competitive nature of the banking industry requires that customer satisfaction be considered. Customers want prompt and accurate servicing of transactions. Thus, accuracy and speed are crucial to the success of First State Bank. How would you suggest the databases and data communications facilities be configured for First State Bank?

6. **Database Authorization Table**
The following information is stored in two relational database files:

Employee Master File
- Social security number
- Name
- Address
- Date hired
- Hourly wage rate
- Marital status
- Number of exemptions

Weekly Payroll File
- Social security number
- Hours worked
- Deductions
- Bonuses

Required:
   a. Bogey works in personnel and Bacall works in payroll. Prepare a database authorization table that you think is appropriate for Bogey and Bacall for these two files.
   b. Discuss any potential exposure if the right prevention devices are not in place or if Bogey and Bacall collude.

7. **Distributed Databases**
The XYZ company is a geographically distributed organization with several sites around the country. Users at these sites need rapid access to common data for read-only purposes. Which distributed database method is best under these circumstances? Explain your reasoning.

8. **Distributed Databases**
The ABC Company is a geographically distributed organization with several sites around the country. Users at these sites need rapid access to data for transaction processing purposes. The sites are autonomous; they do not share the same customers, products, or suppliers. Which distributed database method is best under these circumstances? Explain your reasoning.

CHAPTER 4

Systems Development and Maintenance Activities

Learning Objectives

After studying this chapter, you should:

- Be able to identify the stages in the SDLC.
- Be familiar with common problems that can lead to failure in the systems development process.
- Understand the importance of strategic system planning.
- Have a general understanding of how accountants participate in the SDLC.
- Be able to identify the basic features of both the structured and object-oriented approaches to systems design.
- Be able to identify and discuss the major steps involved in a cost-benefit analysis of proposed information systems.
- Understand the advantages and disadvantages of the commercial software option, and be able to discuss the decision-making process used to select commercial software.
- Understand the purpose of a system walkthrough.
- Be familiar with the different types of system documentation and the purposes they serve.

One of the most valuable assets of the modern business organization is a responsive, user-oriented information system. A well-designed system can increase productivity, reduce inventories, eliminate nonvalue-added activities, improve customer service and management decisions, and coordinate activities throughout the organization.

This chapter begins by describing the roles of the participants involved in developing an organization's information system, including systems professionals, users, and stakeholders. Then it outlines the key activities that constitute the systems development life cycle (SDLC). These include *systems planning, systems analysis, conceptual design, system selection, detailed design, system implementation*, and *systems maintenance*. This multistage procedure is used to guide systems development in many organizations. Finally, it discusses SDLC risks, controls, and audit issues.

Participants in Systems Development

The participants in systems development can be classified into four broad groups: systems professionals, end users, stakeholders, and accountants/auditors.

1. **Systems professionals** are systems analysts, systems engineers, and programmers. These individuals actually build the system. They gather facts about problems with the current system, analyze these facts, and formulate a solution to solve the problems. The product of their efforts is a new system.
2. **End users** are those for whom the system is built. There are many users at all levels in an organization. These include managers, operations personnel, accountants, and internal auditors. In some organizations, it is difficult to find someone who is not a user. During systems development, systems professionals work with the primary users to obtain an understanding of the users' problems and a clear statement of their needs.
3. **Stakeholders** are individuals either within or outside the organization who have an interest in the system but are not end users. These include accountants, internal and external auditors, and the internal steering committee that oversees systems development.
4. **Accountants/Auditors** are those professionals who address the controls, accounting, and auditing issues for systems development. This involvement should include internal auditors, especially IS auditors. However, professional standards and ethics limit the level of involvement in some instances, and outright prohibit the direct involvement of external auditors. Their involvement would be in terms of providing general guidance and input. These limitations are driven by the need for independence on the part of all auditors.

Why Are Accountants and Auditors Involved with SDLC?

The SDLC process is of interest to accountants and auditors for two reasons. First, the creation of an information system entails significant financial transactions. Conceptually, systems development is like any manufacturing process that produces a complex product through a series of stages. Such transactions must be planned, authorized, scheduled, accounted for, and controlled. Accountants are as concerned with the integrity of this process as they are with any manufacturing process that has financial resource implications. Because of their background, experience, and training, accountants and auditors are experts in financial transactions and thus can provide critical input into the system regarding controls, integrity, timeliness, and a number of other important aspects of financial transactions.

The second and more pressing concern for accountants and auditors is with the nature of the products that emerge from the SDLC. The quality of accounting information rests directly on the SDLC activities that produce accounting information systems (AIS). These systems are used to deliver accounting information to internal and external users. The accountant's responsibility is to ensure that the systems employ the proper accounting conventions and rules, and possess adequate controls. Therefore, accountants are greatly concerned with the quality of the process that produces AIS. For example, a sales order system produced by a defective SDLC may suffer from serious control weaknesses that introduce errors into the financial accounting records, or provide opportunity for a fraudster to steal from the organization.

How Are Accountants Involved with the SDLC?

Accountants are involved in systems development in three ways. First, accountants are users. All systems that process financial transactions impact the accounting function in some way. Like all users, accountants must provide a clear picture of their problems and needs to the systems professionals. For example, accountants must specify accounting techniques to be used, internal control requirements (such as audit trails), and special algorithms (such as depreciation models).

Second, accountants participate in systems development as members of the development team. Their involvement often extends beyond the development of strictly AIS applications. Systems that do not process financial transactions directly may still draw from accounting data. The accountant may be consulted to provide advice or to determine if the proposed system constitutes an internal control risk. In all cases, the level of participation by auditors is limited by independence issues in professional standards and ethics.

Third, accountants are involved in systems development as auditors. Accounting information systems must be auditable. Some computer audit techniques require special features that need to be designed into the system. For example, the more paperless a system is, the more logs and information in logs become important, and the more auditors will need log data. The auditor/accountant has a stake in all systems and should be involved early in their design, especially regarding auditability, security, and controls.

Information Systems Acquisition

Organizations usually acquire information systems in two ways: (1) they develop customized systems in-house through formal systems development activities and (2) they purchase commercial systems from software vendors. This section of the text discusses these two alternatives.

In-House Development

Many organizations require systems that are highly tuned to their unique operations. These firms design their own information systems through in-house systems development activities. In-house development requires maintaining a full-time systems staff of analysts and programmers who identify user information needs and satisfy their needs with custom systems.

Commercial Systems

A growing number of systems are purchased from software vendors. Faced with many competing packages, each with unique features and attributes, management must choose the system and the vendor that best serve the needs of the organization. Making the optimal choice requires that this be an informed decision.

Trends in Commercial Software

Four factors have stimulated the growth of the commercial software market: (1) the relatively low cost of general commercial software as compared to customized software; (2) the emergence of industry-specific vendors who target their software to the needs of particular types of businesses; (3) a growing demand from businesses that are too small to afford in-house systems' development staff; and (4) the trend toward downsizing of organizational units and the resulting move toward the distributed data processing environment, which has made the commercial software option more appealing to larger organizations. Indeed, organizations that maintain their own in-house systems' development staff will often purchase commercial software when the need permits. Commercial software packages fall into three basic groups: turnkey systems, backbone systems, and vendor-supported systems.

Types of Commercial Systems

Turnkey Systems. **Turnkey systems** are completely finished and tested systems that are ready for implementation. These are often general-purpose systems or systems customized to a specific industry. Turnkey systems are usually sold only as compiled program modules, and users have limited ability to customize them to their specific needs. Some turnkey systems have software options that allow the user to customize input, output, and some processing through menu choices. Other turnkey system vendors will sell their customers the source code if program changes are desired. For a fee, the user or the vendor can then customize the system by reprogramming the original source code. Some examples of turnkey systems are described next.

General Accounting Systems. **General accounting systems** are designed to serve a wide variety of user needs. By mass-producing a standard system, the vendor is able to reduce the unit cost of these systems to a fraction of in-house development costs. Powerful systems of this sort can be obtained for under $2,000.

To provide as much flexibility as possible, general accounting systems are designed in modules. This allows users to purchase the modules that meet their specific needs. Typical modules include accounts payable, accounts receivable, payroll processing, inventory control, general ledger, financial reporting, and fixed asset.

Special-Purpose Systems. Some software vendors create **special-purpose systems** that target selected segments of the economy. For example, the medical field, the banking industry, and government agencies have unique accounting procedures, rules, and conventions that general-purpose accounting systems do not always accommodate. Software vendors have thus developed standardized systems to deal with industry-specific procedures.

Office Automation Systems. **Office automation systems** are computer systems that improve the productivity of office workers. Examples of office automation systems include word processing packages, database management systems, spreadsheet programs, and desktop publishing systems.

Backbone Systems. **Backbone systems** provide a basic system structure on which to build. Backbone systems come with all the primary processing modules programmed. The vendor designs and programs the user interface to suit the client's needs. Some systems such as Enterprise Resource Planning (ERP) offer a vast array of modules for dealing with almost every conceivable business process, and all are interfaced seamlessly into a single system. By selecting the appropriate modules, the customer can create a highly customized system. Customizing a commercial system, however, is expensive and time consuming. A fully functional ERP system typically takes 18 to 24 months to install and costs anywhere from $10 million to $100 million.

Vendor-Supported Systems. **Vendor-supported systems** are hybrids of custom systems and commercial software. Under this approach, the vendor develops (and maintains) custom systems for its clients. The systems themselves are custom products, but the systems development service is commercially provided. This option is popular in the health care and legal services industries. Since the vendor serves as the organization's in-house systems development staff, the client organization must rely on the vendor to provide custom programming and on-site maintenance of systems. Much of each client's system may be developed from scratch, but by using an object-oriented approach, vendors can produce common modules that can be reused in other client systems. This approach helps to reduce development costs charged to the client firms.

Advantages of Commercial Software

- **Implementaion Time.** Custom systems often take a long time to develop. Months or even years may pass before a custom system can be developed through in-house procedures. Unless the organization successfully anticipates future information needs and schedules application development accordingly, it may experience long periods of unsatisfied need. However, commercial software can be implemented almost immediately once a need is recognized. The user does not have to wait.
- **Cost.** A single user must wholly absorb in-house development costs. However, since the cost of commercial software is spread across many users, the unit cost is reduced to a fraction of the cost of a system developed in-house.
- **Reliability.** Most reputable commercial software packages are thoroughly tested before their release to the consumer market. Any system errors not discovered during testing are likely to be uncovered by user organizations shortly after release and corrected. Although no system is certified as being free from errors, commercial software is less likely to have errors than an equivalent in-house system.

Disadvantages of Commercial Software

- **Independence.** Purchasing a vendor-supported system makes the firm dependent on the vendor for maintenance. The user runs the risk that the vendor will cease to support the system or even go out of business. This is perhaps the greatest disadvantage of vendor-supported systems.
- **The need for customized systems.** The prime advantage of in-house development is the ability to produce applications to exact specifications. This advantage also describes a disadvantage of commercial software. Sometimes, the user's needs are unique and complex, and commercially available software is either too general or too inflexible.
- **Maintenance.** Business information systems undergo frequent changes. If the user's needs change, it may be difficult or even impossible to modify commercial software. In-house development, however, provides users with proprietary applications that can be economically maintained.

THE SYSTEMS DEVELOPMENT LIFE CYCLE

Both the in-house development and the commercial package options have advantages and disadvantages. They are not, however, mutually exclusive propositions. A company may satisfy some of its information needs by purchasing commercial software and develop other systems in-house. Both approaches are enhanced by formal procedures that lend structure to the decision-making process. The systems development life cycle described next is generally associated with in-house development, but many of its phases, particularly those involving needs analysis and system specification, can be effectively employed even when the final system is purchased from an outside vendor.

The objectives and sequence of **systems development life cycle (SDLC)** activities are logical and generally accepted by experts in the systems community, and are generally treated as "best practices" for systems development. However, the number and the names of specific stages within this process are matters of some disagreement. Different authorities have proposed SDLC models with as few as 4 and as many as 14 specific activities. From an auditing point of view, the number of actual stages is of no particular importance. We are concerned about the substance and the consistent application of this process, however it is defined. The SDLC in Figure 4-1 is an eight-phase process consisting of two major stages: new systems development and maintenance.

The first seven phases of the SDLC describe the activities that all new systems should undergo. **New systems development** involves conceptual steps that can apply to any problem-solving process: identify the problem, understand what needs to be done, consider alternative solutions, select the best solution, and, finally, implement the solution. Each phase in the SDLC produces a set of required documentation that together constitutes a body of audit evidence about the overall quality the SDLC.

FIGURE 4-1 **Systems Development Life Cycle**

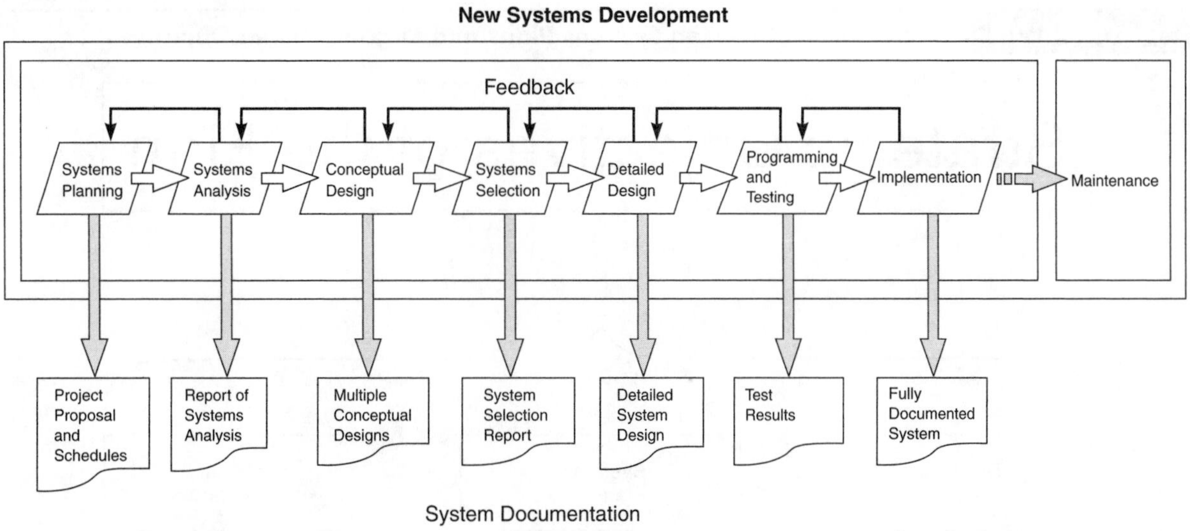

1. Systems planning
2. Systems analysis
3. Conceptual systems design
4. System evaluation and selection
5. Detailed design
6. System programming and testing
7. System implementation

An eighth step, **systems maintenance**, encompasses the majority of the system's life cycle. It begins once the seven phases are complete and the system is fully implemented. Each of the phases is briefly outlined below.

SYSTEMS PLANNING—PHASE I

The objective of **systems planning** is to link individual system projects or applications to the strategic objectives of the firm. In fact, the basis for the systems plan is the organization's business plan, which specifies where the firm plans to go and how it will get there. In particular, systems projects are analyzed by using the IT strategic plan, which is developed from and congruent with the organization's business plan. Figure 4-2 presents the relationship between these plans and the strategic objectives of the firm. There must be congruence between the individual projects and the business plan, or the firm may fail to meet its objectives. Effective systems planning provides this goal congruence.

Who Should Do Systems Planning?

Most firms that take systems planning seriously establish a systems steering committee to provide guidance and review the status of system projects. The composition of the **steering committee** may include the chief executive officer, the chief financial officer, the chief information officer, senior management from user areas, the internal auditor, and senior management from computer services. External parties, such as management consultants and the firm's external auditors, may also

FIGURE 4-2 **Relationship between Systems Plans and Organizational Objectives**

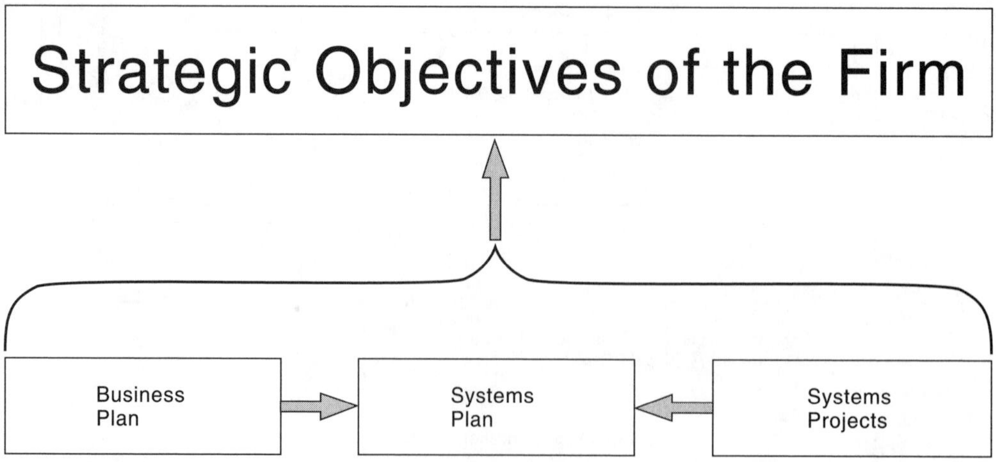

supplement the committee. Typical responsibilities for a steering committee include the following:

- Resolving conflicts that arise from new systems
- Reviewing projects and assigning priorities
- Budgeting funds for systems development
- Reviewing the status of individual projects under development
- Determining at various checkpoints throughout the SDLC whether to continue with the project or terminate it

Systems planning occurs at two levels: strategic systems planning and project planning.

Strategic Systems Planning

Strategic systems planning involves the allocation of systems resources at the macro level. It usually deals with a time frame of three to five years. This process is similar to budgeting resources for other strategic activities, such as product development, plant expansions, market research, and manufacturing technology.

Technically, strategic systems planning is not part of the SDLC because the SDLC pertains to specific applications. The strategic systems plan is concerned with the allocation of such systems resources as employees (the number of systems professionals to be hired), hardware (the number of workstations, minicomputers, and mainframes to be purchased), software (the funds to be allocated to new systems projects and for systems maintenance), and telecommunications (the funds allocated to networking and EDI). It is important that the strategic plan avoid excessive detail. The plan must allow systems specialists to make informed decisions by considering such relevant factors as price, performance measures, size, security, and control.

Why Perform Strategic Systems Planning? Perhaps no aspect of a firm's business activities is as volatile and unpredictable as information systems planning. Who can look five years into the future and accurately predict the state of systems technology? Because of this volatility, any long-term plans a firm makes are likely to change. How, therefore, can a firm do strategic systems planning? Why should it?

There are four justifications for strategic systems planning:

1. *A plan that changes constantly is better than no plan at all.* Strategic planning charts the path the firm will follow to reach its information systems goal. Even if it means making many midcourse adjustments, planning is superior to simply wandering in the wilderness.
2. *Strategic planning reduces the crisis component in systems development.* A formal plan is a model for identifying and prioritizing user needs. It allows management to consider the future needs, recognize problems in their early stages, and even anticipate needs before the symptoms of underlying problems emerge. In the absence of a plan, the trigger that stimulates systems development is the recognition of a problem. Often, problems reach a crisis level before they receive attention, which adversely affects the quality of the solution. Strategic planning provides a structured means of separating legitimate needs from desires, and needs versus problems.
3. *Strategic systems planning provides authorization control for the SDLC.* The strategic systems plan lays out authorization rules to ensure that decisions to

develop specific systems are congruent with the objectives of the firm. Investing in the wrong systems can be just as damaging to a firm as investing in the wrong plant and equipment.

4. *Strategic systems planning works!* Historically, systems planning has proven to be a cost-effective means of managing systems projects and application development.

Project Planning

The purpose of **project planning** is to allocate resources to individual applications within the framework of the strategic plan. This involves identifying areas of user needs, preparing proposals, evaluating each proposal's feasibility and contribution to the business plan, prioritizing individual projects, and scheduling the work to be done. The basic purpose of project planning is to allocate scarce resources to specific projects. The product of this phase consists of two formal documents: the project proposal and the project schedule.

The **project proposal** provides management with a basis for deciding whether to proceed with the project. The formal proposal serves two purposes. First, it summarizes the findings of the study conducted to this point into a general recommendation for a new or modified system. This enables management to evaluate the perceived problem along with the proposed system as a feasible solution. Second, the proposal outlines the linkage between the objectives of the proposed system and the business objectives of the firm, especially those outlined in the IT strategic plan. It shows that the proposed new system complements the strategic direction of the firm.

The **project schedule** represents management's commitment to the project. The project schedule is a budget of the time and costs for all the phases of the SDLC. A project team selected from systems professionals, end users, and other specialists such as accountants and internal auditors will complete these phases. The composition of the team and the competence and dedication of its members are critical to the success of the new system.

The Auditor's Role in Systems Planning

Auditors routinely examine the systems planning phase of the SDLC. History has shown that careful systems planning is a cost-effective control technique in the systems development process. Planning greatly reduces the risk of producing unneeded, unwanted, inefficient, and ineffective systems. Both internal and external auditors are interested in ensuring that adequate systems planning takes place.

Systems Analysis—Phase II

We now move on to the second phase in the SDLC. **Systems analysis** is actually a two-step process involving first a survey of the current system and then an analysis of the user's needs. A business problem must be fully understood by the systems analyst before he or she can formulate a solution. An incomplete or defective analysis will lead to an incomplete or defective solution. Therefore, systems analysis is the foundation for the rest of the SDLC. The deliverable from this phase is a formal systems analysis report, which presents the findings of the analysis and recommendations for the new system.

The Survey Step

Most systems are not developed from scratch. Usually, some form of information system and related procedures are currently in place. The analyst often begins the analysis by determining what elements, if any, of the current system should be preserved as part of the new system. This involves a rather detailed **system survey**. Facts pertaining to preliminary questions about the system are gathered and analyzed. As the analyst obtains a greater depth of understanding of the problem, he or she develops more specific questions for which more facts must be gathered. This process may go on through several iterations. When all the relevant facts have been gathered and analyzed, the analyst arrives at an assessment of the current system. Surveying the current system has both disadvantages and advantages.

Disadvantages of Surveying the Current System

- *Current physical tar pit.* This term is used to describe the tendency on the part of the analyst to be "sucked in" and then "bogged down" by the task of surveying the current dinosaur system.[1]
- *Thinking inside the box.* Some argue that current system surveys stifle new ideas. By studying and modeling the old system, the analyst may develop a constrained notion about how the new system should function. The result is an improved old system rather than a radically new approach.

Advantages of Surveying the Current System

- *Identifying what aspects of the old system should be kept.* Some elements of the system may be functionally sound and can provide the foundation for the new system. By fully understanding the current system, the analyst can identify those aspects worth preserving or modifying for use in the new system.
- *Forcing systems analysts to fully understand the system.* When the new system is implemented, the users must go through a conversion process whereby they formally break away from the old system and move to the new one. The analyst must determine what tasks, procedures, and data will be phased out with the old system and which will continue. To specify these conversion procedures, the analyst must know not only what is to be done by the new system but also what was done by the old one. This requires a thorough understanding of the current system.
- *Isolating the root of problem symptoms.* By surveying the current system, the analyst may determine conclusively the cause of the reported problem symptoms. Perhaps the root problem is not the information system at all; it may be a management or employee problem that can be resolved without redesigning the information system. We may not be able to identify the root cause of the problem if we discard the existing system without any investigation into the symptoms.

Gathering Facts

The survey of the current system is essentially a fact-gathering activity. The facts gathered by the analyst are pieces of data that describe key features, situations, and relationships of the system. System facts fall into the following broad classes.

1 This is perhaps the most compelling argument against surveying the current system.

- **Data sources.** These include external entities, such as customers or vendors, as well as internal sources from other departments.
- **Users.** These include both managers and operations users.
- **Data stores.** Data stores are the files, databases, accounts, and source documents used in the system.
- **Processes.** Processing tasks are manual or computer operations that represent a decision or an action triggered by information.
- **Data flows.** Data flows are represented by the movement of documents and reports between data sources, data stores, processing tasks, and users. Data flows can also be represented in UML diagrams.
- **Controls.** These include both accounting and operational controls and may be manual procedures or computer controls.
- **Transaction volumes.** The analyst must obtain a measure of the transaction volumes for a specified period of time. Many systems are replaced because they have reached their capacity. Understanding the characteristics of a systems transaction volume and its rate of growth are important elements in assessing capacity requirements for the new system.
- **Error rates.** Transaction errors are closely related to transaction volume. As a system reaches capacity, error rates increase to an intolerable level. Although no system is perfect, the analyst must determine the acceptable error tolerances for the new system.
- **Resource costs.** The resources used by the current system include the costs of labor, computer time, materials (such as invoices), and direct overhead. Any resource costs that disappear when the current system is eliminated are called escapable costs. Later, when we perform a cost-benefit analysis, escapable costs will be treated as benefits of the new system.
- **Bottlenecks and redundant operations.** The analyst should note points where data flows come together to form a bottleneck. At peak-load periods, these can result in delays and promote processing errors. Likewise, delays may be caused by redundant operations, such as unnecessary approvals or sign-offs. By identifying these problem areas during the survey phase, the analyst can avoid making the same mistakes in the design of the new system.

Fact-Gathering Techniques

Systems analysts employ several techniques to gather the previously cited facts. Commonly used techniques include observation, task participation, personal interviews, and reviewing key documents.

Observation. Observation involves passively watching the physical procedures of the system. This allows the analyst to determine what gets done, who performs the tasks, when they do them, how they do them, why they do them, and how long they take.

Task Participation. Participation is an extension of observation, whereby the analyst takes an active role in performing the user's work. This allows the analyst to experience first-hand the problems involved in the operation of the current system. For example, the analyst may work on the sales desk taking orders from customers and preparing sales orders. The analyst can determine that documents are improperly designed, that insufficient time exists to perform the required procedures, or that peak-load problems cause bottlenecks and processing errors. With hands-on experience, the analyst can often envision better ways to perform the task.

Personal Interviews. Interviewing is a method of extracting facts about the current system and user perceptions about the requirements for the new system. The instruments used to gather these facts may be open-ended questions or formal questionnaires.

- *Open-ended questions* allow users to elaborate on the problem as they see it and offer suggestions and recommendations. Answers to these questions tend to be difficult to analyze, but they give the analyst a feel for the scope of the problem. The analyst in this type of interview must be a good listener and able to focus on the important facts. Examples of open-ended questions are: "What do you think is the main problem with our sales order system?" and "How could the system be improved?"
- *Questionnaires* are used to ask more specific, detailed questions and to restrict the user's responses. This is a good technique for gathering objective facts about the nature of specific procedures, volumes of transactions processed, sources of data, users of reports, and control issues.

Reviewing Key Documents. The organization's documents are another source of facts about the system being surveyed. Examples of these include the following:

- Organizational charts
- Job descriptions
- Accounting records
- Charts of accounts
- Policy statements
- Descriptions of procedures
- Financial statements
- Performance reports
- System flowcharts
- Source documents
- Transaction listings
- Budgets
- Forecasts
- Mission statements

Following the fact-gathering phase, the analyst formally documents his or her impressions and understanding about the system. This will take the form of notes, system flowcharts, and data flow diagrams.

The Analysis Step

Systems analysis is an intellectual process that is commingled with fact gathering. The analyst is simultaneously analyzing as he or she gathers facts. The mere recognition of a problem presumes some understanding of the norm or desired state. It is therefore difficult to identify where the survey ends and the analysis begins.

Systems Analysis Report

The event that marks the conclusion of the systems analysis phase is the preparation of a formal systems analysis report. This report presents to management or the steering committee the survey findings, the problems identified with the current system, the user's needs, and the requirements of the new system. Figure 4-3 contains a possible format for this report. The primary purpose for conducting a systems analysis is to identify user needs and specify requirements for the new system. The report should set out in detail what the system must do rather than how to do it. The requirements statement within the report establishes an understanding between systems professionals, management, users, and other stakeholders. This document constitutes a formal contract that specifies the objectives and goals of the system. The systems analysis report should establish in clear terms the data sources, users, data files, general processes, data flows, controls, and transaction volume capacity.

The systems analysis report does not specify the detailed design of the proposed system. For example, it does not specify processing methods, storage media, record structures, and other details needed to design the physical system. Rather, the report remains at the objectives level to avoid placing artificial constraints on the conceptual design phase. Several possible designs may serve the user's needs, and the development process must be free to explore all of these.

FIGURE 4-3

Outline of Main Topics in a Systems Analysis Report

Systems Analysis Report

I. Reasons for System Analysis
   A. Reasons specified in the system project proposal
   B. Changes in reasons since analysis began
   C. Additional reasons

II. Scope of Study
   A. Scope as specified by the project proposal
   B. Changes in scope

III. Problems Identified with Current System
   A. Techniques used for gathering facts
   B. Problems encountered in the fact-gathering process
   C. Analysis of facts

IV. Statement of User Requirements
   A. Specific user needs in key areas, such as:
      1. Output requirements
      2. Transaction volumes
      3. Response time
   B. Nontechnical terms for a broad-based audience, including:
      1. End users
      2. User management
      3. Systems management
      4. Steering committee

V. Resource Implications
   A. Preliminary assessment of economic effect
   B. Is economic feasibility as stated in proposal reasonable?

VI. Recommendations
   A. Continue or drop the project
   B. Any changes to feasibility, strategic impact, or priority of the project as a result of analysis

The Auditor's Role in Systems Analysis

The firm's auditors (both external and internal) are stakeholders in the proposed system. In Chapter 8, we will see how certain CAATTs (such as the embedded audit module and the integrated test facility) must be designed into the system during the SDLC. Often, advanced audit features cannot be easily added to existing systems. Therefore, the accountant/auditor should be involved in the needs analysis of the proposed system to determine if it is a good candidate for advanced audit features and, if so, which features are best suited for the system.

Conceptual Systems Design—Phase III

The purpose of the conceptual design phase is to produce several alternative conceptual systems that satisfy the system requirements identified during systems analysis. By presenting users with a number of plausible alternatives, the systems professional avoids imposing preconceived constraints on the new system. The user will evaluate these conceptual models and settle on the alternatives that appear most plausible and appealing. These alternative designs then go to the systems selection phase of SDLC, where their respective costs and benefits are compared and a single optimum design is chosen.

By keeping systems design conceptual throughout these phases of the SDLC, we minimize the investment of resources in alternative designs that, ultimately, will be rejected. The conceptual system that emerges proceeds to the final phases of the SDLC, where it is designed in detail and implemented.

This section describes two approaches to conceptual systems design: the structured approach and the object-oriented approach. The structured approach develops each new system from scratch from the top down. Object-oriented design (OOD) builds systems from the bottom up through the assembly of reusable modules rather than create each system from scratch. OOD is most often associated with the **iterative approach** to SDLC where small "chunks" or modules cycle through all of the SDLC phases rather rapidly, with a short time frame from beginning to end. Then additional modules or chunks are added in some appropriate fashion until the whole system has been developed. These approaches are still emerging concepts in AIS, but are becoming—some say have become—a dominant force in system development.

The Structured Design Approach

The **structured design** approach is a disciplined way of designing systems from the top down. It consists of starting with the "big picture" of the proposed system that is gradually decomposed into more and more detail until it is fully understood. Under this approach, the business process under design is usually documented by data flow and structure diagrams. Figure 4-4 shows the use of these techniques to depict the top-down decomposition of a hypothetical business process.

We can see from these diagrams how the systems designer follows a top-down approach. The designer starts with an abstract description of the system and, through successive steps, redefines this view to produce a more detailed description. In our example, Process 2.0 in the context diagram is decomposed into an intermediate level DFD. Process 2.3 in the intermediate DFD is further decomposed into an elementary DFD. This decomposition could involve several levels to obtain sufficient details. Let's assume that three levels are sufficient in this case. The final step transforms Process 2.3.3 into a structure diagram that defines the program modules that will constitute the process.

FIGURE 4-4 **Top-Down Decomposition of the Structured Design Approach**

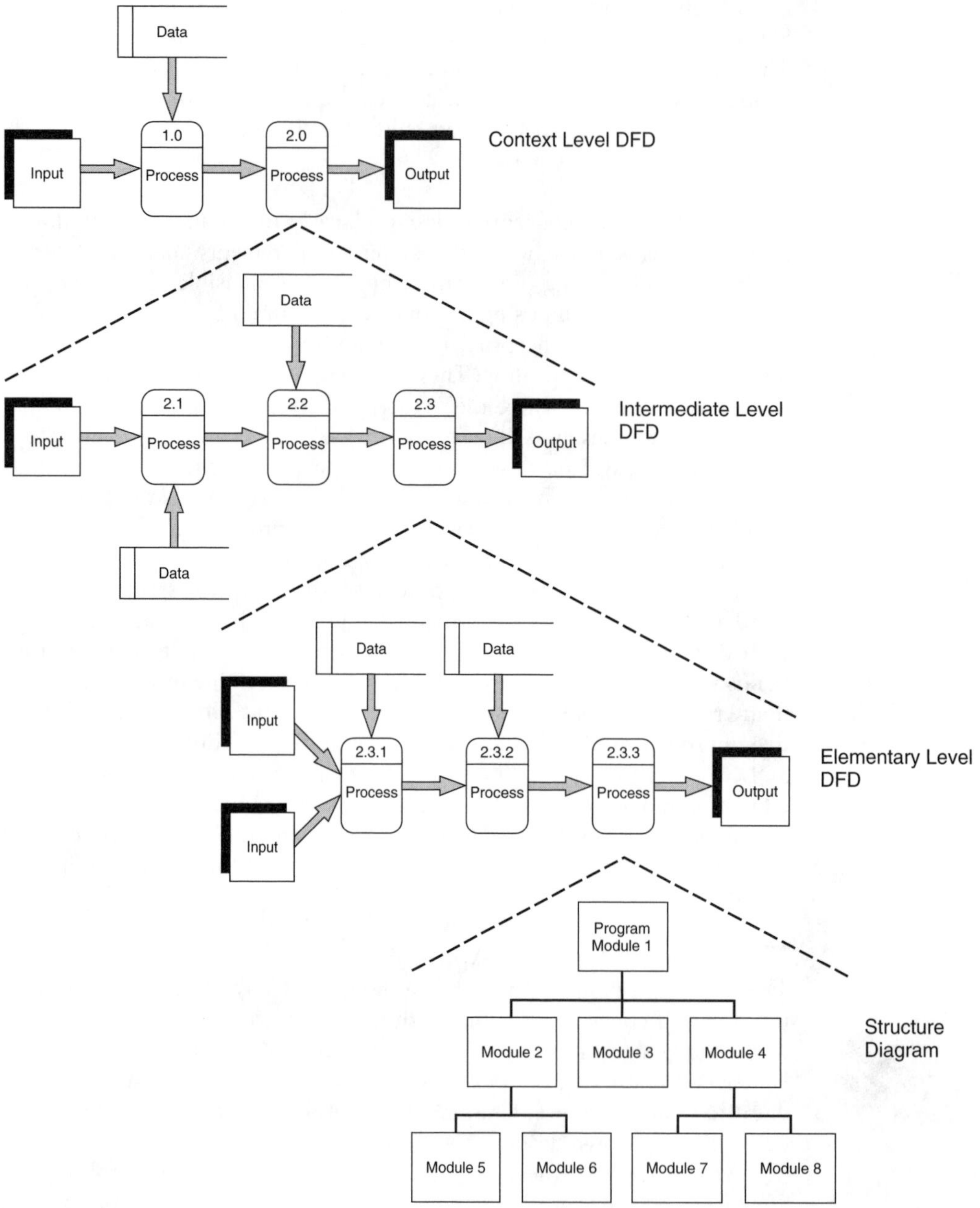

The conceptual design phase should highlight the differences between critical features of competing systems rather than their similarities. Therefore, system designs at this point should be general. The designs should identify all the inputs, outputs, processes, and special features necessary to distinguish one alternative from another. Figure 4-5 presents two alternative conceptual designs

FIGURE 4-5 **Alternative Conceptual Designs for a Purchasing System**

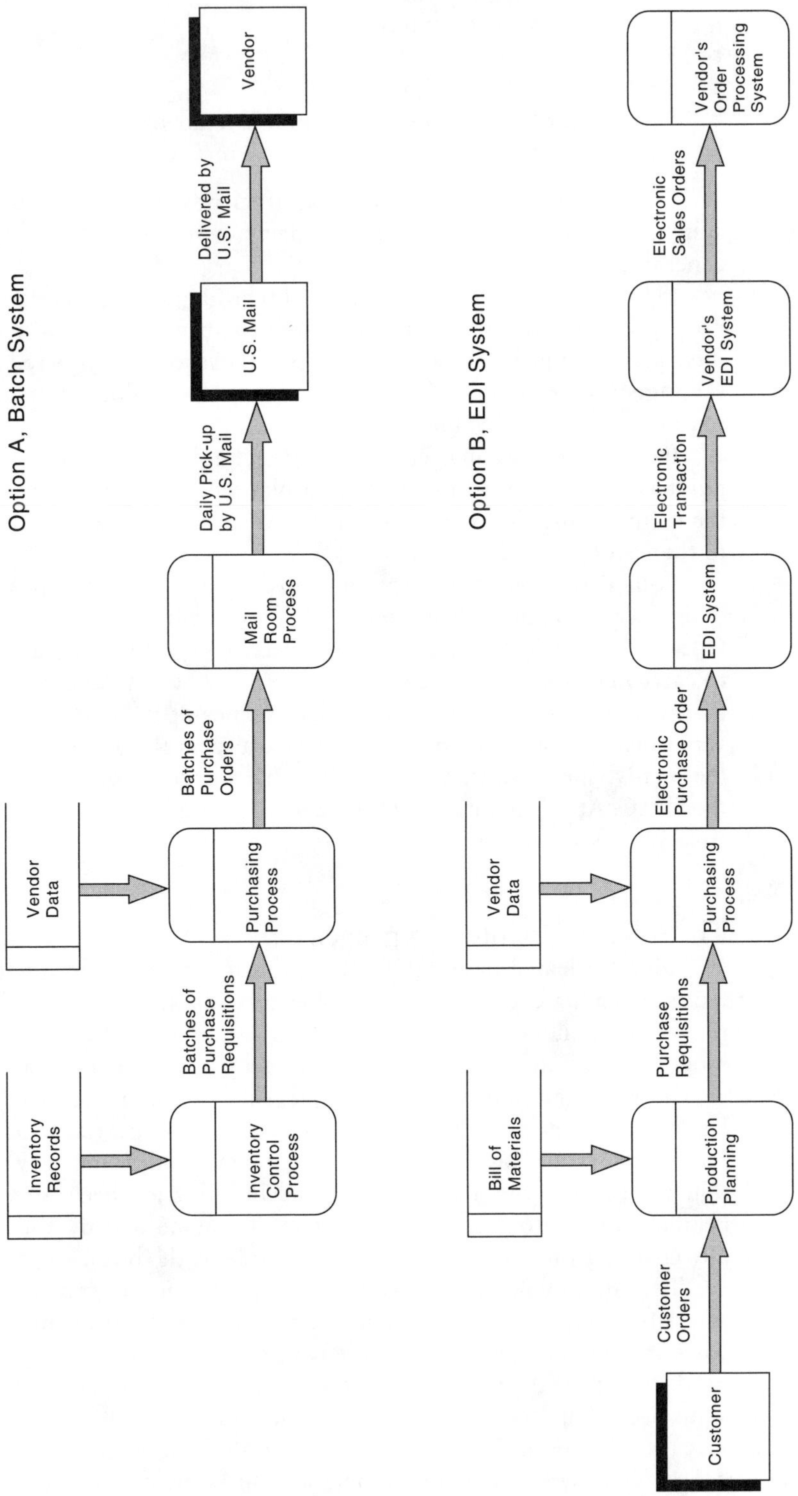

for a purchasing system. These designs lack the details needed to implement the system. For instance, they do not include these necessary components:

- Database record structures
- Processing details
- Specific control techniques
- Formats for input screens and source documents
- Output report formats

The designs do, however, possess sufficient detail to demonstrate how the two systems are conceptually different in their functions. To illustrate, let's examine the general features of each system.

Option A is a traditional batch purchasing system. The initial input for the process is the purchase requisition from inventory control. When inventories reach their predetermined reorder points, new inventories are ordered according to their economic order quantity. Transmittal of purchase orders to suppliers takes place once a day via the U.S. mail.

In contrast, Option B employs EDI technology. The trigger to this system is a purchase requisition from production planning. The purchases system determines the quantity and the vendor and then transmits the order online via EDI software to the vendor.

Both alternatives have pros and cons. A benefit of Option A is its simplicity of design, ease of implementation, and lower demand for systems resources than Option B. On one hand, a negative aspect of Option A is that it requires the firm to carry inventories. On the other hand, Option B may allow the firm to reduce or even eliminate inventories. This benefit comes at the cost of more expensive and sophisticated system resources. It is premature, at this point, to attempt to evaluate the relative merits of these alternatives. This is done formally in the next phase in the SDLC. At this point, system designers are concerned only with identifying plausible system designs.

The Object-Oriented Approach

The **object-oriented design (OOD) approach** is to build information systems from reusable standard components or **objects**. This approach may be equated to the process of building an automobile. Car manufacturers do not create each new model from scratch. New models are actually built from standard components that also go into other models. For example, each model of car produced by a particular manufacturer may use the same type of engine, gearbox, alternator, rear axle, radio, and so on. Some of the car's components will be industry-standard products that are used by other manufacturers. Such things as wheels, tires, spark plugs, and headlights fall into this category. In fact, it may be that the only component actually created from scratch for a new car model is the body.

The automobile industry operates in this fashion to stay competitive. By using standard components, car manufacturers minimize production and maintenance costs. At the same time, they can remain responsive to consumer demands for new products and preserve manufacturing flexibility by mixing and matching components according to the customer's specification.

The concept of reusability is *central* to the object-oriented approach to systems design. Once created, standard modules can be used in other systems with similar needs. Ideally, the organization's systems professionals will create a library (inventory) of modules that can be used by other system designers within the firm. The benefits of this approach include reduced time and cost for development, maintenance, and testing and improved user support and flexibility in the development process.

The OOD methodology most often is also associated with the iterative approach to design phases rather than the *waterfall*, or complete project, approach. The waterfall approach takes the complete project and divides the process into project functions, as outlined in this chapter (analysis, design, etc.). Iterative development uses a discrete subset of the project (e.g., module) and completes the entire SDLC cycle for development that piece of the bigger project. The result is a functioning subset application of the entire project. Certain functions such as training are done at the end of all subsets and iterations. The OO community almost exclusively uses the iterative approach. For example, one UML and OO expert Martin Fowler says, "You should use iterative development only on projects that you want to succeed."

The Auditor's Role in Conceptual Systems Design

The auditor is a stakeholder in all financial systems and, thus, has an interest in the conceptual design stage of the system. The auditability of a system depends in part on its design characteristics. Some computer auditing techniques require systems to be designed with special audit features that are integral to the system. These audit features must be specified at the conceptual design stage.

SYSTEM EVALUATION AND SELECTION—PHASE IV

The next phase in the SDLC is the procedure for selecting the one system from the set of alternative conceptual designs that will go to the detailed design phase. The **systems evaluation and selection** phase is an optimization process that seeks to identify the best system. This decision represents a critical juncture in the SDLC. At this point, there is a great deal of uncertainty about the system, and a poor decision here can be disastrous. The purpose of a formal evaluation and selection procedure is to structure this decision-making process and thereby reduce both uncertainty and the risk of making a poor decision. The evaluation and selection process involves two steps:

1. Perform a detailed feasibility study
2. Perform a cost-benefit analysis

Perform a Detailed Feasibility Study

The following discussion outlines four aspects of project feasibility that need to be considered. Each competing project will be assessed in the same manner. The projects deemed feasible are then compared on a cost-benefit basis. The selected system will then advance to the detailed design phase.

Technical Feasibility. Technical feasibility is concerned with whether the system can be developed under existing technology or if new technology is needed. As a general proposition, the technology in the marketplace is far ahead of most firms' ability to apply it. Therefore, from an availability viewpoint, technical feasibility is not usually an issue. For most firms, the real issue is their desire and ability to apply available technology. Given that technology is the physical basis for most of the system's design features, this aspect bears heavily on the overall feasibility of the competing system.

Legal Feasibility. Legal feasibility identifies any conflicts between the conceptual system and the company's ability to discharge its legal responsibilities. In previous chapters, we have studied the need to comply with the control requirement laid down in the Foreign Corrupt Practices Act of 1977 and SAS 78. In addition, many regulations and statutes deal with invasion of privacy and the confidentiality of stored information. The decision maker must be certain the proposed system falls inside all legal boundaries.

Operational Feasibility. Operational feasibility shows the degree of compatibility between the firm's existing procedures and personnel skills and the operational requirements of the new system. Implementing the new system may require adopting new procedures and retraining operations personnel. The question that must be answered is, can adequate procedural changes be made, sufficient personnel retrained, and new skills obtained to make the system operationally feasible?

Schedule Feasibility. Schedule feasibility relates to the firm's ability to implement the project within an acceptable time. This feasibility factor impacts both the scope of the project and whether it will be developed in-house or purchased from a software vendor. If the project, as conceptually envisioned, cannot be produced internally by the target date, then its design, its acquisition method, or the target date must be changed.

Perform a Cost–Benefit Analysis

Cost–benefit analysis helps management determine whether (and by how much) the benefits received from a proposed system will outweigh its costs. This technique is frequently used for estimating the expected financial value of business investments. However, in this case, the investment is an information system, and the costs and benefits are more difficult to identify and quantify than those of traditional capital projects. Although imperfect for this setting, cost-benefit analysis is employed because of its simplicity and the absence of a clearly better alternative. In spite of its limitations, cost–benefit analysis, combined with feasibility factors, is a useful tool for comparing competing systems designs.

There are three steps in the application of cost–benefit analysis: identify costs, identify benefits, and compare costs and benefits. We discuss each of these steps below.

Identify Costs. One method of identifying costs is to divide them into two categories: one-time costs and recurring costs. One-time costs include the initial investment to develop and implement the system. Recurring costs include operating and maintenance costs that recur over the life of the system. Table 4-1 shows a breakdown of typical one-time and recurring costs.

One-time costs include the following:

- *Hardware acquisition.* This cost includes the cost of mainframe, minicomputers, microcomputers, and peripheral equipment, such as tape drives and disk packs. These cost figures can be obtained from the vendor.
- *Site preparation.* This cost involves such frequently overlooked costs as building modifications (e.g., adding air conditioning or making structural changes), equipment installation (which may include the use of heavy equipment), and

TABLE 4-1

One-Time and Recurring Costs

ONE-TIME AND RECURRING COSTS
One-Time Costs
Hardware acquisition
Site Preparation
Software acquisition
Systems design
Programming and testing
Data conversion from old system to new system
Personnel training
Recurring Costs
Hardware maintenance
Software maintenance contracts
Insurance
Supplies
Personnel

freight charges. Estimates of these costs can be obtained from the vendor and the subcontractors who do the installation.

- *Software acquisition.* These costs apply to all software purchased for the proposed system, including operating system software (if not bundled with the hardware), network control software, and commercial applications (such as accounting packages). Estimates of these costs can be obtained from vendors.
- *Systems design.* These costs are those incurred by systems professionals performing the planning, analysis, and design functions. Technically, such costs incurred up to this point are "sunk" and irrelevant to the decision. The analyst should estimate only the costs needed to complete the detailed design.
- *Programming and testing.* Programming costs are based on estimates of the personnel hours required to write new programs and modify existing programs for the proposed system. System testing costs involve bringing together all the individual program modules for testing as an entire system. This must be a rigorous exercise if it is to be meaningful. The planning, testing, and analysis of the results may demand many days of involvement from systems professionals, users, and other stakeholders of the system. The experience of the firm in the past is the best basis for estimating these costs.
- *Data conversion.* These costs arise in the transfer of data from one storage medium to another. For example, the accounting records of a manual system must be converted to magnetic form when the system becomes computer-based. This can represent a significant task. The basis for estimating conversion costs is the number and size of the files to be converted.
- *Training.* These costs involve educating users to operate the new system. In-house personnel could do this in an extensive training program provided by an outside organization at a remote site or through on-the-job training. The cost of formal training can be easily obtained. The cost of an in-house training program includes instruction time, classroom facilities, and lost productivity. This

cost is often the first one cut to meet budgets, and such an action can be fatal to systems development (e.g., Hershey's ERP implementation disaster was blamed in part on the drastic reduction in employee training before "going live").[2] Accountants and auditors should be aware of the danger of cutting this important part of systems development.

Recurring costs include the following:

- *Hardware maintenance.* This cost involves the upgrading of the computer (increasing the memory), as well as preventive maintenance and repairs to the computer and peripheral equipment. The organization may enter into a maintenance contract with the vendor to minimize and budget these costs. Estimates for these costs can be obtained from vendors and existing contracts.
- *Software maintenance.* These costs include upgrading and debugging operating systems, purchased applications, and in-house developed applications. Maintenance contracts with software vendors can be used to specify these costs fairly accurately. Estimates of in-house maintenance can be derived from historical data.
- *Insurance.* This cost covers such hazards and disasters as fire, hardware failure, vandalism, and destruction by disgruntled employees.
- *Supplies.* These costs are incurred through routine consumption of such items as paper, magnetic disks, CDs, and general office supplies.
- *Personnel costs.* These are the salaries of individuals who are part of the information system. Some employee costs are direct and easily identifiable, such as the salaries of operations personnel exclusively employed as part of the system under analysis. Some personnel involvement (such as the database administrator and computer room personnel) is common to many systems. Such personnel costs must be allocated on the basis of expected incremental involvement with the system.

Identify Benefits. The next step in the cost-benefit analysis is to identify the benefits of the system. These may be both tangible and intangible. Table 4-2 lists several types of tangible benefits.

TABLE 4-2

Tangible Benefits

Tangible Benefits
Increased Revenues
Increased sales within existing markets
Expansion into other markets
Cost Reduction
Labor reduction
Operating cost reduction (such as supplies and overhead)
Reduced inventories
Less expensive equipment
Reduced equipment maintenance

2 ERP systems are discussed in Chapter 6.

Tangible benefits fall into two categories: those that increase revenue and those that reduce costs. For example, assume a proposed EDI system will allow the organization to reduce inventories and at the same time improve customer service by reducing stockouts. The reduction of inventories is a cost-reducing benefit. The proposed system will use fewer resources (inventories) than the current system. The value of this benefit is the dollar amount of the carrying costs saved by the annual reduction in inventory. The estimated increase in sales due to better customer service is a revenue-increasing benefit.

When measuring cost savings, it is important to include only escapable costs in the analysis. Escapable costs are directly related to the system, and they cease to exist when the system ceases to exist. Some costs that appear to be escapable to the user are not truly escapable and, if included, can lead to a flawed analysis. For example, data processing centers often "charge back" their operating costs to their user constituency through cost allocations. The charge-back rate they use for this includes both fixed costs (allocated to users) and direct costs created by the activities of individual users. Figure 4-6 illustrates this technique.

Assume the management in User Area B proposes to acquire a computer system and perform its own data processing locally. One benefit of the proposal is the cost savings derived by escaping the charge-back from the current data processing center. Although the user may see this as a $400,000 annual charge, only the direct cost portion ($50,000) is escapable by the organization as a whole. Should the proposal be approved, the remaining $350,000 of the charge-back does not go away. The remaining users of the current system must now absorb this cost.

FIGURE 4-6

DP Center Cost Charge-Back to User Areas

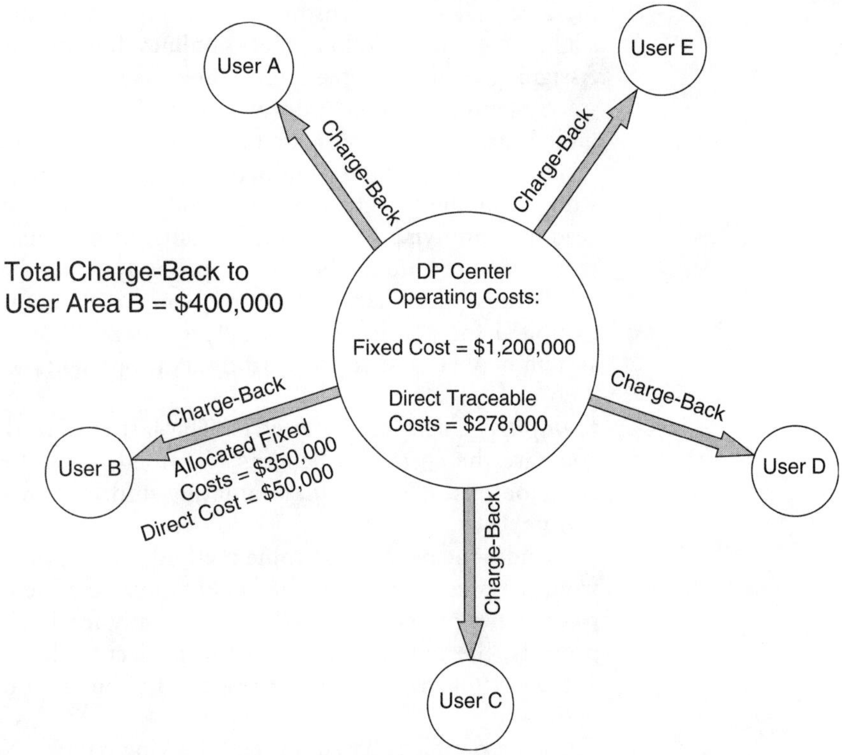

TABLE 4-3

Intangible Benefits

Increased customer satisfaction
Improved employee satisfaction
More current information
Improved decision making
Faster response to competitor actions
More efficient operations
Better internal and external communications
Improved planning
Operational flexibility
Improved control environment

Table 4-3 lists some common categories of **intangible benefits**. Although intangible benefits are often of overriding importance in information system decisions, they cannot be easily measured and quantified. For example, assume that a proposed point-of-sale system for a department store will reduce the average time to process a customer sales transaction from 11 minutes to 3 minutes. The time saved can be quantified and produces a tangible benefit in the form of an operating cost saving. An intangible benefit is improved customer satisfaction; no one likes to stand in long lines to pay for purchases. But what is the true value of this intangible benefit to the organization? Increased customer satisfaction may translate into increased sales. More customers will buy at the store—and may be willing to pay slightly more to avoid long checkout lines. But how do we quantify this translation? Assigning a value is often highly subjective.

Systems professionals draw upon many sources in attempting to quantify intangible benefits and manipulate them into financial terms. Some common techniques include customer (and employee) opinion surveys, statistical analysis, expected value techniques, and simulation models. Though systems professionals may succeed in quantifying some of these intangible benefits, more often they must be content to simply state the benefits as precisely as good judgment permits.

Because they defy precise measurement, intangible benefits are sometimes exploited for political reasons. By overstating or understating these benefits, a system may be pushed forward by its proponents or killed by its opponents.

Compare Costs and Benefits. The last step in the cost–benefit analysis is to compare the costs and benefits identified in the first two steps. The two most common methods used for evaluating information systems are net present value and payback.

Under the **net present value method**, the present value of the costs is deducted from the present value of the benefits over the life of the system. Projects with a positive net present value are economically feasible. When comparing competing projects, the optimal choice is the project with the greatest net present value. Table 4-4 illustrates the net present value method by comparing two competing designs.

The example is based on the following data:

TABLE 4-4 Net Present Value Method of Cost-Benefit Analysis

Year Time	Beginning End Year Outflows	Inflows	Beginning Year Time	End Year Outflows	Inflows
0	$(3,000,000)		0	$(140,000)	
1	(45,000)	170,000	1	(55,000)	135,000
2	(45,000)	170,000	2	(55,000)	135,000
3	(45,000)	170,000	3	(55,000)	135,000
4	(45,000)	170,000	4	(55,000)	135,000
5	(45,000)	170,000	5	(55,000)	135,000
PV Out	$(479,672)		PV Out	$(369,599)	
PV In	$628,428		PV In	$499,089	
NPV	$148,810		NPV	$139,490	
Interest Rate	8.00%				

	Design A	Design B
Project completion time	1 year	1 year
Expected useful life of system	5 years	5 years
One-time costs (thousands)	$300	$140
Recurring costs (thousands) incurred in beginning of Years 1 through 5	$45	$55
Annual tangible benefits (thousands) incurred in end of Years 1 through 5	$170	$135

If costs and tangible benefits alone were being considered, then Design A would be selected over Design B. However, the value of intangible benefits, along with the design feasibility scores, must also be factored into the final analysis.

The **payback method** is a variation of break-even analysis. The **break-even point** is reached when total costs equal total benefits. Figure 4-7(A) and (B) illustrates this approach using the data from the previous example.

The total-cost curve consists of the one-time costs plus the present value of the recurring costs over the life of the project. The total benefits curve is the present value of the tangible benefits. The intersection of these lines represents the number of years into the future when the project breaks even, or pays for itself. The shaded area between the benefit curve and the total-cost curve represents the present value of future profits earned by the system.

In choosing an information system, payback speed is often a decisive factor. With brief product life cycles and rapid advances in technology, the effective lives of information systems tend to be short. Using this criterion, Design B, with a payback period of four years, would be selected over Design A, whose payback will take four and one-half years. The length of the payback period often takes precedence over other considerations represented by intangible benefits.

FIGURE 4-7A

Discounted Payback Method of Cash Flow Analysis

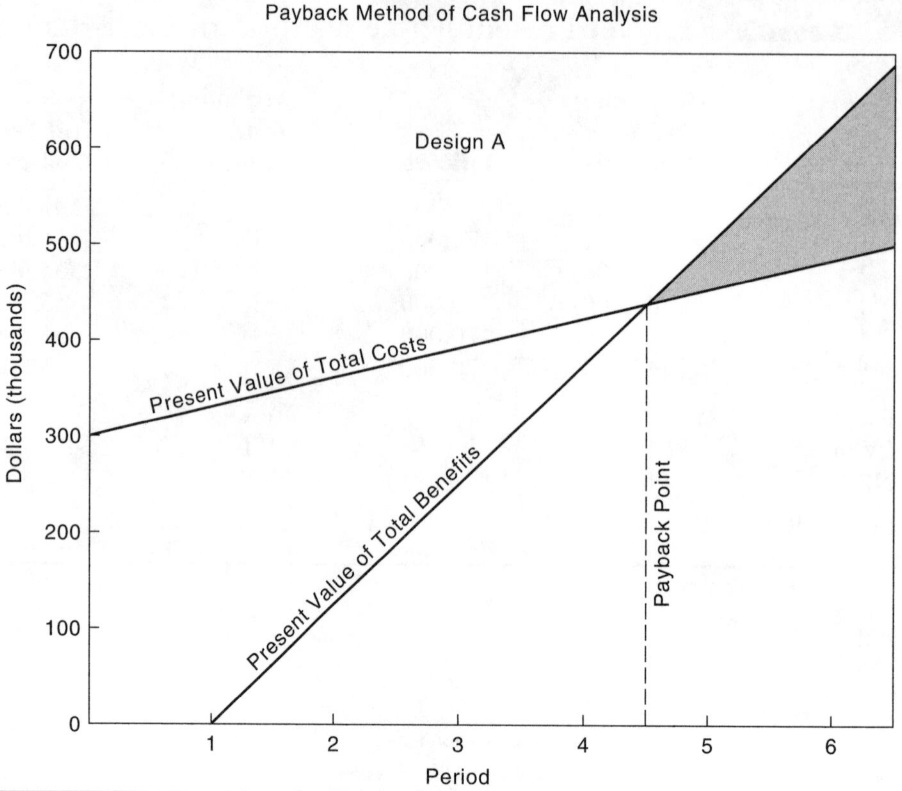

FIGURE 4-7B

Discounted Payback Method of Cost-Benefit Analysis

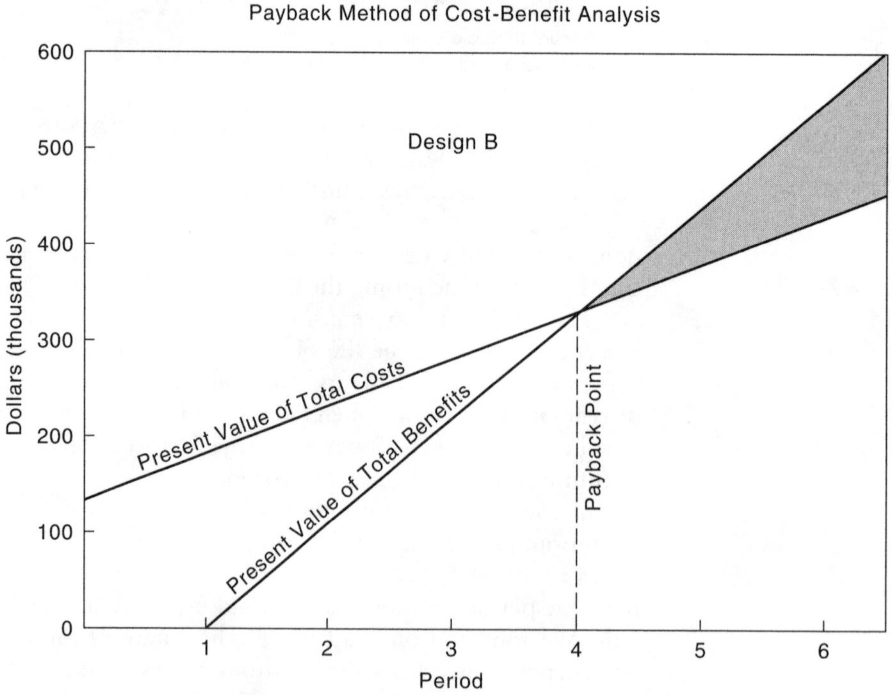

Prepare Systems Selection Report

The deliverable product of the systems selection process is the **systems selection report**. This formal document consists of a revised feasibility study, a cost-benefit analysis, and a list and explanation of intangible benefits for each alternative design. On the basis of this report, the steering committee will select a single system that will go forward to the next phase of the SDLC—detailed design.

The Auditor's Role in Evaluation and Selection

The primary concern for auditors is that the economic feasibility of the proposed system is measured as accurately as possible. Specifically, the auditor should ensure five things:

1. Only escapable costs are used in calculations of cost savings benefits.
2. Reasonable interest rates are used in measuring present values of cash flows.
3. One-time and recurring costs are completely and accurately reported.
4. Realistic useful lives are used in comparing competing projects.
5. Intangible benefits are assigned reasonable financial values.

Errors, omissions, and misrepresentations in the accounting for such items can distort the analysis and may result in a materially flawed decision.

Detailed Design—Phase V

The purpose of the **detailed design** phase is to produce a detailed description of the proposed system that both satisfies the system requirements identified during systems analysis and is in accordance with the conceptual design. In this phase, all system components (user views, database tables, processes, and controls) are meticulously specified. At the end of this phase, these components are presented formally in a detailed design report. This report constitutes a set of blueprints that specify input screen formats, output report layouts, database structures, and process logic. These completed plans then proceed to the final phase in the SDLC—systems implementation—where the system is physically constructed.

Perform a System Design Walkthrough

After completing the detailed design, the development team usually performs a system design **walkthrough** to ensure that the design is free from conceptual errors that could become programmed into the final system. Many firms have formal, structured walkthroughs conducted by a **quality assurance group**. This group is an independent one made up of programmers, analysts, users, and internal auditors. The job of this group is to simulate the operation of the system to uncover errors, omissions, and ambiguities in the design. Most system errors emanate from poor designs rather than programming mistakes. Detecting and correcting errors in the design phase thus reduces costly reprogramming later.

Review System Documentation

The **detailed design report** documents and describes the system to this point. This report includes the following:

- Designs for all screen inputs and source documents for the system.
- Designs of all screen outputs, reports, and operational documents.

- Normalized data for database tables, specifying all data elements.
- Database structures and diagrams: Entity relationship (ER) diagrams describing the data relations in the system, context diagrams for the overall system, low-level data flow diagrams of specific system processes, structure diagrams for the program modules in the system—including including a pseudocode description of each module.
- An updated data dictionary describing each data element in the database.
- Processing logic (flow charts).

The quality control group scrutinizes these documents, and any errors detected are recorded in a walkthrough report. Depending on the extent of the system errors, the quality assurance group will make a recommendation. The system design will either be accepted without modification, accepted subject to modification of minor errors, or rejected because of material errors.

At this point, a decision is made either to return the system for additional design or to proceed to the next phase—system coding and testing. Assuming the design goes forward, the documents in the design report constitute the blueprints that guide application programmers and the database designers in constructing the physical system.

System Programming and Testing—Phase VI

Program the Application Software

The next stage of the SDLC is to select a programming language from among the various languages available and suitable to the application. These include *procedural languages* like COBOL, *event-driven languages* like Visual Basic, or *object-oriented programming (OOP) languages* like Java or C++. This section presents a brief overview of various programming approaches. Systems professionals will make their decision based on the in-house standards, architecture, and user needs.

Procedural Languages. A **procedural language** requires the programmer to specify the precise order in which the program logic is executed. Procedural languages are often called **third-generation languages** (3GLs). Examples of 3GLs include COBOL, FORTRAN, C, and PL1. In business (particularly in accounting) applications, COBOL was the dominant language for years. COBOL has great capability for performing highly detailed operations on individual data records and handles large files very efficiently. However, it is an extremely "wordy" language that makes programming a time-consuming task. COBOL has survived as a viable language because many of the "legacy systems" written in the 1970s and 1980s, which were coded in COBOL, are still in operation today. Major retrofits and routine maintenance to these systems need to be coded in COBOL. Upward of 12 billion lines of COBOL code are executed daily in the United States.

Event-Driven Languages. **Event-driven languages** are no longer procedural. Under this model, the program's code is not executed in a predefined sequence. Instead, external actions or "events" that are initiated by the user dictate the control flow of the program. For example, when the user presses a key, or "clicks" on an icon on the computer screen, the program automatically executes code associated with that event. This is a fundamental shift from the 3GL era. Now, instead of designing applications that execute sequentially from top to bottom in accordance with the way the programmer *thinks* they should function, the user is in control.

Microsoft's Visual Basic is the most popular example of an event-driven language. The syntax of the language is simple yet powerful. Visual Basic is used to create real-time and batch applications that can manipulate flat files or relational databases. It has a screen-painting feature that greatly facilitates the creation of sophisticated *graphical user interfaces (GUI)*.

Object-Oriented Languages. Central to achieving the benefits of the object oriented approach is developing software in an **object-oriented programming (OOP) language**. The most popular true OOP languages are Java and Smalltalk. However, the learning curve of OOP languages is steep. The time and cost of retooling for OOP is the greatest impediment to the transition process. Most firms are not prepared to discard millions of lines of traditional COBOL code and retrain their programming staffs to implement object-oriented systems. Therefore, a compromise, intended to ease this transition, has been the development of hybrid languages, such as Object COBOL, Object Pascal, and C++.

Programming the System. Regardless of the programming language used, modern programs should follow a *modular approach*. This technique produces small programs that perform narrowly defined tasks. The following three benefits are associated with modular programming.

1. *Programming efficiency.* Modules can be coded and tested independently, which vastly reduces programming time. A firm can assign several programmers to a single system. Working in parallel, the programmers each design a few modules. These are then assembled into the completed system.
2. *Maintenance efficiency.* Small modules are easier to analyze and change, which reduces the start-up time during program maintenance. Extensive changes can be parceled out to several programmers simultaneously to shorten maintenance time.
3. *Control.* By keeping modules small, they are less likely to contain material errors of fraudulent logic. Since each module is independent of the others, errors are contained within the module.

Test the Application Software

All program modules must be thoroughly tested before they are implemented. There are some proven concepts about testing that should be followed by the system developers, and considered by auditors in conducting audits.

Testing Methodology. The process itself has structured steps to follow. Figure 4-8 shows a program-testing procedure involving the creation of hypothetical master files and transactions files that are processed by the modules being tested. The results of the tests are then compared against predetermined results to identify programming and logic errors. For example, in testing the logic of the accounts receivable update module illustrated in Figure 4-8, the programmer might create an accounts receivable master file record for John Smith with a current balance of $1,000 and a sales order transaction record for $100. Before performing the update test, the programmer concludes that a new balance of $1,100 should be created. To verify the module's internal logic, the programmer compares the actual results obtained from the run with the predetermined results. This example is a simple one of a program test. Actual testing

FIGURE 4-8

Program-Testing Procedures

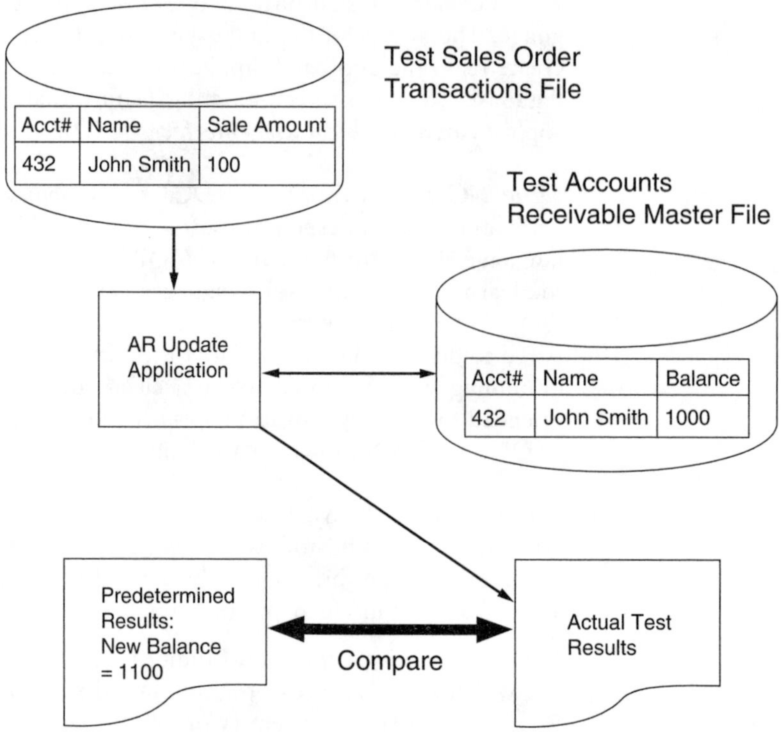

would be extensive and would involve many transactions that test all aspects of the module's logic.

Testing Offline Before Deploying Online. The first point that is critical in testing is to never underestimate the principle of *testing offline before deploying a system online.* Implementing a system without testing offline is an invitation to disaster. One online e-commerce firm went out of business because it implemented a system online without testing it offline first, and accidentally left a vulnerable Web server open to attacks from crackers. A cracker stole thousands of credit card numbers and eventually the online business failed.

Test Data. Creating meaningful test data is an extremely time-consuming aspect of program testing. This activity can, however, provide future benefits. As we shall see in Chapter 7, application auditing sometimes involves program testing. To facilitate future testing, test data prepared during the implementation phase should be retained for reuse. This test data will give the auditor a frame of reference for designing and evaluating future audit tests. For example, if a program has undergone no maintenance changes since its original implementation, the test results from the audit should be identical to the original test results. On one hand, having a basis for comparison, the auditor can thus quickly verify the integrity of the program code. On the other hand, if changes have occurred, the original test data can provide evidence regarding these changes. The auditor can thus focus attention upon those areas. Maintaining test data and its results is also a significant control feature, as future systems development can use the test data and results to test future changes to the application software.

The Auditor's Role in System Testing

The auditor's role is to verify systems personnel and projects used for these testing procedures. In particular, the auditor should inquire into the testing of systems offline prior to deployment online, and test data and test results. As already stated, the auditor may even want to use the test data to test controls in applications.

System Implementation—Phase VII

In the **system implementation** phase of the systems development process, database structures are created and populated with data, equipment is purchased and installed, employees are trained, the system is documented, and the new system is installed. The implementation process engages the efforts of designers, programmers, database administrators, users, and accountants. The activities in this phase entail extensive costs and will often consume more personnel-hours than all other pre-implementaion phases of the SDLC combined.

Testing the Entire System

When all modules have been coded and tested, they must be brought together and tested as a whole. User personnel should direct system-wide testing as a prelude to the formal system implementation. The procedure involves using the system to process hypothetical data. The outputs of the system are then reconciled with predetermined results, and the test is documented to provide evidence of the system's performance. Finally, when those conducting the tests are satisfied with the results, they should then complete a formal acceptance document. This is an explicit acknowledgment by the user that the system in question meets stated requirements. The user acceptance document becomes important in reconciling differences and assigning responsibility during the post-implementation review of the system.

Documenting the System

The system's **documentation** provides the auditor with essential information about how the system works. The documentation requirements of three groups—systems designers and programmers, computer operators, and end users—are of particular importance.

Designer and Programmer Documentation. Systems designers and programmers need documentation to debug errors and perform maintenance on the system. This group is involved with the system on a highly technical level, which requires both general and detailed information. Some of this is provided through data flow diagrams (DFDs), entity relation (ER) diagrams, and structure diagrams. In addition, system flowcharts, program flowcharts, and program code listings are important forms of documentation. The *system flowchart* shows the relationship of input files, programs, and output files. However, it does not reveal the logic of individual programs that constitute the system. The *program flowchart* provides a detailed description of the sequential and logical operation of the program. Each program in the system's flowchart is represented by a separate program flowchart, as shown in Figure 4-9. From these, the programmer can visually review and evaluate the program's logic. The program code should itself be documented with comments that describe each major program segment.

FIGURE 4-9 **System Designer and Programmer Documentation**

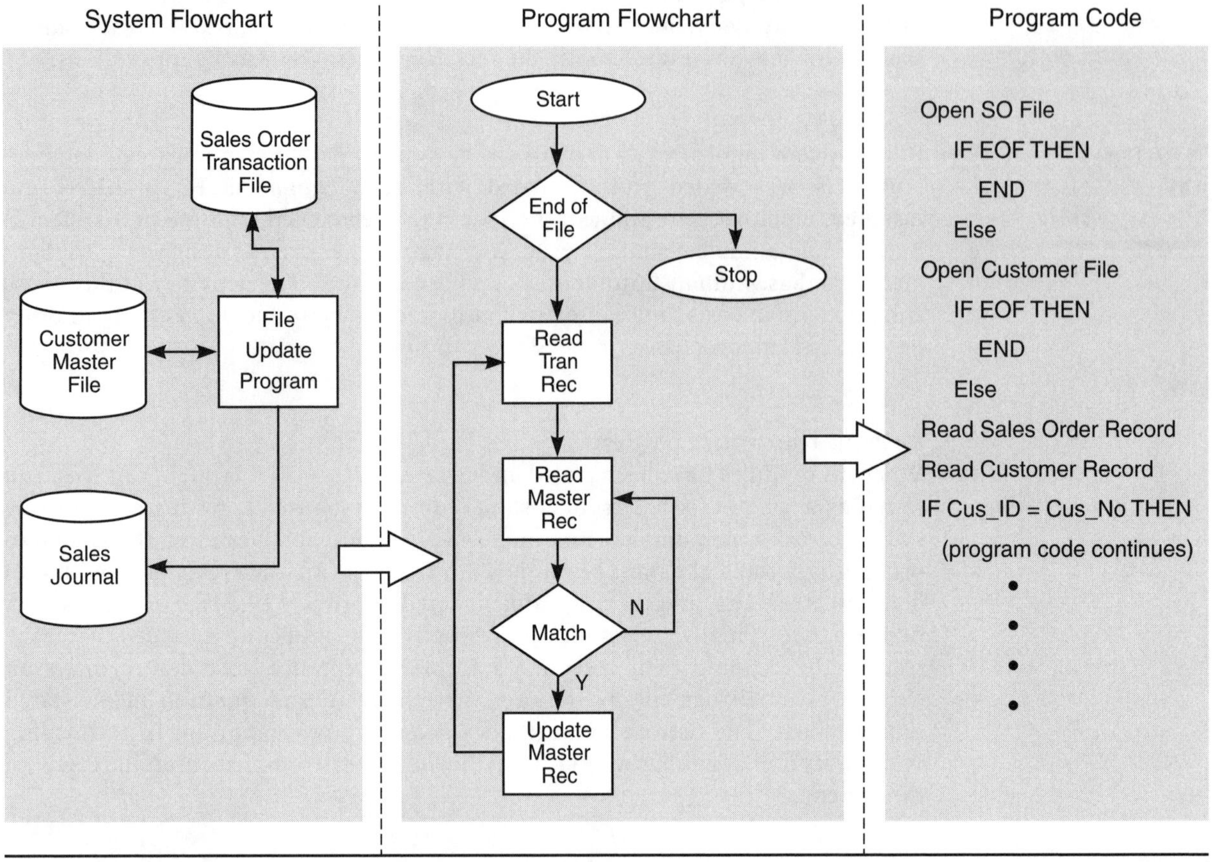

Operator Documentation. Computer operators use documentation called a **run manual**, which describes how to run the system. The typical contents of a run manual include

- The name of the system, such as Purchases System
- The run schedule (daily, weekly, time of day, and so on)
- Required hardware devices (tapes, disks, printers, or special hardware)
- File requirements specifying all the transaction (input) files, master files, and output files used in the system
- Run-time instructions describing the error messages that may appear, actions to be taken, and the name and telephone number of the programmer on call, should the system fail
- A list of users who receive the output from the run

For security and control reasons, system flowcharts, logic flowcharts, and program code listings should not be part of the operator documentation. Operators should not have access to the details of a system's internal logic. We will discuss this point more fully later.

User Documentation. Users need documentation describing how to use the system. User tasks include such things as entering input for transactions, making inquiries of account balances, updating accounts, and generating output reports. The nature of user documentation will depend on the user's degree of sophistication with computers and technology. Thus, before designing user documentation, the systems professional must assess and classify the user's skill level. The following is one possible classification scheme:

- **Novices** have little or no experience with computers and are embarrassed to ask questions. Novices also know little about their assigned tasks. User training and documentation for novices must be extensive and detailed.
- **Occasional users** once understood the system but have forgotten some essential commands and procedures. They require less training and documentation than novices.
- **Frequent light users** are familiar with limited aspects of the system. Although functional, they tend not to explore beneath the surface and lack depth of knowledge. This group knows only what it needs to know and requires training and documentation for unfamiliar areas.
- **Frequent power users** understand the existing system and will readily adapt to new systems. They are intolerant of detailed instructions that waste their time. They like to find shortcuts and use macro commands to improve performance. This group requires only abbreviated documentation.

User Handbook. With these classes in mind, user documentation often takes the form of a **user handbook**, as well as online documentation. The typical **user handbook** will contain the following items:

- An overview of the system and its major functions
- Instructions for getting started
- Descriptions of procedures with step-by-step visual references
- Examples of input screens and instructions for entering data
- A complete list of error message codes and descriptions
- A reference manual of commands to run the system
- A glossary of key terms
- Service and support information

Online documentation will guide the user interactively in the use of the system. Some commonly found online features include tutorials and help features.

Tutorials. Online **tutorials** can be used to train the novice or the occasional user. The success of this technique is based on the tutorial's degree of realism. Tutorials should not restrict the user from access to legitimate functions.

Help Features. Online **help features** range from simple to sophisticated. A simple help feature may be nothing more than an error message displayed on the screen. The user must "walk through" the screens in search of the solution to the problem. More sophisticated help is context-related. When the user makes an error, the system will send the message, "Do you need help?" The help feature analyzes the context of what the user is doing at the time of the error and provides help with that specific function (or command).

Converting the Databases

Database conversion is a critical step in the implementation phase. This is the transfer of data from its current form to the format or medium required by the new system. The degree of conversion depends on the technology leap from the old system to the new one. Some conversion activities are very labor intensive, requiring data to be entered into new databases manually. For example, the move from a manual system to a computer system will require converting files from paper to magnetic disk or tape. In other situations, data transfer may be accomplished by writing special conversion programs. A case in point is changing the file structure of the databases from sequential direct access files. In any case, data conversion is risky and must be carefully controlled. The following precautions should be taken:

1. *Validation.* The old database must be validated before conversion. This requires analyzing each class of data to determine whether it should be reproduced in the new database.
2. *Reconciliation.* After the conversion action, the new database must be reconciled against the original. Sometimes this must be done manually, record by record and field by field. In many instances, this process can be automated by writing a program that will compare the two sets of data.
3. *Backup.* Copies of the original files must be kept as backup against discrepancies in the converted data. If the current files are already in magnetic form, they can be conveniently backed up and stored. However, paper documents can create storage problems. When the user feels confident about the accuracy and completeness of the new databases, he or she may destroy the paper documents.

Converting to the New System

The process of converting from the old system to the new one is called the **cutover**. A system cutover will usually follow one of three approaches: cold turkey, phased, or parallel operation.

Cold Turkey Cutover. Under the **cold turkey cutover** approach (also called the "Big Bang" approach), the firm switches to the new system and simultaneously terminates the old system. When implementing simple systems, this is often the easiest and least costly approach. With more complex systems, it is the riskiest. Cold turkey cutover is akin to skydiving without a reserve parachute. As long as the main parachute functions properly, there is no problem. But things don't always work the way they are supposed to. System errors that were not detected during the walkthrough and testing steps may materialize unexpectedly. Without a backup system, an organization can find itself in serious trouble.

Phased Cutover. Sometimes an entire system cannot, or need not, be cut over at once. The **phased cutover** begins operating the new system in modules. For example, Figure 4-10 shows how we might implement a system, starting with the sales subsystem, followed by the inventory control subsystem, and finally the purchases subsystem.

By phasing in the new system in modules, we reduce the risk of a devastating system failure. However, the phased approach can create incompatibilities between new subsystems and yet-to-be-replaced old subsystems. This problem may be alleviated by implementing special conversion systems that provide temporary interfaces during the cutover period.

FIGURE 4-10

Phased Cutover

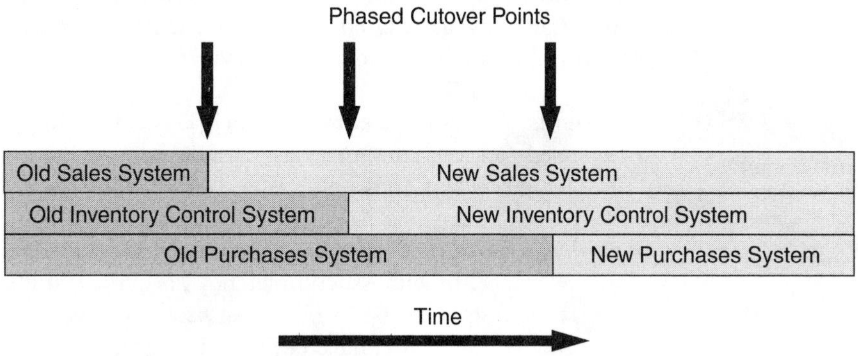

Parallel Operation Cutover. **Parallel operation cutover** involves running the old system and the new system simultaneously for a period of time. Figure 4-11 illustrates this approach, which is the most time consuming and costly of the three. Running two systems in parallel essentially doubles resource consumption. During the cutover period, the two systems require twice the source documents, twice the processing time, twice the databases, and twice the output production.

The advantage of parallel cutover is the reduction in risk. By running two systems, the user can reconcile outputs to identify errors and debug errors before running the new system solo. Parallel operation should usually extend for one business cycle, such as one month. This allows the user to reconcile the two outputs at the end of the cycle as a final test of the system's functionality.

Post-Implementation Review

One of the most important steps in the implementation stage actually takes place some months later in a *post-implementation review*. The review is conducted by an independent team to measure the success of the system and of the process after the dust has settled. Although systems professionals strive to produce systems that are on budget, on time, and meet user needs, this outcome does not always happen. The post-implementation review of the newly installed system can provide insight into ways to improve the process for future systems. The following discussion provides

FIGURE 4-11

Parallel Operation Cutover

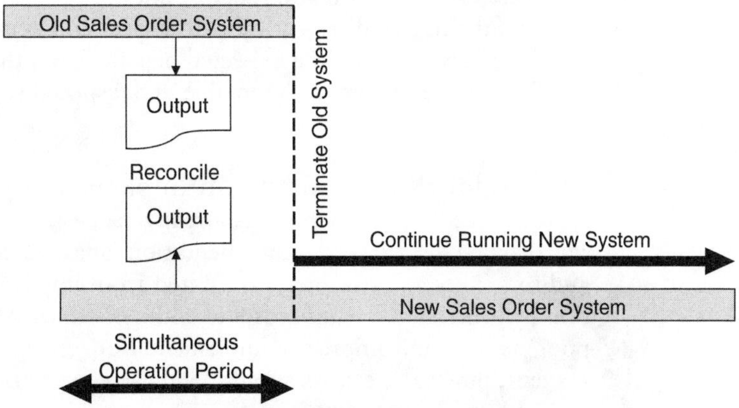

the auditor with valuable evidence regarding the adequacy of the SDLC in general and the risks associated with a particular system. Auditors should be highly involved in post-implementation reviews.

Systems Design Adequacy. The physical features of the system should be reviewed to see if they meet user needs. The reviewer should seek answers to the following types of questions:

- Does the output from the system possess such characteristics of information as relevance, timeliness, completeness, accuracy, and so on?
- Is the output in the format most useful and desired by the user (such as tables, graphs, electronic, hard copy, and so on)?
- Are the databases accurate, complete, and accessible?
- Were data lost, corrupted, or duplicated by the conversion process?
- Are input forms and screens properly designed and meeting user needs?
- Are the users using the system properly?
- Does the processing appear to be correct?
- Can all program modules be accessed and executed properly, or does the user ever get stuck in a loop?
- Is user documentation accurate, complete, and easy to follow?
- Does the system provide the user adequate help and tutorials?

Accuracy of Time, Cost, and Benefit Estimates. The task of estimating time, costs, and benefits for a proposed system is complicated by uncertainty. This is particularly true for large projects involving many activities and long time frames. The more variables in the process, the greater the likelihood for material error in the estimates. History is often the best teacher for decisions of this sort. Therefore, a review of actual performance compared to budgeted amounts provides critical input for future budgeting decisions. From such information, we can learn where mistakes were made and how to avoid them next time. The following questions provide some insight:

- Were actual costs in line with budgeted costs?
- What were the areas of significant departures from budget?
- Were departures from budget controllable (internal) in the short run or noncontrollable (for example, supplier problems)?
- Were estimates of the number of lines of program code accurate?
- Was the degree of rework due to design and coding errors acceptable?
- Are users receiving the expected benefits from the system?
- Were values assigned to tangible and, especially, intangible benefits accurate?

The Auditor's Role in System Implementation

As the preceding discussion has already suggested, the role of internal auditors in the detailed design and implementation phases should be significant. External auditors, however, are now prohibited from involvement in systems implementation by professional standards and codes of ethics. Most system failures are due to poor designs and improper implementation. Being a stakeholder in all financial systems, internal auditors should lend their expertise to this process to guide and shape the finished system. Specifically, internal auditors may get involved in the following ways.

Provide Technical Expertise. The detailed design phase involves precise specifications of procedures, rules, and conventions to be used in the system. In the case of an AIS, these specifications must comply with GAAP, GAAS, SEC regulations, and IRS codes. Failure to so comply can lead to legal exposure for the firm. For example, choosing the correct depreciation method or asset valuation technique requires a technical background not necessarily possessed by systems professionals. The accountant may provide this expertise to the systems design process.

Specify Documentation Standards. In the implementation phase, the auditor plays a role in specifying system documentation. Since financial systems must periodically be audited, they must be adequately documented. The auditor should actively encourage adherence to effective documentation standards.

Verify Control Adequacy. The applications that emerge from the SDLC must possess controls that are in accordance with the provisions of SAS No. 78 (known as the COSO model of internal controls). This process requires the internal auditor's involvement at both the detailed design and implementation phases. Controls may be both programmed and manual procedures. Some controls are part of the daily operation of the system, while others are special actions that precede, follow, or oversee routine processing. Control adequacy is even more important with the passage of the Sarbanes-Oxley Act of 2002 and SAS No. 99, because of the requirement to evaluate internal controls annually, and for external auditors to review those evaluations.

External Auditors. External auditors should be very concerned about the development and implementation of systems as they relate to controls. A materially flawed financial application will eventually corrupt the financial data, which will then be incorrectly reported in the financial statements. Therefore, the accuracy and integrity of these information systems directly affect the accuracy of the client's financial data.

Systems Maintenance—Phase VIII

Once a system is implemented, it enters the second phase in its life cycle—maintenance. **Systems maintenance** involves changing systems to accommodate changes in user needs. Sometime the change is trivial, such as modifying the system to produce a new report or changing the length of a data field. Maintenance can also be extensive, such as making major changes to an application's logic and the user interface. The systems maintenance period can last from 5 to 10 years, depending upon the organization. Systems in highly competitive business environments see much shorter system life spans. When it is no longer feasible for the organization to continue to maintain an aging system, it is scrapped, and a new systems development life cycle begins.

Maintenance represents a significant resource outlay compared to initial development costs. Over a system's life span, as much as 80 to 90 percent of its total cost may be incurred in the maintenance phase. We review the auditing implications of maintenance in the next section.

Controlling and Auditing the SDLC

In this chapter we have reviewed the highly technical and complex processes that constitute the SDLC. Before proceeding, it is useful to place this material in perspective with regard to audit objectives. Simply stated, the purpose of a financial audit is to provide an expert opinion regarding the fair presentation of the financial statements. To render such an opinion, the expert auditor must perform certain audit tests. Naturally, the accuracy of the financial data in the client's databases bears directly on the auditor's opinion. In a CBIS environment, financial data are processed (accessed, stored, and updated) by computer applications. The accuracy and integrity of these programs directly affects the accuracy of the client's financial data. A materially flawed financial application can corrupt financial data, which are then incorrectly reported in the financial statements.

Chapter 7 reviews several techniques for testing application controls. If audit evidence shows that computer applications process data correctly and accurately, the auditor can form the basis for reducing the amount of substantive testing that needs to be performed. Since the client organization could, however, have hundreds of financially significant applications, testing application controls can prove to be a highly technical and time-consuming activity. Auditors, therefore, seek efficient and effective ways to limit the application testing.

The systems development and maintenance process is common to all applications. A properly functioning systems development process ensures that only needed applications are created, that they are properly specified, that they possess adequate controls, and that they are thoroughly tested before being implemented. The systems maintenance process ensures that only legitimate changes are made to applications and that such changes are also tested before being implemented. Together, these processes establish the accuracy of new applications and preserve their integrity throughout the period under review.

If the auditor can verify that these processes are effectively controlled, he or she can limit the extent of application testing that needs to be done. If, however, audit evidence shows SDLC controls to be weak and inconsistently applied, application testing and substantive testing cannot be reduced. In some situations, it may even be necessary to expand the scope of the audit. With this perspective in place, let's now examine the controls, audit objectives, and audit procedures related to these important processes.

Controlling New Systems Development

The first six controllable activities discussed deal with the authorization, development, and implementation of the original system. The last two controllable activities pertain to systems maintenance activities.

Systems Authorization Activities

All systems must be properly authorized to ensure their economic justification and feasibility. As with all material transactions, authorizing the development of a new information system should be a formal step in the process. Typically, this requires that each new system request be submitted in writing by users to systems professionals who have both the expertise and authority to evaluate and approve (or reject) the request.

User Specification Activities

Users must be actively involved in the systems development process. Their involvement should not be stifled because the proposed system is technically complex.

Regardless of the technology involved, the user can and should provide a detailed written description of the logical needs that must be satisfied by the system. The creation of a user specification document often involves the joint efforts of the user and systems professionals. However, it is most important that this document remain a statement of user needs. It should describe the user's view of the problem, not that of the systems professionals.

Technical Design Activities

The technical design activities translate the user specifications into a set of detailed technical specifications of a system that meets the user's needs. The scope of these activities includes systems analysis, general systems design, feasibility analysis, and detailed systems design. The adequacy of these activities is measured by the quality of the documentation that emerges from each phase. Documentation is both a control and evidence of control and is critical to the system's long-term success. Specific documentation requirements were discussed previously.

Internal Audit Participation

The internal auditor plays an important role in the control of systems development activities, particularly in organizations whose users lack technical expertise. The internal auditor can serve as a liaison between users and the systems professionals to ensure an effective transfer of knowledge. An internal audit group, astute in computer technology and with a solid grasp of the business problems of users, can make a valuable contribution to all aspects of the SDLC process. The auditor should become involved at the inception of the process to make conceptual suggestions regarding system requirements and controls. Auditor involvement should continue throughout all phases of the development process and into the maintenance phase.

User Test and Acceptance Procedures

Just before implementation, the individual modules of the system must be tested as a unified whole. A test team comprising user personnel, systems professionals, and internal audit personnel subjects the system to rigorous testing. Once the test team is satisfied that the system meets its stated requirements, the system is formally accepted by the user department(s).

The formal testing and acceptance of the system by the user is considered by many auditors to be the most important control over the SDLC. This is the last point at which the user can determine that the system adequately meets his or her needs. Although discovering a major flaw at this juncture can be costly, discovering the flaw later, during operation, can be devastating. The user's acceptance of the new system should be formally documented.

Audit Objectives

- Verify that SDLC activities are applied consistently and in accordance with management's policies.
- Determine that the system as originally implemented was free from material errors and fraud.
- Confirm that the system was judged to be necessary and justified at various checkpoints throughout the SDLC.
- Verify that system documentation is sufficiently accurate and complete to facilitate audit and maintenance activities.

Audit Procedures

The auditor should select a sample of completed projects (completed in both the current period and previous periods) and review the documentation for evidence of compliance with SDLC policies. Specific points for review should include determining the following:

- User and computer services management properly authorized the project.
- A preliminary feasibility study showed that the project had merit.
- A detailed analysis of user needs was conducted that resulted in alternative general designs.
- A cost–benefit analysis was conducted using reasonably accurate figures.
- The project's documentation shows that the detailed design was an appropriate and accurate solution to the user's problem.
- Test results show that the system was thoroughly tested at both the individual module and the total system level before implementation. (To confirm these test results, the auditor may decide to retest selected elements of the application.)
- There is a checklist of specific problems detected during the conversion period, along with evidence that they were corrected in the maintenance phase.
- Systems documentation complies to organizational requirements and standards.

Controlling Systems Maintenance

The last two controllable activities pertain to systems maintenance. Upon implementation, the system enters the maintenance phase of the SDLC. This is the longest period in the SDLC, often spanning several years. It is important to recognize that systems do not remain static throughout this period. Rather, they may undergo substantial changes that constitute a financial outlay many times their original cost. If an application has undergone maintenance (and even if it has not), its integrity may have been compromised since implementation. The auditor's review may, therefore, extend into the maintenance phase to determine that application integrity is still intact.

In this section, we see how uncontrolled program changes can increase a firm's exposure to financial misstatement due to programming errors. Some programming errors are subtle, resulting in the creation and distribution of incorrect information that goes undetected by the user. Other forms of errors are more apparent and result in system failures that can disrupt data processing and even bring operations to a halt. In addition to these exposures, program fraud may take root in an environment of poorly controlled maintenance and can go undetected for years.

Maintenance Authorization, Testing, and Documentation

The benefits achieved from controlling new system development can be quickly lost during system maintenance if control does not continue into that phase. Access to systems for maintenance purposes increases the possibility of systems errors. Logic may be corrupted either by the accidental introduction of errors or intentional acts to defraud. To minimize the potential exposure, all maintenance actions should require, as a minimum, four controls: formal authorization, technical specification of the changes, retesting the system, and updating the documentation. In other words, maintenance activities should be given essentially the same treatment as new development. The extent of the change and its potential impact on the system should govern the degree of control applied. When maintenance causes extensive changes to program logic, additional controls, such as involvement by the internal auditor and the implementation of user test and acceptance procedures, may be necessary.

Source Program Library Controls

In spite of the preceding maintenance procedures, application integrity can be jeopardized by individuals who gain unauthorized access to programs. The remainder of this section deals with control techniques and procedures for preventing and detecting unauthorized access to application programs.

In larger computer systems, application program source code is stored on magnetic disks called the *source program library (SPL)*. Figure 4-12 illustrates the relationship between the SPL and other key components of the operating environment.

To execute a production application, it must first be compiled and linked to create a load module that the computer can process. As a practical matter, load modules are secure and free from the threat of unauthorized modification. Program changes (both authorized maintenance and unauthorized changes) are accomplished by first making changes to the source code stored on the SPL and then recompiling and linking the program to create a new load module that incorporates the changed code. Therefore, the SPL is a sensitive area, which, to preserve application integrity, must be properly controlled.

The Worst-Case Situation: No Controls

Figure 4-12 shows the SPL without controls. This arrangement has the potential to create the following two serious forms of exposure (see the following list).

1. *Access to programs is completely unrestricted.* Programmers and others can access any programs stored in the library, and there is no provision for detecting an unauthorized intrusion.
2. *Because of these control weaknesses, programs are subject to unauthorized changes.* Hence, there is no basis for relying on the effectiveness of other controls (maintenance authorization, program testing, and documentation). In other words, with no provision for detecting unauthorized access to the SPL, program integrity cannot be verified.

Control is always in conflict with operational flexibility and efficiency. For these reasons, systems professionals who must work daily within this environment sometimes oppose controlling the SPL. To achieve a mutually acceptable control-flexibility trade-off between the needs of systems professionals and auditors, both

FIGURE 4-12 **Uncontrolled Access to the Source Program Library**

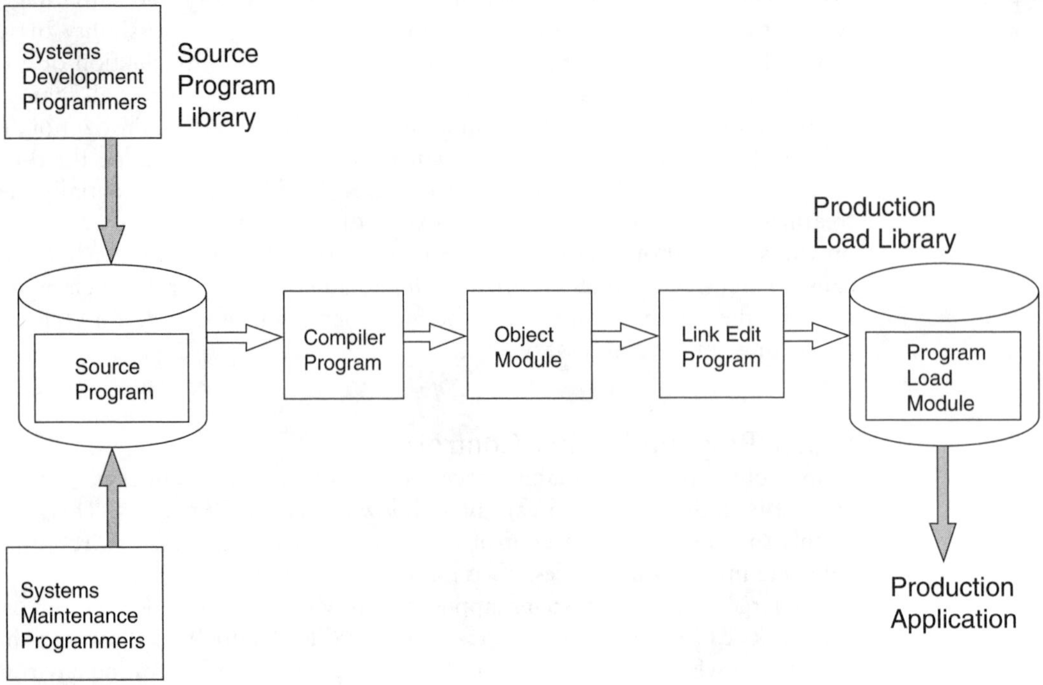

must understand the exposures that are created when control features are not employed or are routinely circumvented. In spite of the exposure just described, the no-controls approach is often the choice (perhaps inadvertently) that management makes.

A Controlled SPL Environment

To control the SPL, protective features and procedures must be explicitly addressed, and this requires the implementation of an *SPL management system (SPLMS)*. Figure 4-13 illustrates the use of this technique. The black box surrounding the SPL signifies the SPLMS. This software is used to control four routine but critical functions: (1) storing programs on the SPL, (2) retrieving programs for maintenance purposes, (3) deleting obsolete programs from the library, and (4) documenting program changes to provide an audit trail of the changes.

You may have recognized the similarities between the SPL management system and a database management system. This is a valid analogy, the difference being that SPL software manages program files and DBMSs manage data files. SPLMSs may be supplied by the computer manufacturer as part of the operating system or may be purchased through software vendors. Some organizations, to provide special control features, develop their own SPL software.

The mere presence of an SPLMS does not guarantee program integrity. Again, we can draw an analogy with the DBMS. To achieve data integrity, the DBMS must be properly used; control does not come automatically, it must be planned. Likewise, an SPL requires specific planning and control techniques to ensure program integrity.

FIGURE 4-13 Source Program Library under the Control of SPL Management Software

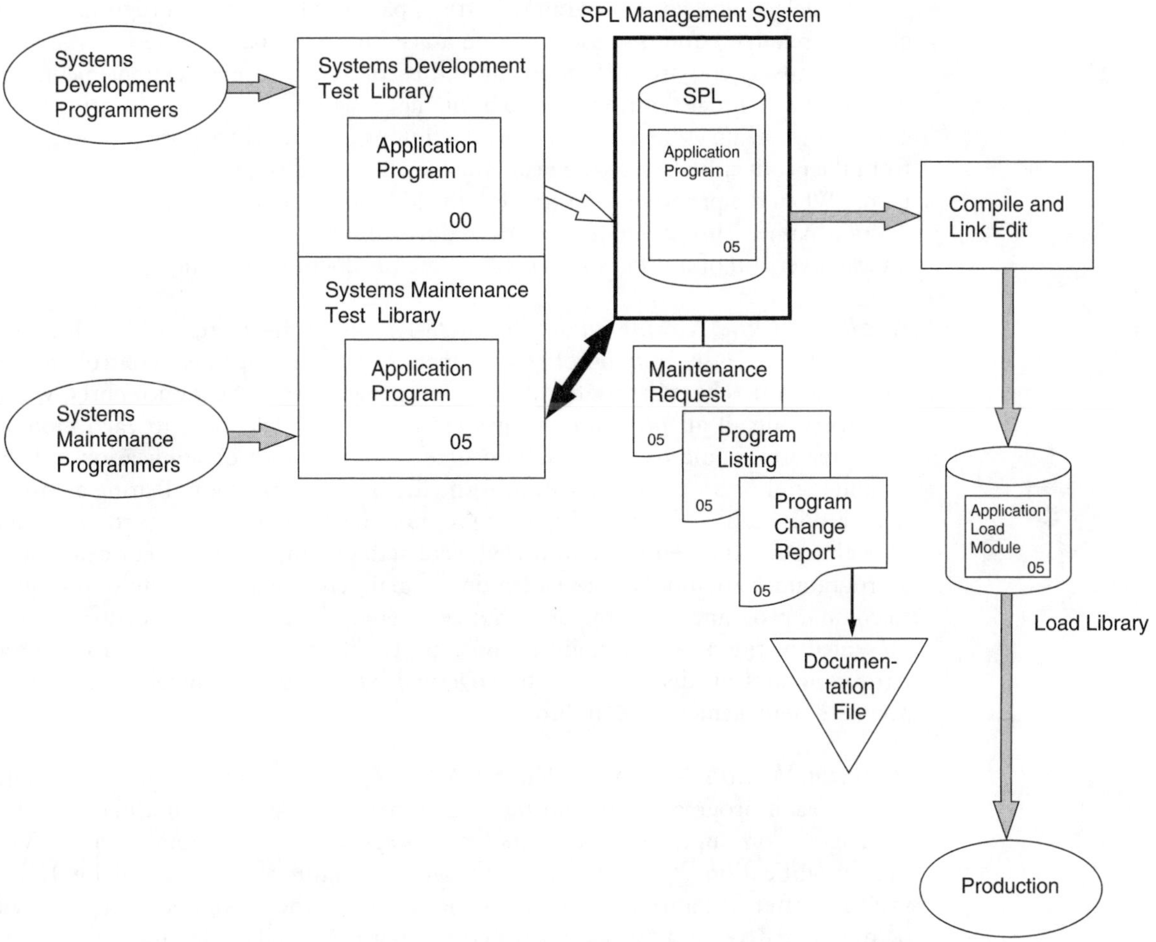

The control techniques discussed in the following paragraphs address only the most vulnerable areas and should be considered minimum control.

Password Control. Assigning passwords provides one form of access control over the SPL. This is similar to password controls used in a DBMS to protect data files. Every financially significant program stored in the SPL can be assigned a separate password. As previously discussed, passwords have drawbacks. When more than one person is authorized to access a program, preserving the secrecy of a shared password is a problem. As more authorized personnel have a need to know the password, the potential for losing control of the password increases. Since responsibility for the secrecy of a shared password lies with the group rather than with an individual, personal accountability is reduced, and individuals within the group may take less care in protecting the password.

Separate Test Libraries. Figure 4-13 illustrates an improvement on the shared password approach through the creation of separate password-controlled libraries (or directories) for each programmer. Under this concept, programs are copied into the programmer's library for maintenance and testing. Direct access to the production SPL is limited to an authorized librarian who must approve all requests to modify, delete, and copy programs. Further, passwords to access programs can be changed regularly and disclosed only on a need-to-know basis.

A relatively cost-free enhancement to this control feature is the implementation of program naming conventions. The name assigned a program clearly distinguishes it as being either a test or a production program. When a program is copied from the production SPL to the programmer's library, it is given a temporary "test" name. When the program is returned to the SPL, it is renamed with its original production name. This technique greatly reduces the risk of accidentally running an untested version of a program in place of the production program.

Audit Trail and Management Reports. An important feature of SPL management software is the creation of reports that enhance management control and the audit function. The most useful of these are program modification reports, which describe in detail all program changes (additions and deletions) to each module. These reports should be part of the documentation file of each application to form an audit trail of program changes over the life of the application. During an audit, these reports can be reconciled against program maintenance requests to verify that only changes requested and authorized were actually implemented. For example, if a programmer attempted to use a legitimate maintenance action as an opportunity to commit program fraud, the unauthorized changes to the program code would be presented in the program modification report. These reports can be produced as hard copy and on disk and can be governed by password control, thus limiting access to management and auditors.

Program Version Numbers. The SPLMS assigns a version number automatically to each program stored on the SPL. When programs are first placed in the libraries (upon implementation), they are assigned a version number of 0. With each modification to the program, the version number is increased by 1. For instance, after five authorized maintenance changes, the production program will be designated version 05, as illustrated in Figure 4-14. This feature, when combined with audit trail reports, provides evidence for identifying unauthorized changes to program modules. An unauthorized change is signaled by a version number on the production load module that cannot be reconciled to the number of authorized changes. For example, if 10 changes were authorized but the production program shows version 12, then one of two possibilities explain this discrepancy: (1) authorized changes occurred that are unsupported by documentation or (2) unauthorized changes were made to the program, which incremented the version numbers.

Controlling Access to Maintenance Commands. SPL management systems use powerful maintenance commands to alter or eliminate program passwords, alter the program version (modification) number, and temporarily modify a program without generating a record of the modification. There are legitimate technical reasons why systems designers and administrators need these commands. However, if not controlled, maintenance commands open the possibility of

FIGURE 4-14 **Auditing SPL Software System**

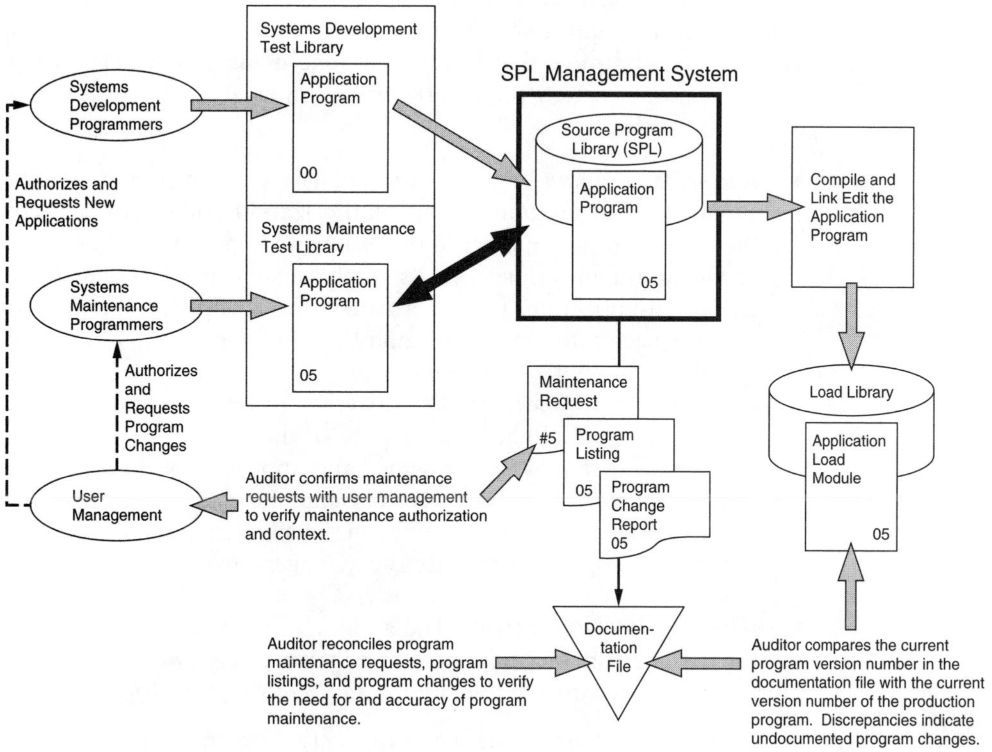

unrecorded, and perhaps unauthorized, program modifications. Hence, access to the maintenance commands themselves should be password-controlled, and the authority to use them should be controlled by management or the security group.

Audit Objectives

- Detect unauthorized program maintenance (which may have resulted in significant processing errors or fraud). Determine that (1) maintenance procedures protect applications from unauthorized changes, (2) applications are free from material errors, and (3) program libraries are protected from unauthorized access.

We will examine each of these objectives in turn, focusing on the tests of controls that are necessary to achieve the objective. The discussion will assume that the organization employs source program library (SPL) software to control program maintenance. It should be noted that without SPL software, it can be difficult to achieve these audit objectives. The procedures described below are illustrated in Figure 4-14.

Audit Procedures

Identify Unauthorized Changes. To establish that program changes were authorized, the auditor should examine the audit trail of program changes for a sample of applications that have undergone maintenance. The auditor can confirm that authorization procedures were followed by performing the following tests of controls.

- *Reconcile program version numbers.* The permanent file of the application should contain program change authorization documents that correspond to the current version number of the production application. In other words, if the production application is in its tenth version, there should be ten program change authorizations in the permanent file as supporting documentation. Any discrepancies between version numbers and supporting documents may indicate that unauthorized changes were made.
- *Confirm maintenance authorization.* The program maintenance authorization documents should indicate the nature of the change requested and the date of the change. It should also be signed and approved by the appropriate management from both computer services and the user departments. The auditor should confirm the facts contained in the maintenance authorization and verify the authorizing signatures with the managers involved.

Identify Application Errors. The auditor can determine that programs are free from material errors by performing three types of tests of controls: reconciling the source code, reviewing the test results, and retesting the program.

- *Reconcile the source code.* Each application's permanent file should contain the current program listing and listings of all changes made to the application. These documents describe in detail the application's maintenance history. In addition, the nature of the program change should be clearly stated on the program change authorization document. The auditor should select a sample of applications and reconcile each program change with the appropriate authorization documents. The modular approach to systems design (creating applications that comprise many small discrete program modules) greatly facilitates this testing technique. The reduced complexity of these modules enhances the auditor's ability to identify irregularities that indicate errors, omissions, and potentially fraudulent programming code.
- *Review test results.* Every program change should be thoroughly tested before being implemented. Program test procedures should be properly documented by test objectives, test data, and processing results, which support the programmer's decision to implement the change. The auditor should review this record for each significant program change to establish that testing was sufficiently rigorous to identify any errors.
- *Retest the program.* The auditor can retest the application to confirm its integrity. We examine several techniques for application testing in Chapter 7.

Test Access to Libraries. The existence of a secure program library is central to preventing errors and program fraud. One method is to assign library access rights exclusively to individuals who act as librarians. Their function is to retrieve applications from the program libraries for maintenance and to restore the modified programs to the library. In this arrangement, programmers perform program maintenance and testing in their own "private" libraries but do not have direct access to the program library.

The auditor should establish that the program library and private libraries are protected from unauthorized access by performing the following tests of controls.

- *Review programmer authority tables.* The auditor can select a sample of programmers and review their access authority. The programmer's authority table will specify the libraries a programmer may access. These authorizations should be matched against the programmer's maintenance authority to ensure that no irregularities exist.
- *Test authority table.* The auditor should simulate the programmer's access privileges and then violate the authorization rules by attempting to access unauthorized libraries. Any such attempts should be denied by the operating system.

SUMMARY

One of the most valuable assets of the modern business organization is a responsive, user-oriented information system. A well-designed system can increase productivity, reduce inventories, eliminate nonvalue-added activities, improve customer service and management decisions, and coordinate activities throughout the organization.

This chapter examined the purpose, control, and audit of the systems development life cycle. It began by describing the roles of the participants involved in systems development, including systems professionals, users, and stakeholders. Then it outlined the key activities associated with SDLC. This process consists of two primary sets of activities: new systems development and maintenance. The former, which is used to guide the development of information systems in many organizations, includes *systems planning, systems analysis, conceptual design, system selection, detailed design, system programming and testing, and system implementation.* A properly functioning systems development process ensures that only needed applications are created, that they are properly specified, that they possess adequate controls, and that they are thoroughly tested before being implemented. Upon implementation, new systems enter the *systems maintenance* phase, where they remain until they are terminated and ultimately replaced. The systems maintenance process ensures that only legitimate changes are made to applications and that such changes are also tested before being implemented.

The systems development and maintenance process is common to all applications. Together, they establish the accuracy of new applications and preserve their integrity throughout the period under review.

The auditor's objective in testing controls over these processes is to establish application integrity and thus limit the tests of application controls and substantive testing that needs to be done.

Key Terms

accountants/auditors
backbone systems
bottlenecks and redundant operations
break-even point
cold turkey cutover
conceptual design
controls
cutover
data flows
data sources
data stores
database conversion
detailed design
detailed design report
documentation
end users
error rates
event-driven languages
frequent light users
frequent power users
general accounting systems
help features
intangible benefits
legal feasibility
net present value method
new systems development
novices
object-oriented design approach
object-oriented programming language
objects
observation
occasional users
office automation systems
operational feasibility
parallel operation cutover
payback method
personal interviews
phased cutover
processes
procedural language
project planning
project proposal
project schedule
quality assurance group
resource costs
reviewing key documents
run manual
schedule feasibility
special-purpose systems
stakeholders
steering committee
strategic systems planning
structured design
system implementation
system survey
systems analysis
systems analysis report
systems development life cycle (SDLC)
systems evaluation and selection
systems maintenance
systems planning
systems professionals
systems selection report
tangible benefits
task participation
technical feasibility
third-generation languages
transaction volumes
turnkey systems
tutorials
user handbook
users
vendor-supported systems
walkthrough

Review Questions

1. Distinguish between systems professionals, end users, and stakeholders.
2. What is the role of the accountant in the SDLC? Why might accountants be called on for input into the development of a nonaccounting information system?
3. What are the three problems that account for most system failures?

4. Why is it often difficult to obtain competent and meaningful user involvement in the SDLC?
5. Who should sit on the systems steering committee? What are their typical responsibilities?
6. Why is strategic systems planning not technically considered to be part of the SDLC?
7. What is strategic systems planning, and why should it be done?
8. What is the purpose of project planning, and what are the various steps?
9. What is the object-oriented design (OOD) approach?
10. What are the broad classes of facts that need to be gathered in the system survey?
11. What are the primary fact-gathering techniques?
12. What are the relative merits and disadvantages of a current systems survey?
13. Distinguish among data sources, data stores, and data flows.
14. What are some of the key documents that may be reviewed in a current systems survey?
15. What is the purpose of a systems analysis, and what type of information should be included in the systems analysis report?
16. What is the primary objective of the conceptual systems design phase?
17. What are two approaches to conceptual systems design?
18. How much design detail is needed in the conceptual design phase?
19. What is an object, and what are its characteristics in the object-oriented approach? Give two examples.
20. What is the auditor's primary role in the conceptual design of the system?
21. Who should be included in the group of independent evaluators performing the detailed feasibility study?
22. What makes the cost–benefit analysis more difficult for information systems than most other investments an organization may make?
23. Classify each of the following as either one-time or recurring costs:
    a. training personnel
    b. initial programming and testing
    c. systems design
    d. hardware costs
    e. software maintenance costs
    f. site preparation
    g. rent for facilities
    h. data conversion from old system to new system
    i. insurance costs
    j. installation of original equipment
    k. hardware upgrades
24. Distinguish between turnkey and backbone systems. Which is more flexible?
25. Discuss the relative merits of in-house programs versus commercially developed software.
26. Why is modular programming preferable to free coding?
27. Why should test data be saved after it has been used?
28. Explain the importance of documentation by the systems programmers.
29. What documents not typically needed by other stakeholders do accountants and auditors need for the new system?

Discussion Questions

1. Comment on the following statement: "The maintenance stage of the SDLC involves making trivial changes to accommodate changes in user needs."
2. Discuss how rushing the system's requirements stage may delay or even result in the failure of a systems development process. Conversely, discuss how spending too long in this stage may result in "analysis paralysis."
3. Is a good strategic plan detail oriented?
4. Distinguish between a problem and a symptom. Give an example. Are these usually noticed by upper-, middle-, or lower-level managers?
5. What purposes does the systems project proposal serve? How are these evaluated and prioritized? Is the prioritizing process objective or subjective?
6. Most firms underestimate the cost and time requirements of the SDLC by as much as 50 percent. Why do you think this occurs? In what

stages do you think the underestimates are most dramatic?

7. A lack of support by top management has led to the downfall of many new systems projects during the implementation phase. Why do you think management support is so important?
8. Many new systems projects grossly underestimate transaction volumes simply because they do not take into account how the new, improved system can actually increase demand. Explain how this can happen and give an example.
9. Compare and contrast the structured design approach and the object-oriented approach. Which do you believe is most beneficial? Why?
10. Do you think legal feasibility is an issue for a system that incorporates the use of machines to sell lottery tickets?
11. Intangible benefits are usually extremely difficult to quantify accurately. Some designers argue that if you understate them, then conservative estimates are produced. Any excess benefits will be greatly welcomed but not required for the new system to be a success. What are the dangers of this viewpoint?
12. If a firm decides early on to go with a special-purpose system, such as SAP, based on the recommendations of the external audit firm, should the SDLC be bypassed?
13. During a test data procedure, why should the developers bother testing "bad" data?
14. If the system is behind schedule and if each program module is tested and no problems are found, is it necessary to test all modules in conjunction with one another? Why or why not?
15. Run manuals for computer operators are similar in theory to the checklists that airplane pilots use for takeoffs and landings. Explain why these are important.
16. Who conducts the post-implementation review? When should it be conducted? If an outside consulting firm were hired to design and implement the new system, or a canned software package were purchased, would a post-implementation review still be useful?
17. Discuss the importance of involving accountants in the detailed design and implementation phases. What tasks should they perform?
18. Discuss the independence issue when audit firms also provide consulting input into the development and selection of new systems.
19. Discuss the various feasibility measures that should be considered. Give an example of each.
20. Discuss three benefits associated with modular programming.

Multiple-Choice Questions

1. CMA 1282 5-9
   The role of an information system steering committee should be to
   a. initiate all computer applications, set computer applications priorities, control access to the computer room, and keep the computer file library.
   b. prepare control totals, maintain systems documentation, and perform follow-up on errors.
   c. assign duties to systems personnel, prepare and monitor system implementation plans, and prepare flowcharts of systems applications.
   d. review systems project proposals, long-range systems plans, and the performance of the systems department and approve major acquisitions in consideration of overall plans.
   e. decide on specific information needs, prepare detailed plans for systems evaluations, set priorities for writing programs, and decide which equipment will be purchased.
2. CIA 582 IV-8
   Many people believe that a data processing department should have a long-range plan. Which of the following is NOT likely to appear in a long-range plan?
   a. organizational goals and objectives
   b. detailed flowcharts for each computer program that will be developed
   c. schedule of the development of each project
   d. identification of the hardware, personnel, and financial resources that will be required
   e. forecast of future hardware developments

3. CIA 584 II-36
In reviewing a feasibility study for a new computer system, the auditor should ascertain that the study
   a. considered costs, savings, controls, profit improvement, and other benefits analyzed by application area.
   b. provided the preliminary plan for converting existing manual systems and clerical operations.
   c. provided management with assurance from qualified, independent consultants that the use of a computer system appeared justified.
   d. included a report by the internal audit department that evaluated internal control features for each planned application.
4. CMA 686 5-2
The most important factor in planning for a system change is
   a. having an auditor as a member of the design team.
   b. using state-of-the-art techniques.
   c. concentrating on software rather than hardware.
   d. involving top management and people who use the system.
   e. selecting a user to lead the design team.
5. CMA 678 5-5
In the context of a feasibility study, technical feasibility refers to whether
   a. a proposed system is attainable, given the existing technology.
   b. the systems manager can coordinate and control the activities of the systems department.
   c. an adequate computer site exists for the proposed system.
   d. the proposed system will produce economic benefits exceeding its costs.
   e. the system will be used effectively within the operating environment of an organization.
6. CMA 1281 5-13
The stage of a systems study that would include up-to-date organizational charts; a description of the present system; complete flowcharts for the present system; forms and layouts of all input and output documents (along with samples) used in the present system; and summaries of interviews, review sessions, and personal observations regarding the present system is
   a. problem definition.
   b. problem analysis.
   c. system design.
   d. program analysis.
   e. documentation and maintenance.
7. CMA 678 5-4
A systems survey is being conducted to obtain an accurate perspective on the existing system and to identify weaknesses that can be corrected by the new system. Which one of the following steps is not considered part of this systems survey?
   a. Interviews are conducted with operating people and managers.
   b. The complete documentation of the system is obtained and reviewed.
   c. Measures of processing volume are obtained for each operation.
   d. Equipment sold by various computer manufacturers is reviewed in terms of capability, cost, and availability.
   e. Work measurement studies are conducted to determine the time required to complete various tasks or jobs.
8. Which of the following is NOT a one-time cost?
   a. site preparation
   b. insurance
   c. software acquisition
   d. data conversion
9. Which of the following is NOT an advantage of commercial software?
   a. independence
   b. cost
   c. reliability
   d. implementation time
10. CMA 1287 5-6
The process of developing specifications for hardware, software, personnel hours, data resources, and information products required to develop a system is referred to as
   a. systems analysis.
   b. systems feasibility study.
   c. systems maintenance.
   d. system implementation.
   e. systems design.
11. CMA 689 5-4
The analysis tool for the systems analyst and steering committee to use in selecting the best systems option is
   a. cost–benefit analysis.
   b. systems design.
   c. decision tree analysis.

d. user selection.
e. pilot testing.

12. CMA 1289 5-8
In determining the need for system changes, several types of feasibility studies can be made. The most commonly recognized feasibility studies are
a. legal, environmental, and economic.
b. environmental, operational, and economic.
c. technical, economic, legal, and practical.
d. practical, technical, and operational.
e. technical, operational, and economic.

13. CMA 1290 4-13
The technique that recognizes the time value of money by discounting the after-tax cash flows for a project over its life to time period zero using the company's minimum desired rate of return is called the
a. net present value method.
b. capital rationing method.
c. payback method.
d. average rate of return method.
e. accounting rate of return method.

14. CMA 691 (Adapted)
Fitzgerald Company is planning to acquire a $250,000 computer that will provide increased efficiencies, thereby reducing annual operating costs by $80,000. The computer will be depreciated by the straight-line method over a five-year life with no salvage value at the end of five years. Assuming a 40 percent income tax rate, the machine's payback period is
a. 3.13 years.
b. 3.21 years.
c. 3.68 years.
d. 4.81 years.
e. 5.21 years.

Questions 15 and 16 are based on the following information and deal with a critique of the cost–benefit analysis portion of the feasibility study.

When management decides to implement a management information system in a segment of the company, the decision is often based upon a feasibility study conducted by the systems department. Following are terms and examples of them used in the section of the study dealing with the cost–benefit analysis:

Terms	*Examples*
Tangible cost	Development cost
Intangible cost	Imputed interest
Tangible benefits	Cost displacement
Intangible benefits	Improved decisions

The feasibility study identifies the major benefits of the new management information system. Many of the benefits are intangible, such as improved decision-making capability and effectiveness, better customer relations, and improved employee morale.

15. CMA Adapted 679 5-9
The estimated category that ordinarily would have the greatest uncertainty as to its precise value is
a. the tangible costs.
b. the intangible costs.
c. the tangible benefits.
d. the intangible benefits.
e. none of the above because they are equally precise.

16. CMA Adapted 679 5-10
Which one of the following statements best describes what is usually true regarding the estimates included in feasibility studies?
a. Development time and costs are usually less than estimated; benefits are stated accurately.
b. Development time and costs are usually less than estimated; benefits are usually greater than estimated.
c. Development costs and benefits are usually greater than estimated; development time is usually less than estimated.
d. Development time and costs are usually greater than estimated; benefits are usually less than estimated.
e. Development time, costs, and benefits are usually greater than estimated.

17. CMA 691 4-29
Errors are most costly to correct during
a. programming.
b. conceptual design.
c. analysis.
d. detailed design.
e. implementation.

18. CMA 1287 5-6
    The process of developing specifications for hardware, software, personnel hours, data resources, and information products required to develop a system is referred to as
    a. systems analysis.
    b. systems feasibility study.
    c. systems maintenance.
    d. system implementation.
    e. systems design.
19. CMA 678 5-2
    When designing a computer-based information system, the initial step in the systems design process is to determine
    a. the required output.
    b. the source documents that serve as the basis for input.
    c. the processing required.
    d. the decisions for which data will be required.
    e. the file information required during processing.
20. CMA 1282 5-12
    Characteristics of an accounting application that might influence the selection of data entry devices and media for a computerized accounting system are
    a. timing of feedback needs relative to input, need for documentation of an activity, and the necessity for reliability and accuracy.
    b. cost considerations, volume of input, complexity of activity, and liquidity of assets involved.
    c. need for documentation, necessity for accuracy and reliability, volume of output, and cost considerations.
    d. relevancy of data, volume of input, cost considerations, volume of output, and timing of feedback needs relative to input.
    e. type of file used, reliability of manufacturer's service, volume of output, and cost considerations.
21. CIA 1187 III-32
    User acceptance is part of which phase of the system development life cycle?
    a. implementation
    b. general systems design
    c. program specification and implementation planning
    d. detailed systems design

PROBLEMS

1. **Systems Planning**
   A new systems development project is being planned for the Reindeer Christmas Supplies Company. The invoicing, cash receipts, and accounts payable modules are all going to be updated. The controller, Kris K. Ringle, is a little anxious about this project. The last systems development project that affected his department was not very successful, and the employees in the accounting department did not accept the new system very well at first. He feels that the systems personnel did not interact sufficiently with the users of the systems in the accounting department. Prepare a memo from Ringle to the head of the information systems department, Sandy Klaus. In this memo, provide some suggestions for including the accounting personnel in the systems development project. Give some very persuasive arguments why prototyping would be helpful to the workers in the accounting department.

2. **Problem Identification**
   The need for a new information system may be manifest in various symptoms. In the early stages of a problem, these symptoms seem innocuous and go unrecognized. As the underlying source of the problem grows in severity, so do its symptoms, until they are alarmingly apparent. Classify each of the following as a problem or a symptom. If it is a symptom, give two examples of a possible underlying problem. If it is a problem, give two examples of a possible symptom that may be detected.
   a. declining profits
   b. defective production process
   c. low-quality raw materials
   d. shortfall in cash balance
   e. declining market share
   f. shortage of employees in the accounts payable department
   g. shortage of raw material due to a drought in the Midwest

h. inadequately trained workers
i. decreasing customer satisfaction

3. **Systems Development and Implementation**
Kruger Designs hired a consulting firm three months ago to redesign the information system used by the architects. The architects will be able to use state-of-the-art CAD programs to help in designing the products. Further, they will be able to store these designs on a network server where they and other architects may be able to call them back up for future designs with similar components. The consulting firm has been instructed to develop the system without disrupting the architects. In fact, top management believes that the best route is to develop the system and then to "introduce" it to the architects during a training session. Management does not want the architects to spend precious billable hours guessing about the new system or putting work off until the new system is working. Thus, the consultants are operating in a back room under a shroud of secrecy.

Required:
a. Do you think that management is taking the best course of action for the announcement of the new system? Why?
b. Do you approve of the development process? Why?

4. **Systems Analysis**
Consider the following dialogue between a systems professional, Joe Pugh, and a manager of a department targeted for a new information system, Lars Meyer:

Pugh: The way to go about the analysis is to first examine the old system, such as reviewing key documents and observing the workers perform their tasks. Then we can determine which aspects are working well and which should be preserved.

Meyer: We have been through these types of projects before and what always ends up happening is that we do not get the new system we are promised; we get a modified version of the old system.

Pugh: Well, I can assure you that will not happen this time. We just want a thorough understanding of what is working well and what is not.

Meyer: I would feel much more comfortable if we first started with a list of our requirements. We should spend some time up-front determining exactly what we want the system to do for my department. Then you systems people can come in and determine what portions to salvage if you wish. Just don't constrain us to the old system!

Required:
a. Obviously, these two workers have different views on how the systems analysis phase should be conducted. Comment on whose position you sympathize with the most.
b. What method would you propose they take? Why?

5. **Systems Design**
Robin Alper, a manager of the credit collections department for ACME Building Supplies, is extremely unhappy with a new system that was installed three months ago. Her complaint is that the data flow from the billing and accounts receivable departments are not occurring in the manner originally requested. Further, the updates to the database files are not occurring as frequently as she had envisioned. Thus, the hope that the new system would provide more current and timely information has not materialized. She claims that the systems analysts spent three days interviewing her and other workers. During that time, she and the other workers thought they had clearly conveyed their needs. She feels as if their needs were ignored and their time was wasted.

Required:
What went wrong during the systems design process? What suggestions would you make for future projects?

6. **Conceptual Design**
Prepare two alternative conceptual designs for both an accounts payable system and an accounts receivable system. Discuss the differences in concept between the different designs. From a cost perspective, which is more economical? From a benefits perspective, which is more desirable? Which design would you prefer and why?

7. **Systems Design**

Robert Hamilton was hired six months ago as the controller of a small oil and gas exploration and development company, Gusher, Inc., headquartered in Beaumont, Texas. Before working at Gusher, Hamilton was the controller of a larger petroleum company, Eureka Oil Company, based in Dallas. The joint interest billing and fixed asset accounting systems of Gusher are outdated, and many processing problems and errors have been occurring quite frequently. Hamilton immediately realized these problems and informed the president, Mr. Barton, that it was crucial to install a new system. Barton concurred and met with Hamilton and Sally Jeffries, the information systems senior manager. Barton instructed Jeffries to make the new system that Hamilton wished to have a top priority in her department. Basically, he told Jeffries to deliver the system to meet Hamilton's needs as soon as possible.

Jeffries left the meeting feeling overwhelmed since the IS department is currently working on two other very big projects, one for the production department and the other for the geological department. The next day, Hamilton sent a memo to Jeffries indicating the name of a system he had 100 percent confidence in—Amarillo Software—and he also indicated that he would very much like this system to be purchased as soon as possible. He stated that the system had been used with much success during the past four years in his previous job.

When commercial software is purchased, Jeffries typically sends out requests for proposals to at least six different vendors after conducting a careful analysis of the needed requirements. However, due to the air of urgency demonstrated in the meeting with the president and the overworked systems staff, she decided to go along with Hamilton's wishes and sent only one RFP (request for proposal) out, which went to Amarillo Software. Amarillo promptly returned the completed questionnaire. The purchase price ($75,000) was within the budgeted amount. Jeffries contacted the four references provided and was satisfied with their comments. Further, she felt comfortable since the system was for Hamilton, and he had used the system for four years.

The plan was to install the system during the month of July and try it for the August transaction cycle. Problems were encountered, however, during the installation phase. The system processed extremely slowly on the hardware platform owned by Gusher. When Jeffries asked Hamilton how the problem had been dealt with at Eureka, he replied that he did not remember having had such a problem. He called the systems manager from Eureka and discovered that Eureka had a much more powerful mainframe than Gusher. Further investigation revealed that Gusher has more applications running on its mainframe than Eureka did, since Eureka used a two-mainframe distributed processing platform.

Further, the data transfer did not go smoothly. A few data elements being stored in the system were not available as an option in the Amarillo system. Jeffries found that the staff at Amarillo was very friendly when she called, but they could not always identify the problem over the phone. They really needed to come out to the site and investigate. Hamilton was surprised at the delays between requesting an Amarillo consultant to come out and the time in which he or she actually arrived. Amarillo explained that it had to fly a staff member from Dallas to Beaumont for each trip. The system finally began to work somewhat smoothly in January, after a grueling fiscal year-end close in October. Hamilton's staff viewed the project as an unnecessary inconvenience. At one point, two staff accountants threatened to quit. The extra consulting fees amounted to $35,000. Further, the systems department at Gusher spent 500 more hours during the implementation process than it had expected. These additional hours caused other projects to fall behind schedule.

Required:

Discuss what could have been done differently during the design phase. Why were most of the problems encountered? How might a detailed feasibility study have helped?

8. **Programming Languages**

Describe the basic features of the following three types of programming languages: procedural, event-driven, and object oriented. Give examples of each type of language.

9. Program Testing
When program modules have been coded and tested, they must be brought together and tested as a whole. Comment on the importance of testing the entire system.

10. Database Conversion
What is database conversion and why is it a risky activity, and what precautions should be taken?

11. System Cutover
Discuss three common approaches to system cutover. Comment on the advantages and disadvantages of each approach.

CHAPTER

5

Networks, Internet, and E-Commerce

Learning Objectives

After studying this chapter, you should:

- Be able to distinguish between the different types of networks.
- Be familiar with the basic components of a network, including network operating systems, terminals, connection devices, the physical transmission path, and the front-end processor (server).
- Be familiar with network topologies and architectures.
- Be familiar with the technologies that support electronic commerce.
- Understand the operational features and risks associated with EDI and Internet commerce.
- Understand the control techniques used to reduce risk in e-commerce systems.
- Understand the audit objectives and procedures used to test controls in networks, the Internet, and e-commerce systems.

Electronic commerce (e-commerce) involves using Internet technologies, network systems, and the electronic processing and transmission of data. It encompasses many diverse activities, including electronic trading of goods and services, online delivery of digital products, electronic funds transfer (EFT), electronic trading of stocks, and direct consumer marketing. E-commerce, however, is not a new phenomenon. For many years, companies have engaged in electronic data interchange (EDI) over private networks. In recent years, driven by the Internet revolution, e-commerce is dramatically expanding and undergoing radical changes. This fast-moving environment is engendering an array of innovative markets and trading communities. Although e-commerce promises enormous opportunities for consumers and businesses, its effective implementation and control are urgent challenges for organization management and auditors.

To properly evaluate the potential exposures and risks in this environment, the modern auditor must be familiar with the technologies and techniques that underlie e-commerce. Hardware failures, software errors, and unauthorized access from remote locations can expose the organization's accounting system to unique threats. For example, transactions can be lost in transit and never processed, electronically altered or rearranged to change their financial effect, corrupted by transient signals on transmission lines, and diverted to or initiated by the perpetrator of a fraud.

This chapter deals with the technologies, risks, controls, and audit issues associated with e-commerce. These include private local area networks (LANs), private and public wide area networks (WANs), electronic data interchange (EDI), and Internet-enabled commerce.

NETWORKS

TYPES

One way of distinguishing between types of networks is the geographic area covered by their distributed sites. Networks are usually classified as either *local area networks* (LANs), *wide area networks* (WANs), or *Internet-worked networks*.

LANs

Local area networks are often confined to a single room in a building, or they may link several buildings within a close geographic area. However, a LAN can cover distances of several miles and connect hundreds of users. LANs are capable of voice and video transmissions, as well as data communications. The nodes connected to a LAN are usually microcomputer-based workstations. Typically, LANs are privately owned and controlled. Over the last decade, they have played a dominant role in the distributed data processing strategy of countless organizations. Their impact on data processing and AIS is certain to grow in the future.

WANs

When networks exceed the geographic limitations of the LAN, they are called **wide area networks**. Because of the distances involved and the high cost of interconnections, WANs typically employ common-carrier facilities (such as telephone lines or microwave channels) between remote nodes. Therefore, WANs are often public networks (at least in part) and are thus subject to Federal Communications Commission regulations. The nodes of a WAN can include microcomputer workstations, minicomputers, mainframes, or LANs. The WAN may be used to link together geographically dispersed segments of a single organization or connect multiple organizations in a trading partner arrangement. Later in the chapter, we see how EDI is made financially viable to many organizations because of value-added networks that employ public WANs.

Internet/Internet-Works

With the advent of the Internet, networks expanded beyond WANs to a global "network of networks." The more people used the Internet, the more people became familiar with the way Internet technologies work—specifically, a Web browser for accessing, viewing, and using Web pages and objects, and e-mail. Internet protocols, especially TCP/IP, made previously disparate systems (different incompatible platforms) virtually compatible on the same network. Combined with the public's familiarity of how Internet technologies work, it became efficient and effective to employ Internet technologies for applications on LANs and WANs. Thus, we get the term **Internet-worked**

networks: networks employing Internet technologies. And obviously, the geographic area became global! This change in application development and system design is a major influence in application development systems such as Microsoft's dot-net. Many, probably most, applications are 'web-enabled' to take advantage of the shorter learning curve for users, and the resulting easy-to-use interface.

Network Topologies

A **network topology** is the physical arrangement of components (terminals, servers, and communications links) in a network. In this section, we examine the features of four basic network topologies: star, hierarchical, ring, and bus. Most networks are a variation on, or combination of, these basic models. However, before proceeding, we must develop a working definition for some of the terms that will be used in the following sections.

Star

The **star topology** shown in Figure 5-1 describes a network of computers with a large central computer (the host) at the hub that has direct connections to a periphery of smaller computers. Communications between the nodes in the star are managed and controlled from the host site.

The star topology is often used for a WAN, in which the central computer is a mainframe. The nodes of the star may be microcomputer workstations, minicomputers, mainframes, or a combination. Databases under this approach may be distributed or centralized. A common model is to partition local data to the nodes and centralize the common data. For example, consider a department store chain that issues its own credit cards. Each node represents a store in a different metropolitan area. In Figure 5-1, these are Dallas, St. Louis, Topeka, and Tulsa. The nodes maintain

FIGURE 5-1

Star Network

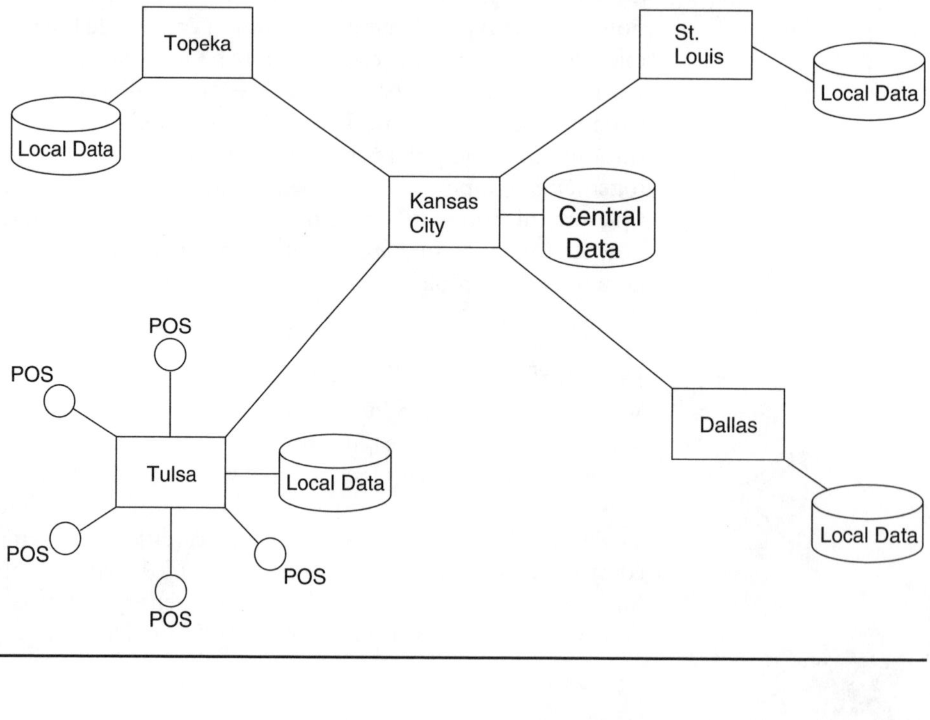

local databases such as records for customers holding credit cards issued in their areas and records of local inventory levels. The central site—Kansas City—maintains data common to the entire regional area, including data for customer billing, accounts receivable maintenance, and overall inventory control. Each local node is itself a LAN, with point-of-sales (POS) terminals connected to a minicomputer at the store.

If one or more nodes in a star network fail, communication between the remaining nodes is still possible through the central site. However, if the central site fails, individual nodes can function locally but cannot communicate with the other nodes. Transaction processing in this type of configuration could proceed as follows. Sales are processed in real time at the POS terminals. Local processing includes obtaining credit approval, updating the customer's available credit, updating the inventory records, and recording the transaction in the transaction file (journal).

At the end of the business day, each of the nodes transmits sales and inventory information to the central site in batches. The central site updates the control accounts, prepares customer bills, and determines inventory replenishment for the entire region.

The assumption underlying the star topology is that primary communication will be between the central site and the nodes. However, limited communication between the nodes is possible. For example, assume a customer from Dallas was in Tulsa and made a purchase from the Tulsa store on credit. The Tulsa database would not contain the customer's record and Tulsa would then send the transaction for credit approval to Dallas via Kansas City. The approved transaction would then be returned by Dallas to Tulsa via Kansas City. Inventory and sales journal updates would be performed at Tulsa.

The preceding transaction processing procedure would differ somewhat, depending on the database configuration. For example, if local databases are partial replicas of the central database, credit queries could then be made directly from Kansas City. However, this configuration would require keeping the central database current with all the nodes.

Hierarchy

A **hierarchical topology** is one in which a host computer is connected to several levels of subordinate smaller computers in a master–slave relationship. This structure is applicable to firms with many organizational levels that must be controlled from a central location. For example, consider a manufacturing firm with remote plants, warehouses, and sales offices, such as the one illustrated in Figure 5-2. Sales orders from the local sales departments are transmitted to the regional level, where they are summarized and uploaded to the corporate level. Sales data, combined with inventory and plant-capacity data from manufacturing, are used to compute production requirements for the period, which are downloaded to the regional production scheduling system. At this level, production schedules are prepared and distributed to the local production departments. Information about completed production is uploaded from the production departments to the regional level, where production summaries are prepared and transmitted to the corporate level.

Ring

The **ring topology** illustrated in Figure 5-3 eliminates the central site. All nodes in this configuration are of equal status; thus, responsibility for managing communications is distributed among the nodes. Every node on the ring has a unique electronic

FIGURE 5-2 **Hierarchical Topology**

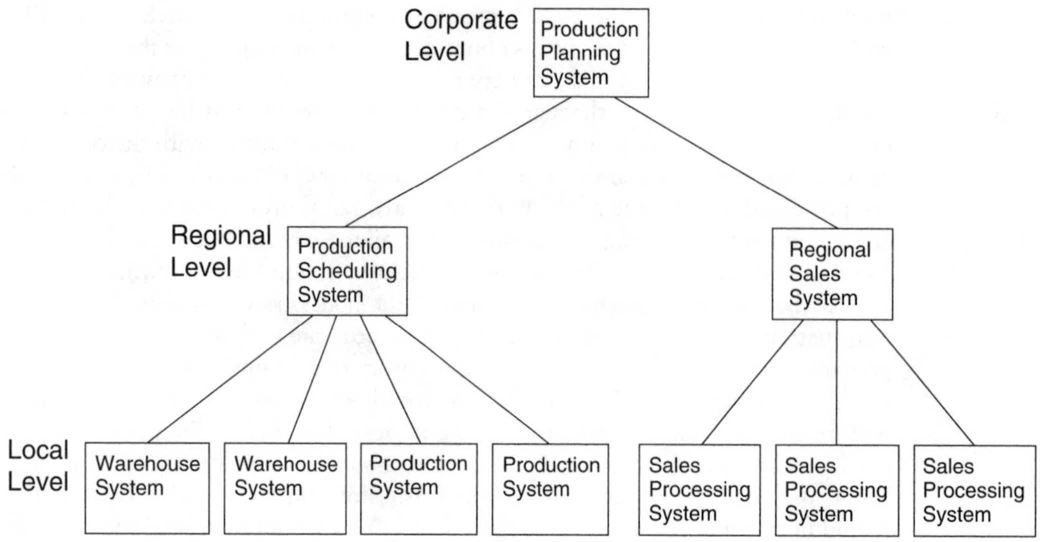

FIGURE 5-3 **Ring Topology**

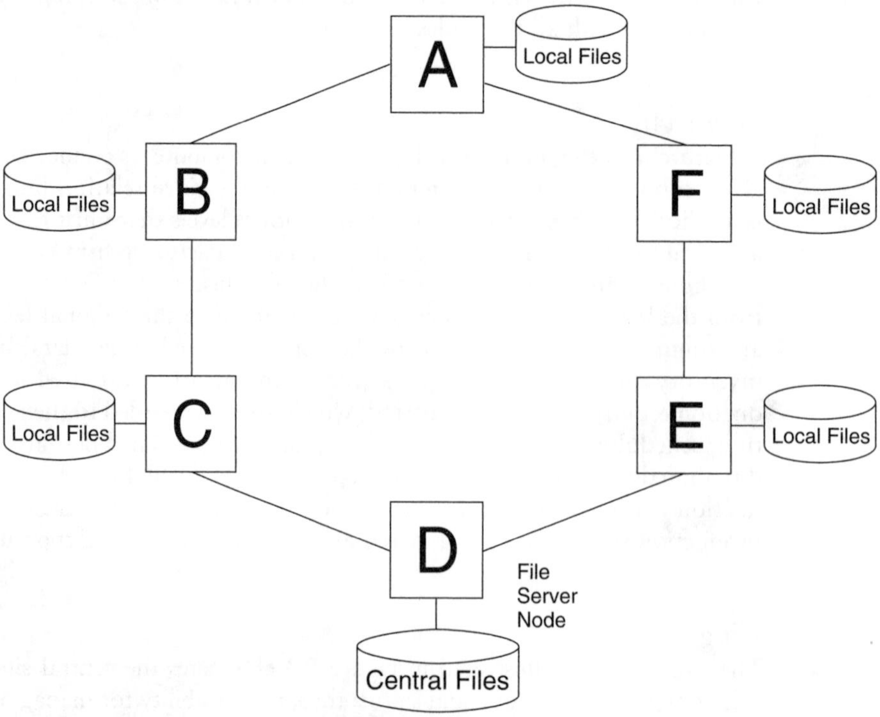

address, which is attached to messages such as an address on an envelope. If Node A wishes to send a message to Node D, the message is received, regenerated, and passed on by Nodes B and C until it arrives at its destination. The ring topology is a peer-to-peer arrangement in which all nodes are of equal status. This topology has been a popular one for LANs. The peer nodes manage private programs and databases locally. However, common resources that are shared by all nodes can be centralized and managed by a file server that is also a node on the network ring.

The ring topology may also be used for a WAN, in which case the databases may be partitioned rather than centralized. For example, consider a company with widely separated warehouses, each with different suppliers and customers and each processing its own shipping and receiving transactions. In this case, where there is little common data, it is more efficient to distribute the database than to manage it centrally. However, when one warehouse has insufficient stock to fill an order, it can communicate through the network to locate the items at another warehouse.

Bus

The **bus topology** illustrated in Figure 5-4 is the current most popular LAN topology. It is so named because the nodes are all connected to a common cable—the bus. Communications and file transfers between workstations are controlled centrally by one or more servers. As with the ring topology, each node on the bus has a unique address, and only one node may transmit at a time. The technique, which has been used for more than two decades, is simple, reliable, and generally less costly to install than the ring topology.

Architectures

The term **architecture** can refer to either hardware or software, or to a combination of hardware and software. The architecture of a system always defines its broad outlines, and may define precise mechanisms as well. Networks can be generally classified as either using peer-to-peer architecture, or client–server architecture.

FIGURE 5-4 **Bus Topology**

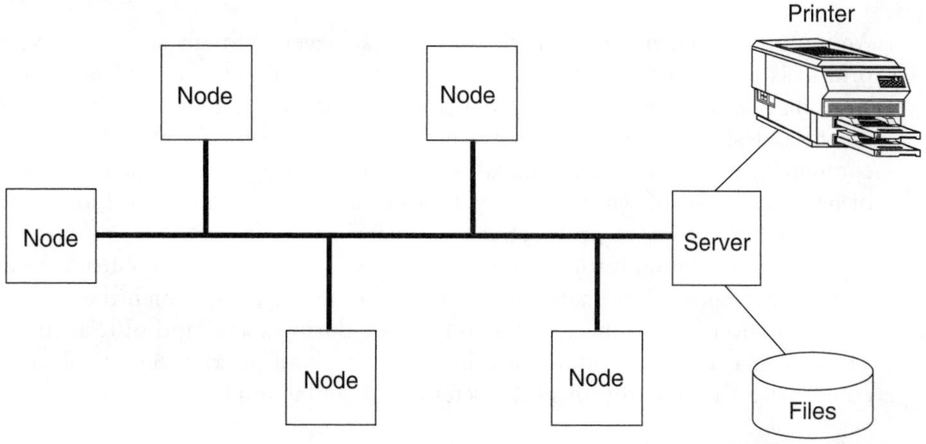

Peer-to-Peer

Peer-to-peer (P2P) is a type of network in which each workstation has equivalent capabilities and responsibilities. This architecture differs from client–server architectures, in which some computers are dedicated to serving the others. Peer-to-peer networks are generally simpler, but they usually do not offer the same performance under heavy loads.[1] Windows operating system for desktops is capable of creating a P2P network.

Client-Server

The term *client–server* is often misused to describe any type of network arrangement. In fact, the **client–server architecture** has specific characteristics that distinguish it from topologies and networks in general. Figure 5-5 illustrates the architecture.

To explain the client–server architecture, let's review the features of a traditional distributed system. We have already seen that DDP can result in considerable data traffic jams. Users competing for access to shared data files experience queues, delays, and lockouts. A factor influencing the severity of this problem is the data structure (file organization and access methods) in use. For example, assume a user at Site A requests a single record from a sequential file located at a central site. To meet this request, the file server at the central site must lock and transmit the entire file to the remote site. The search for the specific record is performed at the remote site by the user's application. When the update is complete, the entire file is then transmitted back to the central site.

The client–server model distributes the processing between the user's (client's) computer and the central file server. Both computers are part of the network, but each is assigned functions that it performs best. For example, the record-searching portion of an application can be placed on the server, and the data manipulation portion can be placed on the client computer. Thus, only a single record, rather than the entire file, must be locked and sent to the client for processing. After processing, the record is returned to the server, which restores it in the file and removes the lock. This approach reduces traffic and allows more efficient use of shared data. Distributing the record-searching logic of the client's application to the server permits other clients to access different records in the same file simultaneously. The client–server approach can be applied to any topology (i.e., ring, star, or bus). Figure 5-5 illustrates the client–server model applied to a bus topology.

PROTOCOLS

An important element of network control is achieved through protocols. Network protocols are the rules and standards governing the design of hardware and software that permit users of networks manufactured by different vendors to communicate and share data. The general acceptance of protocols within the network community provides both standards and economic incentives for the manufacturers of hardware and software. Products that do not comply with prevailing protocols will have little utility to prospective customers.

The data communications industry borrowed the term **protocol** from the diplomatic community. Diplomatic protocols define the rules by which the representatives of nations communicate and collaborate during social and official functions. These formal rules of conduct are intended to avoid international problems that could arise through the misinterpretation of ambiguous signals passed between

1 Taken from *http://pcwebopedia.com/TERM/P/peer_to_peer_architecture.html*.

FIGURE 5-5

Client–Server Architecture

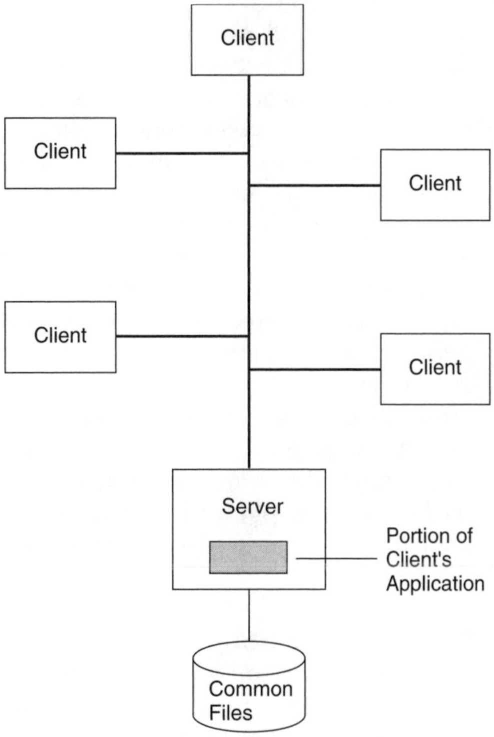

diplomatic counterparts. The greatest potential for error naturally exists between nations with vastly dissimilar cultures and conventions for behavior. Establishing a standard of conduct through protocols that all members of the diplomatic community understand and practice minimizes the risk of miscommunication between nations of different cultures.

An analogy may be drawn to data communications. A communications network is a community of computer users who also must establish and maintain unambiguous lines of communication. If network members all had homogeneous needs and operated identical systems, this communication would not be much of a problem; but networks are characterized by heterogeneous systems components. Typically, network users employ hardware devices (PCs, printers, monitors, data storage devices, modems, and so on) and software (user applications, network control programs, and operating systems) that are produced by a variety of vendors. Passing messages effectively from device to device in such a multivendor environment requires ground rules, or protocols.

The Functitons of Protocols

Protocols serve network functions in several ways.[2] First, they facilitate the physical connection between the network devices. Through protocols, devices are able to identify themselves to other devices as legitimate network entities and thus initiate (or terminate) a communications session.

2 H. M. Kibirige, *Local Area Networks in Information Management* (Westport, CT: Greenwood Press, 1989).

Second, protocols synchronize the transfer of data between physical devices. This process involves defining the rules for initiating a message, determining the data transfer rate between devices, and acknowledging message receipt.

Third, protocols provide a basis for error checking and measuring network performance. This process is done by comparing measured results against expectations. For example, performance measures pertaining to storage device access times, data transmission rates, and modulation frequencies are critical to controlling the network's function. The identification and correction of errors thus depends on protocol standards that define acceptable performance.

Fourth, protocols promote compatibility among network devices. To successfully transmit and receive data, the various devices involved in a particular session must conform to a mutually acceptable mode of operation, such as synchronous or asynchronous and duplex or half duplex. Without protocols to provide such conformity, messages sent between devices would be distorted and garbled.

Finally, protocols promote network designs that are flexible, expandable, and cost-effective. Users are free to change and enhance their systems by selecting from the best offerings of a variety of vendors. Manufacturers must, of course, construct these products in accordance with established protocols.

COMPONENTS

Network Operating System

Each network uses an operating system much like each microcomputer has its own operating system. The **network operating system (NOS)**, like a desktop operating system, manages the functions and data across the network. Different NOSs are available from different vendors, and advanced versions of Windows are capable of performing the NOS functions. Some examples include Windows 2003 Server, Unix, and Novell Netware.

NOS controls communications between the physical devices connected to the network. Its purpose is to perform the following tasks:

1. Establish a communication session between the sender and the receiver.
2. Manage the flow of data across the network.
3. Detect and resolve data collisions between competing nodes.
4. Detect errors in data caused by line failure and signal degeneration.

There are several techniques for managing sessions and controlling transmissions, but most of them are variants of three basic methods: polling, token passing, and carrier sensing.

Polling. **Polling** is the most popular technique for establishing a communication session in WANs. One site, designated the *master*, polls the other *slave* sites to determine if they have data to transmit. If a slave responds in the affirmative, the master site locks the network while the data are transmitted. The remaining sites must wait until they are polled before they can transmit. The polling technique illustrated in Figure 5-6 is well suited to both the star and the hierarchical topologies. There are two primary advantages to polling. First, polling is noncontentious. Because nodes can send data only when requested by the master node, two nodes can never access the network at the same time. Data collisions (the simultaneous transmission of two or more messages that destroy each other) are, therefore, prevented. Second, an organization can set priorities for data communications across the network. Important nodes can be polled more often than other, less-important nodes.

FIGURE 5-6

Polling Method of Controlling Data Collisions

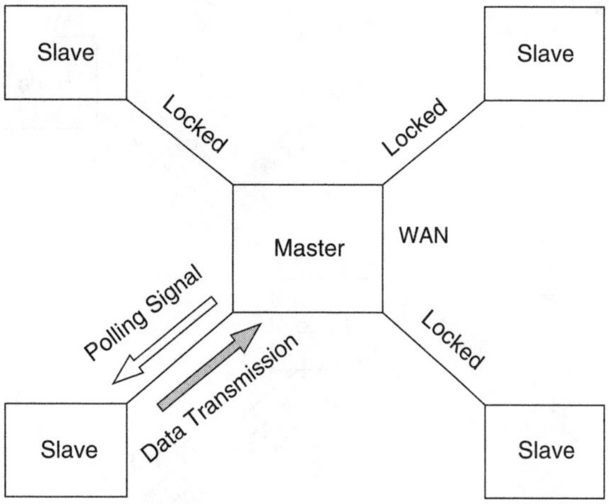

Token Passing. **Token passing** involves transmitting a special signal—the token—around the network from node to node in a specific sequence. Each node on the network receives the token, regenerates it, and passes it to the next node. Only the node possessing the token is allowed to transmit data.

Token passing can be used with either ring or bus topologies. On a ring topology, the token passing sequence is determined by the order in which the nodes are physically connected. With a bus, the sequence is logical, not physical. The token is passed from node to node in a predetermined order to form a logical ring. Token bus and token ring configurations are illustrated in Figure 5-7. Since nodes are permitted to transmit only when they possess the token, the node wishing to send data across the network seizes the token upon receiving it. Holding the token blocks other nodes from transmitting and ensures that no data collisions will occur. After the transmitting node sends its message and receives an acknowledgment signal from the receiving node, it releases the token. The next node in sequence then has the option of either seizing the token and transmitting data or passing the token on to the next node in the circuit.

A major advantage of token passing is its *deterministic* access method, which avoids data collisions. This method is in contrast to the *random* access approach of carrier sensing. IBM's version of token ring is emerging as an industry standard.

Carrier Sensing. **Carrier sensing** is a random access technique that detects collisions when they occur. This technique, which is formally labeled *carrier sensed multiple access with collision detection* (CSMA/CD), is used with the bus topology. The node wishing to transmit "listens" to the bus to determine if it is in use. If it senses no transmission in progress (no carrier), the node transmits its message to the receiving node. This approach is not as fail-safe as token passing. Collisions can occur when two or more nodes, unaware of each other's intent to transmit, do so simultaneously when they independently perceive the line to be clear. When this circumstance happens, the network server directs each node to wait a unique and random period of time and then retransmit the message. In a busy network, data collisions are more likely to occur, thus resulting in delays while the nodes retransmit their messages. Proponents of the token-passing approach point to its collision-avoidance characteristic as a major advantage over the CSMA/CD model.

FIGURE 5-7

Token Passing Approach to Controlling Data Collisions

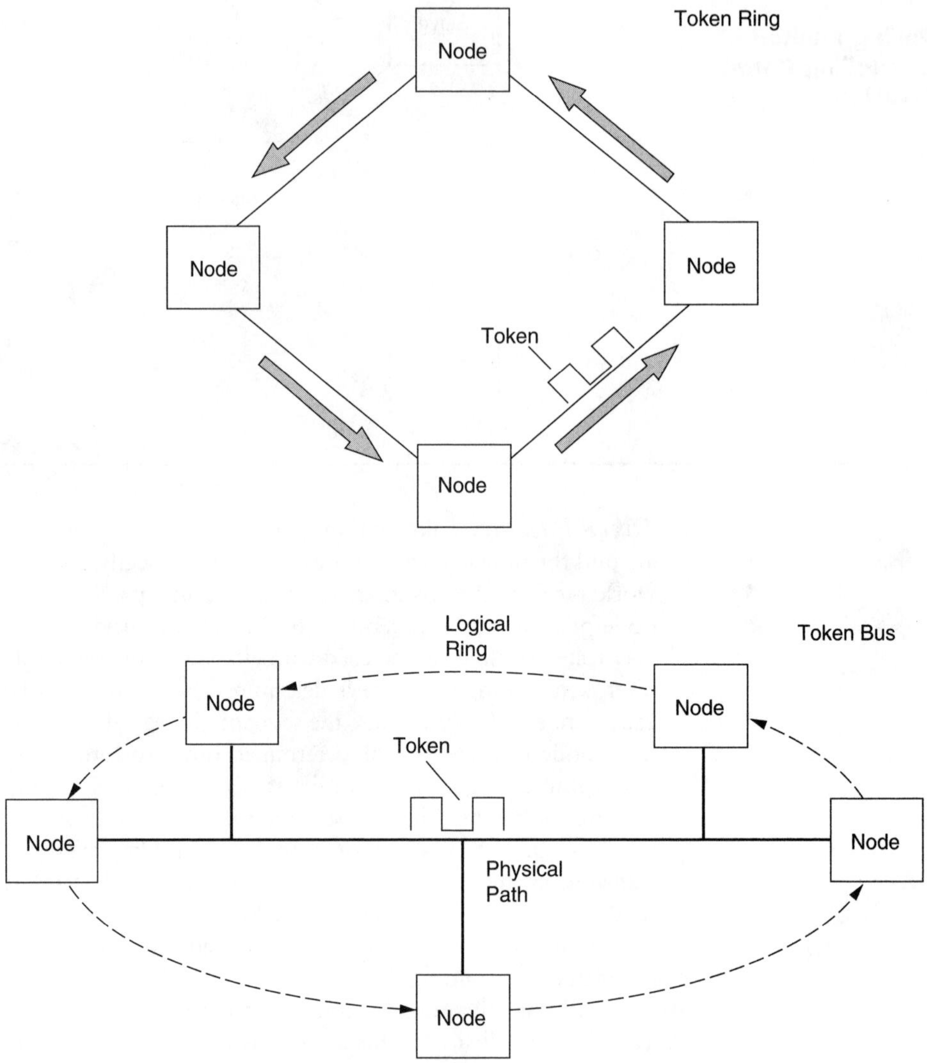

Ethernet is the best-known LAN software that uses the CSMA/CD standard. The Ethernet model was developed by the Xerox Corporation in the 1970s. In 1980, Digital Equipment Corporation, in a joint venture with Intel Corporation, published the specifications for a LAN based on the Ethernet model.[3] The greatest advantage of Ethernet is that it is established, reliable, and well understood by network specialists. Ethernet also has a number of economic advantages over token ring: (1) the technology, being relatively simple, is well suited to the less-costly twisted-pair cabling, whereas token ring works best with more expensive coaxial cable; (2) the network interface cards used by Ethernet are much less expensive than those used in the token ring topology; and (3) Ethernet uses a bus topology, which is easier to expand.

3 The Ethernet, a Local Area Network Version 1.0. Digital Equipment Corporation, Maynard, Mass.; Intel Corporation, Santa Clara, Calif.; and Xerox Corporation, Stanford, Conn.

Nodes/Terminals

Technically, any input-output device connected by a communications line to a computer is a **node**. Many users interact with computers via **terminals**, which come in numerous varieties and are produced by scores of vendors. Millions of terminals are installed in this country; the count varies depending on how we define terminal.

The simplest way to approach a review of this broad topic is to start with the most basic forms of terminals and then move on to the more complex and powerful types. For this purpose, we shall classify terminals as dumb, smart, or programmable. At the end of this section, we discuss the transmission channels that terminals use for communications.

Dumb Terminals. **Dumb terminals** are so called because they can only send and receive data. All processing capability is centralized in the host computer. The most common examples of dumb terminals are teleprinters and cathode ray tubes (CRTs).

- *Teleprinters* The basic dumb terminal consists of a keyboard for data entry and a **teleprinter** for output. Most computer systems use some form of printer to produce hard copy output in readable form. Teleprinters may be impact, ink-jet, or laser devices. A common type of printer is the ink-jet or laser printer, which uses photocopy technology to print the information. Laser printers can print at speeds of several pages per minute. Ink-jet and laser printers produce output of high quality. These devices are also quiet, because they do not impact the paper to print. Large line printers can attain several thousand lines per second using a metal cylinder with embossed characters as the printing element. Laser printers cannot use multipart paper to produce multiple copies of the output simultaneously, as impact printers can. Teleprinters are most useful in batch input-output applications or where interaction between the user and the host computer is minimal.
- *Cathode Ray Tubes* A common form of terminal in the past was the **cathode ray tube** (CRT) or video display terminal (VDT). Used in conjunction with a keyboard, a CRT provides visual display for input-output functions such as data insertions, data deletions, and screen paging through keyboard input. This technology allows the user to view large amounts of data on screen without having to print a hard copy and to access the host computer interactively.

Smart Terminals. **Smart terminals** provide more user features than dumb terminals. For instance, smart terminals can support user applications, such as word processing, spreadsheets, and graphics capabilities, under the control of the host computer. Most smart terminals provide local storage of data and permit data editing before transmission. For certain types of data input, smart terminals using pointing devices provide a more efficient alternative than keyboards. For instance, the tasks of making menu choices, selecting icons from a screen, and performing graphics operations can be greatly simplified. Examples of pointing devices include the electronic mouse, touch-sensitive CRTs, and the light pen.

Smart terminals include a range of optical scanning equipment that read text, graphics, and bar codes and convert them into digital input data. A common example is the optical scanning wand that is used to read product bar codes on food items in supermarkets.

Programmable Terminals. The personal computer (PC) is widely used as a **programmable terminal**. A PC workstation may consist of data storage, commercial software, utility programs, a CRT, printer, and a processor powerful enough to handle extensive business applications.

Transmission Channels

The communications lines connecting the nodes of a network possess far more message-carrying capacity than a single node can use. If separate lines were dedicated to each pair of nodes, they would likely sit idle much of the time. This configuration is not a problem in most LANs, where distances are short and the cost of a line is relatively small. However, efficient line utilization is of far greater importance in WANs that employ expensive, long-distance communication paths.

The terms *synchronous*, *asynchronous*, *simplex*, *half duplex*, and *full duplex* describe various channel-methods by which terminals (and other devices) attached to a network transmit data. The first two terms are associated with the structure and format of the data flow. The last three terms pertain to the direction of the data flow.

The **asynchronous transmission** method is so called because there is no continuous synchronization between the sending and receiving devices. The advantages of asynchronous transmission are that it is simple and inexpensive. The disadvantage is that data transfer rates are slow. This method is used in communications between microcomputers and between microcomputers and mainframes. In contrast, the **synchronous transmission** method uses a separate timing signal to keep the receiving end's device in constant synchronization with the transmitting device. The method requires more costly equipment, but is capable of high-speed data transfer. Mainframe-to-mainframe communications use the synchronous transmission method.

The terms *simplex*, *half duplex*, and *full duplex* characterize transmission by the direction of data flow. Figure 5-8 illustrates the three methods. **Simplex transmission** allows transmission in one direction only. This method is used primarily by output devices. **Half duplex transmission** allows signals to be sent in both directions, but not simultaneously. A transmission can be in only one direction at a time—from terminal to host or vice versa. With **full duplex transmission**, signals can be sent and received simultaneously. This method is the most costly of the three, but permits the greatest volume of data transfer across the network.

The physical transmission path is the connection between the transmitting and receiving devices in the network. These include the cables that plug into the back of the end user's microcomputer as well as radio transmissions that carry thousands of signals simultaneously across the country and around the world. Our discussion examines five common transmission media: *twisted-pair cable*, *coaxial cable*, *fiber optic cable*, *microwave transmissions*, and *communications satellites*.

Twisted Pair. A **twisted-pair cable**, illustrated in Figure 5-9(a) consists of hundreds of sets of copper wires that are twisted together in pairs. The twisting is done in an exact pattern (two twists per foot) to create a better signal transmission than a straight pair of wires can produce. Twisted-pair cables can be shielded or unshielded. Shielded cable is more expensive but provides better protection against signal loss caused by interference from extraneous sources and permits higher data-transmission speeds. Unshielded twisted-pair cables come from the telephone industry and are used as the standard wiring for all business offices. Unshielded

FIGURE 5-8

Simplex, Half Duplex, and Full Duplex Transmission Modes

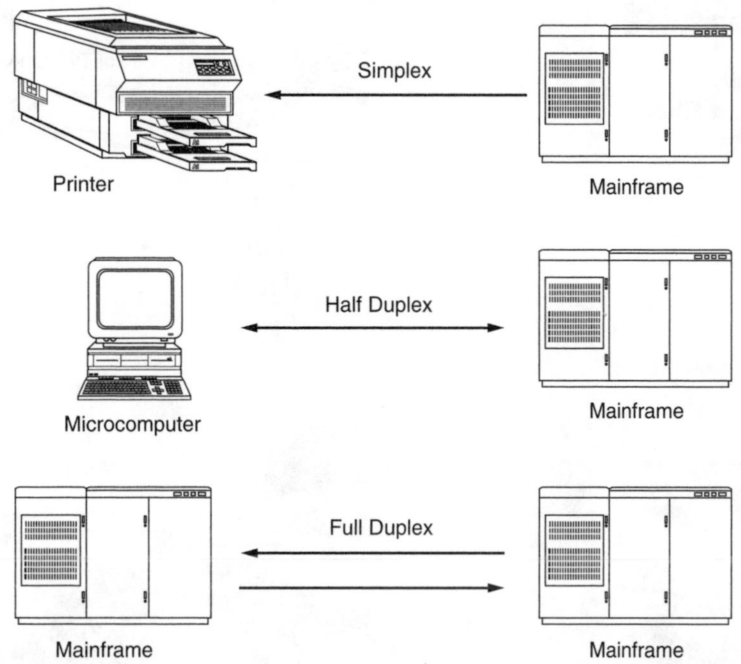

twisted-pair cables provide adequate signal paths at lower transmission rates but are more susceptible to cross-talk (noise) between pairs within the cable.

Coaxial. **Coaxial cable**, as illustrated in Figure 5-9(b), has been around since the 1940s. It consists of a central wire conductor covered by insulation and surrounded by a wire mesh shield. The shielding provides the return (ground) path for the signal and prevents interference from other transmissions and noise.

Coaxial cable is often used for the backbone connections between LANs and for linking LANs to WANs. This medium is capable of high-speed transmissions and is especially applicable where electromagnetic interference is a problem. The most commonly used form of coaxial cable for networks, especially LANs, is CAT-5 cable.

Fiber Optic. The **fiber optic cable** illustrated in Figure 5-9(c) has a glass core surrounded by a glass cladding. Data, in the form of high-speed pulses of light, travel along the core. The light source for the fiber optic cable is either a laser or a light-emitting diode. Data are conveyed as on and off pulses of light to represent the digital bit stream. Since the light can travel in one direction only, two optical cores (two cables or a single cable with two cores) are required to complete a transmit and receive path. Fiber optic cable has several advantages over electromagnetic media.[4]

1. Due to their high frequency range, fiber optic devices have a large capacity for information transmission. A single fiber can carry more than 30,000 voice signals.
2. The signals traveling along glass fibers are unaffected by electromagnetic disturbances caused by electric motors, electric sparks, magnetic devices, lightning, and adjacent cables.

4 U. D. Black, *Data Communications and Distributed Networks,* 2d ed. (Englewood Cliffs, N.J.: Prentice Hall, 1987), p. 56.

FIGURE 5-9

Twisted-Pair, Coaxial, and Fiber Optic Cables

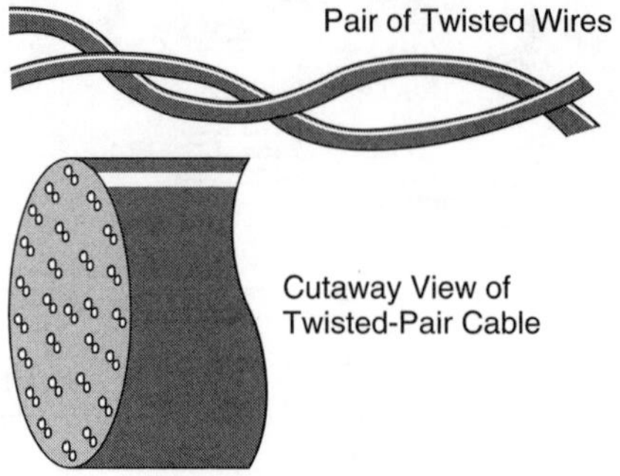

(a) Twisted-Pair Cable

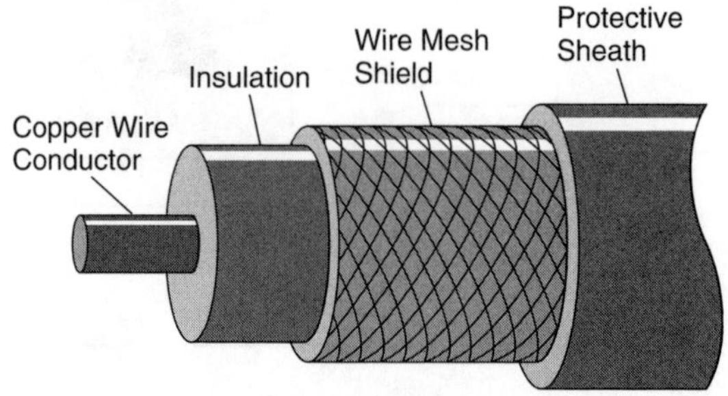

(b) Coaxial Cable

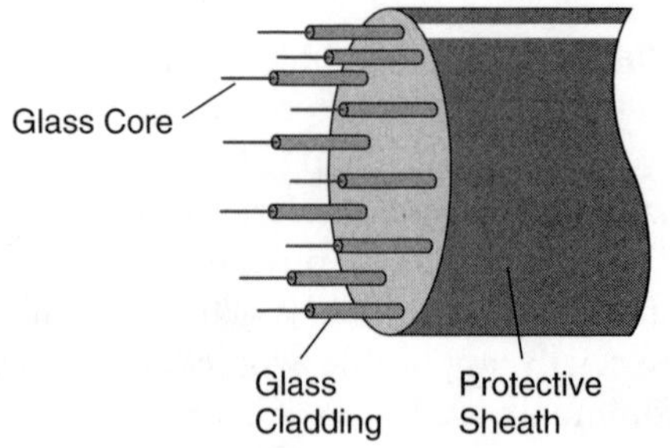

(c) Fiber Optic Cable

3. The signal loss in fiber optic transmissions caused by attenuation is far less than it is in cables that use copper conductors. Two benefits derive from this: repeaters for fiber optic cables can be placed as far as 50 to 100 miles apart, compared to about 3 miles for copper cables; and these improved signal characteristics translate into much lower error rates in data transmissions.
4. Because light transmissions do not emit an electromagnetic field, this form of transmission is much more secure than microwaves or twisted-pair cables. The electromagnetic field surrounding an electronic transmission contains information that can be selectively retrieved by an intruder with the proper equipment. It is very difficult to tap into a fiber optic cable.
5. Fiber optic technology can operate in environments subject to extreme temperatures and temperature variations.

6. Fiber optic cable is physically small—the thickness of a hair—and requires much less physical space than twisted-pair or coaxial cable.

Microwave. Microwaves are extremely high-frequency (above 1 gigahertz) radio waves that follow a line-of-sight transmission path. This medium can carry a large amount of traffic from point to point and commonly provides the long-distance (trunk) communication legs for WANs. **Microwave transmissions** are used for more than half of the telephone and television trunk traffic in this country.

A disadvantage of this medium is that the microwave transmitter and receiver must be able to "see" each other to permit line-of-sight transmissions. Prominent objects, such as tall buildings and trees, and even the curvature of the earth, can interfere with the signal. For this reason, microwave transmitters and receivers are placed on the tops of tall buildings or on specially constructed towers. To cover long distances, repeater stations located at intermediate points (every 50 miles or so) receive and then retransmit the signal to the next site. Thus, a signal can be relayed from point to point across the country, as illustrated in Figure 5-10. The cost of building and maintaining a string of repeater stations is proportional to the distance to be covered, and for most organizations it is prohibitive. Instead, an organization constructing a WAN will usually lease the long-distance facilities from common carriers such as AT&T.

Communications Satellites. **Communications satellites** provide an alternative to ground repeater stations. This technology provides a radio relay station in space, more than 22,000 miles above the transmitting and receiving ends of the signal path. Communications satellites hold a geosynchronous orbit, allowing them to remain positioned over the same point on the earth. Figure 5-11 shows how ground transmitters and receivers can remain in one position because the satellite's movement relative to the earth's is fixed. Communications satellites have the ability to broadcast signals to cover an area of approximately 30 percent of the earth's surface. Thus, a message from a single earth station can be retransmitted to multiple receiving stations across the country and internationally. A practical advantage of this capability is that an organization can achieve database concurrency in a widely distributed system.

FIGURE 5-10

Microwave Transmission

FIGURE 5-11 **Communications Satellites in Fixed Orbit**

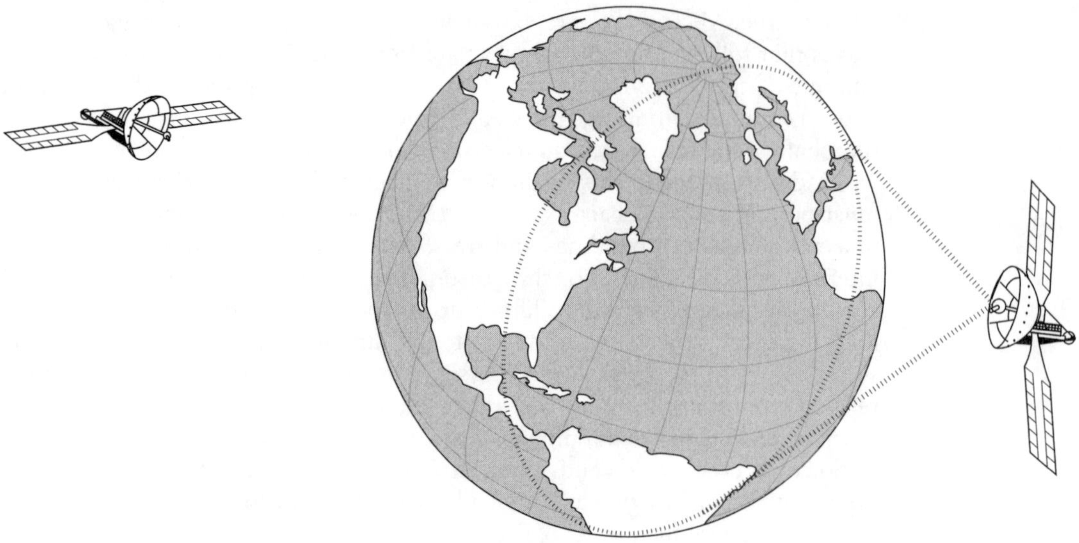

Wireless. In recent years, wireless transmission has become popular, partly because it is less expensive than other transmission methods. In particular, laptops can function more easily using wireless technology. There is an additional risk to wireless because of the risk that wireless transmissions, traveling through the air with a signal strength up to a few hundred feet, can be intercepted. However, wireless encryption protocols (WEP) have been developed that secure wireless transmissions using strong encryption.

Server(s)

LAN nodes often share common resources such as programs, data, and printers, which are managed through special-purpose computers called **servers**, as depicted in Figure 5-12. A *dedicated server* is a single computer in a network reserved for serving a particular function for the network, such as printing, communications, or databases. When the server receives requests for resources, the requests are placed in a queue and are processed in sequence.

When a mainframe (host) computer is connected to a network, it uses a special-purpose computer called a *front-end processor* (FEP) to manage communications between it and the other nodes or IPUs on the network. Figure 5-13 shows the relationship between the host, the FEP, and the connected nodes. In contrast to the host computer, which is a general-purpose processor, the FEP performs a very specific set of tasks to relieve the workload on the host:

- Responding to a host computer's requests to transmit or receive data on the communications lines attached to the FEP.
- Assembling bits into an outgoing message and adding control and synchronization characters to the message.
- Translating the coding schemes of dissimilar devices into a mutually compatible format.

FIGURE 5-12

LAN with File and Print Servers

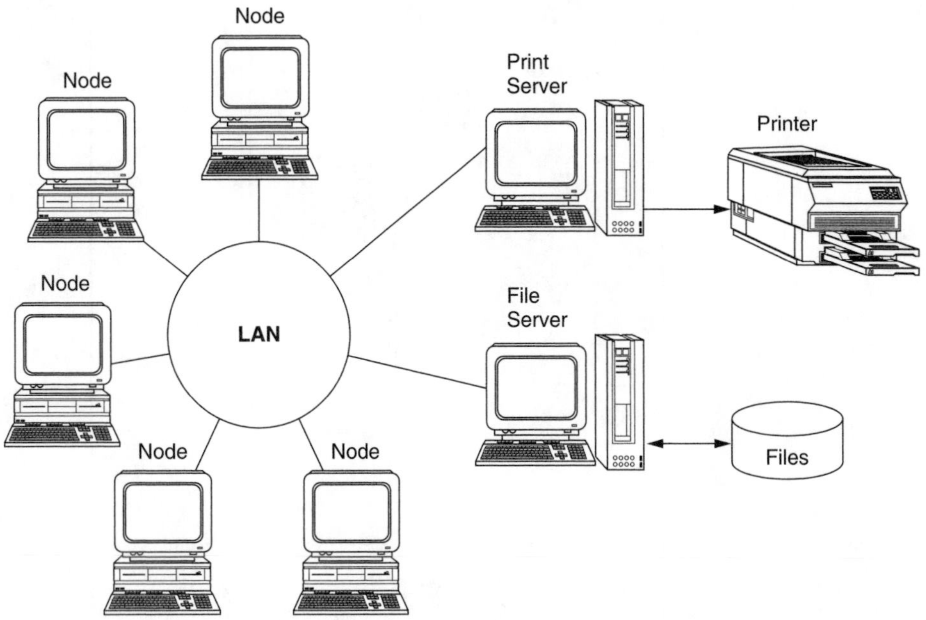

- Managing FEP buffer storage. Messages are temporarily stored in the buffer area before transfer to the host. After transfer is complete, the buffer space must be released for additional incoming messages. The efficient management of the limi ted buffer space is critical to overall network performance.
- Analyzing communications problems by identifying errors, performing diagnostics, testing lines, and selecting alternative paths for failed lines.

These tasks, if performed by the host, would require valuable CPU time that would be taken away from data processing applications. Without an FEP to offload this work, a typical network could consume a substantial portion of the host's capacity.

Connecting Devices

Digital transmission is the dominant trend in communications technology. Rather than being transmitted as analog waves, signals are converted to digital values through a digitizing process and transmitted as pulses. The advantage of digital technology is its ability to better suppress line noise and thus reduce **transmission errors**. Voice-grade transmission circuits suffer from inherent noise from various sources, including adjacent electrical circuits, transient signals, cross-talk, and background or "white" noise, that can distort analog signals and inject errors into the data. Using special regenerative repeaters, digital systems can provide error-free communications over long distances that would cause analog signals to degenerate.

Modems. In the early days of data communications, the telephone system provided the technology infrastructure that connected remote locations in a network. However, the system was designed to transmit voice signals, not computer-generated data.

FIGURE 5-13 Communications System Technology

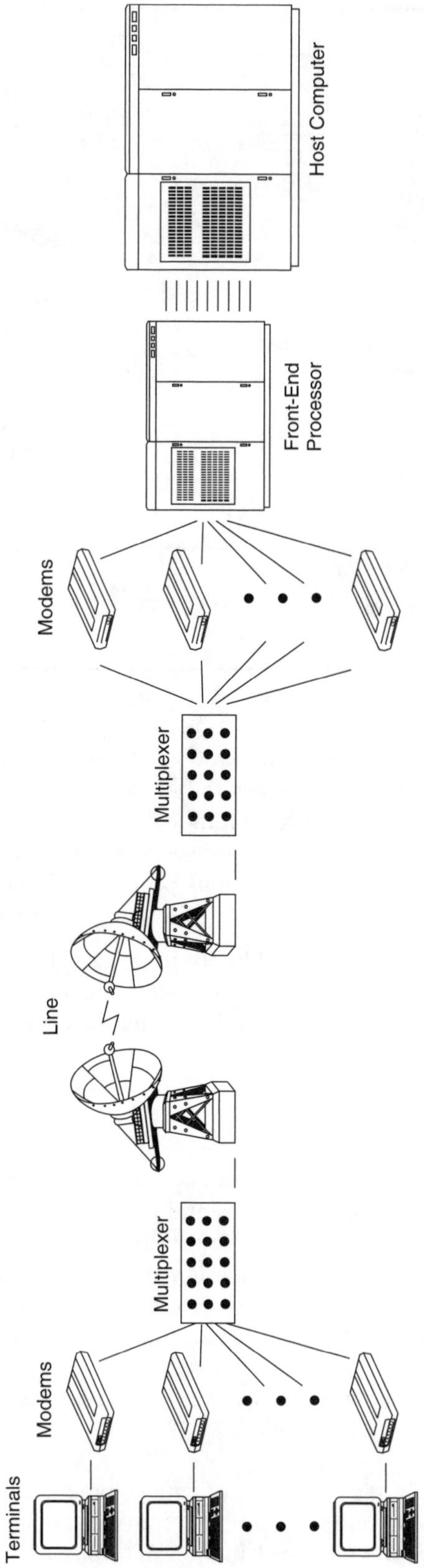

Figure 5-14 shows the differences between voice and data signals. Voice signals are represented as oscillating waveforms, and data signals are represented as digital pulses.

The **wave signal** rises from 0 to some positive maximum level, then swings back through 0 to an equal negative level, and returns to 0 to complete 360 degrees of travel, or one cycle. Wave signals have three characteristics that can be varied to convey message content: amplitude, frequency, and phase. The **amplitude**, or strength of the signal, is represented by the height of its positive (and negative) peaks relative to zero. Amplitude is measured in volts. Signal **frequency** is the number of cycles or oscillations occurring per second. The unit of measure for frequency is the Hertz (Hz). Thus, 1,000 cycles per second is 1,000 Hz. The **phase** of the signal is the point in the cycle to which the signal has advanced. This is expressed in degrees. The cycle begins at 0 degrees of phase and ends at 360 degrees. The points at one-quarter, one-half, and three-quarters through the cycle correspond to 90, 180, and 270 degrees, respectively.

Data stored in computers are represented as *b*inary dig*its*, or **bits**, which assume a numeric value of either 0 or 1. To transmit computer data, the bits are converted into a **digital signal** that represents zeros and ones as a series of electrical pulses.

In concept, a digital signal is similar to turning a flashlight on and off to represent ones and zeros, respectively. When the flashlight switch is turned to the on position, an electrical voltage (a pulse) is produced by the battery, which illuminates the bulb to represent a 1 bit. The pulse ends when the switch is turned to the off position. The off condition signifies the presence of a 0 bit. Figure 5-14(b) illustrates a digital signal coding scheme for representing ones and zeros as electric pulses. The time duration of the signal determines the number of ones or zeros being transmitted in a series. In the example, a pulse spanning three time periods is used to represent a series of three 1 bits.

FIGURE 5-14

Wave and Digital Signals

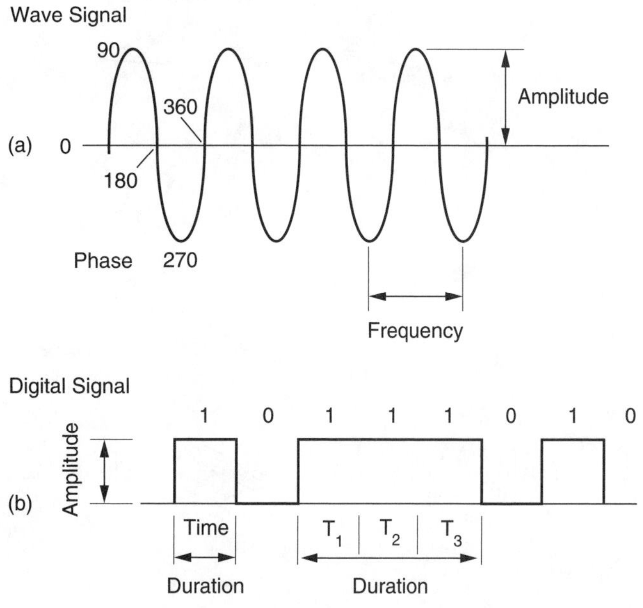

Computers communicate with peripheral devices (such as disk packs, tape drives, printers, and terminal monitors) and with other computers in close proximity through digital signals. However, when data are sent over longer distances to remote locations through the telephone system, the digital signal must be converted to a wave signal. The process of converting from digital to wave form, illustrated in Figure 5-15, is called **modulation.**

Modulation involves mixing an input signal with a base carrier frequency to produce an output signal that has the properties needed for transmission. At the receiving end of the transmission path, a reverse modulation process called *demodulation* regenerates the original input signal. The hardware device that performs the modulator–demodulator task is called a **modem**. Three basic forms of modulation are commonly used: amplitude modulation, frequency modulation, and phase modulation. These are discussed in Section 1 of the chapter appendix.

FIGURE 5-15 The Modulation Process

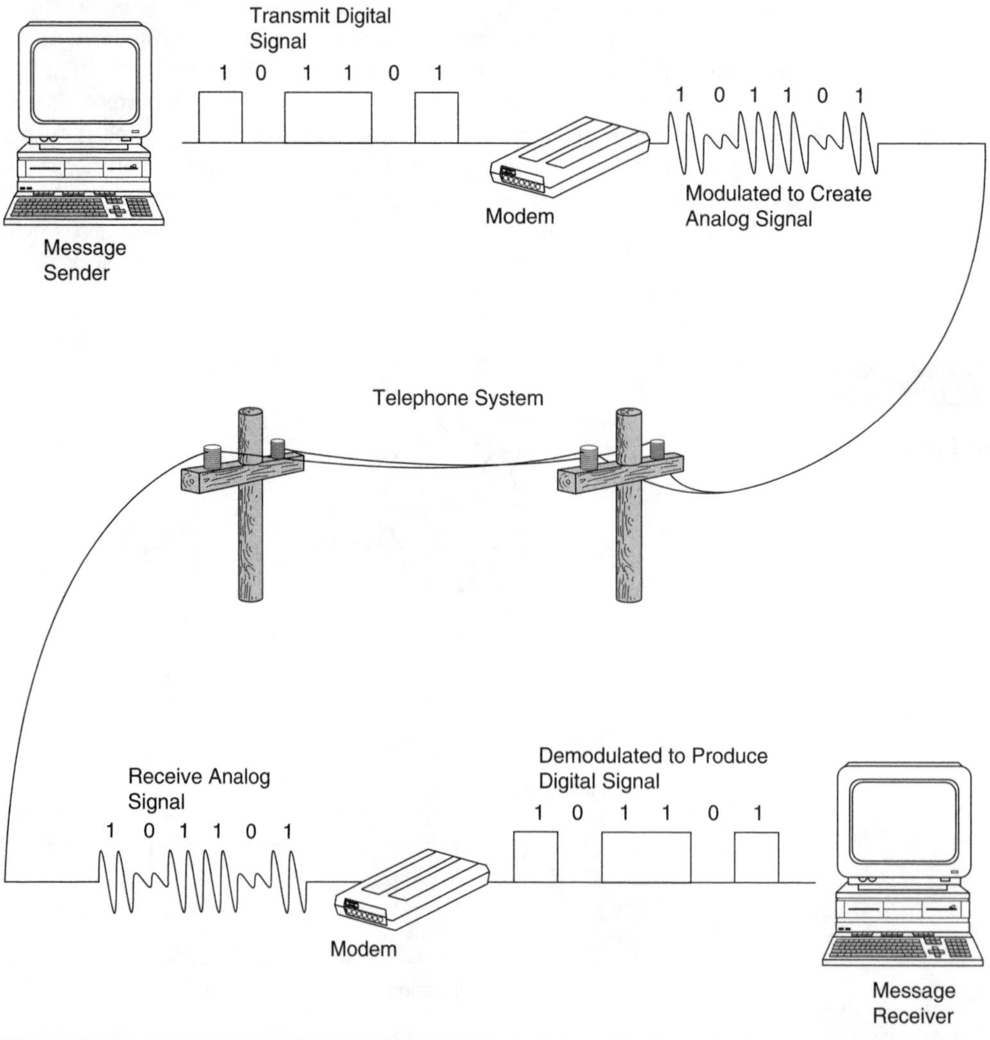

Network Interface Card. The workstation's physical connection to the LAN is achieved through a **network interface card (NIC)**, which fits into one of the expansion slots in the microcomputer. This device provides the electronic circuitry needed for internode communications. The NIC works with the network control program to send and receive messages, programs, and files across the network.

Network Processors. In a distributed environment, there is often a need to link networks together. For example, users of one LAN may wish to share data with users on a different LAN. A LAN user in one organization may wish to transmit data across the country over a public WAN to a user on a LAN with a different topology. Networks can be linked together via combinations of hardware and software devices called *bridges* and *gateways*. Figure 5-16 illustrates this technique. Bridges provide a means for linking LANs of the same type, such as an IBM token ring to another IBM token ring. Gateways connect LANs of different types and are also used to link LANs to WANs.

Switching. Message **switching** is a technique for efficiently connecting the components of a network. Even a relatively small network of, say, 100 components (workstations, printers, file servers, and so on) would require thousands of individual lines if each were to have a direct connection to every other component. The feasible solution to this situation is to use a switched network. Switches are used to establish temporary connections between devices for the duration of the communication session. This technique is similar to a telephone switchboard operator establishing a connection between two parties by inserting a cord with a connector plug at each end into the jacks of each party's line on the switchboard. When the conversation is over, the operator removes the cords from the switchboard and the path is dropped. Modern-day switches replace the operator and the manual switchboard with a high-speed, computer-controlled device. Two types of switches are used in modern networks: the private branch exchange (PBX) and packet switching.

A **private branch exchange (PBX)**, which is illustrated in Figure 5-17, is used for switching data and voice communications locally within a firm. Increasingly, PBXs are digital devices that are actually special-purpose computers. In addition to switching, they translate the data format of transmitting devices to conform to the requirements of the receiving devices. Thus, a number of devices, including telephones, mainframes, PCs, and fax machines, can be connected to a digital PBX.

FIGURE 5-16

Bridges and Gateways Linking LANs and WANs

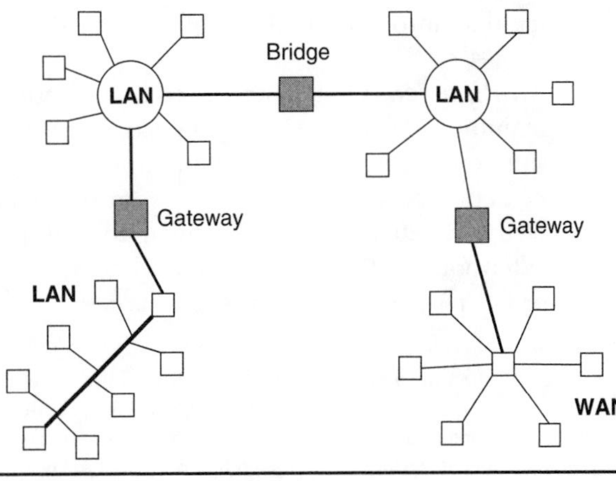

FIGURE 5-17

Digital PBX Various Terminal Devices

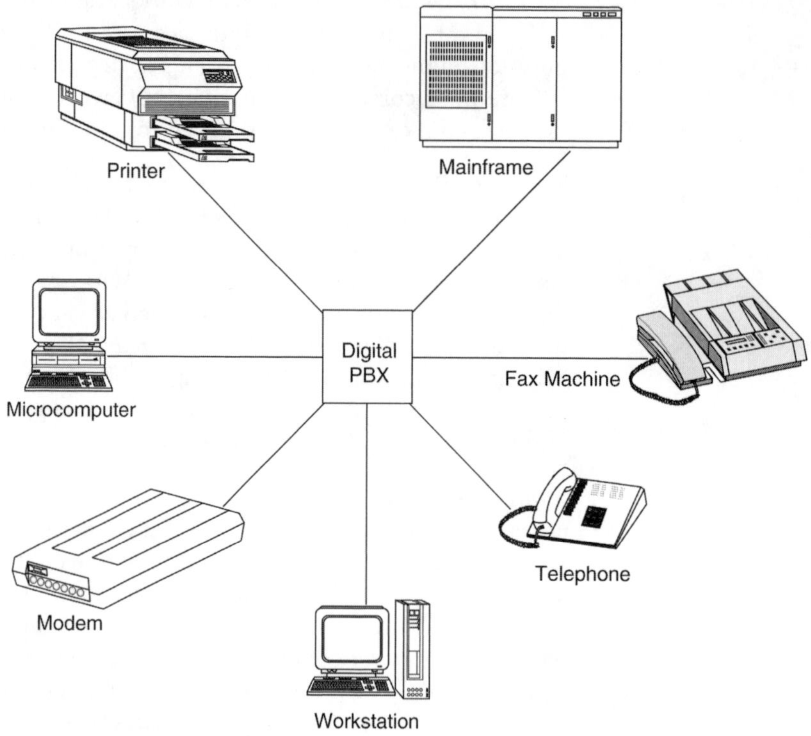

Packet switching is used for long-distance communications in WANs. Figure 5-18 illustrates this technique, whereby messages are divided into small packets for transmission. Individual packets of the same message may take different routes to their destination. Each packet contains address and sequencing codes so they can be reassembled into the original complete message at the receiving end. The choice of transmission path is determined according to criteria that achieve optimum utilization of the long-distance lines, including the degree of traffic congestion on the line, the shortest path between the end points, and the line status of the path (that is, working, failed, or experiencing errors). The network switches provide a physical connection for the addressed packets only for the duration of the message; the line then becomes available to other users. The international standard for organizing data into packets for public switched networks is X.25.[5]

Multiplexer. Long-distance communications lines are extremely expensive to maintain, but have the capacity to carry the signals of many thousands of users simultaneously. To transmit multiple messages simultaneously, each message must be kept separate from the others, or the signals will become commingled and garbled. The effect would be similar to multiple parties talking simultaneously from extensions on the same telephone line. A listener would be unable to distinguish his or her party's message from all the rest.

---

5 The Consultative Committee on International Telephone and Telegraph is a standards-setting body under the auspices of the United Nations. Its search for standards governing international transmissions of data has resulted in the X.25 format. This standard enables LANs and WANs to communicate through packet-switched networks in synchronous mode.

FIGURE 5-18

Message Packet Switching

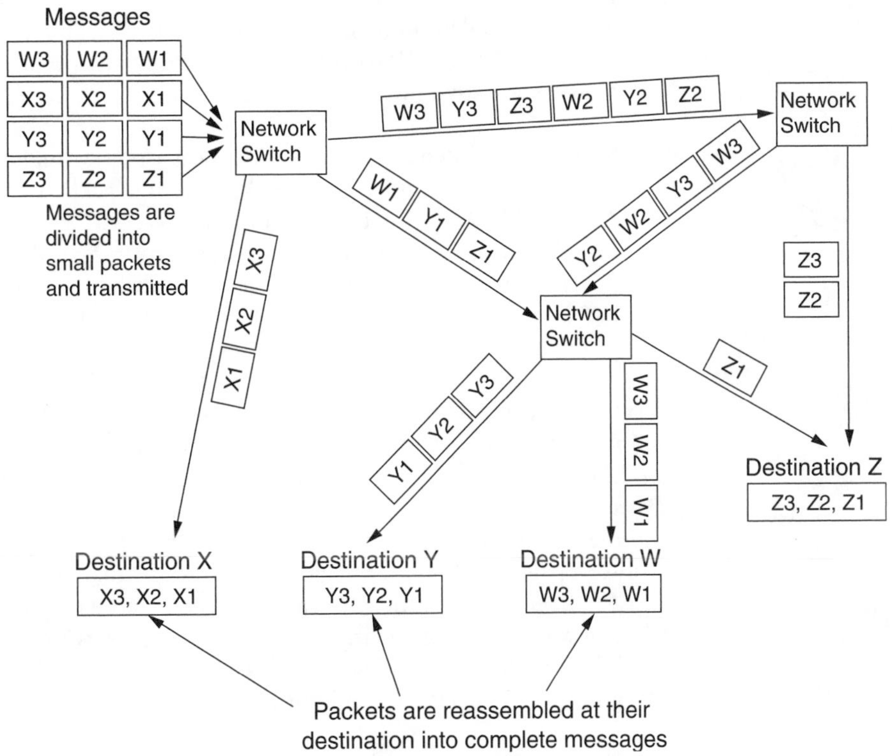

A **multiplexer** is a device that permits the simultaneous transmission of multiple signals while maintaining a separation between each of them. Figure 5-13 illustrates the role of multiplexers in the communications process. Depending on the communications system, thousands of individual terminal messages can be multiplexed and transmitted over a single long-distance line. At the receiving end, the composite signal is de-multiplexed into individual signals, which are then demodulated into digital form.

To achieve message separation over the long-distance line, multiplexers use one of two basic approaches: *frequency division multiplexing (FDM)* or *time division multiplexing (TDM)*. In the former, FDM divides a high-speed channel into multiple slow-speed channels. The FDM method is used to multiplex analog signals, as illustrated in Figure 5-13. In the case of the latter, TDM divides the time each terminal can use the high-speed line into various time slots. Digital systems use the TDM technique. *Statistical TDM* systems allow for dynamic allocation of time slots to active terminals only.

Hubs. **Hubs** are network processors that are commonly used to connect segments of a LAN. They serve as port switching communication devices. A hub contains multiple ports. When a packet arrives at one port, it is copied to the other ports so that all segments of the LAN can see all packets.

Routers. **Routers** are network processors used to interconnect networks with different protocols. They are used for routing messages (i.e., network data packets) to their destination. A router is connected to at least two networks, commonly two

LANs or WANs or a LAN and its ISP's network. Routers use headers and forwarding tables to determine the best path for forwarding the packets, and they use protocols such as ICMP to communicate with each other and configure the best route between any two hosts.

Switches. **Switches** are network processors that make connections between communications circuits in a network, directing packets to their intended destination. A switch is a device that filters and forwards packets between LAN segments. Switches operate at the data link layer (layer 2) and sometimes the network layer (layer 3) of the OSI Reference Model, and therefore support any packet protocol. LANs that use switches to join segments are called *switched LANs* or, in the case of Ethernet networks, switched Ethernet LANs.

Gateways. **Gateways** allow networks with different architectures to be interconnected. Thus, a mainframe network can be interconnected to a PC-based client/server architecture using a gateway. A gateway is a node on a network that serves as an entrance to another network. In enterprises, the gateway is the computer that routes the traffic from a workstation to the outside network that is serving the Web pages. In homes, the gateway is the ISP that connects the user to the Internet.

In enterprises, the gateway node often acts as a proxy server and a firewall. The gateway is also associated with both a router, which use headers and forwarding tables to determine where packets are sent, and a switch, which provides the actual path for the packet in and out of the gateway.[6]

Bridges. **Bridges** are like gateways in that they connects two networks, but in this case, a bridge connects two LANs or two segments of the same LAN that use the same protocol, such as Ethernet or token ring.

INTERNET

INTERNET TYPES/ APPLICATIONS

The **Internet** was originally developed for the U.S. military, and later became widely used for academic and government research. In recent years the Internet has evolved into a worldwide information highway. This growth is attributed to three factors. First, in 1995, national commercial telecom companies such as MCI, Sprint, and UUNET took control of the backbone elements of the Internet and have continued to enhance their infrastructures. Large Internet service providers (ISPs) can link into these backbones to connect their subscribers, and smaller ISPs can either connect directly to the national backbones or into one of the larger ISPs. Second, online services such as MSN and AOL connect to the Internet for e-mail, thus enabling users of different services to communicate with each other. Third, and most significantly, the development of graphics-based Web browsers such as Netscape Navigator and Microsoft's Internet Explorer made accessing the Internet a simple task. The Internet thus became the domain of ordinary people with PCs rather than scientists and computer hackers. The Web has grown exponentially and continues to grow daily. As a result, systems developers and IT professionals have used Internet technologies extensively in building networks and application systems.

6 Taken from *http://pcwebopedia.com/TERM/gateway.html.*

The Internet comprises more than 100,000 interconnected smaller networks located around the world. Unlike corporate networks, which are usually centrally controlled, the Internet is decentralized by design. Each Internet computer, called a *host*, is independent. Its operators can choose which Internet services to use and which local services to make available to the global Internet community. Remarkably, this ad hoc system works extremely well. Via the Internet, organizations conduct business transactions, consumers purchase goods and services, people obtain information quickly and easily, and people communicate virtually instantaneously with others scattered over the globe.

Intranet

One variation of Internet technology is the **intranet**. An intranet's Web sites look and act just like any other Web sites, but the *firewall* surrounding an intranet fends off unauthorized access. It is designed to be accessible only by the organization's members (employees), or others who have proper authorization. Like the Internet itself, intranets are used to share information. Secure intranets are now the fastest-growing segment of the Internet because they are much less expensive to build and manage than private networks based on proprietary protocols.[7]

Extranet

Another variant on Internet technology is the **extranet**. This internet-work is a password-controlled network for private users rather than the general public. Extranets are used to provide access between trading partner internal databases. Internet sites containing information intended for private consumption frequently use an extranet configuration. Extranets are popular for systems that incorporate suppliers, sometimes at multiple levels, business partners, and other entities key to business processes.

Components

The underlying Internet technologies include the network components discussed previously (especially the client–server architecture and servers), Web browsers and Web development technologies, e-mail technologies, file transfer protocol (FTP), and the TCP/IP protocol suite. The client–server architecture is the foundational structure of the Internet technologies used for the Internet and many, if not most, recently deployed LANs. The Web browser (Internet Explorer, Netscape Navigator, etc.) is the universal user interface to not only the Internet and Web, but many of the newer systems and networks based on Internet technologies as well. Web development technologies (such as FrontPage, Quark, Cold Fusion, Dream Weaver, Flash, QuickTime, and a host of multimedia tools) are the tools used to build, maintain, and manage Web sites. E-mail is still the most popular function of the Internet technologies. FTP is used to transfer files across the Internet, and embedded in the download capabilities of Web sites. The TCP/IP protocol suite is the magic wand that enables otherwise disparate systems and computers to communicate seamlessly with each other. TCP/IP works so well, and is so popular, that many, if not most, of the newer networks use TCP/IP as its own WAN protocol.

7 Taken from *http://pcwebopedia.com/TERM/i/intranet.html.*

EDI

To coordinate sales and production operations and to maintain an uninterrupted flow of raw materials, many organizations enter into a trading partner agreement with their suppliers and customers. This agreement is the foundation for a reengineered and fully automated business process called **electronic data interchange (EDI)**. A general definition of EDI is: *the intercompany exchange of computer-processible business information in standard format.*

Description

The definition reveals several important features of EDI. First, EDI is an intercompany endeavor. A firm cannot engage in EDI on its own. Second, the transaction is processed automatically by the information systems of the trading partners. In a pure EDI environment, there are no human intermediaries to approve or authorize transactions. Third, transaction information is transmitted in a standardized format. Therefore, firms with different internal systems can interface and do business.

Figure 5-19 shows an overview of an EDI connection between two companies. Let's assume that the transaction in Figure 5-19 is the purchase of inventory by the

FIGURE 5-19

Overview of EDI

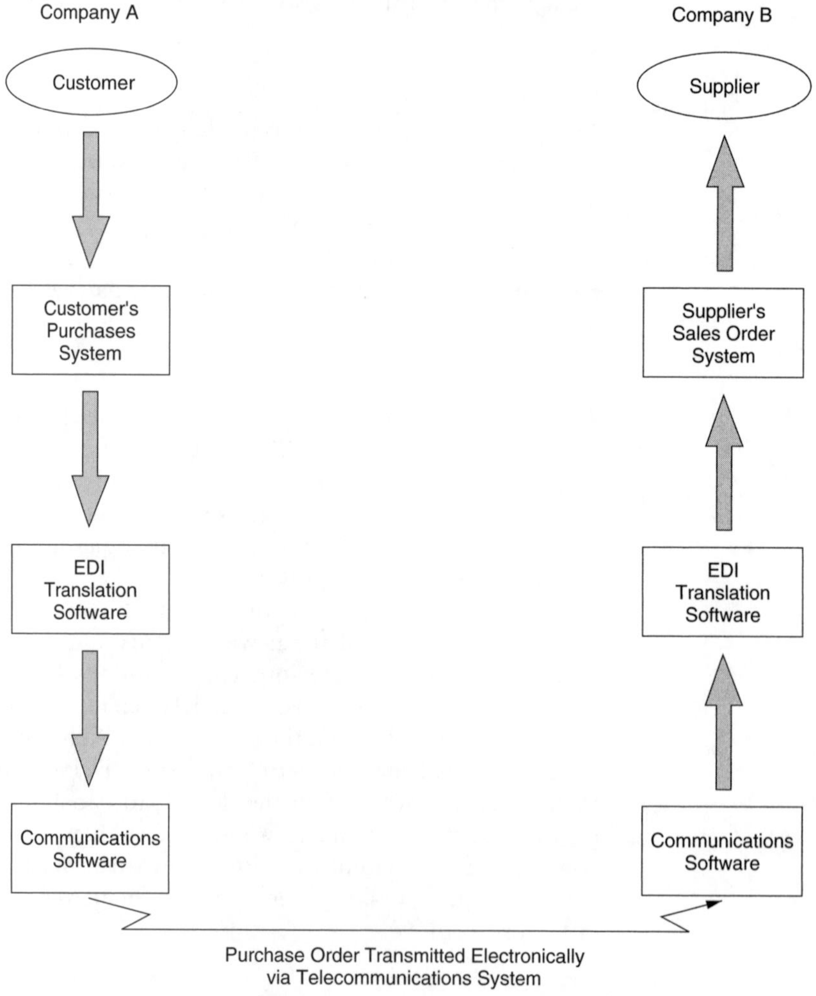

customer (Company A) from the supplier (Company B). Company A's purchases system automatically creates an electronic purchase order (PO), which it sends to its translation software. Here, the PO is converted to a standard format electronic message ready for transmission. The message is transmitted to Company B's translation software, where it is converted to the supplier's internal format. Company B's sales order processing system receives the customer order, which it processes automatically. Figure 5-19 shows a direct communications link between companies. But many companies choose to use a third-party value-added network (VAN) to connect to their trading partners. Figure 5-20 illustrates this arrangement. The originating company transmits its EDI messages to the network rather than directly to the trading partner's computer. The network directs each EDI transmission to its destination and deposits the message in the appropriate electronic mailbox. The messages stay in the mailboxes until the receiving companies connect to the network and retrieve them. The network is called a value-added network because it provides service by managing the distribution of the messages between trading partners. VANs can also provide an important degree of control for EDI transactions.

Protocols

Key to the EDI concept is the use of a standard format for exchanging commerce information between trading partners. Widespread acceptance and growth of EDI did not occur until an acceptable protocol was developed. Over the years, both in the United States and internationally, a number of formats have been proposed. The most popular standard in the United States is the **American National Standards Institute (ANSI)** X.12 format. The standard used internationally is the EDIFACT

FIGURE 5-20

Value-Added Network and EDI

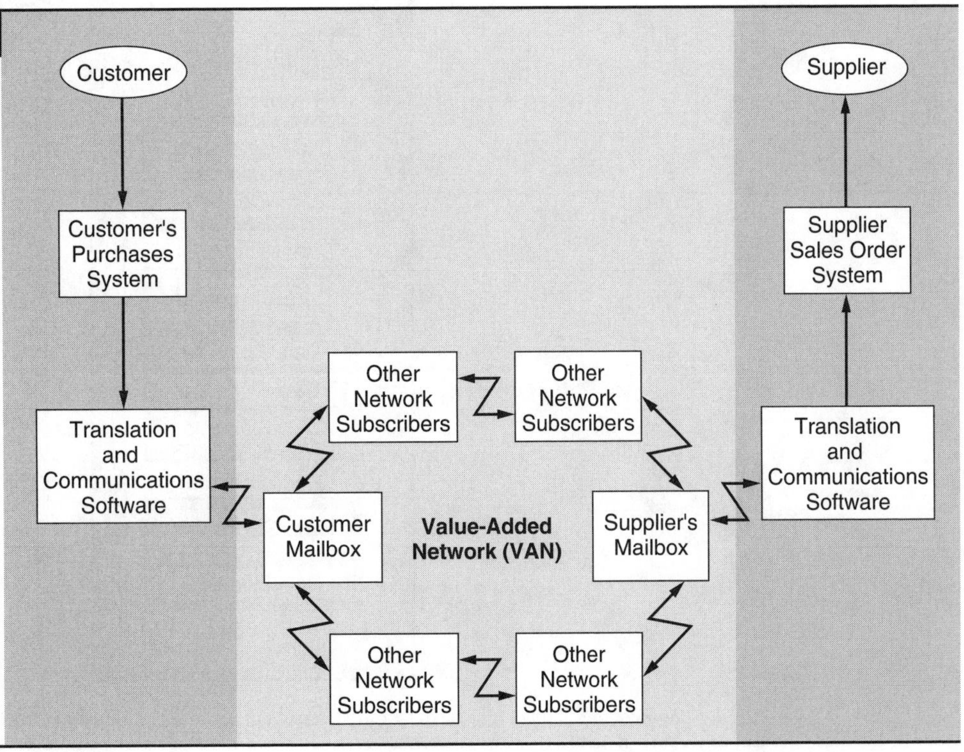

format. This stands for EDI For Administration, Commerce, and Transport. Figure 5-21 presents the X.12 format.

The electronic envelope contains the electronic address of the receiver, communications protocols, and control information. This is the electronic equivalent of a traditional paper envelope. A functional group is a collection of transaction sets (electronic documents) for a particular business application, such as a group of sales invoices or purchase orders. The transaction set is the electronic document and comprises data segments and data elements. Figure 5-22 relates these terms to a

FIGURE 5-21

The X.12 Format

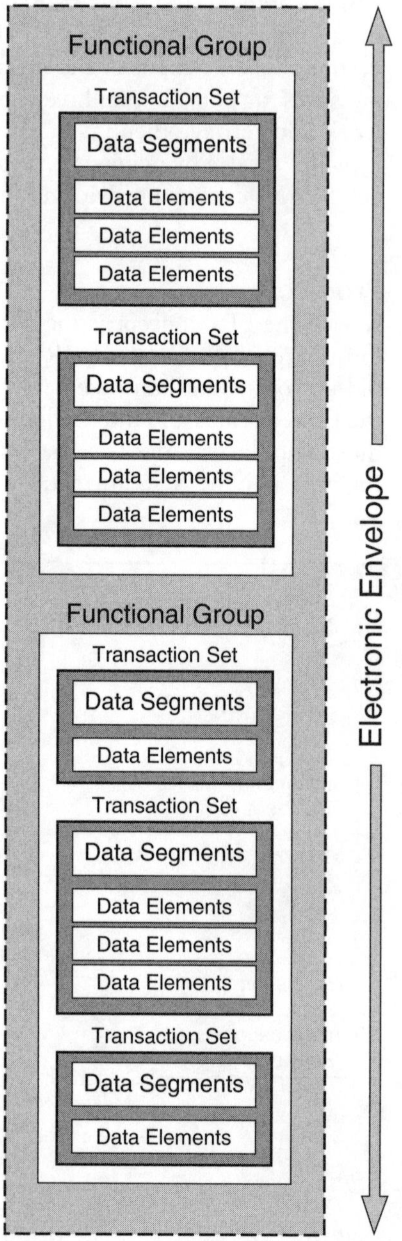

Source: B. K. Stone, *One to Get Ready: How to Prepare Your Company for EDI* (CoreStates, 1988), p. 12.

FIGURE 5-22 **Relationship between X.12 Format and a Conventional Source Document**

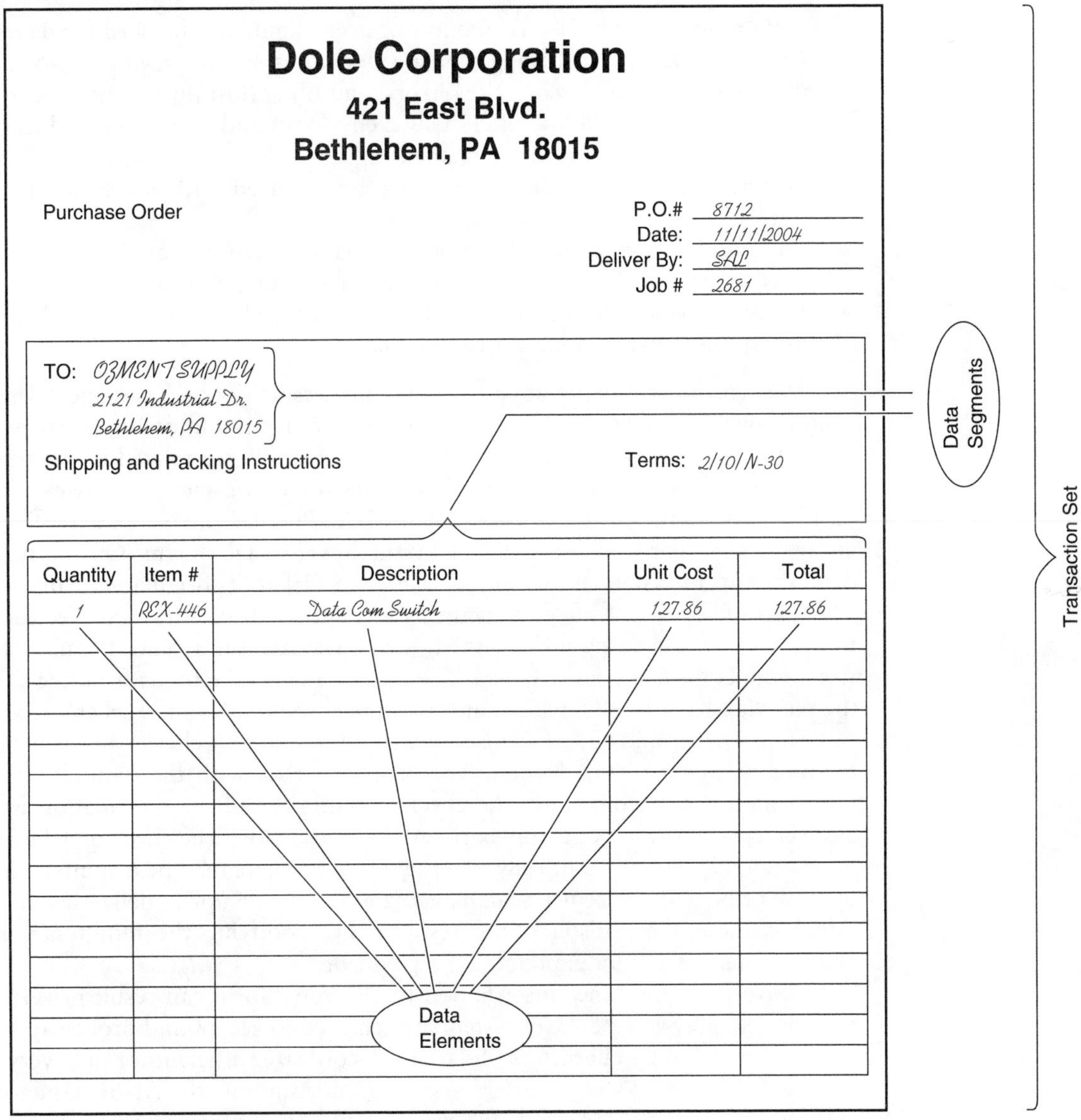

conventional document.[8] Each data segment is an information category on the document, such as part number, unit price, or vendor name. The data elements are specific items of data related to a segment. In the example in Figure 5-22, these include such items as REX-446, $127.86, and Ozment Supply.

Benefits of EDI

Although EDI is often associated with the support of just-in-time manufacturing (JIT), its use is not limited to manufacturing firms. EDI has made considerable inroads

8 J. M. Cathey, "Electronic Data Interchange: What the Controller Should Know," *Management Accounting* (November 1991): 48.

in a number of industries, including automotive, groceries, retail, health care, and electronics. Following are some common EDI cost savings that justify this approach.

- ***Data keying reduction.*** EDI reduces or even eliminates the need for data entry.
- ***Error reduction.*** Firms using EDI see reductions in data keying errors, human interpretation and classification errors, and filing (lost document) errors.
- ***Paper reduction.*** The use of electronic envelopes and documents reduces drastically the paper forms in the system.
- ***Postage reduction.*** Mailed documents are replaced with much cheaper data transmissions.
- ***Procedure automation.*** EDI automates manual activities associated with purchasing, sales order processing, cash disbursements, and cash receipts.
- ***Inventory reduction.*** By ordering directly as needed from vendors, EDI reduces the lag time that promotes inventory accumulation.

The benefits of EDI are apparent in the processing of purchases and sales order transactions. However, using EDI for cash disbursement and cash receipts processing has not seen the same success. The reasons for this are related to the need for intermediary banks in **electronic funds transfer (EFT)** transactions between trading partners. We see this arrangement in Figure 5-23. Purchase invoices are received and automatically approved for payment by the buyer's EDI system. On the payment date, the buyer's system automatically makes an EFT to its originating bank (OBK). The OBK removes funds from the buyer's account and transmits them electronically to the automatic clearing house (ACH) bank. The ACH is a central bank that carries accounts for its member banks. The ACH transfers the funds from the OBK to the receiving bank (RBK), which, in turn, applies the funds to the seller's account.

Transferring funds by EFT poses no special problem. A check can easily be represented within the X.12 format. The problem arises with the remittance advice information that accompanies the check. Remittance advice information is often quite extensive because of complexities in the transaction. The check may be in payment of multiple invoices or only a partial invoice. There may be disputed amounts because of price disagreements, damaged goods, or incomplete deliveries. In traditional systems, these disputes are resolved by modifying the remittance advice and/or attaching a letter explaining the payment.

Converting remittance information to electronic form can result in very large records. Members of the ACH system are required to accept and process only EFT formats limited to 94 characters of data—a record size sufficient for only very basic messages. Most banks in the ACH system do not support the ANSI standard format for remittances—ANSI 820. Therefore, remittance information must be sent to the seller by separate EDI transmission or conventional mail. The seller must then acquire special software and implement separate procedures to match bank and customer EDI transmissions in applying payments to customer accounts.

Recognizing the void between services demanded and those supplied by the ACH system, many banks have established themselves as **value-added banks (VAB)**, to compete for this market. A VAB can accept electronic disbursements and remittance advices from its clients in any format. It converts EDI transactions to the ANSI X.12 and 820 formats for electronic processing. In the case of non–EDI transactions, the VAB writes traditional checks to the creditor. The services offered by VABs allow their clients to employ a single cash disbursement system that can accommodate both EDI and non–EDI customers. The role of the VAB is expected to expand in the future and compete with VANs for nonfinancial EDI business.

FIGURE 5-23 **EFT Transactions between Trading Partners**

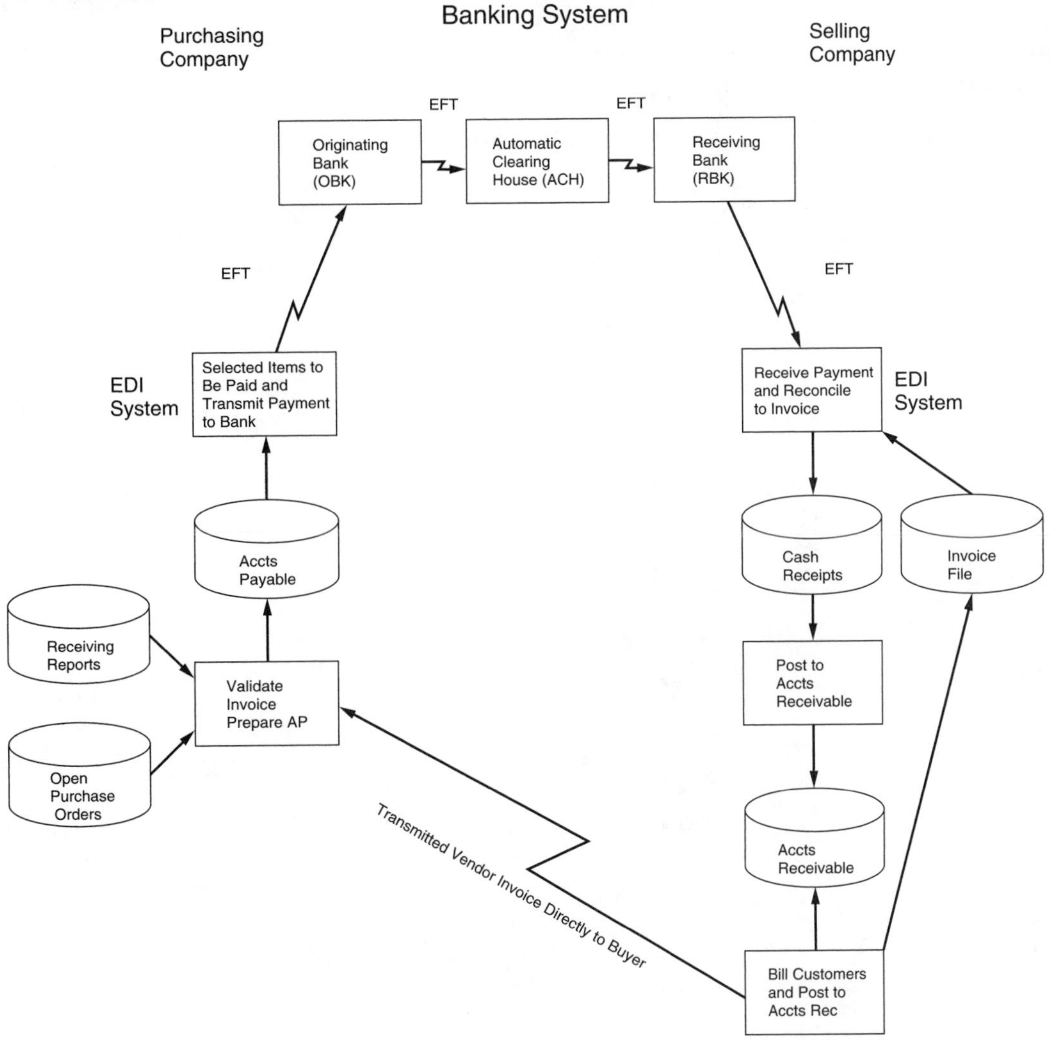

Source: Adapted from B. K. Stone, *One to Get Ready: How to Prepare Your Company for EDI* (CoreStates, 1988), p. 62.

EDI Audit Trail

The absence of source documents in EDI transactions disrupts the traditional audit trail and restricts the ability of accountants to verify the validity, completeness, timing, and accuracy of transactions. One technique for restoring the audit trail is to maintain a control log, which records the transaction's flow through each phase of the EDI system. Figure 5-24 illustrates how this approach may be employed.

As the transaction is received at each stage in the process, an entry is made into the log. In the customer's system, the transaction log can be reconciled to ensure that all transactions initiated by the purchases system were correctly translated and communicated. Likewise, in the vendor's system, the control log will establish that all messages received by the communications software were correctly translated and processed by the sales order system.

FIGURE 5-24

EDI System Using Transaction Control Log for Audit Trail

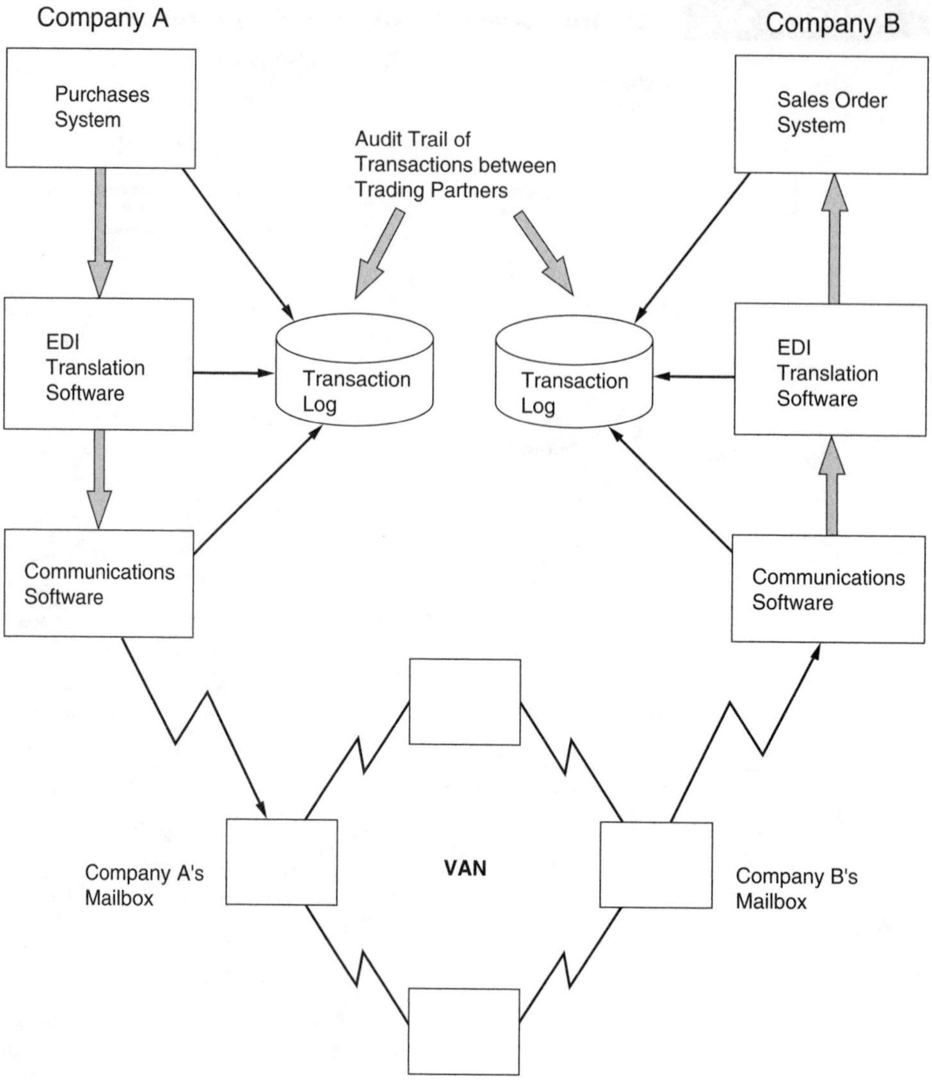

ELECTRONIC COMMERCE

We now turn our attention to the technologies that underlie e-commerce systems. Because we have already examined many of the elements found in LANs, this discussion emphasizes Internet technologies. The section is divided into the following major topics: types, components, and risks.

TYPES

Internet commerce has enabled thousands of business enterprises of all sizes and millions of consumers to congregate and interact in a worldwide virtual shopping mall. Electronic commerce is generally divided into three different categories: Business-to-consumer (B2C), business-to-business (B2B), and consumer-to-consumer (C2C).

B2C

Business-to-consumer (**B2C**) is the exchange of services, information and/or products from a business to a consumer using the Internet and electronic commerce technologies.

B2B

Business-to-business (**B2B**) is the exchange of services, information, and/or products from a business to a consumer using the Internet and electronic commerce technologies. While B2C gets much of the attention from the public media, B2B is by far the largest volume of electronic commerce. B2B is essentially EDI over the Internet using the Web.

C2C

Consumer-to-consumer (**C2C**) is the e-commerce business model where one consumer sells to another consumer using an electronic broker or auction firm. One of the most popular C2C businesses is eBay.com.

COMPONENTS

Electronic Payment Systems

Electronic payment systems are required for any business to sell goods and services online. The business needs some method to receive payment while the customer is online, authenticate the customer (also nonrepudiation), and protect the privacy of the transaction details. Credit/debit cards offer a viable financial approach, and SSL (or other encryption systems) protects the credit card numbers and other transaction data while the transaction is being consummated online.

Protocols

TCP/IP provides most of the protocols necessary to complete a business transaction online, but a special protocol is needed to encrypt the transaction information and maintain the privacy of the customer.

SSL. One commonly used protocol is **Secure Socket Layer** (**SSL**). SSL uses keys, digital certificates/singatures, and encryption to protect the information and to authenticate both the customer and the seller.

SET. Another protocol used is **Secure Electronic Transactions** (**SET**), which was sponsored by VISA, Master Card, and American Express. The difference between SET and SSL is that SET confirms the availability of funds while the two parties are online, and protects information between all three parties (financial institution being the third) on a "need to know" basis. The seller never has the credit card information, and the financial institution never sees what the customer bought. Only the customer knows all the information about the transaction. SET also uses strong encryption and digital certificates/signatures.

Regarding risks, SET's advantages include less exposure of credit card information, protection of customer's privacy, and non-repudiation mitigation.

RISKS

Risks associated with networks and the Internet are often associated with hackers. But the risks go far beyond hackers, and hackers aren't always exactly as they have been portrayed. The risks extend beyond the external threats presented by intruders, such as hackers, and include a firm's own employees!

Internal

There are a number of risks associated with networks, especially the Internet. But surprisingly to most, the majority of malicious activities do not come from outside intruders, but from insiders, and plain, ordinary system failures. Disgruntled employees, recently terminated employees, embezzlers, former contractors or consultants, and others are sometimes bent on revenge and be motivated to perpetrate a malicious attack on his/her (former) employer. In fact, a recent study found that vengeful employees are now the biggest security worry for 90 percent of executive managers.[9] The IT research expert, The Gartner Group, estimates that more than 70 percent of unauthorized access to information systems is committed by employees, as are more than 95 percent of intrusions that result in significant financial losses.[10]

Accidents/System Failures. Of the different kinds of risks associated with system availability or damage, system failure is the most common reason for problems. Accidents also represent a sizable risk to systems.

Ineffective Accountability. Most internal auditors know that although many policies have been developed with good intentions, and many effective procedures were carefully crafted, the major cause of ineffective controls is often the lack of accountability in making sure the procedures are actually working. The lack of accountability on either of these points creates the same risk as if no policy or procedure were ever developed. In fact, it is worse because managers or other responsible parties might be misled into thinking their policies and procedures are working when in fact they are being ignored.

Malicious Activities. One serious aspect of internal risk comes from the entity's own employees, especially when one becomes motivated to get even with the company. For example, if an employee is fired, that person might seek revenge by an act of cyberterrorism or fraud.

Fraud. Recent financial frauds have made the public aware of the scope of fraud in business today. The Association of Certified Fraud Examiners estimates that fraud by employees costs businesses $6 billion in 2002. Thus there is a significant risk that employees will use technology to commit a cyber-crime of fraud.

External

External risks are associated primarily with intruders and their devices.

Intruders. Intruders can be divided into three or four groups: hackers (also *white-hat* hackers), crackers, and script kiddies. *Hacker* was once used as a complimentary term to describe those talented in IT who could "hack" code and run cryptic

---

9 K. Cunningham, "Cyberterrorism: Are We Leaving the Keys Out?" *SC Magazine* (November 2002). Online at *http://www.scmagazine.com/scmagazine/sc-online/2002/article/51/article.html.*

10 *Ibid.*

operating systems. Now it is used by the press to describe all intruders, and used strictly in a negative sense. But a true hacker would disagree, arguing that his/her intent is to take a "joy ride" over the Internet and networks of various organizations, with no intent to actually harm the system. Hackers usually just want to leave their "calling cards"—usually a distinctive alias.

White-hat hackers are experienced hackers who are hired by organizations to play the devil's advocate and uncover any weaknesses in its system of networks and Internet connectivity.

Crackers, by contrast, do come to the system with the intent to "steal, kill, or destroy." They do deliberately attempt to crash the system, steal data or money, or destroy part or all of the system. They represent a great risk from external sources.

Script kiddies are associated with crackers and hackers in that they obtain code written by black-hat hackers or crackers and use basic network and Internet knowledge to execute the scripts or code to invoke some damage or harm to the target—sometimes with the intent of providing "fifteen minutes of fame" as the motive. A script kiddie, for instance, brought eBay, Yahoo!, and Amazon down in a period of a week.

One common script attack is the denial-of-service attack. Malicious external intruders use the code to try to crash an Internet server, bringing the system down —making the system unavailable.

Viruses. Yet the greatest risk from external sources is that presented by viruses. Experts estimate U.S. corporations spent about $12.3 billion to clean up damage from computer viruses in 2001, and many viruses cost more than $1 million per virus. The good news is that there are effective techniques and tools to protect against this risk.

Cyberterrorism/Cyber-Crime. The risk of cyberterrorism is high for certain businesses, but exists to some degree for every business connected to the Internet. Certain tools and techniques have proven to be effective when used appropriately. But the bottom line is that a business needs breadth to their prevention measures because no one method can protect a business against all types of attacks.

CONTROLLING INTERNET/E-COMMERCE

Despite the plethora or risks already mentioned, there are some controls that mitigate those risks. It is the IT auditor's responsibility to ensure a sufficient degree of these controls are in place and effectively working in order to protect the assets and business of the organization. Two major areas of concern are unauthorized access and equipment failure. *Unauthorized access* includes, but is not limited to, a computer criminal intercepting a message transmitted between the sender and the receiver, a computer hacker gaining unauthorized access to the organization's network, and a denial-of-service attack from a remote location of the Internet. EDI operations rely on a great deal of mutual access between trading partners. Without proper controls, trading partners may access other partners' data and/or programs from remote locations to exceed their authority, perpetrate illegal acts, or insert errors into data files. *Equipment failure* includes the fact that transmissions between senders and receivers can be disrupted, destroyed, or corrupted by equipment failures in the communications system. Equipment failure can also result in the loss of databases and programs stored on the network server.

CONTROLS

Controls begin with the best practice of using policies and procedures to address the risks identified in the risk assessments done by the firm or its auditors, and include some sophisticated IT tools to mitigate the risks identified above.

Policies and Procedures

Once the risk assessment team identifies a specific risk, which exceeds some tolerable level of risk and for which a control is cost-effective, then the team (or auditors, and eventually management) should develop a policy to state the organization's intents regarding the risky event (e.g., we intend to collect all invoices billed). That will lead to the choice of procedures (controls) to prevent and detect the event as well (e.g., (1) Do not sell to anyone who is already 90 days past due. (2) Do not sell to anyone until that entity has become an authorized customer. (3) Do not sell to anyone when it takes the balance above the credit limit established by the credit manager.). Now it is easier to develop controls to ensure those procedures work. The same process will work regarding any relevant policy. Therefore, policies and procedures themselves are controls.

SDLC Techniques

One overlooked area is the best practices established in the IT/IS community for decades regarding system development life cycle (SDLC) or systems analysis and design. Practices such as documentation, involvement of endusers, testing of systems off-line before implementing them operationally, etc. have proven to be effective.

Anti-Virus Systems

In Chapter 2, anti-virus software (AVS) and techniques were discussed. Review that section for details on the set of controls necessary for virus protection. Remember that AVS alone is not sufficient, even with regular updates—especially "push" updates. It is necessary these days to also be a part of some alert system or early warning system for emerging viruses, because when a virus is first released, no AVS can protect you until an antidote is perfected and installed into your AVS.

Message Sequence Numbers

An intruder in the communications channel may attempt to delete a message from a stream of messages, change the order of messages received, or duplicate a message. Through **message sequence numbering**, a sequence number is inserted in each message, and any such attempt will become apparent at the receiving end.

Logs

An intruder may successfully penetrate the system by trying different password and user ID combinations. Therefore, all incoming and outgoing messages, as well as attempted (failed) access, should be recorded in a message transaction **log**. The log should record the user ID, the time of the access, and the terminal location or telephone number from which the access originated.

Monitoring Systems

Monitoring routers and gateways have become effective tools to monitor for malicious activities. When combined with graphs that are conscientiously read, any malicious activity could be spotted by radical changes in the trend line of the graph. If a DoS attack were to occur, say on port 80, then the line graphing port 80 would suddenly turn up, much like the picture of a golf club. These tools also help to spot adverse activities, such as poorly timed backups of data (i.e., during high levels of operational activities versus low level traffic times—usually late at night).

Access Control Systems

Access control systems are used to authorize and authenticate users. They use one or more of three basic approaches to security: (1) something you have, (2) something you know, and (3) something you are. Specific controls range from access cards/readers (something you have), to passwords or PINs (something you know), to biometrics (something you are). The more risk that exists, the greater the need to consider multiple approaches (layers) for additional security.

The most general authentication controls are password systems, firewalls, and occasionally access cards or biometrics. The weakness of these former two security methods is that they have been compromised, and intruders have caused great harm and significant financial losses. The latter approach, biometrics, has the potential to provide the greatest level of security because it involves something you are, and because they can be more reliable than the passwords or firewalls—especially standalone password or firewall systems.

Call Back Systems. As we have seen, networks can be equipped with security features such as passwords, authentication devices, and encryption. The common weakness to all of these technologies is that they impose the security measure after the criminal has connected to the LAN server. Many believe that the key to network security is to keep the intruder off the LAN to begin with.

A **call-back device** requires the dial-in user to enter a password and be identified. The system then breaks the connection to perform user authentication. If the caller is authorized, the call-back device dials the caller's number to establish a new connection. This limits access from only authorized terminals or telephone numbers and prevents an intruder masquerading as a legitimate user.

Challenge-Response Systems. An intruder may attempt to prevent or delay the receipt of a message from the sender. When senders and receivers are not in constant contact, the receiver may not know that the communications channel has been interrupted and that messages have been diverted. With the **challenge-response technique**, a control message from the sender and a response from the receiver are sent at periodic, synchronized intervals. The timing of the messages should follow a random pattern that will be difficult for the intruder to determine and circumvent.

Multifaceted Password Systems. While passwords are an effective control and the cornerstone of an effective access control system, good password policy and procedures alone are insufficient in the globally connected world of today. A number of effective tools and techniques can be used to make the traditional password system multifaceted (see Chapter 2 and password policy). The intent is to both authorize (i.e., a valid user name and password), and authenticate (i.e., validate the user is who he/she claims to be) users.

One way to design **multifaceted password systems** is to combine passwords with an extensive access table where each user is granted read-only access to certain fields, read-write access to necessary fields, and no access to all other fields in the database. Another way to add a facet is to combine passwords with other access controls such as biometrics, dynamic PIN systems, advanced security tools, and so on. A dynamic PIN system is one where not only does a person access the system with a valid user name and password, but has to then enter a PIN number that is valid for only a few short minutes (sometimes seconds) before a different PIN is generated. Pager devices are used to transmit the constantly changing PIN. An interesting biometric (see below) is one that can accurately determine the *way* a person enters his or her password. With this control, even when a pretend hacker was allowed to watch the user type in the password and ID, and even when the user gave the password and ID to the pretend hacker, the pretend hacker could not successfully gain access in a test of its effectiveness.

Biometrics. **Biometrics** can be defined as the automated measuring of one or more specific attributes or features of a person, with the objective of being able to distinguish that person from all others. This process is based on using one or more characteristics of the human body as a method to code a unique template (computer file used for comparisons). Physical characteristics like fingerprints, palm prints, voices, retinas and irises, and faces can be used as an access code in biometrics. In other words, biometrics uses one or more attributes of your body as a password. Since these characteristics are unique to each individual, biometrics is known today as the most reliable technology developed to fight against theft and fraud resulting from unauthorized access.

Firewalls. Organizations connected to the Internet or other public networks often implement an electronic *firewall* to insulate their LAN from outside intruders. A **firewall** consists of both software and hardware that provide a focal point for security by channeling all network connections through a control gateway. Firewalls can be used to authenticate an outside user of the network, verify his or her level of access authority, and then direct the user to the program, data, or service requested. In addition to insulating the organization's network from external networks, firewalls can be used to insulate portions of the organization's network from internal access. For example, a LAN controlling access to financial data can be insulated from other internal LANs. A number of firewall products are on the market. Some of these provide a high level of security, while others are less effective. Firewalls fall into two general types: network-level firewalls and application-level firewalls.

Network-level firewalls provide low cost and low security access control. This type of firewall consists of a **screening router** that examines the source and destination addresses that are attached to incoming message packets. The firewall accepts or denies access requests based on filtering rules that have been programmed into it. Similar to an intelligent PBX, the firewall directs incoming calls to the correct internal receiving node. Network-level firewalls are insecure because they are designed to facilitate the free flow of information rather than restrict it. This method does not explicitly authenticate outside users. Employing a technique called **IP spoofing**, hackers can disguise their message packets to look as if they came from an authorized user and thus gain access to the host's network.

Application-level firewalls provide a high level of customizable network security, but can be extremely expensive. These systems are configured to run security applications called **proxies** that permit routine services such as e-mail to pass through the firewall, but can perform sophisticated functions such as logging or user authentication for specific tasks. An important aspect of this is one-time password control, which was discussed in Chapter 2. Application-level firewalls also provide comprehensive transmission logging and auditing tools for reporting unauthorized activity. If an outside user attempts to connect to an unauthorized service or file, the network administrator or security group can be notified immediately.

The highest level of firewall security is provided by a *dual-homed system*. This approach, illustrated in Figure 5-25, has two firewall interfaces. One screens incoming requests from the Internet; the other provides access to the organization's LAN. Direct communication to the Internet is disabled and the two networks are fully isolated. All access is performed by proxy applications that impose separate login procedures.

Choosing the right firewall involves a trade-off between convenience and security. Ultimately, organization management, in collaboration with accountants and network professionals, must come to grips with what constitutes acceptable risk. The more security provided by the firewall, however, the less convenient it is for authorized users to pass through it. An excessive level of control could, therefore, negatively impact the organization's ability to conduct commerce on the Internet.

Intrusion Detection Systems. An **intrusion detection system (IDS)** inspects all inbound and outbound network activity and identifies suspicious patterns that may indicate a network or system attack from someone attempting to break into or compromise a system.

There are several ways to categorize an IDS:

- *Misuse detection versus anomaly detection.* In misuse detection, the IDS analyzes the information it gathers and compares it to large databases of attack signatures. Essentially, the IDS looks for a specific attack that has already been documented. Like a virus detection system, misuse detection software is only as good as the database of attack signatures that it uses to compare packets against. In anomaly detection, the system administrator defines the baseline, or normal, state of the network's traffic load, breakdown, protocol, and typical packet size. The anomaly detector monitors network segments to compare their state to the normal baseline and look for anomalies.
- *Network-based versus host-based systems.* In a network-based system, or NIDS, the individual packets flowing through a network are analyzed. The NIDS can detect malicious packets that are designed to be overlooked by a firewall's simplistic filtering rules. In a host-based system, the IDS examines the activity on each individual computer or host.
- *Passive system versus reactive system.* In a passive system, the IDS detects a potential security breach, logs the information and signals an alert. In a reactive system, the IDS responds to the suspicious activity by logging off a user or by reprogramming the firewall to block network traffic from the suspected malicious source.

FIGURE 5-25 Dual-Homed Firewall

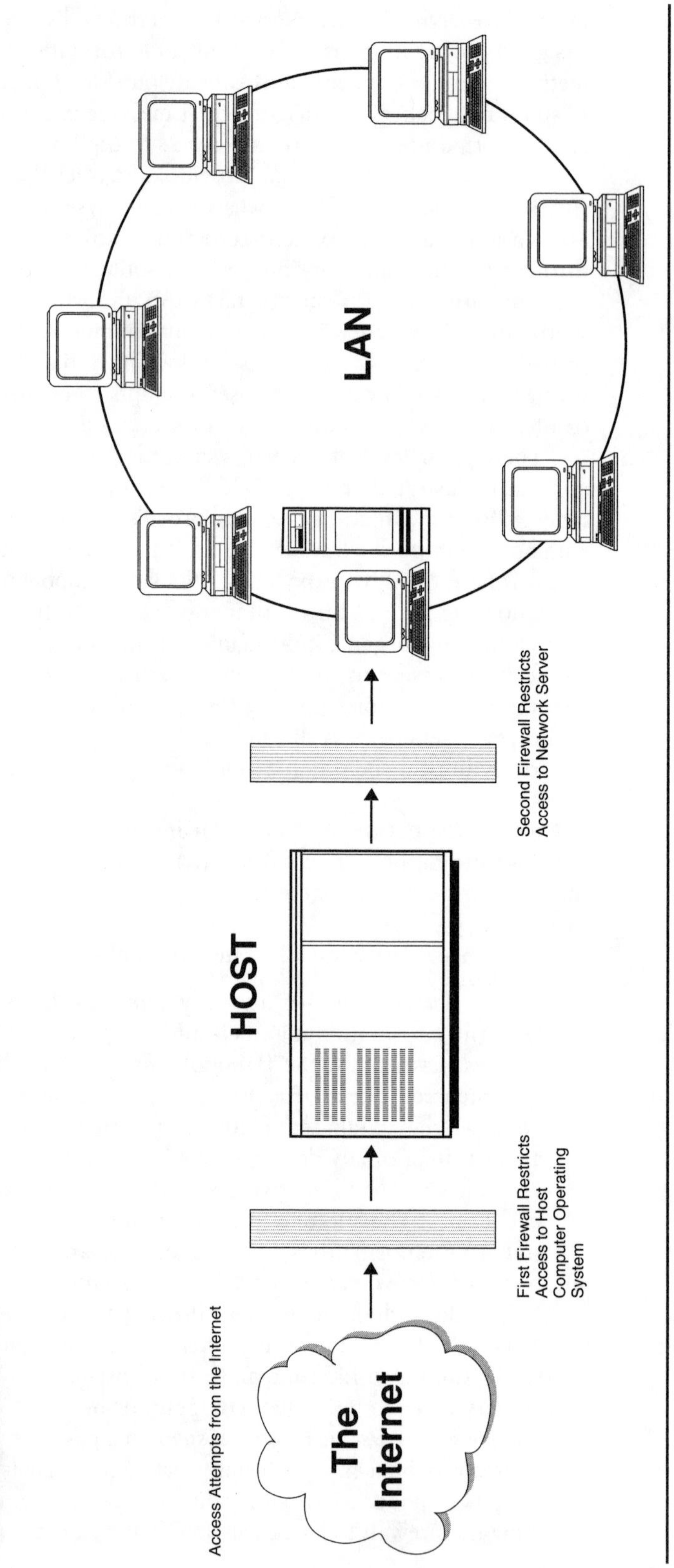

Although they both relate to network security, an IDS differs from a *firewall* in that a firewall looks out for intrusions in order to stop them from happening—that is, it is a *prevention control* (see *PDC model*). The firewall limits the access between networks in order to prevent intrusion and does not signal an attack from inside the network. An IDS evaluates a suspected intrusion once it has taken place and signals an alarm. That is, it is a *detection control* (see *PDC model*). An IDS also watches for attacks that originate from within a system.[10]

Controlling Denial-of-Service Attacks. When a user establishes a connection on the Internet through TCP/IP, a three-way handshake takes place. The connecting server sends an initiation code called a *SYN packet* to the receiving server. The receiving server then acknowledges the request by returning a *SYN/ACK packet*. Finally, the initiating host machine responds with an ACK packet code. Computer hackers and crackers have devised a malicious act called a **denial-of-service attack**, in which the attacker transmits hundreds of SYN packets to the targeted receiver but never responds with an ACK to complete the connection. As a result, the ports of the receiver's server are clogged with incomplete communication requests that prevent legitimate transactions from being received and processed. Organizations under attack have been prevented from receiving Internet messages for days at a time.

If the target organization could identify the server that is launching the attack, the firewall could be programmed to ignore all communication from that site. Such attacks, however, are difficult to prevent because IP spoofing is used to disguise the source of the messages. IP spoofing programs that randomize the source address of the attacker have been written and publicly distributed over the Internet. Therefore, to the receiving site it appears that the transmissions are coming from all over the Internet.

Denial-of-service attacks can severely hamper an organization's ability to use the Internet to conduct commerce. Although this activity cannot currently be prevented, there are two actions that management and accountants can take to limit the exposure. First, Internet sites with firewalls must engage in a policy of social responsibility. The firewalls at the source sites can be programmed to block messages with noninternal addresses. This would prevent attackers from hiding their locations from the targeted site and would assure the organization's management that no undetected attacks could be launched from its site. This strategy will not, however, prevent attacks from areas of the Internet that do screen outgoing transmissions.

Second, security software is available for the targeted sites that scan for half-open connections. The software looks for SYN packets that have not been followed by an ACK packet. The clogged ports can then be restored to allow legitimate connections to be made.

Encryption. Encryption is the conversion of data into a secret code for storage in databases and transmission over networks. The sender uses an encryption algorithm to convert the original message (called *cleartext*) into a coded equivalent (called *ciphertext*). At the receiving end the ciphertext is decoded (decrypted) back into cleartext.

The earliest encryption method is called the **Caesar Cipher**, which is said to have been used by Julius Caesar to send coded messages to his generals in the field. Like modern encryption, the Caesar Cipher has two fundamental components: a **key** and an **algorithm**. The key is a mathematical value that is selected by the sender

10 Taken from *http://pcwebopedia.com/TERM/i/intrusion_detection_system.html.*

of the message. The algorithm is the simple procedure of shifting each letter in the cleartext message the number of positions indicated by the key value. Thus a key value of +3 would shift each letter three places to the right. For example the letter "A" in cleartext would be represented as the letter "D" in the ciphertext message. The receiver of the ciphertext message decodes it and recreates the cleartext by reversing the process, in this case, shifting each chiphertext letter three places to the left. Obviously, both the sender and receiver of the message must know the key.

Modern-day encryption algorithms are far more complex and encryption keys (passwords) are 40 to 128 bits in length. The more bits in the key, the stronger the encryption method. Today, nothing less than 128-bit algorithms are considered truly secure. Two commonly used methods of encryption are *private key encryption* and *public key encryption.*

Private Key Encryption. One commonly used **private key encryption** methodology is the Data Encryption Standard (DES). DES, and private key encryption, uses a single key known to both the sender and the receiver of the message. Figure 5-26 illustrates this technique. To encode a message, the sender provides the encryption program with the key, which the program uses to produce a ciphertext message. The message enters the communication channel and is transmitted to the receiver's location, where it is stored. When the receiver wishes to read the message, he or she must enter the key into the decryption program, which transforms the message to cleartext form.

FIGURE 5-26 **The Data Encryption Standard Technique**

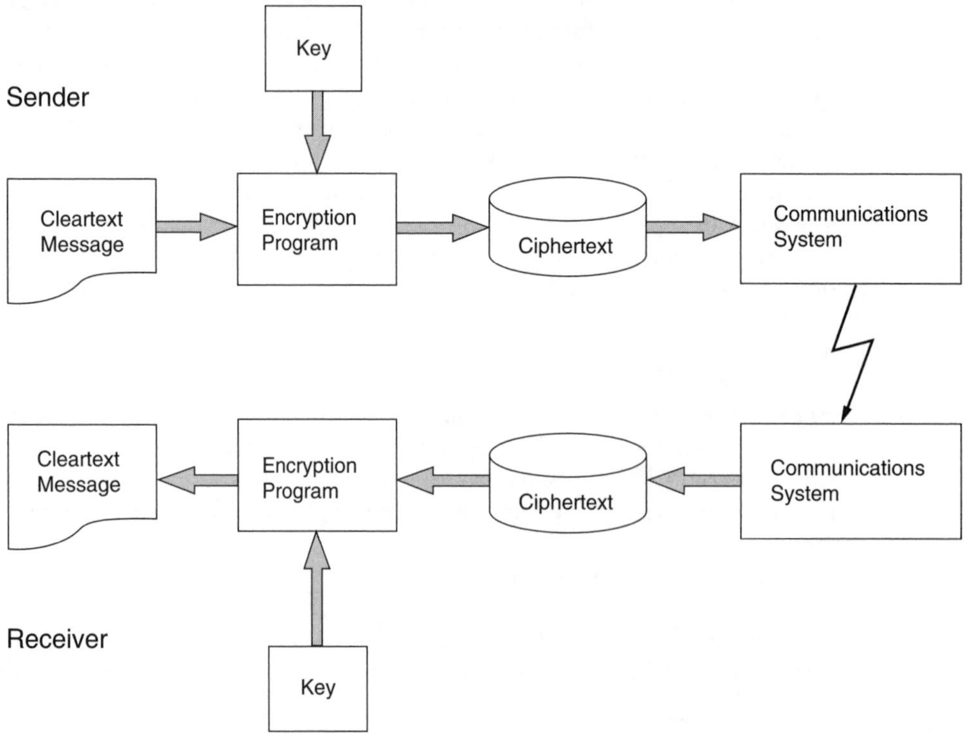

An extension of this technique is to use *double encryption*. The cleartext message undergoes the encryption process twice. Using two different keys greatly reduces the chances of breaking the cipher. The main problem with the DES approach is that a perpetrator may discover the key (or keys) and decipher the intercepted message. The password control issues discussed in Chapter 2 apply here also. The more individuals who need to know the key, the greater the probability of it falling into the wrong hands. One solution to the problem is public key encryption.

Public Key Encryption. The **public key encryption** technique uses two different keys: one for encoding the message, the other for decoding it. The encoding key is distributed to all possible users of the network. If this key falls into the hands of a computer criminal, it can be used only to encode messages, not to decode them. The decoding key thus becomes the focal point of control. This key is retained by the security officer in the organization and is distributed only to the user with the authority to decode the message.

Digital Certificates/Digital Signatures. A **digital certificate** is an attachment to an electronic message used for security purposes. The most common use of a digital certificate is to verify that a user sending a message is who he or she claims to be, and to provide the receiver with the means to encode a reply.

An individual wishing to send an encrypted message applies for a digital certificate from a Certificate Authority (CA). The CA issues an encrypted digital certificate containing the applicant's public key and a variety of other identification information. The CA makes its own public key readily available through print publicity or perhaps on the Internet.

The recipient of an encrypted message uses the CA's public key to decode the digital certificate attached to the message, verifies it as issued by the CA and then obtains the sender's public key and identification information held within the certificate. With this information, the recipient can send an encrypted reply. The most widely used standard for digital certificates is X.509.

A **digital signature** is a code that can be attached to an electronically transmitted message that uniquely identifies the sender. Like a written signature, the purpose of a digital signature is to guarantee that the individual sending the message really is who he or she claims to be. Digital signatures are especially important for electronic commerce and are a key component of most authentication schemes. To be effective, digital signatures must be unforgeable. There are a number of different encryption techniques to guarantee this level of security.

Business Recovery Plan

A **business recovery plan** (also known as disaster recovery plan—DRP) is an effective control for e-commerce firms. The risks are high that someone may deface the Web site, destroy it, invade it, steal from it, etc., and the firm needs to have a good control on how to reestablish business activity should a significant adverse event occur. See Chapter 2 for more details on DRP.

Incident Response Plan

A similar technique is an **incident response plan**. Should the most-feared event occur, some intruder will have stolen a significant asset (information or money), or stopped business activity (e.g., DoS). In either case, the public will eventually find out something significantly adverse occurred. Rather than letting the media dictate information, or relying on a fickle public, a firm would be better suited to prepare and plan for such an event in some detail. Then if it should occur, processes and communications will have been thought out well in advance, and without the pressure of the catastrophe.

Controlling Exposures from Equipment Failure

This section deals with control techniques designed to limit threats from equipment failure that can disrupt, destroy, or corrupt electrical transactions, databases and computer programs.

Line Errors. The most common problem in data communications is data loss due to **line error**. The bit structure of the message can be corrupted through noise on the communications lines. Noise consists of random signals that can interfere with the message signal when they reach a certain level. Electric motors, atmospheric conditions, faulty wiring, defective components in equipment, or noise spilling over from an adjacent communications channel may cause random signals. If not detected, bit structure changes to transmitted data can be catastrophic to the firm. For example, in the case of a database update program, the presence of line errors can result in incorrect transaction values being posted to the accounts. The following two techniques are commonly used to detect and correct such data errors before they are processed.

Echo Check. The **echo check** involves the receiver of the message returning the message to the sender. The sender compares the returned message with a stored copy of the original. If there is a discrepancy between the returned message and the original, suggesting a transmission error, the message is retransmitted. This technique reduces, by one-half, throughput over communications channels. Full duplex channels, which allow both parties to transmit and receive simultaneously, can increase throughput.

Parity Check. The **parity check** incorporates an extra bit (the parity bit) into the structure of a bit string when it is created or transmitted. Parity can be both vertical and horizontal (longitudinal). Figure 5-27 illustrates both types of parity. Vertical parity adds the parity bit to each character in the message when the characters are originally coded and stored in magnetic form. For example, the number of 1 bits in the bit structure of each character is counted. If the number is even (say there are four 1 bits in a given 8-bit character) the system assigns the parity bit a value of 1. If the number of 1 bits is odd, a 0 parity bit is added to the bit structure.

The concern is that during transmission, a 1 bit will be converted to a 0 bit, or vice versa, thus destroying the bit structure integrity of the character. In other words, the original character is incorrectly presented as a different yet valid character. An error of this sort, if it goes undetected, could have a devastating effect on financial numbers. But this error can be detected at the receiving end by a parity check. The 1 bits are again counted by the system and should always equal an odd number. If a 1 bit is added to or removed from the bit structure during transmission, the number of 1 bits for the character will be even, which would signal that an error has occurred.

FIGURE 5-27

Vertical and Horizontal Parity Using Odd Parity

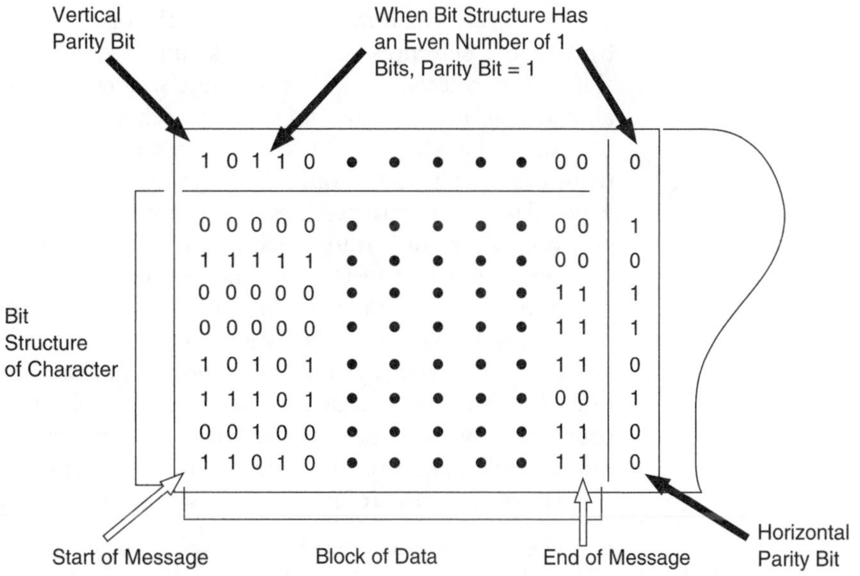

Vertical parity alone cannot detect an error that changes two bits in the structure simultaneously, thus retaining the parity of the character. Some estimates indicate a 40 to 50 percent chance that line noise will corrupt more than one bit within a character. This problem is greatly reduced by using horizontal parity in conjunction with vertical parity. Referring to Figure 5-27, notice the parity bit following each block of characters. The combination of vertical and horizontal parity provides a higher degree of protection from line errors.

AUDIT OBJECTIVES

- *Verify* the security and integrity of the electronic commerce transactions by determining that controls (1) can detect and correct message loss due to equipment failure, (2) can prevent and detect illegal access both internally and from the Internet, and (3) will render useless any data that are successfully captured by a perpetrator.
- *Verify* that backup procedures are sufficient to preserve the integrity and physical security of the databases and other files connected to the network.
- *Determine* that (1) all EDI transactions are authorized, validated, and in compliance with the trading partner agreement; (2) no unauthorized organizations accessed database records; (3) authorized trading partners have access only to approved data; and (4) adequate controls are in place to ensure a complete audit trail of all EDI transactions.

Backup Control for Networks

Data backup in networks is accomplished in several different ways, depending on the network's complexity. In small networks, a single workstation may be assigned the backup and restore functions for the other nodes. As networks grow to include more nodes and increased data sharing, backup is usually assigned at the network server level. Enterprise-level networks can be very large and include multiple servers. These network environments are likely to control mission-critical data, and a server failure could mark disaster for the organization. Because of the large number of users, enterprise-level networks undergo continuous change to accommodate shifts in user needs. In such a dynamic setting, organization management must be able to centrally monitor and control backup procedures.

Restricting access to backup files in enterprise-level networks is a control issue requiring specific attention. The organization's mission-critical backup data are exposed to the same access threats as its production data. Many backup products provide access control features such as encryption and password management. At the very least, user management should ensure that the backup management package under consideration is compatible with the network's existing access control features.

Finally, backup redundancy is advisable in enterprise-level networks. Some top-end products permit dynamic allocation of backup devices and automatic notification of backup status. If an assigned backup device fails, the data are automatically routed to a working device. The backup management system immediately notifies the network administrator of the failure via e-mail or pager.

The procedures are similar to those discussed in previous chapters:

- The auditor should verify that backup is performed routinely and frequently to facilitate the recovery of lost, destroyed, or corrupted data.
- Production databases should be copied at regular intervals (perhaps several times an hour). A balance must be sought between the inconvenience of frequent backup activities and the business disruption caused by excessive reprocessing that is needed to restore the database after a failure.
- The auditor should verify that automatic backup procedures are in place and functioning, and that copies of files and databases are stored off-site for further security.

Transaction Validation

Both the customer and the supplier must establish that a transaction being processed is to (or from) a valid trading partner. This can be accomplished at three points in the process.

- Some VANs have the capability of validating passwords and user ID codes for the vendor by matching these against a valid customer file. Any unauthorized trading partner transactions are rejected by the VAN before they reach the vendor's system.
- Before being converted, the translation software can validate the trading partner's ID and password against a validation file in the firm's database.
- Before processing, the trading partner's application software can validate the transaction by referencing the valid customer and vendor files.

Access Control

The degree of access control in the system will be determined by the trading agreement between the trading partners. For EDI to function smoothly, the trading partners must allow a degree of access to private data files that would be forbidden in a traditional environment. For example, before placing an order, the customer's system may need to access the vendor's inventory files to determine if inventories are available. Also, to prevent the vendor from having to prepare an invoice and the customer having to match it against a purchase order, the partners may agree that the prices on the purchase order will be binding on both parties. In such a scenario, the customer must periodically access the vendor's price list file to keep pricing information current. Alternatively, the vendor may need access to the customer's price list to update prices.

To guard against unauthorized access, each company must establish valid vendor and customer files. Inquiries against databases can thus be validated, and unauthorized attempts at access can be rejected. User authority tables can also be established that specify the degree of access a trading partner is allowed. For example, the partner may be authorized to read inventory or pricing data but not change any values. Again, some VANs can screen and reject unauthorized access attempts by trading partners.

To achieve these control objectives, the auditor may perform the following tests of controls.

Tests of Validation Controls. The auditor should establish that trading-partner identification codes are verified before transactions are processed. To accomplish this objective, the auditor should (1) review agreements with the VAN facility to validate transactions and ensure that information regarding valid trading partners is complete and correct and (2) examine the organization's valid trading-partner file for accuracy and completeness.

Tests of Access Controls. Security over the valid trading-partner file and databases is central to the EDI control framework. The auditor can verify control adequacy in three ways:

1. The auditor should determine that access to the valid vendor or customer file is limited to authorized employees only. The auditor should verify that access to this file is controlled by password and authority tables and that the data are encrypted.
2. The degree of access a trading partner should have to the firm's database records (such as inventory levels and price lists) will be determined by the trading agreement. The auditor should reconcile the terms of the trading agreement against the trading partner's access privileges stated in the database authority table.
3. The auditor should simulate access by a sample of trading partners and attempt to violate access privileges.

Tests of Audit Trail Controls. The auditor should verify that the EDI system produces a transaction log that tracks transactions through all stages of processing. By selecting a sample of transactions and tracing these through the process, the auditor can verify that key data values were recorded correctly at each point.

Audit Procedures

To achieve these audit objectives, the auditor may perform the following tests of controls:

1. Select a sample of messages from the transaction log and examine them for garbled contents caused by line noise. The auditor should verify that all corrupted messages were successfully retransmitted.
2. Review the message transaction logs to verify that all messages were received in their proper sequence.

3. Test the operation of the call-back feature by placing an unauthorized call from outside the installation.
4. Review security procedures governing the administration of data encryption keys.
5. Verify the encryption process by transmitting a test message and examining the contents at various points along the channel between the sending and receiving locations.
6. Review the adequacy of the firewall in achieving the proper balance between control and convenience based on the organization's business objectives and potential risks. Criteria for assessing the firewall effectiveness include
   - *Flexibility.* The firewall should be flexible enough to accommodate new services as the security needs of the organization change.
   - *Proxy services.* Adequate proxy applications should be in place to provide explicit user authentication to sensitive services, applications, and data.
   - *Filtering.* Strong filtering techniques should be designed to deny all services that are not explicitly permitted. In other words, the firewall should specify only those services the user is permitted to access, rather than specifying the services that are denied.
   - *Segregation of systems.* Systems that do not require public access should be segregated from the Internet.
   - *Audit tools.* The firewall should provide a thorough set of audit and logging tools that identify and record suspicious activity.
   - *Probe for weaknesses.* To validate security, the auditor (or a professional security analyst) should periodically probe the firewall for weaknesses just as a computer Internet hacker would do. A number of software products are currently available for identifying security weaknesses.[11]
   - *Review password control procedures.* Ensure that passwords are changed regularly and that weak passwords are identified and disallowed. Reviewing a sample of user passwords taken from the password file can do this. The auditor should also verify that the password file is encrypted and that the encryption key is properly secured.

SUMMARY

Electronic commerce involves the electronic processing and transmission of data. It encompasses many diverse activities, including electronic trading of goods and services, online delivery of digital products, electronic funds transfer (EFT), electronic trading of stocks, and direct consumer marketing. This chapter dealt with the technologies, risks, controls, and audit issues associated with electronic commerce. The topics discussed included private local area networks (LANs), public wide area networks (WANs), electronic data interchange (EDI), and Internet commerce. The chapter began with a review of basic network topologies. The respective features of star, hierarchical, ring, bus, and client-server topologies were each examined. We then turned to communications technologies, which constitute a vital element of network architecture, and focused on a range of important topics. The chapter concluded with a discussion of the risks, controls, and audit of electronic commerce

11 Examples include Security Administrator Tool for Analyzing Networks (SATAN), Internet Security Scanner (ISS), Gabriel, and Courtney.

systems. The risks associated with electronic commerce can be divided into two general areas: risks from unlawful access and risks from equipment failure. Various controls for dealing with these risks were examined. Audit objectives and suggested audit procedures were presented.

Key Terms

access control systems
American National Standards Institute (ANSI)
asynchronous transmission
B2B
B2C
biometrics
bits
bridges
bus topology
business recovery plan
C2C
call-back device
carrier sensing
cathode ray tube
certification authorities (CAs)
challenge-response technique
client-server architecture
cookies
data encryption standard (DES)
denial-of-service attack
digital certificate
digital signal
digital signature
dumb terminals
echo check
electronic data interchange (EDI)
electronic funds transfer (EFT)
extranet
fiber optic cable
firewall
FTP (File Transfer Protocol)
full duplex transmission
gateways
half duplex transmission
hierarchical topology
hubs
incident response plan
intelligent control agents
Internet
Internet-worked networks
intranet
intrusion detection systems (IDS)
IP spoofing
key
line error
local area networks (LANs)
logs
message sequence numbering
modem
modulation
multiplexer
multifaceted password systems
network interface card (NIC)
network operating system (NOS)
network topology
node
packet switching
parity check
peer-to-peer
polling
privacy
private branch exchange (PBX)
private key encryption
protocol
public key encryption
ring topology
routers
screening router
servers
SET (Secure Electronic Transmission)
simplex transmission
smart terminal
SSL (Secure Sockets Layer)
star topology
switches
switching
SYN-ACK (SYNchronize-ACKnowledge)
synchronous transmission
TCP/IP (Transfer Control Protocol/Internet Protocol)

terminals
token passing
transmission errors
twisted-pair cable
value-added banks (VAB)
value-added network (VAN)
Web page
Web sites
wide area networks (WANs)
XBRL (eXtensible Business Reporting Language)
XML (eXtensible Markup Language)
XBRL instance document
XBRL taxonomies

Review Questions

1. What is a network topology?
2. What is a WAN?
3. Distinguish between network bridges and gateways.
4. Define EDI.
5. What is a VAN?
6. What is the X.12 standard?
7. Distinguish between the terms *network*, *network architecture*, and *network topologies*.
8. List four basic network topologies.
9. What purpose does a network interface card serve?
10. Does the star topology foster centralized or distributed data processing? Explain your answer.
11. How do the bus and ring topologies differ?
12. In the client–server mode, which end does the searching of the file, which end does the processing, and what part of the database needs to be locked?
13. What is message packet switching?
14. What are some of the ways in which EDI can generate cost savings for a firm?
15. Explain data collision and discuss three basic methods of avoiding collisions. What are their relative merits?
16. Networks would be inoperable without protocols. Explain the importance of protocols and what functions they perform.
17. Define the Internet.
18. What is the Internet's basic protocol?
19. List and briefly define the privacy conditions inherent to the Safe Harbor agreement

Discussion Questions

1. Explain the purpose of the two elements of the TCP/IP protocol.
2. Discuss the three levels of Internet business models.
3. Discuss risk in an electronic commerce setting.
4. What important factor has contributed to computer crime and what can be done?
5. How can intranet expansion increase risk to an organization?
6. Differentiate between a LAN and a WAN. Do you have either or both at your university or college?
7. What purpose is served by protocols?
8. What is the paradox of networking?
9. As the information superhighway progresses and electronic data interchange increases in popularity, interfaces between organizational computers are becoming a necessity. Discuss what steps are being taken to foster these types of interfaces.
10. Electronic funds transfer is widely used by payroll departments and individuals to pay their personal bills, so why are they so infrequently used by businesses for cash disbursements?
11. EDI systems tied into inventory control models in conjunction with just-in-time inventory systems have been said to be beneficial in many ways; however, a mistake made by one firm in over-ordering can mushroom into

overproduction for many firms. Explain how this can happen.

12. Distinguish between a network-level firewall and an application-level firewall.
13. Discuss the key aspects of the following five seal-granting organizations: Better Business Bureau (BBB), TRUSTe, Veri-Sign, Inc., International Computer Security Association (ICSA), and AICPA/CICA WebTrust.
14. Discuss three audit implications of XBRL.
15. What is a Certification Authority, and what are the implications for the accounting profession?

MULTIPLE-CHOICE QUESTIONS

1. Which of the following statements is correct?
   a. TCP/IP is the basic protocol that permits communication between Internet sites.
   b. TCP/IP controls Web browsers that access the Web.
   c. TCP/IP is the document format used to produce Web pages.
   d. TCP/IP is used to transfer text files, programs, spreadsheets, and databases across the Internet.
   e. TCP/IP is a low-level encryption scheme used to secure transmissions in higher-level (HTTP) format.
2. Which of the following best describes a system of computers that connects the internal users of an organization that is distributed over a wide geographic area?
   a. LAN
   b. Internet
   c. decentralized network
   d. multidrop network
   e. intranet
3. Which of the following statements about the client–server model is correct?
   a. It is best suited to the token-ring topology because the random-access method used by this topology detects data collisions.
   b. It distributes both data and processing tasks to the server node. The client–server model can use the bus or ring topology.
   c. It is most effective when used as a bus topology because its deterministic access method avoids collisions and prevents data loss during transmissions.
   d. It is more efficient than the bus or ring topologies because it transmits an entire file of records to the requesting node rather than only a single record.
   e. It is not used in conjunction with either the bus or ring topologies.
4. Which of the following statements is correct?
   a. A bridge is used to connect a LAN and a WAN.
   b. Packet switching combines the messages of multiple users into a "packet" for transmission. At the receiving end, the packet is disassembled into individual messages and distributed to the user.
   c. The decision to partition a database assumes that no identifiable primary user exists in the organization.
   d. Message switching is used to establish temporary connections between network devices for the duration of a communications session.
   e. A deadlock is a temporary phenomenon that disrupts transaction processing. It will resolve itself when the primary computer completes processing its transaction and releases the data needed by the other nodes.

Problems

1. Encryption

The coded message below is an encrypted message from Brutus to the Roman Senate. It was produced using the Caesar Cipher method in which each letter is shifted by a fixed number of places (determined by the key value).

> OHWV GR MXOLXV RQ PRQGDB PDUFK 48
> GUHVV: WRJD FDVXDO (EBRG)

Required:

Determine the key used to produce the coded message above and decode it.

2. Encryption

Required:

a. Develop a Caesar Cipher-type encryption algorithm with a little more complexity in it. For example, the algorithm could alternatively shift the cleartext letters positive and negative by the amount of the key value. Variations on this are limitless.
b. Select a single digit key.
c. Code a short message using the algorithm and key.
d. Hand in the algorithm, key, cleartext, and ciphertext to your instructor.
e. *Optional:* Your instructor will randomly redistribute to the class the ciphertext messages completed in part 4. You are to decode the message you receive as an additional assignment.

3. Privacy Policies

Required:

Visit 10 Web sites that sell products or services and record the URL of each. Evaluate each site's published privacy policy in terms of the conditions needed for compliance with the State Harbor Agreement. Write a report of your findings.

4. Electronic Data Interchange

The purchase order for one firm is the source document for the sales order of another firm. Consider the following purchase order and sales order data elements stored for two firms. Discuss any differences that may be problematic in transferring information between the two firms.

Purchasing Firm:
GH BETTIS
A Division of Galveston-Houston Corp.
1200 Post Oak Blvd.
P.O. Box 4768
Houston, TX 77637-9877

Data Elements
Vendor Number
Vendor Name
Vendor Address
Vendor City
Vendor State
Vendor Country
Vendor Zip Code
Purchase Order No.
Date
Shipment Destination Code
Vendor Part No.
Item Description
Quantity Ordered
Unit Price
Total

Selling Firm:
Oakland Steel Company
469 Lakeland Blvd.
Chicago, IL 60613-8888

Data Elements
Customer Number
Customer Name
Customer Address
Customer City
Customer State
Customer Country
Customer Zip Code
Purchase Order No.
Sales Order No.
Date

Shipping Company
Vendor Part No.
Item Description
Quantity Ordered
Unit Price
Total
Discount Offered
Tax
Freight Charges

5. **Electronic Fraud**

In a recent financial fraud case, city employees in Brooklyn, New York, accessed electronic databases to defraud the city of $20 million. Several employees in collusion with the former deputy tax collector completely erased or reduced $13 million in property taxes and $7 million in accrued interest owed by taxpayers. In exchange for this service, the taxpayers paid the employees involved bribes of 10 to 30 percent of their bills.

Required:

Discuss the control techniques that could prevent or detect this fraud.

Projects

1. **XBRL**

John Ozment, director of special projects and analysis for Ozment's company, is responsible for preparing corporate financial analyses and monthly statements, and for reviewing and presenting to upper management the financial impacts of proposed strategies. Data for such financial analyses are obtained from operations and financial databases through direct queries by Ozment's department staff. Reports and charts for presentations are then prepared by hand and typed. Multiple copies are then prepared and distributed to various users. The pressure on Ozment's group has intensified as demand for more and more current information increases. A solution to this reporting problem must be found.

The systems department wants to develop a proprietary software package to produce the reports automatically. The project would require a considerable programming investment by the company. Ozment is concerned about the accuracy, completeness, and currency of data in automatically produced reports. He has heard about a reporting system called XBRL and wonders whether a new system based on this technology would not be more effective and reliable.

Required:

a. Research the current state of XBRL and determine if this technology is appropriate for internal reporting projects such as this.
b. Identify the enhancements to current information and reporting that the company could realize by using XBRL.
c. Discuss any data integrity, internal control, and reporting concerns associated with XBRL.

2. **Privacy**

Required:

Visit 10 Web sites that sell products or services and record the URL of each. Evaluate each site's published privacy policy in terms of the conditions need for compliance with the Safe Harbor Agreement. Write a report of your findings.

CASES

1. Internal Controls Assessment and Electronic Data Interchange

Gresko Toys Factory

(Prepared by Robertos Karahannas, Lehigh University)

Gresko Toys was started in the early 1960s by Mr. and Mrs. Gresko. Initially, the company was small and few toys were produced. The talent and skills of Mr. Gresko were by far the major assets of the company. Toys then were mainly made of wood and had few or no electronic parts; they were mainly manually operated and included toy cars, several kinds of dolls, and toy guns. Gresko toys became part of the Pennsylvania tradition. Kids loved them and parents had no choice but to buy them.

Gresko toys quickly expanded, and by 1969 it reported a sales volume of $400,000, $50,000 of which was profit. Such profits caught the attention of other businesspeople, who began entering the market. The innovative spirit of some competitors through the introduction of fancy, battery-operated toys stole some of Gresko's market share. As the competition became more intense, the Greskos saw their market share declining even further. Children liked battery-operated toys.

Mr. Gresko saw this as both a threat and a challenge. He would not give up, however. He knew that he needed better machinery to make competitive toys. With a loan from the local bank and his savings, he sought and bought what he needed. After a period of training and test marketing, Gresko toys were again in the market, boosting sales. The company was generating orders that the factory could not handle. The workforce rose from a low of 50 to a high of 350. Most of the workforce was on the factory floor. More equipment was purchased, and the company has been expanding since then.

Today, the company sells $20 million worth of toys per year. The president of the company is Mrs. Gresko. Mr. Gresko felt that he should be on the factory floor managing production. Under him are the purchasing agent supervising a buyer, the warehouse manager managing two inventory clerks, a chief engineer, and a supervisor who is in charge of the factory workers. The controller of the company is Randi, the Greskos' elder daughter. An accounting clerk, a cashier, and a personnel manager work for her. Finally, Bob, the Greskos' only son, is the sales manager. A credit manager and two salespeople work for him.

Company Information

At present, the company's profit margin is 9 percent, only 2 percent below the industry average. According to Mr. Gresko, $850,000 in sales was lost last year due to insufficient inventory of parts. Due to the seasonal nature of the market and the short popularity span of most toys, Gresko customers require fast delivery of the ordered toys; if the parts are not available, it takes at least two weeks to get the paperwork ready, order the parts, and have them delivered by the suppliers. Some customers cannot wait that long; others order the toys and subsequently cancel the order if it takes too long to complete. Often orders are accepted on the assumption that the parts are readily available in the warehouse; when they are not, orders are delayed for weeks. A missing part not only delays an order but also the whole assembly line.

To alleviate the problem, many parts are rushed in, thus raising tremendously the cost of the toys. The fine quality of the products allows for slight price increases to make up for part of the extra cost, but customers have already complained about such price fluctuations.

The Greskos are on good terms with their suppliers. After all, the market is so competitive that a reliable supplier is crucial to a firm's survival. Most of their major suppliers are located in Pennsylvania, where the Greskos have about 35 percent of the market share. However, those suppliers deal with the Greskos' competitors as well. There are about a dozen suppliers with whom the Greskos deal; eight of them supply about 95 percent of all inventory parts.

Even though good supplier relations are crucial to Gresko Toys, suppliers have often complained about Gresko's promptness in paying. The Greskos demand on-time delivery; the payment of the supplier invoice, however, is usually not timely. Mr. Gresko said that he does not have the time to run from the factory to the accounting department to make sure payments are on time. Late payments, however, also mean a loss of the 2 percent discount offered by the suppliers for early payment.

Besides resulting in lost sales, insufficient inventory of parts also delays the whole assembly line. Workers spend much time switching jobs. A just-in-time inventory system would, according to Mr. Gresko, be more appropriate for the factory. If the parts were available in the warehouse, the machines could be set up on an assembly-line fashion and operated on scheduled runs. But the fact that the necessary parts are frequently missing, forcing production to switch to another job, is a major obstacle to a just-in-time inventory system.

The Purchasing Cycle

Gresko Toys is very involved in purchasing the parts used in the production of toys. The company uses a periodic inventory system. When sales orders are received, Bob Gresko sends a copy to the production floor. This copy is used to trigger production as well as to indicate the potential need of parts not available in inventory. The inventory clerks search for parts; when parts are out of stock, the inventory clerks issue two copies of a purchase requisition. This requisition is approved by Mr. Gresko before a purchase order is issued. One copy is sent to the purchasing manager and the other to the accounting department.

The buyer checks the suppliers' prices for the needed parts. Based on cost as well as past experience with a particular supplier, two suppliers are recommended. The purchasing manager subsequently decides on the supplier, and a purchase order is issued. Four copies of the purchase order are issued. The first copy is sent to the supplier, the second is filed by the purchasing manager, the third is sent to the warehouse, and the fourth is sent to the accounting department. All purchase order copies are filed by supplier number.

Approximately a week after the initiation of the purchase, the parts are received. The warehouse manager along with the inventory clerks inspect and count the received parts. The purchase order copy previously received by the purchasing manager is used as the basis of comparison. A receiving report in three parts is prepared. If prices and quantities received agree with those ordered and with the information on the packing slip received by the carrier, the parts are accepted. If any differences exist, Mr. Gresko is called in to decide whether to accept or reject the parts. On many occasions, acceptance of parts will be delayed for days until the suppliers are informed and an agreement is reached.

One copy of the receiving report is sent to the purchasing manager and another to the accounting department. The original copy is kept at the warehouse. The accounting clerk files the receiving report along with the purchase requisition and the purchase order by supplier number. The clerk also prepares the necessary journal entry and credits the related supplier in the subsidiary ledger. When the supplier sends the invoice, the accounting clerk matches the information to the purchase requisition, purchase order, and receiving report and prepares a disbursement voucher. This voucher is used for two purposes. It initiates the journal entry for the disbursement of cash, and it is used by the cashier to issue a check. Randi Gresko, as well as Mrs. Gresko, must sign the checks before they are sent to the suppliers.

Electronic Data Interchange

In search of anything that could improve the present system at the Gresko Toys factory, Mr. Gresko came across the electronic data interchange (EDI) system. One of his suppliers had attended a conference on EDI and had supplied Mr. Gresko with the conference material. Looking at the present system, Mr. Gresko tried to find EDI applications that would benefit the company's operations and at the same time improve its financial position.

For EDI to be implemented, certain databases will need to be established. An inventory master file with all relevant information is the key to the system. Predetermined order quantities and minimum inventory levels will need to be set for each item based on forecasts. At the warehouse, the inventory clerks will be constantly updating this database. When inventory levels drop below acceptable levels, an EDI purchase requisition will be issued to the purchasing department.

A supplier master file with related information on supplier performance will be accessed to identify potential suppliers. Depending on how advanced the system is, the computer or the purchasing manager will choose the proper supplier and issue an EDI order. This means that the factory's suppliers will also need to be using EDI.

Various ways of developing EDI links with suppliers are available. In the Gresko case, developing an independent system seems more appropriate; it is cheaper and perhaps easier to convince suppliers to join in. Software is readily available in the market and is easy to set up. Someone, however, should help set up the EDI links with the suppliers.

Once an EDI order is issued, the supplier will receive the message instantaneously. The open purchase order will be kept in a database until the receipt of the parts. Any changes to the order can be made by accessing the particular transmitted order and making the change. Suppliers can send the parts as well as their invoices more quickly. An EDI invoice can be sent to the Gresko factory upon shipment.

On arrival of the parts, the receiving clerk will prepare a receiving report and file it in a receiving database file. This report will be used to verify prices by accessing the purchase order. Credit terms, volume discounts, trade allowances, and other adjustments to quoted prices can be settled through EDI transmitted messages. If adjustments due to disagreements occur, the transaction is entered into the adjusted database file. The inventory master file is also updated, and the open purchase order is closed. In addition, the supplier history file and the accounts payable file are updated, and an evaluated receipts settlement (ERS) is established.

An ERS is a database containing records to be used for the payment of suppliers. The EDI order is matched against the receiving and adjusted database files. Such a comparison creates a payment input file that indicates the scheduled payment date within which any discount can be obtained, the latest possible payment date, and the remittance record for such payments.

At the beginning of every day, the treasurer (who presently does not exist) should receive a listing of the payment input file; this listing will indicate what has to be paid and when. The treasurer will initiate an EDI payment pending the approval of Mrs. Gresko. Upon approval and the transmission of the payment, the supplier records as well as the accounts payable records will be automatically updated. For an electronic funds transfer to occur, the banks that serve Gresko and its suppliers will also need to be using EDI. If such intermediary banks are not using EDI, Gresko and its suppliers will need to rely on a manual system of cash disbursement to settle their transactions.

Conclusion

Mr. Gresko has hired you to look at the present accounting system and his suggested EDI implementation plan. He wants you to identify the problem areas and look into the feasibility of setting up EDI links with the company's suppliers.

Required:

a. Draw a document flowchart of the present accounting system at Gresko.
b. What control problems, if any, exist in the accounting system?
c. Draw a document flowchart of the accounting system of the Gresko Toys factory using EDI as suggested by Mr. Gresko.
d. Do some research on your own. What EDI options, other than the one suggested by Mr. Gresko, are available to the Gresko Toys factory?
e. Discuss the possible implementation of an EDI system at the Gresko Toys factory. What areas should Mr. Gresko concentrate on, and what are the related issues associated with implementing EDI at the factory?

2. Santa'sAttic.com

Santa'sAttic.com is an online retailer/manufacturer of children's toys. Its main competitors are larger e-commerce toy companies including Amazon.com; Yahoo Shopping, which includes ToysRUs.com and KBKids.com; and all of the other retail stores with online shopping. It has a low market share compared to the industry leaders, and is possibly a victim of Internet fraud. The CEO of Santa'sAttic.com has noticed that the level of accounts receivable has been quite high in comparison to prior years. He is wondering if this is a sign of weak internal controls. He has also heard through the grapevine that some of his customers were noticing unauthorized charges on their credit cards, and is wondering if there may be online security issues to deal with as well. For this reason, you have been contacted to help Santa'sAttic.com restructure its company to prevent possible company failure.

Santa'sAttic.com employs 100 individuals, 75 of whom work directly on the manufacturing line and 25 of whom hold administrative positions. Its customer base consists mainly of individuals, but also smaller toy stores, day care centers, and schools. Santa'sAttic.com works on a cash basis with its customers and accepts all major credit cards. It has running credit balances with all of its suppliers. Its credit terms are 2/10 n30. Santa'sAttic.com currently has only one warehouse, which is located in Cooperstown, New York. Being the technical genius that he is, the vice president of marketing took it upon himself to design the company Web site. The Web site has pages where customers can view all of the products and prices. There is a virtual shopping cart available for each customer once he or she has set up a demographical information account. A customer choosing to make a purchase simply clicks on the direct link to the shopping cart from the desired product and proceeds to the checkout. Here the customer is prompted to choose a payment method and enter the shipping address. Once this information has been entered, the customer chooses a shipping method. All shipping is done through U.S. Mail, UPS, Federal Express, Airborne Express, or Certified Mail. The customer is then informed of the total price and the date to expect shipment.

Within the purchasing system, Santa'sAttic.com purchases raw materials for production, such as plastics, wood, metal, and certain fabrics. There is no formal purchasing department at Santa'sAttic.com. Judy, the inventory clerk in the warehouse department, is responsible for all purchasing activity. Within the warehouse department, Judy has access to the inventory records and knows when certain materials have to be repurchased. If materials are needed, she prepares a single purchase requisition and also five copies of the purchase order form. Judy includes all of the necessary information on all copies of the form, including the material to be purchased, the price of the material, the quantity needed, and the requested delivery date. Once completed, two copies of the form are sent to the vendor along with the order. One is placed in the open purchase order file in the warehouse, and one is used to update the inventory records that are also kept within the warehouse department. The final copy is forwarded to the receiving department.

The materials are received by Harry, the receiving clerk, who creates four copies of a receiving report based on the packing slip and purchase order information. Two of these receiving reports are forwarded to the warehouse, where one is used to update inventory records and the other is filed. One copy of the receiving report is also maintained within the receiving department and is filed along with the packing slip and the purchase order. The final copy is sent to the accounts payable department, where it is reconciled with the vendor invoice.

Once the receiving report and the vendor invoice are reconciled in the accounts payable department, the liability is posted to the purchases journal and the total amount due is paid to the vendor. Finally, both the receiving report and the invoice are filed within the accounts payable department and the liability is posted to the general ledger by Joanna, the accounts payable clerk.

Santa'sAttic.com's production workers each have timecards that they punch at a punch-in station in the morning when they arrive, and again in the evening when they leave. The punch-in station is located at the entrance to the plant and is not monitored. At the end of the week, the supervisor authorizes the timecards by reviewing them and signing them, and then sends the timecards to cash disbursements. Supervisors do not keep their own attendance records. Rose, in cash disbursements, receives the timecards and reconciles them with personnel records on the company database to verify the timecards for accuracy. All personnel records are maintained in a database. Access to the database is very restricted. Personnel can update the records only once a year. Rose's only view displays employee demographic information and does not allow access to salary information. Rose prepares the paychecks and signs them. She then prepares the payroll register using only information gained from the timecards. Sally in accounts payable receives a copy of the payroll register and uses it to update the general ledger. Accounts payable receives no information besides the payroll register. Rose, in cash disbursements, hands the prepared paychecks to the supervisors of each department for distribution. All checks are written directly from the company's only cash account. Supervisors distribute the checks directly to the employees and themselves.

Engaging in electronic commerce has exposed Santa'sAttic.com to a whole new nature of risks within its real-time revenue cycle. A customer has the option of paying for the product by credit card or personal check. After credit card information is entered, it becomes attached to the customer's e-mail file. This information includes the type of card, the customer's name as it appears on the card, the credit card number, and the expiration date. Once an order is placed, an employee reviews the order in question, verifies credit, and enters the transaction into Santa'sAttic.com's main database.

The main problem with this system is that orders have been placed with the company, but the customers in question honestly deny ever submitting orders. It turned out that many of these orders had been placed by their children, without the customers' knowledge. The children were able to gain access to their parents' accounts after the system recognized cookies in the hard drives. When the children went to the Web site, the page recognized them as the users of the account and gave them authorized access to make purchases.

Another problem with the information in the revenue cycle has been that hackers have been able to enter the database and obtain information concerning customers. This unauthorized access has sent top management in a frenzy knowing that their customer information is insecure.

Required:

a. Discuss the control and security weaknesses in this system.
b. Make specific recommendations for improving controls.

Appendix

Issues of Increasing Importance to the Accounting Profession

The issues discussed in this chapter carry many implications for auditors and the public accounting profession. As key functions such as inventory procurement, sales processing, shipping notification, and cash disbursements are performed automatically, digitally, and in real time, auditors are faced with the challenge of developing new techniques for assessing control adequacy and verifying the occurrence and accuracy of economic events. The following describes issues of increasing importance to auditors in the digital commerce age.

Seals of Assurance

In response to consumer demand for evidence that a Web-based business is trustworthy, a number of "trusted" third-party organizations are offering *seals of assurance* that businesses can display on their Web site home pages. To legitimately bear the seal, the company must show that it complies with certain business practices, capabilities, and controls. This section reviews six seal-granting organizations: *Better Business Bureau (BBB), TRUSTe, Veri-Sign, Inc., International Computer Security Association (ICSA), AICPA/CICA WebTrust*, and *AICPA/CICA SysTrust.*

Better Business Bureau

The Better Business Bureau (BBB) is a nonprofit organization that has been promoting ethical business practices through self-regulation since 1912. The BBB has extended its mission to the Internet through a wholly owned subsidiary called BBBOnline, Inc. To qualify for the BBBOnline seal an organization must do the following:

- Become a member of the BBB.
- Provide information about the company's ownership, management, address, and phone number. This is verified by a physical visit to the company's premises.
- Be in business for at least one year.
- Promptly respond to customer complaints.
- Agree to binding arbitration for unresolved disputes with customers.

The assurance provided by BBBOnline relates primarily to concern about business policies, ethical advertising, and consumer privacy. BBBOnline does not verify controls over transaction processing integrity and data security issues.

TRUSTe

Founded in 1996, TRUSTe is a nonprofit organization dedicated to improving consumer privacy practices among Internet businesses and Web sites. To qualify to display the TRUSTe seal the organization must do the following:

- Agree to follow TRUSTe privacy policies and disclosure standards.
- Post a privacy statement on the Web site disclosing the type of information being collected, the purpose for collecting information, and with whom it is shared.
- Promptly respond to customer complaints.
- Agree to site compliance reviews by TRUSTe or an independent third party.

TRUSTe addresses consumer privacy concerns exclusively and provides a mechanism for posting consumer complaints against it members. If a member organization is found to be out of compliance with TRUSTe standards, its right to display the trust seal may be revoked.

Veri-Sign, Inc.

Veri-Sign, Inc. was established as a for-profit organization in 1995. Veri-Sign, Inc. provides assurance regarding the security of transmitted data. The organization does not verify security of stored data or address concerns related to business policies, business processes, or privacy. Their mission is to "provide digital certificate solutions that enable trusted commerce and communications." Their products allow customers to transmit encrypted data and verify the source and destination of transmissions. Veri-Sign, Inc. issues three classes of certificates to individuals, businesses, and organizations. To qualify for class three certification the individual, business, or organization must provide a third-party confirmation of name, address, telephone number, and Web site domain name.

ICSA

The International Computer Security Association (ICSA) established its Web Certification Program in 1996. ICSA certification addresses data security and privacy concerns. It does not deal with concerns about business policy and business processes. Organizations that qualify to display the ICSA seal have undergone an extensive review of firewall security from outside hackers. Organizations must be recertified on an annual basis and undergo at least two surprise checks each year.

AICPA/CICA WebTrust

The AICPA and CICA established the WebTrust program in 1997. To display the AICPA/CICA WebTrust seal the organization undergoes an examination according to the AICPA's Standards for Attestation Engagements, No. 1, by a specially Web-certified CPA or CA. The examination focuses on the areas of business practices (policies), transaction integrity (business process), and information protection (data security). The seal must be renewed every 90 days.

AICPA/CICA SysTrust

In July 1999, the AICPA/CICA introduced an exposure draft describing a new assurance service called SysTrust. It is designed to increase management, customer, and trading partner confidence in systems that support entire businesses or specific processes. The assurance service involves the public accountant evaluating the system's reliability against four essential criteria: availability, security, integrity, and maintainability.

The potential users of SysTrust are trading partners, creditors, shareholders, and others who rely on the integrity and capability of the system. For example, Virtual Company is considering outsourcing some of its vital functions to third-party organizations. Virtual needs assurance that the third parties' systems are reliable and adequate to provide the contracted services. As part of the outsourcing contract, Virtual requires the servicing organizations to produce a clean SysTrust report every three months.

In theory, the SysTrust service will enable organizations to differentiate themselves from their competitors. Those organizations that undergo a SysTrust engagement will be perceived as competent service providers and trustworthy. They will be more attuned to the risks in their environment and equipped with the necessary controls to deal with the risks.

PRIVACY VIOLATION

Privacy pertains to the level of confidentiality employed by an organization in managing customer and trading partner data. Privacy applies also to data collected by Web sites from visitors who are not customers. Specific concerns include the following:

- Does the organization have a stated privacy policy?
- What mechanisms are in place to assure the consistent application of stated privacy policies?
- What information on customers, trading partners, and visitors does the company capture?
- Does the organization share or sell its customer, trading partner, or visitor information?
- Can individuals and business entities verify and update the information captured about them?

The growing reliance on Internet technologies for conducting business has placed the spotlight on **privacy violation** as a factor detrimental to a client entities' existence. In response to this threat, several firms have developed assurance services for evaluating their client's *privacy violation risk*.[12] A KPMG white paper examines the importance customers place on their privacy. The paper suggests that developing a set of privacy protection policies may prove to be a significant differentiation factor for commercial companies. As such, particular care needs to be exerted by auditor's engaged in certifying management's practices and established privacy policy.

The importance of privacy is reasserted by the Safe Harbor agreement implemented in 1995. The two-way agreement between the United States and the European Union establishes standards for information transmittal. Approved by the European Commission in July 2000, the Safe Harbor principles essentially enable U.S. companies to do business in the European Union by establishing what is deemed to be an "adequate" level of privacy protection. Although the document is still evolving, it establishes that companies need to enter the Safe Harbor Agreement or provide evidence that they are abiding to the privacy regulations set forth in it. Noncompliant organizations may effectively be banned from doing business in the European Union. Compliance with the Safe Harbor Act requires that a company meet six conditions:[13]

---

12 "A New Covenant with Stakeholders: Managing Privacy as a Competitive Advantage," *Privacy Risk Management*, 2001 KPMG LLP, the U.S. member firm of KPMG International, a Swiss association, pp. 22–23.

13 *Ibid.*

1. *Notice.* Organizations must provide individuals with clear notice of "the purposes for which it collects and uses information about them, the types of third parties to which it discloses the information, and how to contact the company with inquiries or complaints."
2. *Choice.* Before any data is collected, an organization must give its customers the opportunity to choose whether to share their sensitive information (e.g., data related to factors such as health, race, or religion).
3. *Onward transfer.* Unless they have the individual's permission to do otherwise, organizations may share information only with those third parties that belong to the Safe Harbor Agreement or follow its principles.
4. *Security and data integrity.* Organizations need to ensure that the data they maintain are accurate, complete, and current, and thus reliable, for use. They must also ensure the security of the information by protecting it against loss, misuse, unauthorized access, disclosure, alteration, and destruction.
5. *Access.* Unless they would be unduly burdened or would violate the rights of others, organizations must give individuals "access to personal data about themselves and provide an opportunity to correct, amend, or delete such data."
6. *Enforcement.* Organizations must "enforce compliance, provide recourse for individuals who believe their privacy rights have been violated, and impose sanctions on their employees and agents for noncompliance."

Audit Implications of XBRL

Although the potential benefits of XBRL and associated Web technologies have been extensively researched, little attention has been given to the audit implications of using XBRL. Areas of specific concern include

- *Taxonomy creation.* Taxonomy may be generated incorrectly, resulting in an incorrect mapping between data and taxonomy elements that could result in material misrepresentation of financial data. Controls must be designed and in place to ensure the correct generation of XBRL taxonomies.
- *Validation of instance documents.* As noted, once the mapping is complete and tags have been stored in the internal database, XBRL instance documents (reports) can be generated. Independent verification procedures need to be established to validate the instance documents to ensure that appropriate taxonomy and tags have been applied before posting to the Web server.
- *Audit scope and timeframe.* Currently, auditors are responsible for printed financial statements and other materials associated with the statements. What will be the impact on the scope of auditor responsibility as a consequence of real time distribution of financial statements across the Internet? Should auditors also be responsible for the accuracy of other related data that accompany XBRL financial statements, such as textual reports?

Continuous Auditing

Continuous auditing techniques need to be developed that will enable the auditor to review transactions at frequent intervals or as they occur. To be effective, such an approach will need to employ **intelligent control agents** (computer programs) that embody auditor-defined heuristics that search electronic transactions for anomalies. Upon finding unusual events, the control agent will first search for similar events to identify a pattern. If the anomaly cannot be explained, the agent alerts the auditor with an alarm or exception report.

Electronic Audit Trails

In an EDI environment, electronic transactions are generated automatically by a trading partner's computer, relayed across a **value added network (VAN)**, and processed by the client's computer without human intervention. In this setting audits may need to be extended to all critical systems of the parties involved in the transactions Validating such transactions may involve the client, its trading partners, and the VAN that connect them. This could take the form of direct review of these systems or collaboration between the auditors of the trading partners and VANs.

Confidentiality of Data

As system designs become increasingly open to accommodate trading partner transactions, mission-critical information is at the risk of being exposed to intruders both from inside and outside the organization. Accountants need to understand the cryptographic techniques used to protect the confidentiality of stored and transmitted data. They need to assess the quality of encryption tools used and the effectiveness of key management procedures used by certification authorities. Furthermore, the term *mission-critical* defines a set of information that extends beyond the traditional financial concerns of accountants. This broader set demands a more holistic approach to assessing internal controls that ensure the confidentiality of data.

Authentication

In traditional systems, the business paper on which it was written determines the authenticity of a sales order from a trading partner or customer. In electronic commerce systems, determining the identity of the customer is not as simple a task. With no physical forms to review and approve, authentication is accomplished through digital signatures and digital certificates. To perform their assurance function, accountants must develop the skill set needed to understand these technologies and their application.

Nonrepudiation

Accountants are responsible for assessing the accuracy, completeness, and validity of transactions that constitute client sales, accounts receivable, purchases, and liabilities. Transactions that can be unilaterally repudiated by a trading partner can lead to uncollected revenues or legal action. In traditional systems, signed invoices, sales agreements, and other physical documents provide proof that a transaction occurred. As with the problem of authentication, electronic commerce systems can also use digital signatures and digital certificates to promote nonrepudiation.

Certification Authority Licensing

The purpose of certification authorities (CA) is to have independent and trusted third parties empowered with responsibility to vouch for the identity of organizations and individuals engaging in Internet commerce. The question then becomes who vouches for the CA? How does one know that the CA who awarded a seal of authenticity to an individual is itself reputable and was meticulous in establishing his or her identity? These questions hold specific implication for the accounting profession. Since they enjoy a high degree of public confidence, public accounting firms are natural candidates for certification authorities.

Data Integrity

A nonrepudiated transaction from an authentic trading partner may still be intercepted and rendered inaccurate in a material way. In a paper-based environment, such alterations are easy to detect. Digital transmissions, however, pose much more of a problem. To assess data integrity, accountants must become familiar with the concept of computing a digest of a document and the role of digital signatures in data transmissions.

A Changing Legal Environment

Accountants have traditionally served their clients by assessing risk (both business and legal) and devising techniques to mitigate and control risk. This risk assessment role is greatly expanded by Internet commerce, whose legal framework is still evolving in a business environment fraught with new and unforeseen risks. To estimate its client's exposure to legal liability in this setting, the public accountant must understand the potential legal implications (both domestic and international) of actions taken by the client's electronic commerce system. The act of creating a Web page from which customers may order goods opens the organization to the national and international business communities and also exposes it to multiple and possibly conflicting legal statutes. Legal issues relating to taxes, privacy, security, intellectual property rights, and libel are of particular concern. For example, if a company has its corporate headquarters and inventory warehouse in one country and its Internet transaction processing systems in another, where did the sale originate for tax purposes?

The legal issues associated with electronic commerce have and will continue to create new opportunities for the profession. Accounting firms will need to provide their clients with rapid and accurate advice on a wide range of legal questions.

CHAPTER

6 Enterprise Resource Planning Systems

LEARNING OBJECTIVES

After studying this chapter, you should:

- Understand the general functionality and key elements of ERP systems.
- Understand the various aspect of ERP configuration including servers, databases, and the use of bolt-on software.
- Understand the purpose of data warehousing as a strategic tool and recognize the issues related to the design, maintenance, and operation of a data warehouse.
- Recognize the risks associated with ERP implementation.
- Be aware of the key considerations related to ERP implementation.
- Understand the internal control and auditing implications associated with ERPs.
- Be able to identify the leading ERP products and be familiar with their distinguishing features.

Until recent years most large and mid-sized organizations designed and programmed custom information systems in-house. This resulted in an array of standalone systems that were designed to the unique needs of specific users. While these systems dealt with their designated tasks efficiently, they did not provide strategic decision support at the enterprise level because they lacked the integration needed for information transfer across organization boundaries. Today the trend in information systems is toward implementing highly integrated enterprise-oriented systems. These are not custom packages designed for a specific organization. Instead, they are generalized systems that incorporate the best business practices in use. Organizations mix and match these prefabricated software components to assemble an **enterprise resource planning (ERP)** system that best meets their business requirements. This means that an organization may need to change the way that it conducts business to take full advantage of the ERP.

This chapter comprises five major sections and an appendix. The first outlines the key features of a generic ERP system by comparing the function and data storage techniques of a traditional flat file or database system to that of an ERP. The second section describes various ERP configurations related to servers, databases and bolt-on software. The third section discusses data warehousing. A data warehouse is a relational or multidimensional database that supports online analytical processing

(OLAP). The fourth section examines risks associated with ERP implementation. The fifth section reviews the internal control and auditing issues related to ERPs. The discussion follows the SAS 78 framework. The chapter appendix reviews the leading ERP software products. Some of the functionality and distinguishing features of these systems are highlighted.

What Is an ERP?

ERP systems are multiple module software packages that evolved primarily from traditional manufacturing resource planning (MRP II) systems. The term ERP was coined by the Gartner Group and has become widely used in recent years. The objective of ERP is to integrate key processes of the organization such as order entry, manufacturing, procurement and accounts payable, payroll, and human resources. By so doing a single computer system can serve the unique needs of each functional area. Designing one system that serves everyone is an undertaking of massive proportions. Under the traditional model each functional area or department has its own computer system optimized to the way that it does its daily business. ERP combines all of these into a single, integrated system that accesses a single database to facilitate the sharing of information and to improve communications across the organization.

To illustrate, consider the traditional model for a manufacturing firm illustrated in Figure 6-1. This company employs a **closed database architecture**, which is similar in concept to the basic flat file model. Under this approach a database management system is used to provide minimal technological advantage over flat file

FIGURE 6-1 **Traditional Information System**

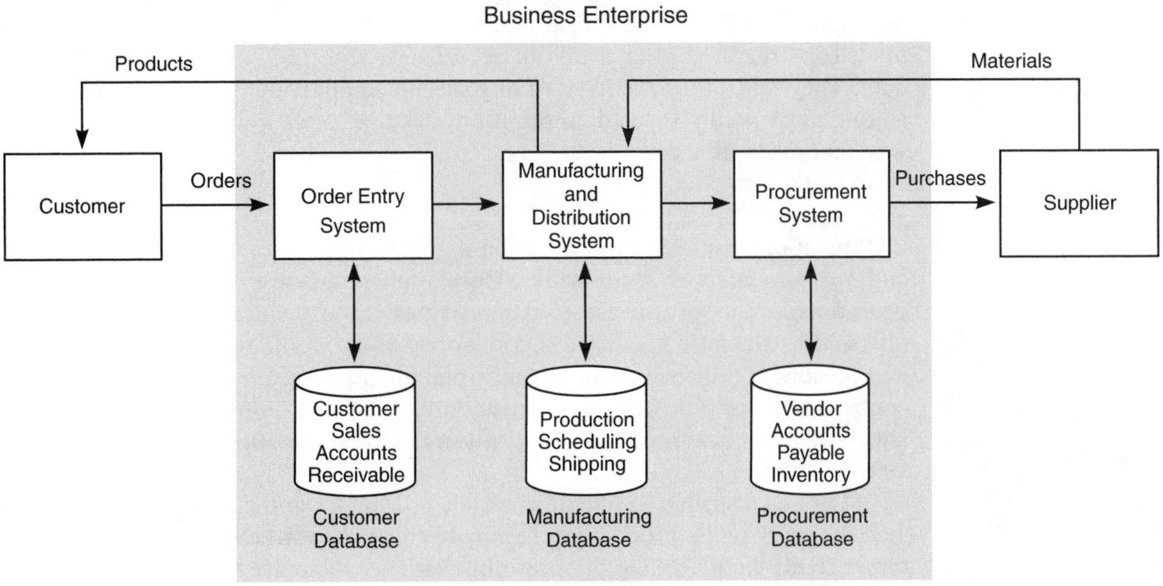

systems. The DBMS is little more than a private but powerful file system. As with the flat file approach, the data remains the property of the application. Thus distinct, separate, and independent databases exist. As is true with the flat file architecture, there is a high degree of data redundancy in a closed database environment.

When a customer places an order, it begins a paper-based journey around the company where it is keyed and rekeyed into the systems of several different departments. These redundant tasks cause delays, lost orders, and promote data entry errors. During transit through the various systems, the status of the order may be unknown at any point in time. For example, responding to a customer query, the marketing department may be unable to look into the production database to determine whether an order has been manufactured and shipped. Instead, the frustrated customer is told, "You will need to call manufacturing." Similarly, the procurement of raw materials from suppliers is not linked to customer orders until they reach the manufacturing stage. This results in delays, as manufacturing awaits the arrival of needed materials, or in excessive investment in inventories to avoid stockouts.

The lack of effective communication between systems in the traditional model is often the consequence of a fragmented systems design process. Each system tends to be designed as a solution to a specific operational problem rather than as part of an overall strategy. Furthermore, since systems designed in-house emerge independently and over time, they are often constructed on different and incompatible technology platforms. Thus special procedures and programs need to be created so that older mainframe systems using flat files can communicate with newer distributed systems that use relational databases. Special software "patches" are also needed to enable commercial systems from different vendors to communicate with each other as well as with custom systems that were developed in-house. While communications between such a hodgepodge of systems is possible, it is highly fragmented and not conducive to efficient operations.

ERP systems support a smooth and seamless flow of information across the organization by providing a standardized environment for a firm's business processes and a common operational database that supports communications. An overview of ERP is presented in Figure 6-2. Data in the operational database are modeled, structured, and stored in accordance with the internal attributes of the data. They remain independent of any specific application. Extensive data sharing among users occurs through application-sensitive views that present the data in a way that meets all user needs.

ERP Core Applications

ERP functionality falls into two general groups of applications: *core applications* and *business analysis applications*. **Core applications** are those applications that operationally support the day-to-day activities of the business. If these applications fail, so does the business. Typical core applications would include but are not limited to sales and distribution, business planning, production planning, shop floor control, and logistics. Core applications are also called *online transaction* processing (OLTP) applications. Figure 6-2 illustrates these functions applied to a manufacturing firm.

Sales and distribution functions handle order entry and delivery scheduling. This includes checking on product availability to ensure timely delivery and verifying customer credit limits. Unlike the previous example, customer orders are entered into the ERP only once. Since all users access a common database, the status of an order

FIGURE 6-2 **ERP System**

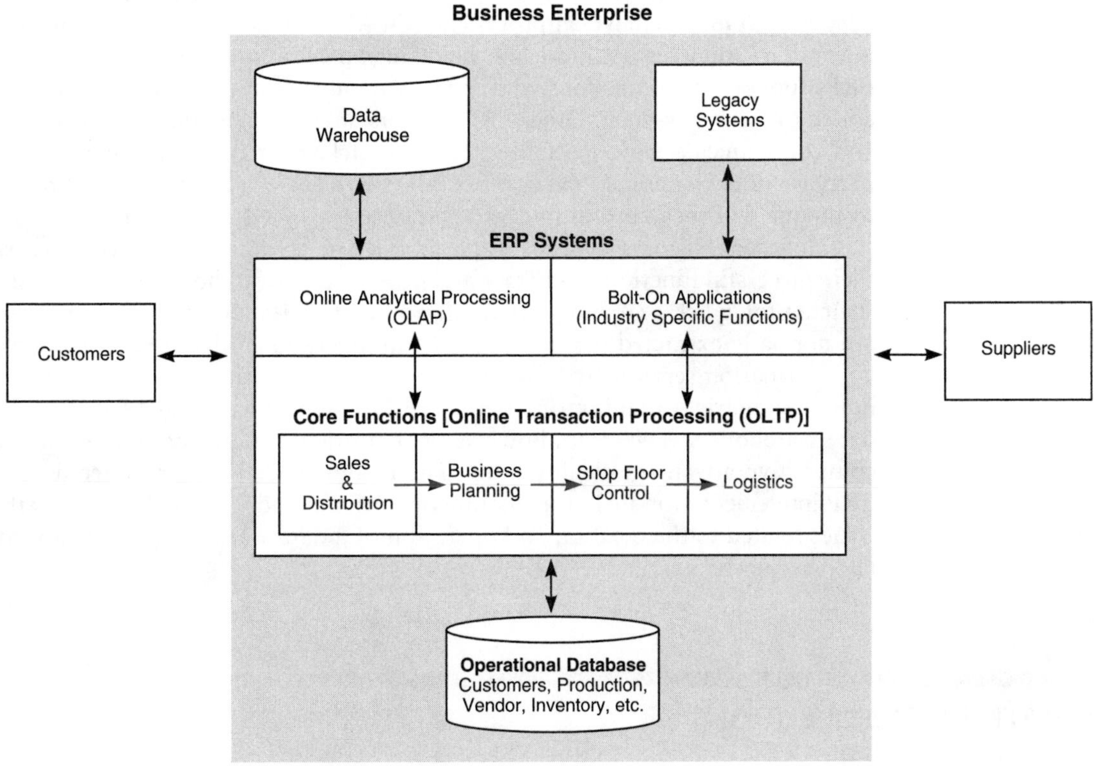

can be determined at any point. In fact, the customer may be able to dial in over the Internet and check the status of the order directly. Such integration reduces manual activities, saves time, and decreases human error.

Business planning consists of forecasting demand, planning product production, and the detailed routing information that describes the sequence and the stages of the actual production process. Capacity planning and production planning can be very complex; therefore, some ERPs provide simulation tools to help managers decide how to avoid shortages in materials, labor, or plant facilities. Once the master production schedule is complete, the data enter the MRP (materials requirements planning) module, which provides three key pieces of information: an exception report, a materials requirements listing, and inventory requisitions. The exception report identifies potential situations such as late delivery of materials that will result in rescheduling production. The materials requirements listing shows the details of vendor shipments and expected receipts of products and components needed for the order. Inventory requisitions are used to trigger material purchase orders to vendors for items not in stock.

Shop floor control involves the detailed production scheduling, dispatching, and job costing activities associated with the actual production process. Finally, the logistics application is responsible for assuring timely delivery to the customer. This consists of inventory and warehouse management, and shipping. Most ERPs also include their procurement activities within the logistics function.

Online Analytical Processing

An ERP is more than simply an elaborate transaction processing system. It is a decision support tool that supplies management with real-time information and permits timely decisions that are needed to improve performance and achieve competitive advantage. **Online analytical processing** (**OLAP**) includes decision support, modeling, information retrieval, ad hoc reporting/analysis, and what-if analysis. Some ERPs support these functions with their own industry-specific modules that can be added to the core system. Other ERP vendors have designed their systems to accept and communicate with specialized *bolt-on* packages that are produced by third-party vendors. Sometimes the user organization's decision support requirements are so unique that they need to integrate in-house legacy systems into the ERP.

However business analysis applications are obtained or derived, central to their successful function is a data warehouse. A **data warehouse** is a database constructed for quick searching, retrieval, ad hoc queries, and ease of use. The data are normally extracted periodically from an operational database or from a public information service. An ERP system could exist without having a data warehouse; similarly, organizations that have not implemented an ERP may deploy data warehouses. The trend, however, is that organizations that are serious about competitive advantage deploy both. The recommended data architecture for an ERP implementation includes separate operational and data warehouse databases. Issues related to the creation and operation of a data warehouse will be examined later in the chapter.

ERP System Configurations

Most ERP systems are based on the **client-server model**, which is discussed in detail in the next chapter. Briefly, the client-server model is a form of network topology in which a user's computer or terminal (the client) accesses the ERP programs and data via a host computer called the server. While the servers may be centralized, the clients are usually located at multiple locations throughout the enterprise. Two basic architectures are the *two-tier model* and the *three-tier model.*

- *Two-Tier Model.* In a typical **two-tier model**, the server handles both application and database duties. Client computers are responsible for presenting data to the user and passing user input back to the server. Some ERP vendors use this approach for local area network (LAN) applications where the demand on the server is restricted to a relatively small population of users. This configuration is illustrated in Figure 6-3.
- *Three-Tier Model.* The database and application functions are separated in the **three-tier model**. This architecture is typical of large ERP systems that use wide area networks (WANs) for connectivity among the users. Satisfying client requests requires two or more network connections. Initially, the client establishes communications with the application server. The application server then initiates a second connection to the database server. Figure 6-4 presents the three-tier model.

OLTP versus OLAP Servers

When implementing an ERP system that will include a data warehouse, a clear distinction needs to be made between the competing types of data processing:

FIGURE 6-3 **Two-Tier Client Server**

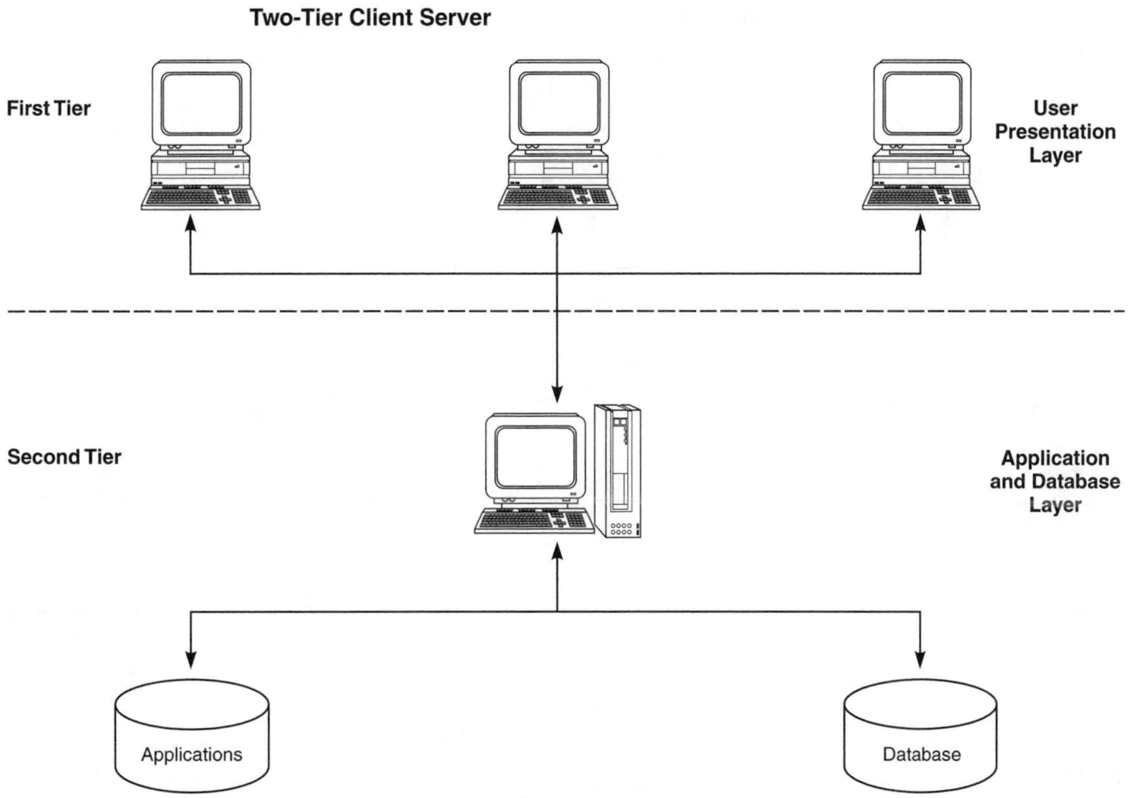

online transaction processing and *online analytical processing*. **Online transaction processing (OLTP)** events consist of large numbers of relatively simple transactions such as updating accounting records that are stored in several related tables. For example, an order entry system retrieves all of the data relating to a specific customer to process a sales transaction. Relevant data are selected from the Customer table, Invoice table, and detail Line Item table. Each table contains an embedded key (i.e., customer number), which is used to relate rows between different tables. The transaction processing activity involves updating the customer's current balance and inserting new records into the Invoice and Line Item tables. The relationships between records in such OLTP transactions are generally simple and only a few records are actually retrieved or updated in a single transaction.

Online analytical processing (OLAP) can be characterized as online transactions that do the following:[1]

- Access very large amounts of data (e.g., several years of sales data).
- Analyze the relationships between many types of business elements such as sales, products, geographic regions, and marketing channels.

1 "Data Mining Techniques," The Queen's University of Belfast, *http://www.pcc.qub.ac.uk/tec/courses/datamining/stu_notes/dm_book_4.html.*

FIGURE 6-4 **Three-Tier Client Server**

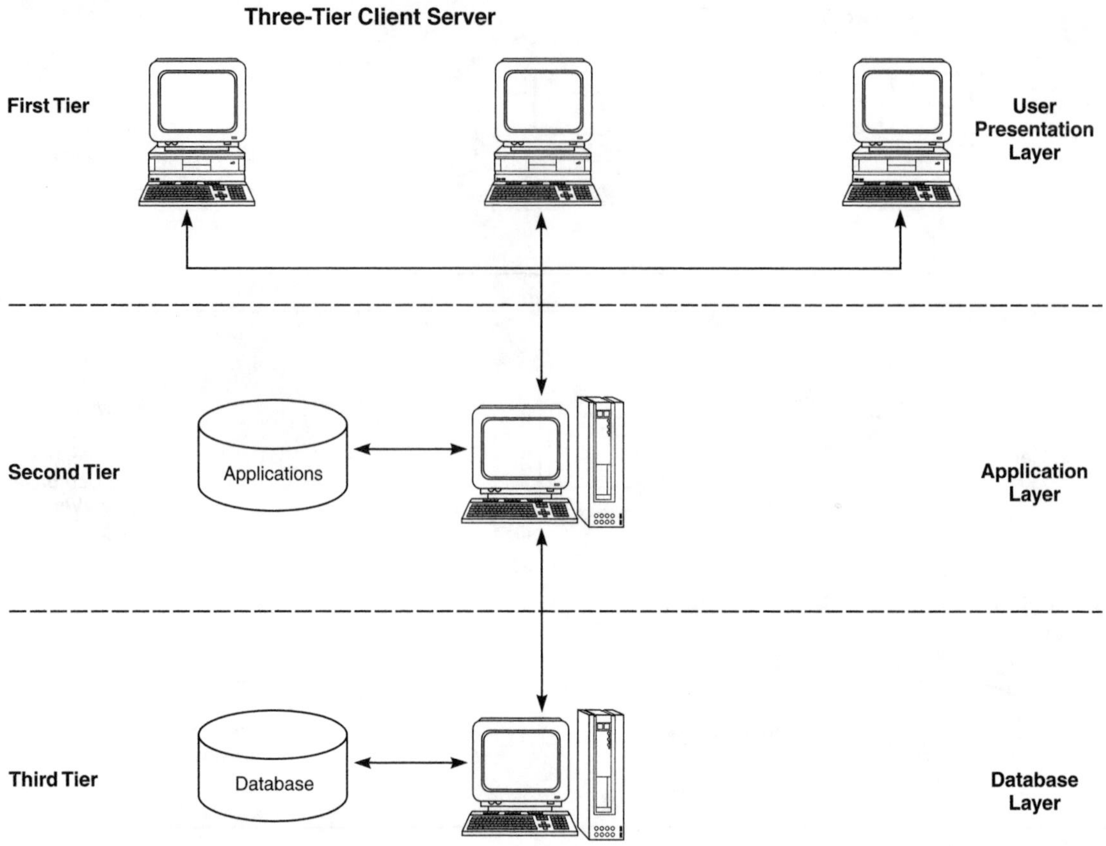

- Involve aggregated data such as sales volumes, budgeted dollars, and dollars spent.
- Compare aggregated data over hierarchical time periods (e.g., monthly, quarterly, yearly).
- Present data in different perspectives such as sales by region, sales by distribution channel, or sales by product.
- Involve complex calculations between data elements, such as expected profit as a function of sales revenue, for each type of sales channel in a particular region.
- Respond quickly to user requests so that they can pursue an analytical thought process without being stymied by system delays.

An example of an OLAP transaction is the aggregation of sales data by region, product type, and sales channel. The OLAP query may need to access vast amounts of sales data over a multiyear period to find sales for each product type within each region. The user can further refine the query to identify sales volume by product for each sales channel within a given region. Finally, the user may decide to perform year-to-year or quarter-to-quarter comparisons for each sales channel. An OLAP application must be able to support this analysis online with rapid response.

The difference between OLAP and OLTP can be summarized as follows. OLTP applications support mission-critical tasks through simple queries of operational databases. OLAP applications support management-critical tasks through analytical investigation of complex data associations that are captured in data warehouses. OLAP and OLTP have specialized requirements that are in direct conflict. Figure 6-5 shows how the client-server architecture enables organizations to deploy separate and specialized application and database servers to resolve these conflicting data management needs. OLAP servers support common analytical operations including *consolidation*, *drill-down*, and *slicing and dicing*.

- **Consolidation** is the aggregation or roll-up of data. For example, sales offices data can be rolled up to districts and districts rolled up to regions.
- **Drill-down** permits the disaggregation of data to reveal the underlying details that explain certain phenomena. For example, the user can drill down from total Sales Returns for a period to identify the actual products returned and the reasons for their return.
- **Slicing and dicing** enables the user to examine data from different viewpoints. One slice of data might show sales within each region. Another slice presents sales by product across regions. Slicing and dicing is often performed along a time axis to depict trends and patterns.

FIGURE 6-5 **OLTP and OLAP Client Server**

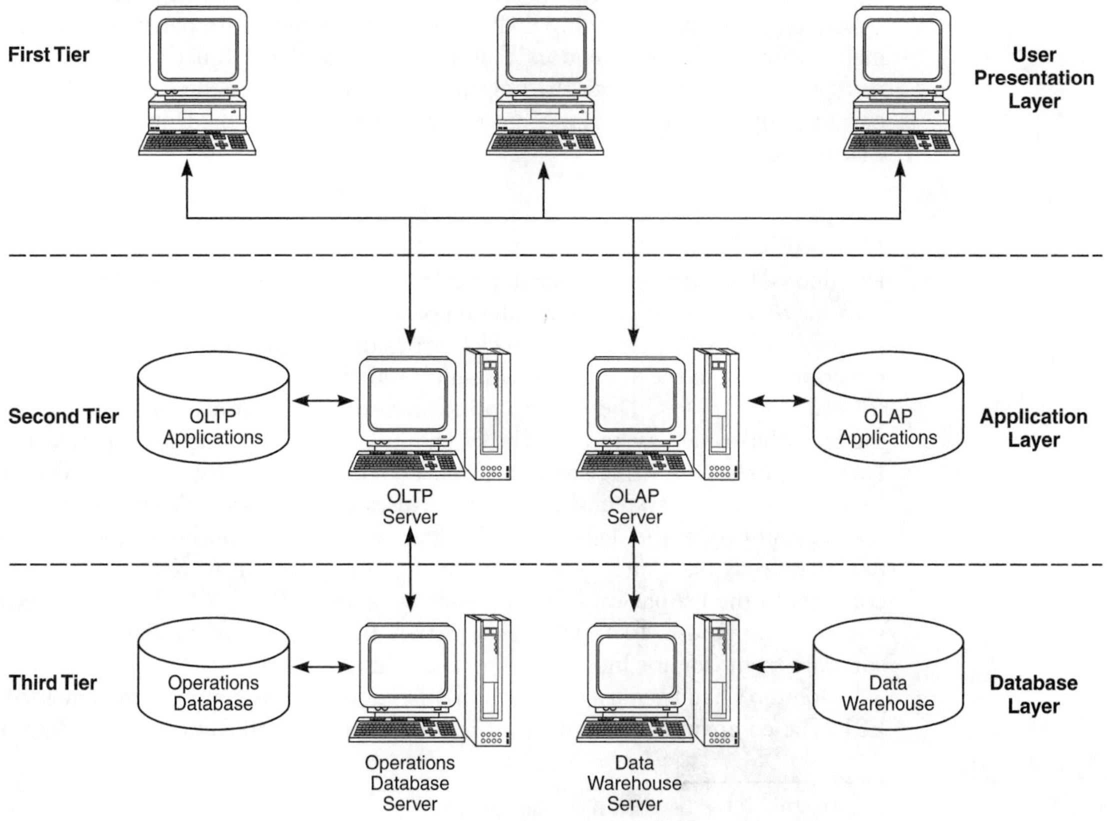

OLAP servers allow users to analyze complex data relationships. The physical database itself is organized in such a way that related data may be rapidly retrieved across multiple dimensions. OLAP database servers thus need to be efficient when storing and processing multidimensional data. Later in the chapter data modeling and storage techniques that improve data warehouse efficiency will be examined. In contrast, relational databases for operations are modeled and optimized to handle OLTP applications. They concentrate on reliability and transaction processing speed, instead of decision support need.

Database Configuration

ERP systems comprise thousands of database tables. Each table is associated with business processes that are coded into the ERP. The ERP implementation team, which includes key users and IT professionals, selects specific database tables and processes by setting switches in the system. Determining how all the switches need to be set for a given configuration requires a deep understanding of the existing processes used in operating the business. Often, however, choosing table settings involves decisions to reengineer the company's processes so that they comply with the best business practices in use. In other words, the company typically changes its processes to accommodate the ERP rather than modifying the ERP to accommodate the company.

Bolt-On Software

Many organizations have found that ERP software alone cannot drive all the processes of the company. These firms use a variety of **bolt-on software** provided by third-party vendors. The decision to use bolt-on software requires careful consideration. Most of the leading ERP vendors have entered into partnership arrangements with third-party vendors that provide specialized functionality. The least risky approach is to choose the bolt-on that is endorsed by the ERP vendor. Some organizations, however, take a more independent approach. Domino's Pizza is a case in point.

Domino's Pizza

Domino's U.S. distribution delivered 338 million pizzas in 1998.[2] The company manufactures an average of 4.2 million pounds of dough per week in its 18 U.S. distribution centers. A fleet of 160 trucks carries the dough along with other food and paper products to the 4,500 U.S. Domino's franchises. Domino's has no cutoff time for ordering supplies. Therefore, a franchise can call and adjust its order even after the truck has rolled away from the distribution center. To help anticipate demand Domino's uses forecasting software from Prescient Systems Inc., which bolts on to its PeopleSoft ERP system. In addition, it uses a system from Manugistics Inc. to schedule and route the delivery trucks. Each truck has an on-board computer system that feeds data into a time-and-attendance system from Kronos Inc., which connects to the PeopleSoft human resources module. Domino's also has an extensive data warehouse. To anticipate its market, Domino's performs data mining with software from Cognos Inc. and Hyperion Solutions Corp.

Domino's had been using these and other applications before it implemented an ERP. The company did not want to retire its existing applications, but discovered

---

2 D. Slater "'The Ties That Bolt,' Enterprise Resource Planning," *CIO Magazine* (April 15, 1999): 4–9.

that the legacy system required data fields that the ERP did not provide. For instance, the routing system tells the truck drivers which stores to visit and in what order. The ERP system did not have a data field for specifying the delivery stop sequence. This information, however, was needed by the warehousing system to tell loaders what to put in the trucks and in what order. Having confidence in its in-house IT staff, Domino's management decided to take the relatively drastic step of modifying the ERP software to include these fields.

Supply Chain Management

Another development regarding the bolt-on software issue is the rapid convergence between ERP and bolt-on software functionality. **Supply chain management (SCM)** software is a case in point. The supply chain is the set of activities associated with moving goods from the raw materials stage through to the consumer. This includes procurement, production scheduling, order processing, inventory management, transportation, warehousing, customer service, and forecasting the demand for goods. SCM systems are a class of application software that supports this task. Successful supply chain management coordinates and integrates these activities into a seamless process. In addition to the key functional areas within the organization, SCM links all of the partners in the chain, including vendors, carriers, third-party logistics companies, and information systems providers. Organizations can achieve competitive advantage by linking the activities in its supply chain more efficiently and effectively than its competitors.

Recognizing this need, ERP vendors have moved decisively to add SCM functionality to their ERP products. ERP systems and SCM systems are now on converging paths. SAP and Oracle have recently added an SCM module, while Baan and PeopleSoft both have acquired smaller SCM vendors to integrate their SCM software into future releases. On the other hand, SCM software vendors are also expanding their functionality to appear more like ERP systems. As larger ERP vendors move into the mid-size company market the smaller SCM and ERP vendors will likely be pushed out of business.

Data Warehousing

Data warehousing is one of the fastest growing IT issues before businesses today. Not surprisingly, data warehousing functionality is being incorporated into all leading ERP systems. A *data warehouse* is a *relational* or *multidimensional* database that may consume hundreds of gigabytes or even terabytes of disk storage. When the data warehouse is organized for single department or function, it is often called a **data mart**. Rather than containing hundreds of gigabytes of data for the entire enterprise, a data mart may have only tens of gigabytes of data. Other than size, we make no distinction between a data mart and a data warehouse. The issues discussed in this section apply to both.

The process of data warehousing involves extracting, converting, and standardizing an organization's operational data from ERP and legacy systems and loading it into a central archive—the data warehouse. Once loaded into the warehouse, data are accessible via various query and analysis tools that are used for *data mining*. Data mining is the process of selecting, exploring, and modeling large amounts of data to uncover relationships and global patterns that exist in large databases but are "hidden" among the vast amount of facts. This involves sophisticated techniques that use *database queries* and *artificial intelligence* to model real-world phenomena from data collected from the warehouse.

Most organizations implement a data warehouse as part of a strategic IT initiative that involves an ERP system. Implementing a successful data warehouse involves installing a process for gathering data on an ongoing basis, organizing it into meaningful information, and delivering it for evaluation. The data warehousing process has the following essential stages:[3]

- Modeling data for the data warehouse.
- Extracting data from operational databases.
- Cleansing extracted data.
- Transforming data into the warehouse model.
- Loading the data into the data warehouse database.

Modeling Data for the Data Warehouse

Good database design stresses the importance of data normalization to eliminate three serious anomalies: the *update anomaly*, the *insertion anomaly*, and the *deletion anomaly*. Normalizing data in an operational database is necessary to accurately reflect the dynamic interactions among entities. Data attributes are constantly updated, new attributes are added, and obsolete attributes are deleted on a regular basis. Although a fully normalized database will yield the flexible model needed for supporting multiple users in this dynamic operational environment, it also adds to complexity that translates into performance inefficiency.

The Warehouse Consists of Denormalized Data

Because of the vast size of a data warehouse, such inefficiency can be devastating. A three-way join between tables in a large data warehouse may take an unacceptably long time to complete and may be unnecessary. In the data warehouse data model, the relationship among attributes does not change. Since historical data are static in nature, nothing is gained by constructing normalized tables with dynamic links.

For example, in an operational database system, Product X may be an element of work-in-process in Department A this month and part of Department B's work-in-process next month. In a properly normalized data model, it would be incorrect to include Department A's work-in-process data as part of a Sales Order table that records an order for Product X. Only the product item number would be included in the Sales Order table as a foreign key linking it to the Product table. Relational theory would call for a join (link) between the Sales Order table and Product table to determine the production status (which department the product is in, currently) and other attributes of the product. From an operational perspective, complying with relational theory is important because the relation changes as the product moves through different departments over time. Relational theory does not apply to a data warehousing system because the Sales Order/Product relation is stable.

Wherever possible, therefore, normalized tables pertaining to selected events may be consolidated into denormalized tables. Figure 6-6 illustrates how sales order

3 P. Fiore, "Everyone Is Talking About Data Warehousing," *Evolving Enterprise*, (1), (Spring 1998): 2.

FIGURE 6-6 **Denormalized Data**

A. Normalized Representation for an Operational Database System

Customer Table

Customer Number	Name	Street	City	State
34675	John Smith	10 Elm	Bath	PA

Invoice Table

Invoice Number	Invoice Date	Shipped Date	Invoice Amount	Customer Number
8866376	06/12/04	06/23/04	600	34675

Line Item Table

Invoice Number	Item Number	Quantity	Price	Extended Price
8866376	j683	2	200	400
8866376	r223	5	40	200

B. Denormalized Representation for Data Warehouse System

Sales Order Table

Customer Number	Name	Street	City	State	Invoice Number	Invoice Date	Shipped Date	Invoice Amount	Item Number	Quantity	Price	Extended Price
34675	John Smith	10 Elm	Bath	PA	8866376	06/12/04	06/23/04	600	j683	2	200	400
34675	John Smith	10 Elm	Bath	PA	8866376	06/12/04	06/23/04	600	r223	5	40	200

data is reduced to a single denormalized Sales Order table for storage in a data warehouse system.

EXTRACTING DATA FROM OPERATIONAL DATABASES

Data extraction is the process of collecting data from operational databases, flat files, archives, and external data sources. Operational databases typically need to be out of service when data extraction occurs to avoid data inconstancies. Because of their large size and the need for a speedy transfer to minimize the downtime, little or no conversion of data occurs at this point. A technique called **changed data capture** can dramatically reduce the extraction time by capturing only newly modified data. The extraction software compares the current operational database with an image of the data taken at the last transfer of data to the warehouse. Only the data that have changed in the interim are captured.

Transaction data stored in the operational database go through several stages as economic events unfold. For example, a sales transaction first undergoes credit approval, then the product is shipped, then billing occurs, and finally payment is received. Each of these events changes the state of the transaction and associated accounts such as inventory, accounts receivable, and cash.

A key feature of a data warehouse is that the data contained in it are in a nonvolatile (stable) state. Typically, transaction data are loaded into the warehouse only when the activity on them has been completed. Potentially important relationships between entities may, however, be absent from data that are captured in this stable state. For example, information about cancelled sales orders will probably not be reflected among the sales orders that have been shipped and paid for before they are placed in the warehouse. One way to reflect these dynamics is to extract the operations data in "slices of time." These slices provide snapshots of business activity. For example, decision makers may want to observe sales transactions approved, shipped, billed, and paid at various points in time along with snapshots of inventory levels at each state. Such data may be useful in depicting trends in the average time taken to approve credit or ship goods that might help explain lost sales.

CLEANSING EXTRACTED DATA

Data cleansing involves filtering out or repairing invalid data prior to being stored in the warehouse. Operational data are "dirty" for many reasons. Clerical, data entry, and computer program errors can create illogical data such as negative inventory quantities, misspelled names, and blank fields. Data cleansing also involves transforming data into standard business terms with standard data values. Data are often combined from multiple systems that use slightly different spellings to represent common terms, such as "cust," "cust_id," or "cust_no." Some operational systems may use entirely different terms to refer to the same entity. For example, a bank customer with a certificate of deposit and an outstanding loan may be called a *Lender* by one system and a *Borrower* by another. The source application may use cryptic or difficult-to-understand terms for a number of reasons. For example, some older legacy systems were designed at a time when programming rules placed severe restrictions on naming and formatting data attributes. Also, a commercial application may assign attribute names that are too generic for the needs of the data warehouse user. Businesses that purchase commercial data, such as competitive performance information or market surveys, need to extract data from whatever format the external source provides and reorganize them according to the conventions used in the data warehouse. During the cleansing process, therefore, the attributes taken from multiple systems need to be transformed into uniform standard business terms. This tends to be an expensive and labor-intensive activity, but one that is critical in establishing data integrity in the warehouse. Figure 6-7 illustrates the role of data cleansing in building and maintaining a data warehouse.

Transforming Data into the Warehouse Model

A data warehouse comprise both detail and summary data. To improve efficiency, data can be transformed into summary views before they are loaded into the warehouse. For example, many decision makers may need to see product sales figures summarized for a week, a month, a quarter, or annually. It may not be practical to summarize information from detail data every time the user needs it. A data warehouse that contains the most frequently requested summary views of data can reduce the amount of processing time during analysis. Referring again to Figure 6-7 we see the creation of summary views over time. These are typically created around business entities such as customers, products, and suppliers. Unlike operational views, which are virtual in nature with underlying base tables, data warehouse views are physical tables. Most OLAP software will, however, permit the user to construct virtual views from detail data when one does not already exist.

A data warehouse will often provide multiple summary views based on the same detailed data such as customers or products. For example, several different summary views may be generated from sales order detail data. These may include summaries by product, by customer, and by region. From such views an analyst can drill down into the underlying detail data. Many business problems require a review of detail data to fully evaluate a trend, pattern, or anomaly exhibited in the summarized reports. Also, a single anomaly in detail data may manifest itself differently in different summary views.

Loading the Data into the Data Warehouse Database

Most organizations have found that data warehousing success requires that the data warehouse be created and maintained separately from the operational (transaction processing) databases. This point is developed further.

Internal Efficiency

One reason for a separate data warehouse is that the structural and operational requirements of transaction processing and data mining systems are fundamentally different, making it impractical to keep both operational (current) and archive data in the same database. Transaction processing systems need a data structure that supports performance, whereas data mining systems need data organized in a manner that permits broad examination and the detection of underlying trends.

Integration of Legacy Systems

The continued influence of legacy systems is another reason that the data warehouse needs to be independent of operations. A remarkably large number of business applications continue to run in the mainframe environment of the 1970s. By some estimates, more than 70 percent of business data for large corporations still resides in the mainframe environment. The data structures employed by these systems are often incompatible with the architectures of modern data mining tools. Hence, transaction data that are stored in navigational databases and VSAM systems often end up in

FIGURE 6-7 Data Warehouse System

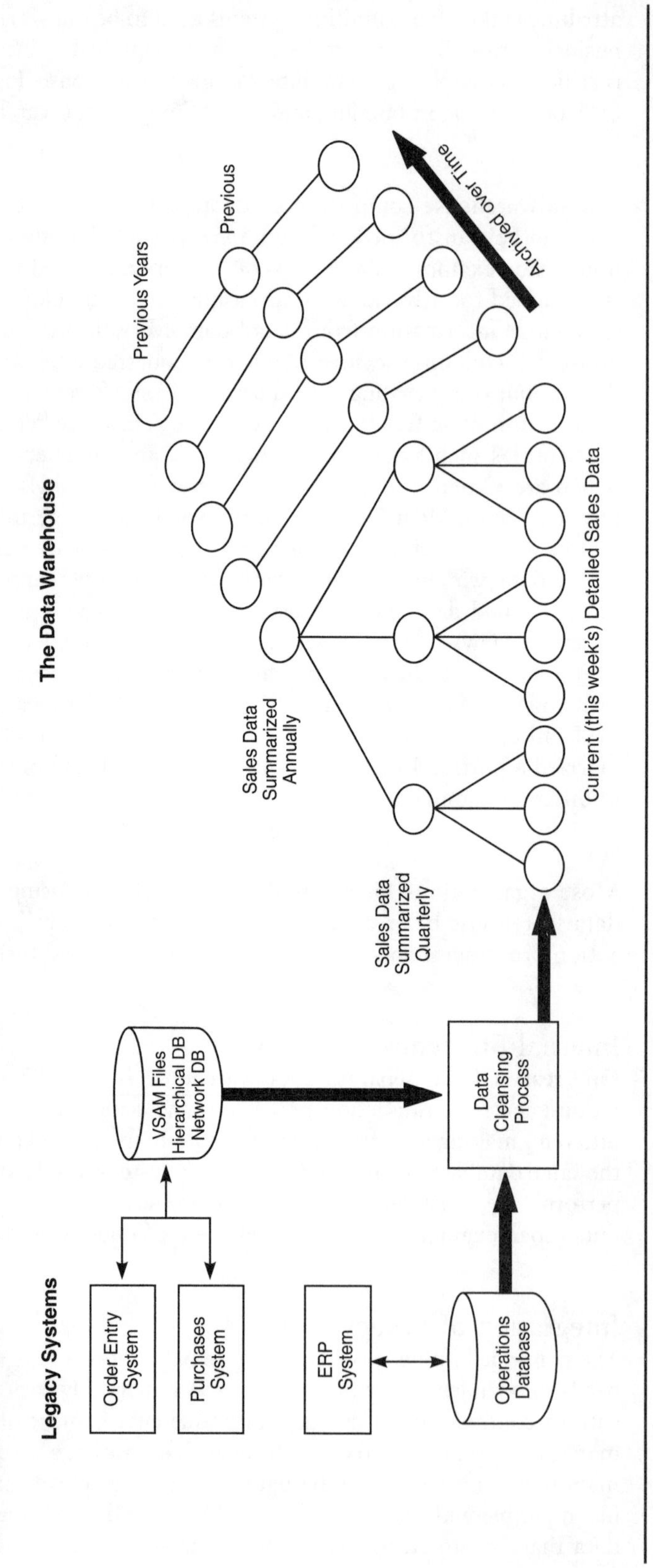

large tape libraries that are isolated from the decision process. A separate data warehouse provides a venue for integrating the data from legacy and contemporary systems into a common structure that supports entity-wide analysis.

Consolidation of Global Data

Finally, the emergence of the global economy has brought about fundamental changes in business organizational structure and has profoundly changed the information requirements of business entities. Decision makers in the global corporation are challenged by unique business complexities. For example, they need to assess the profitability of products built and sold in multiple countries with volatile currencies. Such challenges add complexity to data mining. A separate centralized data warehouse is an effective means of collecting, standardizing, and assimilating data from diverse sources.

In conclusion, the creation of a data warehouse separate from operational systems is a fundamental data warehousing concept. Many organizations now consider data warehouse systems to be key components of their IS strategy. As such, they allocate considerable resources to build data warehouses concurrently with the operational systems being implemented.

Decisions Supported by the Data Warehouse

By making the data warehouse as flexible and friendly as possible, it becomes accessible by many end users. Some decisions supported by a data warehouse are not fundamentally different from those that are supported by traditional databases. Other information uses such as multidimensional analysis and information visualization are not possible with traditional systems. Some users of the data warehouse need routine reports based on traditional queries. When standard reports can be anticipated in advance, they can be provided automatically as a periodic product. Automatic generation of standard information reduces access activity against the data warehouse and will improve its efficiency in dealing with more esoteric needs.

Drill-down capability is a useful data analysis technique associated with data mining. Drill-down analysis begins with the summary views of data described above. When anomalies or interesting trends are observed, the user "drills down" to lower-level views and ultimately into the underlying detail data. Obviously, such analysis cannot be anticipated like a standard report. Drill-down capability is an OLAP feature of data mining tools available to the user. Tools for data mining are evolving rapidly to satisfy the decision maker's need to understand the business unit's behavior in relation to key entities including customers, suppliers, employees, and products. Standard reports and queries produced from summary views can answer many "what" questions, but drill-down capability answers the "why" and "how" questions. Table 6-1 summarizes some of the applications of data mining in decision support.

Supporting Supply Chain Decisions from the Data Warehouse

The primary reason for data warehousing is to optimize business performance. Many organizations feel that more strategic benefit can be gained by sharing data externally. By providing customers and suppliers with the information they need when they need it, the company can improve its relationships and provide better service. The potential gain to the giving organization is seen in a more responsive

TABLE 6-1

Applications of Data Mining

Business Field	Application
Banking/Investments	Detect patterns of fraudulent credit card use
	Identify "loyal" customers and predict those likely to change their credit card affiliation
	Examine historical market data to determine investors' stock trading rules
	Predict credit card spending of key customer groups
	Identify correlations between different financial indicators
Health Care and Medical Insurance	Predict office visits from historical analysis of historical patient behavior
	Identify successful and economical medical therapies for different illnesses
	Identify which medical procedures tend to be claimed together
	Predict which customers will buy new policies
	Identify behavior patterns associated with high-risk customers
	Identify indicators of fraudulent behavior
Marketing	Identify buying patterns based on historical customer data
	Identify relationships among customer demographic data
	Predict response to various forms of marketing and promotion campaigns

and efficient supply chain. Using Internet technologies and OLAP applications an organization can share its data warehouse with its trading partners and, in effect, treat them like divisions of the firm. A few examples of this approach follow.[4]

Western Digital Corporation, a leading manufacturer of hard drives, plans to grant certain suppliers access to its data warehouse so it can view performance data on its parts. Because Western Digital maintains a limited engineering staff, the company relies on its suppliers to act as strategic partners in product development. Providing suppliers with performance data allows it to make improvements and participate in the engineering process. The suppliers improve their parts, which, in turn, improves Western Digital's products.

The company's data warehouse holds more than 600 gigabytes of raw data collected from more than 100,000 drives that it manufactures each day. Approximately 800 attributes are collected on each drive, all of which can be analyzed using OLAP software. The systems feeding the warehouse include ERP applications, data from trouble-call centers, data from failure-analysis systems, and field test data from customer sites and service centers. The company routinely searches

4 B. Davis, "Data Warehouses Open Up," *InformationWeek Online News in Review* (June 28, 1999).

the data warehouse for failure information on every drive that it manufactures. All failures and their causes can be linked back to the supplier.

GM's supply chain data warehouse will be available via the Web to more than 5,000 suppliers worldwide. The suppliers can log on to a secure Web site and query information on the quantities of supplies shipped, delivery times, and prices. This information will help GM suppliers optimize their product planning, their ability to source materials, and their shipping-fulfillment processes.

MIM Health Plans Inc., an independent pharmacy benefits–management company, lets its customers view warehouse data to promote better buying decisions. For instance, benefits managers can view reports and drill down into the warehouse to see claims costs, overall costs, the number of prescriptions ordered in a given time period, the number of brand versus generic drugs, and other decision metrics.

Risks Associated with ERP Implementation

The benefits from ERP can be significant, but they do not come without some risk to the organization. An ERP system is not a silver bullet that will, by its mere existence, solve an organization's problems. If that were the case, there would never be ERP failures, but there have been many. This section examines some of the risk issues that need to be considered.

Big Bang versus Phased-In Implementation

Implementing an ERP system has more to do with changing the way an organization does business than it does with technology. As a result, most ERP implementation failures are due to cultural problems within the firm that stand in opposition to the objective of process reengineering. Strategies for implementing ERP systems to achieve this objective follow two general approaches: the *big bang* and the *phased-in* approach.

The **big bang approach** is the more ambitious and risky of the two. Organizations taking this approach attempt to switch operations from their old legacy systems to the new system in a single event that implements the ERP across the entire company. While this method has certain advantages, it has been associated with numerous system failures. Since the new ERP system means new ways of conducting business, getting the entire organization on board and in sync can be a daunting task. On day 1 of the implementation no one within the organization will have had any experience with the new system. In a sense, everyone in the company is a trainee learning a new job.

The new ERP will initially meet with opposition because using it involves compromise. The legacy systems with which everyone in the organization was familiar had been honed over the years to meet exact needs. In most cases, ERP systems have neither the range of functionality nor the familiarity of the legacy systems that they replace. Also, because a single system is now serving the entire organization, individuals at data input points often find themselves entering considerably more data than they did previously with the more narrowly focused legacy system. As a result, the speed of the new system often suffers, causing disruptions to daily operations. These problems are typically experienced whenever any new system is implemented. The magnitude of the problem is the issue under the big bang approach, because everyone in the company is affected. Once the initial adjustment period has passed and the new culture emerges, however, the ERP becomes an effective operational and strategic tool that provides competitive advantage to the firm.

Because of the disruptions associated with the big bang, the **phased-in approach** has emerged as a popular alternative. It is particularly suited to diversified organizations whose units do not share common processes and data. In these types of companies, independent ERP systems can be installed in each business unit over time to accommodate the adjustment periods needed for assimilation. Common processes and data (such as the general ledger function) can be integrated across the organization without disrupting operations throughout the firm.

Organizations that are not diversified can also employ the phased-in approach. The implementation usually begins with one or more key processes, such as order entry. The goal is to get ERP up and running concurrently with legacy systems. As more of the organization's functions are converted to ERP, legacy systems are systematically retired. In the interim the ERP is interfaced to legacy systems. During this period, the objectives of *system integration* and *process reengineering*, which are fundamental to the ERP model, are not achievable. To take full advantage of the ERP, process reengineering will still need to occur. Otherwise, the organization will have simply replaced its old legacy system with a very expensive new one.

Opposition to Changes to the Businesses Culture

To be successful, all functional areas of the organization need be involved in determining the culture of the firm and in defining the new system's requirements. The firm's willingness and ability to undertake a change of the magnitude of an ERP implementation is an important consideration. If the corporate culture is such that change is not tolerated or desired, then an ERP implementation will not be successful.

The technological culture must also be assessed. Organizations that lack technical support staff for the new system or have a user base that is unfamiliar with computer technology face a steeper learning curve and a potentially greater barrier to acceptance of the system by its employees.

Choosing the Wrong ERP

Since ERP systems are prefabricated systems, users need to determine whether a particular ERP fits their organization's culture and its business processes. A common reason for system failure is when the ERP does not support one or more important business processes. In one example, a textile manufacturer in India implemented an ERP only to discover afterwards that it did not accommodate a basic need. The textile company had a policy of maintaining two prices for each item of inventory that it sold. One price was used for the domestic market and a second price, which was four times higher, was for export sales. The ERP that the user implemented was not designed to allow two different prices for the same inventory item. The changes needed to make the ERP work were both extensive and expensive. Serious system disruptions resulted from this oversight. Furthermore, modifying an ERP program and database can introduce potential processing errors and can make updating the system to later versions difficult.

Goodness of Fit

Management needs to make sure that the ERP it chooses is right for the company. No single ERP system is capable of solving all the problems of all organizations. For example, SAP's R/3 was designed primarily for manufacturing firms with highly predictable processes that are relatively similar to those of other manufacturers. It may not be the best solution for a service-oriented organization that has a great need for customer-related activities conducted over the Internet.

Finding a good functionality fit requires a software selection process that resembles a funnel, which starts broad and systematically becomes more focused. It begins with a large number of software vendors that are potential candidates. Evaluation questions are asked of vendors in iterative rounds. Starting with a large population of vendors and a small number of high-level qualifier questions the number of vendors is reduced to a manageable few. With proper questioning, more than half the vendors are removed from contention with as few as 10 to 20 questions. In each succeeding round, the questions asked become more detailed and the population of vendors decreases.

When a business's processes are truly unique, the ERP system must be modified to accommodate industry-specific (bolt-on) software or to work with custom-built legacy systems. Some organizations, such as telecommunications service providers, have unique billing operations that cannot be satisfied by off-the-shelf ERP systems. Before embarking on the ERP journey, the organization's management needs to assess whether they can and should reengineer their business practices around a standardized model.

System Scalability Issues

If an organization's management expects business volumes to increase substantially during the life of the ERP system, then they have a scalability issue that needs to be addressed. **Scalability** is the system's ability to grow smoothly and economically as user requirements increase. The term *system* in this context refers to the technology platform, application software, network configuration, or database. *Smooth and economical growth* is the ability to increase system capacity at an acceptable incremental cost per unit of capacity without encountering limits that would demand a system upgrade or replacement. *User requirements* pertain to volume-related activities such as transaction processing volume, data entry volume, data output volume, data storage volume, or increases in the user population.

To illustrate scalability, four dimensions of scalability are important: size, speed, workload, and transaction cost. In assessing scalability needs for an organization, each of these dimensions in terms of the ideal of linear scaling must be considered.[5]

- *Size.* With no other changes to the system, if database size increases by a factor of x, then query response time will increase by no more than a factor of x in a scalable system. For example, if business growth causes the database to increase from 100GB to 500GB, then transactions and queries that previously took one second will now take no more than five seconds.
- *Speed.* An increase in hardware capacity by a factor of x will decrease query response time by no less than a factor of x in a scalable system. For example, increasing the number of input terminals (nodes) from 1 to 20 will increase transaction processing time proportionately. Transactions that previously took 20 seconds will now take no more than 1 second in a system with linear scaling.

5 R. Winter, "Scalable Systems: Lexicology of Scale," *Intelligent Enterprise Magazine* (March 2000): 68–74.

- *Workload.* If workload in a scalable system is increased by a factor of x, then response time or throughput can be maintained by increasing hardware capacity by a factor of no more than x. For example, if transaction volume increased from 400 per hour to 4,000 per hour, the previous response time can be achieved by increasing the number of processors by a factor of 10 in a system that is linearly scalable.
- *Transaction cost.* In a scalable system, increases in workload do not increase transaction cost. Therefore, an organization should not need to increase system capacity faster than demand. For example, if the cost of processing a transaction in a system with one processor is 10 cents, then it should still cost no more than 10 cents when the number of processors is increased to handle larger volumes of transactions.

Vendors of ERP systems sometimes advertise scalability as if it were a single dimension factor. In fact, it is a multifaceted issue. Some systems accommodate growth in user populations better than others. Some systems can be scaled to provide more efficient access to large databases when business growth demands it. All systems, however, have their scaling limits. Since infinite scalability is impossible, prospective users need to assess their needs and determine how much scalability they want to purchase up front and what form it should take. The key is to anticipate specific scalability issues before making an ERP investment and before the issues become reality.

Choosing the Wrong Consultant

Implementing an ERP system is an event that most organizations will undergo only once. Success of the projects rests on skills and experience that typically do not exist in-house. Because of this, virtually all ERP implementations involve an outside consulting firm, which coordinates the project, helps the organization to identify its needs, develops a requirements specification for the ERP, selects the ERP package, and manages the cutover. ERP consulting has grown into a $20 billion per year market. The fee for a typical implementation is normally between three and five times the cost of the ERP software license.

Consulting firms with large ERP practices have at times been desperately short of human resources. This was especially true in the mid- to late 1990s when thousands of clients were rushing to implement ERP systems before the new millennium and thus avoid Y2K problems. As demand for ERP implementations grew beyond the supply of qualified consultants, more and more stories of botched projects materialized.

A frequent complaint is that consulting firms promise experienced professionals but deliver incompetent trainees. They have been accused of employing a bait-and-switch maneuver to get contracts. At the initial engagement interview the consulting firm introduces their top consultants who are sophisticated, talented, and persuasive. The client agrees to the deal, incorrectly assuming that these individuals, or others with similar qualifications, will actually implement the system.

The problem has been equated to the airline industry's common practice of overbooking flights. Some suggest that consulting firms, not wanting to turn away business, are guilty of overbooking their consulting staffs. The consequences, however, are far graver than the inconvenience of missing a flight, and a free hotel room and a meal cannot compensate for the damages done. Therefore, before engaging an outside consultant, management should take these steps:

- Interview the staff proposed for the project and draft a detailed contract specifying which members of the consulting team will be assigned to which tasks.
- Establish in writing how staff changes will be handled.
- Conduct reference checks of the proposed staff members.
- Align the consultants' interests with those of the organization by negotiating a pay-for-performance scheme based on achieving certain milestones in the project. For example, the actual amount paid to the consultant may be between 85 to 115 percent of the contracted fee, based on whether a successful project implementation comes in under or over schedule.
- Set a firm termination date for the consultant to avoid consulting arrangements becoming interminable, resulting in dependency and an endless stream of fees.

High Cost and Cost Overruns

Total cost of ownership (TCO) for ERP systems varies greatly from company to company. For medium- to large-sized implementations costs range from hundreds of thousands to hundreds of millions of dollars. TCO includes hardware, software, consulting services, internal personnel costs, installation, and upgrades and maintenance to the system for the first two years after implementation. The risk comes in the form of underestimated and unanticipated costs. Some of the more commonly experienced problems occur in the following areas.

- *Training.* Training costs are invariably higher than estimated because management focuses primarily on the cost of teaching employees the new software. This is only part of the needed training. Employees also need to learn new procedures, which is often overlooked during the budgeting process.
- *System testing and integration.* ERP is a holistic model in which, in theory, one system drives the entire organization. The reality, however, is that many organizations use their ERPs as backbone systems attached to legacy systems and other bolt-on systems, which support unique needs of the firm. Integrating these disparate systems with the ERP may involve writing special conversion programs or even modifying the internal code of the ERP. Integration and testing are done on a case-by-case basis; thus, the cost is extremely difficult to estimate in advance.
- *Database conversion.* A new ERP system usually means a new database. Data conversion is the process of transferring data from the legacy system's flat files to the ERP's relational database. When the legacy system's data are reliable, the conversion process may be accomplished through automated procedures. Even under ideal circumstances, a high degree of testing and manual reconciliation is necessary to ensure that the transfer was complete and accurate. More often, the data in the legacy system are not reliable (sometimes called *dirty*). Empty fields and corrupted data values cause conversion problems that demand human intervention and data rekeying. Also, and more importantly, the structure of the legacy data is likely to be incompatible with the reengineered processes of the new system. Depending on the extent of the process reengineering involved, the entire database may need to be converted through manual data entry procedures.

Since ERPs are extremely expensive to implement, many managers are often dismayed at the apparent lack of cost savings that they achieve in the short term. In fact, a great deal of criticism about the relative success of ERPs relates to whether they provide benefits that outweigh their cost. To assess benefits, management first needs to know what it wants and needs from the ERP. Management should then establish key performance measures, such as reductions in inventory levels, inventory turnover, stockouts, and average order fulfillment time that reflect these expectations. To monitor performance in such key areas, some organizations establish independent *value assessment groups* that report to top management. Although financial break-even on an ERP will take years, management can develop an operational perspective on its successes by developing focused and measurable performance indicators.

Disruptions to Operations

ERP systems can wreak havoc in the companies that install them. In a Deloitte Consulting survey of 64 Fortune 500 companies, 25 percent of the firms surveyed admitted that they experienced a drop in performance in the period immediately following implementation. The reengineering of business processes that often accompanies ERP implementation is the most commonly attributed cause of performance problems. Operationally speaking, when business begins under the ERP system everything looks and works differently from the way it did with the legacy system. An adjustment period is needed for everyone to reach a comfortable point on the learning curve. Depending on the culture of the organization and attitudes toward change within the firm, adjustment may take longer in some firms than in others. The list of major organizations that have experienced serious disruptions includes Dow Chemical, Boeing, Dell Computer, Apple Computer, Whirlpool Corporation, and Waste Management. The most notorious case in the press was Hershey Foods Corporation, which had trouble processing orders through its new ERP system and was unable to ship products.

As a result of these disruptions, Hershey's 1999 third-quarter sales dropped by 12.4 percent compared to the previous year's sales, and earnings were down by 18.6 percent. Hershey's problem was attributed to two strategic errors related to system implementation. First, because of schedule overruns, they decided to cut over to the new system during their busy season. The inevitable snags that arise from implementation of complex systems like SAP's R/3 are easier to deal with during slack business periods. Secondly, many experts feel that Hershey attempted to do too much in a single implementation. In addition to the R/3 system, it implemented a customer relations management system and logistics software from two different vendors, which had to interface with R/3. The ERP and these bolt-on components were all implemented using the big bang approach.

Implications for Internal Control and Auditing

As with any system, the internal control and audit of ERP systems are issues. Key concerns are examined in this section within the framework of SAS 78.

Transaction Authorization

A key benefit of an ERP system is its tightly integrated architecture of modules. This structure, however, also poses potential problems for transaction authorization. For example, the bill of materials drives many manufacturing systems. If the procedures over the creation of the bill of materials are not configured correctly, every component that uses the bill of materials could be affected. Controls need to be built in to the system to validate transactions before they are accepted and acted upon by other modules. Because of their real-time orientation, ERPs are more dependent on programmed controls than on human intervention, as was the case with legacy systems. The challenge for auditors in verifying transaction authorization is to gain a detailed knowledge of the ERP system configuration as well as a thorough understanding of the business processes and the flow of information between system components.

Segregation of Duties

Operational decisions in ERP-based organizations are pushed down to a point as close as possible to the source of the event. Manual processes that normally require segregation of duties are thus often eliminated in an ERP environment. For example, shop supervisors may order inventories from suppliers and receiving dock personnel may post inventory receipts to the inventory records in real time. Furthermore, ERP forces together many different business functions such as order entry, billing, and accounts payable under a single integrated system. Organizations using ERP systems must establish new security, audit, and control tools to ensure duties are properly segregated.

To help resolve the segregation of duties problem, SAP, the leading ERP system, employs a configuration technique called *user role*. Each role is associated with a specific set of activities that are assigned to an authorized user of the ERP system. SAP currently provides over 150 predefined user roles, which limit a user's access to only certain functions and associated data. The system administrator assigns roles to users of the system when it is configured. These can be customized as needed. When the user logs onto the system, a role-based menu appears, which limits the user to the specified tasks. Auditors should ensure that roles are assigned in accordance with job responsibilities on a "need-to-know" basis.

Supervision

An often-cited pitfall of an ERP implementation is that management does not fully understand is impact on business. Too often, after the ERP is up and running, only the implementation team understands how it works. Because their traditional roles will be changed, supervisors need to acquire an extensive technical and operational understanding of the new system. Typically, when an organization implements an ERP many decision-making responsibilities are pushed down to the shop floor level. The employee-empowered philosophy of ERP should not eliminate supervision as an internal control. Instead, it should provide substantial efficiency benefits. Supervisors should have more time to manage the shop floor and, through improved monitoring capability, increase their span of control.

Accounting Records

ERP systems have the ability to streamline the entire financial reporting process. In fact, many organizations can and do close their books daily. OLTP data can be manipulated quickly to produce ledger entries, accounts receivable and payable summaries, and financial consolidation for both internal and external users. Traditional batch controls and audit trails are no longer needed in many cases. This risk is mitigated by improved data entry accuracy through the use of default values, cross-checking, and specified user views of data.

In spite of ERP technology, some risk to accounting record accuracy may still exist. Because of the close interfaces with customers and suppliers, some organizations run the risk that corrupted or inaccurate data may be passed from these external sources and corrupt the accounting database. Additionally, many organizations need to import data from legacy systems into their ERP systems. These data may be laden with problems such as duplicate records, inaccurate values, or incomplete fields. Consequently, strict data cleansing is an important control. Special *scrubber* programs are used as interfaces between the ERP and the exporting systems to reduce these risks and ensure that the most accurate and current data are being received.

Access Controls

Security is perhaps one of the most critical control issues in an ERP implementation. The goal of security in these systems is to provide confidentiality, integrity, and availability of necessary information. Security weaknesses can result in the revealing of trade secrets to competitors and other unauthorized access. Some security professionals argue that computer systems should be restricted to user-specific tasks. Others argue that everyone should have access to all company information. The most sensible resolution to these opposing views is to impose security limitations to data based on a risk assessment. Security administrators should tightly control the more sensitive and risky data within the organization.

Access to the Data Warehouse

Access control is a vital feature of a data warehouse that is shared with customers and suppliers. The organization should establish procedures to oversee the authorization of individuals at customer and supplier sites that will be granted access to their data warehouses. Access privileges should be specified for each outside user and controlled by passwords. User views need to be created to limit outsider access to approved data only. Internet sessions should be managed through firewalls and use encryption and digital signatures to maintain confidentiality. Firewalls, which are a combination of hardware and software that protect the resources of a private network, help to secure data from unauthorized internal and external users. Auditing tools for intrusion detection are available to assist in mitigating security risks. Periodic audits should include a risk assessment and review of access levels granted to both internal and external users based on their job descriptions.

Contingency Planning

In addition to access security, detailed contingency plans that can be invoked instantly in the event of a disaster must be developed for computer and business operations. These plans need to be developed prior to the cutover to a new ERP system. Related to this is the need for backup procedures in the event of a server failure. ERP backup strategies are discussed in the following paragraphs.

Centralized organizations with highly integrated business units may need a single global ERP system that is accessed via the Internet or private lines from around the world to consolidate data from subsidiary systems. A server failure under this model could leave the entire organization unable to process transactions. To control against this, two linked servers can be connected in redundant backup mode. All production processing is done on one server. If it fails, processing is automatically transferred to the other. Organizations that want more security and resilience may arrange servers in a cluster of three or more that dynamically share the workload. Processing can be redistributed if one or more of the servers in the cluster fails.

Companies whose organizational units are autonomous and do not share common customers, suppliers, or product lines often choose to install regional servers. This approach permits independent processing and spreads the risk associated with server failure. For example, BP Amoco implemented SAP's R/3 into 17 separate business groups.

Independent Verification

Since ERP systems employ OLTP, traditional independent verification controls such as reconciling batch control numbers are meaningless. Similarly, process reengineering to improve efficiency also changes the nature of independent verification. For example, the traditional three-way match of the purchase order, receiving report, and invoice serves no purpose in an EDI environment in which the vendor's check is cut when the order is placed. The focus of independent verification needs to be redirected from the transaction level to one that views overall performance. ERP systems come with canned controls and can be configured to produce performance reports that should be used as assessment tools. Internal auditors also play an important role in this new environment and need to acquire a thorough technical background and comprehensive understanding of the ERP system. Ongoing independent verification efforts can be conducted only by a team well versed in ERP technology.

AUDITING THE DATA WAREHOUSE

As part of an information system audit the auditor designs a procedure to gather evidence relating to various management assertions pertaining to the firm's financial statements. As part of this procedure the auditor often performs an **analytical review** of account balances to identify relationships between accounts and risks that are not otherwise apparent. Analytical procedures may indicate trends, even in adequately controlled organizations, that lead the auditor to extend the number and nature of substantive tests that he or she subsequently performs.[6] On the other hand, such evidence can provide assurance that transactions and accounts are reasonably stated and complete and may thus permit the auditor to reduce substantive testing.

The vast amount of data contained in the data warehouse is an excellent resource for performing time-series and ratio analysis. In the case of the revenue cycle, an analytical review will provide the auditor with an overall perspective for trends in sales, cash receipts, sales returns, and accounts receivable. For example, the auditor may compare reported sales for the quarter with those for the same period in previous years. Ratio analysis may be used to compare total sales to cost of goods sold, sales to accounts receivable, and allowance for doubtful accounts to accounts receivable. Significant variations in account balances over time, or unusual ratios, may signify financial statement misrepresentations. Accounts receivable may be examined in time slices for changes in balances relative to sales. This

6 Substantive tests are tests of details as opposed to tests of controls. For example, an auditor may examine the details of invoices to verify that their amounts were properly calculated and recorded in the accounts. Substantive testing can be time consuming. Extensive substantive tests will add cost and delays to the audit. The amount of substantive testing performed is influenced in part by the quality of internal controls in place. Based on evidence provided by testing internal controls and analytical reviews the auditor may decide to reduce or expand the amount of substantive testing to be performed.

can indicate whether the organization's credit policy is being properly and consistently applied. Another useful audit procedure for identifying potential audit risks involves scanning thousands or even millions of records for unusual transactions and abnormal account balances.

In the case of the expenditure cycle, an analytical review can provide the auditor with an overall perspective for trends in accounts payable and related expenses. Current expenses may be compared to historical expenses and management budgets. For example, the auditor may compare current payroll expenses for the quarter with those for the same period in previous years. Unusual trends or variances should be examined for cause.

The auditor may use drill-down techniques to identify unusually high levels of business activity with a particular supplier. Excessive purchases from a single supplier could represent an abnormal business dependency that may prove harmful to the firm if the supplier raises prices or cannot deliver on schedule. It may also signify a fraudulent relationship involving kickbacks to purchasing agents or other management. On the other hand, a large number of vendors with small balances may be evidence of a highly inefficient purchasing process. In such cases management may need to consolidate business activity. Various corporate surveys have estimated the cost of processing a purchase order at between $50 and $125. Restricting the number of vendors with whom the organization does business can reduce this expense.

While an organization's data warehouse is an excellent resource for performing analytical reviews, the auditor needs to understand the procedures used to populate the warehouse. As illustrated, data cleansing is an important phase in the maintenance of a warehouse. To be useful as an OLAP tool the data warehouse needs to be free of contamination. Erroneous data (such as negative inventory values, missing fields, and other clerical errors) that are a natural part of operational databases are identified and repaired (or rejected) in the cleansing process prior to their entering the data warehouse. The auditor must, therefore, be careful of the reliance placed on this resource. Since the data warehouse exists in an artificially pristine state, it may not be a suitable substitute for the operational database when assessing tests of process controls and performing substantive tests.

SUMMARY

This chapter opened by comparing the function and data storage techniques of a traditional flat file or database system to that of an ERP. An important distinction was drawn between OLTP and OLAP applications. Similarly, the differences between the ERP's operational database and the data warehouse were discussed. Next, ERP configurations were examined related to servers, databases, and bolt-on software. Supply chain management (SCM) as an area of contention was discussed. ERP vendors are moving quickly to provide SCM functionality. Simultaneously, SCM vendors are encroaching on traditional ERP territory. The third section discussed data warehousing. A data warehouse is a relational or multidimensional database that supports online analytical processing (OLAP). A number of data warehouse issues were discussed, including data modeling, data extraction from operational databases, data cleansing, data transformation, and loading data into the warehouse. The fourth section examined common risks associated with ERP implementation. Among these are the risks associated with the big bang approach, internal opposition to changing the way a company does its business, choosing the wrong ERP model, choosing the wrong consultant, cost overrun issues, and disruptions to operations. Also presented were a number of issues to consider when implementing an ERP. These include selecting a system that is a good fit for the organization, understanding that the term *scalability* can mean different things to different people, potential problems associated with customizing the software, the need for assigning performance measures, and the need to control outside consultants. The chapter concluded with a review of the internal control and auditing issues related to ERPs.

Key Terms

analytical review
big bang approach
bolt-on software
business activator
changed data capture
client-server model
closed database architecture
consolidation
core applications
data mart
data warehouse
drill-down
enterprise resource planning (ERP)
online analytical processing (OLAP)
online transaction processing (OLTP)
phased-in
scalability
slicing and dicing
supply chain management (SCM)
technology activator
three-tier model
two-tier model

Review Questions

1. Define ERP.
2. What is the closed database architecture?
3. Define core applications and give some examples.
4. Define OLAP and give some examples.
5. What is the client-server model?
6. Describe the two-tier client-server model.
7. Describe the three-tier client-server model.
8. What is bolt-on software?
9. What is SCM software?
10. What is changed data capture?
11. What is a data warehouse?
12. What is data mining?
13. What does data cleansing mean?
14. Why are denormalized tables used in data warehouses?
15. What is the drill-down approach?
16. What is the big bang approach?
17. What is scalability?
18. What is a business activator?
19. What is a technology activator?
20. What is Baan's Evergreen Delivery?
21. How is the Oracle database different from relational databases?
22. What is the OLAP operation called consolidation?
23. What is the OLAP operation of drill-down?
24. What is meant by the term slicing and dicing?

Discussion Questions

1. How are OLTP and OLAP different? Explain, giving some examples.
2. Distinguish between the two-tier and three-tier client-server models. Describe when each would be used.
3. Why do ERP systems need bolt-on software? Give an example of bolt-on software.
4. Your organization is considering acquiring bolt-on software for your ERP system. What approaches are open to you?
5. Explain why the data warehouse needs to be separate from the operational database.
6. Data in a data warehouse are in a stable state. Explain how this can hamper data mining analysis. What can an organization do to alleviate this problem?
7. This chapter stressed the importance of data normalization when constructing a relational database. Why then is it important to denormalize data in a data warehouse?
8. What problems does the data cleansing step attempt to resolve?
9. How are the summary views in a data warehouse different from views in an operational database?
10. Would drill-down be an effective audit tool for identifying an unusual business relationship between a purchasing agent and suppliers in a large organization with several hundred suppliers? Explain.
11. Disruptions to operations are a common side effect of implementing an ERP. Explain the primary reason for this.
12. ERP systems use the best practices approach in designing their applications. Yet goodness of fit is considered to be an important issue when selecting an ERP. Shouldn't the client be able to use just whatever applications the ERP system provides?
13. Explain the issues of size, speed, workload, and transaction as they relate to scalability.
14. Explain how SAP uses roles as a way to improve internal control.
15. How would you deal with the problem of file server backup in a highly centralized organization?
16. How would you deal with the problem of file server backup in a decentralized organization with autonomous divisions that do not share common operational data?
17. Distinguish between the OLAP operations of consolidation and drill-down.
18. When would slicing and dicing be an appropriate OLAP tool? Give an example.

Multiple-Choice Questions

1. Closed database architecture is
   a. a control technique intended to prevent unauthorized access from trading partners.
   b. a limitation inherent in traditional information systems that prevents data sharing.
   c. a data warehouse control that prevents unclean data from entering the warehouse.
   d. a technique used to restrict access to data marts.
   e. a database structure used by many of the leading ERPs to support OLTP applications.
2. Which of the following is typically not part of an ERP's core applications?
   a. OLTP applications
   b. sales and distribution applications
   c. business planning applications
   d. OLAP applications
   e. shop floor control applications
3. Which of the following is typically not part of an ERP's OLAP applications?
   a. decision support systems
   b. information retrieval
   c. ad hoc reporting/analysis
   d. logistics
   e. what-if analysis
4. Which of the following comments describes a data warehouse least well?
   a. It is constructed for quick searching and ad hoc queries.
   b. It contains data that are normally extracted periodically from operational databases.

   c. It contains data from a public information service.
   d. It is an integral part of all ERP systems.
   e. It may be deployed by organizations that have not implemented an ERP.
5. Which statement is not true?
   a. In a typical two-tier client-server architecture, the server handles both application and database duties.
   b. Client computers are responsible for presenting data to the user and passing user input back to the server.
   c. Two-tier architecture is for local area network (LAN) applications where the demand on the server is restricted to a relatively small population of users.
   d. The database and application functions are separated in the three-tier model.
   e. In three-tier client-server architectures, one tier is for user presentation, one is for database and applications access, and the third is for Internet access.
6. Which statement is not true?
   a. Drill-down capability is an OLAP feature of data mining tools available to the user.
   b. The data warehouse should be separate from operational systems.
   c. Denormalization of data involves dividing the data into very small tables that support detailed analysis.
   d. Some decisions supported by a data warehouse are not fundamentally different from those that are supported by traditional databases.
   e. Data cleansing involves transforming data into standard business terms with standard data values.
7. Which statement is least accurate?
   a. Implementing an ERP system has more to do with changing the way an organization does business than it does with technology.
   b. The phased-in approach to ERP implementation is particularly suited to diversified organizations whose units do not share common processes and data.
   c. Since the primary reason for implementing an ERP is to standardize and integrate operations, diversified organizations whose units do not share common processes and data do not benefit and tend not to implement ERPs.
   d. Process reengineering will be necessary in order for the organization to take full advantage of the ERP.
   e. A common reason for ERP failure is that the ERP does not support one or more important business processes of the organization.
8. Which statement is least true?
   a. A defining feature of ERPs is that they are infinitely scalable.
   b. The reengineering of business processes that often accompanies ERP implementation is the most commonly attributed cause of performance problems.
   c. No single ERP system is capable of solving all the problems of all organizations.
   d. When a business's processes are truly unique, the ERP system must be modified to accommodate industry-specific (bolt-on) software or to work with custom-built legacy systems.
   e. Scalability is the system's ability to grow smoothly and economically as user requirements increase.
9. Auditors of ERP systems
   a. need not be concerned about segregation of duties because these systems possess strong computer controls.
   b. focus on output controls such as independent verification to reconcile batch totals.
   c. may be concerned that the data in the data warehouse are too clean and free from errors.
   d. do not see the data warehouse as an audit or control issue at all because financial records are not stored there.
   e. need not review access levels granted to users since these are determined when the system is configured and never change.
10. Which statement is most correct?
   a. SAP is more suited to service industries than manufacturing clients.
   b. J.D. Edwards' ERP is designed to accept the best practices modules of other vendors.
   c. Oracle evolved from a human resources system.
   d. PeopleSoft is the world's leading supplier of software for information management.
   e. Baan's Evergreen Delivery policy ensures free upgrades of bolt-on software.

PROBLEMS

1. **Data Warehouse Access Control**
You are the CEO of a large organization that implemented a data warehouse for internal analysis of corporate data. The operations manager has written you a memo advocating opening the data warehouse to your suppliers and customers. Explain any merit to this proposal. What are the control issues, if any?

2. **Project Implementation**
Your organization is planning to implement an ERP system. Some managers in the organization favor the big bang approach. Others are advocating a phased-in approach. The CEO has asked you, as project leader, to write a memo summarizing the advantages and disadvantages of each approach and to make a recommendation. This is a traditional organization with a strong internal hierarchy. The company was acquired in a merger two years ago and the ERP project is an effort on the part of the parent company to standardize business processes and reporting across the organization. Prior to this, the organization had been using a general ledger package that it acquired in 1979. Most of the transaction processing is a combination of manual and batch processing. Most employees think that the legacy system works well. At this point the implementation project is behind schedule.

3. **Data Warehousing**
EuroTunnel is a company that transports thousands of vehicles and passengers through the Channel Tunnel between Britain and France each day. Initially, the company employed a single Travellog booking system for both its ticketing and marketing operations. As tunnel usage grew, the ticketing sales staff were soon processing more than 5,000 transactions daily. At the same time, EuroTunnel's marketing department was accessing the Travellog system to generate analysis reports and forecast sales. The conflicting demand for marketing analysis data and online ticket sales transactions caused an information gridlock. As large marketing inquiries were running, ticket sales and other online transactions were delayed and the company began to experience an information crisis. EuroTunnel's IS department had to come up with a solution quickly.

Required:
Outline the key elements and operational features of a data warehouse solution that resolves EuroTunnel's conflicting needs for information.

4. **Selecting a Consultant**
You are the chief information officer for a moderate-sized organization that has decided to implement an ERP system. The CEO has met with a consulting ERP firm based on a recommendation from a personal friend at his club. At the interview the president of the consulting firm introduced the chief consultant who was charming, personable, and seemed very knowledgeable. The CEO's first instinct was to sign a contract with the consultant, but he decided to hold off until he had gotten your input.

Required:
Write a memo to the CEO presenting the issues and the risks associated with consultants. Also outline a set of procedures that could be used as a guide in selecting a consultant.

5. **Auditing ERP Databases**
You are an independent auditor attending an engagement interview with the client. The client organization has recently implemented a data warehouse. Management is concerned that the audit tests that you perform will disrupt operations. They suggest that instead of running tests against the live operational database, you draw the data for your analytical reviews and substantive tests of details from the data warehouse. They point out that operational data is copied weekly into the warehouse and everything you need will be contained there. This will enable you to perform your tests without disrupting routine operations. You agree to give this some thought and get back with the client with your answer.

Required:

Draft a memo to the client outlining your response to their proposal. Mention any concerns that you might have.

6. **ERP and People Problems**

Financial executives have found that people problems can cause as many mishaps as flawed technology when installing ERP systems.

Required:

Research this issue and write a brief paper outlining the key issues.

7. **ERP Failure**

When an ERP implementation fails, who is to blame? Is it the software manufacturer, the client firm, or the implementation strategy?

Required:

Research this issue and write a brief paper outlining the key issues

8. **ERP Market Growth**

Since many large corporations implemented ERP systems prior to 2000, what direction will growth of the ERP market take?

Required:

Research this issue and write a brief paper outlining the key issues.

9. **ERP Consultants**

Required:

Do an Internet search of complaints about ERP consultants. Write a report about the most common complaints and cite examples.

10. **ERP Bolt-on Software**

Required:

Go to 10 Web sites of companies that supply bolt-on software. Write a report containing URL's that briefly describes the software features and its compatibility with specific ERP systems.

APPENDIX

LEADING ERP PRODUCTS

The ERP market constitutes products from dozens of vendors of all sizes. This appendix reviews the key features and distinguishing characteristics of the industry leaders, including SAP, J.D.Edwards, Oracle, PeopleSoft, and Baan. The purpose is to provide overview and insight into the underlying philosophies of these vendors. Specific system characteristics and functionality, however, undergo changes on a regular basis. To obtain current and detailed information on these products the reader should visit the vendors' Web pages.

SAP

SAP is the largest of the ERP vendors. At the time of this writing it has an estimated 10 million licensed users worldwide with more than 20,000 installations using its R/3 base product. The customer list consists of firms of all sizes in 19 different industries including aerospace, automobile, banking, chemicals, consumer goods, higher education, and utilities. Currently SAP is expanding its traditional ERP solution to an Internet and e-business approach. Traditionally SAP has targeted larger organization clients but, as is the case for all ERP vendors, they are now focusing on medium-sized and smaller customers.

R/3 employs a three-tier client server architecture. One tier is used for presentation of end-user data. This includes an *Internet enabling layer* that creates an open system providing integration with many different operating systems through Internet data transfer protocols. The second tier is used to host the application and perform data processing. The third tier provides access to the database.

SAP R/3 comprises multiple modules that are fully integrated or can be taken and used individually. The basic functions are organized according to the following categories of applications: financial, logistics, human resources, business process, supply chain management, and electronic commerce support. Each of these is outlined next.

Financial

Financial Accounting. The financial accounting module collects and manages all the financial data for external and internal reporting. This is the backbone system that connects and integrates other SAP business modules. The financial accounting module includes the following general accounting activities: general ledger, accounts payable, accounts receivable, treasury (cash management), foreign exchange, and activity-based cost accounting.

Controlling. This module is a management tool for reporting and controlling costs in support of the following business activities: cost center accounting, job order accounting, project accounting, and profitability analysis.

Fixed Asset Management. This module supports the management of corporate assets including fixed, leased, and real estate. For example, a major purchase could either be assigned as an asset for depreciation, assigned to a project, or declared an expense. The fixed asset module supports the following tasks: asset acquisition, repair, sale of an asset, retirement, and depreciation.

Interactive Requests. This module allows the user to display and maintain current customer data on the Internet. Through this module, customers can be given access to interest rates being charged, account balances, and billing status, and can be provided with current sales and services-rendered information. For example, a utility company can show a customer's current level of electricity, water, or gas usage.

Logistics

The logistics modules support all phases of manufacturing from quoting a job to delivery of the product. The main modules are available-to-promise and sales and distribution.

Available-to-Promise. The available-to-promise (ATP) module allows a customer to obtain information about the manufacturer's production and schedule in real time. The customer connects to SAP via the Internet and enters the product code, quantity, and planned delivery date. The ATP system responds with a quote and a promised delivery date for the product.

Sales and Distribution. This application module supports all the typical tasks associated with the sales and distribution of products to customers including order processing, delivery processing, and billing. In addition, the order entry module allows customers to access the seller's home page over the Internet and access an electronic catalog of products. Product descriptions employ multimedia technology including photographs, audio, and graphics. The system allows the customer to browse, reserve inventory, request production of subassemblies, and enter orders that are built to order. The order status module allows the customer to check the status of the order over the Internet. The system optimizes all the tasks and activities in sales, delivery, and billing, including the following tasks.

- *Product planning.* The product planning module supports a number of manufacturing scenarios including forecasting based on user demand, internal consumption, or sales history. This system connects to MRP II and EDI via the materials management module.
- *Materials management.* The materials management module tells the user what is in stock and defines the procurement and vendor evaluation process. Specific processes supported by this module are material procurement, inventory management, reorder point processing, vendor invoice verification, material valuation, and vendor evaluation.
- *Service calls.* Customers can place product service requests via the Internet into the company's service log by selecting from a list of predefined potential problems. SAP's service module assigns the problem a service number and advises the customer when the problem will be addressed under the terms of the customer's service contract.

- *Preventive maintenance.* The world-class manufacturer cannot afford to have its production equipment fail unexpectedly. The decision to remove plant and equipment from service to perform preventive maintenance (PM), therefore, becomes a critical strategic decision. SAP's PM module permits the collection of equipment usage readings that are used for scheduling PM. Information relating to wear, consumption, or units produced can be automatically collected via counters located at strategic points in the production process. For example, an electricity meter connected to an electrically powered production unit can serve as a usage counter. Personnel at remote sites can enter usage information into the system via the Internet.

Human Resources

The human resources module helps the organization manage its employee resources including hiring, work scheduling, and payroll processing. Management can obtain current information on overtime worked, labor time and costs charged to individual jobs, and travel expenses. The module supports the following routine business tasks: payroll, time management, travel expense accounting, employee benefits, recruitment, and workforce planning.

In addition, SAP's Who Is Who application improves communication among employees by providing personal information on the intranet (the internet used for internal communication). The module maintains current Internet addresses, telephone numbers, fax numbers, and employee photographs, which can be accessed from the Internet using various search criteria.

Business Process Support

Business process support comprises two classes of modules: the workflow management and the industry solution modules. These modules provide a framework for controlling all the application modules discussed previously. Using a centralized data repository, the process support modules permit a smooth flow of information between sales, manufacturing, finance, purchasing, and so on. The workflow management module automates the business process according to specified business procedures and rules. It notifies users of activities that have been successfully completed and of open items that need attention. The industry solution module is a set of SAP processes that have been customized to a specific industry. Customized procedures have been developed for the following industries: consumer packaged goods, utilities and telecommunications, health care, process industries (chemical and pharmaceutical), oil and gas, high technology and electronics, and automotive.

Supply Chain Management

The inclusion of SCM functionality is a recent focus for ERP vendors. The objective is to provide a total-solution system for their clients. SCM components are not included in all ERP systems, but along with improved Internet connectivity (discussed next), SCM issues are at the forefront of ERP development. SAP supports supply chain management with its *advanced planner and optimizer* system. This module helps improve demand forecasting and production efficiencies for the firm. Another module called the *logistics execution system* aids in efficient flow of inventory items along the supply chain and allows integration with outside systems.

Electronic Commerce Support

More and more companies are using electronic commerce to support business-to-business and business-to-consumer processes such as procurement, customer service, and sales order processing. Providing clients with an ERP system that can interact directly with systems used by their customers and suppliers is a primary objective. Many ERP vendors are going the way of Internet order fulfillment to satisfy this requirement. This approach is a departure from the traditional EDI systems in which partnering with another firm was essential for the systems to interact.

R/3 can link to the Internet to execute electronic commerce transactions. For example, a warehouse supervisor can use R/3 to create a requisition for an item of material directly from the shop floor. The system will automatically access the Internet in real time, scan the list of authorized suppliers, select a supplier based on relevant criteria (such as price, quantity needed, terms of trade, and lead time), and then place the order over the Internet.

SAP uses industry standard interfaces such as XML (Extensible Markup Language) to better support integration to outside systems. This helps facilitate the exchange of information with customers and vendors along the supply chain that utilize different ERP systems.

J.D. EDWARDS

J.D. Edwards' ERP philosophy is in sharp contrast to SAP's. Rather than create a highly structured and tightly integrated system, it employs a *configurable network computing* approach, which provides a flexible system that is open enough to accept the best-practices modules of other vendors. In other words, if the client wants to use the SCM system of another vendor, the J.D. Edwards (JDE) system should accommodate it. Its architecture allows highly configurable, distributed applications to run on a variety of platforms without users or analysts knowing which platforms or which databases are involved in any given tasks. JDE's client base is drawn from the following industries: automotive, energy/chemical, government/education/utilities, pharmaceuticals, consumer package goods, industrial fabrication and assembly, architecture/engineering/construction, mining, real estate, and electronics.

JDE is built on a distributed object network-centric architecture with both client server and browser access to enterprise applications. Internet media objects, data marts, and data mining can be incorporated into this environment. Most ERPs offer configurability at the point of system implementation but if the business environment changes in the future, highly structured ERPs may be too rigid accommodate them easily. JDE users can reconfigure after the design phase to adjust for changes in organizational structure, technology, etc. JDE's architecture is written at a high level of abstraction that sorts out platform differences and thus allows the business solution to run in almost any configuration on any platform. This allows simplified configurability and upgrades. Its platform-independent solutions include AS/400 (DB2), RS/6000 (DB2 or Oracle), HP 9000 (DB2 or Oracle), Windows NT servers (SQL Server, DB2, or Oracle), and Internet. JDE has two distinguishing features: flexibility and modularity.

Flexibility

JDE's software flexibility allows business managers to have direct access to configure and change certain system functions. The advantages are that users take immediate ownership of the system and IT professionals do not make business decisions that they are not qualified to make. For example, the business staff has the ability to make changes to user views and output reports without relying on the IT staff to make the changes for them. Business staff can also change the look of input screens through a visually-oriented point-and-click environment. This functionality is based on a separation of *business activators* and *technology activators* that allow the professionals in each area to control their area of expertise.

An example of a **business activator** is the *grid options activator*, which allows business users to control the display and data entry screens. The business users can change the color, size, and style of the font to their preferences. Other business activators JDE provides include charting, navigation, printer/e-mail, security, language, currency, and 19 others. An example of a **technology activator** is the *just-in-time installation* activator that allows a technology professional to distribute user configurations and changes such as a sales order input screen to the users throughout the organization via the network. JDE provides a number of other technology activators, including version control, object configuration manager, EDI, and open data access.

JDE's flexibility differentiates them from their competition by giving business managers the ability to control the business decisions without involving IT unnecessarily. The power of decision making is thus placed into the most qualified hands. Users think of the ERP as their system rather than one that was thrust upon them by others. This sense of ownership is necessary for acceptance of the significant changes that accompany all ERP implementations.

Modularity

Another distinguishing feature of the JDE system software is modularity. Client organizations have the option of implementing one piece of the ERP system or the entire enterprise package. The core function modules include Manufacturing & Distribution Suites, Financial Foundation Suite, and Payroll & Human Resource Suite. JDE has also developed industry-specific applications such as Energy & Chemical Suite, Services Suite, and Public Services Solutions for Government, Education, Utilities, and Not-for-Profits. In addition to these suites, JDE has developed a supply chain management solution called SCOREx. During implementation JDE provides preconfigured Industry Practice Models to allow clients to start with industry standard practices, which they can later modify if necessary.

ORACLE

Oracle was founded in 1977 by Larry Ellison. The Oracle database was the first DBMS to incorporate the SQL language. Now Oracle offers a variety of application development tools and is a major promoter of the network computer. Currently Oracle is the world's leading supplier of software for information management, and the world's second largest independent software company. With annual revenues of about $10 billion, the company offers its database, development tools, and ERP application products, along with related consulting, education, and support services, in more than 145 countries around the world.

Oracle's client list includes many large and mid-sized companies from the following industries: education, telecommunications, chemical/pharmaceutical, high technology, media/Internet, government, energy, financial services, health care, manufacturing, consumer sector, retail, transportation, utilities, aerospace/defense, automotive, and metals. Organizations that employ a competitor's ERP will most likely implement it over an Oracle database. Their core system is organized into modules for manufacturing, supply chain management, financials, projects, human resources, and front office.

Distinguishing Features

Oracle is tailored to an e-business focus. With Oracle's Internet-based applications versus the standard client-server-based applications, its technology easily supports e-business. Internet applications centralize their ERP system into a few professionally managed servers. This technology also consolidates data into a few global databases and distributes information via a global network. The old client-server applications that all of Oracle's competitors are still using (some are developing and starting to use Internet capabilities at this time) distribute complexity onto every user's desktop PC and fragment information into many little database servers spread out in many locations

Internet-Based Software. Oracle's ERP is an Internet-based system rather than a traditional client-server system. Oracle users access the ERP applications via an intranet server using a standard Internet browser. Oracle is the first ERP software company to develop and deploy 100 percent Internet-enabled enterprise software across its entire product line. This approach promotes lower cost of operations, supports thousands of users, and provides a better return on investment because of the rapid implementation and longer software life. Oracle software runs on PCs, workstations, minicomputers, mainframes, and massive parallel computers.

Customizable. During implementation Oracle applications can be customized to the client's needs by the setting of various switches that enable or disable functions and database tables. When upgrades are necessary, the custom parts of the applications are upgraded along with the basic software. Therefore, clients do not need to start from scratch with each new release.

PeopleSoft

When PeopleSoft was founded in 1987, its products supported primarily human resource management and finance functions. Today, PeopleSoft has expanded into an enterprise-wide system. PeopleSoft's core application suite focuses on the functions that are fundamental to most organizations—managing materials, people, finances, and projects. Its product portfolio includes applications that support a wide range of businesses including manufacturing, education, financial services, the public sector, retail, U.S. government, service industries, communications, utilities, and transportation.

PeopleSoft is built on the concept of open architecture, which allows organizations to configure the application to integrate with existing internal systems. Products are supported through three-tier configurations for wide area networks (WANs) and two-tier configurations for local area networks (LANs). Additionally, PeopleSoft gives its customers a choice of leading platforms and is flexible enough to migrate from one to another if necessary. The preferred platforms include DEC Open VMS, IBM DB2, Novell Netware, Informix, OS/400, MS SQL Server, Unix, Oracle, Windows 95/98/NT, Sybase, and IBM S390.

PeopleSoft's distinguishing features are rapid implementation and advanced planning.

Rapid Implementation

The PeopleSoft suite of products was developed on a common platform and employs a modular approach, which allows organizations to implement additional applications rapidly.

Advanced Planning and Scheduling

PeopleSoft was the first ERP vendor to incorporate advanced planning and scheduling directly into its ERP system. This gave the company a competitive advantage in the manufacturing sector by providing an interface for handling multiple constraints in production planning simultaneously.

Baan

Baan is a software company that specializes in enterprise-wide applications. Founded in the Netherlands in 1978 by Jan and Paul Baan, it has become a major ERP vendor operating in more than 80 countries. Baan includes modules for manufacturing, finance, project estimating, and management and distribution. These integrate with other Baan modules including supply chain management. Baan products appear in the following industries: aerospace and defense, automotive, consumer packaged goods, electronics, engineering and construction, forest products, industrial equipment, primary metals, semiconductor, specialty chemicals, and wholesale. Baan's ERP system supports multiple languages, tax structures, and currencies including the Euro. It is built on the concept of open architecture that allows customers to configure applications to work with their existing internal systems. The preferred platforms are UNIX, NT, and AS/400.

Baan's distinguishing features include best-of-class applications, evergreen delivery, and workflow modeling and maintenance modules.

Best-of-Class Applications

The Baan ERP Suite assembles best-of-class components and keeps them current through subsequent releases. This enables enterprises to update their information infrastructure in manageable incremental initiatives. Baan clients are able to choose state-of-the-art software solutions from Baan and hundreds of its technology partner companies. The client organization can effectively configure its ERP's functionality from many different vendors to suit each business need across the company's value chain.

Evergreen Delivery

Baan's partnering arrangements with technology firms provide an ongoing stream of new component applications. Baan customers can implement an "assemble to order" system that grows with business needs. This can prove to be less costly and less risky than the big bang model.

Workflow Modeling and Maintenance Modules

Baan has two unique industry leading modules—Baan DEMse and Baan Maintenance—that allow it to service unique needs. The maintenance module is very useful for industries like aviation, while DEMse provides graphic business control models that are the best in the industry.

CHAPTER

7 Computer-Assisted Audit Tools and Techniques

LEARNING OBJECTIVES

After studying this chapter, you should:

- Be familiar with the classes of transaction input controls used by accounting applications.
- Understand the objectives and techniques used to implement processing controls, including run-to-run, operator intervention, and audit trail controls.
- Understand the methods used to establish effective output controls for both batch and real-time systems.
- Know the difference between black box and white box auditing.
- Be familiar with the key features of the five CAATTs discussed in the chapter.

This chapter examines several issues related to the use of Computer-Assisted Audit Tools and Techniques (CAATTs) for performing tests of application controls and data extraction. It opens with a description of application controls. These fall into three broad classes: input controls, processing controls, and output controls. The chapter then examines the *black box* and *white box* approaches to testing application controls. The latter approach requires a detailed understanding of the application's logic. Five CAATT approaches used for testing application logic are then examined: the test data method, base case system evaluation, tracing, integrated test facility, and parallel simulation.

APPLICATION CONTROLS

Application controls are programmed procedures designed to deal with potential exposures that threaten specific applications, such as payroll, purchases, and cash disbursements systems. Application controls fall into three broad categories: input controls, processing controls, and output controls.

Input Controls

The data collection component of the information system is responsible for bringing data into the system for processing. **Input controls** at this stage are designed to ensure that these transactions are valid, accurate, and complete. Data input procedures can be either source document-triggered (batch) or direct input (real time).

Source document input requires human involvement and is prone to clerical errors. Some types of errors that are entered on the source documents cannot be detected and corrected during the data input stage. Dealing with these problems may require tracing the transaction back to its source (such as contacting the customer) to correct the mistake. Direct input, on the other hand, employs real-time editing techniques to identify and correct errors immediately, thus significantly reducing the number of errors that enter the system.

Classes of Input Control

For presentation convenience and to provide structure to this discussion, we have divided input controls into the following broad classes:

- Source document controls
- Data coding controls
- Batch controls
- Validation controls
- Input error correction
- Generalized data input systems

These control classes are not mutually exclusive divisions. Some control techniques that we shall examine could fit logically into more than one class.

Source Document Controls. Careful control must be exercised over physical source documents in systems that use them to initiate transactions. Source document fraud can be used to remove assets from the organization. For example, an individual with access to purchase orders and receiving reports could fabricate a purchase transaction to a nonexistent supplier. If these documents are entered into the data processing stream, along with a fabricated vendor's invoice, the system could process these documents as if a legitimate transaction had taken place. In the absence of other compensating controls to detect this type of fraud, the system would create an account payable and subsequently write a check in payment.

To control against this type of exposure, the organization must implement control procedures over source documents to account for each document, as described next:

Use Prenumbered Source Documents. Source documents should come prenumbered from the printer with a unique sequential number on each document. Source document numbers permit accurate accounting of document usage and provide an audit trail for tracing transactions through accounting records. We discuss this further in the next section.

Use Source Documents in Sequence. Source documents should be distributed to the users and used in sequence. This requires that adequate physical security be maintained over the source document inventory at the user site. When not in use, documents should be locked away. At all times, access to source documents should be limited to authorized persons.

Periodically Audit Source Documents. Reconciling document sequence numbers should identify missing source documents. Periodically, the auditor should compare the numbers of documents used to date with those remaining in inventory plus those voided due to errors. Documents not accounted for should be reported to management.

Data Coding Controls. Coding controls are checks on the integrity of data codes used in processing. A customer's account number, an inventory item number, and a chart of accounts number are all examples of data codes. Three types of errors can corrupt data codes and cause processing errors: transcription errors, single transposition errors, and multiple transposition errors. **Transcription errors** fall into three classes:

- Addition errors occur when an extra digit or character is added to the code. For example, inventory item number 83276 is recorded as 832766.
- Truncation errors occur when a digit or character is removed from the end of a code. In this type of error, the inventory item above would be recorded as 8327.
- Substitution errors are the replacement of one digit in a code with another. For example, code number 83276 is recorded as 83266.

There are two types of **transposition errors.** *Single transposition errors* occur when two adjacent digits are reversed. For instance, 83276 is recorded as 38276. *Multiple transposition errors* occur when nonadjacent digits are transposed. For example, 83276 is recorded as 87236

Any of these errors can cause serious problems in data processing if they go undetected. For example, a sales order for customer 732519 that is transposed into 735219 will be posted to the wrong customer's account. A similar error in an inventory item code on a purchase order could result in ordering unneeded inventory and failing to order inventory that is needed. These simple errors can severely disrupt operations.

Check Digits. One method for detecting data coding errors is a check digit. A check digit is a control digit (or digits) added to the code when it is originally assigned that allows the integrity of the code to be established during subsequent processing. The check digit can be located anywhere in the code: as a prefix, a suffix, or embedded someplace in the middle. The simplest form of check digit is to sum the digits in the code and use this sum as the check digit. For example, for the customer account code 5372 the calculated check digit would be

$$5 + 3 + 7 + 2 = 17$$

By dropping the tens column, the check digit 7 is added to the original code to produce the new code 53727. The entire string of digits (including the check digit) becomes the customer account number. During data entry, the system can recalculate the check digit to ensure that the code is correct. This technique will detect only transcription errors. For example, if a substitution error occurred and the above code were entered as 52727, the calculated check digit would be 6 ($5 + 2 + 7 + 2 = 16 = 6$), and the error would be detected. However, this technique would fail to identify transposition errors. For example, transposing the first two digits yields the code 35727, which still sums to 17 and produces the check digit 7. This error would go undetected.

There are many check-digit techniques for dealing with transposition errors. A popular method is modulus 11. Using the code 5372, the steps in this technique are as follows:

1. *Assign weights.* Each digit in the code is multiplied by a different weight. In this case, the weights used are 5, 4, 3, and 2, shown as follows:

Digit		Weight
5	×	5 = 25
3	×	4 = 12
7	×	3 = 21
2	×	2 = 4

2. *Sum the products* (25 + 12 + 21 + 4 = 62).
3. *Divide by the modulus.* We are using modulus 11 in this case, giving 62/11 = 5 with a remainder of 7.
4. *Subtract the remainder from the modulus to obtain the check digit* (11 – 7 = 4 [check digit]).
5. *Add the check digit to the original code to yield the new code*: 53724.

Using this technique to recalculate the check digit during processing, a transposition error in the code will produce a check digit other than 4. For example, if the preceding code were incorrectly entered as 35724, the recalculated check digit would be 6.

When Should Check Digits Be Used? The use of check digits introduces storage and processing inefficiencies and therefore should be restricted to essential data, such as primary and secondary key fields. All check digit techniques require one or more additional spaces in the field to accommodate the check digit. In the case of modulus 11, if step three above produces a remainder of 1, the check digit of 10 will require two additional character spaces. If field length is a limitation, one way of handling this problem is to disallow codes that generate the check digit 10. This would restrict the range of available codes by about 9 percent.

Batch Controls. **Batch controls** are an effective method of managing high volumes of transaction data through a system. The objective of batch control is to reconcile output produced by the system with the input originally entered into the system. This provides assurance that:

- All records in the batch are processed.
- No records are processed more than once.
- An audit trail of transactions is created from input through processing to the output stage of the system.

Batch control is not exclusively an input control technique. Controlling the batch continues through all phases of the system. We are treating this topic here because batch control is initiated at the input stage.

Achieving batch control objectives requires grouping similar types of input transactions (such as sales orders) together in batches and then controlling the batches throughout data processing. Two documents are used to accomplish this task: a batch transmittal sheet and a batch control log. Figure 7-1 shows an example of a batch transmittal sheet. The batch transmittal sheet captures relevant information such as the following about the batch.

FIGURE 7-1

Batch Transmittal Sheet

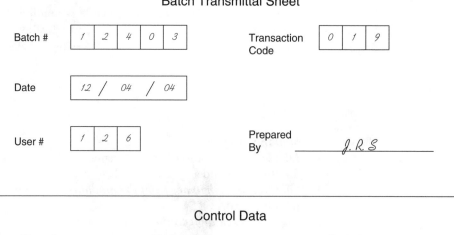

ABC Company
Batch Transmittal Sheet

Batch #	1 2 4 0 3	Transaction Code	0 1 9
Date	12 / 04 / 04		
User #	1 2 6	Prepared By	J. R. S

Control Data

Record Count	Hash Total	Control Total
0 5 0	4 5 3 7 8 3 8	1 2 2 6 7 4 8 7

- A unique batch number
- A batch date
- A transaction code (indicating the type of transactions, such as a sales order or cash receipt)
- The number of records in the batch (record count)
- The total dollar value of a financial field (batch control total)
- The total of a unique nonfinancial field (hash total)

Usually, the batch transmittal sheet is prepared by the user department and is submitted to data control along with the batch of source documents. Sometimes, the data control clerk, acting as a liaison between the users and the data processing department, prepares the transmittal sheet. Figure 7-2 illustrates the batch control process.

The data control clerk receives transactions from users assembled in batches of 40 to 50 records. The clerk assigns each batch a unique number, date-stamps the documents, and calculates (or recalculates) the batch control numbers, such as the total dollar amount of the batch and a hash total (discussed later). The clerk enters the batch control information in the batch control log and submits the batch of documents, along with the transmittal sheet, to the data entry department. Figure 7-3 shows a sample batch control log.

The data entry group codes and enters the transmittal sheet data onto the transaction file, along with the batch of transaction records. The transmittal data may be added as an additional record in the file or placed in the file's internal trailer label. (We will discuss internal labels later in this section.) The transmittal sheet becomes the batch control record and is used to assess the integrity of the batch during processing. For example, the data entry procedure will recalculate the

FIGURE 7-2 **Batch Control Process**

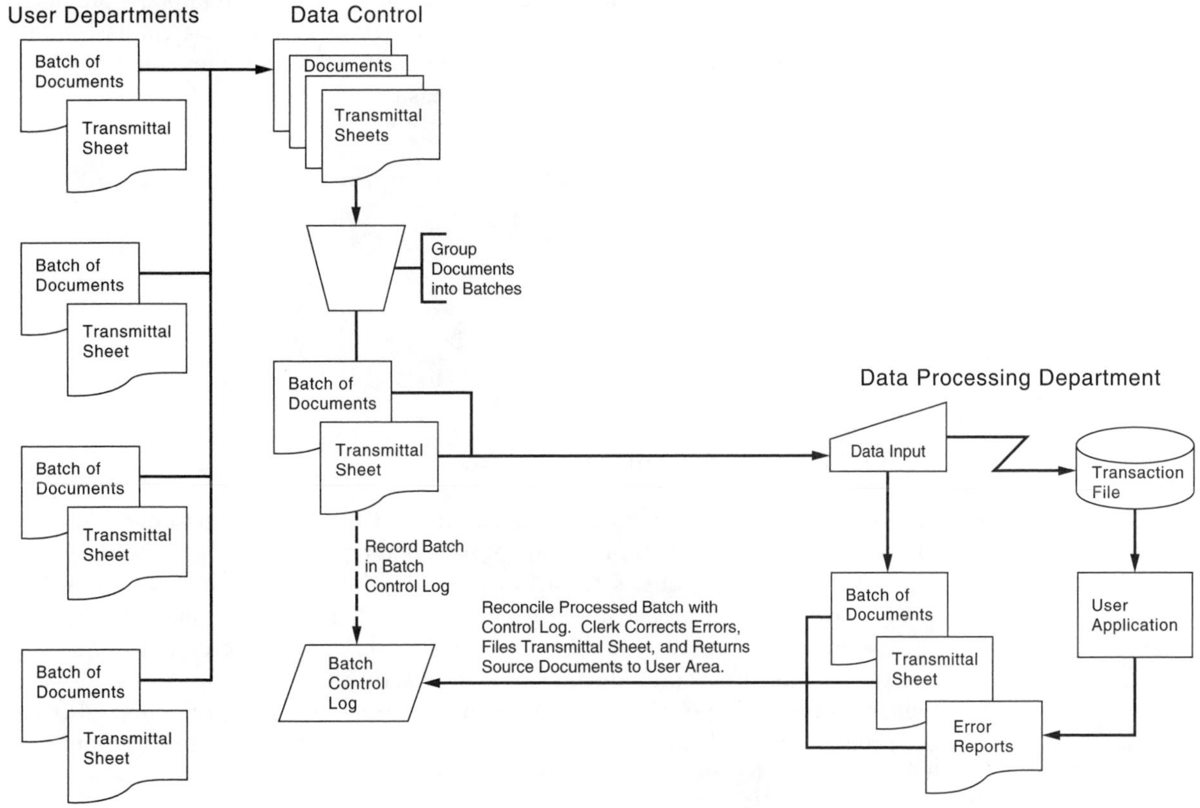

batch control totals to make sure the batch is in balance. The transmittal record shows a batch of 50 sales order records with a total dollar value of $122,674.87 and a hash total of 4537838. At various points throughout and at the end of processing, these amounts are recalculated and compared to the batch control record. If the procedure recalculates the same amounts, the batch is in balance.

After processing, the output results are sent to the data control clerk for reconciliation and distribution to the user. The clerk updates the batch control log to record that processing of the batch was completed successfully.

FIGURE 7-3 **Batch Control Log**

End User							Data Processing					
Batch #	Date	Time	Rec By	Control Total	Hash Total	Record Count	Submitted Date	Submitted Time	Returned Date	Returned Time	Error Code	Reconciled By
12 403	12/4/04	9:05	B.R.	122,674.87	4537838	50	12/4/04	9:55	12/4/04	11:05	0	PMR

Hash Totals. The term **hash total**, which was used in the preceding discussion, refers to a simple control technique that uses nonfinancial data to keep track of the records in a batch. Any key field, such as a customer's account number, a purchase order number, or an inventory item number, may be used to calculate a hash total. In the following example, the sales order number (SO#) field for an entire batch of sales order records is summed to produce a hash total.

SO#	
14327	
67345	
19983	
•	
•	
•	
•	
88943	
96543	
4537838	(hash total)

Let's see how this seemingly meaningless number can be of use. Assume that after this batch of records leaves data control someone replaced one of the sales orders in the batch with a fictitious record of the same dollar amount. How would the batch control procedures detect this irregularity? Both the record count and the dollar amount control totals would be unaffected by this act. However, unless the perpetrator obtained a source document with exactly the same sales order number (which would be impossible, since they should come uniquely prenumbered from the printer), the hash total calculated by the batch control procedures would not balance. Thus, the irregularity would be detected.

Validation Controls. Input **validation controls** are intended to detect errors in transaction data before the data are processed. Validation procedures are most effective when they are performed as close to the source of the transaction as possible. However, depending on the type of CBIS in use, input validation may occur at various points in the system. For example, some validation procedures require making references against the current master file. CBISs using real-time processing or batch processing with direct access master files can validate data at the input stage. Figure 7-4(a) and (b) illustrate these techniques.

If the CBIS uses batch processing with sequential files, the transaction records being validated must first be sorted in the same order as the master file. Validating at the data input stage in this case may require considerable additional processing. Therefore, as a practical matter, each processing module prior to updating the master file record performs some validation procedures. This approach is shown in Figure 7-5.

The problem with this technique is that a transaction may be partially processed before data errors are detected. Dealing with a partially complete transaction will require special error-handling procedures. We shall discuss error-handling controls later in this section.

There are three levels of input validation controls:

1. Field interrogation
2. Record interrogation
3. File interrogation

FIGURE 7-4

Validation during Data Input

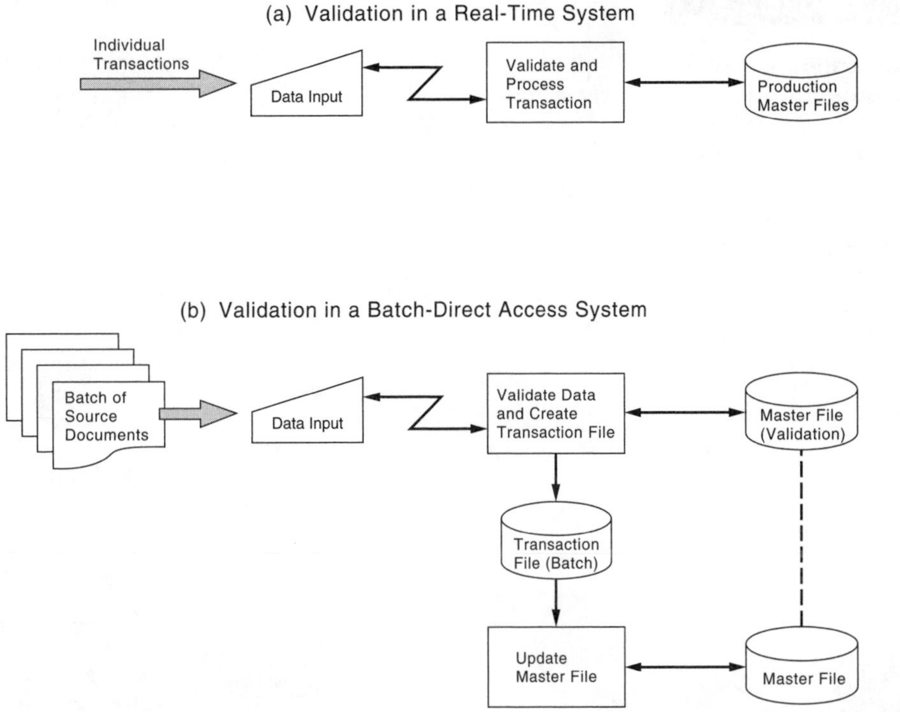

Field Interrogation. **Field interrogation** involves programmed procedures that examine the characteristics of the data in the field. The following are some common types of field interrogation.

Missing data checks are used to examine the contents of a field for the presence of blank spaces. Some programming languages are restrictive as to the justification (right or left) of data within the field. If data are not properly justified or if a character is missing (has been replaced with a blank), the value in the field will be improperly processed. In some cases, the presence of blanks in a numeric data field may cause a system failure. When the validation program detects a blank where it expects to see a data value, this will be interpreted as an error.

Numeric-alphabetic data checks determine whether the correct form of data is in a field. For example, a customer's account balance should not contain alphabetic data. As with blanks, alphabetic data in a numeric field may cause serious processing errors.

Zero-value checks are used to verify that certain fields are filled with zeros. Some program languages require that fields used in mathematical operations be initiated with zeros prior to processing. This control may trigger an automatic corrective control to replace the contents of the field with zero if it detects a nonzero value.

Limit checks determine if the value in the field exceeds an authorized limit. For example, assume the firm's policy is that no employee works more than 44 hours per week. The payroll system validation program can interrogate the hours-worked field in the weekly payroll records for values greater than 44.

Range checks assign upper and lower limits to acceptable data values. For example, if the range of pay rates for hourly employees in a firm is between 8 and

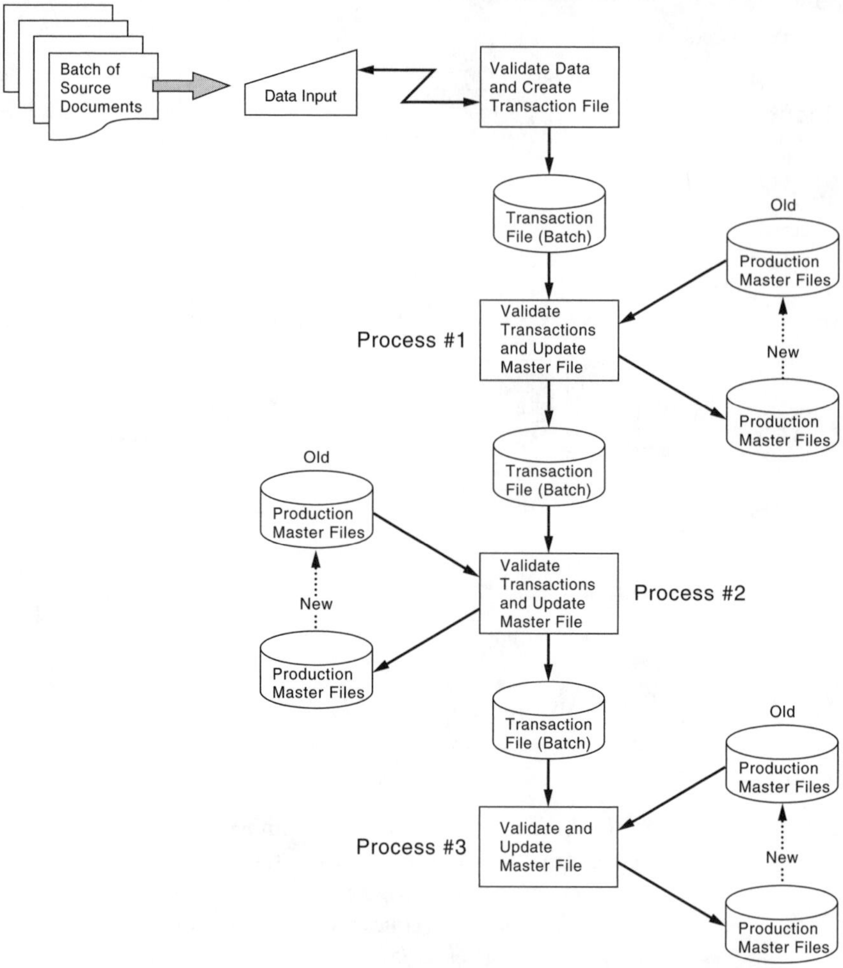

FIGURE 7-5

Validation in Batch Sequential File System *(Note: For simplification, the necessary re-sorting of the transaction file between update processes is not shown.)*

20 dollars, all payroll records can be checked to see that this range is not exceeded. The purpose of this control is to detect keystroke errors that shift the decimal point one or more places. It would not detect an error where a correct pay rate of, say, 9 dollars is incorrectly entered as 15 dollars.

Validity checks compare actual values in a field against known acceptable values. This control is used to verify such things as transaction codes, state abbreviations, or employee job skill codes. If the value in the field does not match one of the acceptable values, the record is determined to be in error.

This is a frequently used control in cash disbursement systems. One form of cash disbursement fraud involves manipulating the system into making a fraudulent payment to a nonexistent vendor. To prevent this, the firm may establish a list of valid vendors with whom it does business exclusively. Thus, before payment of any trade obligation, the vendor number on the cash disbursement voucher is matched against the valid vendor list by the validation program. If the code does not match, payment is denied, and management reviews the transaction.

Check digit controls identify keystroke errors in key fields by testing the internal validity of the code. We discussed this control technique earlier in the section.

Record Interrogation. **Record interrogation** procedures validate the entire record by examining the interrelationship of its field values. Some typical tests are discussed below.

Reasonableness checks determine if a value in one field, which has already passed a limit check and a range check, is reasonable when considered along with other data fields in the record. For example, an employee's pay rate of 18 dollars per hour falls within an acceptable range. However, this rate is excessive when compared to the employee's job skill code of 693; employees in this skill class never earn more than 12 dollars per hour.

Sign checks are tests to see if the sign of a field is correct for the type of record being processed. For example, in a sales order processing system, the dollar amount field must be positive for sales orders but negative for sales return transactions. This control can determine the correctness of the sign by comparing it with the transaction code field.

Sequence checks are used to determine if a record is out of order. In batch systems that use sequential master files, the transaction files being processed must be sorted in the same order as the primary keys of the corresponding master file. This requirement is critical to the processing logic of the update program. Hence, before each transaction record is processed, its sequence is verified relative to the previous record processed.

File Interrogation. The purpose of **file interrogation** is to ensure that the correct file is being processed by the system. These controls are particularly important for master files, which contain permanent records of the firm and which, if destroyed or corrupted, are difficult to replace.

Internal label checks verify that the file processed is the one the program is actually calling for. Files stored on magnetic tape are usually kept off-line in a tape library. These files have external labels that identify them (by name and serial number) to the tape librarian and operator. External labeling is typically a manual procedure and, like any manual task, prone to errors. Sometimes, the wrong external label is mistakenly affixed to a file when it is created. Thus, when the file is called for again, the wrong file will be retrieved and placed on the tape drive for processing. Depending on how the file is being used, this may result in its destruction or corruption. To prevent this, the operating system creates an internal header label that is placed at the beginning of the file. An example of a header label is shown in Figure 7-6.

To ensure that the correct file is about to be processed, the system matches the file name and serial number in the header label with the program's file requirements. If the wrong file has been loaded, the system will send the operator a message and suspend processing. It is worth noting that while label checking is generally a standard feature, it is an option that can be overridden by programmers and operators.

Version checks are used to verify that the version of the file being processed is correct. In a grandparent-parent-child approach, many versions of master files and transactions may exist. The version check compares the version number of the files being processed with the program's requirements.

An *expiration date check* prevents a file from being deleted before it expires. In a GPC system, for example, once an adequate number of backup files is created, the oldest backup file is scratched (erased from the disk or tape) to provide space for new files. Figure 7-7 illustrates this procedure.

FIGURE 7-6

Header Label on Magnetic Tape

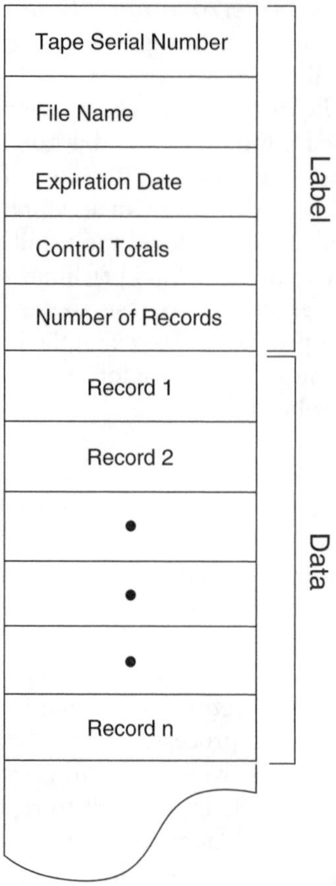

To protect against destroying an active file by mistake, the system first checks the expiration date contained in the header label (see Figure 7-6). If the retention period has not yet expired, the system will generate an error message and abort the scratch procedure. Expiration date control is an optional measure. The length of the retention period is specified by the programmer and based on the number of backup files that are desired. If the programmer chooses not to specify an expiration date, the control against such accidental deletion is eliminated.

Input Error Correction. When errors are detected in a batch, they must be corrected and the records resubmitted for reprocessing. This must be a controlled process to ensure that errors are dealt with completely and correctly. There are three common error handling techniques: (1) correct immediately, (2) create an error file, and (3) reject the entire batch.

Correct Immediately. If the system is using the direct data validation approach (refer to 7-4(a) and (b)), error detection and correction can also take place during data entry. Upon detecting a keystroke error or an illogical relationship, the system should halt the data entry procedure until the user corrects the error.

Create an Error File. When delayed validation is being used, such as in batch systems with sequential files, individual errors should be flagged to prevent them from

FIGURE 7-7 **Scratch Tape Approach Using Retention Date**

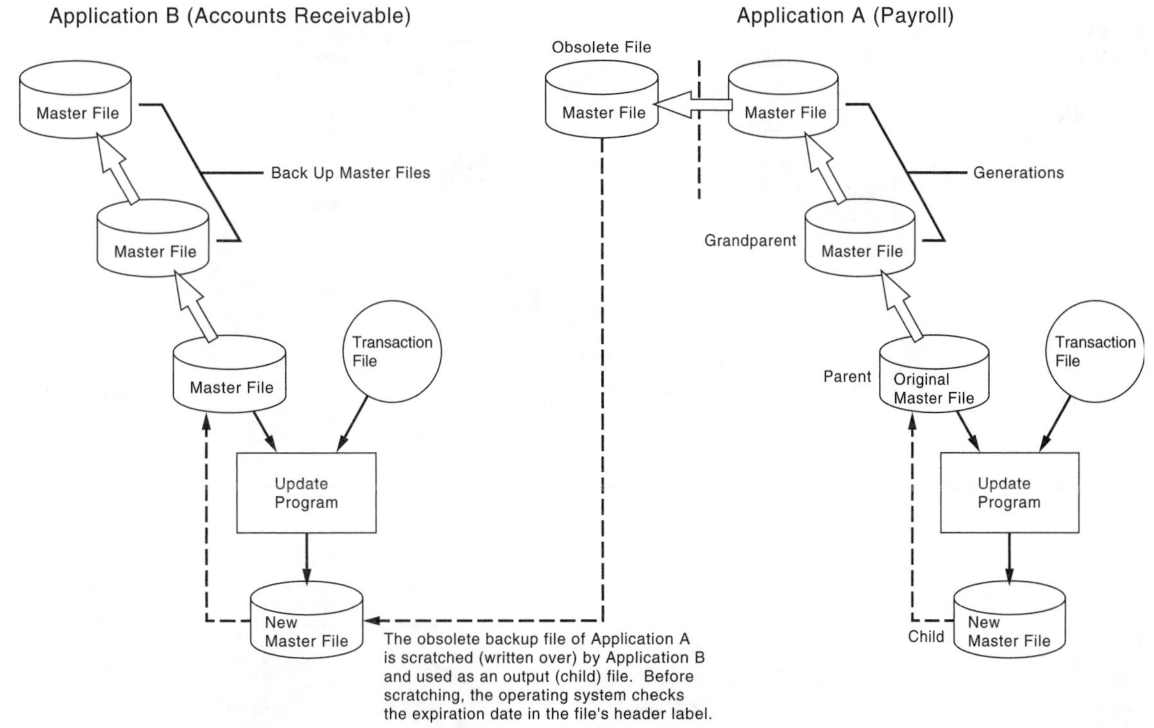

being processed. At the end of the validation procedure, the records flagged as errors are removed from the batch and placed in a temporary error holding file until the errors can be investigated.

Some errors can be detected during data input procedures. However, as was mentioned earlier, the update module performs some validation tests. Thus, error records may be placed on the error file at several different points in the process, as illustrated by Figure 7-8. At each validation point, the system automatically adjusts the batch control totals to reflect the removal of the error records from the batch. In a separate procedure, an authorized user representative will later make corrections to the error records and resubmit them as a separate batch for reprocessing.

Errors detected during processing require careful handling. These records may already be partially processed. Therefore, simply resubmitting the corrected records to the system via the data input stage may result in processing portions of these transactions twice. There are two methods for dealing with this complexity. The first is to reverse the effects of the partially processed transactions and resubmit the corrected records to the data input stage. The second is to reinsert corrected records to the processing stage in which the error was detected. In either case, batch control procedures (preparing batch control records and logging the batches) apply to the resubmitted data, just as they do for normal batch processing.

Reject the Batch. Some forms of errors are associated with the entire batch and are not clearly attributable to individual records. An example of this type of error

FIGURE 7-8

Use of Error File in Batch Sequential File System with Multiple Resubmission Points

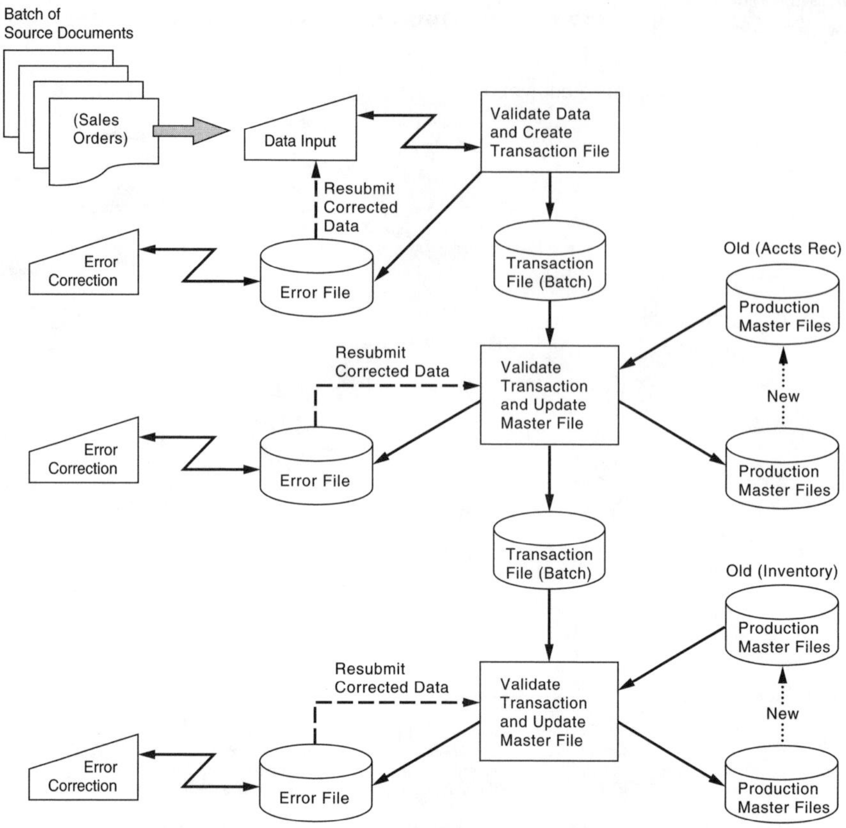

is an imbalance in a batch control total. Assume that the transmittal sheet for a batch of sales orders shows a total sales value of $122,674.87, but the data input procedure calculated a sales total of only $121,454.32. What has caused this? Is the problem a missing or changed record? Or did the data control clerk incorrectly calculate the batch control total? The most effective solution in this case is to cease processing and return the entire batch to data control to evaluate, correct, and resubmit.

Batch errors are one reason for keeping the size of the batch to a manageable number. Too few records in a batch make batch processing inefficient. Too many records make error detection difficult, create greater business disruption when a batch is rejected, and increase the possibility of mistakes when calculating batch control totals.

Generalized Data Input Systems. To achieve a high degree of control and standardization over input validation procedures, some organizations employ a **generalized data input system (GDIS)**. This technique includes centralized procedures to manage the data input for all of the organization's transaction processing systems. The GDIS approach has three advantages. First, it improves control by having one common system perform all data validation. Second, GDIS ensures that each AIS application applies a consistent standard for data validation. Third, GDIS improves systems development efficiency. Given the high degree of commonality in input validation requirements for AIS applications, a GDIS eliminates the need to recreate redundant routines for each new application. Figure 7-9 shows the primary features of this technique. A GDIS has five major components:[1]

1. Generalized validation module
2. Validated data file
3. Error file
4. Error reports
5. Transaction log

Generalized Validation Module. The **generalized validation module** (**GVM**) performs standard validation routines that are common to many different applications. These routines are customized to an individual application's needs through parameters that specify the program's specific requirements. For example, the GVM may apply a range check to the HOURLY RATE field of payroll records. The limits of the range are 6 dollars and 15 dollars. The range test is the generalized procedure; the dollar limits are the parameters that customize this procedure. The validation procedures for some applications may be so unique as to defy a general solution. To meet the goals of the generalized data input system, the GVM must be flexible

FIGURE 7-9

Generalized Data Input System

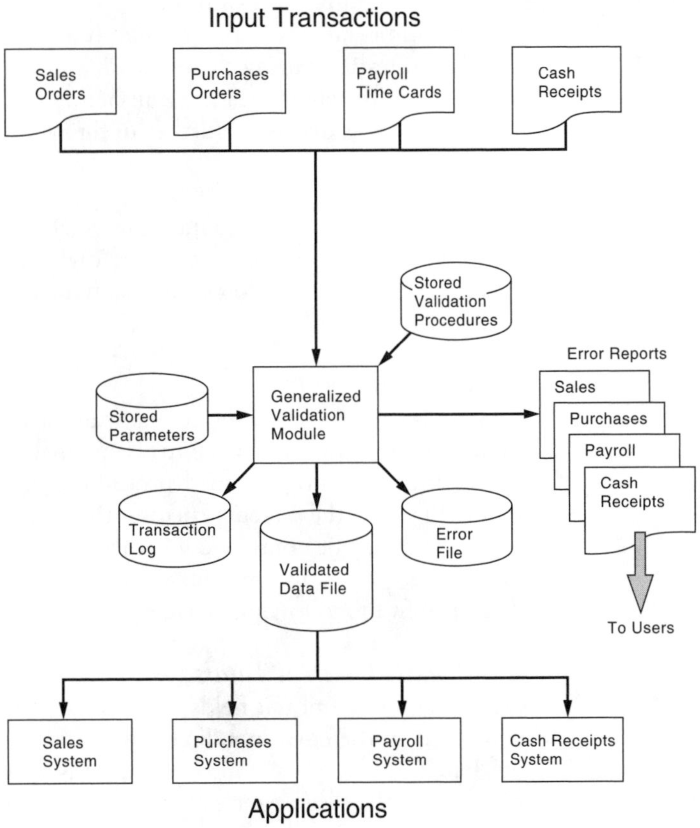

1 Ron Weber, *EDP Auditing: Conceptual Foundations and Practice*, 2d ed. (New York: McGraw-Hill, 1988), pp. 424–427.

enough to permit special user-defined procedures for unique applications. These procedures are stored, along with generalized procedures, and invoked by the GVM as needed.

- *Validated Data File.* The input data that are validated by the GVM are stored on a **validated data file**. This is a temporary holding file through which validated transactions flow to their respective applications. The file is analogous to a tank of water whose level is constantly changing, as it is filled from the top by the GVM and emptied from the bottom by applications.
- *Error File.* The **error file** in the GDIS plays the same role as a traditional error file. Error records detected during validation are stored in the file, corrected, and then resubmitted to the GVM.
- *Error Reports.* Standardized **error reports** are distributed to users to facilitate error correction. For example, if the HOURLY RATE field in a payroll record fails a range check, the error report will display an error message stating the problem so. The report will also present the contents of the failed record, along with the acceptable range limits taken from the parameters.
- *Transaction Log.* The **transaction log** is a permanent record of all validated transactions. From an accounting records point of view, the transaction log is equivalent to the journal and is an important element in the audit trail. However, only successful transactions (those that will be completely processed) should be entered in the journal. If a transaction is to undergo additional validation testing during the processing phase (which could result in its rejection), it should be entered in the transaction log only after it is completely validated. This issue is discussed further in the next section under Audit Trail Controls.

Processing Controls

After passing through the data input stage, transactions enter the processing stage of the system. **Processing controls** are divided into three categories: run-to-run controls, operator intervention controls, and *Audit Trail Controls*.

Run-to-Run Controls

Previously, we discussed the preparation of batch control figures as an element of input control. **Run-to-run controls** use batch figures to monitor the batch as it moves from one programmed procedure (run) to another. These controls ensure that each run in the system processes the batch correctly and completely. Batch control figures may be contained in either a separate control record created at the data input stage or an internal label. Specific uses of run-to-run control figures are described in the following paragraphs.

Recalculate Control Totals. After each major operation in the process and after each run, dollar amount fields, hash totals, and record counts are accumulated and compared to the corresponding values stored in the control record. If a record in the batch is lost, goes unprocessed, or is processed more than once, this will be revealed by the discrepancies between these figures.

Transaction Codes. The **transaction code** of each record in the batch is compared to the transaction code contained in the control record. This ensures that only the correct type of transaction is being processed.

Sequence Checks. In systems that use sequential master files, the order of the transaction records in the batch is critical to correct and complete processing. As the batch moves through the process, it must be re-sorted in the order of the master file used in each run. The **sequence check** control compares the sequence of each record in the batch with the previous record to ensure that proper sorting took place.

Figure 7-10 illustrates the use of run-to-run controls in a revenue cycle system. This application comprises four runs: (1) data input, (2) accounts receivable update, (3) inventory update, and (4) output. At the end of the accounts receivable run, batch control figures are recalculated and reconciled with the control totals passed from the data input run. These figures are then passed to the inventory update run, where they are again recalculated, reconciled, and passed to the output run. Errors detected in each run are flagged and placed in an error file. The run-to-run (batch) control figures are then adjusted to reflect the deletion of these records.

FIGURE 7-10

Run-to-Run Controls

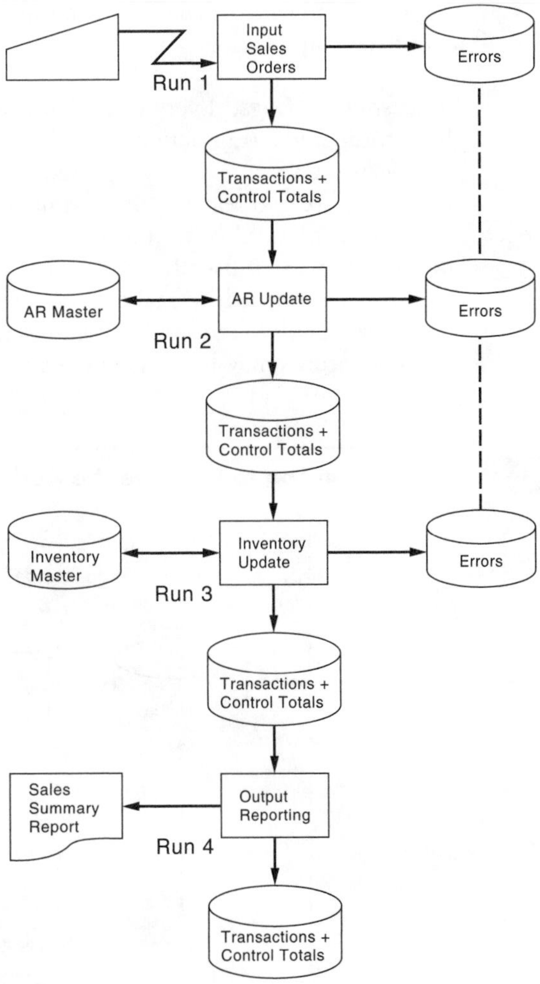

Operator Intervention Controls

Systems sometimes require operator intervention to initiate certain actions, such as entering control totals for a batch of records, providing parameter values for logical operations, and activating a program from a different point when reentering semi-processed error records. Operator intervention increases the potential for human error. Systems that limit operator intervention through **operator intervention controls** are thus less prone to processing errors. Although it may be impossible to eliminate operator involvement completely, parameter values and program start points should, to the extent possible, be derived logically or provided to the system through look-up tables.

Audit Trail Controls

The preservation of an audit trail is an important objective of process control. In an accounting system, every transaction must be traceable through each stage of processing from its economic source to its presentation in financial statements. In a CBIS environment, the audit trail can become fragmented and difficult to follow. It thus becomes critical that each major operation applied to a transaction be thoroughly documented. The following are examples of techniques used to preserve audit trails in a CBIS.

Transaction Logs. Every transaction successfully processed by the system should be recorded on a transaction log, which serves as a journal. Figure 7-11 shows this arrangement.

There are two reasons for creating a transaction log. First, the transaction log is a permanent record of transactions. The validated transaction file produced at the data input phase is usually a temporary file. Once processed, the records on this file are erased (scratched) to make room for the next batch of transactions. Second, not all of the records in the validated transaction file may be successfully processed. Some of these records may fail tests in the subsequent processing stages. A transaction log

FIGURE 7-11 **Transaction Log to Preserve the Audit Trail**

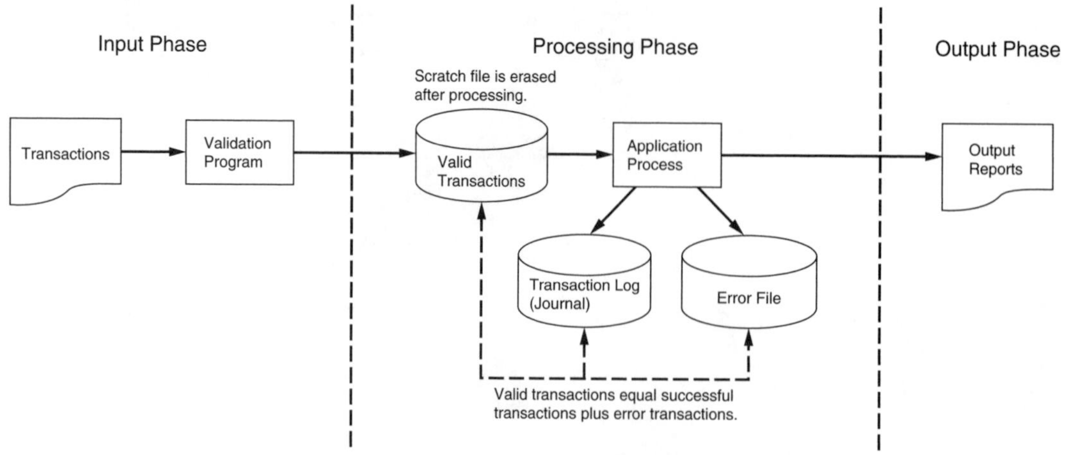

should contain only successful transactions—those that have changed account balances. Unsuccessful transactions should be placed in an error file. The transaction log and error files combined should account for all the transactions in the batch. The validated transaction file may then be scratched with no loss of data.

The system should produce a hard copy transaction listing of all successful transactions. These listings should go to the appropriate users to facilitate reconciliation with input.

Log of Automatic Transactions. Some transactions are triggered internally by the system. An example of this is when inventory drops below a preset reorder point, and the system automatically processes a purchase order. To maintain an audit trail of these activities, all internally generated transactions must be placed in a transaction log.

Listing of Automatic Transactions. To maintain control over automatic transactions processed by the system, the responsible end user should receive a detailed listing of all internally generated transactions.

Unique Transaction Identifiers. Each transaction processed by the system must be uniquely identified with a transaction number. This is the only practical means of tracing a particular transaction through a database of thousands or even millions of records. In systems that use physical source documents, the unique number printed on the document can be transcribed during data input and used for this purpose. In real-time systems, which do not use source documents, the system should assign each transaction a unique number.

Error Listing. A listing of all error records should go to the appropriate user to support error correction and resubmission.

OUTPUT CONTROLS

Output controls ensure that system output is not lost, misdirected, or corrupted and that privacy is not violated. Exposures of this sort can cause serious disruptions to operations and may result in financial losses to a firm. For example, if the checks produced by a firm's cash disbursements system are lost, misdirected, or destroyed, trade accounts and other bills may go unpaid. This could damage the firm's credit rating and result in lost discounts, interest, or penalty charges. If the privacy of certain types of output is violated, a firm could have its business objectives compromised, or it could even become legally exposed. Examples of privacy exposures include the disclosure of trade secrets, patents pending, marketing research results, and patient medical records.

The type of processing method in use influences the choice of controls employed to protect system output. Generally, batch systems are more susceptible to exposure and require a greater degree of control than real-time systems. In this section, we examine output exposures and controls for both methods.

Controlling Batch Systems Output

Batch systems usually produce output in the form of hard copy, which typically requires the involvement of intermediaries in its production and distribution. Figure 7-12 shows the stages in the output process and serves as the basis for the rest of this section.

The output is removed from the printer by the computer operator, separated into sheets and separated from other reports, reviewed for correctness by the data control clerk, and then sent through interoffice mail to the end user. Each stage in this process is a point of potential exposure where the output could be reviewed, stolen, copied, or misdirected. An additional exposure exists when processing or printing goes wrong and produces output that is unacceptable to the end user. These corrupted or partially damaged reports are often discarded in waste cans. Computer criminals have successfully used such waste to achieve their illicit objectives.

Following, we examine techniques for controlling each phase in the output process. Keep in mind that not all of these techniques will necessarily apply to every item of output produced by the system. As always, controls are employed on a cost–benefit basis that is determined by the sensitivity of the data in the reports.

Output Spooling. In large-scale data-processing operations, output devices such as line printers can become backlogged with many programs simultaneously demanding these limited resources. This backlog can cause a bottleneck, which adversely affects the throughput of the system. Applications waiting to print output occupy computer memory and block other applications from entering the processing stream. To ease this burden, applications are often designed to direct their output to a magnetic disk file rather than to the printer directly. This is called **output spooling**. Later, when printer resources become available, the output files are printed.

FIGURE 7-12

Stages in the Output Process

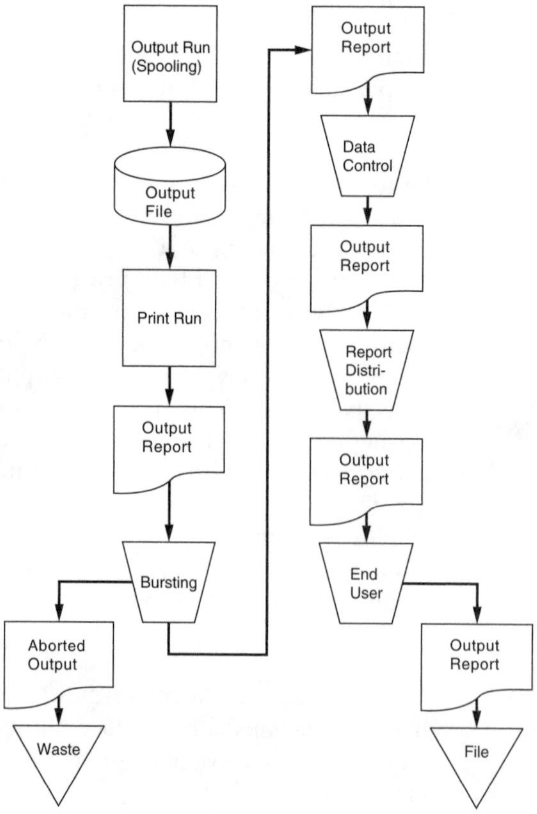

The creation of an output file as an intermediate step in the printing process presents an added exposure. A computer criminal may use this opportunity to perform any of the following unauthorized acts:

- Access the output file and change critical data values (such as dollar amounts on checks). The printer program will then print the corrupted output as if it were produced by the output run. Using this technique, a criminal may effectively circumvent the processing controls designed into the application.
- Access the file and change the number of copies of output to be printed. The extra copies may then be removed without notice during the printing stage.
- Make a copy of the output file to produce illegal output reports.
- Destroy the output file before output printing takes place.

The auditor should be aware of these potential exposures and ensure that proper access and backup procedures are in place to protect output files.

Print Programs. When the printer becomes available, the print run program produces hard copy output from the output file. Print programs are often complex systems that require operator intervention. Four common types of operator actions follow:

1. Pausing the print program to load the correct type of output documents (check stocks, invoices, or other special forms).
2. Entering parameters needed by the print run, such as the number of copies to be printed.
3. Restarting the print run at a prescribed checkpoint after a printer malfunction.
4. Removing printed output from the printer for review and distribution.

Print program controls are designed to deal with two types of exposures presented by this environment: (1) the production of unauthorized copies of output and (2) employee browsing of sensitive data. Some print programs allow the operator to specify more copies of output than the output file calls for, which allows for the possibility of producing unauthorized copies of output. One way to control this is to employ output document controls similar to the source document controls discussed earlier. This is feasible when dealing with prenumbered invoices for billing customers or prenumbered check stock. At the end of the run, the number of copies specified by the output file can be reconciled with the actual number of output documents used. In cases where output documents are not prenumbered, supervision may be the most effective control technique. A security officer can be present during the printing of sensitive output.

To prevent operators from viewing sensitive output, special multipart paper can be used, with the top copy colored black to prevent the print from being read. This type of product, which is illustrated in Figure 7-13, is often used for payroll check printing. The receiver of the check separates the top copy from the body of the check, which contains readable details. An alternative privacy control is to direct the output to a special remote printer that can be closely supervised.

Bursting. When output reports are removed from the printer, they go to the **bursting** stage to have their pages separated and collated. The concern here is that the bursting clerk may make an unauthorized copy of the report, remove a page from the report, or read sensitive information. The primary control against these exposures is supervision. For very sensitive reports, bursting may be performed by the end user.

FIGURE 7-13 **Multipart Check Stock**

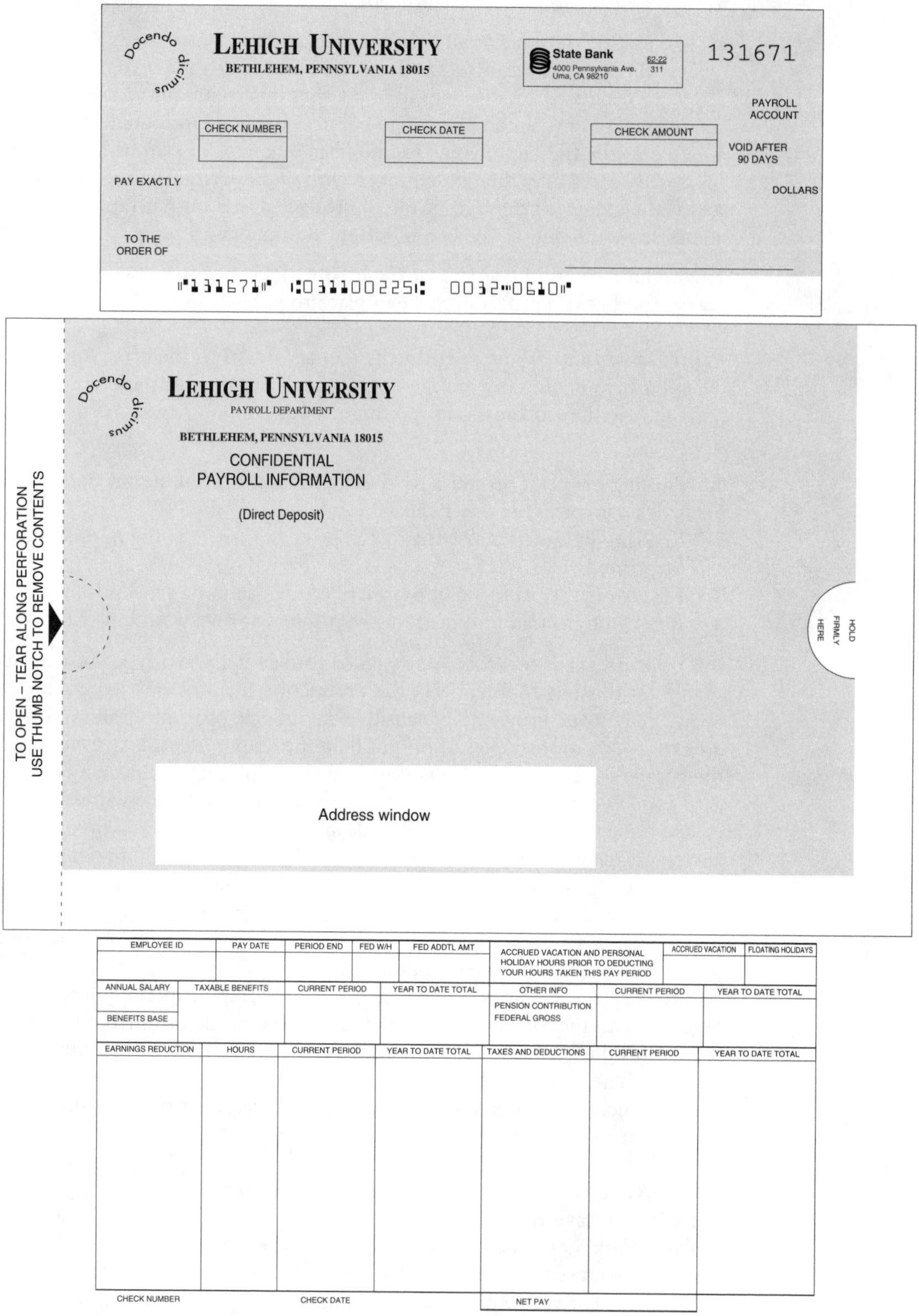

Waste. Computer output waste represents a potential exposure. It is important to dispose of aborted reports and the carbon copies from multipart paper removed during bursting properly. Computer criminals have been known to sift through trash cans searching for carelessly discarded output that is presumed by others to be of no value. From such trash, computer criminals may obtain a key piece of information about the firm's market research, the credit ratings of its customers, or even trade secrets that they can sell to a competitor. Computer waste is also a source of technical data, such as passwords and authority tables, which a perpetrator may use to access the firm's data files. Passing it through a paper shredder can easily destroy sensitive computer output.

Data Control. In some organizations, the **data control** group is responsible for verifying the accuracy of computer output before it is distributed to the user. Normally, the data control clerk will review the batch control figures for balance; examine the report body for garbled, illegible, and missing data; and record the receipt of the report in data control's batch control log. For reports containing highly sensitive data, the end user may perform these tasks. In this case, the report will bypass the data control group and go directly to the user.

Report Distribution. The primary risks associated with report distribution include reports being lost, stolen, or misdirected in transit to the user. A number of control measures can minimize these exposures. For example, when reports are generated, the name and address of the user should be printed on the report. For multicopy reports, an address file of authorized users should be consulted to identify each recipient of the report. Maintaining adequate access control over this file becomes highly important. If an unauthorized individual were able to add his or her name to the authorized user list, he or she would receive a copy of the report.

For highly sensitive reports, the following distribution techniques can be used:

- The reports may be placed in a secure mailbox to which only the user has the key.
- The user may be required to appear in person at the distribution center and sign for the report.
- A security officer or special courier may deliver the report to the user.

End User Controls. Once in the hands of the user, output reports should be reexamined for any errors that may have evaded the data control clerk's review. Users are in a far better position to identify subtle errors in reports that are not disclosed by an imbalance in control totals. Errors detected by the user should be reported to the appropriate computer services management. Such errors may be symptoms of an improper systems design, incorrect procedures, errors inserted by accident during systems maintenance, or unauthorized access to data files or programs.

Once a report has served its purpose, it should be stored in a secure location until its retention period has expired. Factors influencing the length of time a hard copy report is retained include:

- Statutory requirements specified by government agencies, such as the IRS.
- The number of copies of the report in existence. When there are multiple copies, certain of these may be marked for permanent retention, while the remainder can be destroyed after use.
- The existence of magnetic or optical images of reports that can act as permanent backup.

When the retention date has passed, reports should be destroyed in a manner consistent with the sensitivity of their contents. Highly sensitive reports should be shredded.

Controlling Real-Time Systems Output

Real-time systems direct their output to the user's computer screen, terminal, or printer. This method of distribution eliminates the various intermediaries in the journey from the computer center to the user and thus reduces many of the exposures previously discussed. The primary threat to real-time output is the interception, disruption, destruction, or corruption of the output message as it passes along the communications link. This threat comes from two types of exposures: (1) exposures from equipment failure and (2) exposures from subversive acts, whereby a computer criminal intercepts the output message transmitted between the sender and the receiver. Techniques for controlling communications exposures were discussed previously in Chapter 5.

TESTING COMPUTER APPLICATION CONTROLS

This section examines several techniques for auditing computer applications. Control testing techniques provide information about the accuracy and completeness of an application's processes. These tests follow two general approaches: (1) the black box (around the computer) approach and (2) the white box (through the computer) approach. We first examine the black box approach and then review several white box testing techniques.

BLACK-BOX APPROACH

Auditors testing with the **black-box approach** do not rely on a detailed knowledge of the application's internal logic. Instead, they seek to understand the functional characteristics of the application by analyzing flowcharts and interviewing knowledgeable personnel in the client's organization. With an understanding of what the application is supposed to do, the auditor tests the application by reconciling production input transactions processed by the application with output results. The output results are analyzed to verify the application's compliance with its functional requirements. Figure 7-14 illustrates the black box approach.

The advantage of the black-box approach is that the application need not be removed from service and tested directly. This approach is feasible for testing applications that are relatively simple. However, complex applications—those that receive input from many sources, perform a variety of operations, or produce multiple outputs—require a more focused testing approach to provide the auditor with evidence of application integrity.

WHITE-BOX APPROACH

The **white-box approach** relies on an in-depth understanding of the internal logic of the application being tested. The white-box approach includes several techniques for testing application logic directly. These techniques use small numbers of specially created test transactions to verify specific aspects of an application's logic and controls. In this way, auditors are able to conduct precise tests, with known variables,

FIGURE 7-14

Auditing around the Computer—The Black Box Approach

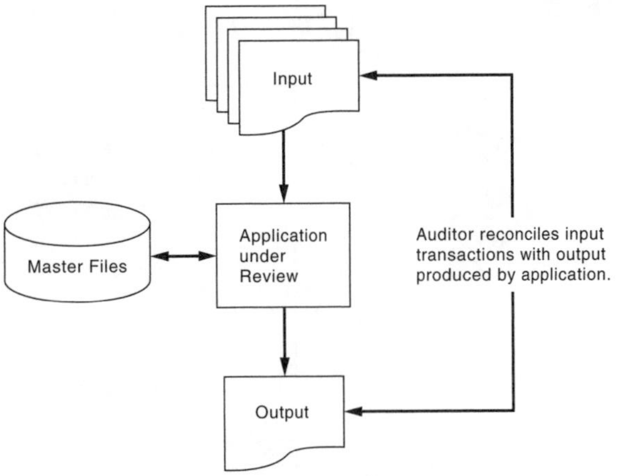

and obtain results that they can compare against objectively calculated results. Some of the more common types of tests of controls include the following:

- **Authenticity tests**, which verify that an individual, a programmed procedure, or a message (such as an EDI transmission) attempting to access a system is authentic. Authenticity controls include user IDs, passwords, valid vendor codes, and authority tables.
- **Accuracy tests**, which ensure that the system processes only data values that conform to specified tolerances. Examples include range tests, field tests, and limit tests.
- **Completeness tests**, which identify missing data within a single record and entire records missing from a batch. The types of tests performed are field tests, record sequence tests, hash totals, and control totals.
- **Redundancy tests**, which determine that an application processes each record only once. Redundancy controls include the reconciliation of batch totals, record counts, hash totals, and financial control totals.
- **Access tests**, which ensure that the application prevents authorized users from unauthorized access to data. Access controls include passwords, authority tables, user-defined procedures, data encryption, and inference controls.
- **Audit trail tests**, which ensure that the application creates an adequate audit trail. This includes evidence that the application records all transactions in a transaction log, posts data values to the appropriate accounts, produces complete **transaction listings**, and generates error files and reports for all exceptions.
- **Rounding error tests**, which verify the correctness of rounding procedures. Rounding errors occur in accounting information when the level of precision used in the calculation is greater than that used in the reporting. For example, interest calculations on bank account balances may have a precision of five decimal places, whereas only two decimal places are needed to report balances. If the remaining three decimal places are simply dropped, the total interest calculated for the total number of accounts may not equal the sum of the individual calculations.

Figure 7-15 shows the logic for handling the rounding error problem. This technique uses an accumulator to keep track of the rounding differences between calculated and reported balances. Note how the sign and the absolute value of the amount

FIGURE 7-15

Rounding Error Algorithm

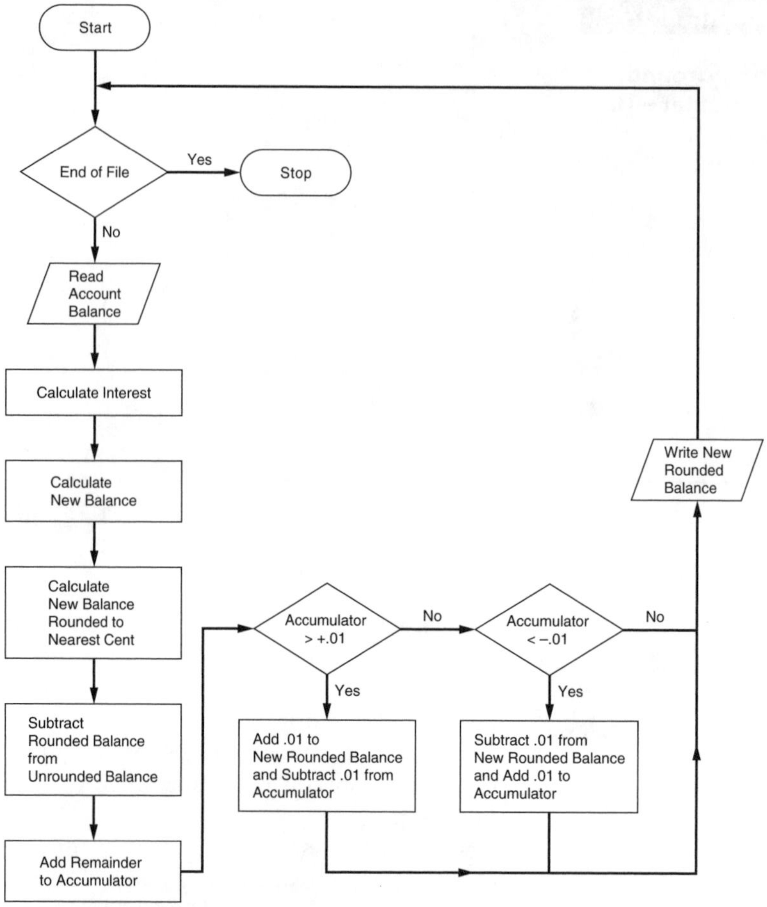

Source: Adapted from R. Weber, *EDP Auditing Conceptual Foundations and Practice,* 2d ed. (New York: McGraw-Hill, 1988), p. 493.

in the accumulator determines how the customer account is affected by rounding. To illustrate, the rounding logic is applied in Table 7-1 to three hypothetical bank balances. The interest calculations are based on an interest rate of 5.25 percent.

Failure to properly account for this rounding difference can result in an imbalance between the total (control) interest amount and the sum of the individual interest calculations for each account. Poor accounting for rounding differences can also present an opportunity for fraud.

Rounding programs are particularly susceptible to salami frauds. **Salami frauds** tend to affect a large number of victims, but the harm to each is immaterial. This type of fraud takes its name from the analogy of slicing a large salami (the fraud objective) into many thin pieces. Each victim assumes one of these small pieces and is unaware of being defrauded. For example, a programmer, or someone with access to the preceding rounding program, can perpetrate a salami fraud by modifying the rounding logic as follows: at the point in the process where the algorithm should increase the customer's account (that is, the accumulator value is > +.01), the program instead adds one cent to another account—the perpetrator's account. Although the absolute amount of each fraud transaction is small, given

TABLE 7-1 Rounding Logic Risk

Record 1	
Beginning accumulator balance	.00861
Beginning account balance	2,741.78
Calculated interest	143.94345
New account balance	2,885.72345
Rounded account balance	2,885.72
Adjusted accumulator balance	.01206 (.00345 + .00861)
Ending account balance	**2,885.73 (round up 1 cent)**
Ending accumulator balance	.00206 (.01206 – .01)
Record 2	
Beginning accumulator balance	.00206
Beginning account balance	1,893.44
Calculated interest	99.4056
New account balance	1,992.8456
Rounded account balance	1,992.85
Adjusted accumulator balance	–.00646 (.00206 – .0044)
Ending account balance	**1,992,85 (no change)**
Ending accumulator balance	–.00234
Record 3	
Beginning accumulator balance	–.00234
Beginning account balance	7,423.34
Calculated interest	389.72535
New account balance	7,813.06535
Rounded account balance	7,813.07
Adjusted accumulator balance	–.00699 (–.00234 –. 00425)
Ending account balance	**7,813.06 (round down 1 cent)**
Ending accumulator balance	.00699

the thousands of accounts processed, the total amount of the fraud can become significant over time.

Operating system audit trails and audit software can detect excessive file activity. In the case of the salami fraud, there would be thousands of entries into the computer criminal's personal account that may be detected in this way. A clever programmer may disguise this activity by funneling these entries through several intermediate temporary accounts, which are then posted to a smaller number of intermediate accounts and finally to the programmer's personal account. By using many levels of accounts in this way, the activity to any single account is reduced and may go undetected by the audit software. There will be a trail, but it can be complicated. A skilled auditor may also use audit software to detect the existence of unauthorized intermediate accounts used in such a fraud.

Computer-Aided Audit Tools and Techniques for Testing Controls

To illustrate how application controls are tested, this section describes five CAATT approaches: the test data method, which includes base case system evaluation and tracing, integrated test facility, and parallel simulation.

TEST DATA METHOD

The **test data method** is used to establish application integrity by processing specially prepared sets of input data through production applications that are under review. The results of each test are compared to predetermined expectations to obtain an objective evaluation of application logic and control effectiveness. The test data technique is illustrated in Figure 7-16. To perform the test data technique, the auditor must obtain a copy of the current version of the application. In addition, test transaction files and test master files must be created. As illustrated in the figure, test transactions may enter the system from magnetic tape, disk, or via an input terminal. Results from the test run will be in the form of routine output reports, transaction listings, and error reports. In addition, the auditor must review the updated master files to determine that account balances have been correctly updated. The test results are then compared with the auditor's expected results to determine if the application is functioning properly. This comparison may be performed manually or through special computer software.

Figure 7-17 lists selected fields for hypothetical transactions and accounts receivable records prepared by the auditor to test a sales order processing application. The figure also shows an error report of rejected transactions and a listing of the updated accounts receivable master file. Any deviations between the actual results obtained and those expected by the auditor may indicate a logic or control problem.

Creating Test Data

When creating test data, auditors must prepare a complete set of both valid and invalid transactions. If test data are incomplete, auditors might fail to examine critical branches of application logic and error-checking routines. Test transactions should test every possible input error, logical process, and irregularity.

Gaining knowledge of the application's internal logic sufficient to create meaningful test data frequently requires a large investment of time. However, the efficiency of this task can be improved through careful planning during systems development. The auditor should save the test data used to test program modules during the implementation phase of the SDLC for future use. If the application has undergone no maintenance since its initial implementation, current audit test results should equal the test results obtained at implementation. However, if the application has been modified, the auditor can create additional test data that focus on the areas of the program changes.

FIGURE 7-16

The Test Data Technique

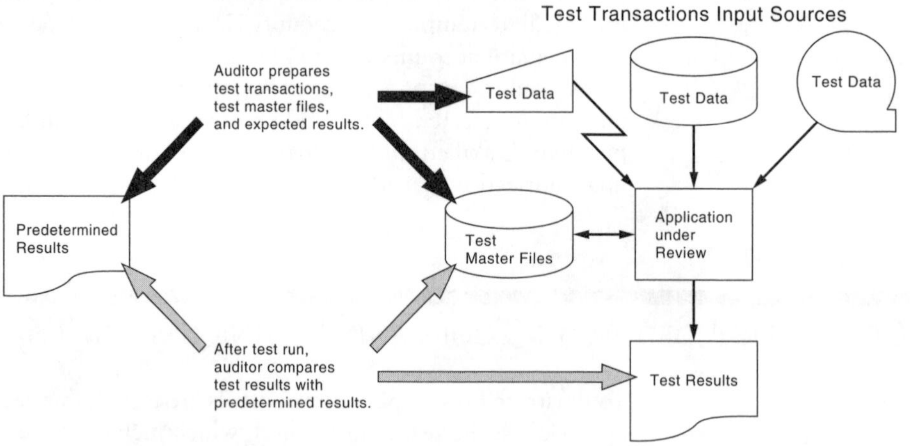

FIGURE 7-17 **Examples of Test Data and Test Results**

Test Transaction File

REC #	CUST #	CUSTOMER NAME	PART #	DESCRIPTION	QNTY	UNIT PRICE	TOTAL PRICE
1	231893	Smith, Joe	AX-612	Water Pump	1	20.00	20.00
2	231893	Azar, Atul	J-912	Gear	3	15.00	45.00
3	245851	Jones, Mary	123-LM	Hose	20	20.00	400.00
4	256519	Lang, Tony	Y-771	Spacer	5	2.00	10.00
5	259552	Tuner, Agnes	U-734	Bushing	5	25.00	120.00
6	175995	Hanz, James	EA-74	Seal	1	3.00	3.00
7	267991	Swindle, Joe	EN-12	Rebuilt Engine	1	1,220.00	1,220.00

Original Test AR Master File

CUST #	CUSTOMER NAME	CUSTOMER ADDRESS	CREDIT LIMIT	CURRENT BALANCE
231893	Smith, Joe	1520 S. Maple, City	1,000.00	400.00
256519	Lang, Tony	18 Etwine St., City	5,000.00	850.00
267991	Swindle, Joe	1 Shady Side, City	3,000.00	2,900.00

Updated Test AR Master File

CUST #	CUSTOMER NAME	CUSTOMER ADDRESS	CREDIT LIMIT	CURRENT BALANCE
231893	Smith, Joe	1520 S. Maple, City	1,000.00	420.00
256519	Lang, Tony	18 Etwine St., City	5,000.00	860.00
267991	Swindle, Joe	1 Shady Side, City	3,000.00	2,900.00

Error Report

REC #	CUST #	CUSTOMER NAME	PART #	DESCRIPTION	QNTY	UNIT PRICE	TOTAL PRICE	EXPLANATION OF ERROR
2	231893	Azar, Atul X	J-912	Gear	3	15.00	45.00	CUSTOMER NAME does not correspond to CUST # 231893
3	245851 X	Jones, Mary	123-LM	Hose	20	20.00	400.00	Check digit error in CUST # field
5	259552	Tuner, Agnes	U-734	Bushing	5	25.00	120.00 X	Price extension error
6	175995 X	Hanz, James	EA-74	Seal	1	3.00	3.00	Record out of sequence
7	267991	Swindle, Joe	EN-12	Rebuilt Engine	1	1,220.00 X	1,220.00 X	Credit limit error

Base Case System Evaluation

There are several variants of the test data technique. When the set of test data in use is comprehensive, the technique is called the **base case system evaluation (BCSE)**. BCSE tests are conducted with a set of test transactions containing all possible transaction types. These are processed through repeated iterations during systems development testing until consistent and valid results are obtained. These results are the base case. When subsequent changes to the application occur during maintenance, their effects are evaluated by comparing current results with base case results.

Tracing

Another type of the test data technique called **tracing** performs an electronic walk-through of the application's internal logic. The tracing procedure involves three steps:

1. The application under review must undergo a special compilation to activate the trace option.
2. Specific transactions or types of transactions are created as test data.
3. The test data transactions are traced through all processing stages of the program, and a listing is produced of all programmed instructions that were executed during the test.

Implementing tracing requires a detailed understanding of the application's internal logic. Figure 7-18 illustrates the tracing process using a portion of the logic for a payroll application. The example shows records from two payroll files—a transaction record showing hours worked and two records from a master file showing pay rates. The trace listing at the bottom of Figure 7-18 identifies the program statements that were executed and the order of execution. Analysis of trace options indicates that Commands 0001 through 0020 were executed. At that point, the application transferred to Command 0060. This occurred because the employee number (the key) of the transaction record did not match the key of the first record in the master file. Then Commands 0010 through 0050 were executed.

FIGURE 7-18

Tracing

Payroll Transaction File

Time Card #	Employee Number	Name	Year	Pay Period	Reg Hrs	OT Hrs
8945	33456	Jones, J.J.	2004	14	40.0	3.0

Payroll Master File

Employee Number	Hourly Rate	YTD Earnings	Dependents	YTD Withhold	YTD FICA
33276	15	12,050	3	3,200	873.62
33456	15	13,100	2	3,600	949.75

Computer Program Logic

```
0001  Read Record from Transaction File
0010  Read Record from Master File
0020  If Employee Number (T) = Employee Number (M)
0030        Wage = (Reg Hrs + (OT Hrs x 1.5) ) x Hourly Rate
0040        Add Wage to YTD Earnings
0050        Go to 0001
0060  Else Go to 0010
```

Trace Listing

0001, 0010, 0020, 0060, 0010, 0020, 0030, 0040, 0050

Advantages of Test Data Techniques

There are three primary advantages of test data techniques. First, they employ through-the-computer testing, thus providing the auditor with explicit evidence concerning application functions. Second, if properly planned, test data runs can be employed with only minimal disruption to the organization's operations. Third, they require only minimal computer expertise on the part of auditors.

Disadvantages of Test Data Techniques

The primary disadvantage of all test data techniques is that auditors must rely on computer services personnel to obtain a copy of the application for test purposes. This entails a risk that computer services may intentionally or accidentally provide the auditor with the wrong version of the application and may reduce the reliability of the audit evidence. In general, audit evidence collected by independent means is more reliable than evidence supplied by the client.

A second disadvantage of these techniques is that they provide a static picture of application integrity at a single point in time. They do not provide a convenient means of gathering evidence about ongoing application functionality. There is no evidence that the application being tested today is functioning as it did during the year under test.

A third disadvantage of test data techniques is their relatively high cost of implementation, which results in audit inefficiency. The auditor may devote considerable time to understanding program logic and creating test data. In the following section, we see how automating testing techniques can resolve these problems.

The Integrated Test Facility

The **integrated test facility (ITF)** approach is an automated technique that enables the auditor to test an application's logic and controls during its normal operation. The ITF is one or more audit modules designed into the application during the systems development process. In addition, ITF databases contain "dummy" or test master file records integrated with legitimate records. Some firms create a dummy company to which test transactions are posted. During normal operations, test transactions are merged into the input stream of regular (production) transactions and are processed against the files of the dummy company. Figure 7-19 illustrates the ITF concept.

ITF audit modules are designed to discriminate between ITF transactions and routine production data. This may be accomplished in a number of ways. One of the simplest and most commonly used is to assign a unique range of key values exclusively to ITF transactions. For example, in a sales order processing system, account numbers between 2000 and 2100 can be reserved for ITF transactions and will not be assigned to actual customer accounts. By segregating ITF transactions from legitimate transactions in this way, routine reports produced by the application are not corrupted by ITF test data. Test results are produced separately on storage media or hard copy output and distributed directly to the auditor. Just as with the test data techniques, the auditor analyzes ITF results against expected results.

Advantages of ITF

The ITF technique has two advantages over test data techniques. First, ITF supports ongoing monitoring of controls as required by SAS 78. Second, applications with

FIGURE 7-19

The ITF Technique

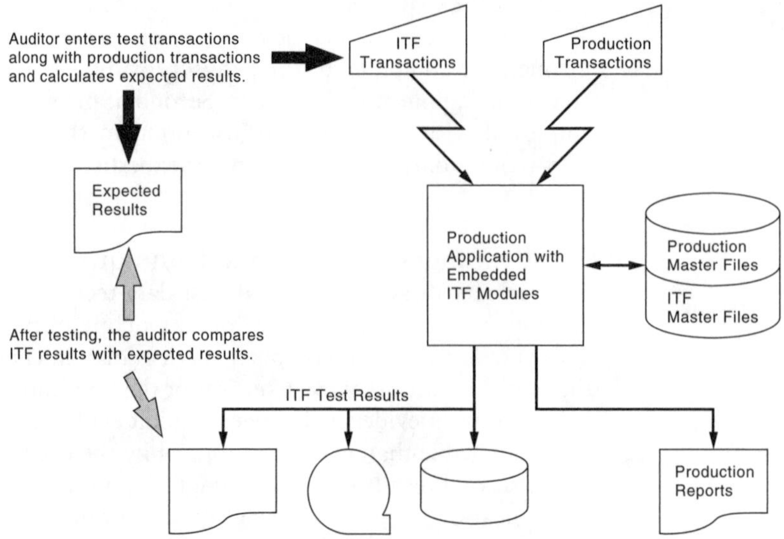

ITF can be economically tested without disrupting the user's operations and without the intervention of computer services personnel. Thus, ITF improves the efficiency of the audit and increases the reliability of the audit evidence gathered.

Disadvantages of ITF

The primary disadvantage of ITF is the potential for corrupting the data files of the organization with test data. Steps must be taken to ensure that ITF test transactions do not materially affect financial statements by being improperly aggregated with legitimate transactions. This problem is remedied in two ways: (1) adjusting entries may be processed to remove the effects of ITF from general ledger account balances or (2) data files can be scanned by special software that remove the ITF transactions.

PARALLEL SIMULATION

Parallel simulation requires the auditor to write a program that simulates key features or processes of the application under review. The simulated application is then used to reprocess transactions that were previously processed by the production application. This technique is illustrated in Figure 7-20. The results obtained from the simulation are reconciled with the results of the original production run to establish a basis for making inferences about the quality of application processes and controls.

Creating A Simulation Program

A simulation program can be written in any programming language. However, because of the one-time nature of this task, it is a candidate for fourth-generation language generators. The steps involved in performing parallel simulation testing are outlined here.

1. The auditor must first gain a thorough understanding of the application under review. Complete and current documentation of the application is required to construct an accurate simulation.

FIGURE 7-20

Parallel Simulation Technique

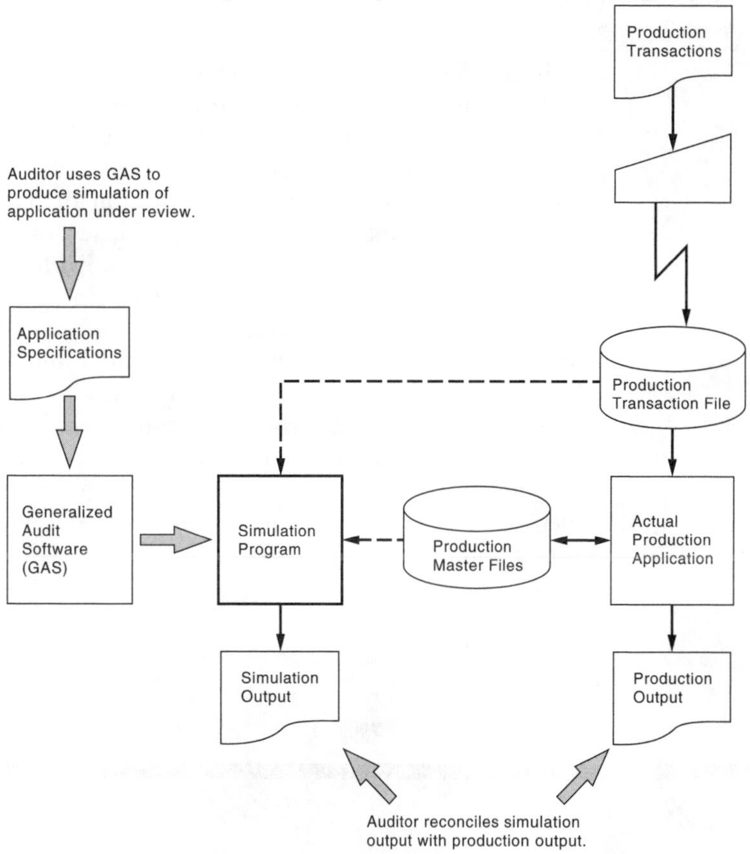

2. The auditor must then identify those processes and controls in the application that are critical to the audit. These are the processes to be simulated.
3. The auditor creates the simulation using a 4GL or **generalized audit software (GAS)**.
4. The auditor runs the simulation program using selected production transactions and master files to produce a set of results.
5. Finally, the auditor evaluates and reconciles the test results with the production results produced in a previous run.

Simulation programs are usually less complex than the production applications they represent. Because simulations contain only the application processes, calculations, and controls relevant to specific audit objectives, the auditor must carefully evaluate differences between test results and production results. Differences in output results occur for two reasons: (1) the inherent crudeness of the simulation program and (2) real deficiencies in the application's processes or controls, which are made apparent by the simulation program.

Summary

This chapter examined issues related to the use of Computer Aided Audit Tools and Techniques (CAATTs) for performing tests of application controls and data extraction. The chapter began by describing three broad classes of application controls: input controls, processing controls, and output controls. Input controls, which govern the gathering and insertion of data into the system, attempt to ensure that all data transactions are valid, accurate, and complete. Processing controls attempt to preserve the integrity of individual records and batches of records within the system and must ensure that an adequate audit trail is preserved. The goal of output controls is to ensure that information produced by the system is not lost, misdirected, or subject to privacy violations. Next, the black box and white box approaches to testing application controls were reviewed. The black box technique involves auditing around the computer. The white box approach requires a detailed understanding of the application's logic. Five types of CAATT that are commonly used for testing application logic were then examined: the test data method, base case system evaluation, tracing, integrated test facility, and parallel simulation.

Key Terms

access tests
accuracy tests
audit trail tests
authenticity tests
base case system evaluation (BCSE)
batch controls
black-box approach
bursting
check digit
completeness tests
data control
error file
error reports
field interrogation
file interrogation
generalized audit software (GAS)
generalized data input system (GDIS)
generalized validation module (GVM)
hash total
input controls
integrated test facility (ITF)
operator intervention controls
output controls
output spooling
parallel simulation
processing controls
record interrogation
redundancy tests
rounding error tests
run-to-run controls
salami frauds
sequence check
test data method
tracing
transaction code
transaction listings
transaction log
transcription errors
transposition errors
validated data file
validation controls
white-box approach

Review Questions

1. What are the broad classes of input controls?
2. Explain the importance of source documents and associated control techniques.
3. Give one example of an error that is detected by a check digit control.
4. What are the primary objectives of a batch control?
5. Classify each of the following as either a field, record, or file interrogation:
   a. Limit check
   b. Validity check
   c. Version check
   d. Missing data check
   e. Sign check
   f. Expiration date check
   g. Numeric-alphabetic data check
   h. Sequence check
   i. Zero-value check
   j. Header label check
   k. Range check
   l. Reasonableness check
6. Compare the three common error-handling techniques discussed in the text.
7. What are the five major components of a GDIS?
8. What are the three categories of processing controls?
9. If all of the inputs have been validated before processing, then what purpose do run-to-run controls serve?
10. What is the objective of a transaction log?
11. How can spooling present an added exposure?

Discussion Questions

1. The field calls for an "M" for married or an "S" for single. The entry is a "2". What control will detect this error?
2. The firm allows no more than 10 hours of overtime a week. An employee entered "15" in the field. Which control will detect this error?
3. The password was "CANARY"; the employee entered "CAANARY." Which control will detect this error?
4. The inventory item number was omitted on the purchase order. Which control will detect this error?
5. The order entry system will allow a 10 percent variation in list price. For example, an item with a list price of $1 could be sold for 90 cents or $1.10 without any system interference. The cost of the item is $3 but the cashier entered $2. Which control would detect this error?
6. How does privacy relate to output control?
7. What are some typical problems with passwords?
8. What are the three categories of processing control?
9. Output controls ensure that output is not lost, misdirected, or corrupted and that privacy is not violated. What are some output exposures, or situations where output is at risk?
10. Input validation includes field interrogation that examines the data in individual fields. List four validation tests and indicate what is checked in each.
11. What is record interrogation? Give two examples.

MULTIPLE-CHOICE QUESTIONS

1. CMA 685 5-28
   Routines that use the computer to check the validity and accuracy of transaction data during input are called
   a. operating systems.
   b. edit programs.
   c. compiler programs.
   d. integrated test facilities.
   e. compatibility tests.
2. CMA 686 5-10
   An edit of individual transactions in a direct access file processing system usually
   a. takes place in a separate computer run.
   b. takes place in an online mode as transactions are entered.
   c. takes place during a backup procedure.
   d. is not performed due to time constraints.
   e. is not necessary.
3. CMA Adapted 686 5-13
   An example of an input control is
   a. making sure that output is distributed to the proper people.
   b. monitoring the work of programmers.
   c. collecting accurate statistics of historical transactions while gathering data.
   d. recalculating an amount to ensure its accuracy.
   e. having another person review the design of a business form.
4. A control designed to validate a transaction at the point of data entry is
   a. recalculation of a batch total.
   b. a record count.
   c. a check digit.
   d. checkpoints.
   e. recalculation of a hash total.
5. CMA 687 5-8
   In a manual system, records of current activity are posted from a journal to a ledger. In a computer system, current records from a(n)
   a. table file are updated to a transaction file.
   b. index file are updated to a master file.
   c. transaction file are updated to a master file.
   d. master file are updated to a year-to-date file.
   e. current balance file are updated to an index file.
6. CMA 1287 5-1
   The primary functions of a computerized information system include
   a. input, processing, and output.
   b. input, processing, output, and storage.
   c. input, processing, output, and control.
   d. input, processing, output, storage, and control.
   e. collecting, sorting, summarizing, and reporting.
7. CMA 1287 5-16
   An employee in the receiving department keyed in a shipment from a remote terminal and inadvertently omitted the purchase order number. The best systems control to detect this error would be a
   a. batch total.
   b. completeness test.
   c. sequence check.
   d. reasonableness test.
   e. compatibility test.
8. CMA 1287 5-15
   In an automated payroll processing environment, a department manager substituted the time card for a terminated employee with a time card for a fictitious employee. The fictitious employee had the same pay rate and hours worked as the terminated employee. The best control technique to detect this action using employee identification numbers would be a
   a. batch total.
   b. record count.
   c. hash total.
   d. subsequent check.
   e. financial total.
9. CMA 1287 5-17
   The reporting of accounting information plays a central role in the regulation of business operations. The importance of sound internal control practices is underscored by the Foreign Corrupt Practices Act of 1977, which requires publicly owned U.S. corporations to maintain systems of internal control that meet certain minimum standards. Preventive controls are an integral part of virtually all accounting processing systems, and much of the information generated by the accounting system is used for preventive control purposes. Which one of the following is

not an essential element of a sound preventive control system?
   a. separation of responsibilities for the recording, custodial, and authorization functions
   b. sound personnel practices
   c. documentation of policies and procedures
   d. implementation of state-of-the-art software and hardware
   e. physical protection of assets
10. Which of the following is *not* a test for identifying application errors?
   a. reconciling the source code
   b. reviewing test results
   c. retesting the program
   d. testing the authority table
11. Which of the following is *not* a common type of white-box test of controls?
   a. completeness tests
   b. redundancy tests
   c. inference tests
   d. authenticity tests
12. All of the following are examples of source document control except
   a. prenumbering source documents.
   b. limiting access to source documents.
   c. supervising the bursting of source documents.
   d. checking the sequence of numbers to identify missing documents.
13. The correct purchase order number, 123456, was incorrectly recorded as shown in the solutions. All of the following are transcription errors except
   a. 1234567
   b. 12345
   c. 124356
   d. 123457
14. Which of the following is correct?
   a. Check digits should be used for all data codes.
   b. Check digits are always placed at the end of data codes.
   c. Check digits do not affect processing efficiency.
   d. Check digits are designed to detect transcription errors.
15. Which statement is NOT correct? The goal of batch controls is to ensure that during processing
   a. transactions are not omitted.
   b. transactions are not added.
   c. transactions are processed more than once.
   d. an audit trail is created.
16. The data control clerk performs all of the following duties except
   a. maintaining the batch control log.
   b. computing (or recomputing) batch control data.
   c. reconciling the output results to the batch control log.
   d. destroying batch control logs when reconciled.
17. An example of a hash total is
   a. total payroll checks—$12,315.
   b. total number of employees—10.
   c. sum of the social security numbers—12,555,437,251.
   d. none of the above.
18. Which statement is NOT true? A batch control log
   a. is prepared by the user department.
   b. records the record count.
   c. indicates any error codes.
   d. is maintained as a part of the audit trail.
19. Which of the following is an example of a field interrogation?
   a. reasonableness check
   b. sign check
   c. sequence check
   d. numeric/alphabetic check
20. Which of the following is an example of record interrogation?
   a. sequence check
   b. zero value check
   c. limit check
   d. range check
21. Which input validation check would detect a payment made to a nonexistent vendor?
   a. missing data check
   b. numeric/alphabetic check
   c. range check
   d. validity check
22. The employee entered "40" in the "hours worked per day" field. Which check would detect this unintentional error?
   a. numeric/alphabetic data check
   b. sign check
   c. limit check
   d. missing data check

23. A specific inventory record indicates that there are 12 items on hand and a customer purchased two of the items. When recording the order, the data entry clerk mistakenly entered 20 items sold. Which check would detect this error?
    a. numeric/alphabetic data check
    b. sign check
    c. sequence check
    d. range check
24. Which check is *not* a file interrogation?
    a. header label
    b. expiration date check
    c. sequence check
    d. version check
25. Which statement is *not* correct?
    a. The purpose of file interrogation is to ensure that the correct file is being processed by the system.
    b. File interrogation checks are particularly important for master files.
    c. Header labels are prepared manually and affixed to the outside of the tape or disk.
    d. An expiration date check prevents a file from being deleted before it expires.
26. A computer operator was in a hurry and accidentally used the wrong master file to process a transaction file. As a result, the accounts receivable master file was erased. Which control would prevent this from happening?
    a. header label check
    b. expiration date check
    c. version check
    d. validity check
27. Which of the following is NOT a component of the Generalized Data Input System?
    a. generalized validation module
    b. validated data file
    c. updated master file
    d. error file
28. Advantages of the Generalized Data Input System include all of the following except
    a. control over quality of data input.
    b. automatic calculation of run-to-run totals.
    c. company-wide standards for data validation.
    d. development of a reusable module for data validation.
29. Run-to-run control totals can be used for all of the following except
    a. to ensure that all data input is validated.
    b. to ensure that only transactions of a similar type are being processed.
    c. to ensure the records are in sequence and are not missing.
    d. to ensure that no transaction is omitted.
30. Methods used to maintain an audit trail in a computerized environment include all of the following except
    a. transaction logs.
    b. unique transaction identifiers.
    c. data encryption.
    d. log of automatic transactions.
31. Risk exposures associated with creating an output file as an intermediate step in the printing process (spooling) include all of the following actions by a computer criminal except
    a. gaining access to the output file and changing critical data values.
    b. using a remote printer and incurring operating inefficiencies.
    c. making a copy of the output file and using the copy to produce illegal output reports.
    d. printing an extra hard copy of the output file.
32. Which statement is NOT correct?
    a. Only successful transactions are recorded on a transaction log.
    b. Unsuccessful transactions are recorded in an error file.
    c. A transaction log is a temporary file.
    d. A hard copy transaction listing is provided to users.

PROBLEMS

1. Input Validation

Identify the types of input validation techniques for the following inputs to the payroll system. Explain the controls provided by each of these techniques.

a. Operator access number to payroll file
b. New employee
c. Employee name
d. Employee number
e. Social security number

f. Rate per hour or salary
g. Marital status
h. Number of dependents
i. Cost center
j. Regular hours worked
k. Overtime hours worked
l. Total employees this payroll period

2. **Processing Controls**
CMA 691 4-2
Unless adequate controls are implemented, the rapid advance of computer technology can reduce a firm's ability to detect errors and fraud. Therefore, one of the critical responsibilities of the management team in firms where computers are used is the security and control of information service activities.

During the design stage of a system, information system controls are planned to ensure the reliability of data. A well-designed system can prevent both intentional and unintentional alteration or destruction of data. These data controls can be classified as (1) input controls, (2) processing controls, and (3) output controls.

Required:
For each of the three data control categories listed, provide two specific controls and explain how each control contributes to ensuring the reliability of data. Use the following format for your answer.

Control Category	Specific Controls	Contribution to Data Reliability

3. **Input Controls and Data Processing**
You have been hired by a catalog company to computerize its sales order entry forms. Approximately 60 percent of all orders are received over the telephone, with the remainder either mailed or faxed in. The company wants the phone orders to be input as they are received. The mail and fax orders can be batched together in groups of 50 and submitted for data entry as they become ready. The following information is collected for each order:

- Customer number (if a customer does not have one, one needs to be assigned)
- Customer name
- Address
- Payment method (credit card or money order)
- Credit card number and expiration date (if necessary)
- Items ordered and quantity
- Unit price

Required:
Determine control techniques to make sure that all orders are entered accurately into the system. Also, discuss any differences in control measures between the batch and the real-time processing.

4. Write an essay explaining the following three methods of correcting errors in data entry: immediate correction, creation of an error file, and rejection of the batch.

5. Many techniques can be used to control input data. Write a one-page essay discussing three techniques.

6. The presence of an audit trail is critical to the integrity of the accounting information system. Write a one-page essay discussing three of the techniques used to preserve the audit trail.

7. Write an essay comparing and contrasting the following audit techniques based on costs and benefits:

- test data method
- base case system evaluation
- tracing
- integrated test facility
- parallel simulation

CHAPTER

8 CAATTs for Data Extraction and Analysis

LEARNING OBJECTIVES

After studying this chapter, you should:

- Understand the components of data structures and how these are used to achieve data-processing operations.
- Be familiar with structures used in flat-file systems, including sequential, indexes, hashing, and pointer structures.
- Be familiar with relational database structures and the principles of normalization.
- Understand the features, advantages, and disadvantages of the embedded audit module approach to data extraction.
- Know the capabilities and primary features of generalized audit software.
- Become familiar with the more commonly used features of ACL.

This chapter examines the use of CAATTs for data extraction and analysis. Auditors make extensive use of these tools in gathering accounting data for testing application controls and in performing substantive tests. In the previous chapter we studied how CAATTs are used to test application controls directly. The data extraction tools discussed in this chapter are used to analyze the data processed by an application rather than the application itself. By analyzing data retrieved from computer files, the auditor can make inferences about the presence and functionality of controls in the application that processed the data.

Another important use of data extraction software is in performing substantive tests. Most audit testing occurs in the substantive-testing phase of the audit. These procedures are called *substantive tests* because they are used for, but not limited to, the following:

- Determining the correct value of inventory.
- Determining the accuracy of prepayments and accruals.
- Confirming accounts receivable with customers.
- Searching for unrecorded liabilities.

In an IT environment, the records needed to perform such tests are stored in computer files and databases. Before substantive tests can be performed, the data need to be extracted from the host system and presented to the auditor in a usable format.

This chapter opens with a review of data structures. Data structures constitute the physical and logical arrangement of data in files and databases. Understanding how data are organized and accessed is central to using data extraction tools. Data extraction software falls into two general categories: embedded audit modules and general audit software. The second section of the chapter describes the features, advantages, and disadvantages of the embedded audit module (EAM) approach. The last section outlines typical functions and uses of generalized audit software (GAS). The section closes with a review of the key features of Audit Command Language (ACL), the leading product in the GAS market.

DATA STRUCTURES

Data structures have two fundamental components: organization and access method. **Organization** refers to the way records are physically arranged on the secondary storage device. This may be either *sequential* or *random*. The records in sequential files are stored in contiguous locations that occupy a specified area of disk space. Records in random files are stored without regard for their physical relationship to other records of the same file. Random files may have records distributed throughout a disk. The **access method** is the technique used to locate records and to navigate through the database or file. While several specific techniques are used, in general, they can be classified as either direct access or sequential access methods.

Since no single structure is best for all processing tasks, different structures are used for storing different types of accounting data. Selecting a structure, therefore, involves a trade-off between desirable features. The criteria that influence the selection of the data structure are listed in Table 8-1.

In the following section, we examine several data structures. These are divided between flat-file and database systems. In practice, organizations may employ any of these approaches in various combinations for storing their accounting data.

FLAT-FILE STRUCTURES

Recall from Chapter 3 that the flat-file model describes an environment in which individual data files are not integrated with other files. End users in this environment own their data files rather than share them with other users. Data processing is thus performed by standalone applications rather than integrated systems. The flat-file approach is a single view model that characterizes legacy systems. Data files are structured, formatted, and arranged to suit the specific needs of the owner or primary user. Such structuring, however, may omit or corrupt data attributes that are essential to other users, thus preventing successful integration of systems across the organization.

Sequential Structure

Figure 8-1 illustrates the **sequential structure**, which is typically called the *sequential access method*. Under this arrangement, for example, the record with key

TABLE 8-1

File Processing Operations

1. Retrieve a record from the file based on its primary key.
2. Insert a record into a file.
3. Update a record in the file.
4. Read a complete file of records.
5. Find the next record in the file.
6. Scan a file for records with common secondary keys.
7. Delete a record from a file.

value 1875 is placed in the physical storage space immediately following the record with key value 1874. Thus, all records in the file lie in contiguous storage spaces in a specified sequence (ascending or descending) arranged by their primary key.

Sequential files are simple and easy to process. The application starts at the beginning of the file and processes each record in sequence. Of the file-processing operations in Table 8-1, this approach is efficient for Operations 4 and 5, which are, respectively, reading an entire file and finding the next record in the file. Also, when a large portion of the file (perhaps 20 percent or more) is to be processed in one operation, the sequential structure is efficient for record updating (Operation 3 in Table 8-1). An example of this is payroll processing, where 100 percent of the employee records on the payroll file are processed each payroll period. However, when only a small portion of the file (or a single record) is being processed, this approach is not efficient. The sequential structure is not a practical option for the remaining operations listed in Table 8-1. For example, retrieving a single record (Operation 1) from a sequential file requires reading all the records that precede the desired record. On average, this means reading half the file each time a single record is retrieved. The sequential access method does not permit accessing a record directly. Files that require direct access operations need a different data structure. The following data structures address this need.

FIGURE 8-1 **Sequential Storage and Access Method**

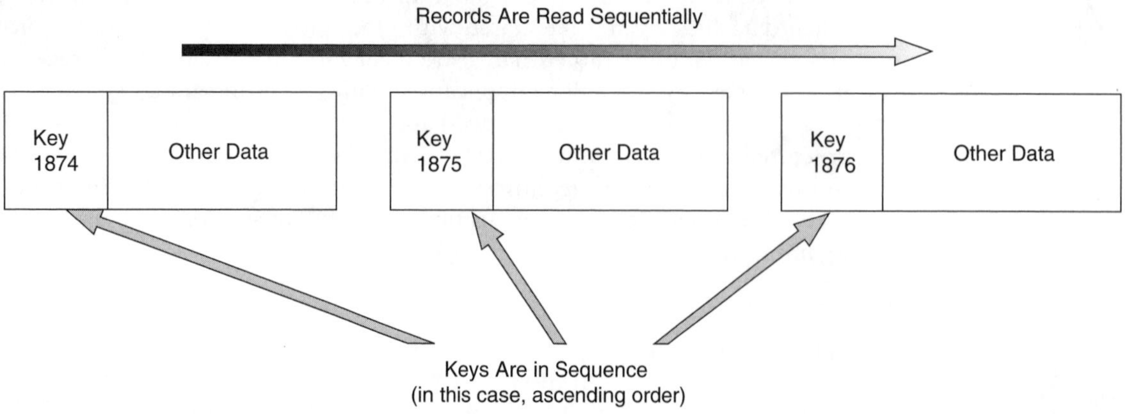

Indexed Structure

An **indexed structure** is so named because, in addition to the actual data file, there exists a separate index that is itself a file of record addresses. This index contains the numeric value of the physical disk storage location (cylinder, surface, and record block) for each record in the associated data file. The data file itself may be organized either sequentially or randomly. Figure 8-2 presents an example of an indexed random file.

Records in an **indexed random file** are dispersed throughout a disk without regard for their physical proximity to other related records. In fact, records belonging to the same file may reside on different disks. A record's physical location is unimportant as long as the operating system software can find it when needed. This locating is accomplished by searching the index for the desired key value, reading the corresponding storage location (address), and then moving the disk read-write head to the address location. When a new record is added to the file, the data management software selects a vacant disk location, stores the record, and adds the new address to the index.

The physical organization of the index itself may be either sequential (by key value) or random. Random indexes are easier to maintain, in terms of adding records, because new key records are simply added to the end of the index without regard to their sequence. Indexes in sequential order are more difficult to maintain because new record keys must be inserted between existing keys. One advantage of a sequential index is that it can be searched rapidly. Because of its logical arrangement, algorithms can be used to speed the search through the index to find a key

FIGURE 8-2 **Indexed Random File Structure**

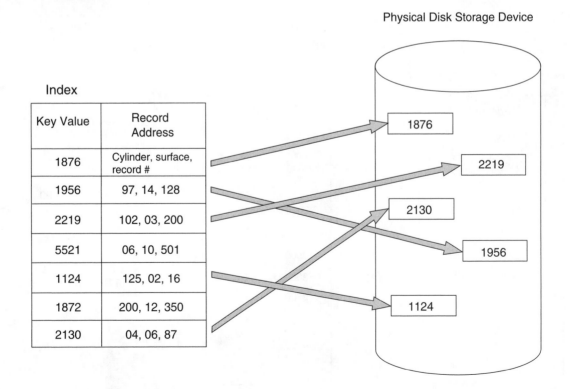

Index

Key Value	Record Address
1876	Cylinder, surface, record #
1956	97, 14, 128
2219	102, 03, 200
5521	06, 10, 501
1124	125, 02, 16
1872	200, 12, 350
2130	04, 06, 87

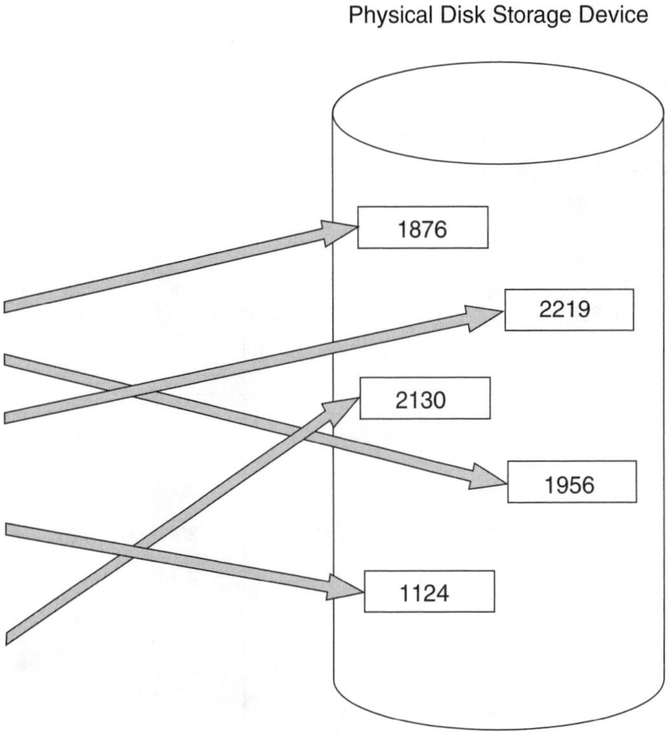

value. This advantage becomes particularly important for large data files with corresponding large indexes.

The principal advantage of indexed random files is in operations involving the processing of individual records (Operations 1, 2, 3, and 6 in Table 8-1). Another advantage is their efficient use of disk storage. Records may be placed wherever there is space without concern for maintaining contiguous storage locations. However, random files are not efficient structures for operations that involve processing a large portion of a file. A great deal of access time may be required to access an entire file of records that are randomly dispersed throughout the storage device. Sequential files are more efficient for this purpose.

The **indexed sequential access method** (ISAM) structure is used for very large files that require routine batch processing and a moderate degree of individual record processing. For instance, the customer file of a public utility company will be processed in batch mode for billing purposes and directly accessed in response to individual customer queries. Because of its sequential organization, the ISAM structure can be searched sequentially for efficient batch processing. Figure 8-3 illustrates how ISAM uses indexes to allow direct access processing.

The ISAM structure is used for files that often occupy several cylinders of contiguous storage on a disk. To find a specific record location, the ISAM file uses a number of indexes that describe in summarized form the contents of each cylinder. For example, in Figure 8-3, we are searching for a record with the key value 2546.

FIGURE 8-3 **ISAM Used for Direct Access**

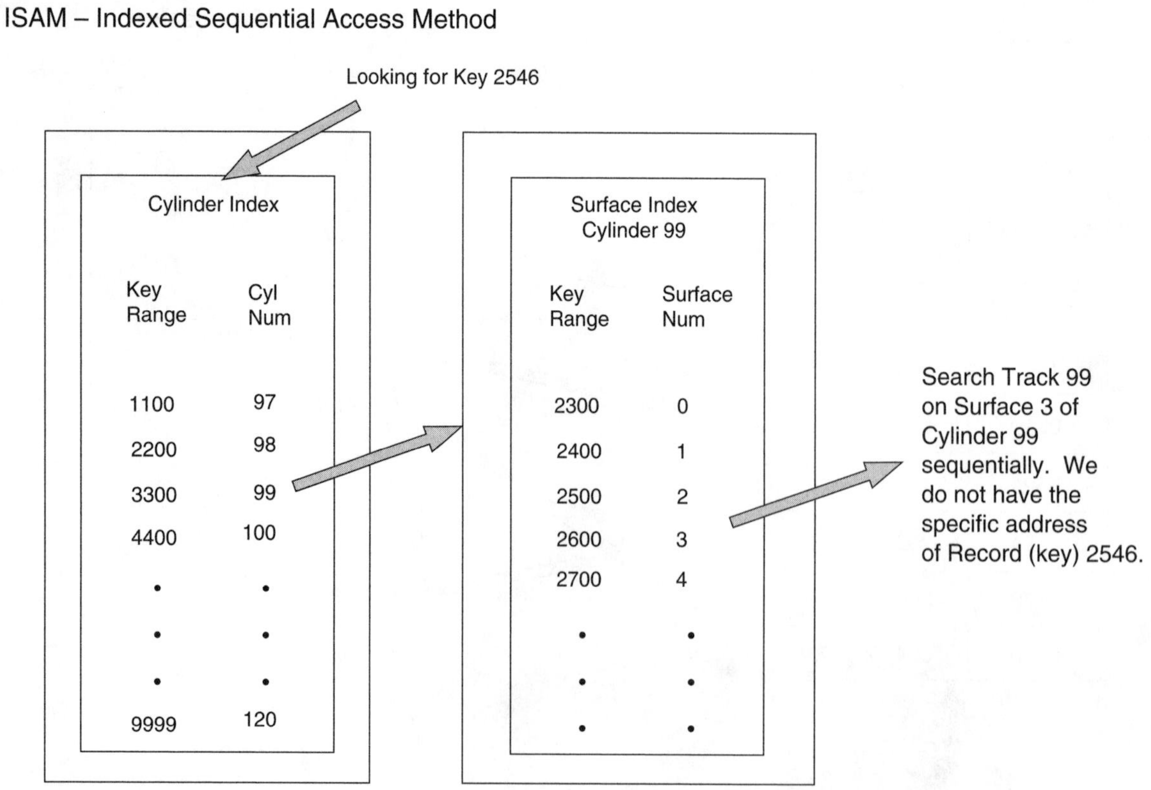

The access method goes first to the overall file index, which contains only the highest key value for each cylinder in the file, and determines that Record 2546 is somewhere on Cylinder 99. A quick scan of the surface index for Cylinder 99 reveals that the record is on Surface 3 of Cylinder 99. ISAM indexes do not provide an exact physical address for a single record. However, they identify the disk track where the record in question resides. The last step is to search the identified track sequentially to find the record with key value 2546.

The ISAM structure is moderately effective for Operations 1 and 3 in Table 8-1. Because ISAM must read multiple indexes and search the track sequentially, the average access time for a single record is slower than the indexed sequential or indexed random structures. Direct access speed is sacrificed to achieve very efficient performance in Operations 4, 5, and 6.

The greatest disadvantage with the ISAM structure is that it does not perform record insertion operations (Operation 2) efficiently. Because the ISAM file is organized sequentially, inserting a new record into the file requires the physical relocation of all the records located beyond the point of insertion. The indexes that describe this physical arrangement must, therefore, also be updated with each insertion. This is extremely time-consuming and disruptive to operations. One method of dealing with this problem is to store new records in an overflow area that is physically separate from the other data records in the file. Figure 8-4 shows how this is done.

FIGURE 8-4 **Inserting a Record into an ISAM File**

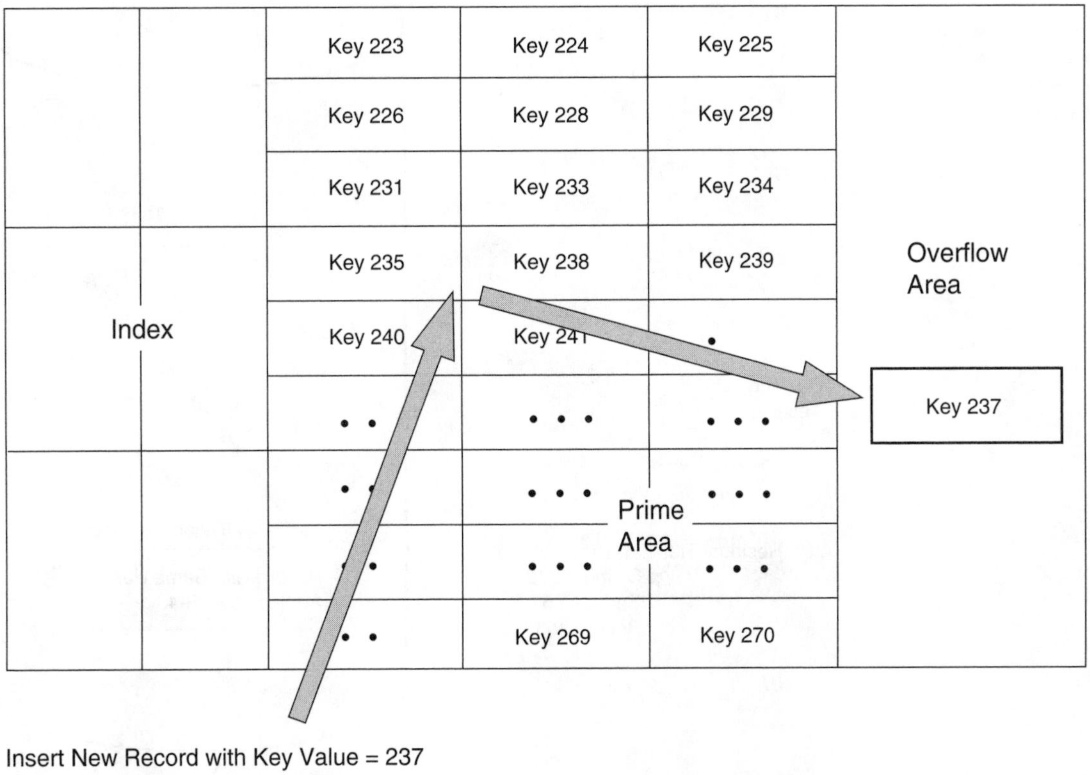

An ISAM file has three physical components: the indexes, the prime data storage area, and the overflow area. Rather than inserting a new record directly into the prime area, the data management software places it in a randomly selected location in the overflow area. It then records the address of the location in a special field (called a *pointer*) in the prime area. Later, when searching for the record, the indexes direct the access method to the track location where the record *should* reside. The pointer at that location reveals the record's *actual* location in the overflow area. Thus, accessing a record may involve searching the indexes, searching the track in the prime data area, and finally searching the overflow area. This slows data access time for both direct access and batch processing.

Periodically, the ISAM file must be reorganized by integrating the overflow records into the prime area and then reconstructing the indexes. This process involves time, cost, and disruption to operations. Therefore, when a file is highly volatile—(records are added or deleted frequently), the maintenance burden associated with the ISAM approach tends to render it impractical. However, for large, stable files that need both direct access and batch processing, the ISAM structure is a popular option.

Hashing Structure

A **hashing structure** employs an algorithm that converts the primary key of a record directly into a storage address. Hashing eliminates the need for a separate index. By calculating the address, rather than reading it from an index, records can be retrieved more quickly. Figure 8-5 illustrates the hashing approach.

FIGURE 8-5

Hashing Technique with Pointer to Relocate the Collision Record

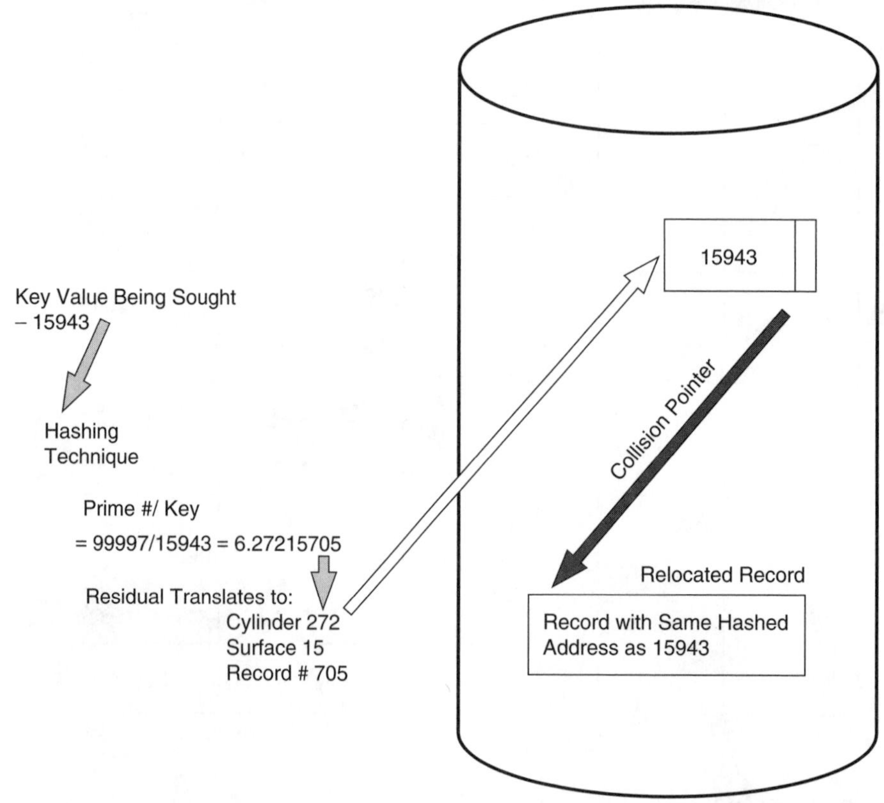

This example assumes an inventory file with 100,000 inventory items. The algorithm divides the inventory number (the primary key) into a prime number. Recall that a prime number is one that can be divided only by itself and 1 without leaving a residual value. Therefore, the calculation will always produce a value that can be translated into a storage location. Hence, the residual 6.27215705 becomes Cylinder 272, Surface 15, and Record number 705. The hashing structure uses a random file organization because the process of calculating residuals and converting them into storage locations produces widely dispersed record addresses.

The principal advantage of hashing is access speed. Calculating a record's address is faster than searching for it through an index. This structure is suited to applications that require rapid access to individual records in performing Operations 1, 2, 3, and 6 in Table 8-1.

The hashing structure has two significant disadvantages. First, this technique does not use storage space efficiently. The storage location chosen for a record is a mathematical function of its primary key value. The algorithm will never select some disk locations because they do not correspond to legitimate key values. As much as one-third of the disk pack may be wasted.

The second disadvantage is the reverse of the first. Different record keys may generate the same (or similar) residual, which translates into the same address. This is called a *collision* because two records cannot be stored at the same location. One solution to this problem is to randomly select a location for the second record and place a pointer to it from the first (the calculated) location. This technique is represented by the dark arrow in Figure 8-5.

The collision problem slows down access to records. Locating a record displaced in this manner involves first calculating its theoretical address, searching that location, and then determining the actual address from the pointer contained in the record at that location. This has an additional implication for Operation 7 in Table 8-1—deleting a record from a file. If the first record is deleted from the file, the pointer to the second (collision) record will also be deleted and the address of the second record will be lost. This can be dealt with in two ways: (1) After deleting the first record, the collision record can be physically relocated to its calculated address, which is now vacant; or (2) The first record is marked "deleted" but is left in place to preserve the pointer to the collision record.

Pointer Structures

Figure 8-6 presents the **pointer structure**, which in this example is used to create a *linked-list file*. This approach stores in a field of one record the address (pointer) of a related record. The records in this type of file are spread over the entire disk without concern for their physical proximity with other related records. The pointers provide connections between the records. In this example, Record 124 points to the location of Record 125, Record 125 points to 126, and so on. The last record in the list contains an end-of-file marker.

Pointers may also be used to link records between files. Figure 8-7 shows an accounts receivable record with three pointers. The first pointer links the AR record to the next AR record within the AR file. The second and third pointers link AR records to sales invoice and remittance advice records, respectively. By accessing an accounts receivable record (for example, Customer 4456), we can locate all sales invoices and remittances pertaining to the account. These records may then

FIGURE 8-6

A Linked-List File

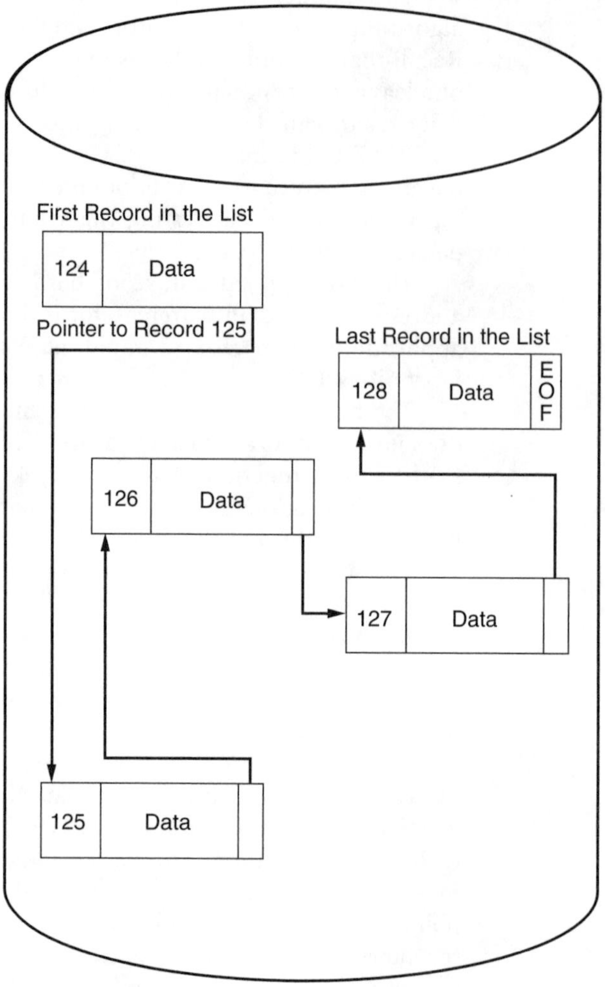

be displayed on a computer screen or printed for review. The next transaction record (a sale or cash receipt) to be processed will be added to the end of the appropriate linked-list. The address of the record will then be stored in the preceding record to provide future access.

Types of Pointers. Figure 8-8 shows three types of pointers: physical address, relative address, and logical key pointer. A **physical address pointer** contains the actual disk storage location (cylinder, surface, and record number) needed by the disk controller. This physical address allows the system to access the record directly without obtaining further information. This method has the advantage of speed, since it does not need to be manipulated further to determine a record's location. However, it also has two disadvantages: First, if the related record is moved from one disk location to another, the pointer must be changed. This is a problem when disks are periodically reorganized or copied. Second, the physical pointers bear no logical relationship to the records they identify. If a pointer is lost or destroyed and cannot be recovered, the record it references is also lost.

FIGURE 8-7 **Pointers within and between Files**

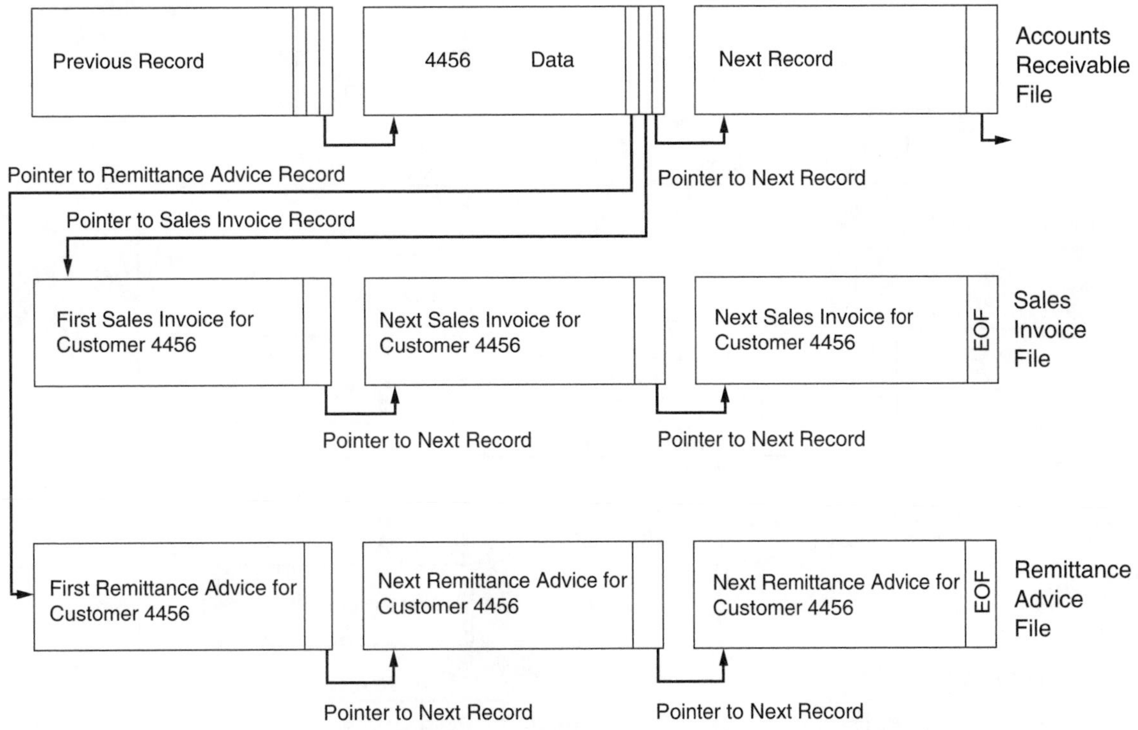

A **relative address pointer** contains the relative position of a record in the file. For example, the pointer could specify the 135th record in the file. This must be further manipulated to convert it to the actual physical address. The conversion software calculates this by using the physical address of the beginning of the file, the length of each record in the file, and the relative address of the record being sought.

A **logical key pointer** contains the primary key of the related record. This key value is then converted into the record's physical address by a hashing algorithm.

HIERARCHICAL AND NETWORK DATABASE STRUCTURES

Early hierarchical and network database models employed many of the preceding flat-file techniques as well as new proprietary database structures. A major difference between the two approaches is the degree of process integration and data sharing that can be achieved. Two-dimensional flat files exist as independent data structures that are not linked logically or physically to other files. Database models were designed to support flat-file systems already in place, while allowing the organization to move to new levels of data integration. By providing linkages between logically related files, a third (depth) dimension is added to better serve multiple-user needs. For example, Figure 8-7 illustrates the use of pointers between files in an example of a simple hierarchical database structure. An example of a complex network database structure is illustrated by Figure 8-9.

Figure 8-9 illustrates a many-to-many association between an inventory file and a vendor file. Each vendor supplies many inventory items and each item is supplied

FIGURE 8-8 **Types of Pointers**

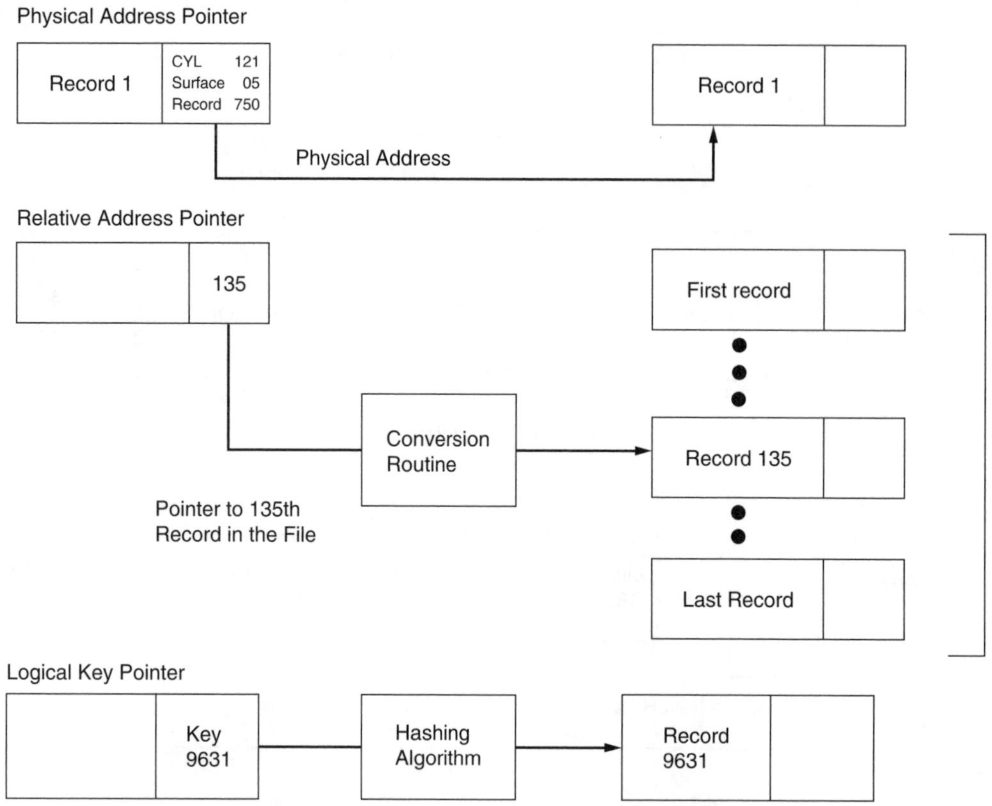

by more than one vendor. Notice that each inventory and vendor record exists only once, but there is a separate link record for each item the vendor supplies and for each supplier of a given inventory item. This arrangement of pointers allows us to find all vendors of a given inventory item and all inventories supplied by each vendor.

Link files may also contain accounting data. For example, the link file in Figure 8-9 shows that the price for Inventory Number 1356 from Vendor Number 1 ($10) is not the same price charged by Vendor Number 3 ($12). Similarly, the delivery time (days-lead time) and discount offered (terms) are different. Transaction characteristics such as these can vary between vendors and even between different items from the same vendor. Data that are unique to the item–vendor associations are stored in the unique link file record, as shown in the figure.

RELATIONAL DATABASE STRUCTURES

In the previous section, we saw how hierarchical and network databases use explicit linkages (pointers) between records to establish relationships. The linkages in the relational model are implicit. Figure 8-10, which was introduced in Chapter 3 (Figure 3-14), illustrates the use of embedded keys to provide a link between related tables. The data structure underlying this model is the *indexed sequential file.*

FIGURE 8-9 **A Link File in a Many-to-Many Relationship**

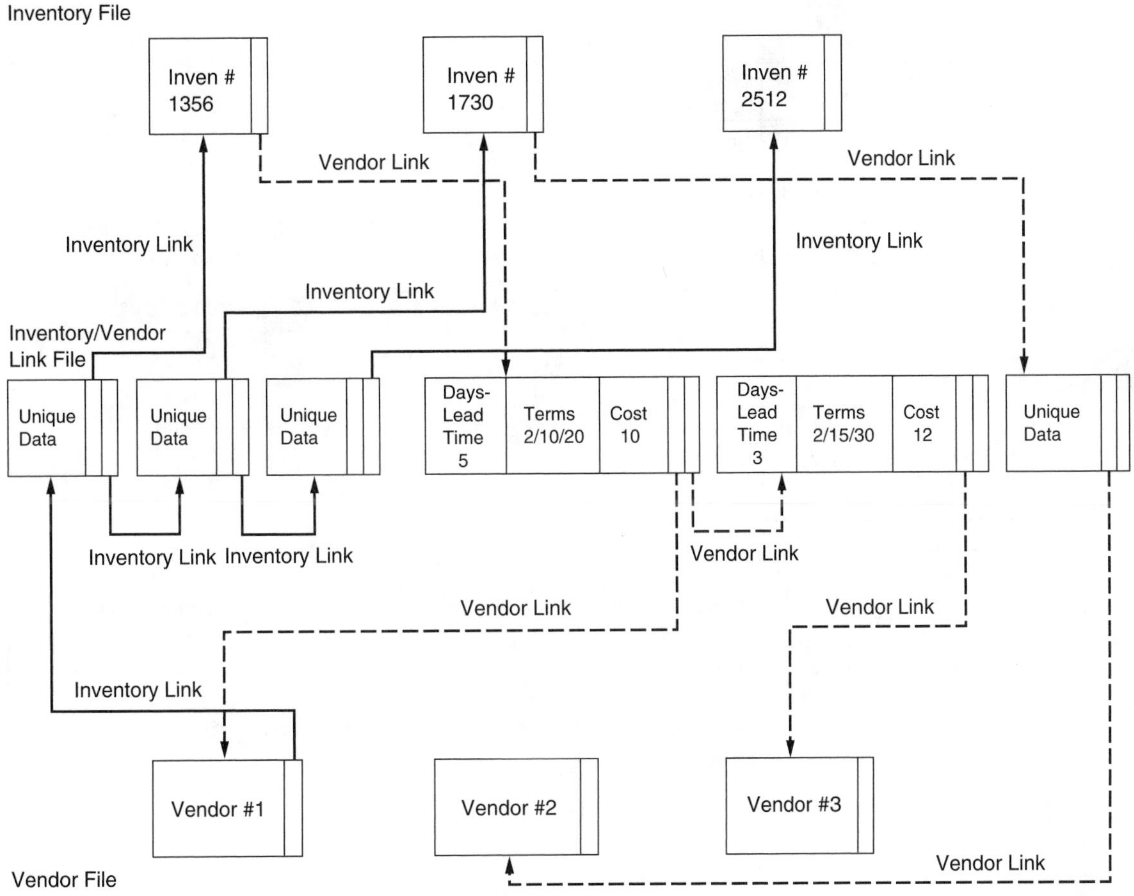

The **indexed sequential file** structure, illustrated in Figure 8-11, uses an index in conjunction with a sequential file organization. This structure allows both direct access to individual records and batch processing of the entire file. Multiple indexes can be used to create a cross-reference called an **inverted list** that allows even more flexible access to data. In Figure 8-11, two indexes are shown. One contains the employee number (primary key) for uniquely locating records in the file. The second index contains record addresses arranged by year-to-date earnings. Using this nonunique field as a secondary key permits all employee records to be viewed in ascending or descending order according to earnings. Alternatively, individual records with selected earnings balances can be displayed. Indexes may be created for each attribute in the table, allowing data to be viewed from multiple perspectives to produce multiple user views.

User Views

A **user view** is the set of data that a particular user needs to achieve his or her assigned tasks. For example, a general ledger clerk's view consists of the organization's chart

FIGURE 8-10 **Linkages between Relational Tables**

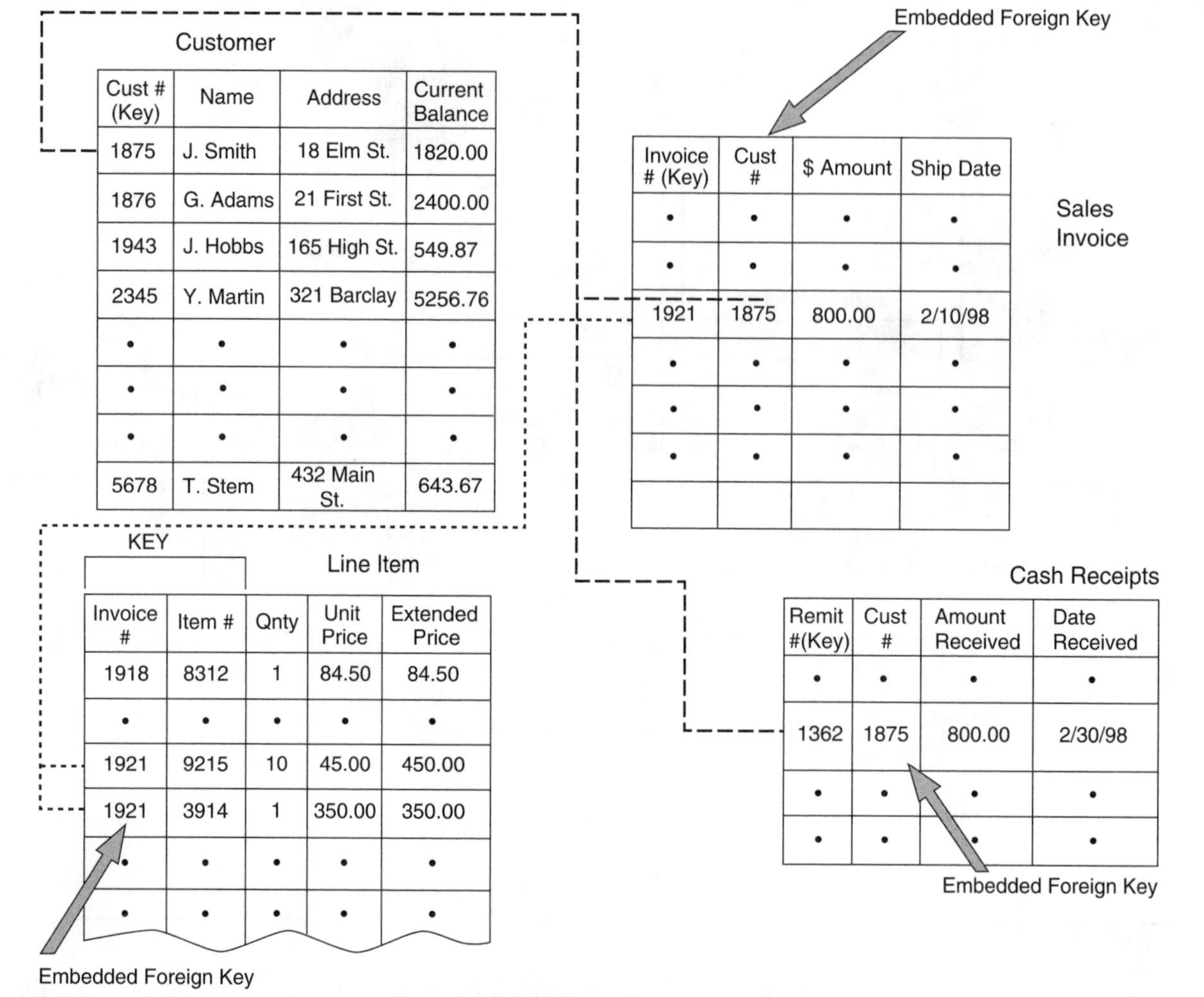
Customer
Cust # (Key) | Name | Address | Current Balance
1875 | J. Smith | 18 Elm St. | 1820.00
1876 | G. Adams | 21 First St. | 2400.00
1943 | J. Hobbs | 165 High St. | 549.87
2345 | Y. Martin | 321 Barclay | 5256.76
5678 | T. Stem | 432 Main St. | 643.67
Embedded Foreign Key
Sales Invoice
Invoice # (Key) | Cust # | $ Amount | Ship Date
1921 | 1875 | 800.00 | 2/10/98
KEY
Line Item
Invoice # | Item # | Qnty | Unit Price | Extended Price
1918 | 8312 | 1 | 84.50 | 84.50
1921 | 9215 | 10 | 45.00 | 450.00
1921 | 3914 | 1 | 350.00 | 350.00
Embedded Foreign Key
Cash Receipts
Remit #(Key) | Cust # | Amount Received | Date Received
1362 | 1875 | 800.00 | 2/30/98
Embedded Foreign Key

FIGURE 8-11 **Indexed Sequential file**

Emp # Index
Key Value | Record Address
101 | 1
102 | 2
103 | 3
104 | 4
105 | 5
Employee Table
Emp # | Name | Address | Skill Code | YTD Earnings
101 | J. Smith | 15 Main St. | 891 | 15000
102 | S. Buell | 107 Hill Top | 379 | 10000
103 | T. Hill | 40 Barclay St. | 891 | 20000
104 | M. Green | 251 Ule St. | 209 | 19000
105 | H. Litt | 423 Rauch Ave. | 772 | 18000
YTD Earnings Index
Key Value | Address
20000.00 | 3
19000 | 4
18000 | 5
15000 | 1
10000 | 2

of accounts; a sales manager's view might include detailed customer sales data organized by product, region, and salesperson; and a production manager's view may include finished goods inventory on hand, available manufacturing capacity, and vendor lead times.

A problem arises in meeting diverse user needs when the collection, summarization, storage, and reporting of transaction and standing data are dominated by a single view that is inappropriate for entity-wide purposes. Traditionally, the accountant's view has dictated the set of financial data used by organizations. However, modern managers need both financial and nonfinancial information in formats and at levels of aggregation that differ from those often accommodated by traditional accounting systems. The trend today is to capture data in sufficient detail and diversity to sustain multiple user views. The tables that support the user views are called **base tables**; to be effective, they must be properly **normalized**. In the next section, we examine the relationship between user views, their underlying base tables, and the process of data normalization.

Creating User Views from Normalized Base Tables

The process of creating a user view begins by designing the output reports, documents, and input screens needed by the user. This usually involves an extensive analysis of user information needs. Once the analysis is complete, the designer can derive the set of data attributes (the conceptual user view) necessary to support these views. Because they are the physical representation of the conceptual user view, reports, documents, and computer screens are called *physical views*. They help the designer understand key relationships among the data.

The discussion that follows is based on the physical views of three users. The first view is for a purchasing agent who needs information about inventory items to be ordered and the suppliers of the inventory. Table 8-2 depicts the inventory status report that conveys this information.

TABLE 8-2 Inventory Status Report

Ajax Manufacturing Co.
Inventory Status Report

Part Number	Description	Quantity On Hand	Reorder Point	Order Quantity	Supplier Number	Name	Address	Telephone
1	Bracket	100	150	500	22 24 27	Ozment Sup Buell Co. B&R Sup	123 Main St. 2 Broadhead Westgate Mall	555-7895 555-3436 555-7845
2	Gasket	440	450	1000	22 24 28	Ozment Sup Buell Co. Harris Manuf	123 Main St. 2 Broadhead 24 Linden St.	555-7895 555-3436 555-3316
3	Brace	10	10	50	22 24 28	Ozment Sup Buell Co. Harris Manuf	123 Main St. 2 Broadhead 24 Linden St.	555-7895 555-3436 555-3316
⋮	⋮	⋮	⋮	⋮	⋮	⋮	⋮	⋮

The second user view is for a sales manager who needs a breakdown of daily sales activity organized by customer and product. Figure 8-12 shows the sales report containing this information. The third view, for the general ledger department, presents a listing of journal vouchers summarizing the day's business activity. The journal voucher report is portrayed in Table 8-3.

Keep in mind that, at this point, the physical views are at the design stage (on paper) only. By working backward from these, and applying normalization principles, conceptual user views will be derived from which we will design a set of base tables. Once this is done, physical tables can be created and transformed into physical reports and documents. We begin this process with the inventory status report in Table 8-2.

FIGURE 8-12 **Sales Report**

Sales Report

Customer Number: 19321
Customer Name : Jon Smith
Address : 520 Main St., City

Invoice #	Date	Invoice Total	Part Num	Quantity	Unit Price	Ext'd Price
12390	11/11/04	$850	2	5	$20	$100
			1	10	50	500
			3	25	10	250
12912	11/21/04	$300	4	10	$30	$300

Customer Total: $1,150

* *

Customer Number: 19322
Customer Name : Mary Smith
Address : 2289 Elm St., City

Invoice #	Date	Invoice Total	Part Num	Quantity	Unit Price	Ext'd Price
12421	11/13/04	$1,000	6	10	$20	$200
			1	2	50	100
			5	7	100	700
12901	11/20/04	$500	4	10	$30	$300
			2	10	20	200

Customer Total: $1,500

* *

Next Customer

•
•
•

Next Customer

TABLE 8-3 Journal Voucher Report

JV #	Date	Title	Acct #	Debit	Credit
1	9/20/04	Cash	101	1000	
		Acct Rec	103	2000	
		Sales	401		3000
2	9/20/04	Cost of Goods Sold	501	2500	
		Inventory	108		2500
⋮	⋮	⋮	⋮	⋮	⋮

The Importance of Data Normalization

Correctly designed database tables are critical to the success of the DBMS. Poorly designed tables can cause operational problems that restrict, or even deny, users access to the information they need. **Data normalization** is a process that promotes effective database design by grouping data attributes into tables that comply with specific conditions associated with best practices in database file design. There are several possible levels of normalization. Usually, designers of accounting databases normalize tables to the level called **third normal form** (3NF).

Tables that have not been normalized are associated with three types of problems called *anomalies*: the update anomaly, the insertion anomaly, and the deletion anomaly. One or more of these anomalies will exist in tables that are normalized at lower levels such as *first normal form* (1NF) and *second normal form* (2NF), but tables in 3NF are free of anomalies. To demonstrate the three anomalies and their implications, the physical view in Table 8-4 is represented as a single unnormalized table called Inventory. This table contains the set of data attributes needed by the purchasing agent. The primary key of the table is Part Num.

Update Anomaly. The **update anomaly** results from data redundancy in an unnormalized table. To illustrate, notice that Supplier Number 22 provides each of the three inventory items (Part Num 1, 2, 3) shown in Figure 8-13. The data attributes pertaining to Supplier Number 22 (Name, Address, and Tele Num) are thus repeated in every record of every inventory item that Supplier Number 22 provides. Any change in the supplier's name, address, or telephone number must be made to each of these records in the table. In our simple example, this means three different updates. To better appreciate the implications of the update anomaly, consider a more realistic situation where the vendor supplies 10,000 different items of inventory. Any update to an attribute must then be made 10,000 times.

Insertion Anomaly. To demonstrate the effects of the **insertion anomaly**, assume that a new vendor has entered the marketplace. The organization does not yet purchase from the vendor, but may wish to do so in the future. In the meantime, the

TABLE 8-4 Unnormalized Database Table

Inventory Table

Primary Key — Nonkey Attributes

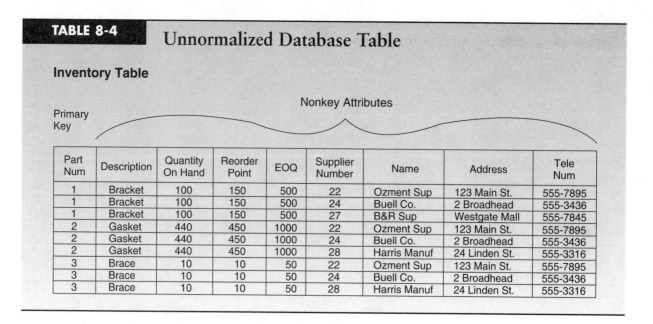

Part Num	Description	Quantity On Hand	Reorder Point	EOQ	Supplier Number	Name	Address	Tele Num
1	Bracket	100	150	500	22	Ozment Sup	123 Main St.	555-7895
1	Bracket	100	150	500	24	Buell Co.	2 Broadhead	555-3436
1	Bracket	100	150	500	27	B&R Sup	Westgate Mall	555-7845
2	Gasket	440	450	1000	22	Ozment Sup	123 Main St.	555-7895
2	Gasket	440	450	1000	24	Buell Co.	2 Broadhead	555-3436
2	Gasket	440	450	1000	28	Harris Manuf	24 Linden St.	555-3316
3	Brace	10	10	50	22	Ozment Sup	123 Main St.	555-7895
3	Brace	10	10	50	24	Buell Co.	2 Broadhead	555-3436
3	Brace	10	10	50	28	Harris Manuf	24 Linden St.	555-3316

FIGURE 8-13 Normalized Database Tables

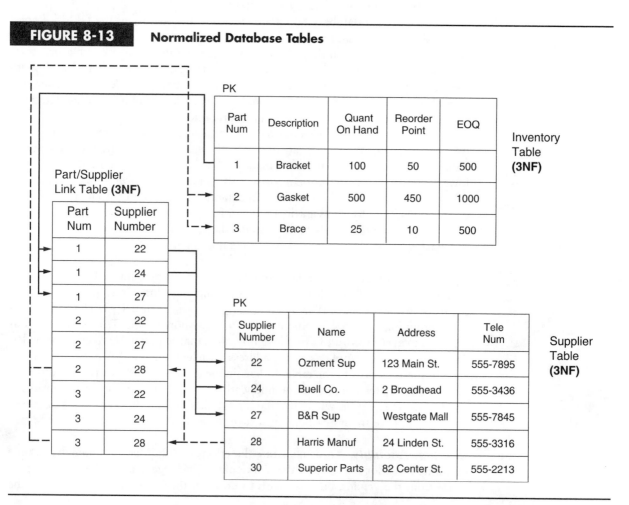

Inventory Table (3NF)

PK

Part Num	Description	Quant On Hand	Reorder Point	EOQ
1	Bracket	100	50	500
2	Gasket	500	450	1000
3	Brace	25	10	500

Part/Supplier Link Table (3NF)

Part Num	Supplier Number
1	22
1	24
1	27
2	22
2	27
2	28
3	22
3	24
3	28

Supplier Table (3NF)

PK

Supplier Number	Name	Address	Tele Num
22	Ozment Sup	123 Main St.	555-7895
24	Buell Co.	2 Broadhead	555-3436
27	B&R Sup	Westgate Mall	555-7845
28	Harris Manuf	24 Linden St.	555-3316
30	Superior Parts	82 Center St.	555-2213

organization wants to add the vendor to the database. This is not possible because the primary key for the inventory record is Part Num. Since the vendor does not supply the organization with any inventory items, it cannot be added to the database.

Deletion Anomaly. The **deletion anomaly** involves the unintentional deletion of data from a table. To illustrate, assume that Supplier Number 27 provides the company with only one item: Part Number 1. If the organization discontinues this inventory item and deletes it from the table, the data pertaining to Supplier Number 27 will also be deleted. Although the company may wish to retain the supplier's information for future use, the current table design prevents it from doing so.

The presence of the deletion anomaly is less conspicuous, but potentially more serious than the update and insertion anomalies. A flawed database design that prevents the insertion of records or requires the user to perform excessive updates attracts attention quickly. However, the deletion anomaly may go undetected, and the user may be unaware of the loss of important data until it is too late. A poorly structured database can result in the unintentional loss of critical accounting records and the destruction of the audit trail. Hence, the design of database tables carries internal control significance that accountants must recognize.

The Normalization Process

Simply stated, eliminating the three anomalies involves a process that systematically splits unnormalized complex tables into smaller tables that meet two conditions:

1. All nonkey attributes in the table are dependent on the primary key.
2. All nonkey attributes are independent of the other nonkey attributes.

Although it is possible to represent simple user views with a single 3NF table, complex views require more than one table. The user view in Table 8-4, for example, cannot be represented by a single table that meets the 3NF conditions.

Two distinct sets of data are contained in the unnormalized table in Table 8-4: data about inventory and data about suppliers. The nonkey attributes of Name, Address, and Tele Num are not dependent on (defined by) the table's primary key (Part Num). Rather, these attributes are dependent on the nonkey attribute—Supplier Number. The solution is to remove the supplier data from the table and place them in a separate table, which we will call Supplier. The two new base tables, Inventory and Supplier, are presented in Figure 8-13, along with a third table, Part/Supplier, which is explained next.

When an unnormalized table is split into two or more normalized tables, the normalized tables must then be linked together by one or more common attributes called *embedded foreign keys*. The degree of association between the tables (i.e., 1:1, 1:M, or M:M) determines how the foreign keys are assigned. The concept of associations and the rules for embedding keys were explained in Chapter 3. As you will recall, when the association is one-to-one, it does not matter which table's primary key is embedded in the other as a foreign key. In one-to-many associations, the primary key on the "one" side is embedded as the foreign key on the "many" side. Embedded keys are not used to link tables that have a many-to-many association. Instead, a separate link table, containing keys for the related tables, is created.

In Figure 8-13, the link table (Part/Supplier) contains the primary keys for the records in the Inventory table (Part Num) and the related Supplier table (Supplier Number). Via the link table, every inventory record can be linked to each supplier of the item, and all suppliers can be linked to the inventory items that they supply. For example, by searching the Inventory table for Part Num 1, we see that suppliers 22, 24, and 27 supply this item. Searching in the opposite direction, supplier 28 provides part numbers 2 and 3. Each unique occurrence of a supplier/inventory relation is represented by a separate record in the link table. For example, if supplier 24 provides 500 different items, 500 link records are needed to depict these relations.

All three tables in Figure 8-13 are in 3NF and, as a result, the three anomalies have been eliminated. First, the update anomaly is resolved because data about each supplier exist in only one location—the Supplier table. Any change in the data about an individual supplier is made only once, regardless of how many items it furnishes the company. Second, the insert anomaly is solved, because new vendors can be added to the supplier table even if they are not currently supplying the organization with inventory. For example, Supplier Number 30 in the table does not supply any inventory items. Finally, the deletion anomaly is eliminated. The decision to delete an inventory item from the database will not result in the unintentional deletion of the supplier data as well, since these data reside independently in different tables.

Applying the same normalization principles to the Sales Report in Figure 8-12, we derive the base tables depicted in Figure 8-14. Four tables emerge: Customer, Invoice, Line-Item, and Inventory. The Customer and Invoice tables have a 1:M association. Similarly, the associations between Invoice and Line-Item and between Inventory and Line-Item are 1:M. The embedded foreign keys that link the tables are assigned in accordance with the rules discussed earlier. Notice that the Line-Item table uses a composite of Invoice Num and Part Num as the primary key. Notice also that both the Inventory Status Report and the Sales Report views use inventory data. The data requirements for both views must be consolidated into a single table. The attribute Unit-Sales Price must therefore be added to the Inventory table.

Figure 8-15 shows the set of base tables and the linkages between them needed to support the three user views in our example. To simplify the illustration, some data attributes are not shown. Note that the Journal Voucher Report view presented in Table 8-3 requires two tables in Figure 8-15: General Journal and Chart of Accounts.

FIGURE 8-14

Normalized Base Tables for Sales Report

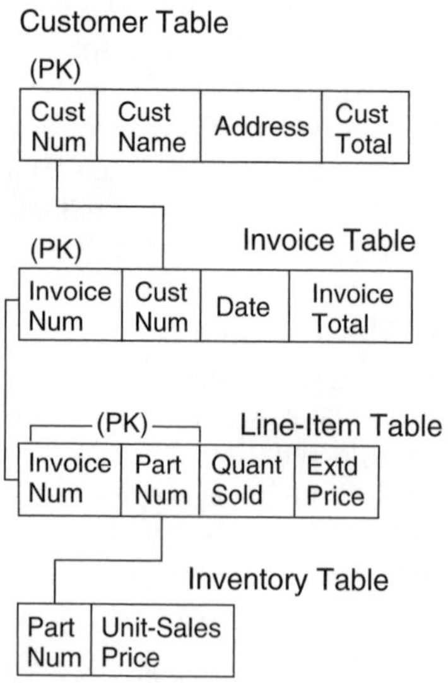

FIGURE 8-15 **Base Users and Links for All Views**

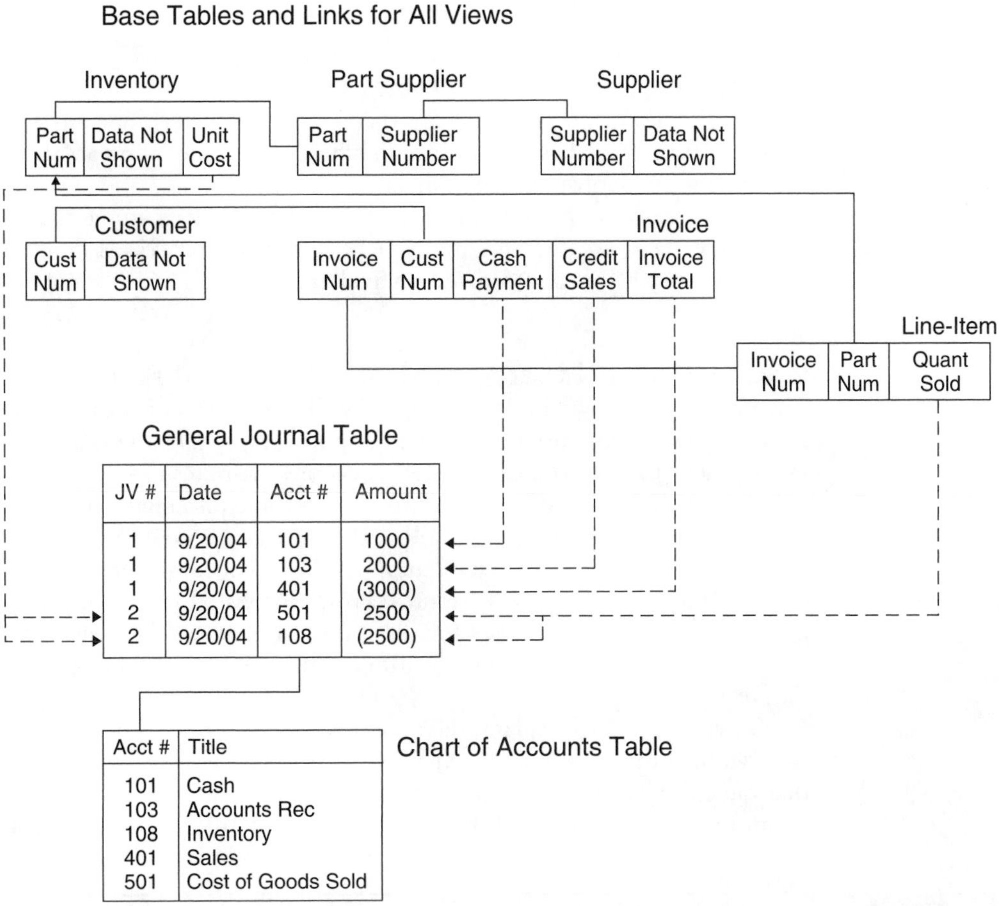

The view also requires summaries of detailed data that are stored in other tables. These are illustrated with dotted lines. The General Journal table receives summary values for cash payments, credit sales, and invoice total from the Invoice table, to produce the following journal voucher recording total cash and credit sales as shown in Table 8-3:

	DR	CR
Cash	1000	
Accts Receivable	2000	
Sales		3000

Since the cash payment and credit sales attributes were not in either of the other two views, they must be added to the Invoice table structure. Summaries are required for Quant Sold from the Line-Item table and Unit Cost from the Inventory table to record cost of goods sold per Figure 8-14:

	DR	CR
Cost of Goods Sold	2500	
Inventory		2500

Unit Cost is also a new attribute that was added to the Inventory table. These summarized values are stored in the General Journal table to produce the Journal Voucher Report.

Creating the Physical Base Tables

The base tables created thus far are theoretical (on paper), not physical. The next step is to create the physical tables and, where applicable, populate them with data. This step is an involved one that must be carefully planned and executed, and may take many months. To continue with this example, let's assume that the physical tables have been created and are in place. Once this process is done, the physical user views can be produced based on available data.

Creating Physical User Views from Normalized Base Tables

The query function of a relational DBMS allows the system designer to easily create user views from base tables. The designer simply tells the DBMS which tables to use, their primary and foreign keys, and the attributes to select from each table. Older DBMSs require the designer to specify these parameters in SQL or another query language. Newer systems allow this process to be done visually through a feature known as Query by Example (QBE). The designer simply points and clicks at the tables and the attributes. From this visual representation, the DBMS generates the SQL commands for the query to produce the view. The SQL commands needed to produce the inventory status report in Table 8-2 are shown in Figure 8-16.

To view and process data, the user executes the query program. Each time this is done, the query builds a new view with current data. The resulting view is a **virtual table** derived from the base tables. A virtual table does not physically exist as a set of rows and columns. It is a partial representation (subrows and subcolumns)

FIGURE 8-16

SQL Query Illustration

```
SELECT inventory.part-num, description, quant-on-hand, reorder-point, EOQ, part-supplier.part-num,
part-supplier.supplier-number, supplier.supplier- number, name, address, tele-num
FROM inventory, part-supplier, supplier
WHERE inventory.part-num=part-supplier.part-num AND part-supplier.
supplier-number=supplier.supplier-number AND quant-on-hand ≤ reorder-point
```

- The SELECT command identifies all the attributes to be contained in the view. When the same attribute appears in more than one table (e.g., part-num) the source table name must also be specified.
- The FROM command identifies the tables used in creating the view.
- The WHERE command specifies how rows in the Inventory, Part-Supplier and Supplier tables are to be matched to create the view. In this case, the three tables are algebraically joined on the primary keys Part Num and Supplier Number. It also serves as a filter to determine which rows in the tables to use in the output.
- LOGICAL OPERATORS: Multiple expressions may be linked with the AND, OR, and NOT operators. In this example, the last expression uses AND to restrict the records to be selected with the logical expression *quant-on-hand ≤ reorder-point*. Only records whose quantities on hand have fallen to or below their reorder points will be selected for the view. The user will not see the many thousands of other inventory items that have adequate quantities available.

of the actual physical base tables. The user perceives the view as his or her personal database. By restricting the user's access to the view, rather than permitting access to the underlying base tables, the user is limited to authorized data only.

A report program is used to make the view visually attractive and easy to use. Column headings can be added, fields summed, and averages calculated to produce a hard copy or computer screen report that resembles the original user report in Table 8-2. The report program can suppress unnecessary data from the view, such as repeating groups (duplicated data) and the key values in the Part-Supplier link table. These keys are necessary to build the view but are not needed for the actual report.

Auditors and Data Normalization

Database normalization is a technical matter that is usually the responsibility of systems professionals. However, the subject has implications for internal control that make it the concern of auditors also. For example, the update anomaly can generate conflicting and obsolete data values; the insertion anomaly can result in unrecorded transactions and incomplete audit trails; and the deletion anomaly can cause the loss of accounting records and the destruction of audit trails. Although most auditors will never be responsible for normalizing an organization's databases, they should have an understanding of the process and be able to determine whether a table is properly normalized.

Furthermore, in order to extract data from tables to perform audit procedures, the auditor first needs to know how the data are structured. The user's view of the data is often very different from its storage structure. For example, Figure 8-17 demonstrates that extracting purchases order data may involve a number of related tables. The circled numbers relate items in the user view to storage locations in the related base tables.

Embedded Audit Module

The objective of the **embedded audit module** (EAM), also known as *continuous auditing*, is to identify important transactions while they are being processed and extract copies of them in real time. An EAM is a specially programmed module embedded in a host application to capture predetermined transaction types for subsequent analysis. The approach is illustrated in Figure 8-18.

As the selected transaction is being processed by the host application, a copy of the transaction is stored in an audit file for subsequent review. The EAM approach allows selected transactions to be captured throughout the audit period. Captured transactions are made available to the auditor in real time, at period end, or at any time during the period, thus significantly reducing the amount of work the auditor must do to identify significant transactions for substantive testing.

To begin data capturing, the auditor specifies to the EAM the parameters and materiality threshold of the transactions set to be captured. For example, let's assume that the auditor establishes a $50,000 materiality threshold for transactions processed by a sales order processing system. Transactions equal to or greater than $50,000 will be copied to the audit file. From this set of transactions, the auditor may select a subset to be used for substantive tests. Transactions that fall below this threshold will be ignored by the EAM.

FIGURE 8-17

Normalized Tables

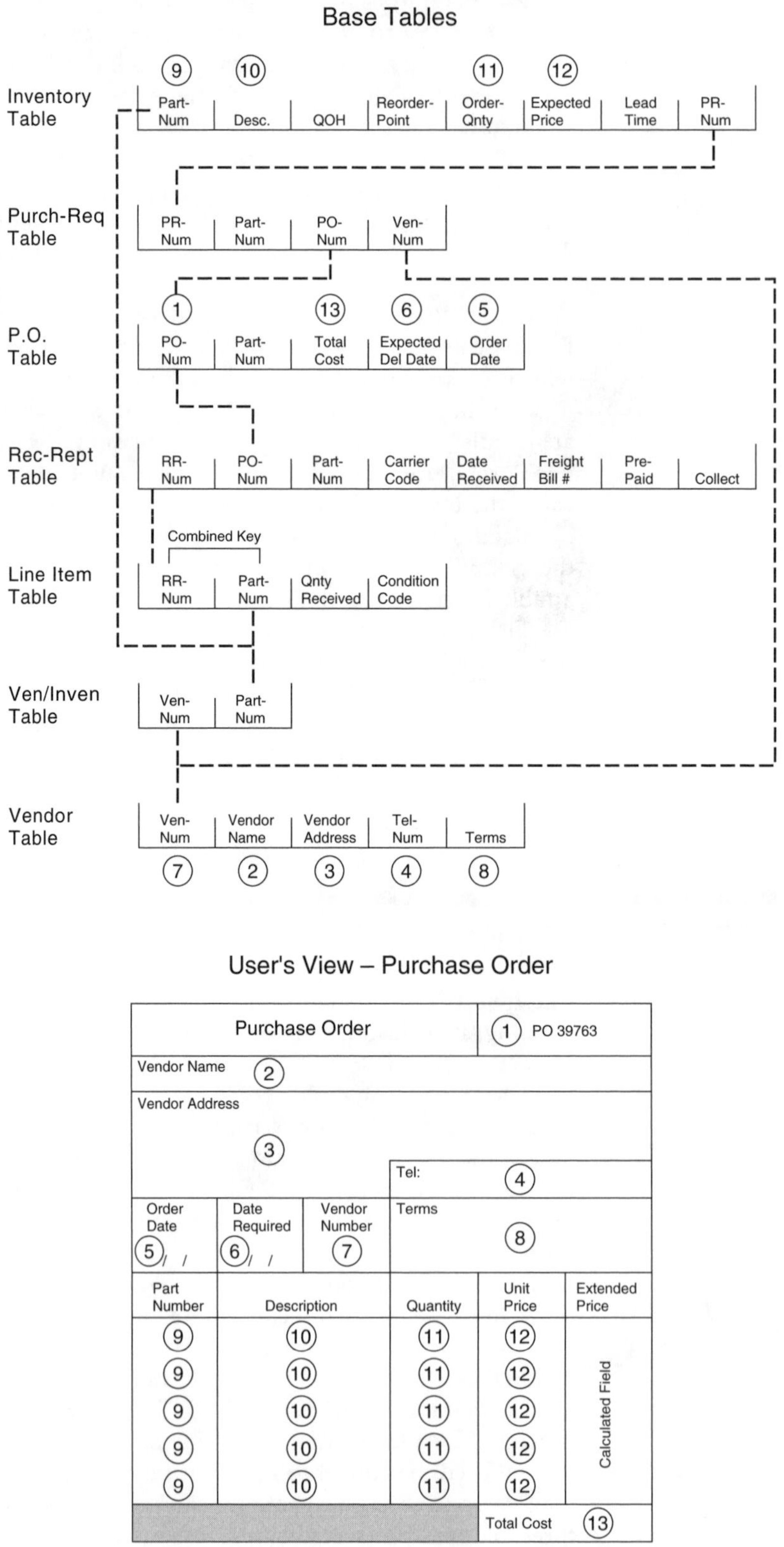

FIGURE 8-18

Embedded Audit Module Technique

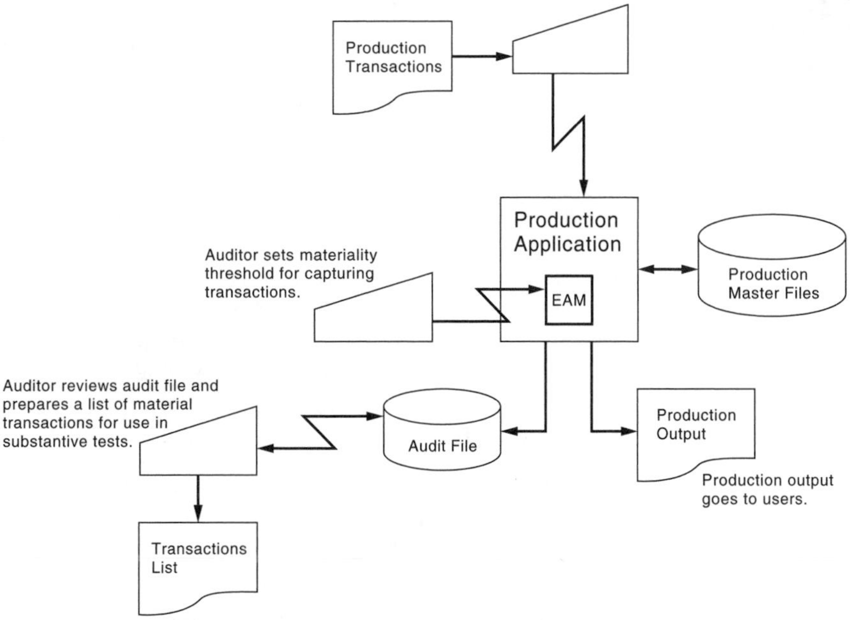

While primarily a substantive testing technique, EAMs may also be used to monitor controls on an ongoing basis as required by SAS 78. For example, transactions selected by the EAM can be reviewed for proper authorization, completeness and accuracy of processing, and correct posting to accounts.

Disadvantages of EAMs

The EAM approach has two significant disadvantages. The first pertains to operational efficiency and the second is concerned with EAM integrity.

Operational Efficiency

From the user's point of view, EAMs decrease operational performance. The presence of an audit module within the host application may create significant overhead, especially when the amount of testing is extensive. One approach for relieving this burden from the system is to design modules that may be turned on and off by the auditor. Doing so will, of course, reduce the effectiveness of the EAM as an ongoing audit tool.

Verifying EAM Integrity

The EAM approach may not be a viable audit technique in environments with a high level of program maintenance. When host applications undergo frequent changes, the EAMs embedded within the hosts will also require frequent modifications. The integrity concerns raised earlier regarding application maintenance apply equally to EAMs. The integrity of the EAM directly affects the quality of the audit process. Auditors must therefore evaluate the EAM integrity. This evaluation is accomplished in the same way as testing the host application controls.

Generalized Audit Software

Generalized audit software (GAS) is the most widely used CAATT for IS auditing. GAS allows auditors to access electronically coded data files and perform various operations on their contents. Some of the more common uses for GAS include:

- Footing and balancing entire files or selected data items
- Selecting and reporting detailed data contained in files
- Selecting stratified statistical samples from data files
- Formatting results of tests into reports
- Printing confirmations in either standardized or special wording
- Screening data and selectively including or excluding items
- Comparing multiple files and identifying any differences
- Recalculating data fields

The widespread popularity of GAS is due to four factors: (1) GAS languages are easy to use and require little computer background on the part of the auditor; (2) many GAS products can be used on both mainframe and PC systems; (3) auditors can perform their tests independent of the client's computer service staff; and (4) GAS can be used to audit the data stored in most file structures and formats.

Using GAS to Access Simple Structures

Gaining access to flat-file structures is a relatively simple process, as illustrated in Figure 8-19. In this example, an inventory file is read directly by the GAS, which extracts key information needed for the audit, including the quantity on hand, the dollar value, and the warehouse location of each inventory item. The auditor's task is to verify the existence and value of the inventory by performing a physical count of a representative sample of the inventory on hand. Thus, on the basis of a materiality threshold provided by the auditor, the GAS selects the sample records and prepares a report containing the needed information.

FIGURE 8-19

Using GAS to Access Simple File Structure

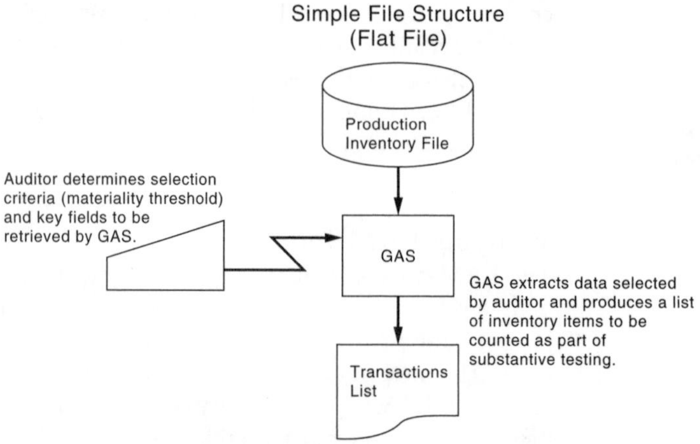
Simple File Structure
(Flat File)
Production
Inventory File
Auditor determines selection
criteria (materiality threshold)
and key fields to be
retrieved by GAS.
GAS
GAS extracts data selected
by auditor and produces a list
of inventory items to be
counted as part of
substantive testing.
Transactions
List

FIGURE 8-20

Using GAS to Access Complex File Structure

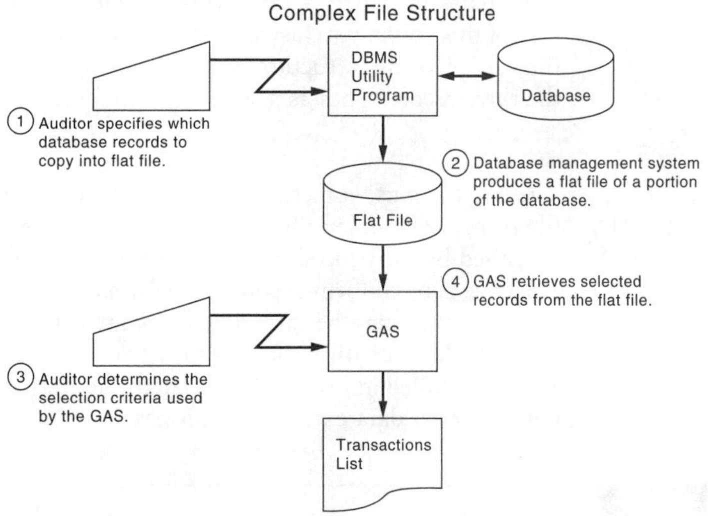

Using GAS to Access Complex Structures

Gaining access to complex structures, such as a hashed file or other form of random file, may pose a problem for the auditor. Not all GAS products on the market may be capable of accessing every type of file structure. If the CAATT in question is unable to deal with a complex structure, the auditor may need to appeal to systems professionals to write a special program that will copy the records from their actual structure to a flat-file sequential structure for easy retrieval. Figure 8-20 illustrates this approach.

Most DBMSs have utility features that can be used to reformat complex structures into flat files suitable for this purpose. To illustrate the file flattening process, consider the complex database structure presented in Figure 8-21. The database structure uses pointers to integrate three related files—Customer, Sales Invoice, and

FIGURE 8-21 **Complex Database Structure**

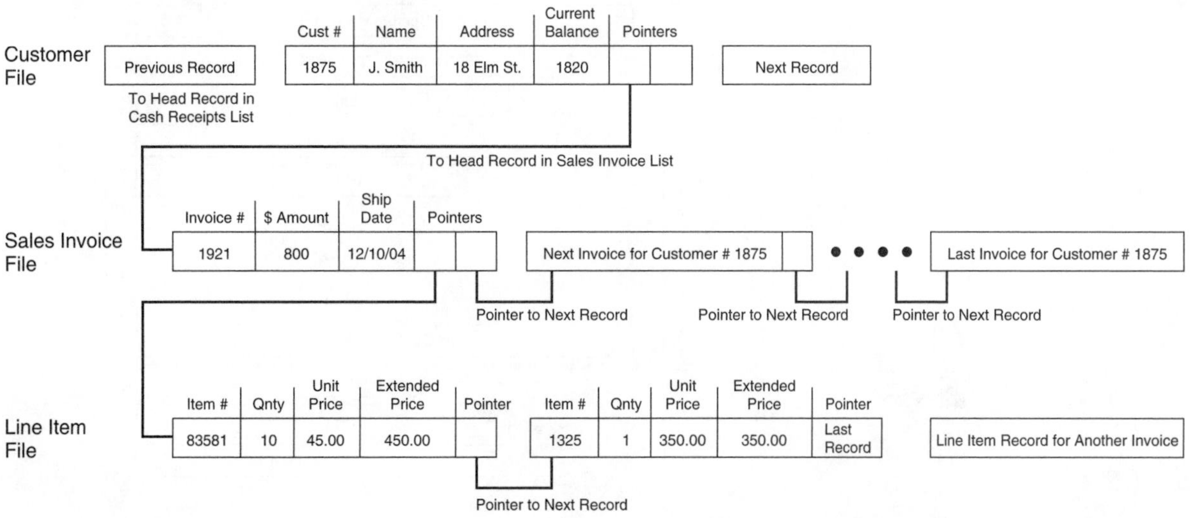

Line Item—in a hierarchical arrangement. Extracting audit evidence from a structure of this complexity using GAS may be difficult, if not impossible. A simpler flat-file version of this structure is illustrated in Figure 8-22. The single flat file presents the three record types as a sequential structure that can be easily accessed by GAS.

Audit Issues Pertaining to the Creation of Flat Files

The auditor must sometimes rely on computer services personnel to produce a flat file from the complex file structures. There is a risk that data integrity will be compromised by the procedure used to create the flat file. For example, if the auditor's objective is to confirm accounts receivable, certain fraudulent accounts in the complex structure may be intentionally omitted from the flat-file copy that is created. The sample of confirmations drawn from the flat file may therefore be unreliable. Auditors skilled in programming languages may avoid this potential pitfall by writing their own data extraction routines.

FIGURE 8-22

Flat Version of a Complex File Structure

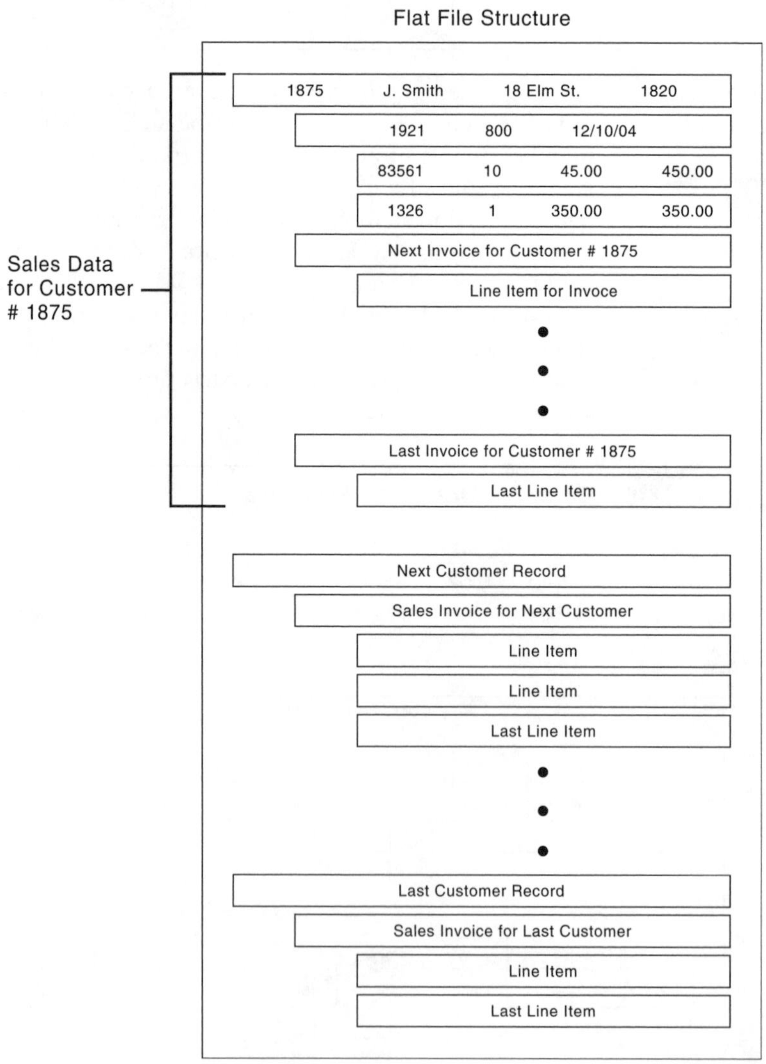

ACL Software

Public accounting firms have in the past developed proprietary versions of GAS, which they used in the audits of their clients. More recently, software companies have serviced this market. Among them, **ACL** (Audit Command Language) is the leader in the industry. ACL was designed as a meta-language for auditors to access most data stored by electronic means and to test them comprehensively. In fact, many of the problems associated with accessing complex data structures have been solved by ACL's Open Data Base Connectivity (ODBC) interface. A student edition of ACL along with sample data files and an instruction manual are stored on the CD that accompanies this text. The remainder of the chapter highlights ACL's more commonly used features. In later chapters, these and other features are demonstrated within the context of specific audit procedures. For a detailed explanation of ACL commands refer to the instruction manual, ACL's extensive online help feature, and the ACL tutorials provided by the authors on the CD.

Data Definition

We have already established that a client's system may store data using a number of flat-file or database structures, including sequential files, ISAM files, linked lists, and relational tables. One of ACL's strengths is the ability to read data stored in most formats. ACL uses the **data definition** feature for this purpose. To create a data definition, the auditor needs to know both where the source file physically resides and its field structure layout. Small files can be imported via text files or spreadsheets. Very large files may need to be accessed directly from the mainframe computer. When this is the case, the auditor must obtain access privileges to the directory in which the file resides. Where possible, however, a copy of the file should be stored in a separate test directory or downloaded to the auditor's PC. This step usually requires the assistance of systems professionals. The auditor should ensure that he or she secures the correct version of the file, that it is complete, and that the file structure documentation is intact. At this point, the auditor is ready to define the file to ACL. Figure 8-23 illustrates ACL's data definition screen.

The data definition screen allows the auditor to define important characteristics of the source file, including overall record length, the name given to each field, the type of data (i.e., numeric or character) contained in each field, and the starting point and length of each field in the file.[1] This definition is stored in a table under a name assigned by the auditor. Since the file in Figure 8-23 contains inventory data, the table shall be named *INVENTORY* for this example. Once the data definition is complete, future access to the table is accomplished simply by selecting *INVENTORY* from ACL's tables folder under the project manager menu. ACL automatically retrieves the file and presents it on screen according to its data definition. For example, Figure 8-24 illustrates the view of the Inventory file after the *INVENTORY.fil* definition is created. As we will see, this view of the data may be changed as needed by the auditor.

Customizing a View

A view is simply a way of looking at data in a file; auditors seldom need to use all the data contained in a file. ACL allows the auditor to customize the original view

1 Refer to "Defining Data" under the Index section of ACL's online Help feature for a detailed explanation of this process.

FIGURE 8-23 **Data File Definition**

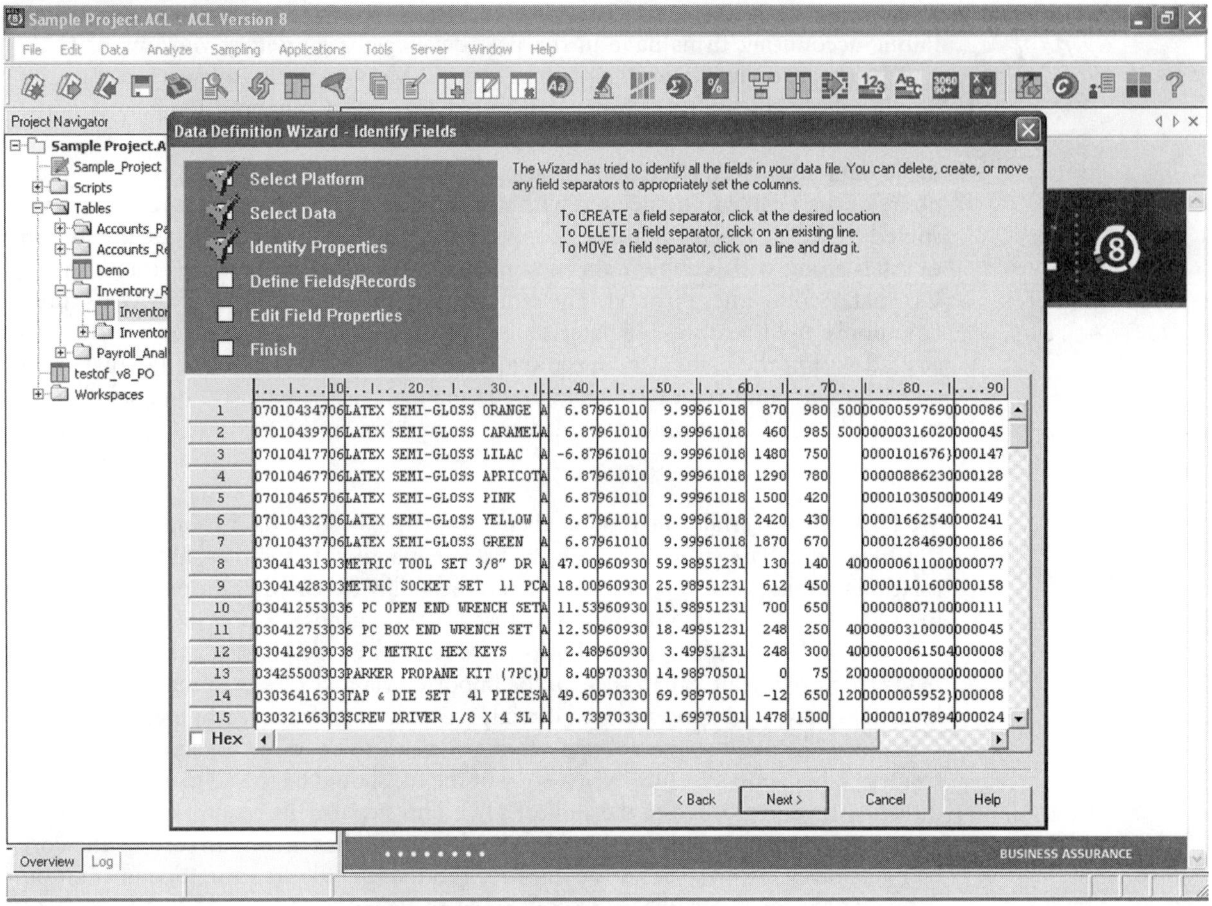

Source: Courtesy ACL Services Ltd.

created during data definition to one that better meets his or her audit needs. The auditor can create and reformat new views without changing or deleting the data in the underlying file. Only the presentation of the data is affected. For example, the inventory file in Figure 8-24 contains a number of fields that are irrelevant to the audit. Also, the key data of interest to the auditor are not organized in contiguous fields. Instead, they are interspersed with irrelevant data, making review of important data difficult. The auditor can easily delete and/or rearrange the data to facilitate effective usage. Figure 8-25 presents a reorganized view of the inventory data that focuses on critical data elements.

FILTERING DATA

ACL provides powerful options for filtering data that support various audit tests. **Filters** are expressions that search for records that meet the filter criteria. ACL's **expression builder** allows the auditor to use logical operators such as AND, OR, <, >, NOT and others to define and test conditions of any complexity and to process only those records that match specific conditions. For example, the auditor

FIGURE 8-24 **View of Inventory Table**

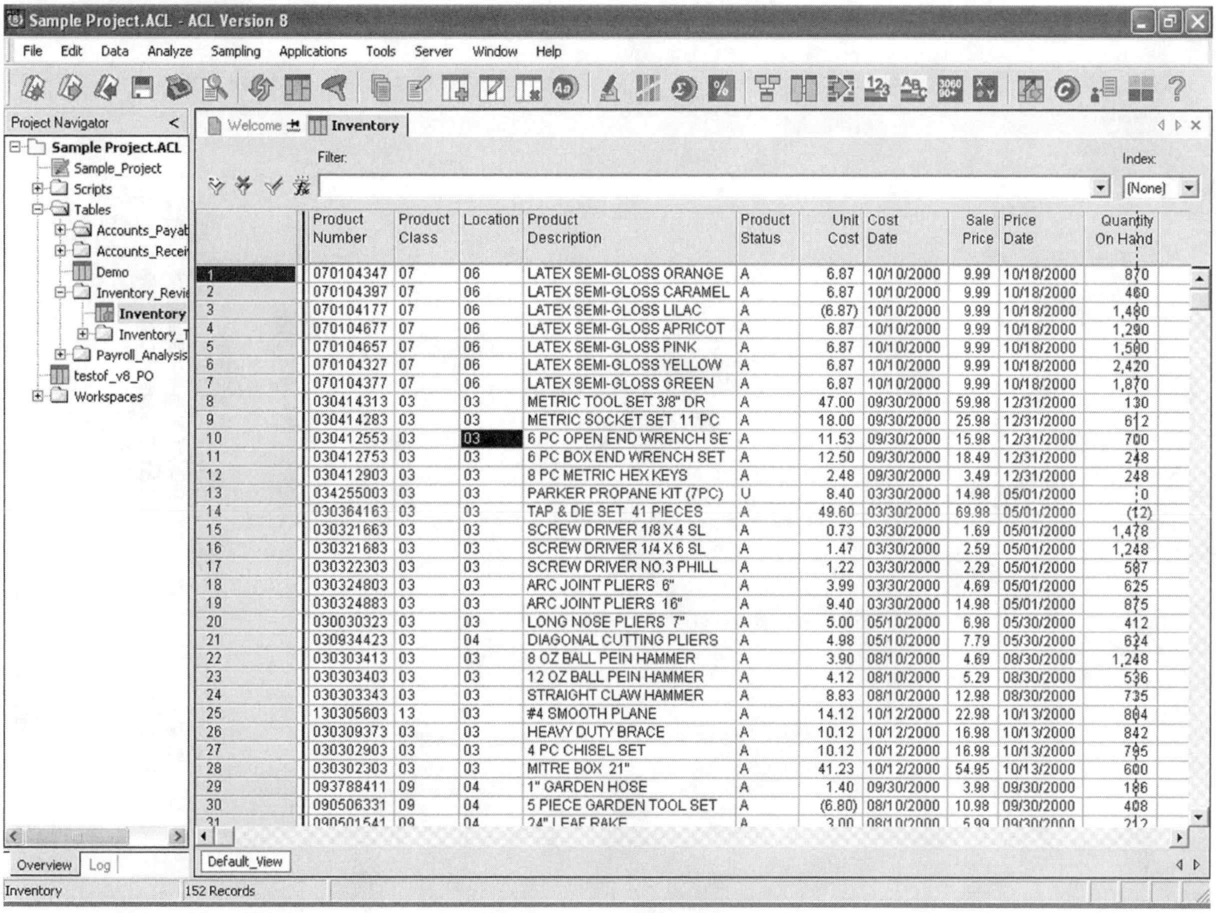

	Product Number	Product Class	Location	Product Description	Product Status	Unit Cost	Cost Date	Sale Price	Price Date	Quantity On Hand
1	070104347	07	06	LATEX SEMI-GLOSS ORANGE	A	6.87	10/10/2000	9.99	10/18/2000	870
2	070104397	07	06	LATEX SEMI-GLOSS CARAMEL	A	6.87	10/10/2000	9.99	10/18/2000	460
3	070104177	07	06	LATEX SEMI-GLOSS LILAC	A	(6.87)	10/10/2000	9.99	10/18/2000	1,480
4	070104677	07	06	LATEX SEMI-GLOSS APRICOT	A	6.87	10/10/2000	9.99	10/18/2000	1,290
5	070104657	07	06	LATEX SEMI-GLOSS PINK	A	6.87	10/10/2000	9.99	10/18/2000	1,500
6	070104327	07	06	LATEX SEMI-GLOSS YELLOW	A	6.87	10/10/2000	9.99	10/18/2000	2,420
7	070104377	07	06	LATEX SEMI-GLOSS GREEN	A	6.87	10/10/2000	9.99	10/18/2000	1,870
8	030414313	03	03	METRIC TOOL SET 3/8" DR	A	47.00	09/30/2000	59.98	12/31/2000	130
9	030414283	03	03	METRIC SOCKET SET 11 PC	A	18.00	09/30/2000	25.98	12/31/2000	612
10	030412553	03	03	6 PC OPEN END WRENCH SE	A	11.53	09/30/2000	15.98	12/31/2000	700
11	030412753	03	03	6 PC BOX END WRENCH SET	A	12.50	09/30/2000	18.49	12/31/2000	248
12	030412903	03	03	8 PC METRIC HEX KEYS	A	2.48	09/30/2000	3.49	12/31/2000	248
13	034255003	03	03	PARKER PROPANE KIT (7PC)	U	8.40	03/30/2000	14.98	05/01/2000	0
14	030364163	03	03	TAP & DIE SET 41 PIECES	A	49.60	03/30/2000	69.98	05/01/2000	(12)
15	030321663	03	03	SCREW DRIVER 1/8 X 4 SL	A	0.73	03/30/2000	1.69	05/01/2000	1,478
16	030321683	03	03	SCREW DRIVER 1/4 X 6 SL	A	1.47	03/30/2000	2.59	05/01/2000	1,248
17	030322303	03	03	SCREW DRIVER NO.3 PHILL	A	1.22	03/30/2000	2.29	05/01/2000	587
18	030324803	03	03	ARC JOINT PLIERS 6"	A	3.99	03/30/2000	4.69	05/01/2000	625
19	030324883	03	03	ARC JOINT PLIERS 16"	A	9.40	03/30/2000	14.98	05/01/2000	875
20	030030323	03	03	LONG NOSE PLIERS 7"	A	5.00	05/10/2000	6.98	05/30/2000	412
21	030934423	03	04	DIAGONAL CUTTING PLIERS	A	4.98	05/10/2000	7.79	05/30/2000	624
22	030303413	03	03	8 OZ BALL PEIN HAMMER	A	3.90	08/10/2000	4.69	08/30/2000	1,248
23	030303403	03	03	12 OZ BALL PEIN HAMMER	A	4.12	08/10/2000	5.29	08/30/2000	536
24	030303343	03	03	STRAIGHT CLAW HAMMER	A	8.83	08/10/2000	12.98	08/30/2000	735
25	130305603	13	03	#4 SMOOTH PLANE	A	14.12	10/12/2000	22.98	10/13/2000	804
26	030309373	03	03	HEAVY DUTY BRACE	A	10.12	10/12/2000	16.98	10/13/2000	842
27	030302903	03	03	4 PC CHISEL SET	A	10.12	10/12/2000	16.98	10/13/2000	795
28	030302303	03	03	MITRE BOX 21"	A	41.23	10/12/2000	54.95	10/13/2000	600
29	093788411	09	04	1" GARDEN HOSE	A	1.40	09/30/2000	3.98	09/30/2000	186
30	090506331	09	04	5 PIECE GARDEN TOOL SET	A	(6.80)	08/10/2000	10.98	09/30/2000	408
31	090501541	09	04	24" LEAF RAKE	A	3.00	08/10/2000	5.99	09/30/2000	212

Source: Courtesy ACL Services Ltd.

can search an inventory file for records with negative or zero quantity on hand. The expression builder screen and the filter needed for this test is illustrated in Figure 8-26.

When the auditor executes this filter procedure, ACL produces a new view of the inventory file (Figure 8-27) containing four records with zero or negative quantity-on-hand levels. This example demonstrates how auditors use ACL to search for anomalies and unusual conditions in accounting files containing thousands of records that defy review by visually scanning their contents.

STRATIFYING DATA

ACL's stratification feature allows the auditor to view the distribution of records that fall into specified strata. Data can be stratified on any numeric field such as sales price, unit cost, quantity sold, and so on. The data are summarized and classified by strata, which can be equal in size (called *intervals*) or vary in size (called *free*). Figure 8-28 illustrates the results of stratifying the inventory table on the unit-cost field. In this example, inventory value is also calculated for each interval.

FIGURE 8-25 **Customized View of Inventory Table**

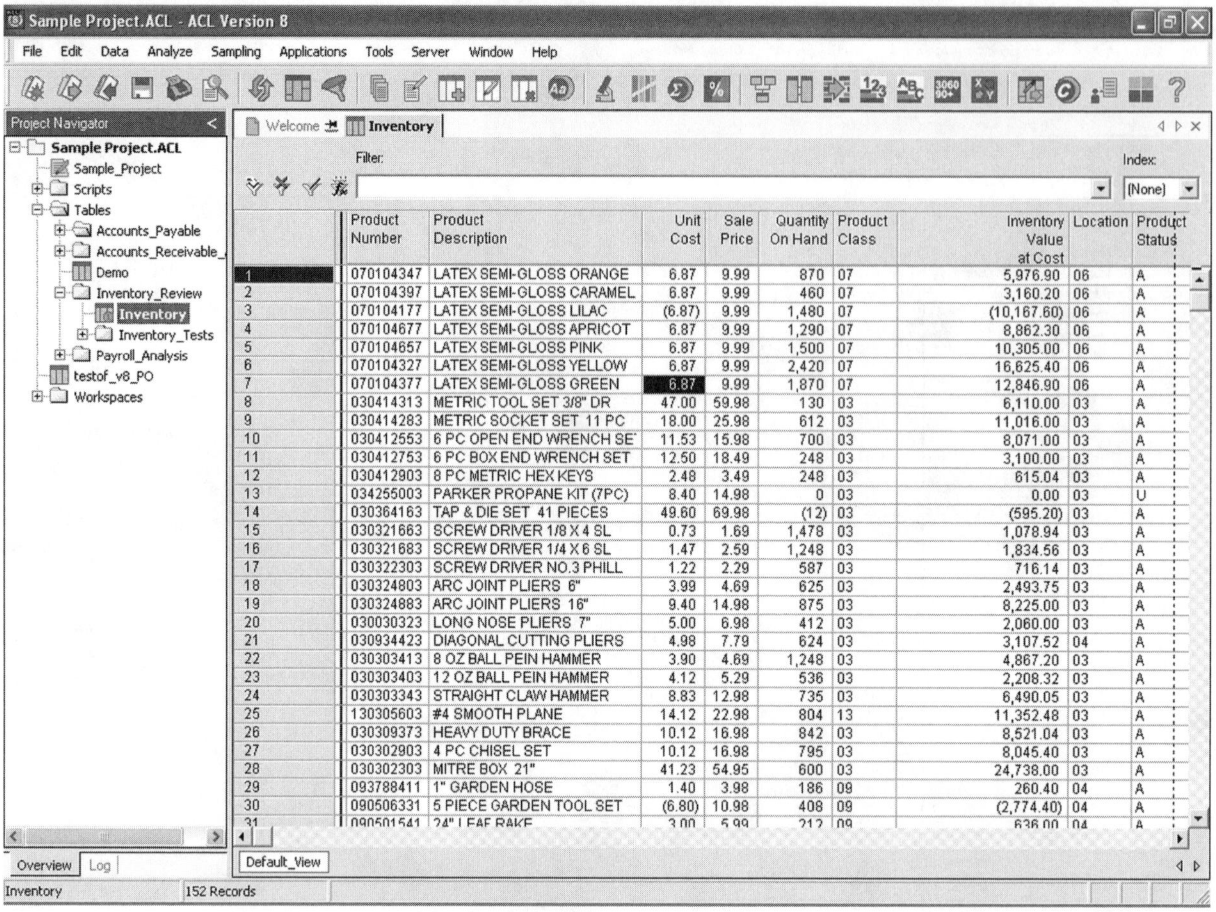

	Product Number	Product Description	Unit Cost	Sale Price	Quantity On Hand	Product Class	Inventory Value at Cost	Location	Product Status
1	070104347	LATEX SEMI-GLOSS ORANGE	6.87	9.99	870	07	5,976.90	06	A
2	070104397	LATEX SEMI-GLOSS CARAMEL	6.87	9.99	460	07	3,160.20	06	A
3	070104177	LATEX SEMI-GLOSS LILAC	(6.87)	9.99	1,480	07	(10,167.60)	06	A
4	070104677	LATEX SEMI-GLOSS APRICOT	6.87	9.99	1,290	07	8,862.30	06	A
5	070104657	LATEX SEMI-GLOSS PINK	6.87	9.99	1,500	07	10,305.00	06	A
6	070104327	LATEX SEMI-GLOSS YELLOW	6.87	9.99	2,420	07	16,625.40	06	A
7	070104377	LATEX SEMI-GLOSS GREEN	6.87	9.99	1,870	07	12,846.90	06	A
8	030414313	METRIC TOOL SET 3/8" DR	47.00	59.98	130	03	6,110.00	03	A
9	030414283	METRIC SOCKET SET 11 PC	18.00	25.98	612	03	11,016.00	03	A
10	030412553	6 PC OPEN END WRENCH SE	11.53	15.98	700	03	8,071.00	03	A
11	030412753	6 PC BOX END WRENCH SET	12.50	18.49	248	03	3,100.00	03	A
12	030412903	8 PC METRIC HEX KEYS	2.48	3.49	248	03	615.04	03	A
13	034255003	PARKER PROPANE KIT (7PC)	8.40	14.98	0	03	0.00	03	U
14	030364163	TAP & DIE SET 41 PIECES	49.60	69.98	(12)	03	(595.20)	03	A
15	030321663	SCREW DRIVER 1/8 X 4 SL	0.73	1.69	1,478	03	1,078.94	03	A
16	030321683	SCREW DRIVER 1/4 X 6 SL	1.47	2.59	1,248	03	1,834.56	03	A
17	030322303	SCREW DRIVER NO.3 PHILL	1.22	2.29	587	03	716.14	03	A
18	030324803	ARC JOINT PLIERS 6"	3.99	4.69	625	03	2,493.75	03	A
19	030324883	ARC JOINT PLIERS 16"	9.40	14.98	875	03	8,225.00	03	A
20	030030323	LONG NOSE PLIERS 7"	5.00	6.98	412	03	2,060.00	03	A
21	030934423	DIAGONAL CUTTING PLIERS	4.98	7.79	624	03	3,107.52	04	A
22	030303413	8 OZ BALL PEIN HAMMER	3.90	4.69	1,248	03	4,867.20	03	A
23	030303403	12 OZ BALL PEIN HAMMER	4.12	5.29	536	03	2,208.32	03	A
24	030303343	STRAIGHT CLAW HAMMER	8.83	12.98	735	03	6,490.05	03	A
25	130305603	#4 SMOOTH PLANE	14.12	22.98	804	13	11,352.48	03	A
26	030309373	HEAVY DUTY BRACE	10.12	16.98	842	03	8,521.04	03	A
27	030302903	4 PC CHISEL SET	10.12	16.98	795	03	8,045.40	03	A
28	030302303	MITRE BOX 21"	41.23	54.95	600	03	24,738.00	03	A
29	093788411	1" GARDEN HOSE	1.40	3.98	186	09	260.40	04	A
30	090506331	5 PIECE GARDEN TOOL SET	(6.80)	10.98	408	09	(2,774.40)	04	A
31	090501541	24" LEAF RAKE	3.00	5.99	212	09	636.00	04	A

Source: Courtesy ACL Services Ltd.

The stratified report presented in Figure 8-28 shows unit cost data allocated across 10 intervals from $-6.8 to $381.20. The auditor may choose to change the size and number of intervals or examine only a subset of the file. For example, the first two strata show that they contain a disproportionate number of items. The auditor can obtain a clearer picture of the inventory cost structure by increasing the number of intervals or by reducing the upper limit of the range to $71.

STATISTICAL ANALYSIS

ACL offers many sampling methods for statistical analysis. Two of the most frequently used are **record sampling** and **monetary unit sampling (MUS)**. Each method allows random and interval sampling. The choice of methods will depend on the auditor's strategy and the composition of the file being audited. On one hand, when records in a file are fairly evenly distributed across strata, the auditor may want an unbiased sample and will thus choose the record sample approach. Using inventory to illustrate, each record, regardless of the dollar amount of the inventory value field, has an equal chance of being included in the sample. On the other hand, if the

FIGURE 8-26

Expression Builder

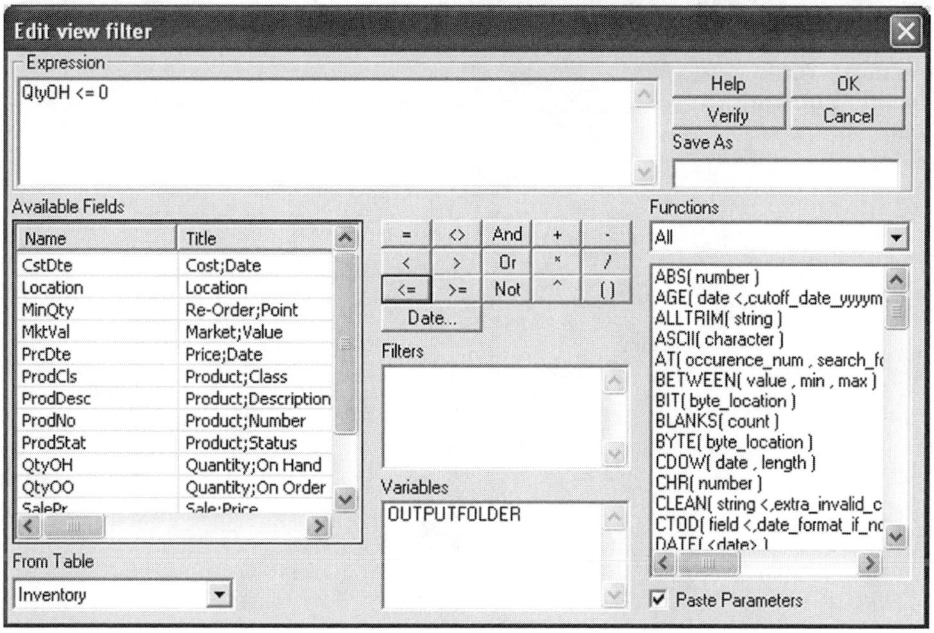

Source: Courtesy ACL Services Ltd.

FIGURE 8-27

View of Filtered Inventory Table

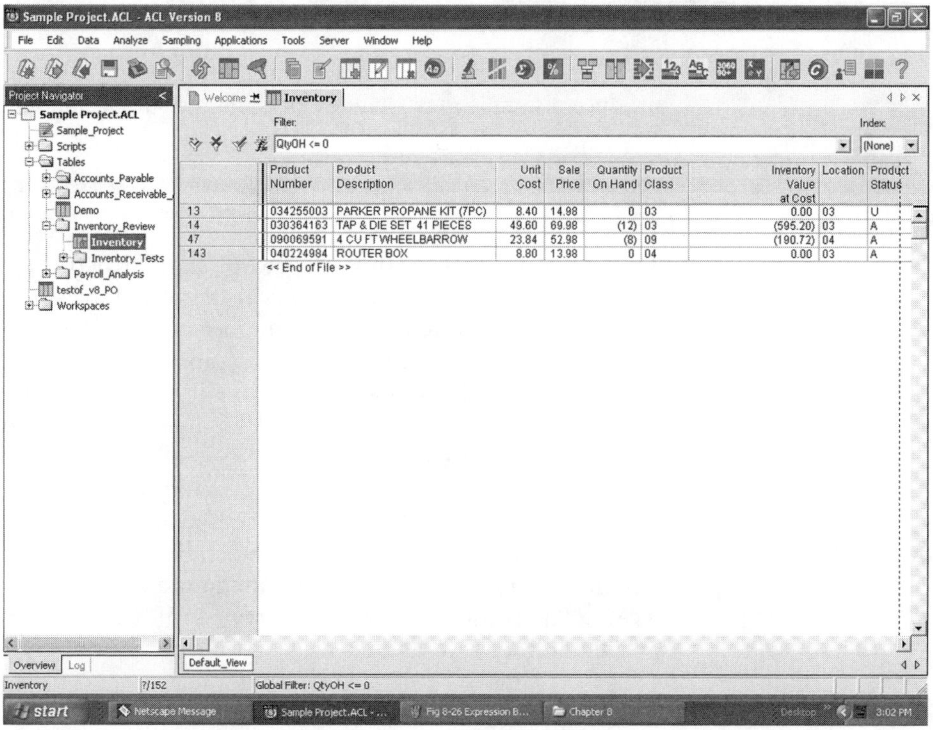

Source: Courtesy ACL Services Ltd.

FIGURE 8-28

Inventory Table Stratified on Unit Cost

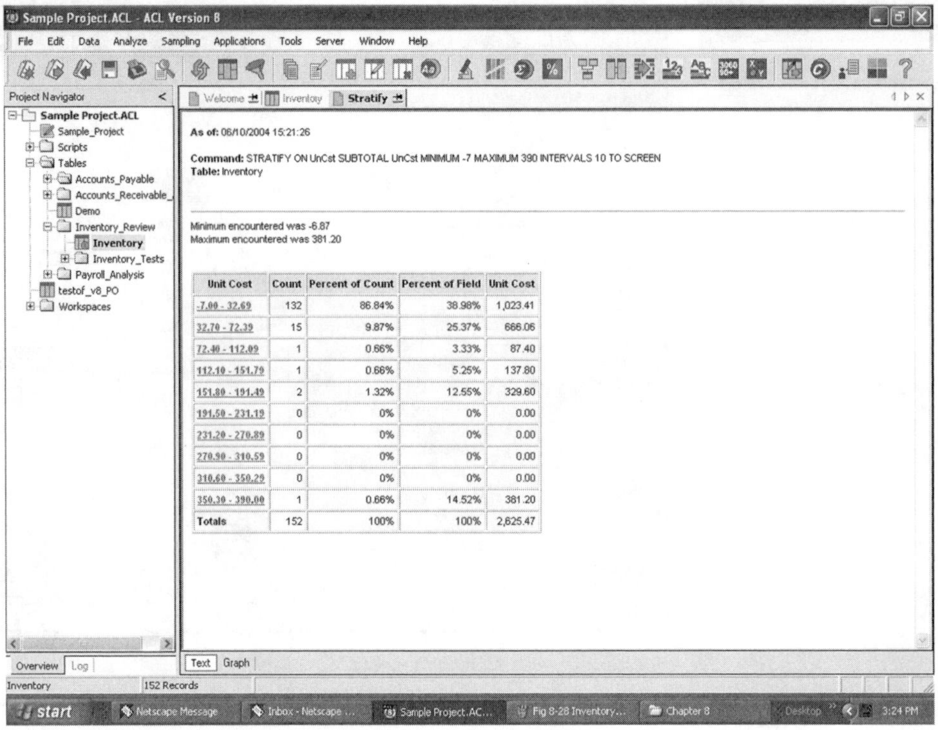

Source: Courtesy ACL Services Ltd.

file is heavily skewed with large value items, the auditor may select MUS, which will produce a sample that includes all the larger dollar amounts.

SUMMARY

This chapter began with a review of data structures, which specify (1) how records are organized in the physical file or database and (2) the access method employed to navigate the file. A number of basic data structures were examined, including sequential, indexed, hashing, and pointers. The chapter then focused on the use of CAATTs for data extraction and analysis. Data extraction can be performed by embedded audit modules and general audit software. Audit software supports two types of audit tests: (1) it allows the auditor to make inferences about application control effectiveness, and (2) it provides access to data needed for substantive tests. The second section of the chapter described the features, advantages, and disadvantages of the embedded audit module (EAM) approach. The third section outlined typical functions and uses of generalized audit software (GAS). The section closed with a review of a few features of ACL, the leading product in the GAS market.

Key Terms

access method
ACL
base tables
data definition
data normalization
data structures
default view
deletion anomaly
embedded audit module (EAM)
expression builder
filters
generalized audit software (GAS)
hashing structure
indexed random file
indexed sequential access method (ISAM)
indexed sequential file
indexed structure
insertion anomaly
inverted list
logical key pointer
monetary unit sampling (MUS)
normalized
organization
physical address pointer
pointer structure
record sampling
relative address pointer
sequential structure
third normal form (3NF)
update anomaly
user view
virtual table

Review Questions

1. What are the two fundamental components of data structures?
2. What are the criteria that influence the selection of the data structure?
3. What are the advantages and disadvantages of using a sequential data structure? Give an example of each.
4. What are the advantages and disadvantages of using an indexed random file structure? An indexed sequential file structure?
5. What are the three physical components of an ISAM file? Explain how a record is searched through these components.
6. What is a pointer? Discuss the three commonly used types of pointers and their relative merits.
7. List the hierarchy of database elements.
8. Discuss and give an example of one-to-one, one-to-many, and many-to-many record associations.
9. Why is a hierarchical database model considered to be a navigational database? What are some limitations of the hierarchical database model?
10. Explain how a separate linking file works in a network model.
11. What is an embedded audit module?
12. Explain what GAS is and why it is so popular with larger public accounting firms. Discuss the independence issue related to GAS.

Discussion Questions

1. Explain how a hashing structure works and why it is quicker than using an index. Give an example. If it is so much faster, why isn't it used exclusively?
2. Explain how an embedded audit module works and why auditors may choose not to use it.
3. Explain the term *navigational data models*. Contrast the hierarchical model and the network model.
4. Explain the three types of anomalies associated with database tables that have not been normalized.
5. Contrast embedded audit modules with generalized audit software.
6. Describe a specific accounting application that could make use of an ISAM file.

7. Explain why auditors should be familiar with the principle of data normalization.
8. How is a virtual table different from a base table?
9. Explain what the term *third normal form* (3NF) means.
10. Explain how a user view differs from a base table.
11. Explain the following three types of pointers: physical address pointer, relative address pointer, and logical key pointer.
12. Explain why GAS technology is popular with most auditors.
13. Explain the risk associated with using GAS to access complex file structures.
14. Explain the purpose of the input file definition feature of ACL.
15. Assume that an auditor is reviewing a file containing 25 fields of data, only 5 of which are relevant to the auditor's objective. Explain how ACL can help in this situation.
16. Explain the purpose of ACL's filter capability.
17. Distinguish between record sampling and monetary unit sampling (MUS).

MULTIPLE-CHOICE QUESTIONS

1. CIA 1186 III-33
   In an inventory system on a database management system, one stored record contains part number, part name, part color, and part weight. These individual items are called
   a. fields.
   b. stored files.
   c. bytes.
   d. occurrences.
2. CIA 586 III-31
   The use of pointers can save time when sequentially updating a
   a. master file.
   b. database management system.
   c. batch file.
   d. random file.
3. It is appropriate to use a sequential file structure when
   a. records are routinely inserted.
   b. a large portion of the file will be processed in one operation.
   c. records need to be scanned using secondary keys.
   d. single records need to be retrieved.
4. Which statement is *not* correct?
   a. The sequential file structure is appropriate for payroll records.
   b. An advantage of a sequential index is that it can be searched rapidly.
   c. The index sequential access method performs record insertion operations efficiently.
   d. The principal advantage of the hashing structure is speed of access.
5. Which of the following statements is *not* true?
   a. Indexed random files are dispersed throughout the storage device without regard for physical proximity with related records.
   b. Indexed random files use disk storage space efficiently.
   c. Indexed random files are efficient when processing a large portion of a file at one time.
   d. Indexed random files are easy to maintain in terms of adding records.
6. Which statement is *not* correct? The indexed sequential access method
   a. is used for very large files that need both direct access and batch processing.
   b. may use an overflow area for records.
   c. provides an exact physical address for each record.
   d. is appropriate for files that require few insertions or deletions.
7. Which statement is true about a hashing structure?
   a. The same address could be calculated for two records.
   b. Storage space is used efficiently.
   c. Records cannot be accessed rapidly.
   d. A separate index is required.
8. In a hashing structure,
   a. two records can be stored at the same address.
   b. pointers are used to indicate the location of all records.
   c. pointers are used to indicate the location of a record with the same address as another record.

d. all locations on the disk are used for record storage.

9. Pointers can be used for all of the following except
   a. to locate the subschema address of the record.
   b. to locate the physical address of the record.
   c. to locate the relative address of the record.
   d. to locate the logical key of the record.
10. An advantage of a physical address pointer is that
   a. it points directly to the actual disk storage location.
   b. it is easily recovered if it is inadvertently lost.
   c. it remains unchanged when disks are reorganized.
   d. all of the above are advantages of the physical address pointer.
11. Pointers are used
   a. to link records within a file.
   b. to link records between files.
   c. to identify records stored in overflow.
   d. all of the above.
12. In a hierarchical model,
   a. links between related records are implicit.
   b. the way to access data is by following a predefined data path.
   c. an owner (parent) record may own just one member (child) record.
   d. a member (child) record may have more than one owner (parent).
13. In a network model
   a. there is one predefined path to a particular record.
   b. many-to-many relationships are supported in a simple network.
   c. management can track and report information by one criterion only.
   d. link files are used to connect records in different files.
14. Which term is *not* associated with the relational database model?
   a. tuple
   b. attribute
   c. collision
   d. relation
15. In the relational database model,
   a. relationships are explicit.
   b. the user perceives that files are linked using pointers.
   c. data are represented on two-dimensional tables.
   d. data are represented as a tree structure.
16. In the relational database model, all of the following are true except
   a. data are presented to users as tables.
   b. data can be extracted from specified rows from specified tables.
   c. a new table can be built by joining two tables.
   d. only one-to-many relationships can be supported.
17. In a relational database,
   a. the user's view of the physical database is the same as the physical database.
   b. users perceive that they are manipulating a single table.
   c. a virtual table exists in the form of rows and columns of a table stored on the disk.
   d. a programming language (COBOL) is used to create a user's view of the database.
18. The update anomaly in unnormalized databases
   a. occurs because of data redundancy.
   b. complicates adding records to the database.
   c. may result in the loss of important data.
   d. often results in excessive record insertions.
19. The most serious problem with unnormalized databases is the
   a. update anomaly.
   b. insertion anomaly.
   c. deletion anomaly.
   d. none of the above.
20. The deletion anomaly in unnormalized databases
   a. is easily detected by users.
   b. may result in the loss of important data.
   c. complicates adding records to the database.
   d. requires the user to perform excessive updates.

Problems

1. **Access Methods**
For each of the following file processing operations, indicate whether a sequential file, indexed random file, indexed sequential access method (ISAM), hashing, or pointer structure works the best. You may choose as many as you wish for each step. Also indicate which would perform the least optimally.
   a. Retrieve a record from the file based on its primary key value.
   b. Update a record in the file.
   c. Read a complete file of records.
   d. Find the next record in a file.
   e. Insert a record into a file.
   f. Delete a record from a file.
   g. Scan a file for records with secondary keys.

2. **File Organization**
For the following situations, indicate the most appropriate type of file organization. Explain your choice.
   a. A local utility company has 80,000 residential customers and 10,000 commercial customers. The monthly billings are staggered throughout the month and, as a result, the cash receipts are fairly uniform throughout the month. For 99 percent of all accounts, one check per month is received. These receipts are recorded in a batch file, and the customer account records are updated biweekly. In a typical month, customer inquires are received at the rate of about 20 per day.
   b. A national credit card agency has 12 million customer accounts. On average, 30 million purchases and 700,000 receipts of payments are processed per day. Additionally, the customer support hot line provides information to approximately 150,000 credit card holders and 30,000 merchants per day.
   c. An airline reservation system assumes that the traveler knows the departing city. From that point, fares and flight times are examined based on the destination. Once a flight is identified as being acceptable to the traveler, then the availability is checked and, if necessary, a seat is reserved. The volume of transactions exceeds one-half million per day.
   d. A library system stocks more than 2 million books and has 30,000 patrons. Each patron is allowed to check out five books. On average, there are 1.3 copies of each title in the library. Over 3,000 books are checked out each day, with approximately the same amount being returned daily. The check-outs are posted immediately, as well as any returns of overdue books by patrons who wish to pay their fines.

3. **Structured Query Language**
The vice president of finance has noticed in the aging of the accounts receivable that the amount of overdue accounts is substantially higher than anticipated. He wants to investigate this problem. To do so, he requires a report of overdue accounts containing the attributes shown in the top half of the of Problem 3 table on page 373. The bottom half of the table contains the data fields and relevant files in the relational database system. Further, he wants to alert the salespeople of any customers not paying their bills on time. Using the SQL commands given in this chapter, write the code necessary to generate a report of overdue accounts that are greater than $5,000 and more than 30 days due. Each customer has an assigned salesperson.

4. **Indexed Sequential Access Method**
Using the index provided explain, step-by-step, how the Key 12987 would be found using the indexed sequential access method. Once a surface on a cylinder is located, what is the average number of records that must be searched?

CYLINDER INDEX		**SURFACE INDEX CYLINDER**	
Key Range	**Cylinder Number**	**Key Range**	**Surface Number**
2,000	44	12,250	0
4,000	45	12,500	1
6,000	46	12,750	2
8,000	47	13,000	3
10,000	48	13,250	4
12,000	49	13,500	5
14,000	50	14,750	6
16,000	51	15,000	7
18,000	52		
20,000	53		

Problem 3: Structured Query Language

Report Attributes

Salesperson Name, Salesperson Branch Office, Customer Number, Customer Name, Amount Overdue, Last Purchase Date, Goods Delivered?, Amount of Last Sales Order, Amount of Last Payment, Date of Last Payment

FILES AVAILABLE:

Salesperson Table	Customer Table	Sales Order Table
Salesperson Name	Customer Number	Sales Order Number
Salesperson Number	Customer Name	Customer Number
Commission Rate	Customer Address 1	Order Date
Rank	Customer Address 2	Amount
Branch	Salesperson Number	Delivery Date
Date of Hire	Last Sales Order Number	
	Year to Date Purchases	
	Account Balance	
	Overdue Balance	
	Amount of Last Payment	
	Date of Last Payment	

5. **Hashing Algorithm**
The systems programmer uses a hashing algorithm to determine storage addresses. The hashing structure is 9,997/key. The resulting number is then used to locate the record. The first two digits after the decimal point represent the cylinder number, while the second two digits represent the surface number. The fifth, sixth, and seventh digits after the decimal point represent the record number. This algorithm results in a unique address 99 percent of the time. What happens the remainder of the time when the results of the algorithm are not unique? Explain in detail the storage process when Key=3 is processed first, Key=2307 at a later date, and shortly thereafter Key=39.

6. **Normalization of Data**
Given below is a table of data for a library. Normalize this data into the third normal form, preparing it for use in a relational database environment. The library's computer is programmed to compute the due date to be 14 days after the check-out date. Document the steps necessary to normalize the data similar to the procedures found in the chapter. Index any fields necessary and show how the databases are related.

Problem 6: Normalization of Data

Student ID Number	Student First Name	Student Last Name	Number of Books Out	Book Call No	Book Title	Date Out	Due Date
678-98-4567	Amy	Baker	3	hf351.j6	Avalanches	09-02-04	09-16-04
678-98-4567	Amy	Baker	4	hf878.k3	Tornadoes	09-02-04	09-16-04
244-23-2348	Ramesh	Sunder	1	i835.123	Politics	09-02-04	09-16-04
398-34-8793	James	Talley	3	k987.d98	Sports	09-02-04	09-16-04
398-34-8793	James	Talley	4	d879.39	Legal Rights	09-02-04	09-16-04
678-98-4567	Amy	Baker	4	p987.t87	Earthquakes	09-03-04	09-17-04
244-23-2348	Ramesh	Sunder	1	q875.i76	Past Heroes	09-03-04	09-17-04

7. **Normalization of Data**
At the right is a table of data for a veterinary practice. Normalize this data into the third normal form, preparing it for use in a relational database environment. Indicate the primary keys and embedded foreign keys in the tables.

8. **Normalization of Data**
Prepare the base tables, in third normal form, needed to produce the user view on the following page.

9. **Normalization of Data**
Prepare the base tables, in third normal form, needed to produce the user view on the following page.

10. **Exposure Identification and Plan of Action**
As the manager of the external audit team, you realize that the embedded audit module writes only "material" invoices to the audit file for the accounts receivable confirmation process. You are immediately concerned that the accounts receivable account may be substantially overstated this year and for the prior years in which this EAM was used.

Required:
Explain why you are concerned since all "material" invoices are candidates for confirmation by the customer. Outline a plan for determining if the accounts receivable are overstated.

11. **Generalized Audit Software**
CMA 1290 4-Y7
The internal audit department of Sachem Manufacturing Company is considering buying computer software that will aid in the auditing process. Sachem's financial and manufacturing control systems are completely automated on a large mainframe computer. Melinda Robinson, the director of internal audit, believes that Sachem should acquire computer audit software to assist in the financial and procedure audits that her department conducts. The types of software packages that Robinson is considering are described below.

- A generalized audit software package that assists in basic audit work, such as the retrieval of live data from large computer

Problem 7: Normalization of Data

Patient ID Number	Patient Name	Owner ID Number	Owner Last Name	Owner First Name	Address1	Address2	Date	Animal Code	Animal Description	Service Code	Service Description	Charge
417	Beau	Magel	Magee	Elaine	23 Elm St	Houston, TX	01/04/05	GR	Golden Retriever	238	Rabies Shot	15.00
417	Beau	Magel	Magee	Elaine	23 Elm St	Houston, TX	01/04/05	GR	Golden Retriever	148	Flea Dip	25.00
417	Beau	Magel	Magee	Elaine	23 Elm St	Houston, TX	01/04/05	GR	Golden Retriever	337	Bloodwork II	20.00
632	Liugi	Cacil	Caciolo	Tony	8 Oak St	Houston, TX	01/09/05	DN	Dalmation	238	Rabies Shot	15.00
632	Luigi	Cacil	Caciolo	Tony	8 Oak St	Houston, TX	01/09/05	DN	Dalmation	500	Kennel–medium	9.00
632	Luigi	Cacil	Caciolo	Tony	8 Oak St	Houston, TX	01/24/05	DN	Dalmation	500	Kennel–medium	9.00
632	Luigi	Cacil	Caciolo	Tony	8 Oak St	Houston, TX	02/01/05	DN	Dalmation	148	Flea Dip	25.00
168	Astro	Jetsl	Jetson	George	3 Air Rd	Sprockley, TX	02/02/05	MX	Canine–mixed	368	Ear Cleaning	17.00

Problem 8: Normalization of Data

User View

Part#	Description	QOH	Reorder Point	EOQ	Unit Cost	Ven #	Ven Name	Ven Address	Tel
132	Bolt	100	50	1000	1.50	987	ABC Co.	654 Elm St	555 5498
143	Screw	59	10	100	1.75	987	ABC Co.	654 Elm St	555 5498
760	Nut	80	20	500	2.00	742	XYZ Co.	510 Smit	555 8921
982	Nail	100	50	800	1.00	987	ABC Co.	654 Elm St	555 5498

Problem 9: Normalization of Data

User View

Part#	Description	QOH	Reorder Point	EOQ	Unit Cost	Ven #	Ven Name	Ven Address	Tel
132	Bolt	100	50	1000	1.50	987	ABC Co.	654 Elm St	555 5498
					1.55	750	RST Co.	3415 8th St	555 3421
					1.45	742	XYZ Co.	510 Smit	555 8921
982	Nail	100	50	800	1.00	987	ABC Co.	654 Elm St	555 5498
					1.10	742	XYZ Co.	510 Smit	555 8921
					1.00	549	LMN Co.	18 Oak St.	555 9987

files. The department would review this information using conventional audit investigation techniques. More specifically, the department could perform criteria selection, sampling, basic computations for quantitative analysis, record handling, graphical analysis, and the printing of output (confirmations).

- An integrated test facility package that uses, monitors, and controls dummy test data through existing programs and checks the existence and adequacy of program data entry controls and processing controls.
- A control flowcharting package that provides a graphical presentation of the data flow of information through a system, pinpointing control strengths and weaknesses.
- A program (parallel) simulation and modeling package that uses actual data to conduct the same systemized process by using a different computer-logic program developed by the auditor. The package can also be used to seek answers to difficult audit problems (involving many comparisons and computations) within statistically acceptable confidence limits.

Required:

a. Without regard to any specific computer audit software, explain to the internal auditor the general advantages of using computer audit software to assist with audits.
b. Describe the audit purpose facilitated and the procedural steps to be followed by the internal auditor to use a(n)
   i. generalized audit software package.
   ii. integrated test facility package.
   iii. control flowcharting package.
   iv. program (parallel) simulation and modeling package.

12. Exposure Identification and Plan of Action

Two years ago an external auditing firm supervised the programming of embedded audit modules for Previts Office Equipment Company. During the audit process this year, the external auditors requested that a transaction log of all transactions be copied to the audit file. The external auditors noticed large gaps in dates and times for transactions being copied to the audit file. When they inquired about this, they were informed that increased processing of transactions had been burdening the mainframe system and that operators frequently had to turn off the EAM to allow the processing of important transactions in a timely fashion. In addition, much maintenance had been performed during the past year on the application programs.

Required:

Outline any potential exposures and determine the courses of action the external auditors should use to proceed.

13. ACL Exercise—Input File Definition

Following the instructions in the Readme.txt file on the CD that accompanies this text, load ACL onto your computer and download the instruction manual. Read pages 1 through 20 and complete the exercises.

14. ACL Exercise—General

Complete the exercises on pages 21 through 34 in the ACL instruction manual.

CHAPTER

9

Auditing the Revenue Cycle

Learning Objectives

After studying this chapter, you should:

- Understand the operational tasks associated with the revenue cycle under different levels of technology.
- Understand audit objectives related to the revenue cycle.
- Be familiar with revenue cycle control issues related to alternative technologies.
- Recognize the relationship between revenue cycle audit objectives, controls, and tests of controls.
- Understand the nature of substantive tests in achieving revenue cycle audit objectives.
- Be familiar with common features and functions of ACL that are used to perform substantive tests.

This chapter examines audit procedures associated with the revenue cycle. The chapter is divided into three main sections. It begins with a review of alternative technologies used in both legacy and modern systems. The focus is on the key operational tasks performed under each technological environment. The second section discusses the revenue cycle audit objectives, controls, and tests of controls that an auditor would perform to gather evidence needed to limit the scope, timing, and extent of substantive tests. The last section describes revenue cycle substantive tests in relation to audit objectives. Specific procedures based on ACL software are illustrated.

Overview of Revenue Cycle Technologies

This section examines alternative information technologies used in the revenue cycle. The first of these is a sales order system that employs batch processing and uses sequential files for storing accounting records. This is an example of an early legacy-type system. This approach characterizes the era of data ownership in which files were designed exclusively for the use of a single user. Data sharing is difficult, if not impossible, in this setting and results in a great deal of data redundancy and data obsolescence. Although archaic, such systems are still used because they continue to add value for organizations. For years, the anticipation was that legacy systems would be replaced before the end of the twentieth century. Instead, many organizations opted to commit significant resources to repair and modify these systems for the next millennium. Once the investments were made, the pressure to replace legacy systems was reduced. Odds favor the likelihood that auditors will be dealing with these technologies for some time to come.

Second, we review the operational features of a cash receipts system that employs batch processing and uses direct access files. This configuration is found in both modern systems and late-era legacy systems. The direct access file approach offers operational advantages over sequential file processing and permits limited data sharing.

The final example depicts a modern real-time sales order entry and cash receipts system that uses database technology. Modern systems design embraces **reengineering** to radically reshape business processes and workflow. The objective of reengineering is to reduce business-processing costs by identifying and eliminating non-value-added tasks. This process involves replacing traditional procedures with procedures that are innovative and sometimes very different from those that previously existed.

You should recognize that the space limitations prohibit a review of all possible configurations of processing technologies, techniques, and file structures. The objective, instead, is to present examples of fundamentally different approaches that are typically found in practice and examine their control and audit implications.

Batch Processing Using Sequential Files—Manual Procedures

Figure 9-1 illustrates an automated sales order system that uses batch processing and sequential files. In this basic system, order taking, credit checking, warehousing, and shipping are performed manually. Computer programs process the accounting records. The following discussion outlines the key features of the system.

Obtaining and Recording the Customers' Orders

The sales process begins in the sales department with the receipt of a **customer order** indicating the type and quantity of merchandise being requested. At this point, the customer order is not in a standard format and may not be a physical document. Orders may arrive by mail, by telephone, or from a field representative who visited the customer's place of business. When the customer is also a business entity, the order is usually a copy of the customer's purchase order.

The primary objective of this step is to ensure that relevant data about the transaction are transcribed into a standard format that can be processed by the selling entity's system. The document prepared in this procedure is the **sales order**, an example of which is presented in Figure 9-2.

The sales order captures such vital information as the name and address of the customer; the customer's account number; the name, number, and description of the items sold; the quantities and unit prices of each item sold; and other financial information such as taxes, discounts, and freight charges. In manual systems, multiple copies of sales orders are produced to serve different purposes. The number of copies created will vary from system to system, depending on the operations to be supported. The hypothetical system in Figure 9-2 uses sales order copies for credit authorizations,

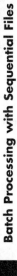

FIGURE 9-1 Batch Processing with Sequential Files

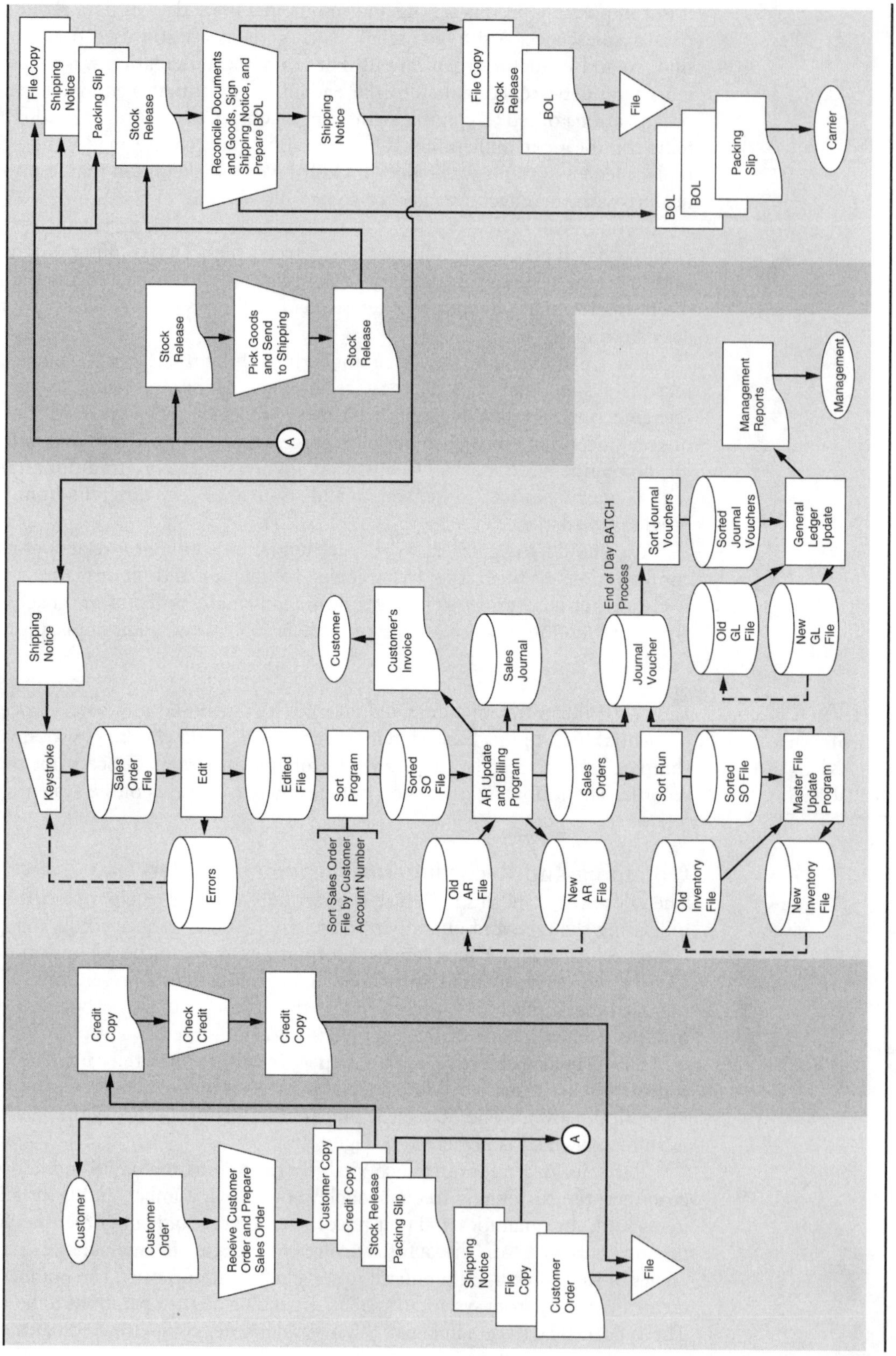

FIGURE 9-2

Sales Order

CHARGE SALE INVOICE

MONTEREY PENINSULA CO-OP
527 River Road
Chicago, IL 60612
(312) 555-0407

INVOICE NUMBER ________

SOLD TO
FIRM NAME ________
ATTENTION OF ________
ADDRESS ________
CITY ________
STATE ____ ZIP ________

INVOICE DATE ________
PREPARED BY ________
CREDIT TERMS ________

CUSTOMER PURCHASE ORDER
NUMBER ________
DATE ________
SIGNED BY ________

SHIPMENT DATE ________
SHIPPED VIA ________
BOL NO. ________

QUANTITY ORDERED	PRODUCT NUMBER	DESCRIPTION	QUANTITY SHIPPED	UNIT PRICE	TOTAL
			TOTAL SALE		
			CUSTOMER ACCT. NO.		
			VERIFICATION		

packing slips, stock release documents, and shipping notices. Customer invoicing and ledger posting are performed by the computer system. In an actual system, the various sales order copies would be numbered or color-coded to signify their purpose and distribution. Copies that are used for more than one purpose, and that go to several locations, sometimes have routing information printed on them.

After preparing the sales order, the sales clerk files one copy of it in the **customer open order file** for future reference. Filling the order and getting the product to the customer may take days or even weeks. Customers frequently contact their suppliers by telephone to check the status of their orders. To facilitate customer inquiries, the open order file is often organized alphabetically by customer name. Although customer name is not an efficient primary key for accessing data, it is often used as a secondary key to cross-reference orders because customers do not always know their account numbers and may not have copies of their invoices handy. In these situations, the customer file enables the clerk to find the sales order and respond to the customer's questions.

Approving Credit

The next step in the revenue cycle is transaction authorization, which involves verifying the customer's creditworthiness. The circumstances of the sale will determine the nature of the credit check. For example, a seller may perform a full financial investigation on new customers to establish a line of credit. However, once a credit limit is set, credit checking on subsequent sales may involve nothing more than ensuring that the current sale does not exceed the limit. In our hypothetical system, the **credit authorization** copy of the sales order is sent to the credit department for approval. The returned approval triggers the release of the other sales order copies simultaneously to various departments. The credit copy is filed in the customer open order file until the transaction is completed.

Processing Shipping Orders

The sales department sends the **stock release** (also called the *picking ticket*) copy of the sales order to the warehouse. This document identifies the items of inventory that must be located and picked from the warehouse shelves. It also provides formal authorization for the warehouse clerk to release custody of the specified assets. After picking the stock, the clerk initials the stock release copy to indicate that the order is complete and accurate. Any out-of-stock items are noted on the stock release copy. One copy of the stock release travels with the goods to the shipping department, and the other is filed in the warehouse to provide a record of the transaction.

The clerk then adjusts the stock records to reflect the reduction in inventory. The stock records are *not* the formal accounting records for these assets. Assigning the warehouse clerk asset custody and recordkeeping responsibility would violate internal control. Updating the inventory accounting records is an automated procedure that is described later.

Before the arrival of the goods and the stock release copy, the shipping department receives the **packing slip** and **shipping notice** copies from the sales department. The packing slip travels with the goods to the customer to describe the contents of the order. These are either placed inside the shipping container or attached to the outside in a special plastic pouch. The shipping notice informs the billing department that the customer's order has been filled and shipped. This document contains such pertinent facts as the date of shipment, items and quantities shipped, the carrier, and freight charges. In some systems, the shipping notice is a separate document prepared by the shipping clerk.

Upon receiving the goods from the warehouse, the shipping clerk reconciles the physical items with the stock release documents, the packing slip, and the shipping notice to verify the correctness of the order. This control is important because it is the last opportunity to detect errors before shipment. The shipping clerk packages the goods, attaches the packing slip to the container, completes the shipping notice, and prepares a **bill of lading**. The bill of lading is a formal contract between the seller and the shipping company (carrier) to transport the goods to the customer. This document establishes legal ownership and responsibility for assets in transit. Figure 9-3 shows a bill of lading.

The shipping clerk transfers custody of the goods, the packing slip, and two copies of the bill of lading to the carrier, then performs the following tasks:

1. Records the shipment in the shipping log.
2. Sends the stock release document and the shipping notice to the billing department as proof of shipment.
3. Files one copy each of the bill of lading and the shipping document.

Batch Processing Using Sequential Files—Automated Procedures

In the last section, we noted that order taking, credit checking, warehousing, and shipping are manual operations. These are illustrated in Figure 9-1. The figure also illustrates a fifth operation—data processing. This is an automated operation, and is discussed in this section in greater detail. The computer system described here is an example of a *legacy* system that employs the sequential file structure for its accounting records. Both tapes and disks can be used as the physical storage medium for such systems. However, the use of tapes has declined considerably in recent years. For day-to-day operations, tapes are inefficient because they must be physically mounted on a tape drive and then dismounted when the job ends. This approach is labor intensive and expensive. The constant decline in the cost of disk storage in recent years has eliminated the economic advantage once associated with tapes. Most organizations that still use sequential files store them on disks that are permanently connected (online) to the computer system and require no human intervention. The operational features of sequential files described earlier are the same for both tape and disk media. Today, tapes are used primarily as backup devices and for storing archive data. For these purposes, they provide an efficient and effective storage medium for a large system.

Keypunch/Data Entry

The process begins with the arrival of batches of shipping notices from the shipping department. These documents are copies of the sales orders that contain accurate information about the number of units shipped and information about the carrier. The data processing (DP) clerk converts the shipping notices to magnetic media to produce a transaction file of sales orders. Typically, this process is continual. Throughout the day, the DP clerks receive and convert batches of shipping notices to magnetic media. The resulting transaction file will thus contain many separate batches of sales orders. **Batch control totals** are calculated for each batch on the file.

Edit Run

Periodically, the batch sales order system is executed. Depending on the volume of transaction and computer resource constraints, the process make take place only once or several times each day. The edit program is the first run in the batch process. This program validates transactions by testing each record for the existence of clerical or logical errors. Typical tests include field checks, limit tests, range tests, and price times quantity extensions. Recall from Chapter 7 that detected errors are removed from the batch and copied to a separate error file. Later, these are corrected

FIGURE 9-3

Bill of Lading

UNIFORM STRAIGHT BILL OF LADING — Domestic

Monterey Peninsula Co-op
527 River Road
Chicago, IL 60612
(312) 555-0407

Document No.__________

Shipper No.__________

Carrier No.__________

Date__________

TO:

Consignee __________

Street __________

City/State Zip Code __________

____
(Name of Carrier)

Route: Vehicle

No. Shipping Units	Kind of packaging, description of articles, special marks and exceptions	Weight	Rate	Charges

TOTAL CHARGES $

The agreed or declared value of the property is hereby specifically stated by the shipper to be not exceeding:

$ _________ per__________

IF WITHOUT RECOURSE:
The carrier shall not make delivery of this shipment without payment of freight

____
(Signature of Consignor)

FREIGHT CHARGES
Check appropriate box:
[ ] Freight prepaid
[ ] Collect
[ ] Bill to shipper

Signature below signifies that the goods described above are in apparent good order, except as noted. Shipper hereby certifies that he is familiar with all the bill of lading terms and agrees with them.

SHIPPER Monterey Peninsula Co-op | CARRIER

PER | PER DATE

(This bill of lading is to be signed by the shipper and agent of the carrier issuing same.)
CONSIGNEE

by an authorized person and resubmitted for processing with the next day's business. The edit program recalculates the batch control totals to reflect changes due to the removal of error records. The "clean" transaction file is then passed to the next run in the process.

Sort Run

At this point, the sales order file is in no useful sequence. To process a sequential transaction file, it must be placed in the same sequence as the master file that it is updating. Since the first master file to be updated in the systems is accounts receivable, the sort run physically arranges the sales order transaction file sequentially by Account Number, which is one of its secondary keys.

AR Update and Billing Run

The AR update program posts to accounts receivable by sequentially matching the Account Number key in each sales order record with the corresponding record in the AR-SUB master file. This procedure creates a new AR-SUB master file that incorporates all the changes to the customer accounts that are affected by transaction records. The original AR-SUB master file remains complete and unchanged by the process. The creation of a new and separate master file is a characteristic of sequential file processing. A side benefit of this is the automatic creation of a backup version of the file being updated. Figure 9-4 illustrates this method with some sample records.

Each sales transaction record processed is added to the sales journal file. At the end of the run, these are summarized and an entry is made to the journal voucher file to reflect total sales and total increases to accounts receivable.

To spread the billing task evenly over the month, some firms employ **cycle billing** of their customers. The update program searches the billing date field in the AR-SUB master file for those customers to be billed on that day of the month and prepares statements for the selected accounts. The statements are then mailed to the customer.

Sort and Inventory Update Runs

The procedures for the second sort and inventory update runs are similar to those just described. The sort program sorts the sales order file on the other secondary key—Inventory Number. The inventory update program reduces the Quantity-on-Hand field in the affected inventory records by the Quantity Sold field in each sales order record. A new inventory master file is created in the process. Figure 9-5 illustrates the process.

In addition, the program compares values of the Quantity-on-Hand and the Reorder Point fields to identify inventory items that need to be replenished. This information is sent to the purchasing department. Finally, a journal voucher is prepared to reflect cost of goods sold and the reduction in inventory.

General Ledger Update Run

Under the sequential file approach, the general ledger master file is not updated after each batch of transactions. To do so would result in the recreation of the entire general ledger every time a batch of transactions (such as sales orders, cash receipts,

FIGURE 9-4 Update of Accounts Receivable from Sales Orders

Sales Order Transaction File

PK SK

Order #	Acct Num	Inven Num	Order Date	Ship Date	Carrier Code	Shipping Charges	Qnty Sold	Unit Price	Invoice Amount
3	1	17	12/22	12/24	011	10	25	10	250
1	4	14	12/22	12/24	011	5	10	2	20
2	7	16	12/22	12/24	011	20	100	5	500

Transaction file sorted by secondary key to primary key of master file

Original Account Receivable Master File

Update Fields

PK

ACCT NUM	Address	Current Balance	Credit Limit	Last Payment Date	Billing Date
1	123 Elm St., City	350	1000	12/8/04	1
2	35 Main S.	600	1500	12/12/04	1
3	510 Barclay Dr. Beth.	1000	1500	12/5/04	1
4	26 Taylo Rd. Alltn.	100	2000	12/16/04	8
5	4 High St., Naz.	800	1000	12/9/04	1
6	850 1st, Beth.	700	2000	12/7/04	8
7	78 Market Alltn.	150	2000	12/17/04	15

New Account Receivable Master File

ACCT NUM	Address	Current Balance	Credit Limit	Last Payment Date	Billing Date
1	123 Elm St., City	600	1000	12/8/04	1
2	35 Main S.	600	1500	12/12/04	1
3	510 Barclay Dr. Beth.	1000	1500	12/5/04	1
4	26 Taylo Rd. Alltn.	120	2000	12/16/04	8
5	4 High St., Naz.	800	1000	12/9/04	1
6	850 1st, Beth.	700	2000	12/7/04	8
7	78 Market Alltn.	650	2000	12/17/04	15

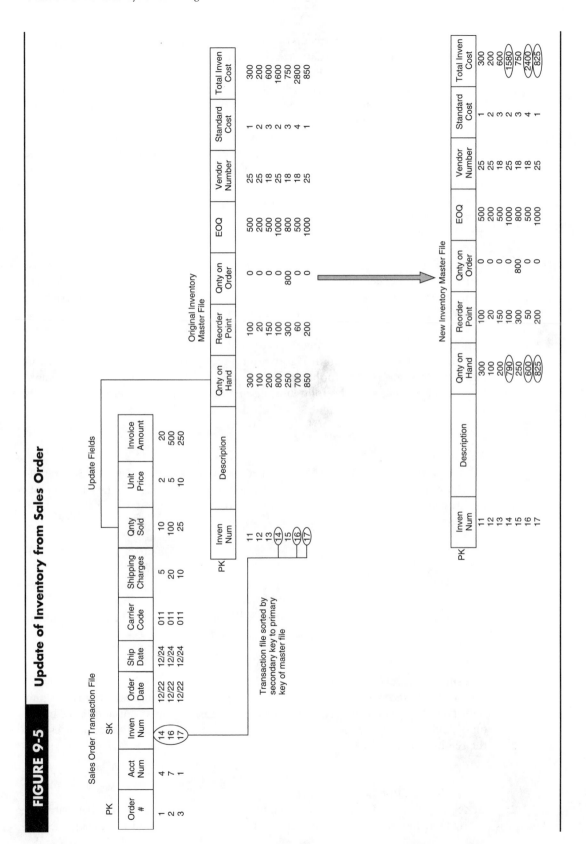

FIGURE 9-5 **Update of Inventory from Sales Order**

Sales Order Transaction File

PK: Order #; SK: Inven Num; Update Fields: Qnty Sold → Qnty on Hand

Order #	Acct Num	Inven Num	Order Date	Ship Date	Carrier Code	Shipping Charges	Qnty Sold	Unit Price	Invoice Amount
1	4	14	12/22	12/24	011	5	10	2	20
2	7	16	12/22	12/24	011	20	100	5	500
3	1	17	12/22	12/24	011	10	25	10	250

Transaction file sorted by secondary key to primary key of master file

Original Inventory Master File

PK: Inven Num

Inven Num	Description	Qnty on Hand	Reorder Point	Qnty on Order	EOQ	Vendor Number	Standard Cost	Total Inven Cost
11		300	100	0	500	25	1	300
12		100	20	0	200	25	2	200
13		200	150	0	500	18	3	600
14		800	100	0	1000	25	2	1600
15		250	300	800	800	18	3	750
16		700	60	0	500	18	4	2800
17		850	200	0	1000	25	1	850

New Inventory Master File

PK: Inven Num

Inven Num	Description	Qnty on Hand	Reorder Point	Qnty on Order	EOQ	Vendor Number	Standard Cost	Total Inven Cost
11		300	100	0	500	25	1	300
12		100	20	0	200	25	2	200
13		200	150	0	500	18	3	600
14		790	100	0	1000	25	2	1580
15		250	300	800	800	18	3	750
16		600	50	0	500	18	4	2400
17		825	200	0	1000	25	1	825

purchases, and cash disbursements) is processed. Firms using sequential files typically employ separate end-of-day procedures to update the general ledger accounts. This technique is depicted in Figure 9-1.

At the end of the day, the general ledger system accesses the journal voucher file. This file contains journal vouchers reflecting all of the day's transactions processed by the organization. The journal vouchers are sorted by general ledger account number and posted to general ledger in a single run, and a new general ledger is created.

The end-of-day procedures will also generate a number of management reports. These may include sales summaries, inventory status reports, transaction listings, journal voucher listings, and budget and performance reports. Quality management reports play a key role in helping management monitor operations to ensure that controls are in place and functioning properly.

Batch Cash Receipts System with Direct Access Files

Cash receipts procedures are natural batch systems. Unlike sales transactions, which tend to occur continuously throughout the day, cash receipts are discrete events. Checks and remittance advices arrive from the postal service in batches. Likewise, the deposit of cash receipts in the bank usually happens as a single event at the end of the business day. Because of these characteristics, many firms see no significant benefit from investing in costly real-time cash procedures.

The cash receipts system in Figure 9-6 on page 389 uses direct access files and batch processing. The technology employed in this example is used to automate traditional procedures. The following discussion outlines the main points of this system.

Mailroom

The mailroom separates the checks and remittance advices and prepares a remittance list. These checks and a copy of the remittance list are sent to the cash receipts department. The remittance advices and a copy of the remittance list go to the accounts receivable department.

Cash Receipts Department

The cash receipts clerk reconciles the checks and the remittance list and prepares the deposit slips. Via terminal, the clerk creates a journal voucher record of total cash received. The clerk files the remittance list and one copy of the deposit slip. At the end of the day, the clerk deposits the cash in the bank.

Accounts Receivable Department

The accounts receivable clerk receives and reconciles the remittance advices and remittance list. Via terminal, the clerk creates the cash receipts transaction file based on the individual remittance advices. The clerk then files the remittance advices and the remittance list.

Data Processing Department

At the end of the day, the batch program reconciles the journal voucher with the transaction file of cash receipts, and updates the AR-SUB and the general ledger

FIGURE 9-6 Computer-Based Cash Receipts System

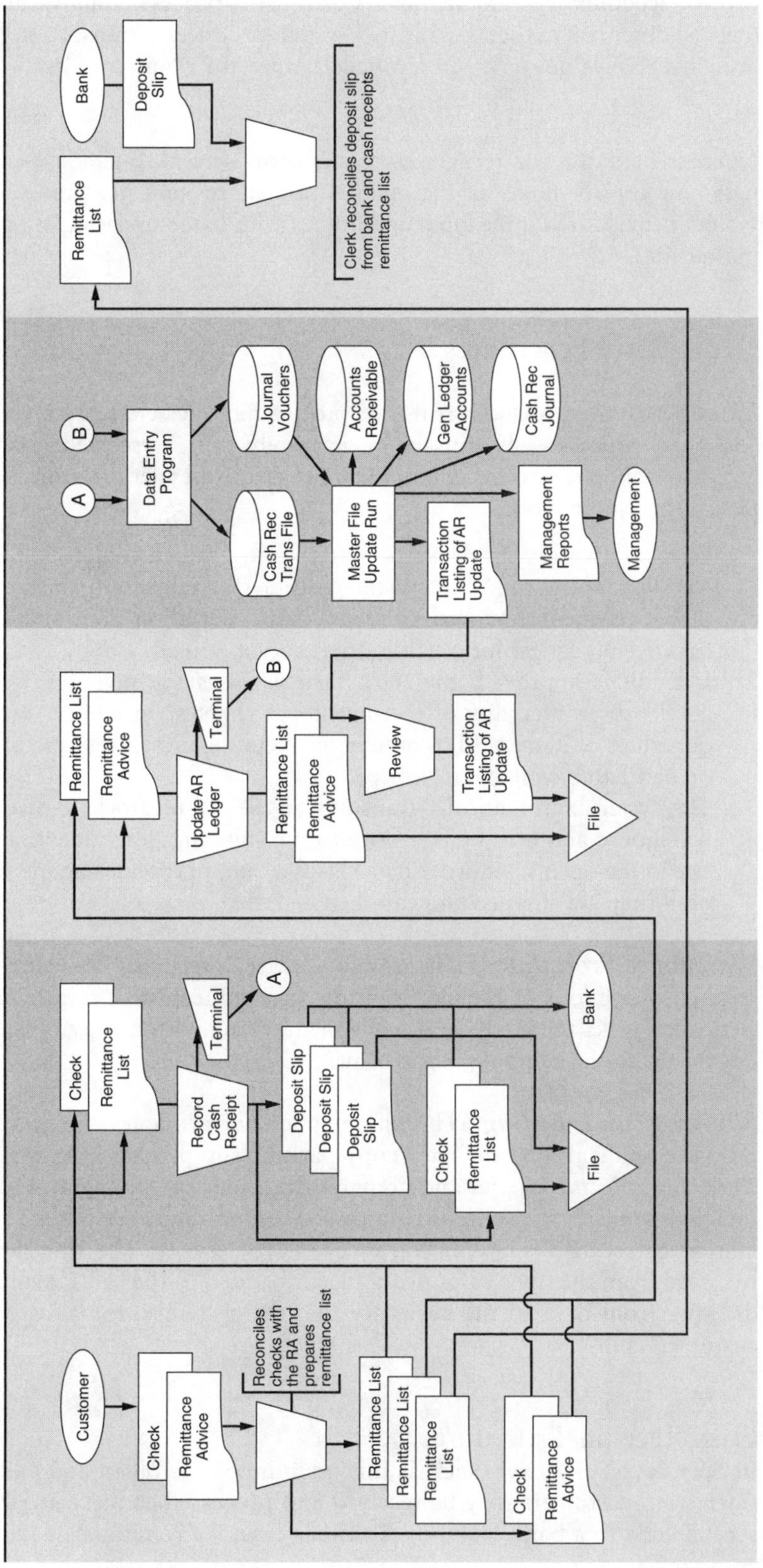

control accounts (AR-Control and Cash). This process employs the direct access method described earlier. Finally, the system produces a transaction listing that the accounts receivable clerk will reconcile against the remittance list.

Real-Time Sales Order Entry and Cash Receipts

Figure 9-7 illustrates a reengineered sales order system. Interactive computer terminals now replace many of the manual procedures and physical documents. This system provides real-time input and output with batch updating of only some of the master files.

Order Entry Procedures

Sales Procedures. Under real-time processing, sales clerks receiving orders from customers process each transaction separately as it is received. Using a computer terminal connected to an edit/inquiry program, the clerk performs the following tasks in real-time mode:

1. Perform a credit check online by accessing the customer credit file. This file contains information such as the customer's credit limit, current balance, date of last payment, and current credit status. Based on programmed criteria, the customer's request for credit is approved or denied.
2. If credit is approved, the clerk then accesses the inventory master file and checks the availability of the inventory. The system reduces inventory by the quantities of items sold to present an accurate and current picture of inventory on hand and available for sale.
3. The system automatically transmits an electronic stock release record to the warehouse and a shipping notice to the shipping department, and records the sale in the open sales order file. This is a temporary holding file for sales orders until they are shipped and can then be billed.

Warehouse Procedures. The warehouse clerk's terminal immediately produces a hard copy printout of the electronically transmitted stock release document. The clerk then picks the goods and sends them, along with a copy of the stock release document, to the shipping department.

Shipping and Billing. The shipping clerk reconciles the goods, the stock release document, and the hard copy packing slip produced on the terminal. The clerk then selects a carrier and prepares the goods for shipment. From a terminal, the clerk transmits a shipping notice containing invoice, date, and carrier information to create a shipping log record of the event. The transaction record is removed from the open sales order file and added to the sales invoice file. Finally, drawing from data in the customer file, the system automatically prepares the customer's bill.

Cash Receipts Procedures

In open invoice systems, such as this, each invoice is billed and paid individually. Cash from customers may be received and processed as just described or may be sent directly to a bank lock-box. In either case, the remittance advices (and credit

FIGURE 9-7 Real-Time Sales Order Entry and Cash Receipts

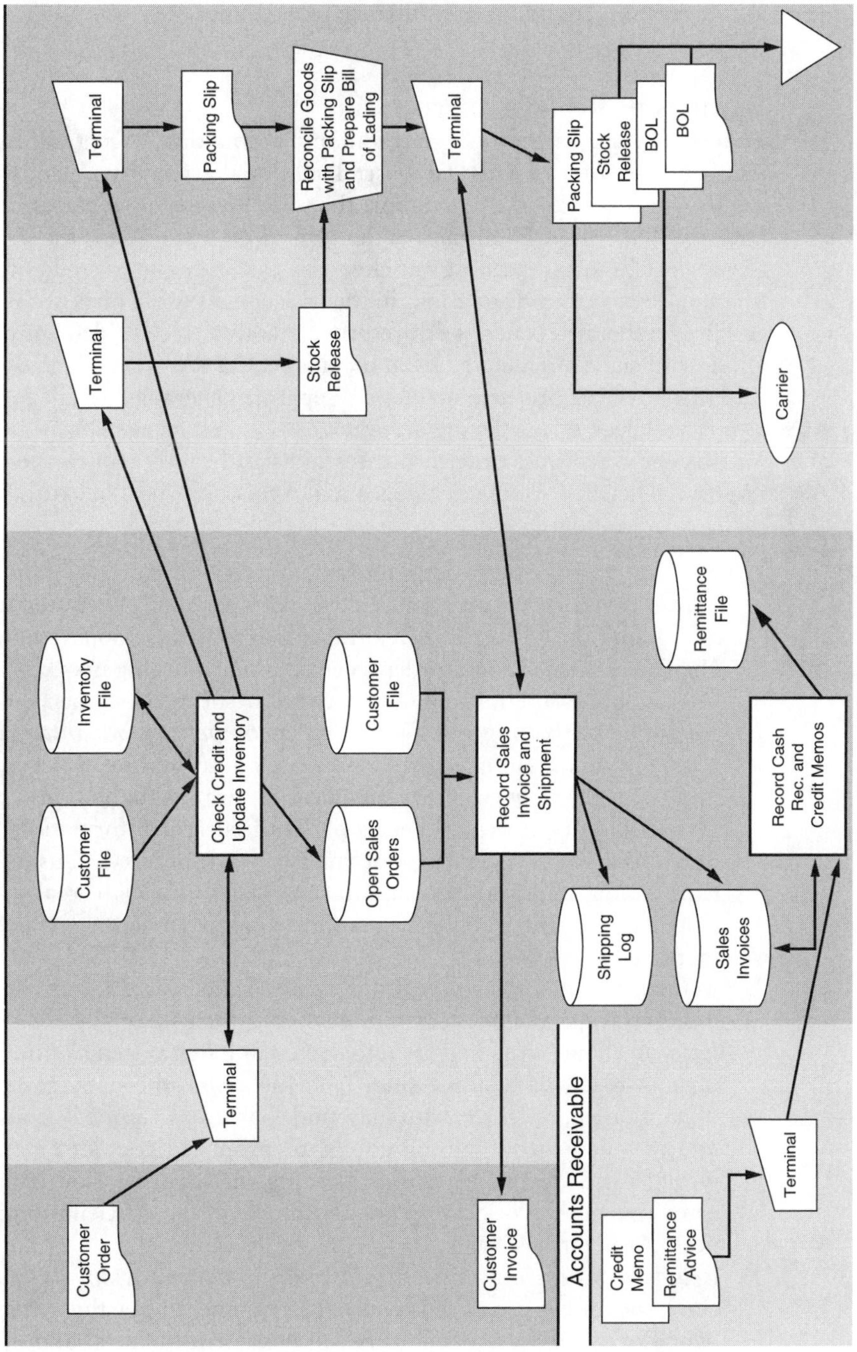

memos to reflect returns and allowances) are sent to the accounts receivable function, where the clerk enters them into the system via a terminal. Each remittance record is assigned a unique remittance number and is added to the remittance file. Placing the remittance number and the current date in the respective fields then closes the corresponding open invoice record.

Features of Real-Time Processing

This system is a departure from traditional accounting. A central feature of the system is the use of an **events database**. Traditional accounting records may not exist per se. For instance, in this example the sales invoice file replaces the sales journal and AR-SUB ledger. Total sales is the sum of *all* invoices for the period. Summing the *open* sales invoices (those not closed by cash receipts or credit memos) provides accounts receivable information. In theory, such a system does not even need a general ledger because sales, sales returns, accounts receivable-control, and cost of goods sold can all be derived from the invoices in the events database. Most organizations, however, prefer to maintain a separate general ledger file for efficiency and as a cross check of processing accuracy.

Reengineered sales order processes can significantly reduce operating costs and improve efficiency. Four advantages make this approach an attractive option for many organizations:

1. *Real-time processing greatly shortens the cash cycle of the firm.* Lags inherent in traditional systems can cause delays of several days between taking an order and billing the customer. A real-time system with remote terminals reduces or eliminates these lags. An order received in the morning may be shipped by early afternoon, thus permitting same-day billing of the customer.
2. *Real-time processing can give a firm a competitive advantage in the marketplace.* By maintaining current inventory information, sales staff can determine immediately whether inventories are available. In contrast, batch systems do not provide salespeople with current information. As a result, a portion of the order must sometimes be back-ordered, causing customer dissatisfaction. Current information provided through real-time processing enhances the firm's ability to maximize customer service, which translates to increased sales.
3. *Manual procedures tend to produce clerical errors, such as incorrect account numbers, invalid inventory numbers, and price–quantity extension miscalculations.* These errors may go undetected in batch systems until the source documents reach data processing, by which time the damage may already be done. For example, the firm may find that it has shipped goods to the wrong address, shipped the wrong goods, or promised goods to a customer at the wrong price. Real-time editing permits the identification of many kinds of errors when they occur and greatly improves the efficiency and the effectiveness of operations.
4. *Real-time processing reduces the amount of paper documents in a system.* Hard copy documents are expensive to produce and clutter the system. The permanent storage of these documents can become a financial and operational burden. Documents in electronic format are efficient, effective, and adequate for most audit trail purposes.

Revenue Cycle Audit Objectives, Controls, and Tests of Controls

Chapter 1 introduced the concept of audit objectives for transactions and account balances that are derived from management assertions about financial statement presentation. The assertions are existence or occurrence, completeness, accuracy, rights and obligations, valuation or allocation and presentation and disclosure. Table 9-1 shows how these translate to specific revenue cycle audit objectives.[1]

Achieving these audit objectives requires designing audit procedures to gather evidence that either corroborates or refutes the management assertions. Generally, this process involves a combination of tests of controls and substantive tests of details. The specific controls we address here are based on the more-extensive discussion of application controls issues contained in Chapter 7. The discussion in this section presumes that the reader is familiar with that material. Recall that computer

TABLE 9-1

Relationship between Management Assertions and Revenue Cycle Audit Objectives

Management Assertions	Revenue Cycle Audit Objectives
Existence or Occurrence	Verify that the accounts receivable balance represents amounts actually owed to the organization at the balance sheet date. Establish that revenue from sales transactions represent goods shipped and services rendered during the period covered by the financial statements.
Completeness	Determine that all amounts owed to the organization at the balance sheet date are reflected in accounts receivable. Verify that all sales for shipped goods, all services rendered, and all returns and allowances for the period are reflected in the financial statements.
Accuracy	Verify that revenue transactions are accurately computed and based on current prices and correct quantities. Ensure that the accounts receivable subsidiary ledger, the Sales Invoice file, and the Remittance file are mathematically correct and agree with general ledger accounts.
Rights and Obligations	Determine that the organization has a legal right to recorded accounts receivable. Customer accounts that have been sold or factored have been removed from the accounts receivable balance.
Valuation or Allocation	Determine that accounts receivable balance states its net realizable value. Establish that the allocation for uncollectible accounts is appropriate.
Presentation and Disclosure	Verify accounts receivable and revenues reported for the period are properly described and classified in the financial statements.

1 Adapted from Montgomery's Auditing, 12th ed. (New York: Cooper's & Lybrand, L.L.P., 1998), p. 18.

application controls fall into three broad categories: input controls, process controls, and output controls. Within this framework, we examine application controls, tests of controls, and the audit objectives to which they relate. Substantive tests and their relationship to audit objectives are considered later in the chapter.

Input Controls

Input controls are designed to ensure that transactions are valid, accurate, and complete. Control techniques vary considerably between batch and real-time systems. The following input controls relate to revenue cycle operations.

Credit Authorization Procedures

The purpose of the credit check is to establish the creditworthiness of the customer. Only customer transactions that meet the organization's credit standards are valid and should be processed further. In batch systems with manual credit authorization procedures, the credit department (or credit manager) is responsible for implementing the firm's credit policies. When credit checks are computerized, the organization's credit policy is implemented through decision rules that have been programmed into the system. For routine transactions, this typically involves determining if the current transaction plus the customer's current account receivable balance exceeds a pre-established credit limit. If the credit limit is exceeded by the transaction, it should be rejected by the program and passed to an exception file, where it can be reviewed by management. The credit manager will decide either to disapprove the sale or to extend the credit limit consistent with the manager's authority.

Testing Credit Procedures

Failure to apply credit policy correctly and consistently has implications for the adequacy of the organization's allowance for uncollectible accounts. The following tests provide evidence pertaining to the *valuation/allocation* audit objectives and, to a lesser extent, the *accuracy* objective.

The auditor needs, therefore, to determine that effective procedures exist to establish appropriate customer credit limits; communicate this information adequately to the credit policy decision makers; review credit policy periodically and revise it as necessary; and monitor adherence to current credit policy.

The auditor can verify the correctness of programmed decision rules by using either the *test data* or *integrated test facility (ITF)* approaches to directly test their functionality. This testing is easily accomplished by creating several dummy customer accounts with various lines of credit and then processing test transactions that will exceed some of the credit limits. The auditor can then analyze the rejected transactions to determine if the computer application correctly applied the credit policy.

The integrity of reference data is an important element in testing credit policy controls. A correctly functioning computer application cannot successfully apply credit policy if customer credit limits are excessively high or can be changed by unauthorized personnel. The auditor needs to verify that authority for making line-of-credit changes is limited to authorized credit department personnel. Performing substantive tests of detail to identify customers with excessive credit limits can do this. Substantive tests traditionally follow tests of controls because the results of tests of controls are used to determine the nature, timing, and extent of the substantive tests. In this case, however, substantive tests may be the most efficient way to verify if credit policy is being properly applied.

Data Validation Controls

Input validation controls are intended to detect transcription errors in transaction data before they are processed. Since errors detected early are less likely to infiltrate the accounting records, validation procedures are most effective when they are performed as close to the source of the transaction as possible. In the batch system depicted in Figure 9-1, data validation occurs only after the goods have been shipped. Extensive error logs, error correction, and transaction resubmission procedures characterize such systems. By contrast, validity tests performed in real time, as shown in Figure 9-7, can deal with most errors as they occur. This approach also minimizes human data entry and thus reduces the risk of data entry errors. For example, when the clerk enters the customer's account number, the system automatically retrieves his or her name and mailing address. When the clerk enters the product number and quantity sold, the data entry system automatically retrieves the product description and price, and then calculates the extended price plus tax and shipping charges.

Chapter 7 presented a number of general types of validation tests. Examples that are relevant to the revenue cycle include the following:

- *Missing data checks* are used to examine the contents of a field for the presence of blank spaces. Missing product numbers, missing customer account numbers, or incomplete mailing or billing addresses will cause the transaction to be rejected. When the validation program detects a blank where it expects to see a data value, this will be interpreted as an error.
- *Numeric-alphabetic data checks* determine whether the correct form of data is in a field. For example, an invoice total should not contain alphabetic data. As with blanks, alphabetic data in a numeric field may cause serious processing errors.
- *Limit checks* determine if the value in the field exceeds an authorized limit. For example, an organization may allow its sales personnel to negotiate prices with customers up to a maximum discount percentage. The order entry validation program can interrogate the discount field in the sales order records for values that exceed the threshold.
- *Range checks* assign upper and lower limits to acceptable data values. For example, the actual sales price charged for a product can be compared to a range of acceptable prices. The purpose of this control is to detect keystroke errors that shift the decimal point one or more places.
- *Validity checks* compare actual values in a field against known acceptable values. This control is used to verify such things as product codes, shipping company codes, and state abbreviations in customer addresses. If the value in the field does not match one of the acceptable values, the record is determined to be in error.
- *Check digit* controls identify keystroke errors in key fields by testing their internal validity. This check is often used to control data entry errors that would otherwise cause the wrong customer's account to be charged for a transaction.

Testing Validation Controls

Data entry errors that slip through edit programs undetected can cause recorded accounts receivable and revenue amounts to be materially misstated. The audit procedures described here provide evidence about the *accuracy* assertion.

The central audit issue is whether the validation programs in the data editing system are functioning correctly and have continued to function as intended throughout the period. Testing the logic of a validation program, however, represents a significant undertaking. The auditor may decide to rely on the quality of other controls to provide the assurance needed to reduce substantive testing. For example, after reviewing systems development and maintenance controls, the auditor may determine that controls over original program design and testing and subsequent changes to programs are effective. This evidence permits the auditor to assess the risk of material program errors at a low level and thus reduce the substantive tests related to the audit objective of accuracy.

If controls over systems development and maintenance are weak, however, the auditor may decide that testing the data editing controls would be more efficient than performing extensive substantive tests of details. In such a case, ITF or the test data approach would enable the auditor to perform explicit tests of the logic. This type of testing would require the auditor to gain a familiarity with all of the validation procedures in place. The auditor would need to create a comprehensive set of test transactions that include both valid and erroneous data values that fall within and outside of the test parameters. An analysis of the test results will show the auditor which types of errors, if any, can pass undetected by the validation program. This evidence will help the auditor determine the nature, timing, and extent of subsequent substantive tests.

In addition to direct testing of program logic, the auditor can achieve some degree of assurance by reviewing error listings and error logs. These documents provide evidence of the effectiveness of the data entry process, the types and volume of errors encountered, and the manner in which the errors are corrected and reentered into the system. Error listings and logs do not, however, provide evidence of undetected errors. An analysis of error conditions not present in the listing can be used to guide the auditor in designing substantive tests to perform. For example, assume that the error listing of the sales invoice file contains no price limit errors. On the one hand, this situation might simply mean that sales personnel strictly adhere to pricing guidelines. On the other hand, it may mean that the validation program does not test for this type of error. To determine whether material price discrepancies exist in the sales invoice file, the auditor can perform substantive tests that compare the actual price charged with the suggested retail price.

Batch Controls

Batch controls are used to manage high volumes of transaction data through a system. The objective of batch control is to reconcile output produced by the system with the input originally entered into the system. While initiated at the data input stage, batch control continues through all phases of data processing. For example, in the revenue cycle sales invoices are gathered together and enter the system at data entry. After each subsequent processing stage in the system, the batch is reviewed for completeness. An important element of batch control is the batch transmittal sheet, which captures relevant information about the batch, such as the following:

- A unique batch number
- A batch date
- A transaction code (indicating the type of transactions, such as a sales order or cash receipt)
- The number of records in the batch (record count)

- The total dollar value of a financial field (batch control total)
- The total of a unique nonfinancial field (hash total)

The information contained in the transmittal sheet is entered as a separate control record that the system uses to verify the integrity of the batch. The task of reconciling processing with the control record provides assurance that:

- All sales invoices and cash receipts records that were entered into the system were processed.
- No invoices or cash receipts were processed more than once.
- All invoices and cash receipts entered into the system are accounted for as either successfully processed or rejected because of errors.

Testing Batch Controls. The failure of batch controls to function properly can result in records being lost or processed multiple times. Tests of batch controls provide the auditor with evidence relating to the management assertions of *completeness* and *accuracy*.

Testing batch controls involves reviewing transmittal records of batches processed throughout the period and reconciling them to the batch control log. The auditor needs to investigate out-of-balance conditions to determine the cause. For example, assume that a batch's transmittal record shows 100 sales invoices with a total dollar value of $182,674.87 were entered into the system, but the completed batch log shows that only 96 records were processed with a batch total of $172,834.60. What caused this? Is the problem due to lost or changed invoices? Did the data entry clerk incorrectly calculate the batch control totals? Were error records rejected in processing and removed from the batch? Were rejected records corrected and resubmitted for processing?

The auditor should be able to obtain answers to these questions by reviewing and reconciling transaction listings, error logs, and logs of resubmitted records. Gathering such evidence, however, could involve scanning literally thousands of transactions. In modern systems, batch control logs are stored online in text files that can be read by word processing and spreadsheet programs. Modern audit software such as ACL is capable of searching log files for out-of-balance conditions.

Batch control totals, such as those on the batch transmittal sheet, are also a valuable tool in doing IT audits and fraud audits. For example, it is typical in IT audits to download a copy of the database or sets of data files from a real-time, online system to a microcomputer for analysis and audit procedures by the auditor. One technique for assuring that the data being downloaded are the same data as those being analyzed and tested is to perform batch controls on the live system, which will then be used as control totals for the data loaded on a separate system. Thus, throughout the audit processes, the auditor can be assured that the data are the same (i.e., they have integrity) by checking totals of the test data against the control totals obtained from the live system. This process is particularly helpful to auditors who use generalized audit software, such as ACL. Batch controls can serve as one means of obtaining "custody of evidence" in a fraud audit. Securing the data, obtaining batch controls, and then running tests that can be used as forensic evidence can be an effective process for fraud audits. Commands such as PROFILE, TOTAL, and COUNT will provide the kind of information necessary to adequately develop a set of batch controls. See Figure 9-8 for a screen shot of ACL using the AR table, and Figure 9-9 to see the results in the log file of running PROFILE, TOTAL, and COUNT on AR.

FIGURE 9-8

ACL View of an AR Table

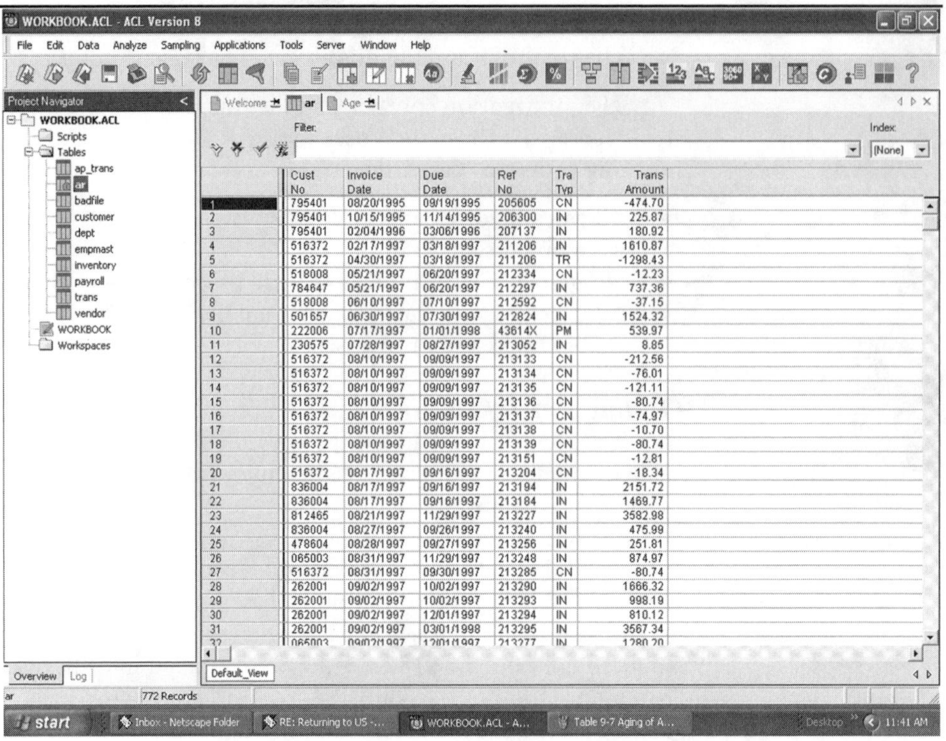

Process Controls

Process controls include computerized procedures for file updating and restricting access to data. Depending on the level of computer technology in place, process controls may also include physical manual tasks. We begin by examining three control techniques related to file updating. Access and physical controls are then examined.

File Update Controls

Run-to-run controls use batch control data discussed in the previous section to monitor the batch as it moves from one programmed procedure (run) to another.

FIGURE 9-9

ACL Screen of Command Log Results

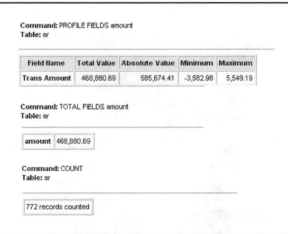

Command: PROFILE FIELDS amount
Table: ar

Field Name	Total Value	Absolute Value	Minimum	Maximum
Trans Amount	468,880.69	585,674.41	-3,582.98	5,549.19

Command: TOTAL FIELDS amount
Table: ar

amount	468,880.69

Command: COUNT
Table: ar

772 records counted

These controls ensure that each run in the system processes the batch correctly and completely. After each major operation in the process, key fields such as invoice amount and record counts are accumulated and compared to the corresponding values stored in the control record. A discrepancy may indicate that a record was lost in processing, a record in the batch went unprocessed, or a record was processed more than once.

Transaction Code Controls. Revenue cycle systems are often designed to process multiple record types. For example, the order entry application may process both sales orders and returns and allowances transactions. The actual tasks performed by the application are determined by a transaction code assigned to each record. Errors in transaction codes, or in the program logic that interprets them, can cause incorrect processing of transactions and may result in materially misstated sales and accounts receivable balances.

Sequence Check Control. In systems that use sequential master files, the order of the transaction records in the batch is critical to correct and complete processing. As the batch moves through the process, it must be re-sorted in the order of the master file used in each run. An out-of-sequence sales order record in a batch may prevent the remaining downstream records from being processed. A more serious problem can occur when the sequencing error is not detected and the downstream records are processed against the wrong customer accounts. A sequence check control should be in place to compare the sequence of each record in the batch with the previous record to ensure that proper sorting took place. Out-of-sequence records should be rejected and resubmitted for subsequent processing to allow the other records in the batch to be properly processed.

Testing File Update Controls. The failure of file update controls to function properly can result in records going unprocessed, being processed incorrectly (i.e., returns are treated as sales), or being posted to the wrong customer's account. Tests of file update controls provide the auditor with evidence relating to the assertions of *existence*, *completeness*, and *accuracy*.

We examined the audit procedures for reviewing batch controls previously as part of the discussion of input controls. Testing run-to-run controls is a logical extension of these procedures and needs no further explanation. Tests of transaction codes and sequence checks can be performed using ITF or the tests–data approach. The auditor should create test data that contain records with incorrect transaction codes and records that are out of sequence in the batch and verify that each was handled correctly. Implicit in this test is verifying the mathematical correctness of the computer operation. For example, consider a sales order for 5 units of product valued at $100. Assume that before the transaction is processed, the current value of the customer's account is $1,000 and the inventory in question shows 250 units on hand. After processing, this transaction should increase the customer balance to $1,100 and reduce the inventory to 245 units.

The efficient use of logic-testing CAATTs like ITF requires careful planning. By determining in advance the input and process controls to be tested, a single audit procedure can be devised that performs all tests in one operation. For example, a single test designed to examine credit authorization controls, transaction code controls, and the mathematical accuracy of the update program can provide evidence that supports multiple audit objectives.

Access Controls

Access controls prevent and detect unauthorized and illegal access to the firm's assets. Inventories and cash are the physical assets of the revenue cycle. Traditional techniques used to limit access to these assets include the following:

- Using warehouse security, such as fences, alarms, and guards
- Depositing cash daily in the bank
- Using a safe or night deposit box for cash
- Locking cash drawers and safes in the cash receipts department

Controlling access to accounting records is no less important. An individual with unrestricted access to data can manipulate the physical assets of the firm and cause financial statements to be materially misstated. Accounting files stored on magnetic media are particularly vulnerable to unauthorized access, whether its cause is accidental, an act of malice by a disgruntled employee, or an attempt at fraud. The following are examples of risks specific to the revenue cycle:

1. An individual with access to the AR subsidiary ledger could remove his or her account (or someone else's) from the books. With no record of the account, the firm would not send the customer monthly statements.
2. Access to blank sales orders may enable an unauthorized individual to trigger the shipment of a product.
3. An individual with access to both cash and accounting records could remove cash from the firm and cover the act by adjusting the cash account.
4. An individual with access to physical inventory and inventory records could steal products and adjust the records to cover the theft.

Testing Access Controls. Access control is at the heart of accounting information integrity. In the absence of controls, invoices can be deleted, added, or falsified. Individual account balances can be erased, or the entire accounts receivable file can be destroyed. Evidence gathered about the effectiveness of access controls tests the management assertions of *existence, completeness, accuracy, valuation and allocation, right and obligations*, and *presentation and disclosure*.

Computer access controls are both system-wide and application-specific. Access control over revenue cycle applications depends on effectively controlling access to the operating systems, the networks, and the databases with which they interact. The control techniques discussed in previous chapters—including passwords, data encryption, firewalls, and user views—apply also in preventing unauthorized access to revenue cycle processes. The auditors will typically test these controls as part of their review of general controls.

Physical Controls

Segregation of Duties. Proper segregation of duties ensures that no single individual or department processes a transaction in its entirety. The number of employees in the organization and the volume of transactions being processed will influence how tasks are divided. In general, the following three rules apply:

- **Rule 1.** Transaction authorization should be separate from transaction processing. For example, within the revenue cycle, the credit department is segregated from the rest of the process, so that the formal authorization of material transactions is an independent event. The importance of this separation is clear when one considers the potential conflict in objectives between the individual salesperson and the organization. Often, sales staff compensation is based on their sales levels. To achieve their personal objective of maximizing sales volume, sales personnel may not always consider the creditworthiness of the prospective customer. The credit department, acting as an independent authorization group, detects risky customers and discourages poor and irresponsible sales decisions.

- **Rule 2.** Asset custody should be separate from the recordkeeping task. In the sales-order processing system, the inventory warehouse clerk with custody of the physical assets should not also maintain the inventory records. Similarly, the cash receipts clerk (with custody of cash) should not record accounts receivable.
- **Rule 3.** The organization should be so structured that the perpetration of a fraud requires collusion between two or more individuals. The recordkeeping functions must be carefully divided. Specifically, the subsidiary ledgers (AR and inventory), the journals (sales and cash receipts), and the general ledger should be separately maintained. An individual with total recordkeeping responsibility, in collusion with someone with asset custody, is in a position to perpetrate fraud. By separating these tasks, collusion must involve more people, which increases the risk of detection and is, therefore, less likely to occur.

Supervision. Some firms have too few employees to achieve an adequate separation of functions and must rely on supervision as a compensating control. By closely supervising employees who perform potentially incompatible functions, a firm can compensate for the exposure inherent in a system.

Supervision can also provide control in systems that are properly segregated. For example, the mailroom is a point of exposure for any firm. The individual who opens the mail has access both to cash (the asset) and to the remittance advice (the record of the transaction). A dishonest employee may use this opportunity to steal the check, cash it, and destroy the remittance advice, thus leaving no evidence of the transaction. Ultimately, this sort of fraud will come to light when the customer receives another bill and, in response, produces the canceled check. However, by the time the firm gets to the bottom of this problem, the perpetrator may have committed the crime many times over and left the organization. Detecting crimes after the fact accomplishes little. Prevention is the best solution. The deterrent effect of supervision can provide an effective preventive control.

Independent Verification. The purpose of independent verification is to review the work performed by others at key junctures in the process to identify and correct errors. Following are two examples in the revenue cycle:

1. The shipping department verifies that the goods sent from the warehouse are correct in type and quantity. Before the goods are sent to the customer, the stock release document and the packing slip are reconciled to identify discrepancies.
2. The billing department reconciles the shipping notice with the sales invoice to ensure that customers are billed only for the items and quantities that were actually shipped.

Testing Physical Controls. Inadequate segregation of duties and the lack of effective supervision and independent verification can result in fraud and material errors. The exposure issues here are similar to the access control issues discussed earlier. Inappropriate access privileges are often associated with incompatible duties. Similarly, the purpose of collusion is to achieve unauthorized access to assets as well as the information needed to conceal the crime. In the absence of supervision and independent verification activities, errors and fraud may go undetected. Evidence gathered from reviewing job descriptions and organizational charts, and by observing physical processes, could be used to test *all* of the management assertions presented in Table 9-1.

The auditor's review of organizational structure should disclose the more egregious examples of incompatible tasks, such as one individual opening the mail, depositing the check, and recording receipts in the customer accounts. Covert relationships that lead to collusion may not be apparent from an organizational chart. For example, married employees (or those otherwise related) who work in incompatible areas go unnoticed. The auditor should verify that the organization has rules for appropriately dealing with nepotism issues.

Many tasks that are normally segregated in manual systems are consolidated in the data-processing function of computer-based systems. Computer programs in the revenue cycle perform inventory control, accounts receivable, billing, and general ledger tasks. In this situation, the auditor's concern should focus on the integrity of the computer programs that perform these tasks. The following questions need answers: Is the logic of the computer program correct? Has anyone tampered with the application since it was last tested? Have changes been made to the program that could have caused an undisclosed error?

Answers to these questions come from the auditor's review of systems development and maintenance controls and by reviewing organizational structure. Recall from earlier chapters that duties pertaining to the design, maintenance, and operation of computer programs need to be separated. Programmers who write the original computer programs should not be responsible for making program changes. Also, individuals who operate the computer system should not be involved in systems design, programming, or maintenance activities. Personal relationships (i.e., marriage) between individuals in these incompatible areas may require further investigation.

Output Controls

Output controls are designed to ensure that information is not lost, misdirected, or corrupted and that system processes function as intended. For example, managers receive daily summaries of sales orders placed by customers, goods shipped, and cash received, and use such data to monitor the status of their operations. Output control can be designed to identify potential problems. For example, an exception report derived from the customer open order file listing end-of-day open sales orders can identify orders placed but not shipped. Such a report can help management assess the operational performance of the shipping process.

Reconciling the general ledger is an output control that can detect certain types of transaction processing errors. For example, the total of all credit sales recorded by billing should equal the total increases posted to the accounts receivable subsidiary accounts. A sales transaction that is entered in the journal but not posted to the customer's account would be detected by an imbalance in the general ledger. The specific cause of an out-of-balance condition could not be determined at this point, but the error would be noted. Finding the error may require examining all the transactions processed during the period. This could be time consuming. For this reason, rather than summarizing an entire day's transactions in a single batch, entities often group transactions into small batches of 50 to 100 items. This facilitates reconciling balances by isolating a problem to a specific batch.

Another important element of output control is the maintenance of an **audit trail**. To resolve transaction processing errors, each detected error needs to be traced to its source. It is not sufficient to know that 100 transactions entered the system and only 99 came out. Details of transaction processing produced at intermediate points can provide an audit trail that reflects activity through every stage of operations. The following are examples of audit trail output controls.

Accounts Receivable Change Report

This is a summary report that shows the overall change to accounts receivable from sales orders and cash receipts. These numbers should reconcile with total sales, total cash receipts (on account), and the general ledger.

Transaction Logs

Every transaction successfully processed by the system should be recorded on a transaction log, which serves as a journal. A transaction log serves two purposes. First, the transaction log is a permanent record of valid transactions. The original transaction file produced at the data input phase is usually only a temporary file. Once processed, the records on this file are erased (scratched) to make room for the next batch of transactions. Second, not all of the records in the temporary transaction file will always be successfully processed. Some of these records may fail validity tests and will be rejected. A transaction log should contain only successful transactions. Rejected transactions should be placed in an error file. The transaction log and error files combined should account for all the transactions in the batch. The validated transaction file may then be scratched with no loss of data.

Transaction Listings

The system should produce a (hard copy) transaction listing of all successful transactions. These listings should go to the appropriate users to facilitate reconciliation with input. For example, a listing of cash receipts processed will go to the controller to be used for a bank reconciliation.

Log of Automatic Transactions

Some transactions are triggered internally by the system. For example, EDI sales orders are accepted and processed without human authorization. To maintain an audit trail of these activities, all internally generated transactions must be placed in a transaction log, and a listing of these transactions should be sent to the appropriate manager.

Unique Transaction Identifiers

Each transaction processed by the system must be uniquely identified with a transaction number. This control is the only practical means of tracing a particular transaction through a database of thousands or even millions of records. In systems that use physical source documents, the unique number printed on the document can be transcribed during data input and used for this purpose. In real-time systems, which do not use source documents, each transaction should be assigned a unique number by the system.

Error Listing

A listing of all error records should go to the appropriate user to support error correction and resubmission.

Testing Output Controls

The absence of adequate output controls has adverse implications for operational efficiency and financial reporting. Evidence gathered through tests of output controls relates to the *completeness* and *accuracy* assertions.

Testing output controls involves reviewing summary reports for accuracy, completeness, timeliness, and relevance to the decisions that they are intended to support. In addition, the auditor should trace sample transactions through audit trail reports, including transaction listings, error logs, and logs of resubmitted records. Gathering such evidence, however, may involve sorting through thousands of transactions.

In modern systems, audit trails are usually stored online in text files. Data extraction software such as ACL can be used to search log files for specific records to verify the completeness and accuracy of output reports. Alternatively, the auditor can test output controls directly using ITF. A well-designed ITF system will permit the auditor to produce a batch of sample transactions, including some error records, and trace them through all phases of processing, error detection, and output reporting.

Substantive Tests of Revenue Cycle Accounts

This section deals with the substantive tests that an auditor may perform to achieve audit objectives related to the revenue cycle. The strategy used in determining the nature, timing, and extent of substantive tests derives from the auditor's assessment of inherent risk, unmitigated control risk, materiality considerations, and the need to conduct the audit in an efficient manner.

Revenue Cycle Risks and Audit Concerns

In general, the auditor's concerns in the revenue cycle pertain to the potential for overstatement of revenues and accounts receivable rather than their understatement. Overstatement of accounts can result from material errors in the processing of normal transactions that occur throughout the year. In addition, the auditor should focus attention on large and unusual transactions at or near period-end. Examples of specific issues that give rise to these concerns include these following:

- Recognizing revenues from sales transactions that did not occur
- Recognizing sales revenues before they are realized (i.e., billing customers for items still being manufactured at period-end)
- Failing to recognize period-end cutoff points, thus allowing reported sales revenues for the current period to be inflated by post-period transactions

- Underestimating the allowance for doubtful accounts, thus overstating the realizable value of accounts receivable
- Shipping unsolicited products to customers in one period that are returned in a subsequent period
- Billing sales to the customer that are held by the seller (Special terms associated with such transactions may require no payment for a lengthy period of time.)

In resolving these concerns, the auditor will seek evidence by performing a combination of tests of internal controls and substantive tests. Tests of controls include testing both general controls (discussed in Chapters 2 through 7) and application controls specifically related to revenue cycle procedures. Various application control techniques were examined in Chapter 7. For example, the auditor may use an integrated test facility (ITF) to test the accuracy of sales transaction postings to the accounts receivable file. Although positive results from such a test may enable the auditor to reduce the degree of substantive testing needed to gain assurance about the mathematical accuracy of account processing, they offer no assurance about the collectibility of those accounts receivable. Similarly, ITF can be used to test the credit-limit logic of the edit program to provide assurance that the organization's credit policy is being properly implemented. This test, however, provides no evidence that proper cutoff procedures were followed in calculating the total value of accounts receivable.

From these examples, we see that in addition to tests of controls, the auditor must perform substantive tests to achieve audit objectives. The remainder of this chapter deals with audit objectives related to the revenue cycle and the substantive tests most commonly performed. Keep in mind that the quality of internal controls bears on the nature and extent of substantive tests determined by the auditor to be necessary. Normally, not all of the tests described will be performed.

Understanding Data

The following tests involve accessing and extracting data from accounting files for analysis. To do this, the auditor needs to understand the systems and controls that produced the data, as well as the physical characteristics of the files that contain them. Much of this chapter has been devoted to explaining alternative revenue cycle configurations and their control implications. The previous chapter described several common file structures and their audit implications. The discussion that follows presumes that the auditor is using ACL for performing the audit tests. Before we proceed, however, we need to review a few salient points regarding file preparation.

First, the auditor must verify that he or she is working with the correct version of the file to be analyzed. To do so the auditor must understand the file backup procedures and, whenever possible, work with the original files. Second, ACL can read most sequential files and relational database tables directly, but esoteric and/or complex file structures may require "flattening" before they can be analyzed. This process may involve additional procedures and special programs to produce a copy of the original file in a format that ACL can accept. If the client organization's systems personnel perform the flattening process, the auditor must verify that the correct version of the original file was used and that all relevant records from the original were transferred to the copy for analysis.

The discussion that follows presumes that any joining of tables or file copying necessary to produce test data was done so under adequate controls to preserve data integrity. These files may reside on either a mainframe or a PC. The audit tests described next are applicable to both environments. The focus is on explaining the logic underlying various substantive tests and on illustrating the functionality of ACL in achieving audit objectives. The audit procedures described are based on the file structure in Figure 9-10. These structures indicate the key data and logical linkages between files. A description of each file follows.

Customer File

The Customer master file contains address and credit information about customers. The Credit Limit value is used to validate sales transactions. If the sum of the customer's outstanding account balance and the amount of current sales transaction exceeds the pre-established credit limit, then the transaction is rejected.

Sales Invoice File

This file, along with the Line Item file, captures sales transaction data for the period. The **Sales Invoice file** contains summary data for each invoice. When an order is shipped to a customer, a record is added to the file. Summing Invoice Amount for all records in the file yields total sales (sale journal) for the period. When cash receipts are received, they are matched to the open invoice record, which is then closed by placing the current date in the Closed Date field. Also, the Remittance Number, which is the primary key of the cash receipt record, is added to the invoice record as a cross reference. The accounts receivable balance for a particular customer is calculated by summing the Invoice Amount fields for all of the customer's open invoices. Total accounts receivable for financial reporting purposes is the sum of all the open invoice records in the file.

Line Item File

The Line Item file contains a record of every product sold. Since a single transaction can involve one or more products, each record in the Sales Invoice file is associated with (linked to) one or more records in this file. Notice that the file contains two primary keys—Invoice Number and Item Number. Both keys are needed to uniquely define each record in the file. They also provide links to related records in the Sales Invoice and Inventory files. Although financial reporting of sales and accounts receivable information requires only the data contained in the Sales Invoice file, the Line Item file is needed for operational tasks such as billing, customer service, marketing, and auditing. For example, sales details in the file allow marketing to evaluate the demand for its products. These data also provide audit evidence needed to corroborate the accuracy of price times quantity calculations that are summarized in the **sales invoices**.

Inventory File

The Inventory file contains quantity, price, supplier, and warehouse location data for each item of inventory. When products are sold, the Quantity on Hand field in the associated records is reduced by the value of the Quantity field in the Line Item record. The Quantity on Hand field is increased by inventory receipts from suppliers. This activity is discussed in the next chapter.

FIGURE 9-10 File Structures for the Revenue Cycle

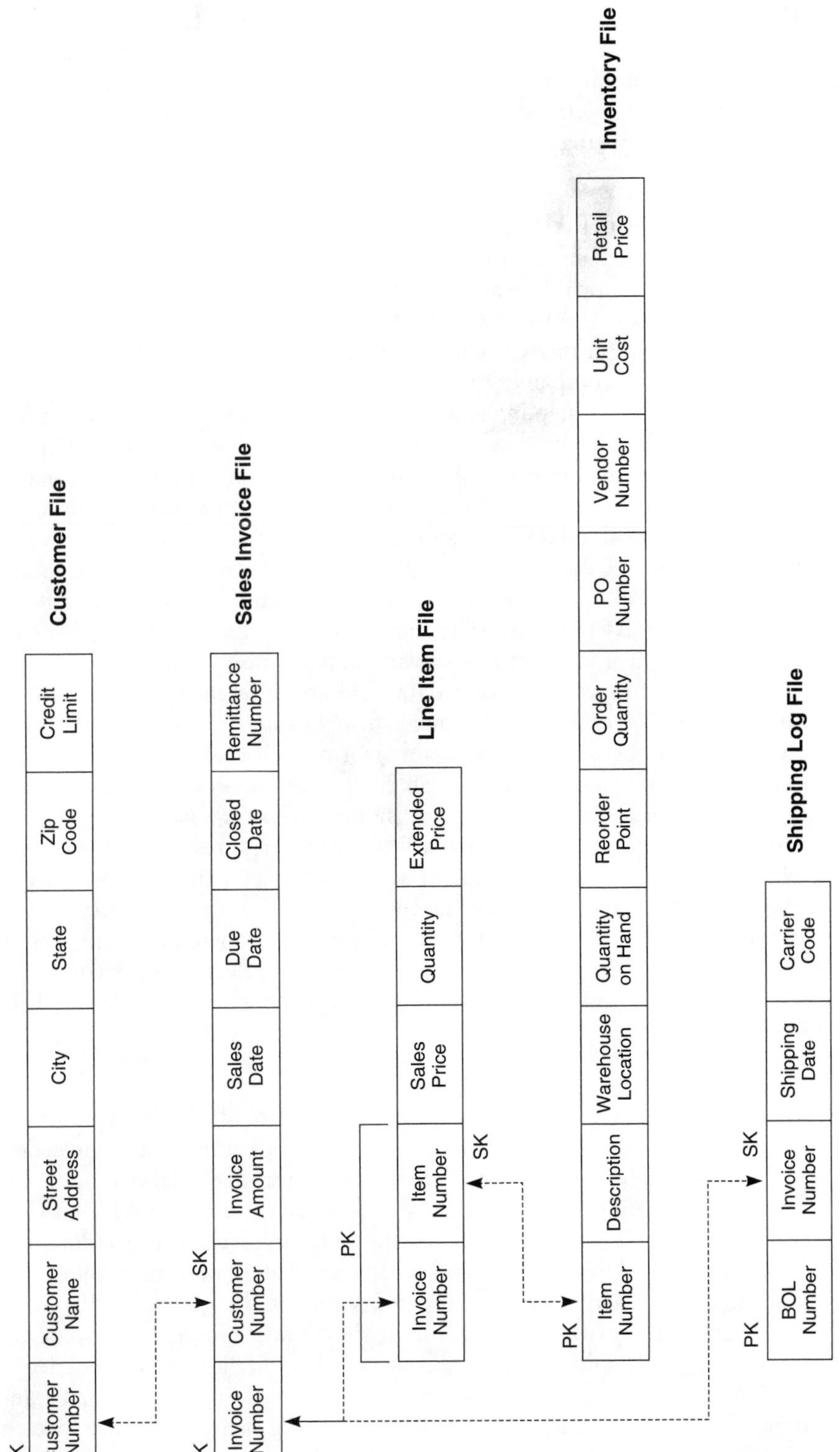

Shipping Log File

The shipping log is a record of all sales orders shipped to customers. The primary key of the file is the bill of lading (BOL) number. The data in this file are useful for verifying that all sales reflected in the Sales Invoice file were shipped in the period under review. As an efficiency tool, these data can also be used to determine if customer orders are being shipped in a timely manner.

File Preparation Procedures

The data contained in the files shown in Figure 9-10 provide evidence that may either corroborate or refute audit objectives. Most of the tests described in the following section involve using ACL to access and extract data from these files. For a detailed explanation of ACL commands, review the instruction manual contained on the CD that accompanies this text and consult ACL's online Help feature.

As a preliminary step in using ACL, each file needs to be defined in terms of its physical location and its structure. Through a series of easy-to-use pop-up menus, the auditor specifies the name of the file and where it resides on the mainframe or PC. ACL then prompts the auditor to define the file's structure in terms of the length of each field and the data type contained in each field (i.e., numeric, character, or date). When the file definition is completed, it is saved under a unique name assigned by the auditor. All future file access is accomplished by simply selecting the file definition from an ACL menu. ACL automatically locates the file and presents it on screen, where the auditor can review and manipulate its contents.

Sometimes the contents of a data field are different from what they are supposed to be. For example, a numeric field in one or more records may contain alphabetic data because of a program error or a clerical mistake. Also, a field may contain corrupted data because of an error in the file-flattening process. Whatever the cause, prior to performing any substantive tests on a new file, it is important to validate its contents. Invalid data will distort the test results and may cause a system failure. ACL's *Verify* command analyzes the data fields in the selected file to ensure that their contents are consistent with the field type in the file definition. Any validity errors detected by ACL need to be traced to their source and resolved. The auditor may also find batch control totals to be an effective means of verifying data integrity. For purposes of discussion, we will assume that the files used in all tests described hereafter have been properly defined and verified.

Testing the Accuracy and Completeness Assertions

The audit procedures described in this section provide evidence relating to management assertions of *accuracy* and *completeness*. Auditors often precede substantive tests of details with an **analytical review** of account balances. In the case of the revenue cycle, an analytical review will provide the auditor with an overall perspective for trends in sales, cash receipts, sales returns, and accounts receivable. Analytical procedures do not necessarily require computer technology. For example, the auditor may compare reported sales for the quarter with those for the same period in previous years. Ratio analysis may be used to compare total sales to cost of goods sold, sales to accounts receivable, and allowance for doubtful accounts to accounts receivable. Significant variations in account balances over time, or unusual ratios, may signify financial statement misrepresentations. However, analytical procedures can provide assurance that transactions and accounts are reasonably stated and complete and may thus permit the auditor to reduce substantive tests of details on these accounts.

A medium-to-large sized organization's sales and accounts receivable data may constitute thousands or perhaps millions of records. Substantive tests of details of such volumes of data cannot be effectively accomplished using manual techniques. The following examples of substantive tests that can be performed using ACL are based on the file structures depicted in Figure 9-10.

Review Sales Invoices for Unusual Trends and Exceptions

A useful audit procedure for identifying potential audit risks involves scanning data files for unusual transactions and account balances. For example, scanning accounts receivable for excessively large balances may indicate that the organization's credit policy is being improperly applied. Credit balances in accounts receivable may suggest unusual sales return activity or errors in the application of cash receipts to customer accounts. The auditor can use ACL's *Stratify* feature to identify such anomalies as shown in the table below. The stratify function groups data into predetermined intervals and counts the number of records that fall into each interval. Using data similar to the sample data illustrated in the table on the next page for the Sales Invoice file, the stratify function will produce the report presented in Figure 9-11.

Invoice Number	Customer Number	Invoice Sales Amount	Due Date	Closed Date	Remittance Date
214088	065003	13.08	12/04/03	12/14/03	12/11/03
611243					
214114	065003	9.76	12/04/03	12/14/03	
214129	065003	116.72	12/04/03	12/14/03	
214121	165006	29.40	12/04/03	12/14/03	12/12/03
613457					
214185	165009	9.17	12/04/03	12/14/03	12/23/03
614476					
213309	376005	–931.55	12/04/03	12/14/03	
213355	376005	–374.71	12/04/03	12/14/03	

The report groups the Invoice Amount field into ten intervals based upon the upper and lower limits of the data in the field. Analysis of the results allows the auditor to identify unusual trends and exceptions. For example:

- The minimum invoice amount was –$3,582.98 and the maximum was $5,549.19.
- Forty-nine items constitute $49,283 of negative sales.
- Fifty-three percent of the sales are between $310 and $1,620.
- Only two items were sales over $4,894.

The auditor can use other ACL features to seek answers to questions raised by the preceding analysis. For example, since this is a Sales Invoice file, it should normally contain only positive numbers. Negative numbers may have been inserted into the records in a number of ways. For example, they could be the result of a defective computer program, unintentional clerical errors, an effort to reverse the effects of erroneous sales transactions, or a fraudulent attempt to reduce a customer's accounts receivable balance. Although the auditor cannot specifically identify from the stratification which records are causing the anomalies, the potential problem has been flagged. The auditor will probably want to pursue this matter further, but to do so will require more detailed information.

ACL provides a *filter capability* that can be used to select or ignore specific records from an entire file. Using this feature, the auditor can select from the Sales Invoice file only those records with negative invoice amounts. The resulting view of the file is much smaller and provides the auditor with the details needed to investigate these anomalies. Sample records from the filtered file are listed below. With knowledge of specific customer account numbers, invoice numbers, and sales dates, the questionable items can be traced to their sources for resolution.

Invoice Number	Customer Number	Invoice Sales Amount	Due Date	Closed Date	Remittance Date
213309	376005	–931.55	12/04/03	12/14/03	
213355	376005	–374.71	12/04/03	12/14/03	
212297	784647	–537.36	12/04/03	12/14/03	
214389	262001	–300.39	12/10/03	12/20/03	
214390	641464	–46.77	12/10/03	12/20/03	
214391	222006	–62.15	12/10/03	12/20/03	
213699	878035	–378.45	12/07/03	12/20/03	
213700	878035	–742.75	12/07/03	12/20/03	

Review Sales Invoice and Shipping Log Files for Missing and Duplicate Items

Searching for missing and/or duplicate transactions is another important test that helps the auditor corroborate or refute the completeness and accuracy assertions. Duplicate and missing transactions in the revenue cycle may be evidence of over- or understated sales and accounts receivable. Duplicate sales invoice records may indicate a computer program error that materially overstates sales and accounts receivable. On one hand, a missing sales invoice may point to an unrecorded sale that was shipped but not billed, thus understating these accounts. On the other

FIGURE 9-11

Stratification of Sales Invoice File

As of: 06/10/2004 10:27:33

Command: STRATIFY ON amount MINIMUM -1000 MAXIMUM 5549.19 INTERVALS 10 TO SCREEN
Table: ar

Minimum encountered was -3,582.98
Maximum encountered was 5,549.19

Trans Amount	Count	Percent of Count	Percent of Field	Trans Amount
<-1,000.00	20	2.59%	-6.81%	-31,928.54
-1,000.00 - -345.09	29	3.76%	-3.7%	-17,355.17
-345.08 - 309.83	216	27.98%	0.48%	2,250.97
309.84 - 964.75	308	39.9%	40.23%	188,622.25
964.76 - 1,619.67	129	16.71%	33.99%	159,371.25
1,619.68 - 2,274.59	42	5.44%	16.81%	78,824.30
2,274.60 - 2,929.51	12	1.55%	6.58%	30,835.20
2,929.52 - 3,584.43	11	1.42%	7.64%	35,840.18
3,584.44 - 4,239.35	2	0.26%	1.6%	7,490.28
4,239.36 - 4,894.27	1	0.13%	0.94%	4,426.14
4,894.28 - 5,549.19	2	0.26%	2.24%	10,503.83
Totals	772	100%	100%	468,880.69

hand, it may indicate nothing more than an invoice that was issued and voided because of a clerical error.

ACL is capable of testing a designated field for out-of-sequence records, gaps in sequence numbers, and duplicates for the entire file. Using this feature, the auditor can scan the Invoice Number field of all records in the Sales Invoice file. The ACL system would return an on-screen report similar to Table 9-2.

The partial report below shows that 242 records in the Sales Invoice file are either duplicated or missing. In resolving this issue, the auditor will need to interview management and employees involved in the process and seek answers to the following types of questions:

- Are procedures in place to document and approve voided invoices?
- How are gaps in sales invoices communicated to management?
- What physical controls exist over access to sales invoice source documents?
- Are batch totals used to control total transactions during data processing?
- Are transaction listings reconciled and reviewed by management?

Tests for missing and duplicate documents can also be performed on the Shipping Log file. Consider the sample data in the table below, which is based on the file structure in Figure 9-10.

BOL Number	Invoice Number	Shipping Date	Carrier Code
50449	214088	11/29/03	538
50450	214090	11/29/03	530
50451	214089	11/30/03	531
50452	214087	11/30/03	532
50453	214092	12/14/03	533
50455	214093	12/10/03	523

TABLE 9-2

@ Gaps on Invoice Duplicates Error Limit 10 to Screen

As of: 06/10/2004 10:59:15

Command: GAPS ON ref DUPLICATES TO SCREEN PRESORT
Table: ar

0 sequence errors detected
243 gaps and/or duplicates detected

Duplicates:

Record Number	Ref No
5	13452X
10	211206
12	212297
13	212297
17	212824
31	213227
34	213248
48	213309
55	213328
61	213355
73	213392
75	213398
81	213418
85	213423

Gaps Found Between:

Ref No
10,000 - 12,284
12,284 - 13,065
13,065 - 13,452
13,452 - 205,805
205,805 - 206,300
206,300 - 207,137
207,137 - 211,206
211,206 - 212,297
212,297 - 212,334
212,334 - 212,592
212,592 - 212,824
212,824 - 213,052

In this example, the auditor would test the Invoice Number field for gaps and duplicate records. A duplicate record may indicate that the same product was shipped to the customer twice. If we presume that the customer was billed only once, then the organization has forfeited the revenue from the second shipment. Missing invoices may denote that some customer orders are not shipped at all. Depending on the circumstances, sales and accounts receivable may be overstated.

Here is an example of how a single test procedure can support more than one audit objective. Invoices missing from the shipping log provide evidence that tests the *valuation/allocation* assertion. The auditor seeks assurance that sales revenue is recognized only when appropriate criteria are met. In most organizations, this means that sales are recognized only when the products are shipped. The auditor should review the shipping log for the following period to determine if the missing invoice numbers are recorded there. If so, this would indicate that the merchandise was shipped after the cut-off period. It may be necessary to adjust the sales and accounts receivable balances accordingly.

Review Line Item and Inventory Files for Sales Price Accuracy

Evidence from testing the product prices charged to customers supports the audit objective of *accuracy*. Sometimes sales personnel are given limited authority to negotiate prices with customers. Significant discrepancies between the suggested retail price and the price actually charged, however, may indicate incompetence, clerical errors, or sales personnel exceeding their authority. A retail outlet such as a department store will usually establish a nonnegotiable pricing policy. Sales prices are calculated automatically by the point-of-sale system to eliminate salesperson intervention and clerical errors. Pricing inconsistency in such a setting may indicate a computer program error or the use of obsolete pricing data.

Traditionally, auditors would verify pricing accuracy by comparing sales prices on the invoices with the published price list. But because of the physical effort involved with this approach, it could be done only on a sample basis. Therefore, out of thousands of sales records, perhaps only one or two hundred would be tested. ACL allows the auditor to compare the prices charged on every invoice in the file for the period under review. Based on the file structures for the Line Item and Inventory files presented in Figure 9-10, we can illustrate this procedure using the sample data on the next page.

This procedure involves a few simple steps. First, notice that the actual sales price charged is stored in the Sales Price field in the Line Item file. The suggested retail price for each product is the Retail Price field in the Inventory file. In addition, the two files have Item Number as a common field. This field is the key field on which the two files are related. Using this common field, the objective of the test is to match each record in the Line Item file with the corresponding record in the Inventory file. We can compare the Sales Price and Retail Price fields for constancy. Significant discrepancies can then be identified and investigated. The actual steps in this test are described next.

First, both files need to be ordered according to their common key. Item number is the primary key of the inventory master file, and we will assume that this file is already in the proper sequence. Since the Line Item file contains the details of the Invoice file, it is probably organized by Invoice Number at this time. It is therefore necessary to sort this file on the Item Number field to place it in the same order as the Inventory file. This process involves simply opening the file and invoking ACL's *Sort* feature.

LINE ITEM FILE

Invoice Number	Item Number	Sales Price	Quantity	Extended Price
214297	030303413	4.69	20	93.88
214297	030303403	5.29	10	52.90
214297	030303343	12.98	2	25.96
214298	130305603	16.00	5	80.00
214298	030302303	44.95	12	539.40

INVENTORY FILE

Item Number	Description	Warehouse Location	Quantity on Hand	Reorder Point	Order Quantity	PO Number	Unit Cost	Retail Price	Vendor Number
030303413	8 oz. Ball-Peen Hammer	03	1,248	510	1,500		3.90	4.69	10879
030303403	12 oz. Ball-Peen hammer	03	536	550	1,200	111104	4.12	5.29	12248
030303343	Straight Claw Hammer	03	735	550	1,600		8.83	12.98	10951
130305603	#4 Smooth Plane	03	804	800	2,000	107427	14.12	22.98	10879
030309373	Heavy Duty Brace	03	842	900	1,200	108123	10.12	16.98	10951
030302903	4 pc. Chisel Set	03	795	620	1,200		10.12	16.98	13411
030302303	Mitre Box 21″	03	600	650	1,200	129124	41.23	54.95	11182

The next step is to combine the two files to create a third. ACL accomplishes this with its *Join* feature. The auditor has several options when joining files. The one most relevant to this test is to create a third file that consists only of matched records. In other words, the new file will contain only the Line Item and Inventory records whose value for the Item Number field match. Any Inventory records that are not matched with a Line Item record will not be part of the new file.

ACL's Join feature permits the auditor to specify the fields from the two input files that are to be passed to the new output file. Usually, it is neither necessary nor desirable to include all fields from both of the original files. In this example, the fields needed from the Line Item file to verify pricing accuracy are Invoice Number, Item Number, and Sales Price; from the Inventory file, the fields are Description and Retail Price. The file structure of the new file and some sample records are presented in the table below.

Invoice Number	Item Number	Description	Sales Price	Retail Price
214297	030303413	8 OZ. BALL PEEN HAMMER	4.69	4.69
214297	030303403	12 OZ. BALL PEEN HAMMER	5.29	5.29
214297	030303343	STRAIGHT CLAW HAMMER	12.98	12.98
214298	130305603	#4 SMOOTH PLANE	16.00	22.98
214298	030302303	MITRE BOX 21″	44.95	54.95

At this point, the resulting file may still be very large. Scanning the file visually for price differences could be time-consuming and ineffective. Here again is an application for a *filter*. Through a series of pop-up menus, the auditor can easily create a filter that will ignore all records in which Sales Price and Retail Price are equal. The resulting file will thus contain only price discrepancies. Using other ACL features, the auditor can calculate the total price variance and make a determination as to its materiality. If material, this issue would need to be pursued with management.

Testing for Unmatched Records

A variation on the preceding test can be used to address some related issues. By selecting a different join option, the auditor can produce a new file of only unmatched records. There are two possible causes for unmatched records. The first is because the value of the Item Number field in the Line Item record is incorrect and does not match an Inventory record. Since the operational assumption is that the inventory master file is correct, then any Line Item records in the unmatched file are errors. The presence (or absence) of such errors is evidence that refutes or corroborates the accuracy assertion.

The second source of unmatched records is the Inventory file. The presence of Inventory records in the unmatched file means that there were no corresponding records in the Line Item file. This result is not an error; it means that these products did not sell during the period. After adjusting for any seasonal influences on sales, such evidence may refute the valuation assertion. The auditor may require that the inventory be written down to reflect its market value.

Testing the Existence Assertion

One of the most widely performed tests of existence is the **confirmation of accounts receivable**. This test involves direct written contact between the auditors and the client's customers to confirm account balances and transactions. *Statement on Auditing Standards No. 67* (SAS67), *The Confirmation Process*, states that auditors should request confirmations of accounts receivable except in the following three situations: (1) accounts receivable are immaterial; (2) based on a review of internal controls, the auditor has assessed control risk to be low; or (3) the confirmation process will be ineffective.

This last point is worthy of further explanation. Because of the way some organizations account for their liabilities, they may be unable to respond to requests for confirmation. For example, government agencies and large industrial organizations often use an **open-invoice system** for liabilities. Under this approach, invoices are recorded individually rather than being summarized or grouped by creditor. In this environment, no accounts payable subsidiary ledger exists. Each invoice is paid (closed) as it comes due. For financial reporting purposes, total accounts payable is calculated simply by summing the open (unpaid) invoices. Determining the liability due to a particular creditor, which may consist of multiple open invoices, is not such a simple task. The auditor should not assume that an organization using this approach would invest the time needed to respond to the confirmation request. Under such circumstances, the confirmation process would be ineffective.

In the discussion that follows, we assume that accounts receivable are material and that the auditor has decided to request confirmations from the client's customers. The confirmation process involves three stages: selecting the accounts to confirm, preparing confirmation requests, and evaluating the responses.

Selecting Accounts to Confirm

Given the file structures used in our example, selecting accounts receivable for confirmation involves processing data that are contained in both the Customer and the Sales Invoice files. Each customer record is associated with one or more sales invoice records. Recall from a previous discussion that the accounts receivable balance for a particular customer is calculated by summing the open sales invoices (those with no values in the Closed Date and Remittance Number fields) for the customer. Once cash is received in payment of an invoice, it is closed by placing the payment date and the cash receipt number in the respective fields. Thus, the Sales Invoice file provides the financial information needed for the confirmation requests, and the customer mailing information is contained in the Customer file. Obtaining a set of accounts for confirmation requires three steps: consolidate the invoices by customer, join the data from the two files, and select a sample of accounts from the joined file.

Consolidate Invoices. The first step in the process is to consolidate all the open invoices for each customer. Using the sample data presented in Table 9-3, ACL's *Classify* command allows the auditor to set a filter to select only the open sales invoices (those with blanks in the Remittance Number field) and to summarize the Invoice Amount field for each record based on the Customer Number. The summarized records are then passed to a new file called Classified Invoices, presented in Table 9-4.

TABLE 9-3 Sales Invoice File

Invoice Number	Customer Number	Invoice Amount	Sales Date	Due Due	Closed Date	Remittance Number
212209	376005	931.55	12/04/03	12/14/03		
212255	376005	377.71	12/04/03	12/14/03		
212297	784647	537.36	12/04/03	12/14/03		
214088	065003	13.08	12/04/03	12/14/03	12/11/01	611243
214389	262001	300.39	12/10/03	12/20/03		
214100	641464	46.77	12/10/03	12/20/03		
214114	065003	9.76	12/04/03	12/14/03		
214129	262001	116.72	12/04/03	12/14/03		
214121	165006	29.40	12/04/03	12/14/03	12/12/01	613457
214185	165009	9.17	12/04/03	12/14/03	12/23/01	614476

TABLE 9-4 Classified Invoices File

Customer Number	Invoice Amount
376005	1,279.26
784647	537.36
262001	417.11
641464	46.77
065003	9.76

Join the Files. The next step in the confirmation process is to join the Classified Invoices file and the Customer file (illustrated in Table 9-5 with sample data) to produce another new file called Accounts Receivable, which is presented in Table 9-6. Recall that when using ACL's Join feature both files must be ordered on the same key. This requires first sorting the Classified Invoices file by Customer Number to place it in the same sequence as the Customer master file. As noted previously, the join feature allows the auditor to select only relevant fields from each of the input files when creating the new file. In this example, Credit Limit, which is not needed for preparing the confirmations, has been dropped from the new Accounts Receivable file structure.

Select a Sample of Accounts. In a moderate-to-large-sized organization, the Accounts Receivable file may contain thousands of records. Rather than confirming all of these accounts, the auditor will probably choose to select a sample of records. To assist the auditor in this task, ACL's Sample feature offers two basic sampling methods: *random (record) sampling* and *monetary unit sampling (MUS)*. The choice of methods will depend on the auditor's strategy and the composition of the Accounts Receivable file. If the account balances are fairly evenly distributed, the auditor may want an unbiased sample and will thus choose the random sample approach. Under this method, each record, regardless of the size of the accounts receivable balance, has an equal chance of being included in the sample. If, on the other hand, the file is heavily skewed with large customer account balances, the auditor may select MUS, which will produce a sample biased toward the larger dollar amounts.

ACL's *Size* command helps the auditor calculate sample size and sampling intervals based on the auditor's desired confidence level, the size of the population being sampled, and the assessed materiality threshold. These parameters are entered into

TABLE 9-5 Customer File Structure with Sample Data

Customer Number	Customer Name	Street Address	City	State	Zip Code	Credit Limit
065003	Accel Enterprises	1000 Strayer Rd.	Brookline	MA	02167	72,000
262001	Connecticut Corp.	600 Paragon Dr.	Brooklyn	NY	11201	80,000
376005	Bully Industries	8 West Street	Las Vegas	NV	89109	53,000
641464	First Healthcare	88 State St.	Austin	TX	78752	28,000
784647	Salt Bank of Amer.	401 N. Broadway	Bentonville	AR	72712	27,000

TABLE 9-6 Accounts Receivable File Structure

Customer Number	Customer Name	Street Address	City	State	Zip Code	Invoice Amount
065003	Accel Enterprises	1000 Strayer Rd.	Brookline	MA	02167	9.76
262001	Connecticut Corp.	600 Paragon Dr.	Brooklyn	NY	11201	417.11
376005	Bully Industries	8 West Street	Las Vegas	NV	89109	1,279.26
641464	First Healthcare	88 State St.	Austin	TX	78752	46.77
784647	Salt Bank of Amer.	401 N. Broadway	Bentonville	AR	72712	537.36

ACL to draw a physical sample from the Accounts Receivable file that is sent to a new output file called AR-Sample. The structure of this file is the same as the Accounts Receivable file, but it contains far fewer records. For example, from the several thousand records in the accounts receivable population, perhaps only 150 records are selected for the sample.

Preparing Confirmation Requests

The next stage in the confirmation process involves preparing confirmation requests that contain the information captured in the AR-Sample file. The requests, which usually take the form of letters, are drafted and administered by the auditor, but are written in the client entity's name. A sample confirmation letter is presented in Figure 9-12.

The letter shown in Figure 9-12 is an example of a **positive confirmation**. Recipients are asked to respond whether their records agree or disagree with the amount stated. Positive confirmations are particularly useful when the auditor suspects that a large number of accounts may be in dispute. They are also used when confirming unusual or large balances or when a large proportion of total accounts receivable arises from a small number of significant customers.

A problem with positive confirmations is poor response rate. Customers that do not dispute the amount shown in the confirmation letter may not respond. The auditor cannot assume, however, that lack of response means agreement. To obtain the highest response rate possible, second and even third requests may need to be sent to nonrespondents.

Negative confirmations request the recipients to respond only if they disagree with the amount shown in the letter. This technique is used primarily when accounts receivable consist of a large number of low-value balances and the control risk of misstatement is considered to be low. The sample size for this type of test is typically large and may include the entire population. Evidence from nonreturned negative confirmations selected from a large population provides indirect evidence to support the auditor's expectation that accounts receivable are not materially misstated.

FIGURE 9-12

Confirmation Letter

CLIENT LETTERHEAD
(CLIENT NAME AND ADDRESS)

(Name and Address of Client's Customer)

To whom it may concern:

In accordance with the request from our external auditors, we ask that you confirm your outstanding account balance with our organization. Our records indicate that your account balances as of **(end-of-period date)** amounted to **($ amount)**.

If your records agree with this balance, please indicate by signing in the space provided below and return this letter directly to our auditors using the enclosed envelope. Your prompt compliance with this request is greatly appreciated.

If the amount indicated is not in agreement with your records, inform the auditors directly using the enclosed envelope. In your response, please show the amount owed according to your records and include full details of the discrepancy.

Sincerely,
(Name of Entity)

The amount stated above is correct: **(Customer Name)**

Responses to negative confirmations, particularly if they are widespread in a large population, may indicate a potential problem. Since the negative confirmations approach does not prove that the intended recipients actually received and reviewed the confirmation letters, evidence of individual misstatements provided by returned responses cannot be projected to the entire population. In other words, responses to negative confirmations cannot be used as a basis for determining the total dollar amount of the misstatement in the account. Such evidence can be used, however, to reinforce the auditor's prior expectation that the account balance may be materially misstated and that additional testing of details is needed to determine the nature and amount of the misstatement.

Once the auditor decides upon the nature and the wording of the confirmation letter, he or she can create it using a word processor. ACL's *Export* feature can greatly facilitate the physical task of inserting the relevant financial data for each customer into the individual letters. Using this option, the auditor can produce a text version of the AR-Sample file that can be integrated with the confirmation letter text using the mail/merge feature of a word processing package such as Microsoft Word or WordPerfect. This facility greatly reduces the clerical effort traditionally associated with confirmation activities.

Evaluating and Controlling Responses

Maintaining control over the confirmation process is critical to its integrity. Evidence provided through confirmations is less reliable when contact between the auditor and the debtor is disrupted by client intervention. The auditor should take all reasonable steps to ensure the following procedures are observed:

- The auditor should retain custody of the confirmation letters until they are mailed.
- The confirmation letters, together with self-addressed stamped envelopes, should be addressed to the auditor, rather than the client organization.
- The confirmation request should be mailed by the auditor. If client mailroom personnel participate in the process, they should be adequately supervised.

When responses are returned to the auditor, discrepancies in the amount owed should be investigated. The auditor should evaluate exceptions to determine if they represent isolated instances or signify a larger potential problem. For example, frequent complaints by debtors that the client is slow to record cash payments may indicate misappropriations of cash and the lapping of accounts receivable. Lapping is discussed in Chapter 12.

Nonresponses to positive confirmations also need to be investigated. SAS 67 requires auditors to use alternative procedures to resolve this issue. A commonly used procedure is to review the following period's closed invoices to determine if the accounts were actually paid. Since it is unlikely that a customer will pay an account that is not owed, subsequent cash payments provide good evidence of the *existence*, *accuracy*, and *valuation* objectives.

Testing the Valuation/Allocation Assertion

The auditor's objective regarding proper valuation and allocation is to corroborate or refute that accounts receivable are stated at net realizable value. This objective rests on the reasonableness of the allowance for doubtful accounts, which is derived from aged accounts receivable balances. To achieve this objective, the auditor needs to review the accounts receivable aging process to determine that the allowance for doubtful accounts is adequate.

Aging Accounts Receivable

As accounts age, the probability that they will ultimately be collected is decreased. Hence, as a general rule, the larger the number of older accounts that are included in an organization's accounts receivable file, the larger the allowance for doubtful accounts needs to be to reflect the risk. Historical trends in collection success also play an important part in estimating the bad debt losses for the period. A key issue for auditors to resolve, therefore, is whether the allowance calculated by the client is consistent with the composition of their organization's accounts receivable portfolio and with prior years. In addition, the auditor needs to determine that the allowance is consistent with current economic conditions. For example, an organization entering into a period of economic decline may experience an increased percentage of bad debts relative to prior, more prosperous, years. Under such circumstances, a larger portion of past-due accounts may need to be included in the allowance calculation than had previously been the case. As a starting point in an attempt to gain assurance on these issues, the auditor may decide to recalculate the aging schedule.

The following describes ACL's Accounts Receivable Aging feature using the Sales Invoice file presented in Table 9-3. The key data fields used in calculation are Invoice Amount and Due Date. The system compares the Due Date in the record with a specified cutoff date to produce aged summaries of the Invoice Amount data. The default intervals used are 30, 60, 90, and 120 days past due. These, however, can be changed to any values that better suit the auditor's needs.

Keep in mind that the Sales Invoice file contains all sales invoices for the period. Only the open sales invoices (those with blanks in the Remittance Number field) as of the cutoff date should be considered in the calculation. By filtering on the Remittance Number field, ACL will ignore all closed invoices. Upon executing the Age command, a report similar to Table 9-7 will be produced.

The aging report provides a clear picture of the accounts receivable composition. The total balance of accounts receivable outstanding at the end of the audit period is $468,880.69. As of the cutoff date, $217,113.27 of the outstanding balance is not past due. However, 17 invoices are between 90 and 120 days past due, and 13 invoices are over 120 days past due. The auditor should review past-due balances with the credit manager to obtain information for basing an opinion on

TABLE 9-7

Aging of Accounts Receivable Produced with ACL

As of: 06/10/2004 11:28:00

Command: AGE ON due CUTOFF 20031231 INTERVAL 0,30,60,90,120,10000 TO SCREEN
Table: ar

Minimum encountered was -124
Maximum encountered was 834

Days	Count	Percent of Count	Percent of Field	Trans Amount
<0	255	33.03%	46.3%	217,113.27
0 - 29	259	33.55%	38.66%	181,252.50
30 - 59	170	22.02%	11.66%	54,676.94
60 - 89	58	7.51%	1.81%	8,496.10
90 - 119	17	2.2%	1.52%	7,137.88
120 - 10,000	13	1.68%	0.04%	204.00
Totals	772	100%	100%	468,880.69

their collectibility. The auditor's objective is not to assess the collectibility of each account, but to determine that the methods used by the credit manager to estimate the allowance for doubtful accounts is adequate and that the overall allowance is reasonable.

SUMMARY

This chapter examined audit procedures associated with the revenue cycle. The chapter began with a review of alternative technologies used in both legacy and modern systems. The emphasis was on key operational tasks under alternative technologies. The second main section of the chapter presented revenue cycle audit objectives and controls. In this section, we examined the tests of controls that an auditor may perform. Evidence gathered from tests of controls contributes to audit objectives and may permit the auditor to limit the scope, timing, and extent of substantive tests. The last section described the use of ACL in performing the more common substantive tests. The tests were presented in relation to the management assertions that they were designed to corroborate or refute.

KEY TERMS

analytical review
audit trail
batch control totals
bill of lading
confirmation of accounts receivable
credit authorization
customer open order file
customer order
cycle billing
events database
negative confirmation
open-invoice system
packing slip
positive confirmation
reengineering
sales invoice
Sales Invoice file
sales order
shipping notice
stock release (picking ticket)

REVIEW QUESTIONS

1. What document initiates the sales process?
2. Distinguish among a packing slip, a shipping notice, and a bill of lading.
3. What are three input controls?
4. What are the three rules that ensure that no single employee or department processes a transaction in its entirety?
5. What is automation, and why is it used?
6. What is the objective of reengineering?
7. Distinguish among an edit run, sort run, and update run.
8. How is the record's primary key critical in preserving the audit trail?
9. What are the advantages of real-time processing?
10. Why does billing receive a copy of the sales order when the order is approved but does not bill until the goods are shipped?
11. How do tests of controls relate to substantive tests?
12. List the audit objectives (derived from management assertions) that pertain to the revenue cycle.

Discussion Questions

1. Distinguish among the sales, billing, and accounts receivable departments. Why can't the sales or accounts receivable departments prepare the bills?
2. Explain the risks associated with mailroom procedures.
3. How could an employee embezzle funds by issuing an unauthorized sales credit memo if the appropriate segregation of duties and authorization controls were not in place?
4. What task can the accounts receivable department engage in to verify that all checks sent by the customers have been appropriately deposited and recorded?
5. Why is access control over revenue cycle documents just as important as the physical control devices over cash and inventory?
6. For a batch processing system using sequential files, describe the intermediate and permanent files that are created after the edit run has successfully been completed when processing the sales order file and updating the accounts receivable and inventory master files.
7. Why has the use of magnetic tapes as a storage medium declined in recent years? What are their primary uses currently?
8. Discuss both the tangible and intangible benefits of real-time processing.
9. Distinguish between positive and negative confirmations.
10. What is the purpose of analytical reviews in the audit of revenue cycle accounts?
11. Explain the open-invoice system. What effect might it have on confirmation responses?

Multiple-Choice Questions

1. Which document is *not* prepared by the sales department?
   a. packing slip
   b. shipping notice
   c. bill of lading
   d. stock release
2. Which document triggers the update of the inventory subsidiary ledger?
   a. bill of lading
   b. stock release
   c. sales order
   d. shipping notice
3. Which function should *not* be performed by the billing department?
   a. Recording the sales in the sales journal
   b. Sending the ledger copy of the sales order to accounts receivable
   c. Sending the stock release document and the shipping notice to the billing department as proof of shipment
   d. Sending the stock release document to inventory control
4. When will a credit check approval most likely require specific authorization by the credit department?
   a. When verifying that the current transaction does not exceed the customer's credit limit
   b. When verifying that the current transaction is with a valid customer
   c. When a valid customer places a materially large order
   d. When a valid customer returns goods
5. Which type of control is considered to be a compensating control?
   a. segregation of duties
   b. access control
   c. supervision
   d. accounting records
6. Which of the following is *not* an output control?
   a. The shipping department verifies that the goods sent from the warehouse are correct in type and quantity.
   b. General ledger clerks reconcile journal vouchers that were independently prepared in various departments.
   c. The use of pre-numbered sales orders
   d. The billing department reconciles the shipping notice with the sales invoice to ensure that customers are billed only for the quantities shipped.

7. CMA Adapted 684 3-29
Which one of the following poses the biggest threat with respect to potential losses?
   a. The petty cash custodian has the opportunity to steal petty cash. Documentation for all disbursements from the fund must be submitted with the request for replenishment of the fund.
   b. An inventory control clerk at a manufacturing plant has the ability to steal one completed television set from inventory a year. The theft probably will never be detected.
   c. An accounts receivable clerk, who approves sales returns and allowances, receives customer remittances and deposits them in the bank. Limited supervision is maintained over the employee.
   d. A clerk in the invoice processing department fails to match a vendor's invoice with its related receiving report. Checks are not signed unless all appropriate documents are attached to a voucher.
   e. An accounting clerk has the ability to record unauthorized journal entries. All journal entries are reviewed by an accounting department supervisor each month.
8. CMA 1288 3-26
In a well-designed internal control structure in which the cashier receives remittances from the mailroom, the cashier should not
   a. endorse the checks.
   b. prepare the bank deposit slip.
   c. deposit remittances daily at a local bank.
   d. prepare a list of mail receipts.
   e. post the receipts to the accounts receivable subsidiary ledger cards.
9. CMA 689 3-15
Which one of the following situations represents an internal control weakness in accounts receivable?
   a. Internal auditors confirm customer accounts periodically.
   b. Only the sales manager reviews delinquent accounts.
   c. The cashier is denied access to customers' records and monthly statements.
   d. Customers' statements are mailed monthly by the accounts receivable department.
   e. Customers' subsidiary records are maintained by someone who has no access to cash.

PROBLEMS

1. Describe the procedures, documents, and departments involved when insufficient inventory is available to fill a customer's approved order.

2. Refer to Figure 9-1 and explain where the batch totals come from and which accounts in the general ledger are affected by the end-of-day batch process.

3. Document Flowchart Analysis
CMA Adapted 1287 5-7 through 5-12
Use the Problem 3 flowchart to answer the following questions:
   a. The customer checks accompanied by the control tape (refer to Symbol A) would be forwarded to whom?
   b. What appropriate description should be placed in Symbol B?
   c. What is the next action to take with the customer remittance advices (refer to Symbol C)?
   d. The appropriate description that should be placed in Symbol D would be what?
   e. What appropriate description should be placed in Symbol E?
   f. The flowchart can be best described as representing what type of processing system?

4. Document Authorization and Transfer
CMA Adapted 690 5-1 through 5-5
Marport Company is a manufacturing company that uses forms and documents in its accounting information systems for recordkeeping and internal control. The departments in Marport's organizational structure and their primary responsibilities are shown in the Problem 4 table on the following page. Using this information, answer the following questions:

Problem 3: Document Flowchart Analysis

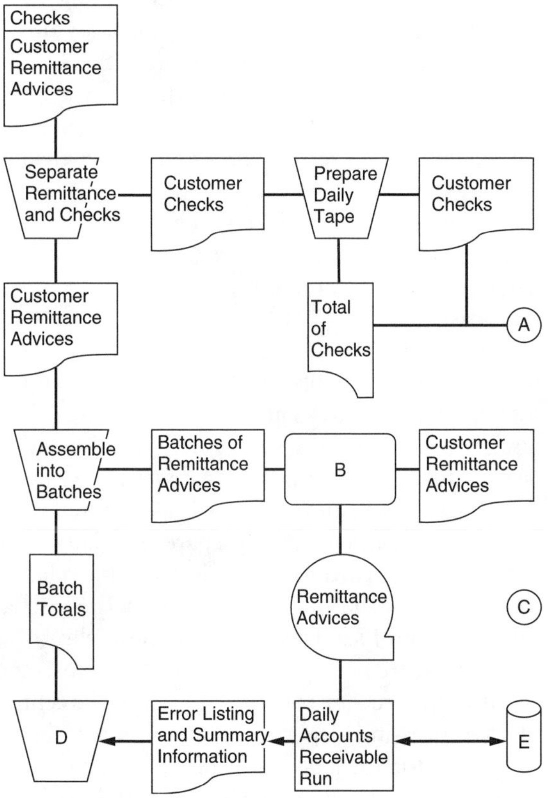

a. The initiation of the purchase of materials and supplies would be the responsibility of what department?
b. The document generated by the department identified in (a) above to initiate the purchasing process would be what?
c. Multiple copies of the purchase order are prepared for recordkeeping and distribution with one copy sent to the vendor and one retained by the purchasing department. In addition, for proper information flow and internal control purposes, a version of the purchase order would be distributed to what other departments?
d. What documents must the accounts payable department review before it can properly authorize payment for the purchase of materials and supplies?
e. Which document is used to transfer responsibility for goods between the seller of goods and a common carrier?

Problem 4: Document Authorization and Transfer

Accounts payable—authorize payments and prepare vouchers	Payroll—compute and prepare the company payroll
Accounts receivable—maintain customer accounts	Personnel—hire employees, as well as maintain records on job positions and employees
Billing—prepare invoices to customers for goods sold	Purchasing—place orders for materials and supplies
Cashier—maintain a record of cash receipts and disbursements	Production—manufacture finished goods
Credit department—verify the credit rating of customers	Production planning—decide the types and quantities of products to be produced
Cost accounting—accumulate manufacturing costs for all goods produced	Receiving—receive all materials and supplies
Finished goods storeroom—maintain the physical inventory and related stock records of finished goods	Sales—accept orders from customers
General accounting—maintain all records for the company's general ledger	Shipping—ship goods to customers
Internal audit—appraise and monitor internal controls, as well as conduct operational and management audits	Stores control—safeguard all materials and supplies until needed for production
Inventory control—maintain perpetual inventory records for all manufacturing	Timekeeping—prepare and control time worked by hourly employees
Mailroom—process incoming, outgoing, and interdepartmental mail	

5. **Segregation of Functions**
CMA Adapted
Refer to the Marport Company in Question 4 and determine whether the following situations represent a proper segregation of functions in the processing of orders from customers.
   a. Invoice preparation by the billing department and posting to the customers' accounts by the accounts receivable department
   b. Approval of a sales credit memo because of a product return by the sales department with subsequent posting to the customer's account by the accounts receivable department
   c. Shipping of goods by the shipping department that have been retrieved from stock by the finished goods storeroom department
   d. Posting to the appropriate general ledger accounts by general accounting on the basis of batch totals prepared and verified by the billing department

6. **Internal Controls**
CMA 688 5-2
Jem Clothes, Inc., is a 25-store chain, concentrated in the Northeast, that sells ready-to-wear clothes for young men and women. Each store has a full-time manager and an assistant manager, both of whom are paid a salary. The cashiers and sales personnel are typically young people working part-time who are paid an hourly wage plus a commission based on sales volume. The Problem 6 flowchart on the next page depicts the flow of a sales transaction through the organization of a typical store. The company uses unsophisticated cash registers with four-part sales invoices to record each transaction. These sales invoices are used regardless of the payment type (cash, check, or bank card).

On the sales floor, the salesperson manually records his or her employee number and the transaction (clothes, class, description, quantity, and unit price), totals the sales invoice, calculates the discount when appropriate, calculates the sales tax, and prepares the grand total. The salesperson then gives the sales invoice to the cashier, retaining one copy in the sales book.

The cashier reviews the invoice and inputs the sale. The cash register mechanically validates the invoice by automatically assigning a consecutive number to the transaction. The cashier is also responsible for getting credit approval on charge sales and approving sales paid by check. The cashier gives one copy of the invoice to the customer and retains the second copy as a store copy and the third for a bank card, if a deposit is needed. Returns are handled in exactly the reverse manner, with the cashier issuing a return slip.

At the end of each day, the cashier sequentially orders the sales invoices and takes cash register totals for cash, bank card, and check sales, and cash and bank card returns. These totals are reconciled by the assistant manager to the cash register tapes, the total of the consecutively numbered sales invoices, and the return slips. The assistant manager prepares a daily reconciliation report for the store manager's review.

Cash, check, and bank card sales are reviewed by the manager, who then prepares the daily bank deposit (bank card sales invoices are included in the deposit). The manager makes the deposit at the bank and files the validated deposit slip.

The cash register tapes, sales invoices, and return slips are then forwarded daily to the central data processing department at corporate headquarters for processing. The data processing department returns a weekly sales and commission activity report to the manager for review.

Required:
   a. Identify six strengths in the Jem Clothes system for controlling sales transactions.
   b. For each strength identified, explain what problem(s) Jem Clothes has avoided by incorporating the strength in the system for controlling sales transactions.

Use the following format in preparing your answer.

1. *Strength* 2. *Problem(s) Avoided*

7. **Stewardship**
Identify which department has stewardship over the following journals, ledgers, and files:
   a. Customer open order file
   b. Sales journal
   c. Journal voucher file
   d. Cash receipts journal
   e. Inventory subsidiary ledger
   f. Accounts receivable subsidiary ledger
   g. Sales history file
   h. Shipping report file

Problem 6: Internal Controls

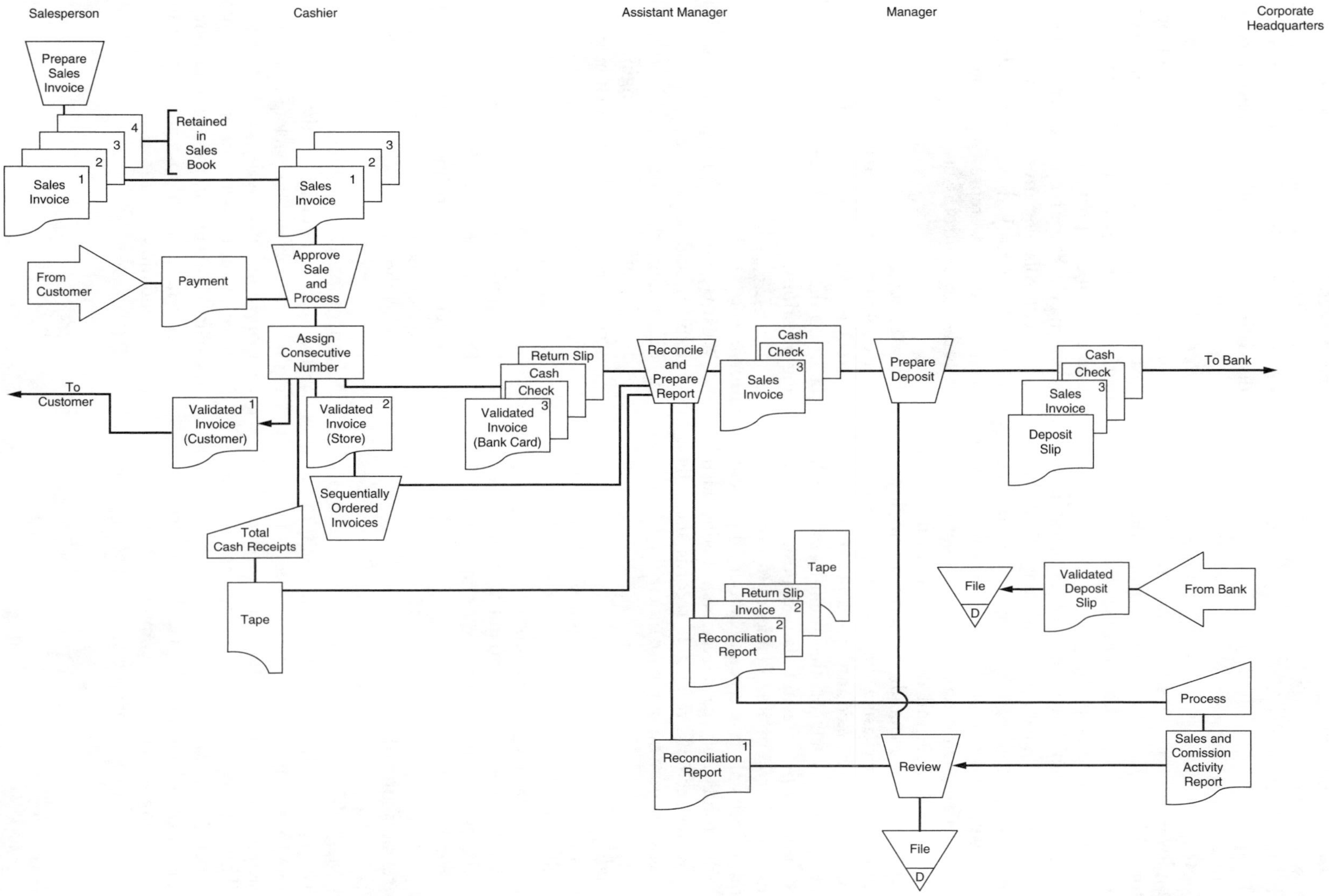

i. Credit memo file
j. Sales order file
k. Closed sales order file

8. **Control Weaknesses**
For the past 11 years, Elaine Wright has been an employee of the Star-Bright Electrical Supply store. Elaine is a very diligent employee who rarely calls in sick and takes her vacation days staggered throughout the year so that no one else gets bogged down with her tasks for more than one day. Star-Bright is a small store that employs only four people other than the owner. The owner and one of the employees help customers with their electrical needs. One of the employees handles all receiving, stocking, and shipping of merchandise. Another employee handles the purchasing, payroll, general ledger, inventory, and accounts payable functions. Elaine handles all of the point-of-sale cash receipts and prepares the daily deposits for the business. Furthermore, Elaine opens the mail and deposits all cash receipts (about 30 percent of the total daily cash receipts). Elaine also keeps the accounts receivable records and bills the customers who purchase on credit.

Required:
a. Point out any control weaknesses you see in the above scenario.
b. List some recommendations to remedy any weaknesses you have found working under the constraint that no additional employees can be hired.

9. **Internal Control**
Iris Plant owns and operates three floral shops in Magnolia, Texas. The accounting functions have been performed manually. Each of the shops has a manager who oversees the cash receipts and purchasing functions for the shop. All bills are sent to the central shop and are paid by a clerk who also prepares payroll checks and maintains the general journal. Iris is seriously considering switching to a computerized system. With so many information systems packages on the market, Iris is overwhelmed. Advise Iris as to which business modules you think her organization could find beneficial. Discuss advantages, disadvantages, and internal control issues.

10. **Internal Control**
You are investing your money and opening a fast-food Mexican restaurant that accepts only cash for payments. You plan on periodically issuing coupons through the mail and in local newspapers. You are particularly interested in access controls over inventory and cash. Design a carefully controlled system and draw a document flowchart to represent it. Identify and discuss the key control issues.

11. **Data Processing**
The computer processing portion of a sales order system is represented by the Problem 11 flowchart on the following page. Answer the following questions:

Required:
a. What type of data processing system is this? Explain, and be specific.
b. The auditor suggests that this system can be greatly simplified by changing to direct access files. Explain the major operational changes that would occur in the system if this were done.
c. The auditor warns of control implications from this change that must be considered. Explain the nature of the control implications.
d. Sketch a flowchart (the computerized portion only) of the proposed new system. Use correct symbols and label the diagram.

12. **Microcomputer AIS packages**
Visit a microcomputer store that carries accounting information system packages. Examine and compare four packages on cost, capabilities (number of business modules), file constraints, flexibility, built-in controls, and support. Rank these systems and write a report supporting your recommendation.

Problem 11: Data Processing

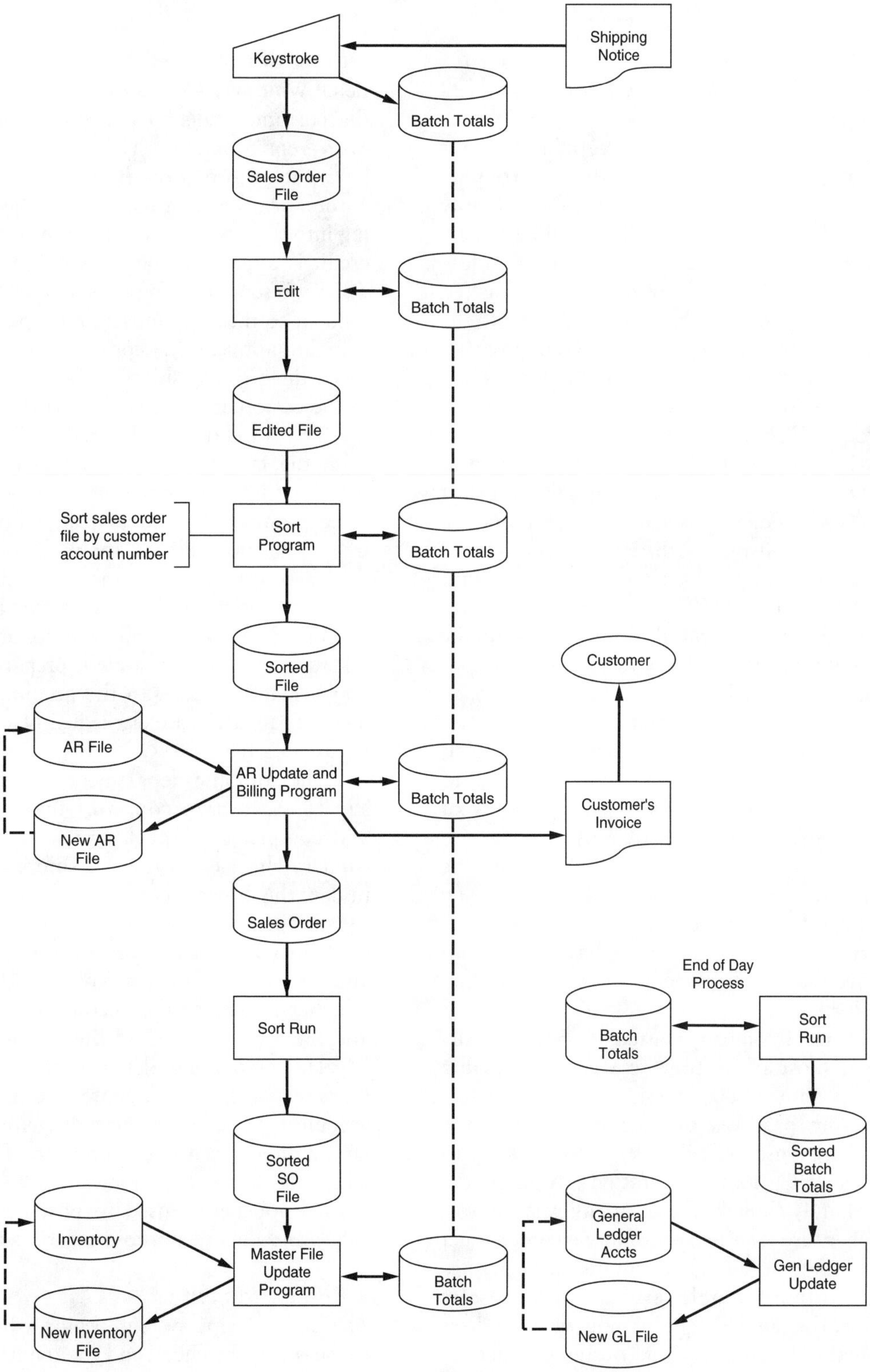

Internal Control Cases

1. **Bella Windows Co.**
(Prepared by Priscilla Law, Lehigh University)
Bella Windows Co. is a window manufacturer located in eastern Pennsylvania with roughly 150 employees in its facility. The Smith family founded it in 1994 because their children, who were architects, needed a specific window design that did not exist in the current market. The parents thought this window would be very successful, so they started a company that made specialty windows. Bella Windows Co.'s motto became "Quality Products, Quick Delivery." This drew a lot of retail customers from their competitors, which allowed them to rapidly grow to $50 million in sales the last three years. Bella Windows Co. developed a strong relationship with its customers and allowed them to purchase windows on account with the terms 2/10/30.

In the past, the Smith family has had the purchasing agent purchase parts from a list of acceptable suppliers. In the beginning of each year, the Smith family researches different suppliers to find which have the parts best suited to their needs. When the purchasing agent needs to reorder wood, glass, or metal pieces, the agent uses a low-cost strategy to choose which supplier to purchase parts from. Recently the Smiths noticed that customers are not getting their products on time due to stockouts in the factory. In addition, customers have been complaining about a lot of incorrect charges on their accounts.

When the company started, the Smith family devoted most of its time to designing quality products and did not invest much time into its accounting practices or computer technology. The Smiths use only low-level technology to facilitate their normal operations. At first, the Smith family thought the company was unprofitable because it spent a lot of money on product design and branding, but now that it has remained unprofitable even with the sales increase, the family is questioning whether there is something wrong with its business structure. Therefore, they hired a consulting firm.

Sales Processing System

Bella Windows Co. sales process begins when the customer calls to place an order with the sales representative. The sales representative keys the information into a terminal, which automatically performs a credit check by looking into the customer's account history. After the credit is approved, the sales order is prepared. The representative prepares a stock release and sends it to the warehouse; and a packing slip, a shipping notice, a file copy, and an invoice, and sends them to the shipping department. A copy of the customer order is also filed.

The warehouse is located in a lot separate from the factory. There is an alarm system in place, but it has been malfunctioning for the past three months. The supervisor, who frequently travels, has not called in the problem yet. Inside, the warehouse clerk uses the stock release to pick up the goods to send to the carrier and updates the direct access inventory account file. After updating the account, a clerk prepares a journal voucher and sends it to the accounting department. The warehouse clerk then places the stock release in a file.

The shipping department uses the packing slip to create two copies of the bill of lading and completes the packing slip to send to the carrier. The clerk uses the shipping notice to update the direct access shipping log. (The copy file of the shipping notice will be filed.) The clerk also updates the direct access sales journal and prepares a journal voucher. The journal voucher is sent to the accounting department, and the invoice is sent to the customer.

The accounting department uses the sales journal voucher to update the direct access account receivable subsidiary ledger and prepares an account receivable summary. The account receivable summary, along with the inventory journal voucher, is used to post to the general ledger and then filed into a control accounts file.

Cash Receipt System

The cash receipt system begins when the customer sends the check and the remittance advice to the mailroom. The mailroom clerk has sole responsibility to reconcile the two documents and prepares three remittance lists in his assigned computer terminal. Because he has worked for the Smiths for many years, there is limited verification on his duties. The check and a remittance list are sent to the cash receipts department to process. The remittance advice and remittance list are sent to the accounting department. A copy of the remittance list is filed.

The cash receipt clerk uses the check and remittance list and inputs this data in order to process the cash receipt. The clerk prepares three deposit slips. Two deposit slips, along with the check, are sent to the bank, and the third deposit slip is filed, along with the remittance list. The clerk updates the direct access cash-receipt journal and prepares a journal voucher to send to the accounting department.

The accounting department uses the remittance advice and the remittance list to update the direct access account receivable subsidiary ledger through the use of a computer terminal, and prepares the account receivable summary. Both the remittance advice and remittance list are filed. The account receivable summary, along with the cash receipt journal voucher, is used to post to the general ledger, which is stored on magnetic tape. After the posting, the summary and voucher are filed into a control accounts file.

Required:

a. Create a data flow diagram of the current system.
b. Create a document flowchart of the existing system.
c. Analyze the internal control weaknesses in the system. Model your response according to the six categories of physical control activities specified in SAS 78.
d. Prepare a system flowchart of a redesigned computer-based system that resolves the control weaknesses that you identified.

2. University Designs
(Prepared by Bentley Hall, Lehigh University)

University Designs originally started out as a small family-run business. The family created silk-screened T-shirts for Lehigh Carbon Community College's bookstore. However, within the past couple of years, the business rapidly expanded. University Designs is now a business of about 125 employees and has expanded to serving colleges within the entire Pennsylvania and New Jersey area. In addition to T-shirts, University Designs applies silk-screening technology to sweatshirts, hats, boxer shorts, and other garments.

Business Description

University Designs buys its clothing in bulk from wholesalers. Next, the company manually designs the logos and then enters them into a microcomputer. The computer controls silk-screening machines that print the selected design on the clothing items. Employees fold and pack the shirts in their shipping boxes. Currently, various departments are equipped with their own microcomputers. Each computer is installed with QuickBooks software, which allows employees to enter data and update the related accounts. These computers are backed up onto secondary storage disks at the end of each week.

Will runs the warehouse. He has proven to be a very dependable employee for the past several years. He is responsible for all of the inventory that comes in and out of the company. Will made spare keys to the warehouse for the supervisor in each department in case of emergency. In addition, the company employs one security guard to watch the warehouse and equipment from 9:00 A.M. until 5:00 P.M. during the weekdays. The mailroom is run by one retired postal employee who is unsupervised. Sally is one of five salespeople. Her salary is based on commission, and she has gotten three bonuses within the last year for highest sales.

Revenue Cycle (Including Cash Receipts)

The customer calls in to order the selected merchandise, specifying quantity and type. The salesperson at the office, Sally, for example, searches the customer files and pulls up the customer information. If the client is new, then Sally simply enters the information into the database. All orders require a credit check to ensure that the customer is allowed to order on credit, and that the credit limit is not being exceeded. Sally then prints out five copies of the sales order: one form that is immediately returned to the customer to ensure accuracy and one copy that is filed in a fireproof filing cabinet. The other three copies consist of a stock release form that is sent to the warehouse and a packing slip and shipping notice that are both sent to the shipping department.

The stock release is sent to the warehouse, where the goods are picked and sent along with the stock release to the shipping department. The warehouse clerk, Will, then uses the workstation to update the accounting records. At the shipping department, Shawn reconciles the packing slip and shipping notice with the incoming stock release. He then prepares three copies of the bill of lading and a remittance advice. One is filed away while the other two copies are sent along with the remittance advice to the shipping company. Once the goods have been picked up by the shipping company the shipping notice is forwarded to Amy at the accounting department where she updates the computer records including the general ledger accounts (cash, inventory, etc.) and the accounts receivable subsidiary account. After each order the computer system automatically reviews the inventory records and quantity on hand. If the inventory has fallen below the reorder point, a purchase requisition form is created, printed, and sent to the purchases system in the expenditure cycle.

Within the next 30 days the customer sends a check paying for the goods along with the remittance advice that was sent with the goods. The mailroom forwards the check and the remittance advice to the accounting department. The accounting department uses the remittance advice amount to update the appropriate records on the microcomputer and creates a deposit slip. It then deposits the check into the company's account at the local bank.

Required:

a. Create a data flow diagram of the current system.
b. Create a document flowchart of the existing system.
c. Analyze the internal control weaknesses in the system. Model your response according to the six categories of physical control activities specified in SAS 78.
d. Prepare a system flowchart of a redesigned computer-based system that resolves the control weaknesses that you identified.

3. Fence, Inc.

(Prepared by Chris Banta and Mike Diana, Lehigh University)

Fence, Inc. was established in 1993 in the Lehigh Valley and is currently one of the fastest-growing wooden fence installers in the industry. The company's headquarters is located in Bethlehem, Pennsylvania and it has a warehouse in Allentown, Pennsylvania to store and customize the fence. The sales staff and purchasing staff are located at the headquarters and sends sales and purchasing information directly to the warehouse. At the warehouse the installation team then takes the stored fence and installs it on the customer's site.

There are approximately 15 warehouse workers, 45 installers (team leaders and general installers), 25 sales and purchasing employees, and 15 other headquarter employees in the company. The general installers, however, are much younger and less experienced than the other employees, and thus have a high employee turnover rate.

Fence, Inc. offers its customers a huge variety of products, including aluminum, vinyl (PVC), chain link, wood split rail, wood board fencing, and other similar items, including guardrails and arbors.

Fence, Inc. uses only one vendor due to its great relationship with a local wood and metal distributor (Royal, Inc.). Royal, Inc. has asked Fence, Inc. if it could organize a better purchasing and receiving system, as it is very large and technologically advanced compared to Fence, Inc. This could lead to an EDI relationship between Fence, Inc. and Royal, Inc. in the near future as technology becomes cheaper and both companies continue to grow from a successful relationship.

Due to the seasonality of the business, Fence, Inc. has decided that this winter during the off-season (December through March) it will be looking into revising its low-level computer technology and some of the manual procedures in its accounting system. This will ensure the company's future relationship with Royal, Inc. and enable it to better handle new accounts. It also wants a control expert or auditor to visit the company and give recommendation on how its processes can be better regulated.

The Plan

The vendor currently used by the fence company wishes to use EDI technology in its relationship with the company. Therefore, during this update, EDI technology will be implemented. This will change the form of the company's computer operations from a standard terminal available in each department to a new automatic sale, inventory update, and reorder point system. Also, professional accountant software will be used to help facilitate management reporting when the daily batches of sales order and cash receipts are processed. This system should be at least 15 times as fast as the old system and allow new opportunities to develop with the single vendor situation Fence, Inc. is in. Lastly, computer consultant from XYZ services will be hired to help update processes and tasks to eliminate control issues in the company.

Description of Current Revenue Cycle

The sales-order processing system for Fence, Inc. currently employs a low level of technology surrounding one main computer that is used for all revenue activities in the business. The first step in this process is when a customer contacts a sales clerk, who generates a customer order. This customer order is then put into an open sales order file to indicate that the order has not yet been completed.

The sales clerk creates from the customer order four documents: the stock release, ledger copy, packing slip, and customer bill. The stock release is sent to the warehouse clerk, who picks the needed goods out of storage and updates the manual inventory record. This inventory record is sent at the end of each day to the computer operations for update in the revenue computer. Once the goods are selected the stock release is sent to inventory control.

The original packing slip from the sales clerk is sent to inventory control as well and here the inventory control clerk reconciles the stock release and packing slip. After reconciliation he prepares two installation invoices. One copy of the installation invoice and the packing slip are sent to the installation team who then installs the fence at the customer site. The other installation invoice and the stock release are used to update and close the open sales order file. The closed sales order file is then sent to computer operations for entry into the revenue computer.

Lastly, the ledger copy provided by the sales order clerk is also sent to computer operations to provide reconciliation throughout the three departments: sales, warehouse, and inventory control. The customer bill generated by the sales clerk is sent to the customer directly.

In the computer operations department the clerk reconciles the inventory records, closed sales order file, and the ledger copy of the customer order and updates all of the general ledger accounts via the revenue computer. This concludes the flow of documents for the sales order processing system.

The cash receipt system begins when the customer sends a check and remittance advice (customer bill) to Fence, Inc. The cash receipts department receives these two documents and reconciles the check with the remittance advice. The clerk then prepares a remittance list that contains all the received checks for the given business day. The cash receipts clerk prepares four documents: the check, two remittance lists, and a deposit slip.

The check, a remittance list, and a deposit slip are all sent to the controller. The controller takes the three documents and brings the check and deposit slip to the bank. He then updates the general ledger accounts on the revenue computer. The second copy of the remittance list in the cash receipts department is sent to the account receivable department where a clerk reconciles and updates accounts via the revenue computer. This concludes the flow of documents for the cash receipts system.

Required:

a. Create a data flow diagram of the current system.
b. Create a document flowchart of the existing system.
c. Analyze the internal control weaknesses in the system. Model your response according to the six categories of physical control activities specified in SAS 78.
d. Prepare a system flowchart of a redesigned computer-based system that resolves the control weaknesses that you identified.

4. Sports Rush, Inc

(Prepared by David Crockett and Antonio Marino, Lehigh University)

Sports Rush, Inc is a large supplier of quality athletic equipment, footwear, and apparel, featuring major brands such as Nike, Reebok, Spalding, Links, Wilson, Bauer, North Face, Adidas, and New Balance. Established to meet the performance needs of high school and college athletes, its mission is to provide the best available athletic equipment to enhance the performance of these athletes. Its products range from sneakers, running shoes, cleats, equipment, clothing, weights, and all general accessories for all types of sports. Gross sales range from \$100.5 million to \$103.5 million a year, averaging \$41.7 million over the past three years. Sports Rush operates a distribution center that takes sales orders by phone and mail-in catalog and has about 250 employees. The company has contracts and agreements to supply many universities and sports teams with equipment and accessories. Some of these universities include the University of Florida, Florida State University, and Lehigh University. Its major competitors are Eastbay catalog and the retail sporting stores such as Sports Authority and Modell's. Because of its call-in and mail-in service, the company provides a service that helps it rise above retail stores. Its general customer ranges from the average, everyday athlete to the world-class athlete, incorporating all ages, types of sports teams, and universities

Recently Sports Rush has been experiencing complaints from customers because their products are arriving later than usual. The lead time was five days from the time the order was placed until the order was received. Now the lead time is about seven to eight days. The company feels that the warehouse clerk has too much responsibility, which has been causing problems in its ability to have the correct equipment in stock. It is also slowing down its shipment process. Sports Rush also feels that this could be the reason why sales have been on a slow rise over the past three years instead of a more steady gain as in previous years. Sports Rush wants to bring in an audit team to evaluate this situation.

Sales Order and Cash Receipts Process

A sale begins when a customer contacts a sales representative in one of three ways: online order, mail-in order, or by phone. Here, the sales representative converts the customer's requests into a sales order. Using this information, he is then able to create the following documents: a customer copy, a stock release, a packing slip, the shipping notice, a file copy, and the original sales order.

The customer copy is simply sent back to the customer as a record of the order. The stock release is then sent to the warehouse where the warehouse clerk uses this document to pick the goods. After picking the goods, he sends them to the shipping department, along with the stock release. After sending out the goods, the warehouse clerk updates the inventory subsidiary file.

The sales department then sends the packing slip, shipping notice, and the file copy to the shipping department. The shipping clerk uses these three documents, in addition to the stock release, to reconcile the goods received from the warehouse with the information from the sales department to ensure the order meets customer specifications. After this reconciliation is complete, he signs the shipping notice, authorizing the shipping, and then prepares the bill of lading (two copies). The shipping notice is then sent to the computer department, a copy of the bill of lading and the packing slip are given to the carrier delivering the goods. The other bill of lading, the file copy of the sales order, and the stock release are filed in the shipping department.

Lastly, a data entry employee enters the data from the shipping notice into a computer terminal. The computer automatically puts the data into the sales order file. This data is then edited and stored in the edited sales order file. Next, after a direct access update procedure is performed, the accounts receivable file and the general ledger file are updated. When this task is completed, management reports are created, the sales journal is updated, and a customer invoice is also created. The management reports are sent to management and the customer invoice is sent to the customer to signify the end of the sales order processing system.

Cash Receipts System

The cash receipts portion of the revenue cycle begins when a customer sends a check and the remittance advice to the company. The mailroom clerk takes these documents and uses them to prepare a remittance list (three copies).

One copy of the remittance list, along with the customer's check, is sent to the cash receipts department. These are entered into a computer terminal, which automatically updates the cash receipts journal and creates a journal voucher. Three copies of a deposit slip are also created. One copy of the deposit slip is put on file in the cash receipts department, along with the remittance list and the check, while the other two copies of the deposit slip are sent to the bank.

Another copy of the remittance list, along with the remittance advice from the mailroom, is sent over to the accounts receivable department. They are then entered into the accounts receivable sub-ledger computer terminal, where the accounts receivable sub-ledger is updated and an account summary is created. The remittance list and remittance advice are filed in the A/R department. The account summary is sent over to the general ledger department along with the journal voucher from the cash receipts department. The data from these documents are entered into the general ledger computer terminal, the general ledger is updated, and the account summary and journal voucher are filed.

The third and final copy of the remittance list (from the mailroom) is sent over to the controller. He then obtains this remittance list, along with a copy of the deposit slip, which is sent from the bank, the account summary, and the journal voucher from the general ledger file. The controller then reconciles the documents to ensure their correctness. With this reconciliation, the cash receipts process is completed.

Required:

a. Create a data flow diagram of the current system.
b. Create a document flowchart of the existing system.
c. Analyze the internal control weaknesses in the system. Model your response according to the six categories of physical control activities specified in SAS 78.

ACL Assignments

The **AR** and **Customer** files used for the following assignments are located in the *workbook.acl* document on the CD that accompanies this text. The AR file is actually an invoice file that contains several related records as designated by the Trans Type field:

IN = Sales invoice
PM = Payment from customer
CN = Credit note (Credit memo)
TR = Transfer (write off)

Sales invoices should be represented by positive Trans Amount values, while the other transaction types are negative.

Some of the following assignments employ the ACL's *Relation* and *Join* features. For detailed information on the use of these and other commands, consult ACL's online Help.

1. Open the **AR** file, *Profile* the data, and *Stratify* on the Trans Amount field. Print the Last Results window and write an analysis providing possible explanations for the results obtained.

2. Open the **AR** file, stratify the file on the Trans Amount field, and use the expression builder to create filters that limit the strata to
   a. sales invoice transactions only
   b. credit note (memo) transactions only
   c. payment transactions only
   d. transfer (write off) transactions

3. Open the **AR** file and use the expression builder to create a filter that screens for invalid transaction types. Print the results and comment.

4. Using the *Relation* feature create a view from data in both the **AR** and **Customer** files that shows customer details (**name** and **street address**) for payment transactions with abnormal (positive) amount values. Print the view and comment on the results.

5. Using the *Join* feature create a view from data in both the **AR** and **Customer** files that show customer details (**name** and **address**) for payment transactions with abnormal (positive) amount values. Print the view and comment on the results.

   The following Assignments are located in the **ACL Tutorial** folder on the CD accompanying this text.

6. Tutorial 2 relates to the following commands: TOTAL, PROFILE, STATISTICS, SAMPLE, SEQUENCE, SORT, DUPLICATES, GAPS

7. Tutorial 5 relates to the following commands: AGE, JOIN, MERGE

8. Tutorial 6 relates to the following commands: TOTAL, COUNT, EXTRACT, EXPORT, SORT, INDEX

9. Brandmark Comprehensibe Case

Required:

Access the Brandmark folder on the CD accompanying this text. The Brandmark case is a word file located in a sub-folder named CASE. The data used to solve the case is located in the DATA sub-folder. Your instructor will tell you which questions to answer.

CHAPTER

10 Auditing the Expenditure Cycle

Learning Objectives

After studying this chapter, you should:

- Understand the primary tasks associated with the expenditure cycle under different levels of technology.
- Understand audit objectives related to the expenditure cycle.
- Be familiar with expenditure cycle control issues related to alternative technologies.
- Recognize the relationship between expenditure cycle audit objectives, controls, and tests of controls.
- Understand the nature of substantive tests in achieving expenditure-cycle audit objectives.
- Be familiar with common features and functions of ACL that are used to perform substantive tests.

This chapter examines audit procedures associated with the expenditure cycle. The chapter is divided into three main sections. It begins with a review of computer technologies used in both legacy and modern systems. The focus is on the way that key operational tasks are performed under different technological environments. The second section discusses the expenditure cycle audit objectives, controls, and tests of controls that an auditor would normally perform to gather the evidence needed to limit the scope, timing, and extent of substantive tests. The last section describes substantive tests in relation to expenditure cycle audit objectives that can be performed using ACL software.

Overview of Expenditure Cycle Technologies

This section examines alternative information technologies used in the expenditure cycle. The first of these is a purchases and cash system that employs batch processing and uses sequential files for storing accounting records. This type of system is an example of an early legacy system. This approach characterizes the era of data ownership in which files were designed exclusively for the use of a single user. Data sharing is virtually impossible in this setting and results in a great deal of data redundancy and data obsolescence. Second, we review the operational features of a modern system that employs real-time processing and uses direct access files or databases. The final example depicts a modern payroll system that uses real-time processing and database technology.

You should recognize that space limitations prohibit a review of all possible configurations of processing technologies, techniques, and file structures. The objective, instead, is to present examples of fundamentally different approaches that are typically found in practice and examine their control and audit implications.

Purchases and Cash Disbursement Procedures Using Batch Processing Technology

Many of the manual functions in the batch system presented in Figure 10-1 are the same as those found in manual purchase systems. The principal difference is that the routine accounting tasks are automated. The following section describes the sequence of events as they occur in this system.

Data Processing Department: Step 1

The purchasing process begins in the data processing department, where the inventory control function is performed. The revenue cycle (in retailing firms) or the conversion cycle (in manufacturing firms) actually initiates this activity. When inventories are reduced by sales to customers or usage in production, the system determines if the affected items in the **inventory subsidiary file** have fallen to their reorder points.[1] If so, a record is created in the open requisition file. Each record in the open requisition file defines a separate inventory item to be replenished. The record contains the inventory item number, a description of the item, the quantity to be ordered, the standard unit price, and the vendor number of the primary supplier. The information needed to create the requisition record is selected from the inventory subsidiary record. The inventory subsidiary record is then flagged "On Order" to prevent the item from being ordered again before it arrives.

At the end of the day, the system sorts the open requisition file by vendor number and consolidates multiple items from the same vendor onto a single requisition. Next, vendor mailing information is retrieved from the valid vendor file to produce purchase requisition documents. Copies of these documents go to manual procedures in the purchasing and accounts payable departments.

Purchasing Department. Upon receipt of the purchase requisition, the purchasing department prepares a five-part purchase order. Copies go to the vendors, accounts payable, receiving, data processing, and the purchasing department's own file.

The system in Figure 10-1 employs manual procedures to control the ordering process. A computer program identifies inventory requirements and prepares traditional purchase requisitions, thus allowing the purchasing agent to verify the purchase transaction before placing the order. Some firms use this technique to

1 This may be batch or real time, depending on the revenue and conversion cycle systems that interface with the expenditure cycle. The raw materials and finished goods inventory files link these three transaction cycles together. The design of one system influences the others. For example, if sales processing (revenue cycle) reduces inventories in real time, the system will naturally identify inventory requirements in real time also. This is true even if the purchases system is batch oriented.

FIGURE 10-1 Batch Purchases System

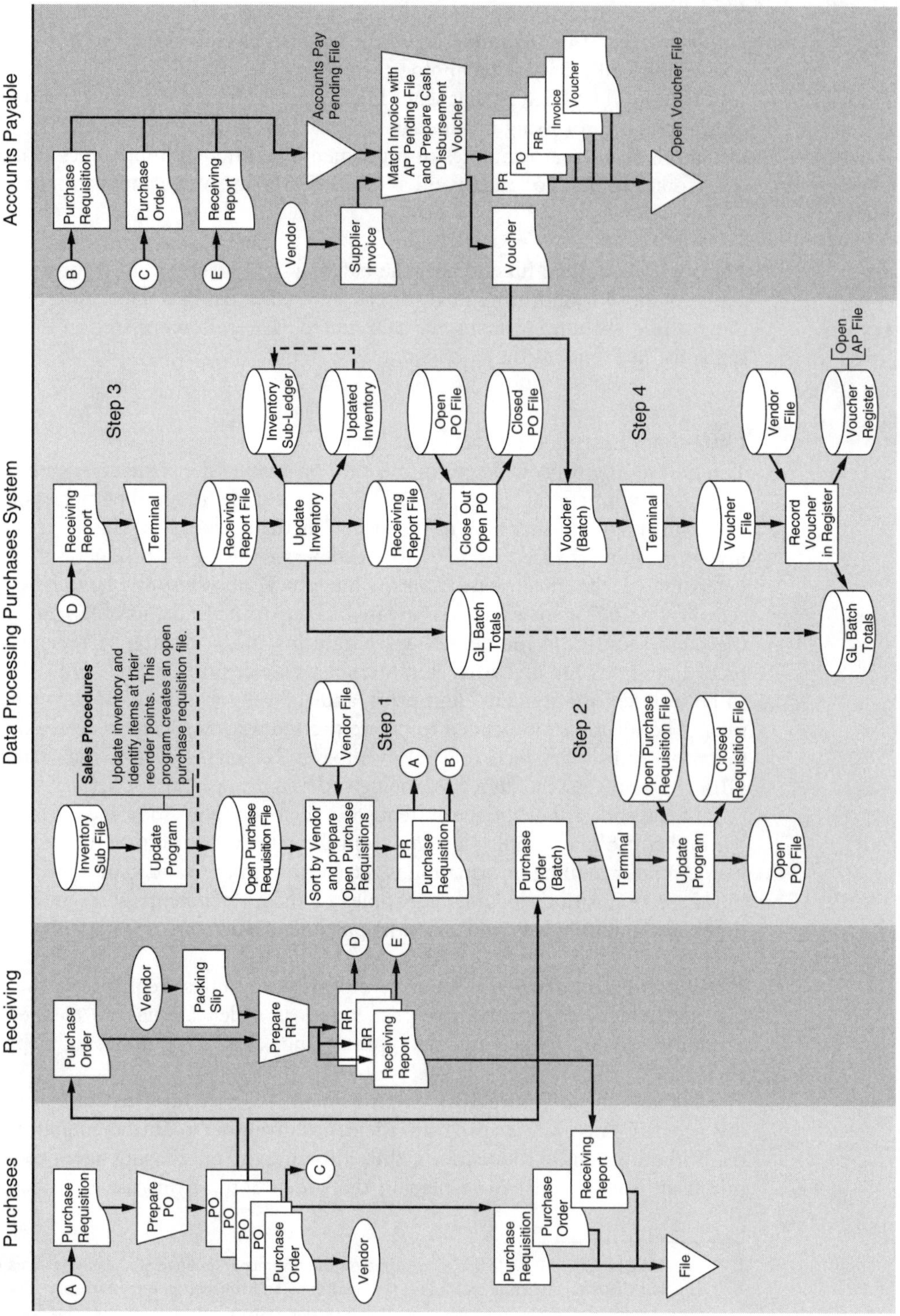

FIGURE 10-1 (continued)

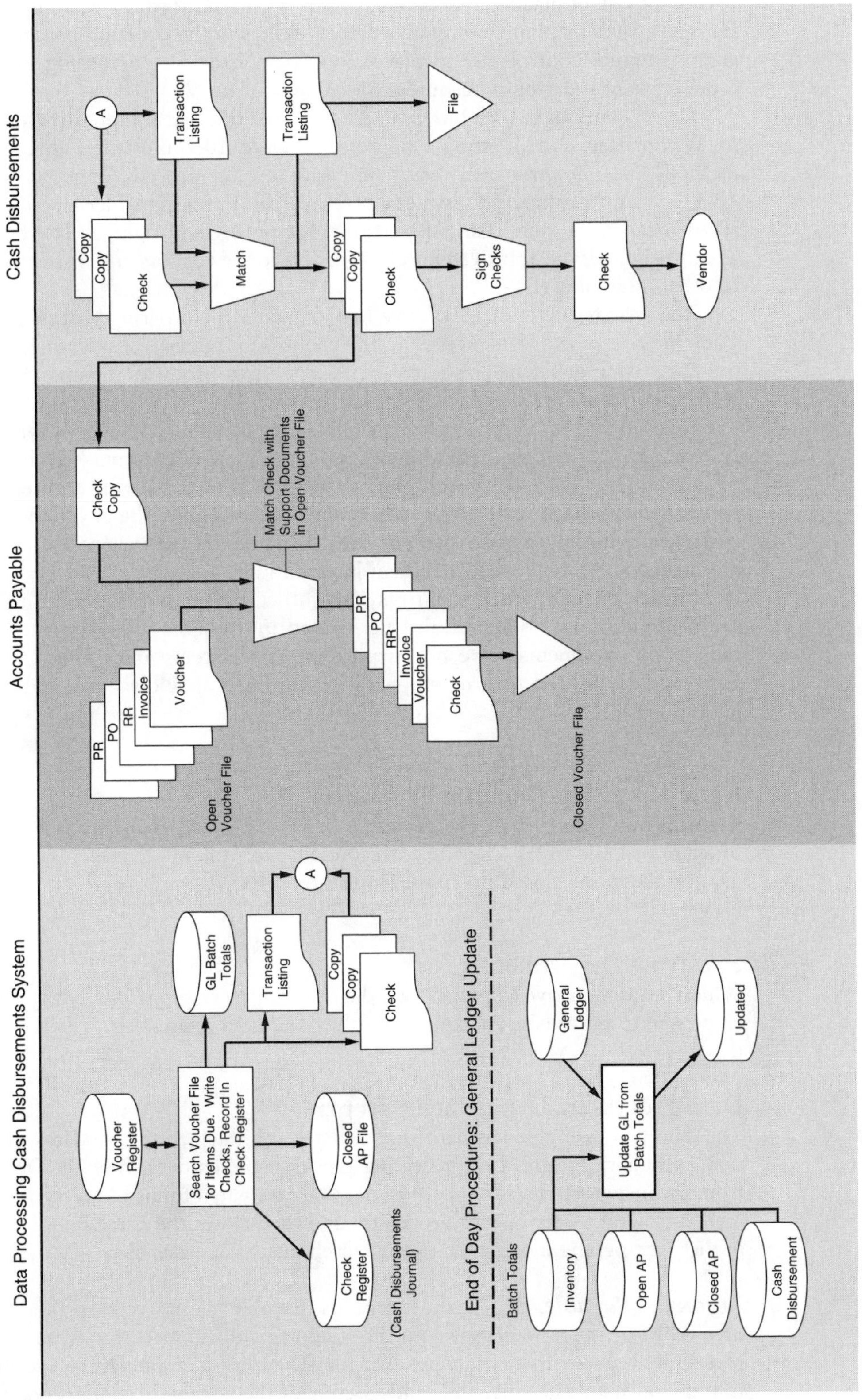

reduce the risk of placing unnecessary orders with vendors due to a computer error. However, such manual intervention creates delays in the ordering process. If sufficient computer controls are in place to prevent or detect purchasing errors, then more efficient ordering procedures can be implemented.

Before continuing with our example, we need to discuss alternative approaches for authorizing and ordering inventories. Figure 10-2 illustrates three different methods. In *alternative one*, the system advances the procedures shown in Figure 10-1 one-step further. This system prepares the purchase order documents and sends them to the purchasing department for review and signing. The purchasing agent then mails the approved purchase orders to the vendors and distributes copies to other internal users.

The system shown in *alternative two* expedites the ordering process by distributing the purchase orders directly to the vendors and internal users, thus bypassing the purchasing department completely. This system produces a transaction list of items ordered for the purchasing agent's review.

Alternative three represents a reengineering system that uses *electronic data interchange (EDI)*. This method produces no physical documents (purchase orders or sales orders). Instead, the computer systems of both the buying and selling companies are connected via a special telecommunications link. The buyer and seller are parties in a trading partner arrangement in which the entire ordering process is automated and unimpeded by human intervention.

In each of the three alternatives, the authorization and the ordering steps in the process are consolidated and performed by the computer system. Purchase requisition documents serve no purpose in such systems and are not produced. However, requisition records may still exist on magnetic disk or tape to provide an audit trail.

Data Processing Department: Step 2

Returning to Figure 10-1, the purchase order is used to create an open purchase order record and to transfer the corresponding record(s) in the open purchase requisition file to the closed purchase requisition file.

Receiving Department

When the goods arrive from vendors, the receiving clerk prepares a receiving report. Copies go to purchasing, accounts payable, and data processing.

Data Processing Department: Step 3

The data processing department runs a batch job (Step 3) that updates the inventory subsidiary file from the receiving reports and removes the "On Order" flag from the inventory records. The system calculates batch totals of inventory receipts for the general ledger update procedure and then closes the corresponding records in the open purchase order file to the closed purchase order file.

Accounts Payable. When the accounts payable clerk receives the supplier's invoice, he or she reconciles it with the supporting documents that were previously placed in the accounts payable pending file. The clerk then prepares a voucher, files it in the open voucher file, and sends a copy of the voucher to data processing.

FIGURE 10-2 **Alternative Inventory Ordering Procedures**

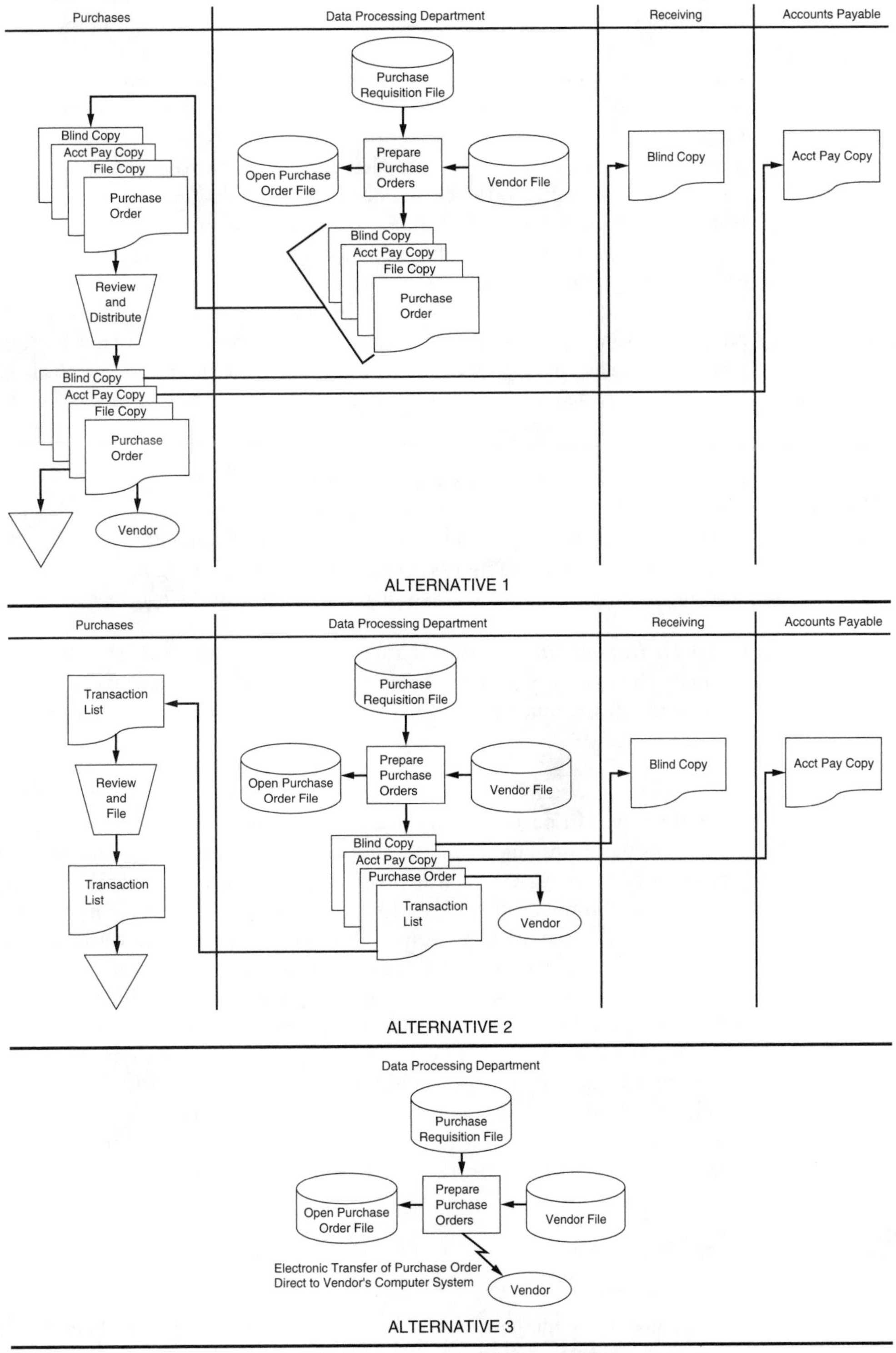

Data Processing Department: Step 4

A batch program validates the voucher records against the valid vendor file, adds them to the voucher register (or open accounts payable subsidiary file), and prepares batch totals for posting to the accounts payable control account in the general ledger.

Cash Disbursement: Data Processing Department. Each day, the system scans the Due Date field of the voucher register for items due. Checks are printed for these items, and each check is recorded in the check register (cash disbursements journal). The check number is recorded in the voucher register to close the voucher and transfer the items to the **closed accounts payable file**. The checks, along with a transaction listing, are sent to the cash disbursements department. Finally, batch totals of closed accounts payable and cash disbursements are prepared for the general ledger update procedure.

At the end of the day, batch totals of open (unpaid) and closed (paid) accounts payable, inventory increases, and cash disbursements are posted to the accounts payable control, inventory control, and cash accounts in the general ledger. The totals of closed accounts payable and cash disbursements should balance.

Cash Disbursement: Cash Disbursements Department

The cash disbursements clerk reconciles the checks with the transaction listing and submits the negotiable portion of the checks to management for signing. The checks are then mailed to the suppliers. One copy of each check goes to accounts payable, and the other copy is filed in cash disbursements along with the transaction listing.

Cash Disbursement: Accounts Payable. Upon receipt of the check copies, the accounts payable clerk matches them with open vouchers and transfers these closed items to the closed voucher file. The expenditure cycle process concludes with this step.

Reengineering the Purchases/Cash Disbursement System

The automated system just described simply replicates many of the procedures in a manual system. In particular, the accounts payable task of reconciling supporting documents with supplier invoices is labor intensive and costly. The following example shows how reengineering this process can produce considerable savings.

The Ford Motor Company employed more than 500 clerks in its North American accounts payable department. Analysis of the function showed that a large part of Ford's accounts payable clerks' time was devoted to reconciling discrepancies between supplier invoices, receiving reports, and purchase orders. The first step in solving the problem was to bring about fundamental changes in the business environment. Ford initiated trading partner agreements with suppliers in which they agreed in advance to terms of trade such as price, quantities to be shipped, discounts, and lead times. With these sources of discrepancy eliminated, Ford reengineered the workflow to take advantage of the new environment. The flowchart in Figure 10-3 depicts key features of a reengineered system.

Data Processing

The following tasks are performed automatically:

1. The inventory file is searched for items that have fallen to their reorder point.
2. A record is entered in the purchase requisition file for each item to be replenished.

FIGURE 10-3 **Reengineered Purchases/Cash Disbursement System**

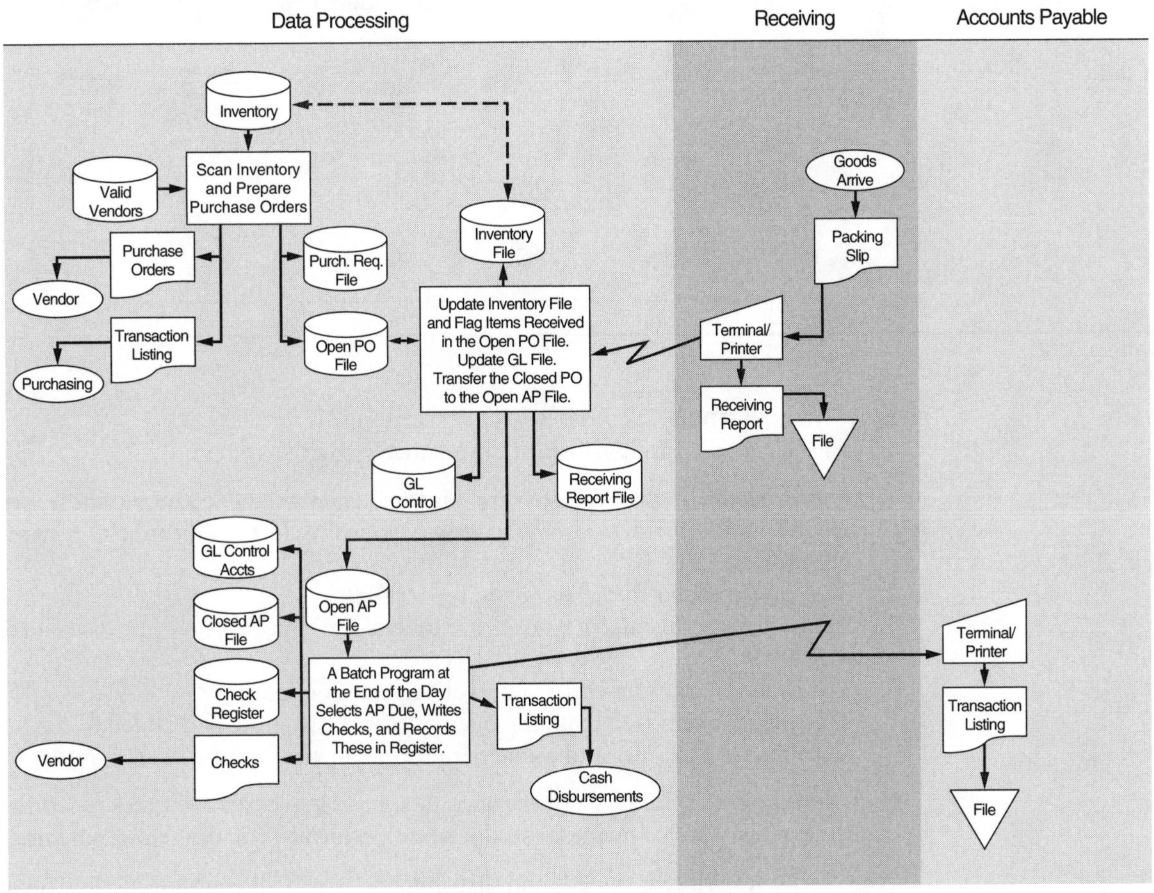

3. Requisitions are then consolidated according to vendor number.
4. Vendor mailing information is retrieved from the valid vendor file.
5. Purchase orders are prepared and sent to the vendor. Alternatively, these may be transmitted using EDI technology.
6. A record of each transaction is added to the open purchase order file.
7. A transaction listing of purchase orders is sent to the purchasing department for review.

Receiving Department

When the goods arrive, the receiving clerk accesses the open purchase order file in real time by entering the purchase order number taken from the packing slip. The receiving screen, illustrated in Figure 10-4, then prompts the clerk to enter the quantities received for each item on the purchase order.

FIGURE 10-4

Receiving Screen

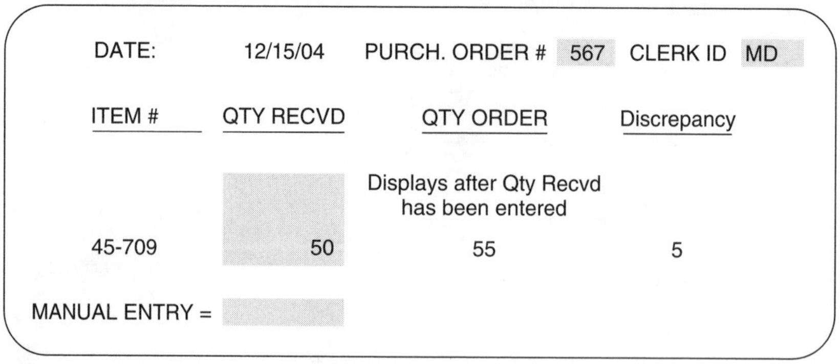

Data Processing

The following tasks are performed automatically by the system:

1. Quantities of items received are matched against the open purchase order record, and a "Y" value is placed in a logical field to indicate the receipt of inventories.
2. A record is added to the receiving report file.
3. The inventory subsidiary records are updated to reflect the receipt of the inventory items.
4. The general ledger inventory control account is updated.
5. The record is removed from the open purchase order file and added to the open accounts payable file, and a due date for payment is established.

Each day, the Due Date fields of the accounts payable records are checked for items due to be paid. The following procedures are performed for the selected items:

1. Checks are printed, signed, and distributed to the mailroom for mailing to vendors. EDI vendors receive payment electronically.
2. The payments are recorded in the check register file.
3. Items paid are transferred from the open accounts payable file to the closed accounts payable file.
4. The general ledger accounts payable and cash accounts are updated.
5. Reports detailing these transactions are transmitted via terminal to the accounts payable and cash disbursements departments for management review and filing.

Since the financial information about purchases is known in advance from the trading partner agreement, the **vendor's invoice** provides no critical information that cannot be derived from the receiving report. By eliminating this source of potential discrepancy, Ford was able to eliminate the task of reconciling vendor invoices with the supporting documents for the majority of purchase transactions. As a result of its reengineering effort, the company was able to reduce its accounts payable staff from 500 to 125.

Control Implications

The technology control issues (i.e., those pertaining to the use of sequential files versus direct access files) are general in nature. The points made in the last chapter apply to the expenditure cycle also. Therefore, let's examine only the issues specific to this cycle by focusing on the differences between an automated versus a reengineered system.

The Automated System

Improved Inventory Control. The greatest advantage of the automated (batch) system over its manual counterpart is its improved ability to manage inventory needs. Inventory requirements are detected as they arise and are processed automatically. As a result, the risks of accumulating excessive inventory or of running out of stock are reduced. However, with this advantage comes a control concern. Authorization rules governing purchase transactions are consolidated within a computer program. Program errors or flawed inventory models can cause firms to be suddenly inundated with inventories or desperately short of stock. Therefore, it is extremely important to monitor automated decisions. A well-controlled system will provide management with adequate summary reports on inventory purchases, inventory turnover, spoilage, and slow-moving items.

Better Cash Management. This type of system promotes effective cash management by scanning the voucher file daily for items due, thus avoiding early payments and missed due dates. In addition, by writing checks automatically, the firm reduces labor cost, saves processing time, and promotes accuracy.

As a control against unauthorized payments, comparing the vendor number on the voucher with a valid vendor file validates all entries in the voucher file. If the vendor number is not on file, the record is presumed to be invalid and is diverted to an error file for management review.

In this system, a manager in the cash disbursements department physically signs the checks, thus providing control over the disbursement of cash. However, many computer systems automate check signing with special printing equipment, which is more efficient when check volume is high, but relinquishes some control. To offset this exposure, firms often set a materiality threshold for check writing. Checks for amounts below the threshold are signed automatically, and an authorized manager or the treasurer signs those above the threshold.

Less Time Lag. A lag exists between the arrival of goods in the receiving department and recording inventory receipts in the inventory file. Depending on the type of sales order system in place, this lag may affect sales negatively. Because of this time lag, sales clerks will not know the current status of inventory, and sales may be lost.

Better Purchasing Time Management. In this hypothetical batch system, the purchasing department is directly involved with all purchase decisions. For many firms, this creates additional work that extends the time lag in the ordering process. A vast number of routine purchases could be automated. By freeing purchasing agents from routine work, such as preparing purchase orders and mailing them to the vendors, attention can be focused on problem orders (such as special items or those in short supply), and the purchasing staff can be reduced.

Reduction of Paper Documents. The basic batch system is laden with paper documents. All operations departments create documents, which are sent to data processing and which data processing must then convert to magnetic media. A number of costs are associated with paper documents, since the paper must be purchased and the documents filed, stored, handled by internal mail carriers, and converted by data processing personnel. Organizations with high volumes of transactions benefit considerably from reducing or eliminating paper documents in their systems.

The Reengineered System

This system addresses many of the operational weaknesses found in the basic batch system. Specifically, the improvements in this system are that (1) it uses real-time procedures and direct-access files to shorten the lag time in recordkeeping; (2) it eliminates routine manual procedures through automation; and (3) it achieves a significant reduction in paper documents by using electronic communications between departments and by storing records on direct-access media. These operational improvements, however, carry control implications.

Segregation of Duties. This system removes the fundamental separation between authorization and transaction processing. Here, computer programs authorize and process purchase orders, and authorize and issue checks to vendors. To compensate for this exposure, the system needs to provide management with detailed transaction listings and summary reports. These documents describe the automated actions taken by the system and allow management to spot errors and any unusual events that warrant investigation.

Accounting Records and Access Controls. This system maintains accounting records exclusively on magnetic disks. To preserve the integrity of these records, the organization must implement controls that limit access to the disks. Unauthorized access to magnetic records carries the same consequences as access to source documents, journals, and ledgers in a manual environment. Organizations can employ a number of physical and software techniques to provide adequate access control. However, keep in mind that some techniques are costly, and management must justify these costs against their expected benefits.

Overview of Payroll Procedures

Payroll processing is actually a special expenditure system. In theory, payroll checks could be processed through the regular accounts payable and cash disbursements system. However, as a practical matter, this approach would have a number of drawbacks:

- *General expenditure procedures that apply to all vendors will not apply to employees.* Payroll procedures differ greatly among classes of employees. For example, different procedures are used for hourly employees, salaried employees, piece workers, and commissioned employees. Also, payroll processing requires special accounting procedures for employee deductions and withholdings for taxes. Cash disbursements for trade accounts do not require special processing. Therefore, general expenditure systems are not designed to deal with these complications.
- *Writing checks to employees requires special controls.* It is easier to conceal payroll fraud when payroll checks are combined with trade account checks.

- *General expenditure procedures are designed to accommodate a relatively smooth flow of transactions.* Business enterprises are constantly purchasing inventories and disbursing funds to vendors. Naturally, they design systems to deal adequately with their normal level of transaction activity. Payroll activities are discrete rather than continuous. Disbursements to employees occur weekly, biweekly, or monthly. To periodically impose this processing burden on the general system may have an overwhelming peak-load effect.

Because payroll systems run infrequently (weekly or monthly), they are often well suited to batch processing and sequential files. Figure 10-5 shows a flowchart for such a system. The data processing department receives the personnel action forms and time cards, which it converts to sequential files. Batch computer programs perform the detailed record-keeping, check-writing, and general ledger functions.

Control Implications

The strengths and weaknesses of this system are similar to those in the batch system for general expenditures discussed earlier. This system promotes accounting accuracy and reduces check-writing errors. Beyond this, it does not significantly enhance operational efficiency; however, for many types of organizations, this level of technology is adequate.

Reengineering the Payroll System

For moderate-sized and large organizations, payroll processing is often integrated within the **human resource management (HRM) system**. The HRM system captures and processes a wide range of personnel-related data, including employee benefits, labor resource planning, employee relations, employee skills, personnel actions (pay rates, deductions, and so on), as well as payroll. HRM systems must support real-time access to personnel files for purposes of direct inquires and recording changes in employee status as they occur. Figure 10-6 illustrates a payroll system as part of an HRM system.

This system differs from the simple automated system described previously in the following ways: (1) operations departments transmit transactions to data processing via terminals, (2) direct access files are used for data storage, and (3) many processes are now performed in real time. We discuss the key operating features of this system as follows:

Personnel. The personnel department makes changes to the employee file in real time via terminals. These changes include additions of new employees, deletions of terminated employees, changes in dependents, changes in withholding, and changes in job status (pay rate).

Cost Accounting. The cost accounting department enters job cost data (real time or daily) to create the **labor usage file.**

Timekeeping. Upon receipt of the approved timecards from the supervisor at the end of the week, the timekeeping department creates the current **attendance file.**

FIGURE 10-5 Batch Payroll System with Sequential Files

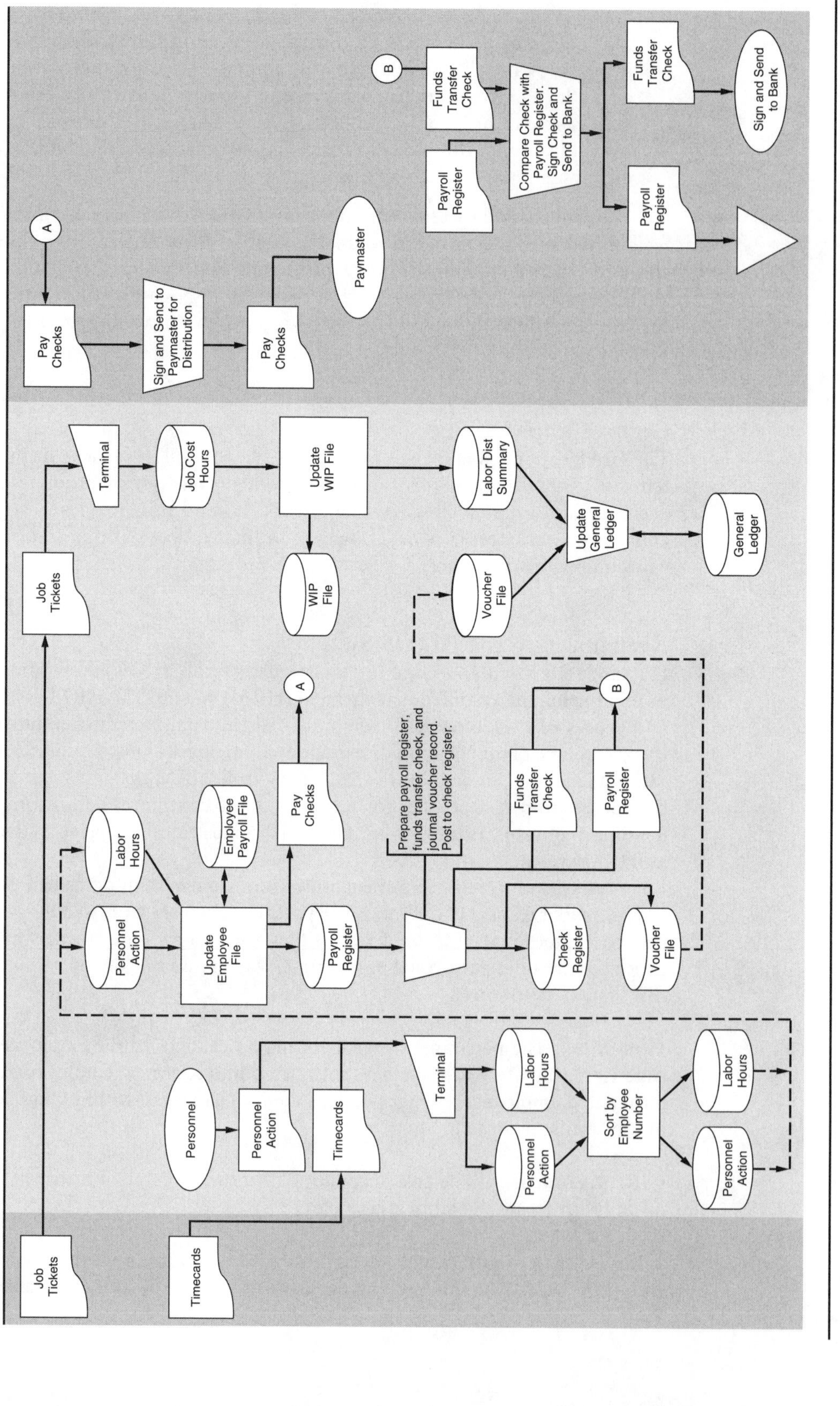

FIGURE 10-6 Payroll System with Real-Time Elements

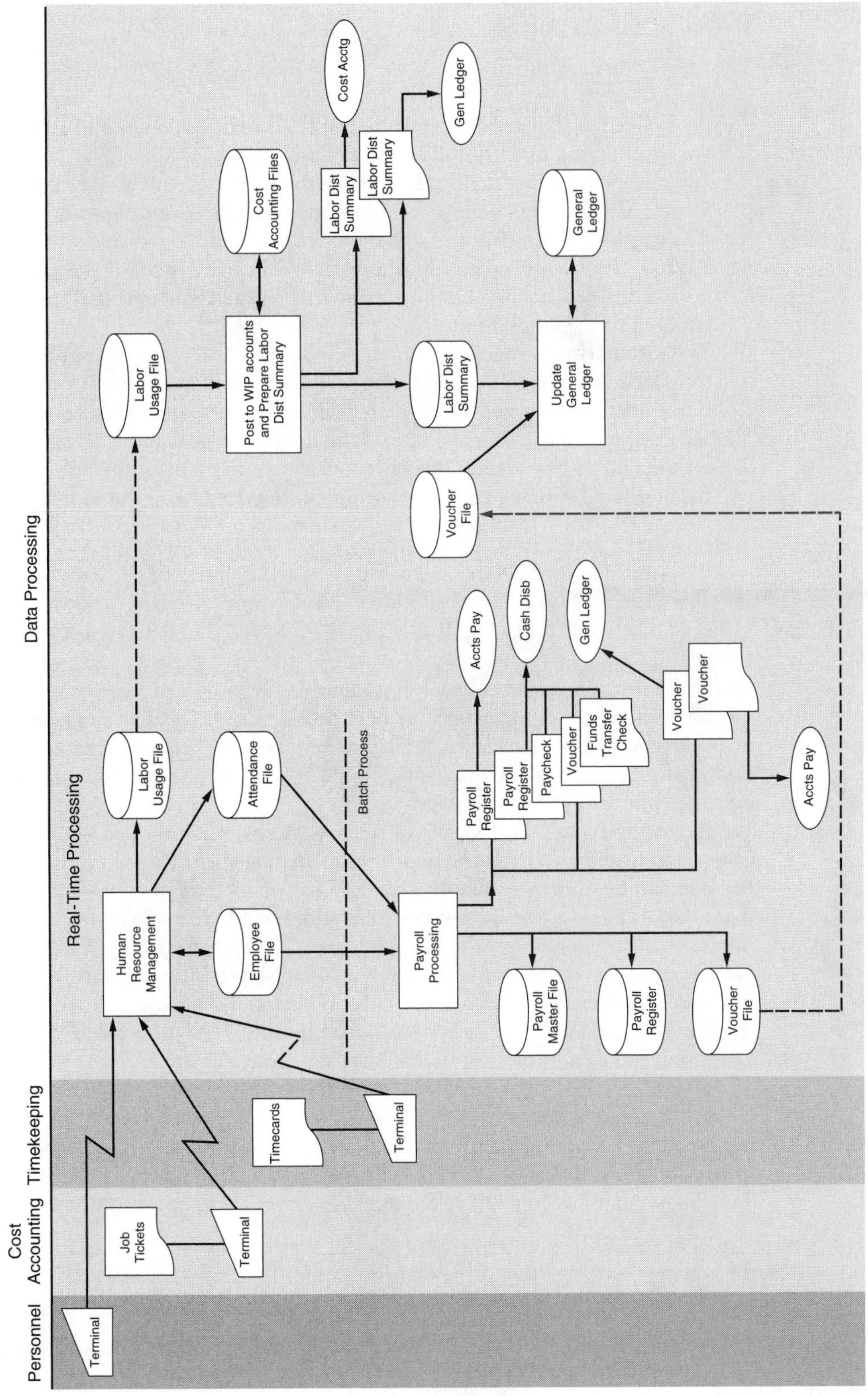

Data Processing. At the end of the work period, the following tasks are performed in a batch process:

1. Labor costs are distributed to various work-in-process, overhead, and expense accounts.
2. An online labor distribution summary file is created. Copies of the file go to the cost accounting and general ledger departments.
3. An online payroll register is created from the attendance file and the **employee file.** Copies of the files go to the accounts payable and cash disbursements departments.
4. The employee records file is updated.
5. Payroll checks are prepared and signed. They are sent to the treasurer for review and reconciliation with the payroll register. The paychecks are then distributed to the employees.[2]
6. The disbursement voucher file is updated and a check is prepared for the funds transfer to the payroll imprest account.[3] The check and a hard copy of the disbursement voucher go to cash disbursements. One copy of the voucher goes to the general ledger department, and the final copy goes to accounts payable.
7. At the end of processing, the system retrieves the labor distribution summary file and the disbursements voucher file and updates the general ledger file.

Expenditure Cycle Audit Objectives, Controls, and Tests of Controls

Chapter 1 introduced the concept of audit objectives derived from general management assertions about financial statement presentation. The assertions are existence or occurrence, completeness, accuracy, rights and obligations, valuation or allocation, and presentation and disclosure. Table 10-1 shows how these translate to specific expenditure cycle audit objectives.

Achieving these audit objectives requires designing audit procedures to gather evidence that either corroborates or refutes management assertions. As we saw in the last chapter, this often involves a combination of tests of controls and substantive tests of details. The specific controls addressed here are based on the application controls framework presented in Chapter 7, which classifies controls into three broad categories: input controls, process controls, and output controls. Within this framework, we examine application controls, tests of controls, and the audit objectives to which they relate. Substantive tests and their relationship to management assertions and corresponding audit objectives are considered later in the chapter.

Input Controls

Input controls are designed to ensure that transactions are valid, accurate, and complete. Control techniques vary considerably between batch and real-time systems. The following input controls relate to expenditure cycle operations.

2 For added internal control, many companies encourage their employees to have their checks directly deposited in their bank accounts.

3 An imprest account is established at a specified, predetermined amount of the total payroll. When all paychecks clear, the account balance is 0.

TABLE 10-1 Relationship Between Management Assertions and Expenditure Cycle Audit Objectives

Management Assertions	Expenditure Cycle Audit Objectives
Existence or Occurrence	Verify that the accounts payable balance represents amounts actually owed by the organization at the balance sheet date. Establish that purchases transactions represent goods and services actually received during the period covered by the financial statements. Determine that payroll transactions represent wages for services actually performed during the period covered by the financial statements.
Completeness	Determine that accounts payable represent all amounts owed by the organization for purchases of goods and services as of the balance sheet date. Ensure that the financial statements reflect all goods and services received by the organization, less returns, for the period covered. Verify that the financial statements reflect all wages for services performed during the period covered.
Accuracy	Establish that purchases transactions are accurately computed and based on correct prices and correct quantities. Ensure that the accounts payable subsidiary ledger is mathematically correct and agrees with the general ledger accounts. Verify that payroll amounts are based on correct pay rates and hours worked and are accurately computed.
Rights and Obligations	Establish that the accounts payable and accrued payroll recorded at the balance sheet date are legal obligations of the organization.
Valuation or Allocation	Verify that accounts payable are stated at correct amounts owed.
Presentation and Disclosure	Ensure that accounts payable, accrued payroll, and expenses reported for the period are properly described and classified in the financial statements.

Data Validation Controls

Input validation controls are intended to detect transcription errors in transaction data before they are processed. Since errors detected early are less likely to infiltrate the accounting records, validation procedures are most effective when they are performed as close to the source of the transaction as possible. In the batch purchases system depicted in Figure 10-1, validation of purchase orders occurs only after they have been sent to the vendor. Because of inevitable transcription errors that occur in preparation of source documents, such systems are characterized by the need for extensive error correction and transaction resubmission procedures. On the other hand, the real-time input of timecard data illustrated in Figure 10-6 can identify and resolve most errors as they occur. This approach also minimizes human data entry and thus reduces the risk of data entry errors. For example, when the clerk enters the employee number, the system automatically retrieves his or her name, mailing address, pay rate, and other relevant data from the employee file.

Chapter 7 presented a number of general types of validation tests. Examples that are relevant to the expenditure cycle are reviewed in the following paragraphs.

Missing data checks are used to examine the contents of a field for the presence of blank spaces. An employee number missing from an attendance record, the quantity-received value missing from a receiving report, or an incomplete mailing address in a purchase order record will cause the transaction to be rejected. When the validation program detects a blank where it expects to see a data value, this situation will be interpreted as an error.

Numeric-alphabetic data checks determine whether the correct form of data is in a field. For example, the quantity field in a purchase order should not contain alphabetic data. As with blanks, alphabetic data in a numeric field may cause serious processing errors.

Limit checks determine if the value in the field exceeds an authorized limit. For example, if the firm has a policy that no employee works more than 44 hours per week, the payroll system validation program can interrogate the hours-worked field in the weekly payroll records for values greater than 44.

Range checks assign upper and lower limits to acceptable data values. This technique can be used to control orders placed with vendors. For example, a range of 500 to 1,000 units can be set as the normal order quantity for a particular class of product. A range check is also useful for controlling payroll transactions. If the range of pay rates for hourly employees in a firm is between $8 and $20, all payroll records can be checked to see that this range is not exceeded. The purpose of this control is to detect keystroke errors that shift the decimal point one or more places. It would not detect an error where a correct pay rate of, say, $9 is incorrectly entered as $15.

Validity checks compare actual values in a field against known acceptable values. This control is used to verify such things as state abbreviations or employee job skill codes. If the value in the field does not match one of the acceptable values, the record is determined to be in error.

Check digit controls identify keystroke errors in key fields by testing their internal validity. A check digit could be used to verify a vendor number on a purchase order record.

Testing Validation Controls

Data entry errors that slip through edit programs undetected can cause recorded accounts payable and expense amounts to be materially misstated. The following audit procedures provide evidence about the accuracy assertion.

The central audit issue is whether the validation programs in the data editing system are functioning correctly and have functioned as intended throughout the period. Testing the logic of a validation program, however, represents a significant undertaking. The auditor may decide to rely on the quality of other controls to provide the assurance needed to reduce substantive testing. For example, after reviewing systems development and maintenance controls, the auditor may determine that controls over original program design and testing and subsequent changes to programs are effective. This evidence permits the auditor to assess the risk of material program errors at a low level and thus reduce the substantive tests related to the audit objective of accuracy.

If controls over systems development and maintenance are weak, however, the auditor may decide that testing data editing controls will be more efficient than performing extensive substantive tests of details. In such a case, ITF or the test data approach can enable the auditor to perform explicit tests of the validation logic. This testing would require the auditor to gain a familiarity with all of the validation procedures in place. The auditor would need to create a comprehensive set of test transactions that include both valid and erroneous data values that fall within and outside of the test parameters. An analysis of the test results will show the auditor which types of errors, if any, can pass undetected by the validation program. This evidence will help the auditor determine the nature, timing, and extent of subsequent substantive tests.

In addition to direct testing of program logic, the auditor can achieve some degree of assurance by reviewing error listings and error logs. These documents provide evidence of the effectiveness of the data entry process, the types and volume of errors encountered, and the manner in which the errors are corrected and reentered into the system. Recall from the last chapter that error listings and logs do not provide evidence of undetected errors. An analysis of error conditions not present in the listing can, however, guide the auditor in designing substantive tests to perform. For example, assume that the error listing of the purchase order file contains no order-quantity range errors. This fact may simply mean that data entry personnel are skilled and no transcription errors of that sort occurred. On the other hand, it may mean that the validation program does not test for this type of error. To determine whether material order-quantity discrepancies existed, the auditor can perform substantive tests that compare the actual quantity ordered on purchase orders with the order-quantity data stored in the inventory records.

Batch Controls

Batch controls are used to manage high volumes of transaction data through a system. The objective of batch control is to reconcile output produced by the system with the input originally entered into the system. Batch control is initiated at the data input stage and continues through all phases of data processing. For example, a batch of supplier invoices enters the system at the data entry stage; after each subsequent processing stage, the batch is reviewed for completeness.

The information contained in the transmittal sheet is entered as a separate control record that the system uses to verify the integrity of the batch. Periodic reconciliation between the data in the transmittal record and actual processing results provides assurance of the following:

- All invoices that were entered into the system were processed.
- No invoices were processed and paid more than once.
- All invoices entered into the system are accounted for as either successfully processed or rejected because of errors.

Testing Batch Controls

The failure of batch controls to function properly can result in records being lost or processed multiple times. Tests of batch controls provide the auditor with evidence relating to the assertions of *completeness* and *accuracy*.

Testing batch controls involves reviewing transmittal records of batches processed throughout the period and reconciling them to the batch control log. The auditor needs to investigate out-of-balance conditions to determine their cause. For example, assume that the transmittal record for a batch of supplier invoices shows that 100 records with an invoice total of $285,458.86 entered the system. The completed batch log, however, shows that 101 records were processed with a batch total of $288,312.50. What caused this anomaly? Did the system process one record twice, due to a programming error? Was an extra record entered into the system during processing? Did the data entry clerk incorrectly calculate the batch control totals? By reviewing and reconciling transaction listings and error logs, the auditor should be able to obtain answers to these questions.

Purchases Authorization Controls

Purchases authorization actually occurs in the revenue cycle when goods are sold to customers. At that time, the system compares the quantity on hand with the reorder point to determine if the inventory needs to be reordered. If so, a purchases requisition for the standard order quantity is created and the item is flagged "On Order" to prevent subsequent orders from being placed. In the expenditure cycle, the purchase requisition file is sorted by vendor number and purchases orders are then prepared.

Testing Purchases Authorization Controls

Incorrectly functioning purchase authorization controls can cause unnecessary and incorrect orders to be placed with vendors. The following tests of controls provide evidence pertaining to the *accuracy* and *valuation* assertions.

Since purchase requisitions are internally generated, they should be free from clerical errors and do not need validating. However, computer logic errors in this procedure can cause negative operational and financial consequences that may go undetected. Two concerns are of particular importance. First, the auditor needs to verify that the correct order quantity is used when a requisition is created. Errors in programming logic (or data entry) may cause an intended order quantity of 1,000 to be recorded as 100 or 10,000. This sort of error can result in unanticipated stockouts, excessive ordering costs, or overinvestment in inventory. Second, the auditor should verify that the inventory record is flagged "On Order" when a requisition is first prepared. Failure to do so will result in overinvestment in inventory due to multiple orders being placed for the same item. Testing these controls using CAATTs involves creating test inventory records and sales transactions that reduce the inventory items below their reorder point. The resulting purchase requisitions and inventory records can then be examined for evidence of properly functioning controls.

Employee Authorization

The personnel department prepares and submits personnel action forms to the payroll department. These documents are used to effect changes in hourly pay rates, payroll deductions, and job classification. They also identify employees who are authorized to receive a paycheck. This information plays an important role in preventing errors and payroll fraud. A common form of fraud is to submit timecards on behalf of employees who are not employed by the firm. To prevent this kind of fraud, someone in the payroll department should be designated to compare timecards with the list of authorized employees sent from personnel. Another common fraud is to create checks for "ghost" employees. The authorization of employees should be done in such a way as to help prevent this kind of fraud.

When employee authorization procedures are computerized, the payroll program matches each attendance record with a corresponding record in the current personnel action file. Any attendance records that do not match should be rejected and investigated by management.

Testing Employee Authorization Procedures

Failure to implement employee authorization procedures can result in payroll distributions to unauthorized individuals. The following tests of controls provide evidence pertaining to the *existence, accuracy, valuation,* and *rights and obligation* assertions.

The auditor needs to determine that effective procedures exist in the personnel department to identify current employees, communicate their status completely and correctly to the payroll function, and monitor adherence to employee authorization procedures. Using either the test data or integrated test facility (ITF) approaches, the auditor can assess the correctness of programmed procedures that validate employee authenticity. This testing involves creating a dummy authorized employee file and a corresponding attendance file containing both records that match and some that do not. The auditor can analyze the processing results to determine if the payroll application correctly identified and rejected the invalid transactions.

The integrity of standing data is an important consideration in the preceding test. A correctly functioning payroll application cannot successfully validate payroll transactions if the authorized employee file is itself invalid. The auditor can obtain assurance that the file has integrity when the following controls exist: access to the authorized employee file is password controlled; additions to and deletions from the file are restricted to authorized individuals in the personnel department; and the employee records stored on the file are encrypted.

PROCESS CONTROLS

Process controls include computerized procedures for updating files and restricting access to data. Depending on the level of computer technology in place, process controls may also include physical controls associated with manual activities. We begin by examining three control techniques related to file updating. Access and physical controls are examined later.

File Update Controls

Run-to-run controls use batch control data discussed in the previous section to monitor the batch as it moves from one programmed procedure (run) to another. These controls ensure that each run in the system processes the batch correctly and completely. After each major operation, key fields such as invoice amount and record counts are accumulated and compared to the corresponding values stored in the transmittal record. A discrepancy may indicate that a record was lost in processing, a record in the batch went unprocessed, or a record was processed more than once.

Sequence Check Control. In systems that use sequential master files (mostly legacy systems), the order of the transaction records in the batch is critical to correct and complete processing. As the batch moves through the process, it must be re-sorted in the order of the master file used in each run. An out-of-sequence supplier's invoice record in a batch will prevent other downstream records from being processed. In more serious cases, the downstream records may be processed against the wrong suppliers' accounts. A sequence check control needs to be in place to compare the sequence of each record in the batch with the previous record to ensure that proper sorting took place. Out-of-sequence records should be rejected and resubmitted, thus allowing the other records in the batch to be processed.

Liability Validation Control. An important control in purchases/accounts payable systems is the validation of the liability prior to making payment. The process involves reconciling supporting documents including the purchase order, receiving report, and supplier's invoice. When these documents agree as to the items and quantities ordered and received, and the prices charged match the expected prices, then a liability (account payable) should be recognized and recorded. At a future date, cash will be disbursed to pay the liability.

In business environments where discrepancies in prices charged and quantities received are commonplace, the validation process is difficult to automate. Programmed decision rules must be implemented to accept less-than-perfect matches between supporting documents. For example, the system may be designed to accept invoice prices that are within five percent of expected prices. Discrepancies in the items and quantities ordered and received, however, are more difficult to resolve. Dealing with these problems often requires reordering inventory and/or making adjustments to accounts payable records. In this type of business setting, many organizations employ manual procedures for reconciling supporting documents and validating the liability.

Trading partner relationships (such as the Ford example described earlier) stabilize the business environment and permit organizations to depart from traditional accounting procedures. Because prices, quantities, and product quality are guaranteed by the trading partner agreement, the liability validation process can be greatly simplified and automated. For example, matching the receiving report to the original purchase order is all that is necessary to establish the liability.

Valid Vendor File. The **valid vendor file** is similar to the authorized employee file discussed earlier. This file consists of a list of vendors with whom the organization normally does business. Fraudulent transactions in the expenditure cycle often culminate in a payment to someone posing as a legitimate vendor. Before payment, the recipient of the cash disbursement should be validated against the valid vendor file. Any record that does not match should be rejected and investigated by management.

Testing File Update Controls. Failure of file update controls to function properly can result in transactions (1) not being processed (liabilities are not recognized and recorded), (2) being processed incorrectly (i.e., payments are approved for unauthorized recipients), or (3) being posted to the wrong supplier's account. Tests of file update controls provide the auditor with evidence relating to the management assertions of *existence, completeness, rights and obligations,* and *accuracy*.

Tests of sequence checks can be performed using either ITF or the test data approach. The auditor should create test data that contain records that are out of sequence in the batch and verify that each was handled correctly. In addition, the auditor needs to verify the mathematical correctness of the procedure. For example, a receiving report record of 1,000 units of product costing $10,000 should increase the quantity-on-hand of that inventory item by 1,000 units and increase its total carrying value by $10,000. Similarly, a payroll record of $1,000 updating an employee's year-to-date earnings record of $10,000 should produce a new balance of $11,000.

Testing the liability validation logic requires understanding the decision rule for matching supporting documents. By creating test purchase orders, receiving reports, and supplier invoices, the auditor can verify whether decision rules are being correctly applied. Similarly, the ITF and test data methods can be used to test the effectiveness of valid vendor control. This testing involves creating a reference file of valid vendors and a file of supplier invoices (accounts payable) to be paid. Invoice records with vendor numbers that do not match a valid vendor record should be rejected by the program and passed to an error file for management review.

The efficient use of logic-testing CAATTs such as ITF requires determining in advance the input and process controls to be tested. A single audit procedure can be devised that performs many or all of the needed tests. For example, when testing payroll, a single transaction that tests employee authorization controls, sequence checks, and mathematical accuracy can provide evidence that supports multiple audit objectives.

Access Controls

Access controls prevent and detect unauthorized and illegal access to the firm's assets. Inventories and cash are the physical assets of the expenditure cycle. Traditional techniques used to limit access to these assets include:

- Warehouse security, such as fences, alarms, and guards.
- Moving assets promptly from the receiving dock to the warehouse.
- Paying employees by check rather than cash.

Controlling access to accounting records is no less important. An individual with unrestricted access to data can manipulate the physical assets of the firm and cause financial statements to be materially misstated. Accounting files stored on magnetic media are particularly vulnerable to unauthorized access, whether its cause is accidental, an act of malice by a disgruntled employee, or an attempt at fraud. The following are examples of risks specific to the expenditure cycle:

1. An individual with access to the AP subsidiary ledger (and supporting documents) could add his or her account (or someone else's) to the file. Once recognized by the system as a legitimate liability, the account will be paid even though no purchase transaction transpired.
2. Access to employee attendance cards may enable an unauthorized individual to trigger an unauthorized paycheck.
3. An individual with access to both cash and accounts payable records could remove cash from the firm and record the act as a legitimate disbursement.
4. An individual with access to physical inventory and inventory records can steal products and adjust the records to cover the theft.

Testing Access Controls

Access control lies at the heart of accounting information integrity. In the absence of adequate controls, supplier invoices can be deleted, added, or falsified. Individual payroll account balances can be erased or the entire accounts payable file can be destroyed. Evidence gathered about the effectiveness of access controls tests the management assertions of *existence, completeness, accuracy, valuation and allocation, rights and obligations*, and *presentation and disclosure.*

Since payments to false vendors carries such potential for material loss, the auditor is concerned about the integrity of the valid vendor file. By gaining access to the file, a computer criminal can place his or her name on it and masquerade as an authorized vendor. The auditor should therefore assess the adequacy of access controls protecting the file. These include password controls, restricting access to authorized managers, and using data encryption to prevent the file contents from being read or changed.

As discussed in previous chapters, computer access controls are both system-wide and application-specific. Access control includes controlling access to the operating systems, the networks, and the databases with which all applications interact. The auditors will typically test these controls as part of their review of general controls.

Physical Controls

Physical controls include manual activities and human actions to initiate computer procedures to safeguard the assets of the organization. The relevant physical controls for the purchases and payroll systems follow.

Purchases System Controls

- *Segregation of inventory control from the warehouse.* The primary assets at risk in the expenditure cycle are inventory and cash. Warehouse clerks responsible for asset custody should not be given responsibility for maintaining inventory records. Otherwise, inventory could be removed from the warehouse and the accounting records adjusted to conceal the event.
- *Segregation of the general ledger and accounts payable from cash disbursements.* An individual with the combined responsibilities of writing checks, posting to the cash account, and maintaining accounts payable could perpetrate fraud against the firm. An individual with such access could withdraw cash and then adjust the cash account accordingly to hide the transaction. Also, he or she could establish fraudulent accounts payable (to an associate in a nonexistent vendor company) and then write checks to discharge the phony obligations. By segregating these functions, the organization's management can greatly reduce this exposure.
- *Supervision of receiving department.* Large quantities of valuable assets flow through the receiving department on their way to the warehouse. Close supervision here reduces the chances of two types of exposure: failure to properly inspect the assets and the theft of assets.
    - *Inspection of assets.* When goods arrive from the supplier, receiving clerks must inspect items for proper quantities and condition (damage, spoilage, and so on). For this reason, the receiving clerk receives a blind copy of the original purchase order from purchasing. A blind purchase order has all the relevant information about the goods being received except for the quantities and prices. To obtain the information on quantities, which is needed for the receiving report, the receiving personnel are forced to physically count and inspect the goods. If receiving clerks were provided with quantity information through formal documentation (i.e., the purchase order), they may be tempted to transfer this information to the receiving report without performing a physical count. Inspecting and counting the items received protects the firm from incomplete orders and damaged goods. Supervision is critical at this point to ensure that the clerks properly carry out these important duties. Incoming goods are accompanied by a packing slip containing quantity information that could be used to circumvent the inspection process. A supervisor should take custody of the packing slip while receiving clerks count and inspect the goods.
    - *Theft of assets.* Receiving departments are sometimes hectic and cluttered during busy periods. In this environment, incoming inventories are

exposed to theft until they are securely placed in the warehouse. Improper inspection procedures coupled with inadequate supervision can create a situation that is conducive to the theft of inventories in transit.

- *Reconciliation of supporting documents.* The accounts payable department plays a vital role in controlling the disbursement of cash to vendors. Copies of supporting documents flow into this department for review and comparison. Each document contains unique facts about the purchase transaction, which the accounts payable clerk needs to verify before the obligation is recognized.
    - *The purchase order*, which shows that the purchasing agent ordered only the needed inventories from a valid vendor.[4]
    - *The receiving report*, which is evidence of the physical receipt of the goods, their condition, and the quantities received. The reconciliation of this document with the purchase order signifies the point of realization of the obligation.
    - *The supplier's invoice*, which provides the financial information needed to record this obligation as an account payable. The accounts payable clerk verifies that the prices on the invoice are reasonable (in compliance with organizational policy) compared with the expected prices stated on the purchase order.

Payroll System Controls

- *Verification of timecards.* The **timecard** is the formal record of daily attendance. Each day at the beginning of the shift, employees place their timecards in a special clock that records arrival. They clock out for their lunch period and at the end of the shift. Before sending timecards to payroll, the supervisor must verify their accuracy and sign them.
- *Supervision.* Sometimes an employee will clock in for another worker who is late or absent. Supervisors should observe the clocking process and reconcile the timecards with actual attendance.
- *Paymaster.* The use of an independent **paymaster** to distribute checks (rather than the normal supervisor) helps verify the existence of the employees. This control is useful in uncovering a fraud whereby the supervisor is pretending to distribute paychecks to nonexistent employees.
- *Payroll imprest account.* Employee paychecks are drawn on a special **payroll imprest** bank account, which is used only for payroll. Funds must be transferred from the general cash account to this imprest account before the paychecks can be cashed. The amount of the funds transfer is determined from the payroll register, which is reviewed for correctness and approved by accounts payable. The imprest account technique physically limits the organization's exposure. Individual checks that exceed the imprest amount will not clear. This result will expose the existence of checks written in error (duplicates) or created through fraudulent activities.

---

4 Firms often establish a list of valid vendors with whom they do regular business. Purchasing agents must acquire inventories only from valid vendors. This technique deters certain types of fraud such as an agent buying from suppliers with whom he or she has a relationship (a relative or friend) or buying at excessive prices from vendors in exchange for a kickback or bribe.

Testing Physical Controls

Inadequate segregation of duties and lack of supervision can result in fraud and errors that can cause financial statements to be materially misstated. The exposure issues here are similar to the access control issues discussed earlier. Granting inappropriate access privileges is often due to assigning incompatible duties to an individual. Similarly, the purpose of collusion is to achieve unauthorized access to assets as well as the information needed to conceal the crime. Evidence gathered by reviewing the segregation of duties can be used to test *all* of the management assertions outlined in Table 10-1.

The auditor's review of organizational structure should disclose the more egregious examples of incompatible tasks, such as one individual opening and approving timecards, authorizing employee payments, and receiving and distributing the paychecks. Covert relationships that may lead to collusion may not be apparent from an organizational chart. For example, married employees (or those otherwise related) who work in incompatible areas may go unnoticed. The auditor should determine whether the organization has an effective policy for dealing with nepotism.

Many tasks that are normally segregated in manual systems are consolidated in the data processing function of computer-based systems. Computer programs in the expenditure cycle authorize purchases, place orders, update inventory records, approve payments to vendors, and write the checks. In automated environments, the auditor's concern should focus on the integrity of the computer programs that perform these tasks. The following questions need to be answered: Is the logic of the computer program correct? Has anyone tampered with the application since it was last tested? Have changes been made to the program that could have caused an undisclosed error? Are there adequate formal procedures (i.e., supervision) to compensate for the lack of segregation of duties? These formal procedures could be reports, especially error reports, sent directly to the supervisor.

Answers to these questions come from the auditor's review of systems development and maintenance controls and by reviewing organizational structure. Recall from earlier chapters that duties pertaining to the design, maintenance, and operation of computer programs need to be separated. Programmers who write the original computer programs should not be responsible for making program changes. Also, individuals who operate the computer system should not perform systems design, programming, or maintenance activities. Personal relationships (i.e., marriage) between individuals in these incompatible areas may require further investigation.

Output Controls

Output controls are designed to ensure that information is not lost, misdirected, or corrupted and that system processes function as intended. For example, daily summaries of cash disbursements to vendors and inventory receipts should go to managers to report the status of their operations. Output control can be designed to identify operational and internal control problems. For example, an exception report derived from the Suppliers Invoice (accounts payable) file listing past-due liabilities can identify discounts lost and help management assess the operational performance of the accounts payable process. Output, however, is not limited to end-of-day reporting. System output is also needed at intermediate junctures where processing accuracy can be reviewed and verified and errors can be detected quickly and corrected.

Reconciling the general ledger can detect certain types of transaction processing errors. For example, the total of all reductions to accounts payable should equal the total cash disbursements to vendors. A cash disbursement that is entered in the journal but not posted to the vendor's account would be detected by an imbalance in the general ledger. The specific cause of an out-of-balance condition may not be apparent at this point, but the error would be noted. Finding the error may require examining all the transactions processed during the period and could be time consuming. For this reason, rather than summarizing an entire day's transactions in a single batch, entities often group transactions into small batches of 50 to 100 items. This process facilitates reconciling balances by isolating a problem to a specific batch.

Another important element of output control is the maintenance of an audit trail. Details of transaction processing produced at intermediate points can provide an audit trail that reflects activity through every stage of operations. The following are examples of audit trail output controls.

Accounts Payable Change Report

This document is a summary report that shows the overall change to accounts payable. These figures should reconcile with total vendor invoices received, total cash disbursements, and the general ledger.

Transaction Logs

Every transaction successfully processed by the system should be recorded on a **transaction log**, which serves as a journal. Transactions rejected because of input errors should be placed in an error file, corrected, and resubmitted. The transaction log and error files together thus account for all economic activity.

Transaction Listing

The system should produce a (hard copy) **transaction listing** of all successful transactions. Listings should go to the appropriate users to facilitate reconciliation with input. For example, a listing of cash disbursements processed will go to the controller to be used for the bank reconciliation.

Log of Automatic Transactions

Some transactions are triggered internally by the system. For example, EDI purchase orders are initiated and processed without human authorization. To maintain an audit trail of these activities, all internally generated transactions must be placed in a transaction log, and a listing of these transactions should be sent to the appropriate manager for review.

Unique Transaction Identifiers

Each transaction processed by the system must be uniquely identified with a transaction number. This feature is the only practical means of tracing a particular transaction through a database of thousands or even millions of records. In systems that use physical purchase orders, the unique number printed on the document can be transcribed during data input and used for this purpose. In real-time systems, which do not use source documents, each purchase order should be assigned a unique number by the system.

Error Listing

A listing of all error records should go to the appropriate user to support error correction and resubmission.

Testing Output Controls

The absence of adequate output controls has adverse implications for operational efficiency and financial reporting. Evidence gathered through tests of output controls relates to the *completeness* and *accuracy* assertions.

Testing output controls involves reviewing summary reports for accuracy, completeness, timeliness, and relevance to the decision that they are intended to support. In addition, the auditor should trace sample transactions through audit trail reports, including transaction listings, error logs, and logs of resubmitted records. Gathering such evidence, however, may involve sorting through thousands of transactions.

In modern systems, audit trails are usually stored online as text files that can be read by word processing and spreadsheet programs. Data extraction CAATTs such as ACL are capable of searching log files for specific records to verify completeness and accuracy of the output reports. Alternatively, the auditor can test output controls directly using ITF. A well-designed ITF system will permit the auditor to produce a batch of sample transactions, including some error records, and trace them through all phases of processing, error detection, and output reporting.

SUBSTANTIVE TESTS OF EXPENDITURE CYCLE ACCOUNTS

This section deals with the substantive tests that an auditor may perform to achieve audit objectives related to the expenditure cycle. The strategy used in determining the nature, timing, and extent of substantive tests derives from the auditor's assessment of inherent risk, unmitigated control risk, materiality considerations, and the need to conduct the audit in an efficient manner.

EXPENDITURE CYCLE RISKS AND AUDIT CONCERNS

Taking the most narrow attest-function view, external auditors are concerned primarily with the potential for understatement of liabilities and related expenses. Reported balances usually consist of items that have been reviewed, validated, and acknowledged by management. Attempts to improve financial statement presentation may involve actions to suppress the recognition and reporting of valid liabilities related to the period under review. Substantive tests of expenditure cycle accounts are therefore directed toward gathering evidence of understatement and omission of material items rather than their overstatement. Broader operational audit concerns, however, include process efficiency, fraud, and losses due to errors. Within this context, overstatement of liabilities and related expenses are also important.

In resolving these concerns, the auditor will seek evidence by performing a combination of tests of internal controls and substantive tests. Tests of controls include testing both general controls (discussed in Chapters 2 through 7) and application controls specifically related to the expenditure cycle. Various application control-testing techniques were examined in Chapter 8 and specific tests related to the expenditure cycle were described in this chapter. In addition to tests of controls, the auditor must perform substantive tests to achieve audit objectives. The remainder of this chapter deals with audit objectives related to expenditure cycle accounts and the substantive tests most commonly performed. Keep in mind that the quality of internal controls bears on the nature and extent of substantive tests determined by the auditor to be necessary. Ordinarily, not all of the following tests will be performed.

Understanding Data

The substantive tests described in this section involve extracting data from accounting files for analysis. To do this task, the auditor needs to understand the systems and controls that produced the data as well as the physical characteristics of the files that contain them. Much of this chapter was devoted to explaining various expenditure cycle configurations and their control implications. Chapter 8 described several common file structures and their audit implications. The discussion that follows presumes that the auditor is using ACL for performing the audit tests. Before we proceed, however, we need to review a few salient points regarding file preparation.

First, the auditor must verify that he or she is working with the correct version of the file to be analyzed. To do so, the auditor must understand the file backup procedures and, whenever possible, work with the original files. Second, ACL can read most sequential files and relational database tables directly, but esoteric and/or complex file structures may require "flattening" before they can be analyzed. This process may involve additional procedures and special programs to produce a copy of the original file in a format that ACL can accept. If the organization's systems personnel perform the flattening process, the auditor must verify that the correct version of the original file was used and that all relevant records from the original were transferred to the copy for analysis.

The discussion that follows presumes that any file copying necessary to produce test data was performed under adequate controls to preserve data integrity. Furthermore, the tests described are applicable to both mainframe and PC environments. The focus of this material is on explaining the logic underlying various substantive tests and on illustrating the functionality of ACL in achieving audit objectives. The audit procedures described are based on the file structure in Figure 10-7. These structures indicate the key data and logical linkages between files. A description of each file follows.

Inventory File

The Inventory file contains quantity, price, supplier, and warehouse location data for each item of product inventory. The purchasing process begins with a review of the inventory records to identify inventory items that need to be ordered. In a retail organization, this step is performed when sales of finished goods to customers are recorded in the inventory records. In this case, the purchasing process involves replenishing the finished goods inventory. Purchasing systems of manufacturing firms replenish raw materials inventory as these items are used in the production process. In either case, when inventory items are sold or used in production, the Quantity-On-Hand field is reduced accordingly by a computer application. With each inventory reduction, the system tests for a "reorder" condition, which occurs when the quantity-on-hand falls below the reorder point. At that time, the system prepares a purchase order, which is sent to the vendor, and adds a record to the Purchase Order file. The quantity-on-hand value will remain below the reorder-point until the inventory is received from the supplier. This process may

FIGURE 10-7 File Structures for the Expenditure Cycle

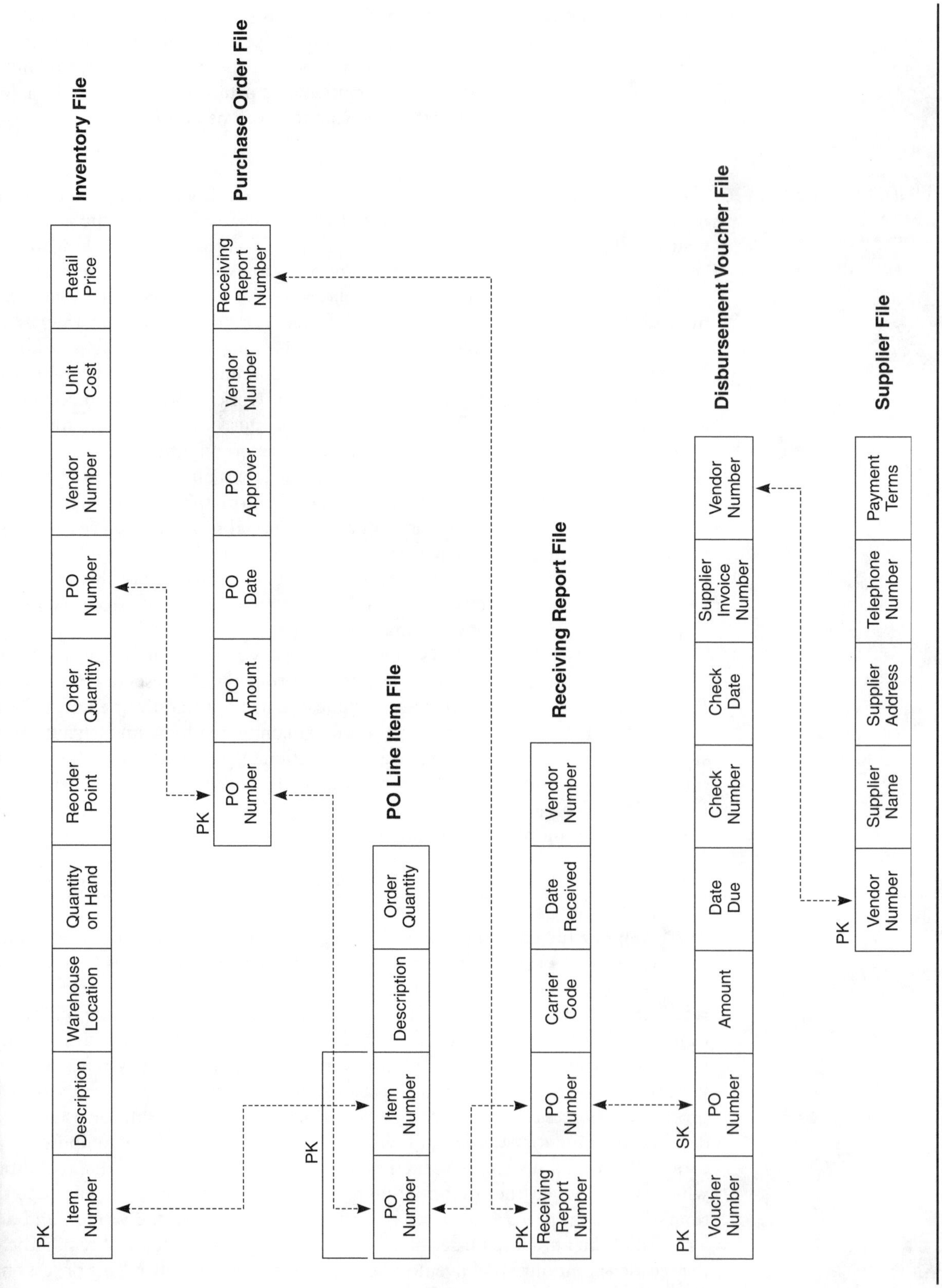

take days or even weeks. To signify that the item is on order and to prevent it from being reordered each time the computer application detects the same reorder condition, a computer-generated purchase order number is placed in the PO-Number field of the inventory record. Normally, this field is blank.

Purchase Order File

This file contains records of purchases placed with suppliers. The record remains open until the inventory arrives. Placing the receiving report number in the dedicated field closes the record.

Purchase Order Line Item File

The Line Item file contains a record of every item ordered. Since a single transaction can involve one or more products, each record in the Purchase Order file is associated with (linked to) one or more records in this file. Notice that the file contains two primary keys—Purchase Order Number and Item Number. Both keys are needed to uniquely define each record in the file. They also provide links to related records in the Purchase Order and Inventory files.

Receiving Report File

When the ordered items arrive from the supplier, they are counted and inspected, and receiving documents are prepared. Via terminal, the receiving clerk enters information about the items received. The system automatically performs the following tasks: (1) increases the Quantity-on-Hand field in the inventory record(s); (2) removes the reorder condition by resetting the PO-Number field to its normal blank state; (3) creates a receiving report record of the event; and (4) closes the purchase order record by placing the receiving report number in the designated field.

Disbursement Voucher File

For most companies, discrepancies between amounts ordered, received, and billed are legitimate concerns that must be resolved before payment to the vendor is approved. Because of its complexity, this reconciliation is often a manual process that is triggered by receipt of the supplier's invoice. The accounts payable clerk reviews the supporting records in the Purchase Order and Receiving Report files and compares them to the invoice. If the items, quantities, and prices match, then a cash disbursement voucher is created. Based on the supplier's terms of trade and the company's payment policy, the payment due date is determined and placed in the voucher record.

Each payment day, the Cash Disbursement application selects the items due, flags them *paid* by entering the current date in the Check-Date field, and cuts the check, which is then mailed to the supplier. The **Disbursement Voucher file** provides three important pieces of information for the auditor: (1) it is a record of the timing and amount of vendor invoices received; (2) it is a journal of checks written in payment of trade accounts for the period; and (3) at any point in time, the open items (unpaid vouchers) in the file constitute the company's outstanding accounts payable balance.

File Preparation Procedures

The data contained in the preceding files provide evidence that may either corroborate or refute audit objectives. Most of the tests described in the following section involve using ACL to access and extract data from these files. Recall from the previous chapter that each file needs to be defined in terms of its physical location and its structure. Through a series of easy-to-use pop-up menus, the auditor specifies the name of the file and where it resides on the mainframe or PC. ACL then prompts the auditor to define the file's structure in terms of the length of each field and the data type contained in each field (i.e., numeric, character, or date). When the data definition is completed, it is saved under a unique name assigned by the auditor. All future file access is accomplished by simply selecting the data definition from an ACL menu. ACL automatically locates the file and presents it on screen, where the auditor can review and manipulate its contents. Figure 10-8 shows a sample ACL data definition screen.

Sometimes the contents of a data field are different from what they are supposed to be. For example, a numeric field in one or more records may contain alphabetic data because of a program error or a clerical mistake. Also, a field may contain corrupted data because of an error in the file-flattening process. Whatever

FIGURE 10-8 **ACL Data Definition Screen**

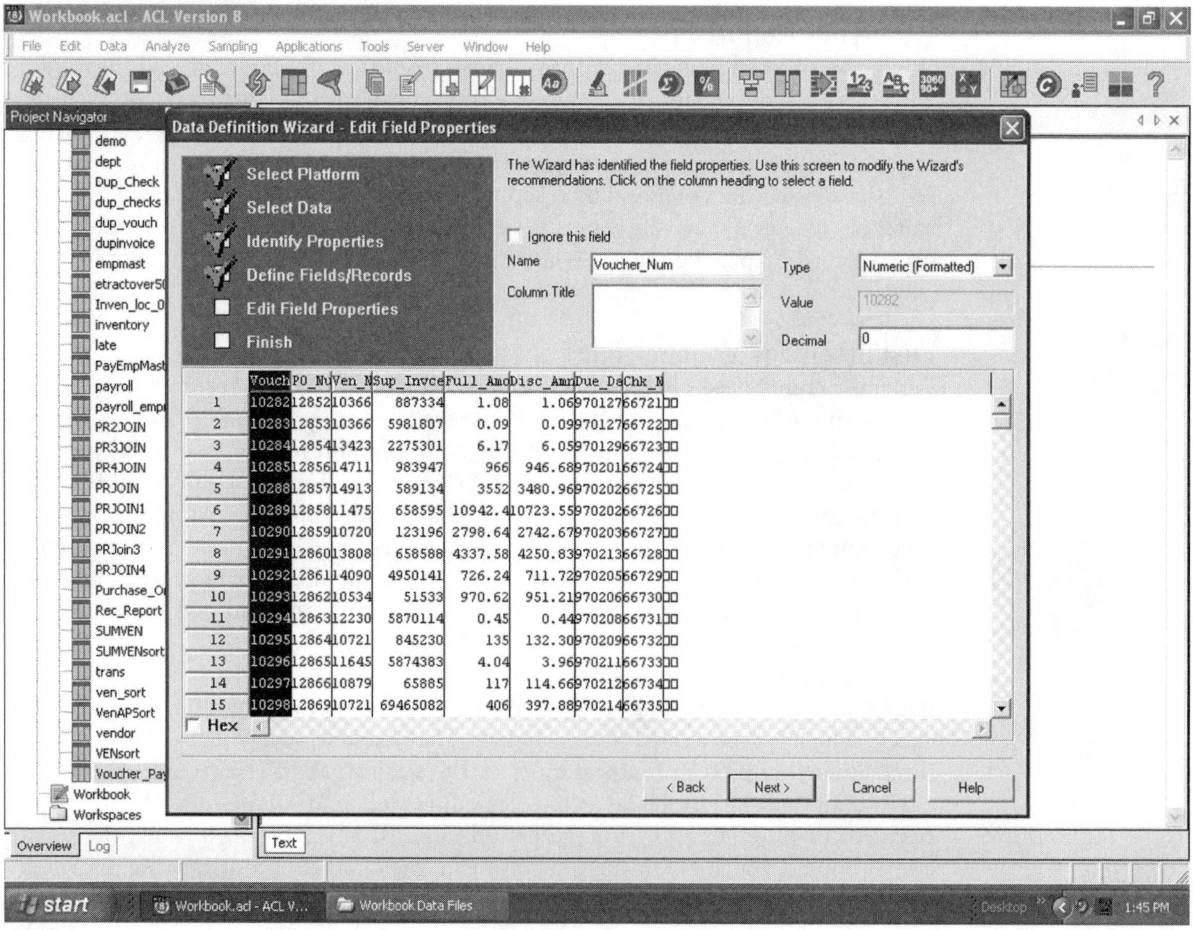

the cause, prior to performing any substantive tests on a new file, it is important that the auditor validate its contents. Invalid data will distort the test results and may cause a system failure. ACL's *Verify* command analyzes the data fields in the selected file to ensure that their contents are consistent with the field type in the file definition. Any validity errors detected by ACL need to be traced to their source and resolved. For purposes of discussion, we will assume that the files used in all tests described hereafter have been properly defined and verified. Figure 10-9 shows the ACL Verify command box.

Testing the Accuracy and Completeness Assertions

The audit procedures described in this section provide evidence relating to management assertions of *accuracy* and *completeness*. We saw in the last chapter that auditors often precede substantive tests of details with an *analytical review* of account balances. Analytical procedures can identify relationships between accounts and risks that are not otherwise apparent. In the case of the expenditure cycle, an analytical review can provide the auditor with an overall perspective for trends in accounts payable and related expenses. Current expenses may be compared to

FIGURE 10-9 ACL Verify Command Box

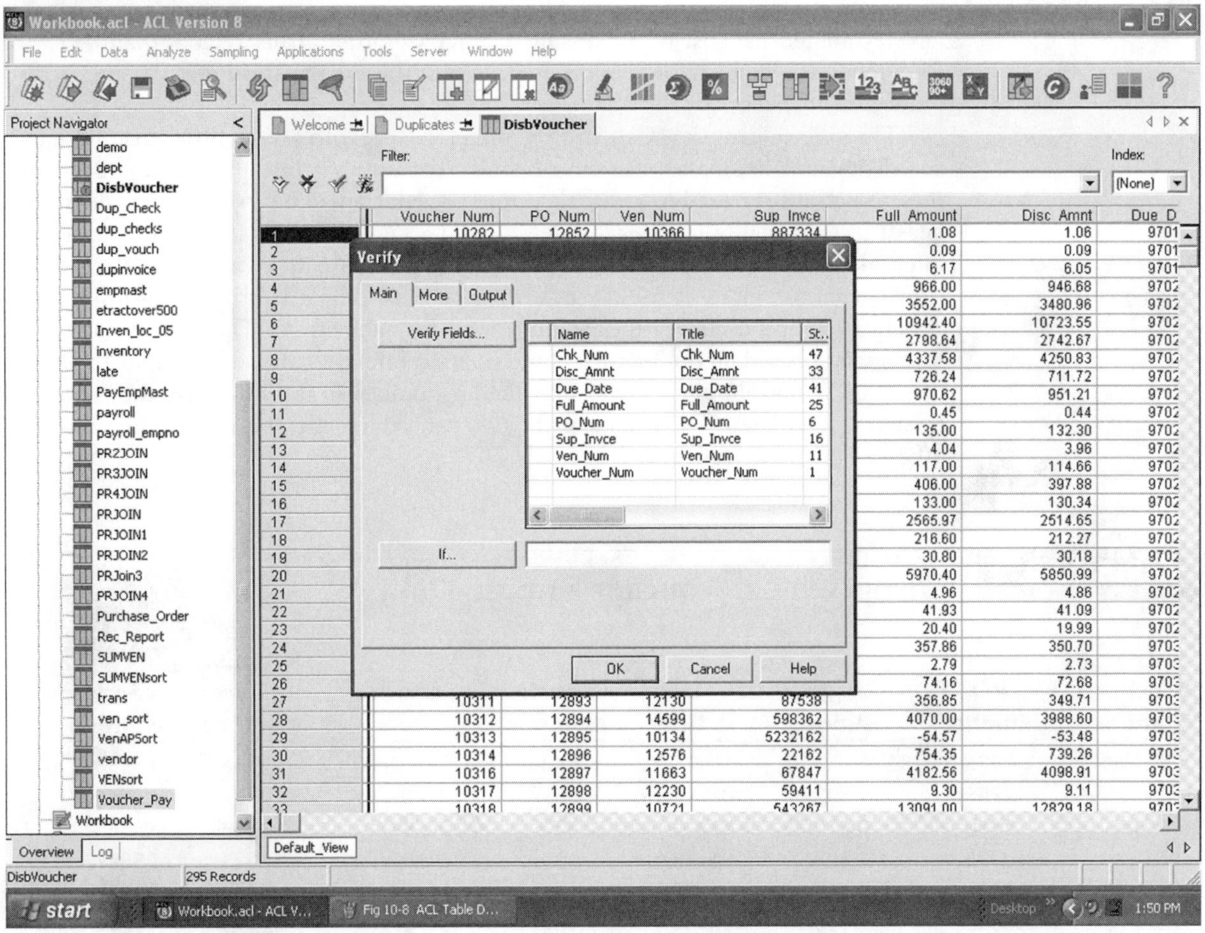

historical expenses and management budgets. For example, the auditor may compare current payroll expenses for the quarter with those for the same period in previous years. Unusual trends or variances should be noted and examined for cause. On the one hand, analytical procedures may indicate trends, even in adequately controlled organizations, that lead the auditor to extend substantive tests. On the other hand, they can provide assurance that transactions and accounts are reasonably stated and complete and may thus permit the auditor to reduce substantive testing.

A medium- to large-sized organization's expenses and accounts payable data may constitute thousands or perhaps millions of records. Unlike analytical procedures, which can be performed without CAATTs, substantive tests of details of such volumes of data cannot be effectively accomplished without using CAATTs. The following substantive tests that can be performed using ACL are based on the file structures depicted in Figure 10-7.

REVIEW DISBURSEMENT VOUCHERS FOR UNUSUAL TRENDS AND EXCEPTIONS

A useful audit procedure for identifying potential audit risks involves scanning data files for unusual transactions and account balances. For example, scanning accounts payable for excessively large balances may indicate abnormal dependency on a particular supplier. However, a high number of vendors with small balances may indicate the need to consolidate business activity. Various corporate surveys have estimated the cost of processing a purchase order at between $50 and $125. Restricting the number of vendors with whom the organization does business can reduce this expense.

The auditor can use ACL's *stratify* and *classify* features to identify various characteristics and anomalies associated with accounts payable procedures. Both of these functions are used to group data into predetermined intervals, count the number of records that fall into each interval, and accumulate a financial value for each interval. The stratify function groups financial data into specific strata. Using data similar to those in Table 10-2, we demonstrate its use for stratifying disbursement vouchers by accumulating the Amount field for each strata. The classify function forms strata based on nonfinancial (and nonnumeric) data. In our example, this feature is used to group the vouchers by vendor number. In this case also, the Amount field is accumulated. The results of the two procedures are presented in Figures 10-10 and 10-11, respectively.

TABLE 10-2 Disbursement Voucher Sample Data

Voucher Number	PO Number	Amount	Due Date	Check Number	Check Date	Supplier Invoice Number	Vendor Number
12655	12923	158.32	12/21/03	6484	01/02/04	1223467	28788
512973	12958	1,802.63	01/15/04	6537	01/09/04	67783pl	15545
511810	12960	10,815.75	01/12/04	6567	01/09/04	88746pl	15545
1064	12998	4,427.99	01/15/04	6571	01/09/04	667223	28847
1060	13002	117,667.60	01/03/04	6611	01/09/04	844001	28847
77696	13006	150.95	12/04/03	6641	01/09/04	po2298	1564485

FIGURE 10-10

Stratified Disbursement Voucher Data

As of: 06/09/2004 14:53:14

Command: STRATIFY ON Full_Amount MINIMUM -7000 MAXIMUM 120000 INTERVALS 10 TO SCREEN
Table: DisbVoucher

Minimum encountered was -584.22
Maximum encountered was 110,035.04

Full_Amount	Count	Percent of Count	Percent of Field	Full_Amount
-7,000.00 - 5,699.99	268	90.85%	15.25%	164,962.05
5,700.00 - 18,399.99	14	4.75%	11.68%	126,341.70
18,400.00 - 31,099.99	0	0%	0%	0.00
31,100.00 - 43,799.99	3	1.02%	10.35%	111,997.56
43,800.00 - 56,499.99	3	1.02%	12.71%	137,496.48
56,500.00 - 69,199.99	3	1.02%	17.31%	187,256.91
69,200.00 - 81,899.99	2	0.68%	14.38%	155,598.63
81,900.00 - 94,599.99	1	0.34%	8.14%	88,051.68
94,600.00 - 107,299.99	0	0%	0%	0.00
107,300.00 - 120,000.00	1	0.34%	10.17%	110,035.04
Totals	295	100%	100%	1,081,740.05

The first report gives the auditor an overall perspective for the nature of the purchasing process. Notice that 91 percent of the total number of disbursement vouchers constitutes only 15 percent of the business volume for the period. The second report shows the business activity associated with individual vendors. Over 40 percent of the organization's purchases are from a single vendor, while most of the other vendors receive only a small percentage of the total business. These findings may reflect a natural business phenomenon, or they may signify potential risks.

Excessive purchases from a single supplier may reflect an unusual business dependency that may prove harmful to the firm if the supplier raises prices or cannot deliver on schedule. This situation may also signify a fraudulent relationship involving kickbacks to purchasing agents or other management.

The large number of small volume suppliers is evidence of a highly inefficient purchasing process. Management may consider reducing the number of suppliers and increasing the size of their order quantities to reduce the number of orders placed. This situation may also be a signal to the auditor that a valid vendor approach to purchasing is *not* in use. It is unlikely that an organization would add vendors to the file for control purposes unless they expect significant levels of business.

Reviewing for Accurate Invoice Prices

Comparing prices on supplier invoices to original purchase order prices provides evidence for testing the management assertion of *accuracy*. Significant discrepancies between expected prices and the prices actually charged may be due to clerical errors, failure to review supporting documents before authorizing payment, or accounts payable personnel exceeding their authority in dealing with price discrepancies.

FIGURE 10-11

Disbursement Voucher Data Classified on Vendor Number

As of: 06/09/2004 14:40:31

Command: CLASSIFY ON Ven_Num SUBTOTAL Full_Amount TO SCREEN
Table: DisbVoucher

Ven_Num	Count	Percent of Count	Percent of Field	Full_Amount
10001	12	4.07%	0.78%	8,441.85
10025	3	1.02%	0%	40.23
10101	1	0.34%	0.01%	120.33
10134	1	0.34%	-0.01%	-54.57
10366	48	16.27%	40.79%	441,293.98
10559	4	1.36%	0.61%	6,548.21
10656	2	0.68%	0.03%	357.54
10787	7	2.37%	0.27%	2,950.73
10879	13	4.41%	0.65%	7,008.51
10951	6	2.03%	0.01%	108.59
11009	1	0.34%	0.01%	72.72
11182	6	2.03%	0.18%	1,964.99
11213	1	0.34%	0%	11.53
11247	7	2.37%	7.27%	78,608.55
11435	4	1.36%	0.06%	651.10
11475	5	1.69%	1.49%	16,091.94
11645	12	4.07%	0.19%	2,068.54
11663	18	6.1%	11.19%	121,010.48
11837	7	2.37%	0.04%	458.52

Traditionally, auditors verify pricing accuracy by comparing invoice prices with the purchase orders on a sample basis only. Of the thousands of invoices processed during the period, perhaps only one or two hundred can be tested manually. ACL allows the auditor to compare the prices charged on every invoice in the file for the period under review. The test will involve the Disbursement Voucher file and the Purchase Order file, which is illustrated with some sample data in Table 10-3.

Testing pricing accuracy involves matching records from the two files using ACL's *Join* feature. This can be accomplished in a few simple steps. First, recall from Chapter 9 that both files being joined need to be ordered on a common key. In this example, PO Number is a common secondary key. Reorganizing both files on this field requires opening each file separately, invoking ACL's sort function, specifying the sort field, and designating the file name to receive the sorted output. The results of this process will be two new files ordered in the same sequence.

TABLE 10-3 Purchase Order File

PO Number	PO Amount	PO Date	PO Approver	Vendor Number	Rec. Rpt Number
12821	493.05	12/16/03	Controller	25152	10134
12838	138.95	01/24/04	PurchMgr	25152	10101
12848	14,463.75	01/10/04	Controller	28847	10787
12891	2,845.57	01/30/04	Controller	28847	11663
12894	252.54	12/06/03	PurchMgr	28529	11922
12946	238.65	12/13/03	PurchMgr	28529	11475
12958	1,802.63	12/16/03	Controller	15545	11668

The next step is to combine the two files to create a third output file. The auditor achieves this with the *Join* command. Several options are available when joining files. The relevant option in this case is to create an output file that consists only of matched records from the two files. ACL's *join* feature permits the auditor to specify the fields from the two input files that are to be passed to the new output file. Usually, it is neither necessary nor desirable to include all fields from both of the original files. In this example, the fields needed from the Purchase Order file to verify pricing accuracy are PO Number and PO Amount; from the Disbursement Voucher file the fields are Voucher Number, Amount, Check Number, and Vendor Number. The file structure of the new combined PO/Disbursement file with some sample records is presented in Table 10-4.

At this point, the resulting file may be quite large. Scanning the file visually for price differences can be time consuming and ineffective. Here again is an application for a *filter*. Using ACL's *Expression Builder* feature, the auditor can easily create a filter that will select only records where PO Amount and Amount are not equal. The resulting file will thus contain only records with price discrepancies. Using other ACL features, the auditor can calculate the total price variance and make a determination as to its materiality. If material, the matter should be pursued with management. Figure 10-12, presents ACL's Expression Builder window.

TABLE 10-4 Combined PO/Disbursement File

PO Number	PO Amount	Voucher Number	Amount	Check Number	Vendor Number
12821	493.05	121655	493.05	6484	25152
12838	138.95	512973	138.95	6537	25152
12848	14,463.75	511810	14,463.75	6537	28847
12891	2,845.57	105436	2,845.57	6541	28847
12894	252.54	102360	252.54	6544	28529
12946	238.65	776756	238.65	6555	28529
12958	1,802.63	514760	1,802.63	6652	15545

FIGURE 10-12 **ACL's Expression Builder**

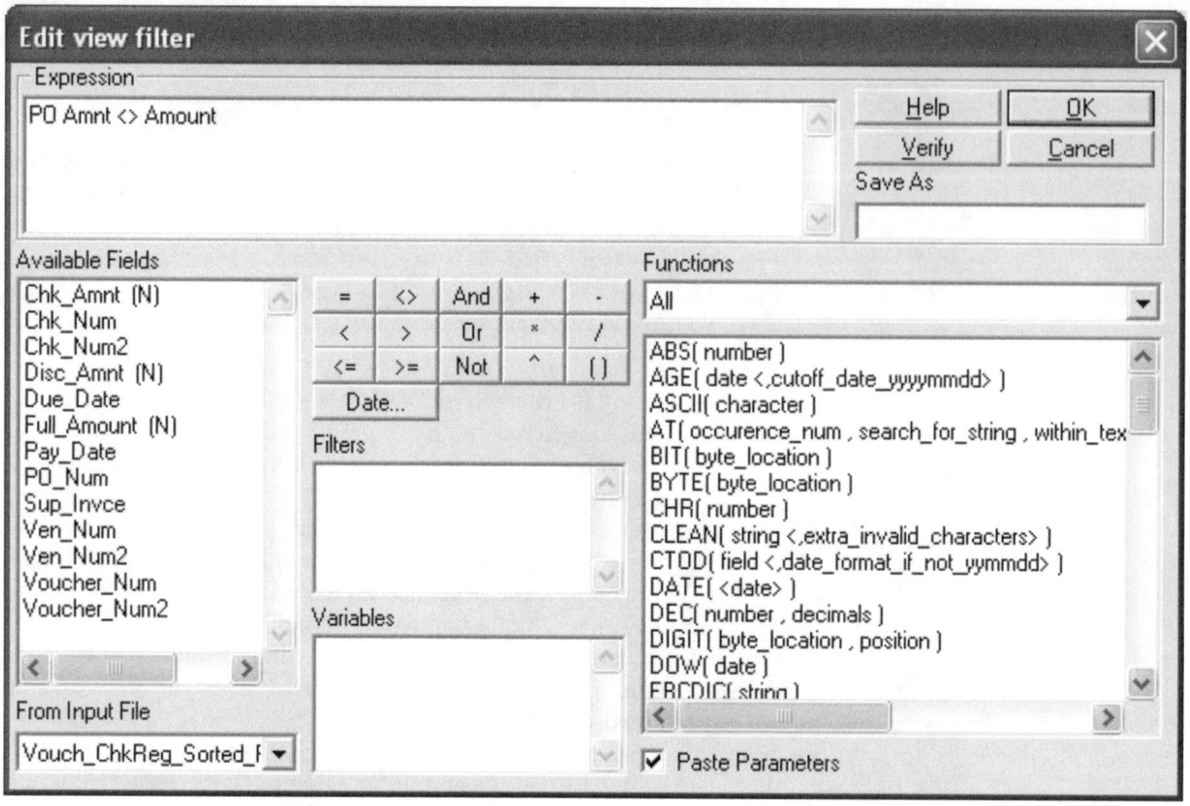

Testing the Completeness, Existence, and Rights and Obligations Assertions

Inventories received from valid suppliers in response to authorized purchase orders constitute liabilities. In most systems, however, the trigger that causes the liability to be recognized and recorded as an account payable (in our example, a disbursement voucher) is the receipt of the supplier's invoice, which often lags the receipt of the merchandise. Normally, the time lag between liability realization and recognition does not impact financial reporting. At period-end closing, however, it becomes an issue requiring special attention. Items of inventory received at the end of the audit period, whose related invoice is not received until early into the following period, may not be included as an accounts payable. Management should have procedures for identifying invoices received in a subsequent period that relate to the audit period and adjusting the liabilities accordingly. The search for unrecorded liabilities described in the following paragraphs provides evidence that tests the *completeness*, *existence*, and *rights and obligations* assertions.

Searching for Unrecorded Liabilities

The search for unrecorded liabilities involves the Disbursement Voucher and Receiving Report files, illustrated without data in Table 10-5. Each record of an inventory receipt contained in this file for the period should match a corresponding

TABLE 10-5 Disbursement Voucher and Receiving Report Files

Disbursement Voucher File

Voucher Number	PO Number	Amount	Due Date	Check Number	Check Date	Invoice Number	Vendor Number

Receiving Report File

Rec. Rpt Number	PO Number	Carrier Code	Date Received	Vendor Number

record in the Disbursement Voucher file. Again, using the *join* feature, the two files can be compared for the existence of mismatched records.

As in the previous example, the two files being joined need to be ordered on a common key, which, again, is PO Number. Since the Disbursement Voucher file was previously sorted on this key, that sorted output file can be used for this test also. Therefore, only the Receiving Report file needs to be reorganized. The next step is to join the two files to create a combined output file. This time, however, the output option is different from the previous example. The relevant option in this case is to create an output file that consists only of *unmatched* records from the *primary* file. Remember, the auditor is attempting through this test to identify receiving report records that have not been recorded as liabilities. The primary file in this instance is the Receiving Report file, and the Disbursement Voucher file is the secondary file. In choosing this option, all the inventory receipts that were correctly recorded as liabilities will be ignored by the *join* process. Only the unmatched receiving report records will be contained in the new output file. The structure of the file is the same as the Receiving Report file in Table 10-5. If the output file contains any records, the auditor needs to review this information with management to determine if the appropriate adjustments were made to the accounts payable balance.

Searching for Unauthorized Disbursement Vouchers

A variation on the preceding test can be used to address questions pertaining to overstated accounts payable. By selecting the Disbursement Vouchers file as the primary file and the Receiving Report file as the secondary file, the preceding test will produce a file of vouchers for which the organization has no record of inventory receipts. This might indicate that payments are approved solely on the basis of receiving a supplier's invoice rather than also verifying that inventories were ordered and actually received. Unsupported disbursement vouchers may signify an attempt at fraud or a poor control environment in which multiple payments are made for the same purchase. The latter situation is now examined further.

Review for Multiple Checks to Vendors

Corporate losses from multiple payments to vendors for the same merchandise have been estimated to be in the hundreds of millions of dollars per year. Malfunctioning computer programs, data entry errors, and the failure of authorization controls are usually the basis for duplicate payments. Occasionally, however, they are the result of dishonest vendors who attempt to circumvent internal controls by sending two supplier invoices with different invoice numbers for the same purchase. Sometimes they send multiple copies of the same invoice or simply add a letter behind one of the invoice numbers to differentiate them. The auditor can test for duplicate records in a large file by employing ACL's *duplicate* feature. This technique is demonstrated below using the Disbursement Voucher file in Table 10-5.

Any field or combination of fields can be used to test for duplicate records. The auditor, however, needs to understand the relationship between the files to draw meaningful conclusions from the test results. For instance, in our example each disbursement voucher is issued in payment of a single supplier's invoice, and each supplier invoice relates to a single purchase order. Recognizing this relationship, the auditor can conclude that the same PO Number value should not normally exist in two or more records in the Disbursement Voucher file. A search for duplicate records in the file produces the report in Figure 10-13.

The report indicates that two records (voucher numbers 10392 and 10393) have the same purchase order number. The cause of this situation will require further examination in consultation with the appropriate management. The explanation may simply be that vouchers were created in error, voided, and resubmitted. However, the results may signify that, on two occasions, duplicate checks were issued for the same merchandise. This anomaly may be due to a computer error or an internal control problem in the voucher approval process, or it could be a result of fraud.

Auditing Payroll and Related Accounts

Testing accrued payroll and related accounts for completeness and accuracy consist primarily of analytical procedures and reviews of cash disbursements made in the following period. The auditor should test the mathematical accuracy of payroll summaries and trace totals to the payroll records and to the general ledger accounts. The average salary per employee in the current period can be compared to the previous year's averages. ACL's *stratify* feature can help the auditor detect unusual trends and abnormal balances in the payroll file. Substantive tests of

FIGURE 10-13

Duplicate Records Report

As of: 06/09/2004 13:28:45

Command: DUPLICATES ON PO_Num OTHER Voucher_Num TO SCREEN PRESORT
Table: Voucher_Pay

0 sequence errors detected
1 gap or duplicate detected

Duplicates:

PO_Num	Voucher_Num
12977	10392
12977	10393

details, however, are normally not performed on payroll expense accounts unless analytical procedures or severe weaknesses in internal controls indicate the need for additional testing.

SUMMARY

This chapter examined audit procedures associated with the expenditure cycle. It began with a review of alternative technologies used in both legacy and modern systems. The focus was on the key operational tasks that constitute the purchases, cash disbursement, and payroll procedures. The second section explained expenditure cycle audit objectives, controls, and tests of controls that an auditor normally performs. Evidence from such procedures is used to determine the nature, timing, and extent of substantive tests. The last section described substantive tests in relation to expenditure cycle assertions based upon ACL software applications.

KEY TERMS

attendance file
closed accounts payable file
closed voucher file
disbursement voucher file
employee file
file definition
human resource management (HRM) system
inventory subsidiary file
labor usage file
log of automatic transactions
paymaster
payroll imprest account
supplier's (vendor's) invoice
timecard
transaction listing
transaction log
valid vendor file
vendor's invoice

REVIEW QUESTIONS

1. Differentiate between a purchase requisition and a purchase order.
2. What purpose does a purchasing department serve?
3. Distinguish between an accounts payable file and a vouchers payable file.
4. What are the three logical steps of the cash disbursements system?
5. What general ledger journal entries are triggered by the purchases system?
6. What two types of exposure can close supervision of the receiving department reduce?
7. What steps of independent verification does the general ledger department perform?
8. What is (are) the purpose(s) of maintaining a valid vendor file?
9. How do computerized purchasing systems help to reduce the risk of purchasing bottlenecks?
10. What is a personnel action form?
11. What tasks does a payroll clerk perform upon receipt of hours-worked data from the production department?
12. What documents constitute the audit trail for payroll?

Discussion Questions

1. What is the importance of the job ticket? Illustrate the flow of this document and its information from inception to impact on the financial statements.
2. What documents support the payment of an invoice? Discuss where these documents originate and the resulting control implications.
3. Discuss the time lags between realizing and recognizing economic events in the purchase and payroll systems. What is the accounting profession's view on this matter as it pertains to these two systems?
4. Discuss the importance of supervision controls in the receiving department and the reasons behind blind fields on the receiving report, such as quantity and price.
5. How does the procedure for determining inventory requirements differ between a basic batch processing system and batch processing with real-time data input of sales and receipts of inventory?
6. What advantages are achieved in choosing:
   a. a basic batch computer system over a manual system?
   b. a batch system with real-time data input over a basic batch system?
7. Discuss the major control implications of batch systems with real-time data input. What compensating procedures are available?
8. Discuss some specific examples of how information systems can reduce time lags that positively affect an organization.
9. Discuss some service industries that may require their workers to use job tickets.
10. Payroll is often used as a good example of batch processing using sequential files. Explain why.

Multiple-Choice Questions

1. Which document helps to ensure that the receiving clerks actually count the number of goods received?
   a. packing list
   b. blind copy of purchase order
   c. shipping notice
   d. invoice
2. When the goods are received and the receiving report has been prepared, which ledger may be updated?
   a. standard cost inventory ledger
   b. inventory subsidiary ledger
   c. general ledger
   d. accounts payable subsidiary ledger
3. Which statement is *not* correct for an expenditure system with proper internal controls?
   a. Cash disbursements maintain the check register.
   b. Accounts payable maintains the accounts payable subsidiary ledger.
   c. Accounts payable is responsible for paying invoices.
   d. Accounts payable is responsible for authorizing invoices.
4. Which duties should be segregated?
   a. matching purchase requisitions, receiving reports, and invoices and authorizing payment
   b. authorizing payment and maintaining the check register
   c. writing checks and maintaining the check register
   d. authorizing payment and maintaining the accounts payable subsidiary ledger
5. Which documents would an auditor most likely choose to examine closely in order to ascertain that all expenditures incurred during the accounting period have been recorded as a liability?
   a. invoices
   b. purchase orders
   c. purchase requisitions
   d. receiving reports
6. Which task must still require human intervention in an automated purchases/cash disbursements system?
   a. determination of inventory requirements
   b. preparation of a purchase order
   c. preparation of a receiving report
   d. preparation of a check register

7. CMA 686 3-12
In a well-designed internal control structure, two tasks that should be performed by different persons are
   a. preparation of purchase orders and authorization of monthly payroll.
   b. preparation of bank reconciliations and recording of cash disbursements.
   c. distribution of payroll checks and approval of credit sales.
   d. posting of amounts from both the cash receipts journal and cash disbursements journal to the general ledger.
   e. posting of amounts from the cash receipts journal to the general ledger and distribution of payroll checks.

8. CMA 689 3-17
Which one of the following situations represents a strength in the internal control for purchasing and accounts payable?
   a. Prenumbered receiving reports are issued randomly.
   b. Invoices are approved for payment by the purchasing department.
   c. Unmatched receiving reports are reviewed on an annual basis.
   d. Vendors' invoices are matched against purchase orders and receiving reports before a liability is recorded.
   e. The purchasing department reconciles the accounts payable subsidiary vendor ledger with the general ledger control account.

PROBLEMS

1. Payroll Fraud

John Smith worked in the stockyard of a large building supply company. One day he unexpectedly and without notice left for California, never to return. His foreman seized the opportunity to continue to submit timecards for John to the payroll department. Each week, as part of his normal duties, the foreman received the employee paychecks from payroll and distributed them to the workers on his shift. Since John Smith was not present to collect his paycheck, the foreman forged John's name and cashed it.

Required:

Describe two control techniques to prevent or detect this fraud scheme.

2. Payroll Controls

Refer to the Problem 2 flowchart in the next column.

Required:

a. What risks are associated with the payroll procedures depicted in the flowchart?
b. Discuss two control techniques that will reduce or eliminate the risks.

Problem 2: Payroll Controls

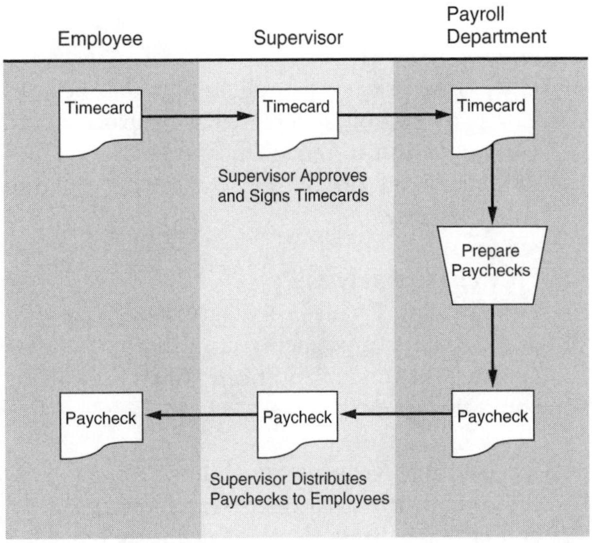

3. Payroll Controls

Sherman Company employs 400 production, maintenance, and janitorial workers in eight separate departments. In addition to supervising operations, the supervisors of the departments are responsible for recruiting, hiring, and firing workers within their areas of responsibility. The organization attracts casual labor and experiences a 20 to 30 percent turnover rate in employees per year. A portion of Sherman Company's payroll procedures are as follows:

Employees clock on and off the job each day to record their attendance on timecards. Each department has its own clock machine that is located in an unattended room away from the main production area. Each week, the supervisors gather the timecards, review them for accuracy, and sign and submit them to the payroll department for processing. In addition, the supervisors submit personnel action forms to reflect newly hired and terminated employees. From these documents, the payroll clerk prepares payroll checks and updates the employee records. The supervisor of the payroll department signs the paychecks and sends them to the department supervisors for distribution to the employees. A payroll register is sent to accounts payable for approval. Based on this approval, the cash disbursements clerk transfers funds into a payroll clearing account.

Required:

Discuss the risks for payroll fraud in the Sherman Company payroll system. What controls would you implement to reduce the risks? Use the SAS 78 framework of control activities to organize your response.

4. **Flowchart Analysis**

Examine the Problem 4 diagram on page 479 and indicate any incorrect initiation and/or transfer of documentation. What problems could this cause?

5. **Accounting Records and Files**

Indicate which department—accounts payable, cash disbursements, data processing, purchasing, inventory, or receiving—has ownership over the following files and registers:

a. Open Purchase Order file
b. Purchase Requisition file
c. Open Purchase Requisition file
d. Closed Purchase Requisition file
e. Inventory file
f. Closed Purchase Order file
g. Valid Vendor file
h. Voucher register
i. Open Vouchers Payable file
j. Receiving Report file
k. Closed Voucher file
l. Check register (cash disbursements journal)

6. **Source Documents Identification**

Refer to the Problem 6 figure on page 480, which shows typical expenditure cycle files and attributes. Explain, in detail, the process by which these data are obtained and used in the requisition, purchase, and payment to inventory.

7. **Internal Control**

Using the Problem 7 flowchart of a purchases system on page 481, identify six major control weaknesses in the system. Discuss and classify each weakness in accordance with SAS 78.

8. **Purchase Discounts Lost**

Estimate the money that could be saved by the accounts payable and cash disbursements departments if a basic batch processing system were implemented. Assume that the clerical workers cost the firm \$12 per hour, that 13,000 vouchers are prepared, and that 5,000 checks are written per year. Assume that total cash disbursements to vendors amount to \$5 million per year. Due to sloppy bookkeeping, the current system takes advantage of only about 25 percent of the discounts offered by vendors for timely payments. The average discount is 2 percent if payment is made within 10 days. Payments are currently made on about the 15th day after the invoice is received. Make your own assumptions (and state them) regarding how long specific tasks will take. Also discuss any intangible benefits of the system. (Don't worry about excessive paper documentation costs.)

9. **Data Processing Output**

Using the information provided in Problem 8, discuss all transaction listings and summary reports that would be necessary for a batch system with real-time input of data.

Problem 4: Flowchart Analysis

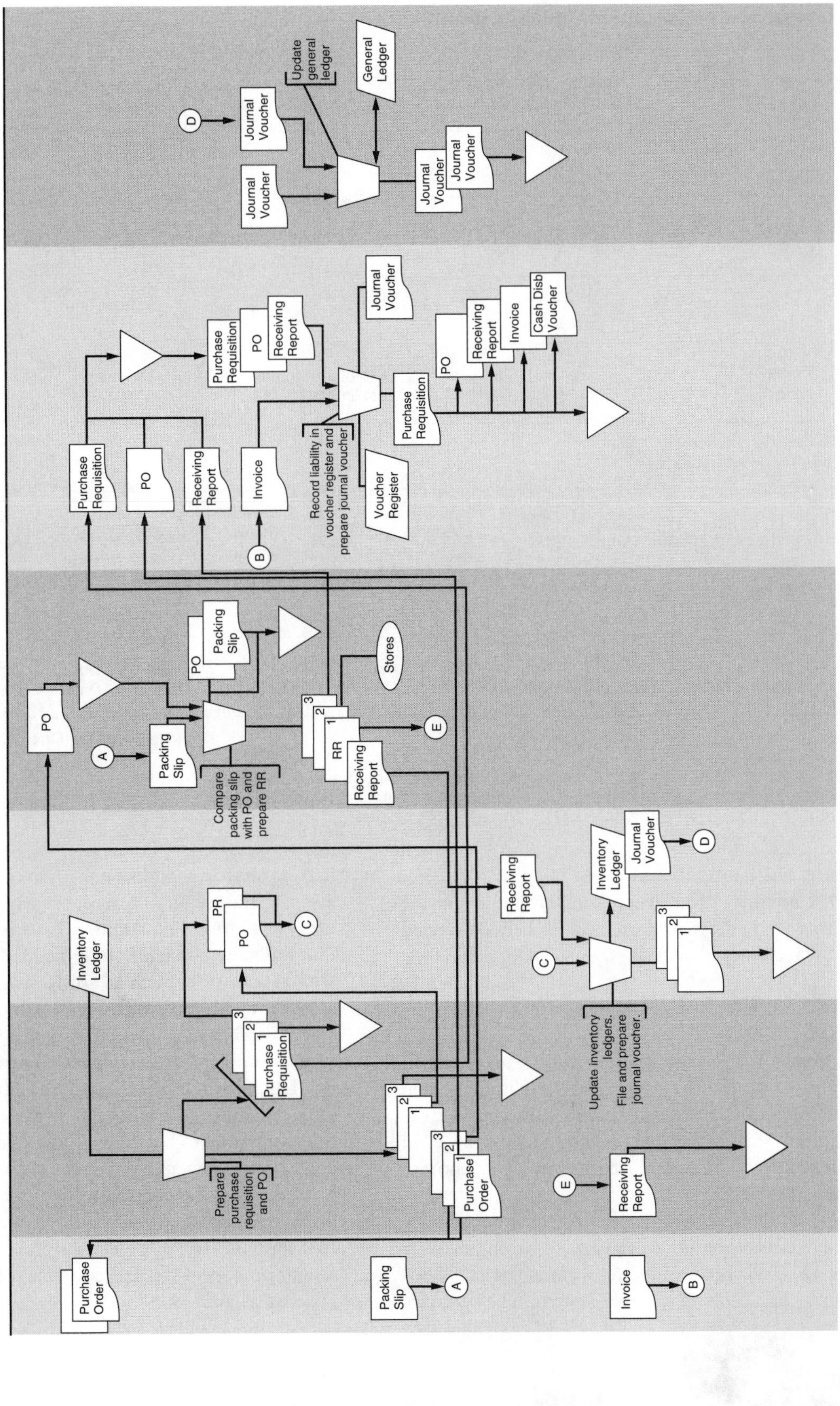

Problem 6: Source Documents Identification

Inventory Master File

Inven Num	Description	Qnty on Hand	Reorder Point	Qnty On Order*	EOQ	Vendor Number	Standard Cost	Total Inven. Cost

Purchase Requisition File

Pur Req Number	Inven Num	Qnty on Order	Vendor Number	Unit Standard Cost

Vendor File

Vendor Number	Address	Terms of Trade	Date of Last Order	Lead Time

Open (and Closed) Purchase Order File

PO Num	Pur Req Number	Inven Num	Qnty on Order	Vendor Number	Address	Standard Cost	Expected Invoice Amount	Rec Flag	Inven Flag

Voucher Number	Check Num	Invoice Num	Invoice Amount	Acct Cr	Acct DR	Vendor Number	Open Date	Due Date	Close Date

Voucher Register (Open AP File)

* A value in this field is a "flag" to the system not to order item a second time. When inventories are received, the flag is removed by changing this value to zero.

10. Internal Control

Discuss any control weaknesses found in the Problem 10 flowchart on page 482. Recommend any necessary changes.

11. Internal Control

CMA 1288 5-3

Lexsteel is a leading manufacturer of steel furniture. Although the company has manufacturing plants and distribution facilities throughout the United States, the purchasing, accounting, and treasury functions are centralized at corporate headquarters.

While discussing the management letter with the external auditors, Ray Lansdown, controller of Lexsteel, became aware of potential problems with the accounts payable system. The auditors had to perform additional audit procedures to attest to the validity of accounts payable and cut-off procedures. The auditors have recommended that a detailed systems study be made of the current procedures. Such a study would not only assess the exposure of the company to potential embezzlement and fraud, but would also identify ways to improve management controls.

Lansdown has assigned the study task to Dolores Smith, a relatively new accountant in the department. Because Smith could not find adequate documentation of the accounts payable procedures, she interviewed those employees involved and constructed a flowchart of the current system. The Problem 11 flowchart is presented on page 483. A description of the current procedures follows.

Problem 7: Internal Control

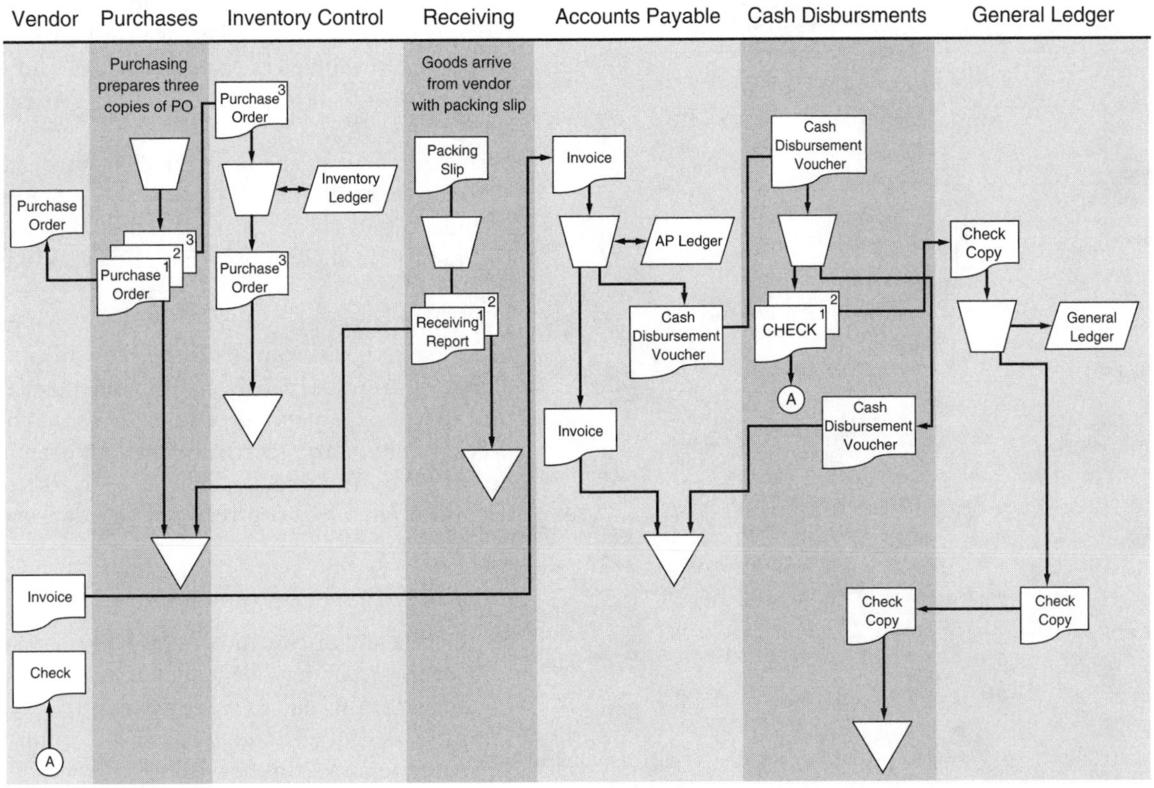

Computer Resources Available

The host computer mainframe is located at corporate headquarters with interactive, remote job-entry terminals at each branch location. In general, data entry occurs at the source and is transmitted to an integrated database maintained on the host computer. Data transmission is made between the branch offices and the host computer over leased telephone lines. The software allows flexibility for managing user access and editing data input.

Procedures for Purchasing Raw Materials

Production orders and appropriate bills of materials are generated by the host computer at corporate headquarters. Based on these bills of materials, purchase orders for raw materials are generated by the centralized purchasing function and mailed directly to the vendors. Each purchase order instructs the vendor to ship the materials directly to the appropriate manufacturing plant. Assuming that the necessary purchase orders have been issued, the manufacturing plants proceed with the production orders received from corporate headquarters.

When goods are received, the manufacturing plant examines and verifies the count with the packing slip and transmits the receiving data to accounts payable at corporate headquarters. In the event that raw material deliveries fall behind production, each branch manager is given the authority to order materials and issue emergency purchase orders directly to the vendors. Data about the emergency orders and verification of materials receipt are transmitted via computer to accounts payable at corporate headquarters. Because the company employs a computerized perpetual inventory system, physical counts of raw materials are deemed not to be cost effective and are not performed.

Accounts Payable Procedures

Vendor invoices are mailed directly to corporate headquarters and entered by accounts payable

Problem 10: Internal Control

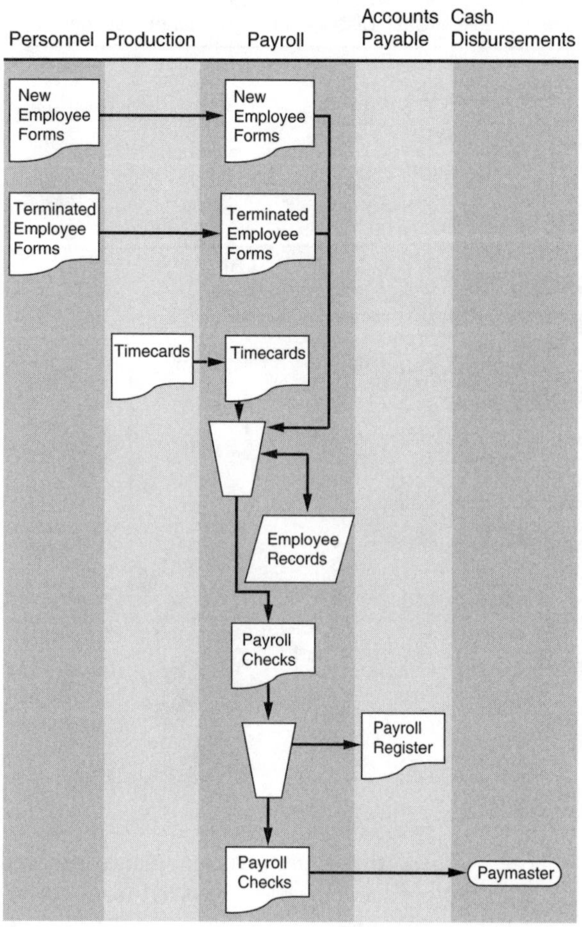

personnel when received; this often occurs before the receiving data are transmitted from the branch offices. The final day of the invoice term for payment is entered as the payment due date. This due date must often be calculated by the data entry person using information listed on the invoice.

Once a week, invoices due the following week are printed in chronological entry order on a payment listing, and the corresponding checks are drawn. The checks and the payment listing are sent to the treasurer's office for signature and mailing to the payee. The check number is printed by the computer and displayed on the check, and the payment listing is validated as the checks are signed. After the checks are mailed, the payment listing is returned to accounts payable for filing. When there is insufficient cash to pay all the invoices, certain checks and the payment listing are retained by the treasurer until all checks can be paid. When the remaining checks are mailed, the listing is then returned to accounts payable. Often, weekly check mailings include a few checks from the previous week, but rarely are there more than two weekly listings involved.

When accounts payable receives the payment listing back from the treasurer's office, the expenses are distributed, coded, and posted to the appropriate plant or cost center accounts. Weekly summary performance reports are processed by accounts payable for each cost center and branch location reflecting all data entry to that point.

Required:

a. Identify and discuss three areas where Lexsteel Corporation may be exposed to fraud or embezzlement due to weaknesses in the procedures described, and recommend improvements to correct these weaknesses.
b. Describe three areas where management information could be distorted due to weaknesses in the procedures, and recommend improvements to correct these weaknesses.
c. Identify three strengths in the procedures described and explain why they are strengths.

12. Human Resource Data Management

In a payroll system with real-time processing of human resource management data, control issues become very important. List some items in this system that could be very sensitive or controversial. Also describe what types of data must be carefully guarded to ensure that they are not altered. Discuss some control procedures that might be put into place to guard against unwanted changes to employees' records.

Problem 11: Internal Control

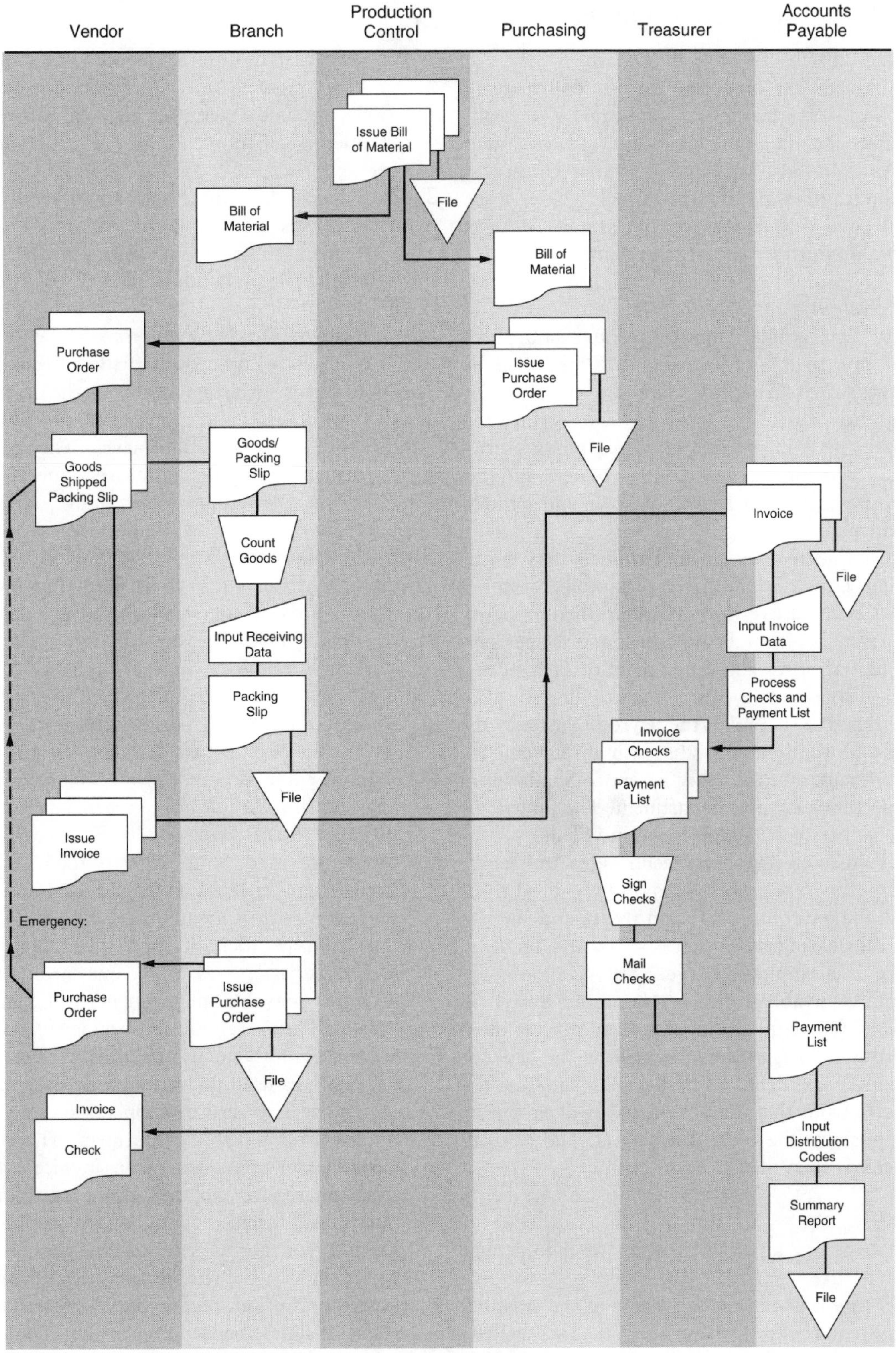

INTERNAL CONTROL CASES

1. Price Right Inc.—Payroll System

The Price Right Company consists of five retail clothing stores in the Tri-State area. The headquarters and main store are located in Manhattan. Price Right sells high-quality sports clothes at discount prices. As of December 31, 2002, Price Right had 130 employees consisting of sales staff, administrative staff, and management.

Payroll System

Every two weeks employees enter data from their timecards into a terminal located in each of the stores. After the data are entered, the computer runs a check on the employees through an employee history file. Upon verification, a personnel action form is created, and the data are transmitted to Giorgio in the payroll department.

Giorgio remains at his terminal every other Friday because he must oversee payroll data coming in from all five stores. Giorgio then prepares the paychecks from the timecards and the personnel action forms, and sends them to Fred in the cash disbursements department. Giorgio also prepares three copies of the payroll registers: one is filed, one is sent to the cash disbursements department, and the other is sent to Shannon in the accounts payable department. The timecards and the personnel action forms are filed.

Fred in cash disbursements signs and sends the checks to the employees directly. Fred then takes the payroll register and writes and signs a payroll clearing check that is sent to the bank to cover the employee paychecks. Shannon, in accounts payable, verifies and copies the payroll register. One copy of the payroll register is filed and the other is sent to Michelle in the general ledger department. Michelle uses the payroll register from the accounts payable department and posts to the control accounts. The payroll register is then filed.

Required:

a. Create a data flow diagram of the current system.
b. Create a document flowchart of the existing system.
c. Analyze the internal control weaknesses in the system. Model your response according to the six categories of physical control activities specified in SAS 78.

2. Rex Records—Purchases and Payroll Procedures

(Prepared by Kara Winne and Andrea Brown, Lehigh University)

Purchases and Cash Payments

The purchases procedures at Rex Records begin when a purchasing agent reviews the inventory in the warehouse and finds that products have diminished to a certain level. The purchases department prepares a purchase requisition form, which signals the preparation of five copies of the purchase order. Two are sent to the vendor, one is filed, a blind copy is sent to the receiving department, and the last copy is filed along with the purchase requisition form in the inventory control department. Because Rex has a small staff, sometimes no one is available to inspect and sign for goods at the receiving dock. As a result, occasionally a clerk will sign for the goods without inspection when the carrier drops them off.

After the ordered products arrive with a packing slip, a clerk in the receiving department prepares the receiving report. Four copies of the report are made. One copy is filed within the department for future reference, and one copy is sent to inventory control to be reconciled with the purchase order and used to update the inventory records. The last two copies are sent to the accounts payable department and the warehouse. The receiving report is filed in the accounts payable department. In the warehouse, the report is used to constitute an audit trail.

Invoices are sent by suppliers and received by the accounts payable department. The accounts payable clerk reconciles the invoice with the receiving report and then posts a liability. The purchases journal is consequently updated and a journal voucher is sent to the general ledger department. The liabilities created are also posted to the voucher register and three copies of a cash disbursements voucher are prepared.

The general ledger department utilizes the summary information created in the inventory control department and the journal voucher from the accounts payable department to update the general ledger control accounts. Finally, the summary information and the journal voucher are filed within the general ledger department.

An accounts payable clerk searches for any items on which payment is due. These items are sent along with their supporting documents over to the cash disbursements department. A clerk in charge of the department prepares the checks, compares the appropriate records and signs and mails the checks to the vendors. A journal voucher is prepared and sent over to the general ledger department. One check is sent to the appropriate vendor, while the other is filed. Summary information is sent to the general ledger department where it is reconciled with journal vouchers to complete the purchasing process.

Description of Payroll Procedures

When Rex Records employees report to work each morning, they are required to punch a timecard to record their hours. The production manager sends this timecard information to the payroll process department on a biweekly basis. There is no supervisor at the timecard station and, as a result, management has been under the impression that some warehouse employees are clocking in for their late or absent co-workers. The production department, which is responsible for submitting the timecard information, also sends summary information to the cost accounting department. The clerk at this department uses the job ticket information to post to the various work-in-progress accounts and create a labor distribution summary, which will later be sent to the accounts payable department.

The personnel action form that is prepared in the production department is sent to the payroll department to be reconciled with time cards and authorize the payment of Rex Records employees. The clerk in charge at the payroll department sends paychecks to employees and sends payroll summary information to the accounts payable department through the preparation of a payroll register.

The accounts payable department sends the summary labor distribution information to the general ledger department where it is posted. The department uses the payroll register to prepare vouchers. Two voucher copies are prepared and the payroll register is sent to the general ledger department. One voucher is sent to the cash disbursements department and the final copy is sent with the payroll register to the general ledger department.

In the cash disbursements department, a clerk signs the checks and sends a copy to his supervisor. The voucher sent over from the accounts payable department is reviewed and used to write an amount for the imprest account, which is then deposited in the bank. Employees cash their checks upon receipt.

Required:

a. Create a data flow diagram of the current system.
b. Create a document flowchart of the existing system.
c. Analyze the internal control weaknesses in the system. Model your response according to the six categories of physical control activities specified in SAS 78.
d. Prepare a system flowchart of a redesigned computer-based system that resolves the control weaknesses that you identified.

3. Green Leaf Produce Company—Comprehensive Case

(Prepared by Glenn Adams and Nausheena Rahim, Lehigh University)

Green Leaf Produce Company, a wholesale distributor nestled away in the coal-mining regions of Pennsylvania, generates revenues of $90 million per year and currently employs 187 people while servicing the northeastern United States. Its customer base is comprised of restaurants, public schools, universities, and hospitals. This family-owned operation competes against the likes of national food distributors Sysco and U.S. Foods. The competition among these rivals can be fierce at times as pricing strategies are employed to gain market share.

Green Leaf Produce Company first opened its doors to the general public in the 1930s. The local ice company in town rented a small storefront to Green Leaf, giving birth to this Mom-and-Pop operation. During this time, small-merchant businesses were on the rise as individuals who had lost their jobs in the Depression tried their hands at entrepreneurship. Green Leaf succeeded, as it captured the local market selling fruits and vegetables to the people of bustling Main Street.

Through the 1930s up until the late 1950s, Green Leaf Produce continued to expand its operations to meet the ever-changing demand of the customers it served. Land, building, trucks, and equipment were purchased as revenues and earnings increased substantially. Over the years its product base was expanded to include a line of frozen foods, seafood, and fresh meats to enhance the company's product mix.

Green Leaf Produce purchases inventory items from growers, manufacturers, and processors domestically and from around the world. Since the company's inception, Green Leaf Produce has formed strategic partnerships with more than 47 different suppliers that include some of the industry giants, such as Frosty Acres, Tyson Food, H.J. Heinz, and Iceland Seafood.

Following another 40 years of growth, servicing restaurants, public schools, universities, and hospitals, Green Leaf Produce relocated once again to its new 100,000-square-foot state-of-the-art distribution center. The new facility has a refrigeration capacity of more than two million cubic feet, which will position it to meet the challenges of the twenty-first century.

Sales Order Processing

Green Leaf's credit approval system operates in a real-time processing environment. The sales order process begins with the receipt of customer orders indicating the type of product and quantity being requested. Green Leaf receives customer orders two ways, via an 800 number in which a customer service representative keys the order into the computer system, and from a sales representative located in the field who transmits the order back to the plant from a wireless laptop. Customer records are then matched with the company's database and checked for flags and credit limits before an approval is generated. If the customer's account has been flagged, a message appears that notifies the representative that the account is under review by the credit department. The customer is notified at this point that a decision will be rendered within the hour. In real time the flagged account is transmitted to the credit manager's queue to ensure that proper application of the firm's credit policies and procedures are followed. (One aspect of the credit manager's job function is to review customer accounts regularly for creditworthiness and to set appropriate high credit limits. A *second look,* performed by the credit manager, is a process of reviewing customer orders for possible missed sales opportunities or to give proper attention to past due accounts.) Once a decision has been made regarding the order placed, the credit manager overrides the system, the sales order file is updated, and the customer is notified of the decision made.

A normal business day ends at 5 P.M. and no new orders are accepted for delivery the next day. A manager in the computer operations department who maintains and operates the system sorts and compiles the orders that were processed and approved during the course of that day's business transactions. At this point the sales journal is updated. Once the orders have been compiled, records are matched against inventory levels to confirm that items are in stock or unavailable. An inventory report is then generated and sent to purchasing notifying them of unavailable items to replenish inventory levels.

The sorted and compiled sales orders are then downloaded to the logistics department, where the sales orders are segregated according to geographical area. The groupings of sales orders are determined by the logistic program and then are assigned to a truck. Once the sales orders have been routed they are uploaded back to the mainframe in computer operations and stored in the routed deliveries file. The manager of the logistics department then runs the billing/invoice program from his terminal. The billing program accesses the records in computer operations and produces a three-part invoice along with the truck summary report detailing the customer stops. Part 1 of the invoices is sent to the credit department, is temporarily filed, and acts as a control copy in case of missing invoices.

Copies 2 and 3 of the invoice and the truck summary report are sent to shipping and temporarily filed. When the billing/invoice program is run, the accounts receivable and inventory records are updated in computer operations, along with the journal voucher file.

The clerk in the computer operation department then accesses the routed delivery file and runs the order-picking program that generates the stock release and picking labels that go to the warehouse.

The labels, which contain customer number, name, truck to be loaded, product name, number, and quantity, are distributed to warehouse workers. Based on the information contained on the labels, goods are picked and loaded onto skids and shrink-wrapped. The stock release is filed in the warehouse and the picked goods are sent directly to shipping, where the skids are then loaded onto the trucks in reverse of customer delivery.

Once the trucks are loaded with the customer orders, the shipping clerk pulls invoice copies 2 and 3, along with the truck summary report, and hands them to the driver with the deliveries for the day. After the driver unloads an order, he or she has the customer sign part 2 of the invoice. This acts as Green Leaf's binding contract. Part 3 of the invoice goes to the customer. At the end of the day, the driver returns with the truck summary report and part 2 of all the invoices, and delivers them to the credit department.

A clerk in the credit department then reconciles the truck summary report and the invoice copy. Once they have been reconciled, the invoice is imaged into the optical control reader and stored in the imaged file. This allows invoices to be viewed online for answering customer questions about billing. In addition, this added feature provides internal controls by affording Green Leaf the capability of running spot checks by querying invoices by account number, customer name, amount, or date of invoice.

At 4 A.M., the computer operations manager begins the end-of-day batch update process. The journal vouchers are sorted and the general ledger program is run to update the general journal for previous day business transactions. After the general journal is updated, three management reports are produced. The sales recap report and the truck recap report go to the controller, and the accounts receivable control summary is distributed to the credit manager.

Cash Receipts Procedures

Green Leaf's receptionist, Helen, is located at the front of the plant's facility. She greets all incoming visitors as they arrive through the front doors. Each day the postal carrier delivers all the mail for the entire plant, which includes customer payments from orders previously delivered. Helen then sorts through the entire batch of mail, separating customer payments from the rest of the mail. As Helen opens each payment, she carefully records the account number along with the business name in the memo section of the check and disposes of the remittance advice. Helen then delivers all the checks documented with customer account number and name to the accounting department to be posted to the respective accounts.

The accounts receivable clerk posts the payments to each of the customer's accounts and updates the accounts receivable ledger and cash receipts journal by entering the information into the computer terminal. All records and files are stored in the data processing department. After all the payments are posted, two copies of the payment posting summary are then generated. One, which will later be reconciled with the validated deposit slip from the bank, will go to the controller's office, and the other will go to the manager of the accounts receivable department. Next the clerk prepares three deposit slips, one of which will accompany the deposit to the bank. One of the copies is filed in the department and the other is sent with the summary report to the controller's office. When the validated deposit slip arrives from the bank, the controller reconciles the payment summary report deposit slip against the validated deposit slip from the bank. The general journal and control accounts are updated.

Purchases System

The purchasing agent reviews stock reports by category to determine what needs to be ordered based on sales demand and seasonal demand. The order quantity is determined by sales demand/frequency and quantity on hand from the inventory file via a terminal. A full weekly stock reorder report is prepared. The purchasing agent then calls all the suppliers on the supplier list for prices. The supplier with the best price is contracted and a purchase order is sent. Two copies of the purchase order are made: one is attached to the stock reorder report and permanently filed, and the other purchase order is sent to the receiving area.

Once the goods arrive in the receiving area, the receiving clerk compares the purchase order to the goods and notes any discrepancies. A receiving report is prepared and a copy is made. The receiving report, packing slip, and bill of lading are sent to the accounts payable department, where they are temporarily filed awaiting the invoice. The copy is sent to the purchasing department, with the purchase order, where they are reconciled with the stock reorder report in the open purchase file and the documents are permanently filed. Inventory records are then updated via a terminal to the inventory file and the goods are sent to warehousing. A journal voucher is prepared by the receiving clerk and sent to the general accounting clerk to key in to the general ledger control account file.

After the invoice is received from the supplier by the accounts payable department, it is reconciled with the packing slip and receiving report. Once reconciled, the purchases journal is posted to and the supplier's account is updated in the accounts payable subsidiary ledger. The invoice is then filed by due date. The accounts payable clerk prepares a summary of the entries in journal voucher form. which is then sent to the general accounting clerk to key it in to the general ledger control account file.

Current Cash Disbursement System

As the due dates approach, the accounts payable clerk writes out a check to the supplier indicating the invoice number and amount due. The check is sent to the general accounting department comptroller for a signature. The check is signed, a copy made, and the check mailed. The check copy is stamped as "paid" and is sent back to the accounts payable. The accounts payable clerk then updates the accounts payable subsidiary ledger to reflect the payments, prepares and sends an account summary to the general ledger, and permanently files the documents. The accounts payable clerk also updates the check register, summarizes it, and sends a journal voucher to the general accounting clerk for keying in to the general ledger control account file via a terminal.

The Fixed Asset System

Daniel Jefferson has been the fixed asset manager for 16 years. He is a trusted employee of Green Leaf Produce, and has been given greater responsibility in recent years. Daniel is in charge of the acquisition, maintenance, and time logging of the fixed assets that the company owns. In his tenure, he has implemented a program to buy all delivery trucks rather than lease them. The added equity that owning provides over leasing has allowed Green Leaf Produce to employ leverage into acquiring new assets. Recently, however, management has become concerned about the rise in maintenance costs. The average maintenance bill has increased by 15 percent over the last two years. Management is considering leasing once again, and selling the trucks that they now own. Before taking any major steps, they have decided to investigate the fixed asset department.

Daniel Jefferson is responsible for selecting repair companies and negotiating maintenance and repair contracts with them. Daniel selected Fix 'Em All Repairs for all the needed work. Jessica Jefferson, his wife, is the office manger of the repair shop. Daniel fills out the work orders as maintenance comes due and repairs are needed. Fix 'Em All Repairs bills Green Leaf Produce at the end of the month for services rendered. Upon receipt of the bill, the accounts payable department processes the payment, which takes five business days. Daniel makes the necessary entries to the general ledger.

Payroll System

Management at Green Leaf Produce trusts the employees to be accurate in recording hours worked. Jim Richmond, treasurer of the company, has been working in the accounting department since the early 1960s. Because of his extended service, he has been entrusted with many responsibilities. One of his responsibilities is to maintain the personnel files. He supplies this information for payroll processing purposes.

The employees prepare their timesheets when they arrive and note when they leave. At the end of the workweek, each department sends the employee timesheets to Jim for approval. After he approves all the timesheets, he sends them and the personnel action form to the payroll office to be processed. The paychecks are drawn on the company's general cash account. After preparing the payroll register, the payroll department sends the paychecks and the payroll register to the accounts payable department for review. Accounts payable then sends a journal voucher to the general ledger department, files the payroll register, and sends the paychecks to Jim for signing and distribution to the employees.

Required:

a. Create a data flow diagram for all systems.
b. Create a document flowchart for all systems.
c. Analyze the internal control weaknesses in the system. Model your response according to the six categories of physical control activities specified in SAS 78.
d. Prepare a system flowchart for all systems that resolves the control weaknesses that you identified.

4. Fence, Inc.

(Prepared by Chris Banta and Mike Diana, Lehigh University)

Fence, Inc. was established in 1993 in the Lehigh Valley and is currently one of the fastest-growing wooden-fence installers in the industry. The company's headquarters is located in Bethlehem, Pennsylvania, and it has a warehouse in Allentown, Pennsylvania, to store and customize the fence. The sales staff and purchasing staffs are located at the headquarters and send sales and purchasing information directly to the warehouse. At the warehouse the installation team then takes the stored fence and installs it on the customer's site.

There are approximately 15 warehouse workers, 45 installers (team leaders and general installers), 25 sales and purchasing employees, and 15 other headquarter employees in the company. The general installers are much younger and less experienced than the other employees, which leads to a higher turnover rate in this position.

Fence, Inc. offers its customers a huge variety of products, including aluminum, vinyl (PVC), chain link, wood split rail, and wood board fences, and related items, including guardrails and arbors.

Fence, Inc. uses only one vendor due to its great relationship with a local wood and metal distributor (Royal, Inc.). Royal, Inc. has asked Fence, Inc. if it could organize a better purchasing and receiving system, as it is very large and technologically advanced compared to Fence, Inc. This could lead to an EDI relationship between Fence, Inc. and Royal, Inc. in the near future as technology becomes cheaper and both companies continue to grow with successful relationship.

Due to the seasonality of the business, Fence, Inc. has decided that this winter, during the off-season (December through March), it will be looking into revising its low-level computer technology and some of the manual procedures in its accounting system to ensure the company's future relationship with Royal, Inc. and to better handle new accounts in the future. It also wants a control expert or auditor to visit the company and give recommendations on how its processes can be better regulated.

The Plan

The vendor currently used by Fence, Inc. wishes to use EDI technology in its relationship with the company. Therefore, during this update, EDI technology will be implemented. This will change the form of the company's computer operations from a standard terminal available in each department to a new, automatic sale, inventory update, and reorder point system. Also, professional accounting software will be used to help facilitate management reporting after each day when the batches of sales order and cash receipts are processed. This system should be at least 15 times faster than the old system and allow new opportunities to develop with the single-vendor situation Fence is in. Lastly, a computer consultant from XYZ services will be hired to help update processes and tasks to eliminate control issues in the company.

Description of Current Expenditure Cycle

The expenditure cycle for Fence, Inc. begins when a purchasing agent reviews the records in the inventory computer and finds a low level of one or several inventory items. He or she then fills out three copies of a purchase requisition. The first copy is used to prepare a purchase order. The second copy is placed in the Accounts Payable Pending file, while the third is used to update inventory records after the goods are received.

Five copies of the purchase order are made, with the first two being sent to the supplier. A third is placed in the AP Pending file, and the fourth is used to update inventory records later. The final copy of the purchase order goes to the receiving department, where it is used, along with the packing slip from the supplier, to assure accuracy of the shipment on the receiving dock.

After confirming the accuracy of the shipment, the receiving clerk enters the receiving information into the inventory computer (password: fencesrgood). The inventory computer generates four copies of the receiving report, one of which is combined with a copy of the purchase order and packing slip and filed in the receiving department.

The second copy of the receiving report travels with the goods to the warehouse. The third copy is placed into the AP Pending file, while the last copy is used, along with the purchase requisition and purchase order, to update and confirm the records in the inventory computer.

In the accounts payable department, the invoice from the supplier is combined with the AP Pending file and entered into the accounts payable computer (password: fencesrgood). The information is entered into the purchases journal and a journal voucher is prepared and sent on to the general ledger department.

The general ledger department utilizes the summary information generated by the inventory computer in the purchasing department along with the journal voucher from accounts payable to update the general ledger computer (password: fencesrgood) and assure accuracy throughout the process. Finally, the summary information and journal voucher are filed in the general ledger department.

To set the cash disbursements system into action, the accounts payable clerk looks for any items on which payment is due in the accounts payable computer. They send these items and their supporting documents over to the cash disbursements department. Royal, Inc.'s account is debited in the AP ledger and summary information is sent to the general ledger department.

The cash disbursements clerk then confirms the accuracy of the supporting documents and prepares the necessary checks. She prepares a journal voucher for these checks and sends it over to the general ledger department. She then signs the checks and sends one copy to the vendor and files the other.

The general ledger clerk receives the summary information from accounts payable and the journal voucher from cash disbursements and inputs this information into the general ledger computer. The summary information and journal voucher are filed in the general ledger department to complete the purchasing process.

Required:

a. Create a data flow diagram of the current system.
b. Create a document flowchart of the existing system.
c. Analyze the internal control weaknesses in the system. Model your response according to the six categories of physical control activities specified in SAS 78.

5. Green Mountain Coffee Roasters, Inc. *(Prepared by Ronica Sharma, Lehigh University)*

Green Mountain Coffee Roasters, Inc. was founded in 1981 and began as a small cafe in Waitsfield, Vermont, roasting and serving premium coffee on the premises. Green Mountain blends and distributes coffee to a variety of customers, including cafés, delis, and restaurants, and currently has about 6,700 customer accounts reaching states across the nation. As the company has grown, several beverages have been added to its product line, including signature blends, light and heavy roasts, decaffeinated coffee and teas, and an assortment of herbal teas. Green Mountain Coffee Roasters, Inc. has been publicly traded since 1993 and had sales in excess of $84 million for the fiscal year ended September 2002.

Green Mountain Coffee has a warehouse and manufacturing plant located in Wilton, Vermont, where it presently employees 250 full- and part-time workers. The company receives its beans in bulk from a select group of distributors located across the world, with its largest supplier being Columbia Beans Co. Green Mountain Coffee also sells accessories that complement its products, such a mugs, thermoses, and coffee containers, which it gets from its supplier, Coffee Lovers, Inc. In addition to selling coffee and accessories, Green Mountain uses paper products such as coffee bags, coffee cups, and stirrers to distribute to its customers and to package the coffee. Green Mountain purchases its paper products from Save the Trees Inc.

Purchases System

Currently, Green Mountain employs a manual purchases system with minimal computer technology. Green Mountain Coffee purchases beans and blends from other companies and then sells them to other stores. Bean inventory fluctuates with respect to sales of blends to stores. Sara Katherine Smothers in the warehouse is in charge of inventory management. She reviews periodic inventory status reports to identify inventory needs and when items fall to their preestablished reorder point, she prepares a purchase requisition. She keeps a copy for herself in her department, files one in the open purchase requisition file, and sends a copy to accounts payable. At the end of the day, a three-part purchase order is prepared. One copy is filed and two are sent to the supplier.

When the goods arrive, Sara inspects and counts them and sends the packing slip to Fayth Burns in the accounting department. Using a PC, Sara updates the inventory subsidiary ledger and, at the end of day, sends an account summary to Vic in the general ledger department. After checking to see that the purchase requisitions exist to support the packing slip, Fayth files the documents in the Account Payable Pending file. The supplier's invoice is mailed directly to Fayth who checks it against the documents in the pending file. Using a PC system, she updates the accounts payable subsidiary ledger and records the transaction in the purchases journal. At the end of the day she prepares a journal voucher, which goes to Vic in the general ledger department. Using a separate PC-based system, Vic updates the control accounts affected by the transactions and files the summary and journal vouchers.

Cash Disbursements System Summary

Using the PC system, Fayth reviews the Accounts Payable file for items due for payment, waiting for the last date she can make a payment but still take advantage of the discount. She then updates (closes) the appropriate AP subsidiary record, prints a two-part check, and records the payment in the check register file. Fayth has signature authority for payments under $5,000. Checks for amounts greater than $5,000 are sent to Stuart, Green Mountain Coffee's treasurer, who co-signs them and returns them to Fayth. At the close of day, Fayth mails the check to the supplier, files a copy, and prepares a journal voucher, which goes to Vic. Vic records the transaction in the affected general ledger accounts and files journal voucher.

Required:

a. Create a data flow diagram of the current system.
b. Create a document flowchart of the existing system.
c. Analyze the internal control weaknesses in the system. Model your response according to the six categories of physical control activities specified in SAS 78.
d. Prepare a system flowchart of a redesigned computer-based system that resolves the control weaknesses that you identified.

6. USA Cycle Company

(Prepared by Kim Hancy, Lehigh University)

USA Cycle Company is one of the fastest-growing bicycle distributors in the United States, with headquarters in Chicago, Illinois. Its primary business is the distribution of bicycles assembled in China, but it also has a smaller, custom-order business for which it builds bicycles from parts purchased from various suppliers. Its product line includes mountain, road, and comfort bikes, as well as a juvenile line with up to 24" frames. It also distributes BMX bicycles, tricycles, and trailer bikes. In addition, it distributes various bicycle accessories such as helmets, clothing, lights, and spare parts for all models they carry.

Established in 1975, the company's first warehouses were in Illinois and Wisconsin and supplied retail bicycle outlets primarily in the Midwest. One year ago, USA Cycle Company expanded, adding two additional facilities in Sacramento, California, and Redmond, Washington, to meet the growing demand for its bicycles. Taking advantage of the increase in Internet technology, it now also sells customized bicycles direct to retailers through the Internet as well as by conventional means.

Its expansion to the west coast was coupled with a planned increase in reliance on suppliers in China. Although this resulted in decreased costs, some problems regarding inventory levels arose due to unexpected delays in shipping, primarily attributable to miscommunication and shipping conditions. Since the company does not want to carry excess inventory, it is sometimes forced to seek local suppliers at an increased cost.

USA Cycle Company uses limited computer technology to process business transactions and record accounting data, but the data is distributed and not shared throughout the company. This has caused data redundancy and associated problems of data currency, and these problems have been exacerbated by the company's recent rapid expansion on the west coast.

Initially, USA Cycle Company was a family-owned business. In need of capital for expansion, the company went public when it added the two facilities on the west coast. The number of employees rose from 100 to 200 during the expansion. Gross sales also rose from $10 to $20 million.

Description of Purchases Procedures

The USA Cycle purchases process begins when a clerk in the warehouse reviews inventory records. When it is determined that inventory is needed, the clerk inputs the information on the warehouse department microcomputer. This automatically inserts the information into a purchase record file. Four copies of the purchase order are subsequently printed. One copy is filed in the Open Purchase Order file. Two copies are sent to the supplier. The last copy is forwarded to the accounts payable department and filed in the Accounts Payable Pending file.

When the goods are received in the warehouse, the purchase order is pulled from the Open Purchase Order file and a clerk inspects, counts, and reconciles the goods to the packing slip and what was ordered. If many orders are received at the same time, the clerk tends to skip the reconciliation process in order to save some time. He places the goods on the warehouse shelves and then uses the computer to prepare the receiving report. The information is saved in the receiving record file and two copies of the receiving report are printed. One copy is forwarded to the accounts payable department. The other copy, along with the purchase order and packing slip, is used to update the inventory subsidiary records. The general ledger is automatically updated when changes are made to these records. The source documents are then filed in the Closed Purchase Order file.

When the receiving report is received in the accounts payable department it is filed in the Accounts Payable Pending file with the purchase order. When the invoice is received from the supplier, both documents are pulled from the Accounts Payable Pending file. A clerk uses these documents to add the record to the purchases journal and post the liability. The purchase order, receiving report, and invoice are filed in the Open Accounts Payable file. When the liability is recorded, the accounts payable subsidiary ledger, purchases journal, and general ledger are automatically updated.

Description of Cash Disbursements Process

Using the Open Accounts Payable file, in which the source documents are arranged by payment date, a clerk in the Accounts Payable/Cash Disbursement department searches for accounts coming due. When payments are due, the clerk removes the purchase order, receiving report, and invoice from the file to prepare the checks. The checks are used to subsequently update the check register and accounts payable subsidiary ledger. The general ledger is automatically updated. The checks are sent to be signed by the supervisor, who generally signs the check without much examination. A copy of the check is filed with the purchase order, receiving report, and invoice in the Closed Accounts Payable file. The supervisor then mails the checks to the supplier.

Required:

a. Create a data flow diagram of the current system.
b. Create a document flowchart of the existing system.
c. Analyze the internal control weaknesses in the system. Model your response according to the six categories of physical control activities specified in SAS 78.
d. Prepare a system flowchart of a redesigned computer-based system that resolves the control weaknesses that you identified.

ACL ASSIGNMENTS

The files used for the following assignments are located in the **workbook.acl** document on the CD that accompanies this text. Some of the assignments employ the ACL's Relation and Join features. For detailed information on the use of these and other commands, consult ACL's online Help.

1. Open the **AP_Trans** (purchases) file and stratify it on the Quantity field. Print the last results window and comment on the action to be taken by the auditor.
2. Using the *Relation* feature create a view from data in both the **AP_Trans** (purchases) and **Inventory** files that shows product details (**product description** and **quantity on-hand**). Print the view and comment on the results.
3. Open the **EMPMAST** (employee master file) and test for duplicate employee records. Prepare a last-results report that identifies anomalies or potential errors. Print the report and comment on the results.
4. Using the *Relation* feature create a view of data from both the **Empmast** and **Payroll** files that test for paychecks to non-existent employees.
5. Using the *Join* feature create a view of data from both the **Empmast** and **Payroll** files that tests for paychecks to nonexistent employees.

CHAPTER

11

Introduction to Business Ethics and Fraud

LEARNING OBJECTIVES

After studying this chapter, you should:

- Understand the broad issues pertaining to business ethics.
- Know why the subject of ethics is important to the study of accounting information systems.
- Have a basic understanding of ethical issues related to the use of information technology.
- Understand what constitutes fraudulent behavior.
- Be able to distinguish between management fraud and employee fraud.
- Be able to explain fraud-motivating forces.
- Be familiar with anti-fraud legislation and the anti-fraud profession in general.

Fraud, it seems, is as old as crime itself. Recent major financial frauds, such as Enron and Worldcom, have heightened the public awareness of frauds and the extent of the damage that can be done by them. The U.S. Congress passed the Sarbanes-Oxley Act of 2002 in response to the giant frauds as an attempt to bring into legislation certain requirements to deter fraud and increase punishment for executives who commit financial frauds.

This chapter examines the two closely related subjects of ethics and fraud and their implications for auditing. We begin with a survey of ethical issues that highlight an organization's conflicting responsibilities to its employees, shareholders, customers, and the general public. Organization managers have an ethical responsibility to seek a balance between the risks and benefits to these constituents that result from their decisions. Similarly, employees have an ethical responsibility to their employers. Management, employees, and auditors need to recognize the implications of new information technologies for such historic issues as working conditions, the right to privacy, and the potential for fraud.

Although the term *fraud* is very familiar in today's financial press, it is not always clear what constitutes fraud. In this section, we examine the nature and meaning of fraud, differentiate between employee fraud and management fraud, explain fraud-motivating forces, and discuss the anti-fraud profession in general.

ETHICS

With scandals in the banking industry, stories of computer crimes and viruses, and almost daily charges of impropriety and illegalities by government officials, one cannot help but wonder about the current state of ethics in America. Such business activities as kickbacks, fraud, consumer deception, conflicts of interest, and the selling of products that are banned in the United States to Third World countries are all too common. Countless journal and newspaper articles, books, television programs, and movies are concerned with ethics or, more precisely, the *lack of ethics* in business, politics, education, and everyday life.

Ethical standards are derived from societal mores, religious teachings, and deep-rooted personal beliefs about issues of right and wrong that are not universally agreed upon. It is quite possible for two individuals, both of whom consider themselves to be acting ethically, to be on opposite sides of an issue. Often, we confuse ethical issues with legal issues. When the Honorable Gentleman from the state of ———, who is charged with ethical misconduct, stands before Congress and proclaims that he is "guilty of no wrongdoing," is he really saying that he did not *break the law*?

WHAT IS BUSINESS ETHICS?

Ethics pertains to the principles of conduct that individuals use in making choices and guiding their behavior in situations that involve the concepts of right and wrong. More specifically, **business ethics** involves finding the answers to two questions:

1. How do managers decide on what is right in conducting their business?
2. Once managers have recognized what is right, how do they achieve it?

Ethical issues in business can be divided into four areas: equity, rights, honesty, and the exercise of corporate power. Table 11-1 identifies some of the business practices in each of these areas that have ethical implications.

Although interest in business ethics has increased significantly over the last decade, the subject has concerned both scholars and the public since the beginnings of the Western economy. Concerns about the moral shortcomings of financiers, bankers, and investors are found in many historical writings. In fact, many contemporary debates about the nature of business ethics are centuries old.[1]

John F. Akers, the former chairman of the board and CEO of IBM Corporation, states: "Our ethical standards come out of the past—out of our inheritance as a people: religious, philosophical, historical. And the more we know of that past, the more surefootedly we can inculcate ethical conduct in the future."[2]

Ethical behavior and personal gain are closely related issues. Medieval Catholicism deemed capitalism and money making to be morally wrong: "A Catholic could no more have been an ethical moneylender six centuries ago than he could be a socially responsible drug dealer today."[3] Many medieval merchants did act unscrupulously by any standards. But if their business was thought to be fundamentally immoral, why should they try to perform it ethically? How could they?

---

1 D. Vogel, "Business Ethics Past and Present," *Public Interest* (Winter 1991): 49–64.

2 J. F. Akers, "Ethics and Competitiveness—Putting First Things First," *Sloan Management Review* (Winter 1989): 69–71.

3 Vogel, "Business Ethics Past and Present."

TABLE 11-1

Ethical Issues in Business

Equity	Executive salaries Comparable worth Product pricing Corporate due process Employee health screening Employee privacy
Rights	Sexual harassment Affirmative action Equal employment opportunity Whistleblowing Employee and management conflicts of interest Security of organization data and records
Honesty	Misleading advertising Questionable business practices in foreign countries Accurate reporting of shareholder interests Political action committees Workplace safety
Exercise of Corporate Power	Product safety Environmental issues Divestment of interests Corporate political contributions Downsizing and plant closures

The Protestant Reformation made it possible for the successful businessperson to be an ethical individual as well. Profit and heaven were thus no longer mutually exclusive pursuits. A diligent worker could be rewarded financially as a sign of God's favor. Further, the acquisition of personal wealth could be socially beneficial. Hence, businesspeople were rewarded with profits for fulfilling the needs and expectations of their customers, employees, and investors.

Protestant business ethics has had a significant impact on Western culture. Nineteenth-century Americans were very concerned with the relationship between the moral character of individuals and success in business. Contemporary business ethics shifts the focus away from the individual's character to the organization's actions. In addition, current discussions about business ethics have taken on a secular tone. Nonetheless, we remain preoccupied with the relationship of ethics and profit.

In today's world, many people believe that the term *business ethics* is an oxymoron. However, good ethical behavior should also be good for business. This does not mean that firms that act ethically will prosper. Ethical behavior is a necessary but not a sufficient condition for business success. An equally important corollary is that firms that act *unethically* should be punished.

How Some Firms Address Ethical Issues

In 1990, the Business Roundtable, composed of the chief executive officers of 200 major corporations, set up a task force that included several ethicists as consultants. The group studied ethics programs at 10 companies and made recommendations that would help to ensure ethical practices within organizations. These included greater commitment of top management to improving ethical standards, written codes that clearly communicate management expectations, programs to implement ethical guidelines, and techniques to monitor compliance.[4]

Some very successful companies have long emphasized ethics. For example, Boeing uses line managers to lead ethics training sessions and maintains a toll-free number to enable employees to report violations. General Mills has published guidelines for dealing with vendors, competitors, and customers, and emphasizes open decision making. Johnson & Johnson's credo of corporate values is integral to its culture. It holds companywide meetings that challenge the credo tenets and uses surveys to ascertain compliance.[5]

The Role of Management in Maintaining the Ethical Climate

Organization managers must create and maintain an appropriate ethical atmosphere; they must limit the opportunity and temptation for unethical behavior within the firm. It is not enough for managers to appeal to each individual's conscience. The individual must be made aware of the firm's commitment to ethics above short-term increases in profit and efficiency.[6]

Although top management's attitude toward ethics sets the tone for business practice, in many situations it is up to lower-level managers to uphold a firm's ethical standards. Poor ethical standards among employees are a root cause of employee fraud and other abuses. Reported abuses in Wall Street scandals have typically been perpetrated by relatively junior employees. Methods need to be developed for including lower-level managers and employees in the ethics schema of the firm. Managers and employees alike should be made aware of the firm's code of ethics, be given decision models, and participate in training programs that explore ethical issues.

Ethical Development

Most individuals develop a code of ethics as a result of their family environment, formal education, and personal experiences. Behavioral stage theory suggests that we all go through several stages of moral evolution before settling on one level of ethical reasoning.[7] The levels in the stage theory model are presented in Figure 11-1. Managers who achieve Stage 6 are guided by self-chosen ethical principles and are not influenced by social pressure, fear, or guilt in their decisions.

Making Ethical Decisions

Business schools can and should be involved in the ethical development of future managers. Business programs can teach students analytical techniques to use in trying to understand and put into perspective a firm's conflicting responsibilities to its employees, shareholders, customers, and the public.

---

4 J. A. Byrne, "Businesses Are Signing up for Ethics 101," *BusinessWeek*, 15 February 1988, pp. 56–57.

5 *Ibid.*

6 S. W. Gellerman, "Managing Ethics from the Top Down," *Sloan Management Review* (Winter 1989): 73–79.

7 G. Baxter and C. Rarick, "Education for the Moral Development of Managers: Kohlberg's Stages of Moral Development and Integrative Education," in James A. O'Brien, *Management Information Systems: A Managerial End User Perspective* (Boston: Irwin, 1993), p. 545.

FIGURE 11-1 **Behavioral Stage Theory**

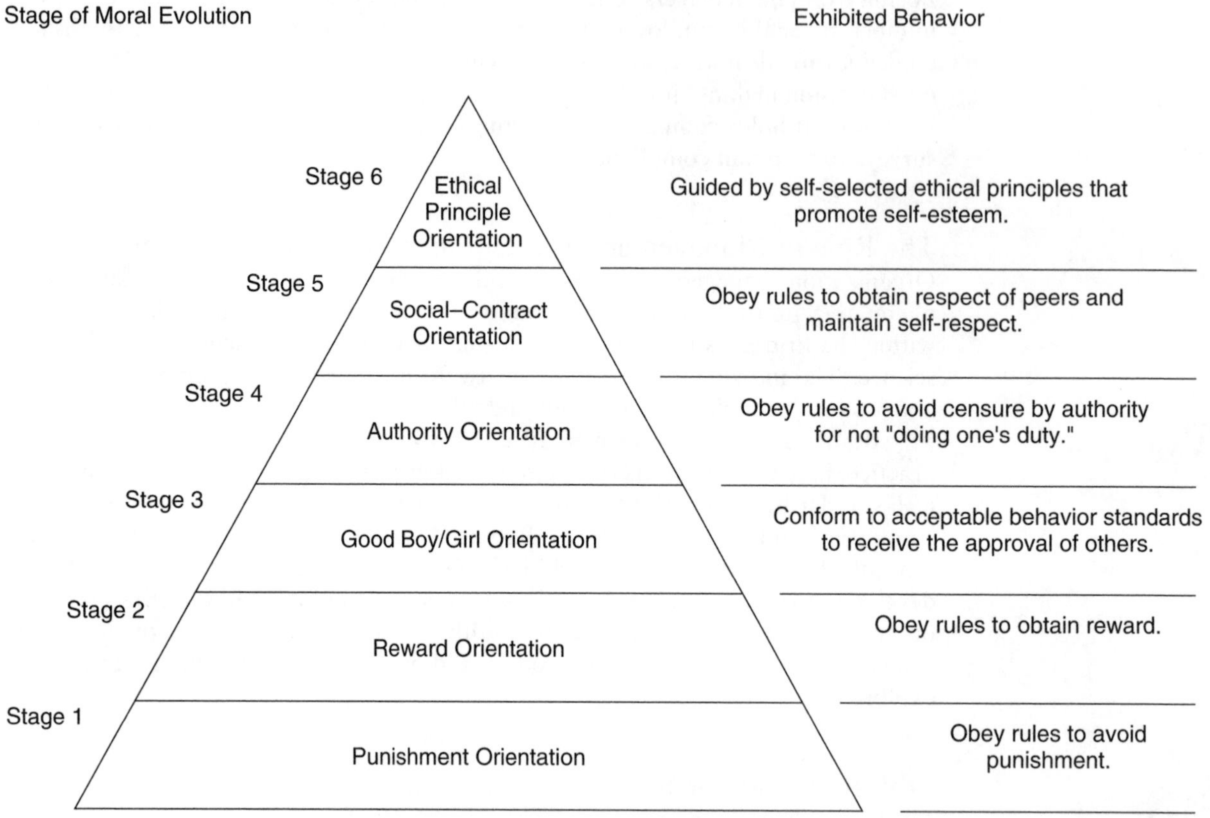
Stage of Moral Evolution
Exhibited Behavior
Stage 6
Ethical Principle Orientation
Guided by self-selected ethical principles that promote self-esteem.
Stage 5
Social–Contract Orientation
Obey rules to obtain respect of peers and maintain self-respect.
Stage 4
Authority Orientation
Obey rules to avoid censure by authority for not "doing one's duty."
Stage 3
Good Boy/Girl Orientation
Conform to acceptable behavior standards to receive the approval of others.
Stage 2
Reward Orientation
Obey rules to obtain reward.
Stage 1
Punishment Orientation
Obey rules to avoid punishment.

Every ethical decision has both risks and benefits. For example, implementing a new computer-based information system in an organization may cause some employees to lose their jobs, while those who remain enjoy the benefit of improved working conditions. Seeking a balance between these consequences is the managers' **ethical responsibility**. The following ethical principles provide some guidance in the discharge of this responsibility.[8]

- *Proportionality.* The benefit from a decision must outweigh the risks. Furthermore, there must be no alternative decision that provides the same or greater benefit with less risk.
- *Justice.* The benefits of the decision should be distributed fairly to those who share the risks. Those who do not benefit should not carry the burden of risk.
- *Minimize Risk.* Even if judged acceptable by the above principles, the decision should be implemented so as to minimize all of the risks and avoid any unnecessary risks.

8 M. McFarland, "Ethics and the Safety of Computer System," *Computer*, February 1991.

What Is Computer Ethics?

The use of information technology in business has had a major impact on society and thus raises significant ethical issues regarding computer crime, working conditions, privacy, and more. **Computer ethics** is "the analysis of the nature and social impact of computer technology and the corresponding formulation and justification of policies for the ethical use of such technology . . . [This includes] concerns about software as well as hardware and concerns about networks connecting computers as well as computers themselves."[9]

Bynum has defined three levels of computer ethics: pop, para, and theoretical.[10] ***Pop* computer ethics** is simply the exposure to stories and reports found in the popular media regarding the good or bad ramifications of computer technology. The society at large needs to be aware of such things as computer viruses and computer systems designed to aid handicapped persons. ***Para* computer ethics** involves taking a real interest in computer ethics cases and acquiring some level of skill and knowledge in the field. All systems professionals need to reach this level of competency so they can do their jobs effectively. Students of accounting information systems should also achieve this level of ethical understanding. The third level, ***theoretical* computer ethics**, is of interest to multidisciplinary researchers who apply the theories of philosophy, sociology, and psychology to computer science with the goal of bringing some new understanding to the field.

A New Problem or Just a New Twist on an Old Problem?

There are many ethical issues to which students should be exposed. Some will argue that the pertinent issues have already been examined in some other domain. For example, the issue of property rights has been explored and has resulted in copyright, trade secret, and patent laws. Although computer programs are a new type of asset, many believe that they should not be considered as different from other forms of property. So a fundamental question is whether computers present new ethical problems or just create new twists on old problems. Where the latter is the case, we need only to understand the generic values that are at stake and the principles that should then apply.[11] However, a large contingent vociferously disagrees with the premise that computers are no different than other technology. For example, many reject the notion of intellectual property being the same as real property. There is, as yet, no consensus on this matter.

This section touches on several issues of concern for the student of accounting information systems. This listing is not presumed to be exhaustive, and a full discussion of each of the issues is beyond the scope of this chapter. Instead, it provides several trigger questions. It is hoped that these questions will serve as discussion starters in the classroom. To give each of them a label and separate treatment, some overlap between issues is unavoidable.

---

9 J. H. Moor, "What Is Computer Ethics?" *Metaphilosophy* 16 (1985): 266–275.

10 T. W. Bynum, "Human Values and the Computer Science Curriculum" (Working paper for the National Conference on Computing and Values, August 1991).

11 G. Johnson, "A Framework for Thinking about Computer Ethics" in J. Robinette and R. Barquin (eds.), *Computers and Ethics: A Sourcebook for Discussions* (Brooklyn: Polytechnic Press, 1989), pp. 26–31.

Privacy

People desire to be in full control of what and how much information about themselves is available to others, and to whom it is available. This is the issue of **privacy**. "[P]rivacy is a matter of the restricted access to persons or information about persons."[12] The creation and maintenance of huge, shared databases makes it necessary to protect people from the potential misuse of data. This raises the issue of **ownership** in the personal information industry.[13] Should the privacy of individuals be protected through policies and systems? No laws currently govern this industry, yet the demand for personal information (for targeted mailing lists, for example) is ever-growing. What information about oneself does the individual "own"? Why can firms that are unrelated to individuals buy and sell information about these individuals without their permission?

Security (Accuracy and Confidentiality)

Computer security is an attempt to avoid such undesirable events as a loss of confidentiality or data integrity. Security systems attempt to prevent fraud and other misuse of computer systems; they act to protect and further the legitimate interests of the system's constituencies. The ethical issues involving security arise from the emergence of shared, computerized databases that have the potential to cause irreparable harm to individuals by disseminating inaccurate information to authorized users, such as through incorrect credit reporting.[14] There is a similar danger in disseminating accurate information to persons unauthorized to receive it. However, increasing security can actually cause other problems. For example, security can be used both to protect personal property and to undermine freedom of access to data, which may have a deleterious effect on some individuals. Which is the more important goal? Automated monitoring can be used to detect intruders or other misuse, yet it can also be used to spy on legitimate users, thus diminishing their privacy. Where is the line to be drawn? What is an appropriate use and level of security? Which is most important: security, accuracy, or confidentiality?

Ownership of Property

Laws designed to preserve real property rights have been extended to cover what is referred to as intellectual property—that is, software. The question here becomes, what can an individual (or organization) own? Ideas? Media? Source code? Object code? A related question is whether owners and users should be constrained in their use or access. Copyright laws have been invoked in an attempt to protect those who develop software from having it copied. Unquestionably, the hundreds and thousands of program development hours should be protected from piracy. However, many believe the copyright laws can cause more harm than good. For example, should the "look and feel" of a software package be granted copyright protection? The League for Programming Freedom argues that this flies in the face of the original intent of the law. Whereas the purpose of copyrights is to "promote the

---

12 J. H. Moor, "The Ethics of Privacy Protection," *Library Trends* 39 (1990): 69–82.

13 W. Ware, "Contemporary Privacy Issues" (Working paper for the National Conference on Computing and Human Values, August 1991).

14 K. C. Laudon, "Data Quality and Due Process in Large Interorganizational Record Systems," *Communications of the ACM* (1986): 4–11.

progress of science and the useful arts," allowing a user interface to have the protection of copyright may do just the opposite.

The best interest of computer users is served when industry standards emerge; copyright laws work to disallow this. This same group also argues against the use of patents for software. Patents protect the holder against anyone using the same basic process, even if it is independently developed. Since patent searches are very expensive and quite unreliable, programmers may be sued for inadvertently using a process on which someone else holds the patent. Firms exist whose only mission is to obtain patents, then sue software developers for patent infringement. In trying to resolve these issues, social goals (such as preservation and dissemination of information, justice of distribution, and maximum potential of resources) are found to conflict with personal goals (recognition and credit, control, empowerment). Part of the problem lies in the uniqueness of software, its ease of dissemination, and the possibility of exact replication. Does software fit with the current categories and conventions regarding ownership?

Race

While African Americans and Hispanics constitute about 20 percent of the U.S. population, they make up only 7 percent of management information systems (MIS) professionals.[15] What causes this difference? Our society often tries to make restitution for past social wrongs. Should something special be done in this situation? If so, what, and how can reverse discrimination then be avoided? Or should it?

Equity in Access

Some barriers to access are intrinsic to the technology of information systems, but some are avoidable through careful system design. Several factors, some of which are not unique to information systems, can limit access to computing technology. The economic status of the individual or the affluence of an organization will determine the ability to obtain information technology. Culture also limits access, for example, where documentation is prepared only in one language or is poorly translated. Safety features, or the lack thereof, have limited access to pregnant women, for example. How can hardware and software be designed with consideration for differences in physical and cognitive skills? What is the cost of providing equity in access? For what groups of society should equity in access become a priority?

Environmental Issues

Computers with high-speed printers allow for the production of printed documents faster than ever before. It is probably easier just to print a document than to consider seriously whether it should be printed and how many copies really need to be made. It may be more efficient or more comforting to have a hard copy in addition to the electronic version. However, paper comes from trees, a precious natural resource, and ends up in landfills if not properly recycled. Should organizations limit nonessential hard copies? Can *nonessential* be defined? Who can and should define it? Should proper recycling be required? How can it be enforced?

---

15 J. S. Bozman, "MIS Dream Jobs Still Elude Blacks," *Computerworld*, 18 January 1988, p. 1.

Artificial Intelligence

A new set of social and ethical issues has arisen out of the popularity of expert systems. Because of the way these systems have been marketed, that is, as decision makers or replacements for experts, some people rely on them significantly. Therefore, both knowledge engineers (those who write the programs) and domain experts (those who provide the knowledge about the task being automated) must be concerned about their responsibility for faulty decisions, incomplete or inaccurate knowledge bases, and the role given to computers in the decision-making process.[16] Additionally, the proliferation of knowledge-based systems has the potential to cause a displacement of "experts" (most of whom are in middle management positions) similar to that which occurred to artisans during the Industrial Revolution. Further, since expert systems attempt to clone a manager's decision-making style, an individual's prejudices may implicitly or explicitly be included in the knowledge base. Several questions need to be explored: Who is responsible for the completeness and appropriateness of the knowledge base? Who is responsible for a decision made by an expert system that causes harm when implemented? Who owns the expertise once it is coded into a knowledge base?

Unemployment and Displacement

Many jobs have been and are being changed as a result of the availability of computer technology. People unable or unprepared to change are displaced and are finding it difficult to obtain new jobs. Should employers be responsible for retraining workers who are displaced as a result of the computerization of their functions? Even white-collar professionals are at risk for displacement. Should there be a concern over the exploitation of experts? How can the good provided by information systems be reconciled with their potential for harm?

Misuse of Computers

Computers can be misused in many ways. Copying proprietary software, using a company's computer for personal benefit, and snooping through other people's files are just a few obvious examples.[17] Although copying proprietary software (except to make a personal backup copy) is clearly illegal, it is commonly done. Why do people feel that it is not necessary to obey this law? Are there any good arguments for trying to change this law? What harm is done to the software developer when people make unauthorized copies? A computer is not an item that deteriorates with use, so is there any harm to the employer if it is used for an employee's personal benefit? Does it matter if the computer is used during company time or outside of work hours? Is there a difference if some profit-making activity takes place rather than, for example, using the computer to write a personal letter? Does it make a difference if a profit-making activity takes place during or outside of working hours? Is it okay to look through paper files that clearly belong to someone else? Is there any difference between paper files and computer files?

---

16 R. Dejoie, G. Fowler, and D. Paradice (eds.), *Ethical Issues in Information Systems* (Boston: Boyd & Fraser, 1991).

17 K. A. Forcht, "Assessing the Ethic Standards and Policies in Computer-Based Environments," in R. Dejoie, G. Fowler, and D. Paradice (eds.), *Ethical Issues in Information Systems* (Boston: Boyd & Fraser, 1991).

Internal Control Responsibility

A business cannot meet its financial obligations or achieve its objectives if its information is unreliable. Therefore, managers must establish and maintain a system of appropriate internal controls to ensure the integrity and reliability of their data.[18] Because much of the internal control system relates to the transaction processing system, information systems professionals and accountants are central to ensuring control adequacy.

Deadlines for putting new systems into place often become unachievable. For example, cutting corners by omitting audit trails and other controls might be suggested as a way to complete a project on time.[19] What are the ramifications of cutting certain corners? Is it ever appropriate? What is the purpose of an audit trail? What are the consequences for a system without one? How much control is adequate?

FRAUD AND ACCOUNTANTS

Perhaps no major aspect of the independent auditor's role has caused more controversy for the public accounting profession than the responsibility for the detection of fraud during an audit. Over the last 20 years, the structure of the U.S. financial reporting system has become the subject of congressional inquiries, and the issue of the auditor's role in detecting fraud has gathered momentum to the point where the public accounting profession today faces a crisis in public confidence in its ability to perform the independent attestation function. This situation is represented most vividly by the Enron crisis and subsequent collapse of Arthur Andersen.

The Securities and Exchange Commission, the courts, and the public, along with Congress, are focusing more and more on business failures and questionable practices by the management of corporations that engage in alleged fraud. The question consistently being asked is, "Where were the auditors?"

Although fraud is a very familiar term in today's financial press, its meaning is not always clear. For example, in cases of bankruptcies and business failures, alleged fraud is often poor management decisions or adverse business conditions. Under such circumstances, it becomes necessary to clearly define and understand the nature and meaning of fraud.

Fraud denotes a false representation of a material fact made by one party to another party with the intent to deceive and induce the other party to justifiably rely on the fact to his or her detriment. According to common law, a fraudulent act must meet the following five conditions:

1. ***False representation.*** There must be a false statement or a nondisclosure.
2. ***Material fact.*** A fact must be a substantial factor in inducing someone to act.
3. ***Intent.*** There must be the intent to deceive or the knowledge that one's statement is false.

18 All companies registered with the Securities and Exchange Commission are required by law (Foreign Corrupt Practices Act of 1977) to maintain such a system of internal control.

19 E. Cohen and L. Cornwell, "A Question of Ethics: Developing Information Systems Ethics," *Journal of Business Ethics* 8 (1989): 431–437.

4. ***Justifiable reliance.*** The misrepresentation must have been a substantial factor on which the injured party relied.
5. ***Injury or loss.*** The deception must have caused injury or loss to the victim of the fraud.

Fraud in the business environment has a more specialized meaning. It is an intentional deception, misappropriation of a company's assets, or manipulation of its financial data to the advantage of the perpetrator. In the accounting literature, fraud is also commonly known as *white-collar crime*, *defalcation*, *embezzlement*, and *irregularities*. The auditor deals with fraud typically at two levels: *employee fraud* and *management fraud*. Since each form of fraud has different implications for auditors, we need to distinguish between the two.

Employee fraud, or fraud by nonmanagement employees, is generally designed to directly convert cash or other assets to the employee's personal benefit. Employee fraud usually involves the misappropriation of assets, which is a three-step process: (1) stealing something of value (an asset), (2) converting the asset to a usable form (cash), and (3) concealing the crime to avoid detection. The third step is often the most difficult. It may be relatively easy for a storeroom clerk to steal inventories from the employer's warehouse, but altering the inventory records to hide the theft is more of a challenge. To perpetrate such a fraud, the employee must circumvent the company's internal control system. If a company has an effective system of internal control, employee fraud can usually be prevented or detected.

Management fraud is more insidious than employee fraud because it often escapes detection until irreparable damage or loss has been suffered by the organization. Usually management fraud does not involve the direct theft of assets. Top management may engage in fraudulent activities to obtain a higher stock value. This may be done to meet investor expectations or to take advantage of stock options that have been loaded into the manager's compensation package. This is also called **performance fraud**, which often involves deceptive practices to inflate earnings or to forestall the recognition of either insolvency or a decline in earnings. Lower-level management fraud typically involves materially misstating financial data and internal reports to gain additional compensation, to garner a promotion, or to escape the penalty for poor performance. Management fraud typically contains three special characteristics:[20]

1. The fraud is perpetrated at levels of management above the one to which internal control structures generally relate.
2. The fraud frequently involves using the financial statements to create an illusion that an entity is more healthy and prosperous than it actually is.
3. If the fraud involves misappropriation of assets, it frequently is shrouded in a maze of complex business transactions, often involving related third parties.

The preceding characteristics of management fraud suggest that management can often perpetrate irregularities by overriding an otherwise effective internal control structure that would prevent similar irregularities by other employees.

---

20 R. Grinaker, "Discussant's Response to a Look at the Record on Auditor Detection of Management Fraud," *Proceedings of the 1980 Touche Ross University of Kansas Symposium on Auditing Problems* (Kansas City: University of Kansas, 1980).

Factors That Contribute to Fraud

According to one study by Donald Cressey, people engage in fraudulent activity as a result of an interaction of forces both within an individual's personality and in the external environment. These forces are classified into three major categories: (1) **situational pressures**, (2) **opportunities**, and (3) **personal characteristics (integrity)**. These circumstances have come to be known as the "fraud triangle." Figure 11-2 graphically displays the interplay of these three fraud-motivating forces.[21]

Figure 11-2 suggests that a person with a high level of personal integrity and limited pressure and opportunity to commit fraud is most likely to behave honestly. Similarly, an individual with less personal integrity, when placed in situations with increasing pressure and given the opportunity, is most likely to commit fraud.

Although these factors, for the most part, fall outside of the auditors' sphere of influence, auditors can develop a *red-flag* checklist to detect possible fraudulent activity. To that end, a questionnaire approach could be used to help external auditors uncover motivations for committing fraud. Some of the larger public accounting firms have developed checklists to help uncover fraudulent activity during an

FIGURE 11-2 **Fraud Motivating Forces**

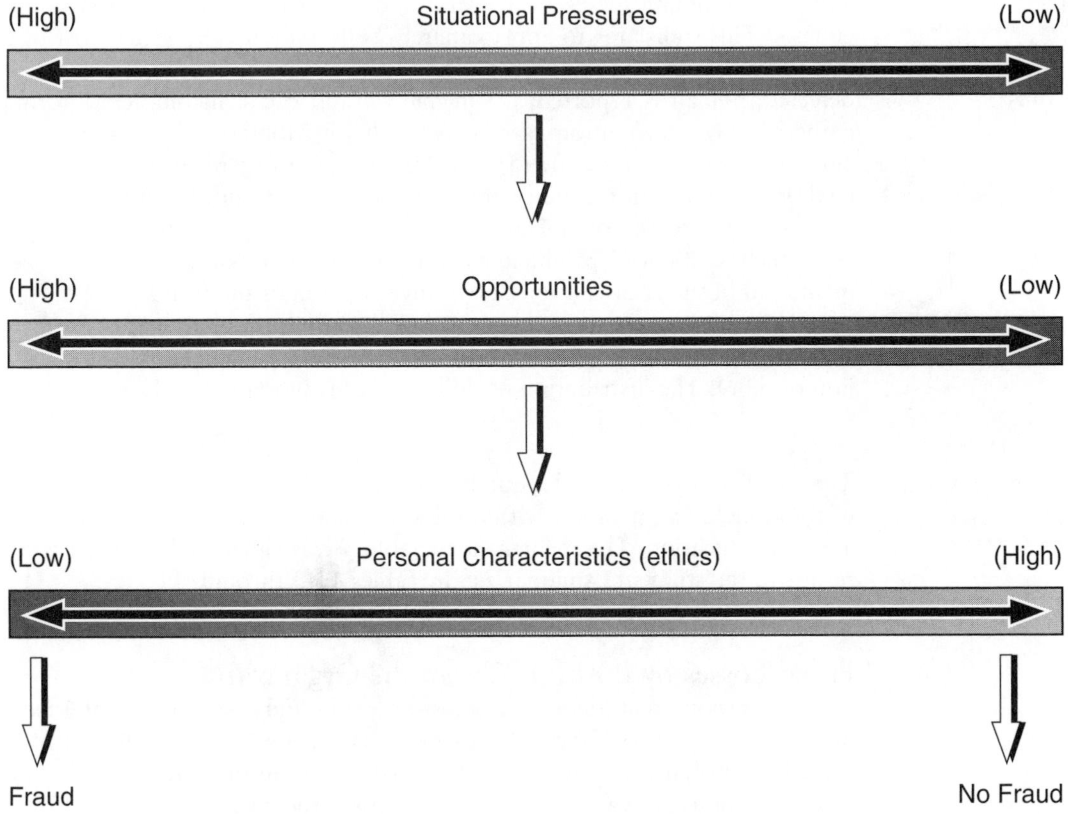

21 M. Romney, W. S. Albrecht, and D. J. Cherrington, "Auditors and the Detection of Fraud," *Journal of Accountancy* (May 1980).

audit. Questions for such a checklist related to management fraud, or financial fraud as it is sometimes called, might include the following:[22]

- Do key executives have unusually high personal debt?
- Do key executives appear to be living beyond their means?
- Do key executives engage in habitual gambling?
- Do key executives appear to abuse alcohol or drugs?
- Do any of the key executives appear to lack personal codes of ethics?
- Are economic conditions unfavorable within the company's industry?
- Does the company use several different banks, none of which sees the company's entire financial picture?
- Do any key executives have close associations with suppliers?
- Is the company experiencing a rapid turnover of key employees, either through quitting or being fired?
- Do one or two individuals dominate the company?

A review of some of these questions suggests that the contemporary auditor may use special investigative agencies to run a complete but confidential background check on the key managers of existing and prospective client firms.

Financial Losses from Fraud

Studies conducted by the **Association of Certified Fraud Examiners (ACFE)** in 1996 and 2002 estimate losses from fraud and abuse to be 6 percent of annual revenues.[23] This translates to approximately $600 billion. The actual cost of fraud is difficult to quantify for a number of reasons: (1) not all fraud is detected; (2) of that detected, not all is reported; (3) in many fraud cases, incomplete information is gathered; (4) information is not properly distributed to management or law enforcement authorities; and (5) too often, business organizations decide to take no civil or criminal action against the perpetrator(s) of fraud. In addition to the direct economic loss to the organization, the total cost of fraud includes many indirect costs such as reduced productivity, the cost of legal action, increased unemployment, and business disruption due to investigation of the fraud.

Of the 620 cases examined in the ACFE study, more than half of the frauds cost their victim organizations at least $100,000, and 16 percent caused losses of $1 million or more. The distribution of dollar losses is presented in Table 11-2.

The Perpetrators of Fraud

The ACFE study examined a number of factors that characterized the perpetrators of fraud including position within the organization, collusion with others, gender, age, and education. The median financial loss was calculated for each factor. The results of the study are summarized in Tables 11-3 through 11-7.

Fraud Losses by Position Within the Organization

Table 11-3 shows that 58 percent of the reported fraud cases were committed by nonmanagerial employees, 36 percent by managers acting alone, and 6 percent by managers in collusion with employees. The median loss in the cases involving manager/employee collusion was $500,000. This is twice the median loss caused by schemes

22 *Ibid.*

23 *Report to the Nation: Occupational Fraud and Abuse,* Association of Fraud Examiners, 2004.

TABLE 11-2

Distribution of Losses

Amount of Loss	Percent of Frauds
$1–$999	2.3%
$1,000–$9,999	10.2%
$10,000–$49,999	22.9%
$50,000–$99,999	12.1%
$100,000–$499,999	27.6%
$500,000–$999,999	8.5%
$1,000,000–$9,999,999	13.2%
$10,000,000 +	3.2%

TABLE 11-3

Losses from Fraud by Position

Position	Percent of Frauds	Loss
Manager and employee	6	$500,000
Manager alone	36	$250,000
Employees alone	58	$60,000

in which managers acted alone and nearly eight times the loss when employees acted alone.

Collusion among employees in the commission of a fraud is difficult to both prevent and detect. This is particularly true when the collusion is between managers and their subordinate employees. Management plays a key role in the internal control structure of an organization. They are relied upon to prevent and detect fraud among their subordinates. When they participate in fraud with the employees over whom they are supposed to provide oversight, the organization's control structure is weakened, or completely circumvented, and the company becomes more vulnerable to losses. More on the effect of collusion is examined next.

Fraud Losses and the Collusion Effect

As already noted, fraud losses involving collusion tend to be greater than those where the perpetrator acts alone. Table 11-4 compares the median losses from frauds (regardless of position) committed by a single individual and those involving collusion. This includes both internal collusion and schemes where an employee or manager colludes with an outsider such as a vendor or a customer. Although fraud committed by a single perpetrator is far more common (68 percent of cases), the median loss from collusion is $450,000. This represents a median loss almost seven times greater than that caused by lone perpetrators.

Fraud Losses by Gender

Table 11-5 shows that the median loss per case caused by males ($200,000) was more than three times that caused by females ($60,000).

TABLE 11-4

Losses from Fraud by Collusion

Perpetrators	Loss
Two or more (32.4%)	$450,000
One (67.6%)	67,000

TABLE 11-5

Losses from Fraud by Gender

Gender	Loss
Male	$200,000
Female	60,000

Fraud Losses by Age

Table 11-6 indicates that perpetrators 25 years of age or younger cause median losses of about $18,000, while employees 60 and older perpetrated frauds that were, on average, 28 times larger—$500,000.

Fraud Losses by Education

Table 11-7 shows the median loss from frauds relative to the perpetrator's education level. Frauds committed by high school graduates averaged only $70,000, while those with bachelor's degrees averaged $245,000. Perpetrators with advanced degrees were responsible for frauds with a medial loss of $162,000. This last result

TABLE 11-6

Losses from Fraud by Age

Age Range	Loss
< 25	$18,000
26–30	27,000
31–35	100,000
36–40	100,000
41–50	150,000
51–60	285,000
> 60	500,000

TABLE 11-7

Losses from Fraud by Education Level

Education Level	Loss
High school	$70,000
College	243,000
Post-graduate	162,000

is inconsistent with the ACFE's 1996 report, which showed that the level of fraud loss increased with the number of years of education received.

Conclusions to Be Drawn

Unless we intend to eliminate all managers, and male employees over the age of 25 who have received degrees in higher education, the fraud classification scheme above provides little in the way of anti-fraud decision-making criteria. There is, however, a common threat that can be identified from this study. Notwithstanding the importance of personal ethics and situational pressures, *opportunity* is the factor that engenders fraud. Opportunity can be defined as control over assets or access to assets. Indeed, control and access are essential elements of opportunity. The financial loss differences associated with the classifications are explained by the opportunity factor.

- *Gender.* While the demographic picture is changing, more men than women occupy positions of authority in business organizations, which provides them greater access to assets.
- *Position.* Those in the highest positions have the greatest access to company funds and assets.
- *Age.* Older employees tend to occupy higher-ranking positions and therefore generally have greater access to company assets.
- *Education.* Generally, those with more education occupy higher positions in their organizations and therefore have greater access to company funds and other assets.
- *Collusion.* One reason for segregating occupational duties is to deny potential perpetrators the opportunity to commit fraud. When individuals in critical positions collude, they create opportunities to control or gain access to assets that otherwise would not exist.

The Underlying Problems

The underlying problems that permit and aid these frauds are found in the boardroom, not the mailroom. In this section we examine some prominent corporate governance failures and the legislation designed to remedy them.

The series of events symbolized by the Enron, Worldcom, and Adelphia debacles caused many to question whether our existing federal securities laws were adequate to assure full and fair financial disclosures by public companies. The following underlying problems are at the root of this concern.

Lack of Auditor Independence

Auditing firms that are also engaged by their clients to perform nonaccounting activities such as actuarial services, internal audit outsourcing services, and consulting lack independence. They are essentially auditing their own work. This risk is that as auditors they will not bring to management's attention detected problems that might adversely affect their consulting fees. For example, Enron's auditors—Arthur Andersen—were also Enron's internal auditors and management consultants.

Lack of Director Independence

Many boards of directors comprise individuals who are not independent. Examples of lack of independence are directors who: have a personal relationship by serving on the boards of other directors companies; have a business trading relationship as key customers or suppliers of the company; have a financial relationship as primary stockholders or have received personal loans from the company; have an operational relationship as employees of the company.

A notorious example of corporate inbreeding is Adelphia Communications, a telecommunication company. Founded 1952, it went public 1986 and grew rapidly through a series of acquisitions and became the sixth largest cable provider in the United States before an accounting scandal came to light. The founding family (John Rigas, CEO and chairman of the board, Timothy Rigas, CFO, CAO and chairman of audit committee, Michael Rigas, VP for operation, and J. P. Rigas, VP for strategic planning) perpetrated the fraud. Between 1998 and May 2002, the Rigas family successfully disguised transactions, distorted the company's financial picture, and engaged in embezzlement that resulted in a loss of more than $60 billion to shareholders.

While it is neither practical nor wise to establish a board of directors that is totally void of self-interest, popular wisdom suggests that a healthier board of directors is one in which the majority of directors are independent outsiders with the integrity and the qualifications to understand the company and objectively plan its course.

Questionable Executive Compensation Schemes

A survey by Thompson Financial revealed the strong belief that executives have abused stock-based compensation.[24] The consensus is that fewer stock options should be offered than currently is the practice. Excessive use of short-term stock options to compensate directors and executives may result in short-term thinking and strategies aimed at driving up stock prices at the expense of the firm's long-term health. In extreme cases, financial statement misrepresentation has been the vehicle to achieve the stock price needed to exercise the option.

As a case in point, Enron's management was a firm believer in the use of stock options. Almost all employees had some type of arrangement where they could purchase shares at a discount, or were granted options based on future share prices. At Enron's headquarters in Houston, TVs were installed in the elevators so employees could track Enron's (and their own portfolio's) success. Before the firm's collapse, Enron executives added millions of dollars to their personal fortunes by exercising stock options.

Inappropriate Accounting Practices

The use of inappropriate accounting techniques is a characteristic common to many financial statement fraud schemes. Enron made elaborate use of Special Purpose Entities (SPE) to hide liabilities through off-balance-sheet accounting. SPEs are legal, but their application in this case was clearly intended to deceive the market. Enron also employed income-inflating techniques. For example, when the company sold a contract to provide natural gas for a period of two years, it would recognize all the future revenue in the period when the contract was sold.

---

24 Howard Stock, "Institutions Prixe Good Governance: Once Bitten, Twice Shy, Investors Seek Oversight and Transparency," *Investor Relations Business*; New York (November 4, 2002).

WorldCom was another culprit of the improper accounting practices. In April 2001, WorldCom management decided to transfer transmission-line costs from current expense accounts to capital accounts. This allowed WorldCom to defer some operating expenses and report higher earnings. Also, through acquisitions, it seized the opportunity to raise earnings. WorldCom reduced the book value of hard assets of MCI by $3.4 billion and increased goodwill by the same amount. Had the assets been left at book value, they would have been charged against earnings over four years. Goodwill, on the other hand, was amortized over much longer period. In June 2002, the company declared a $3.8 billion profits overstatement due to falsely recorded expenses over the previous five quarters. The size of this fraud increased to $9 billion over the following months as additional evidence of improper accounting came to light.

Sarbanes-Oxley Act

To address plummeting institutional and individual investor confidence triggered in part by business failures and accounting restatements, Congress enacted and President Bush signed into law the **Sarbanes-Oxley Act** in July 2002. This landmark piece of legislation will fundamentally change the way public companies do business and how the accounting profession performs its attest function. The act establishes a framework to modernize and reform the oversight and regulation of public company auditing. Its principal reforms pertain to: (1) the creation of an accounting oversight board; (2) auditor independence; (3) corporate governance and responsibility; (4) disclosure requirements; and (5) penalties for fraud and other violations.

Accounting Oversight Board

The Sarbanes-Oxley Act creates a **Public Company Accounting Oversight Board (PCAOB)**. The PCAOB is empowered to set auditing, quality control, and ethics standards, to inspect registered accounting firms, to conduct investigations, and to take disciplinary actions.

Auditor Independence

The act addresses auditor independence by creating more separation between a firm's attestation and nonauditing activities. This is intended to specify categories of services that a public accounting firm cannot perform for its client. These include the following nine functions:

1. Bookkeeping or other services related to the accounting records or financial statements
2. Financial information systems design and implementation
3. Appraisal or valuation services, fairness opinions, or contribution-in-kind reports
4. Actuarial services
5. Internal audit outsourcing services
6. Management functions or human resources
7. Broker or dealer, investment adviser, or investment banking services
8. Legal services and expert services unrelated to the audit; and
9. Any other service that the PCAOB determines is impermissible

While the Sarbanes-Oxley Act prohibits auditors from providing these services to their audit clients, they are not prohibited from performing such services for nonaudit clients or privately held companies.

Corporate Governance and Responsibility

The Sarbanes-Oxley Act requires all audit committee members to be independent and requires the audit committee to hire and oversee the external auditors. This provision is consistent with many investors who consider the board composition to be a critical investment factor. For example, a Thompson Financial survey revealed that most institutional investors want corporate boards to be comprised of at least 75 percent independent directors.[25]

Two other significant provision of the act relate to corporate governance: (1) public companies are prohibited from making loans to executive officers and directors; and (2) the act requires attorneys to report evidence of a material violation of securities laws or breaches of fiduciary duty to the CEO, CFO, or PCAOB.

Issuer and Management Disclosure

The Sarbanes-Oxley Act imposes new corporate disclosure requirements, including:

- Public companies must report all off-balance-sheet transactions.
- Annual reports filed with the SEC must now include a statement by management asserting that it is responsible for creating and maintaining adequate internal controls and asserting to the effectiveness of those controls. This new requirement is of special importance to internal auditors because they are likely to be heavily involved in the development of the controls statement.
- Officers must certify that the company's accounts "fairly present" the firm's financial condition and results of operations. Knowingly filing a false certification is a criminal offense.

Fraud and Criminal Penalties

The Sarbanes-Oxley Act imposes a range of new criminal penalties for fraud and other wrongful acts. In particular, the Sarbanes-Oxley Act creates new federal crimes relating to the destruction of documents or audit work papers, securities fraud, tampering with documents to be used in an official proceeding, and actions against whistleblowers.

Anti-Fraud Profession

Persons pursuing a career in anti-fraud have filled a wide variety of jobs and positions. Many are assistants to attorneys in various civil or criminal legal cases. In this role, the forensic accountant or fraud auditor serves as an expert in either the investigation or presenting of evidence in court. Many do fraud audits for the public. Clearly all major public accounting firms have accountants and CPAs on staff who could be considered fraud auditors. Internal audit and IT audit also generally include specialized fraud auditors in the larger firms. Thus, there is a wide array of potential job opportunities or fields in which a fraud auditor or forensic accountant could be employed.

25 *Ibid.*

Perhaps *the* organization that serves the anti-fraud profession in a manner similar to the way the AICPA serves public accounting is the Association of Certified Fraud Examiners (ACFE). The ACFE provides education, training, literature, support, and certification for the anti-fraud profession and is arguably its greatest champion in the last few years. A Certified Fraud Examiner (CFE) would be an expert in these mentioned concepts, and additionally in areas such as interview, legal evidence, and criminology of the white-collar criminal.

SUMMARY

This chapter examined the two closely related subjects of ethics and fraud and their implications for auditing. It began by examining ethical issues that societies have pondered for centuries. Good ethics is a necessary condition for the long-term profitability of a business. This requires that ethical issues be understood at all levels of the firm, from top management to line workers. In this section, we identified several ethical issues for auditors to consider in their fraud risk assessment. The second section of the chapter examined a number of fraud issues. Although the term *fraud* is familiar in today's financial press, what constitutes fraud is not always clear. In this chapter, we examined the nature and meaning of fraud, differentiated between employee fraud and management fraud, explained fraud-motivating forces, and discussed recent anti-fraud legislation and the anti-fraud profession in general.

KEY TERMS

Association of Certified Fraud Examiners (ACFE)
business ethics
computer ethics
computer fraud
computer security
conflict of interest
employee fraud
ethical responsibility
ethics
false representation
fraud
fraud triangle
injury or loss
intent
justice
justifiable reliance
management fraud
material fact
minimize risk
opportunity
ownership
para computer ethics
performance fraud
personal characteristics (integrity)
pop computer ethics
privacy
proportionality
Public Company Accounting Oversight Board (PCAOB)
situational pressures
theoretical computer ethics

Review Questions

1. What is ethics?
2. What is business ethics?
3. What are the four areas of ethical business issues?
4. What is a business code of ethics?
5. What are three ethical principles that may provide some guidance for ethical responsibility?
6. What is computer ethics?
7. How do the three levels of computer ethics—pop, para, and theoretical—differ?
8. Are computer ethical issues new problems, or just a new twist on old problems?
9. What are the computer ethical issues regarding privacy?
10. What are the computer ethical issues regarding security?
11. What are the computer ethical issues regarding ownership of property?
12. What are the computer ethical issues regarding race?
13. What are the computer ethical issues regarding equity in access?
14. What are the computer ethical issues regarding the environment?
15. What are the computer ethical issues regarding artificial intelligence?
16. What are the computer ethical issues regarding unemployment and displacement?
17. What are the computer ethical issues regarding misuse of computers?
18. What are the computer ethical issues regarding internal control responsibility?
19. What are the five conditions that constitute fraud under common law?
20. What is fraud in the business environment?
21. What is management fraud?
22. What is employee fraud?
23. What are the three forces within an individual's personality and the external environment that interact to promote fraudulent activity?
24. How can external auditors attempt to uncover motivations for committing fraud?

Discussion Questions

1. Distinguish between ethical issues and legal issues.
2. Some argue against corporate involvement in socially responsible behavior because the costs incurred by such behavior place the organization at a disadvantage in a competitive market. Discuss the merits and flaws of this argument.
3. Although top management's attitude toward ethics sets the tone for business practice, sometimes it is up to lower-level managers to uphold a firm's ethical standards. John, an operations-level manager, discovers that the company is illegally dumping toxic materials and is in violation of environmental regulations. John's immediate supervisor is involved in the dumping. What action should John take?
4. When a company has a strong internal control structure, stockholders can expect the elimination of fraud. Comment on the soundness of this statement.
5. Distinguish between employee fraud and management fraud.
6. The estimates of losses annually due to computer fraud vary widely. Why do you think obtaining a good estimate of this figure is difficult?
7. Explain the characteristics of management fraud.
8. The text discusses many questions about personal traits of employees that might help uncover fraudulent activity. Name three.
9. Why are the computer ethics issues of privacy, security, and property ownership of interest to accountants?
10. Explain the five conditions necessary for an act to be considered fraudulent.
11. Explain the problems associated with lack of auditor independence.
12. Explain the problems associated with lack of director independence.

13. Explain the problems associated with questionable executive compensation schemes.
14. Explain the problems associated with inappropriate accounting practices.
15. Explain the purpose of the PCAOB.
16. Why is an Independent Audit Committee important to a company?
17. What are the key points of the "Issuer and Management Disclosure" of the Sarbanes-Oxley Act?

MULTIPLE-CHOICE QUESTIONS

1. Which ethical principle states that the benefit from a decision must outweigh the risks, and that there is no alternative decision that provides the same or greater benefit with less risk?
   a. minimize risk
   b. justice
   c. informed consent
   d. proportionality
2. Individuals who acquire some level of skill and knowledge in the field of computer ethics are involved in which level of computer ethics?
   a. para computer ethics
   b. pop computer ethics
   c. theoretical computer ethics
   d. practical computer ethics
3. All of the following are issues of computer security except
   a. releasing incorrect data to authorized individuals.
   b. permitting computer operators unlimited access to the computer room.
   c. permitting access to data by unauthorized individuals.
   d. providing correct data to unauthorized individuals.
4. Which characteristic is not associated with software as intellectual property?
   a. uniqueness of the product
   b. possibility of exact replication
   c. automated monitoring to detect intruders
   d. ease of dissemination
5. For an action to be called fraudulent, all of the following conditions are required except
   a. poor judgment.
   b. false representation.
   c. intent to deceive.
   d. injury or loss.
6. One characteristic of employee fraud is that the fraud
   a. is perpetrated at a level to which internal controls do not apply.
   b. involves misstating financial statements.
   c. involves the direct conversion of cash or other assets to the employee's personal benefit.
   d. involves misappropriating assets in a series of complex transactions involving third parties.
7. Forces that may permit fraud to occur do not include
   a. a gambling addiction.
   b. lack of segregation of duties.
   c. centralized decision-making environment.
   d. questionable integrity of employees.
8. Who is responsible for establishing and maintaining the internal control system?
   a. the internal auditor
   b. the accountant
   c. management
   d. the external auditor
9. Which of the following indicates a strong internal control environment?
   a. The internal audit group reports to the audit committee of the board of directors.
   b. There is no segregation of duties between organization functions.
   c. There are questions about the integrity of management.
   d. Adverse business conditions exist in the industry.
10. Employee fraud involves three steps. Of the following, which is not involved?
    a. concealing the crime to avoid detection
    b. stealing something of value
    c. misstating financial statements
    d. converting the asset to a usable form
11. The importance to the accounting profession of the Sarbanes-Oxley Act of 2002 is that
    a. bribery will be eliminated.
    b. management will not be able to override the company's internal controls.
    c. firms are required to have an effective internal control system.
    d. firms will not be exposed to lawsuits.

12. The board of directors consists entirely of the CEO's close business associates and management of the organization. This
    a. indicates a weakness the accounting system.
    b. is incompliant with the Sarbanes-Oxley Act.
    c. is a red flag for auditors to review and report on executive compensation.
    d. is a normal board structure and not an issue of audit concern.
13. Business ethics involves
    a. how managers decide on what is right in conducting business.
    b. how managers achieve what they decide is right for the business.
    c. both a and b.
    d. only a.
14. All of the following are conditions for fraud except
    a. false representation.
    b. injury or loss.
    c. intent.
    d. material reliance.

PROBLEMS

1. CMA 1289 3-Y6 Causes of Fraud

The studies conducted by the National Commission on Fraudulent Financial Reporting (the Treadway Commission) revealed that fraudulent financial reporting usually occurs as the result of certain environmental, institutional, or individual influences and opportune situations. These influences and opportunities, present to some degree in all companies, add pressures and motivate individuals and companies to engage in fraudulent financial reporting. The effective prevention and detection of fraudulent financial reporting requires an understanding of these influences and opportunities, while evaluating the risk of fraudulent financial reporting that these factors can create in a company. The risk factors to be assessed include not only internal ethical and control factors but also external environmental conditions.

Required:

a. Identify two situational pressures in a public company that would increase the likelihood of fraud.
b. Identify three corporate circumstances (opportune situations) where fraud is easier to commit and detection is less likely.
c. For the purpose of assessing the risk of fraudulent financial reporting, identify the external environmental factors that should be considered in the company's
    i. industry.
    ii. business environment.
    iii. legal and regulatory environment.
d. List several recommendations that top management should incorporate to reduce the possibility of fraudulent financial reporting.

2. Kickback Fraud

The kickback is a form of fraud often associated with purchasing. Most organizations expect their purchasing agents to select the vendor that provides the best products at the lowest price. To influence the purchasing agent in his or her decision, vendors may grant the agent financial favors (cash, presents, football tickets, and so on). This activity can result in orders being placed with vendors that supply inferior products or charge excessive prices.

Required:

Describe the controls that an organization can employ to deal with kickbacks. Classify each control as either preventive, detective, or corrective.

3. A recent survey of institutional investors reveals that most of them want corporate boards to be composed of at least 75 percent independent directors.

Required:

Write an essay explaining why director independence has become such a high profile issue and one of great importance.

4. The Sarbanes-Oxley Act addresses auditor independence by creating more separation between a firm's attestation and nonauditing activities.

   Write an essay outlining the services that a public accounting firm cannot perform for its client. Conduct research to explain the rationale behind each of these prohibitions.

5. The Sarbanes-Oxley Act created a Public Company Accounting Oversight Board (PCAOB). The PCAOB is empowered to set auditing, quality control, and ethics standards, to inspect registered accounting firms, to conduct investigations, and to take disciplinary actions.

   Required:

   Write an essay comparing the powers of the PCAOB with those of the AICPA. Describe how this initiative might affect the accounting profession.

6. A number of factors have been used to characterized the perpetrators of the frauds, including position within the organization, collusion with others, gender, age, and education.

   Required:

   Write an essay summarizing the usefulness of these factors as predictors of fraud within an organization.

7. **CMA 1289 3-4**
   Evaluation of Internal Control

   Oakdale, Inc. is a subsidiary of Solomon Publishing and specializes in the publication and distribution of reference books. Oakdale's sales for the past year exceeded $18 million, and the company employed an average of 65 employees. Solomon periodically sends a member of the internal audit department to audit the operations of each of its subsidiaries, and Katherine Ford, Oakdale's treasurer, is currently working with Ralph Johnson of Solomon's internal audit staff. Johnson has just completed a review of Oakdale's investment cycle and prepared the following report.

General

Throughout the year, Oakdale has made both short-term and long-term investments in securities; all securities are registered in the company's name. According to Oakdale's bylaws, long-term investment activity must be approved by its board of directors, while short-term investment activity may be approved by either the president or the treasurer.

Transactions

All purchases and sales of short-term securities were made by the treasurer. The long-term security purchases were approved by the board, while the long-term security sales were approved by the president. Because the treasurer is listed with the broker as the company's contact, all revenue from these investments (dividends and interest) is received by this individual, who then forwards the checks to accounting for processing.

Documentation

Purchase and sale authorizations, along with the broker's advices, are maintained in a file by the treasurer. The certificates for all long-term investments are kept in a safe deposit box at the local bank; only the president of Oakdale has access to this box. An inventory of this box was made, and all certificates were accounted for. Certificates for short-term investments are kept in a locked metal box in the accounting office. Other documents, such as long-term contracts and legal agreements, are also kept in this box. There are three keys to the box held by the president, the treasurer, and the accounting manager. The accounting manager's key is available to all accounting personnel should they require documents kept in this box. Documentation for two of the current short-term investments could not be located in this box; the accounting manager explained that some of the investments are for such short periods of time that formal documentation is not always provided by the broker.

Accounting Records

The accounting department records deposits of checks for interest and dividends earned on investments, but these checks could not be traced to the cash receipts journal, which is maintained by the individual who normally opens, stamps, and logs incoming checks. These amounts are journalized monthly in an account for investment revenue. The treasurer authorizes checks drawn for investment purchases. Both the treasurer and the president must sign checks in excess of $15,000. When securities are sold, the broker deposits the proceeds directly in Oakdale's bank account by an electronic funds transfer.

Each month, the accounting manager and the treasurer prepare the journal entries required to adjust the short-term investment account. There was insufficient backup documentation attached to the journal entries reviewed to trace all transactions; however, the balance in the account at the end of last month closely approximates the amount shown on the statement received from the broker. The amount in the long-term investment account is correct, and the transactions can be clearly traced through the documentation attached to the journal entries. There are no attempts made to adjust either account to the lower of aggregate cost or market.

Required:

To achieve Solomon Publishing's objective of sound internal control, the company believes the following four controls are basic for an effective system of accounting control:

- Authorization of transactions
- Complete and accurate record keeping
- Access control
- Internal verification

a. For each of the four controls listed above, describe its purpose.
b. Identify an area in Oakdale's investment procedures that violates each of the four controls.
c. For each of the violations identified, describe how Oakdale can correct each weakness.

CHAPTER

12 Fraud Schemes and Fraud Detection

Learning Objectives

After studying this chapter, you should:

- Be familiar with typical fraud schemes perpetrated by managers and employees.
- Be familiar with the common anti-fraud techniques used in both manual systems and computer-based systems.
- Be familiar with auditors' responsibilities under SAS No. 99.
- Be familiar with the use of ACL in the detection of fraud.

Over the centuries, the practice of auditing developed concurrently with accounting because it was considered useless to keep accounts unless it was possible to ensure that they were kept accurately. Although auditing is a comparatively modern profession, the necessity for some independent check (attestation) of the accounts was consistently felt in ancient Egypt, the Roman Empire, and the great mercantile establishments of the Middle Ages.[1]

This chapter is devoted to the subject of fraud schemes and fraud detection. No major aspect of the independent auditor's role has caused more concern for the public accounting profession than the auditor's responsibility for detecting fraud during an audit. The adoption of SAS No. 99 and passage of the Sarbanes-Oxley Act of 2002 has caused new requirements to be placed on external auditors. This chapter outlines the most common fraud schemes and presents audit procedures to detect fraud. It concludes with a review of ACL tests that can be performed to detect fraud.

Fraud Schemes

Fraud schemes can be classified in a number of different ways. For purposes of discussion, this section presents the classification format derived by the Association of

1 R. Lindberg and T. Cohn, *Operation Auditing* (New York: American Management Association, 1972).

Certified Fraud Examiners. Three broad categories of fraud schemes are defined: fraudulent statements (management fraud), corruption, and asset misappropriation (employee fraud).[2]

FRAUDULENT STATEMENTS

Fraudulent statements are associated with management fraud discussed in Chapter 11. Although all fraud involves some form of financial misstatement, to meet the definition under this class of fraud scheme, the statement itself must bring direct or indirect financial benefit to the perpetrator. In other words, the statement is not simply a vehicle for obscuring or covering a fraudulent act. For example, misstating the cash account balance to cover the theft of cash does not fall under this class of fraud scheme. By contrast, understating liabilities to present a more favorable financial picture of the organization to drive up stock prices does qualify.

Table 12-1 shows that while fraudulent statements account for only 5 percent of the fraud cases covered in the ACFE fraud study, the median loss due to this type of fraud scheme is significantly higher than losses from corruption and asset misappropriation.

Appalling as this type of fraud loss appears on paper, these numbers fail to reflect the human suffering that parallels them in the real world. How does one measure the impact on stockholders as they watch their life savings and retirement funds evaporated after news of the fraud breaks?

CORRUPTION

Corruption is perhaps the oldest of the white-collar crimes. It includes bribery, conflicts of interest, illegal gratuities, and economic extortion. It is an act of an official or fiduciary person who unlawfully and wrongfully uses his station or character to procure some benefit for himself or for another person, contrary to duty and the rights of others.[3] According to the Association of Certified Fraud Examiners (ACFE), corruption accounts for about 10 percent of occupational fraud cases. Almost 90 percent of losses in the corruption category are due to bribery schemes.

TABLE 12-1

Losses from Fraud by Scheme Type

Scheme Type	Percent of Frauds[a]	Loss
Fraudulent Statements	5	$4,250,000
Corruption	13	$530,000
Asset Misappropriation	85	$80,000

a The sum of the percentages exceeds 100 percent because some of the reported frauds in the ACFE study involved more than one type of fraud.

2 *Report to the Nation: Occupational Fraud and Abuse*, Association of Fraud Examiners, 1996, pp. 31-34.

3 According to *Black's Law Dictionary*, p. 331.

Bribery

Bribery involves giving, offering, soliciting, or receiving things of value to influence an official in the performance of his or her lawful duties. Officials may be employed by government (or regulatory) agencies or by private organizations. Bribery defrauds the entity (business organization or government agency) of the right to honest and loyal services from those employed by it. The following is an example of bribery.

> The manager of a meat-packing company offers a U.S. health inspector a cash payment. In return, the inspector suppresses his report of health violations discovered during a routine inspection of the meat-packing facilities. In this situation, the victims are those who rely on the honest reporting of the inspector. The loss is salary paid to the inspector for work not performed and any damages that result from failure to perform.

Illegal Gratuities

An **illegal gratuity** involves giving, receiving, offering, or soliciting something of value because of an official act that has been taken. This is similar to a bribe, but the transaction occurs after the fact. The following is an example of an illegal gratuity.

> The plant manager in a large corporation uses his influence to ensure that a request for proposals is written in such a way that only one contractor will be able to submit a satisfactory bid. As a result, the favored contractor's proposal is accepted at a noncompetitive price. In return, the contractor secretly makes a financial payment to the plant manager. The victims in this case are those who expect a competitive procurement process. The loss is the excess costs incurred by the company because of the noncompetitive pricing of the construction.

Conflicts of Interest

Every employer should expect that his or her employees will conduct their duties in a way that serves the interests of the employer. A **conflict of interest** occurs when an employee acts on behalf of a third party during the discharge of his or her duties or has self-interest in the activity being performed. When the employee's conflict of interest is unknown to the employer and results in financial loss, then fraud has occurred. The preceding examples of bribery and illegal gratuities also constitute conflicts of interest. This type of fraud can exist, however, when bribery and illegal payments are not present, but the employee has an interest in the outcome of the economic event. The following is an example.

> A purchasing agent for a building contractor is also part owner in a plumbing supply company. The agent has sole discretion in selecting vendors for the plumbing supplies needed for buildings under contract. The agent directs a disproportionate number of purchase orders to his company, which charges above-market prices for its products. The agent's financial interest in the supplier is unknown to his employer.

Economic Extortion

Economic extortion is the use (or threat) of force (including economic sanctions) by an individual or organization to obtain something of value. The item of value could be a financial or economic asset, information, or cooperation to obtain a favorable decision on some matter under review. The following is an example of economic extortion.

> A contract procurement agent for a state government threatens to blacklist a highway contractor if he does not make a financial payment to the agent. If the contractor fails to cooperate, the blacklisting will effectively eliminate him from consideration for future work. Faced with a threat of economic loss, the contractor makes the payment.

Asset Misappropriation

The most common form of fraud scheme involves some type of asset misappropriation. Eighty-five percent of the frauds included in the ACFE study fall into this category. Assets can be misappropriated either directly or indirectly for the perpetrator's benefit. Certain assets are more susceptible than others to misappropriation. Transactions involving cash, checking accounts, inventory, supplies, equipment, and information are the most vulnerable to abuse. Examples of fraud schemes involving asset misappropriation are described below.

Charges to Expense Accounts

The theft of an asset creates an imbalance in the basic accounting equation (Assets = Equities), which the criminal must adjust if the theft is to go undetected. The most common way to conceal the imbalance is to charge the asset to an expense account and reduce equity by the same amount. For example, the theft of $20,000 cash could be charged to a miscellaneous operating expense account. The loss of the cash reduces the firm's assets by $20,000. To offset this, equity is reduced by $20,000 when the miscellaneous expense account is closed to retained earnings, thus keeping the accounting equation in balance. This technique has the advantage of limiting the criminal's exposure to one period. When the expense account is closed to retained earnings, its balance is reset to zero to begin the new period.

Lapping

Lapping involves the use of customer checks, received in payment of their accounts, to conceal cash previously stolen by an employee. For example, the employee first steals and cashes a check for $500 sent by Customer A. To conceal the accounting imbalance caused by the loss of the asset, Customer A's account is not credited. Later (the next billing period), the employee uses a $500 check received from Customer B and applies this to Customer A's account. Funds received in the next period from Customer C are then applied to the account of Customer B, and so on.

Employees involved in this sort of fraud often rationalize that they are simply borrowing the cash and plan to repay it at some future date. This kind of accounting cover-up must continue indefinitely or until the employee returns the funds. Lapping is usually detected when the employee leaves the organization or becomes sick and must take time off work. Unless the fraud is perpetuated, the last customer to have funds diverted from his or her account will be billed again, and the lapping technique will be detected. Employers can deter lapping by periodically rotating employees into different jobs and forcing them to take scheduled vacations.

Transaction Fraud

Transaction fraud involves deleting, altering, or adding false transactions to divert assets to the perpetrator. This technique may be used to ship inventories to the perpetrator in response to a fraudulent sales transaction or to disburse cash in payment of a false liability. A common type of transaction fraud involves the distribution of fraudulent paychecks to nonexistent employees. For example, an employee who has left the organization is kept on the payroll by her immediate supervisor. Each week, the supervisor continues to submit time cards to the payroll department just as if the employee was still working for the firm. The fraud works best in organizations that distribute employee paychecks to the supervisor, who then distributes them to the employees. The supervisor forges the ex-employee's signature and then cashes the check. Although the organization has lost cash, the fraud can go undetected because the credit to the cash account is offset by a debit to payroll expense.

Computer Fraud Schemes

Since computers lie at the heart of most organizations' accounting information systems today, the topic of **computer fraud** is of special importance to auditors. Although the objectives of the fraud are the same—misappropriation of assets—the techniques used to commit computer fraud vary greatly.

No one knows for sure how much business loses each year to computer fraud, but estimates reaching $100 billion per year give some indication of the problem's magnitude. One reason for the discrepancy between these estimates is that computer fraud is not well defined. For example, we saw in the ethics section of this chapter that some people do not view copying commercial computer software to be unethical. On the other side of this issue, software vendors consider this to be a criminal act. Regardless of how narrowly or broadly computer fraud is defined, most agree that it is a rapidly growing phenomenon.

For our purposes, computer fraud includes the following:

- The theft, misuse, or misappropriation of assets by altering computer-readable records and files.
- The theft, misuse, or misappropriation of assets by altering the logic of computer software.
- The theft or illegal use of computer-readable information.
- The theft, corruption, illegal copying, or intentional destruction of computer software.
- The theft, misuse, or misappropriation of computer hardware.

The general model for accounting information systems shown in Figure 12-1 portrays, conceptually, the key stages of an information system. Each stage in the model—data collection, data processing, database management, and information generation—is a potential area of risk for certain types of computer fraud.

Data Collection. **Data collection** is the first operational stage in the information system. The objective is to ensure that event data entering the system are valid, complete, and free from material errors. In many respects, this is the most important stage in the system. Should transaction errors pass through data collection undetected, the organization runs the risk that the system will process the errors and generate erroneous and unreliable output. This, in turn, could lead to incorrect actions and poor decisions by the users.

FIGURE 12-1 **The General Model for Accounting Information Systems**

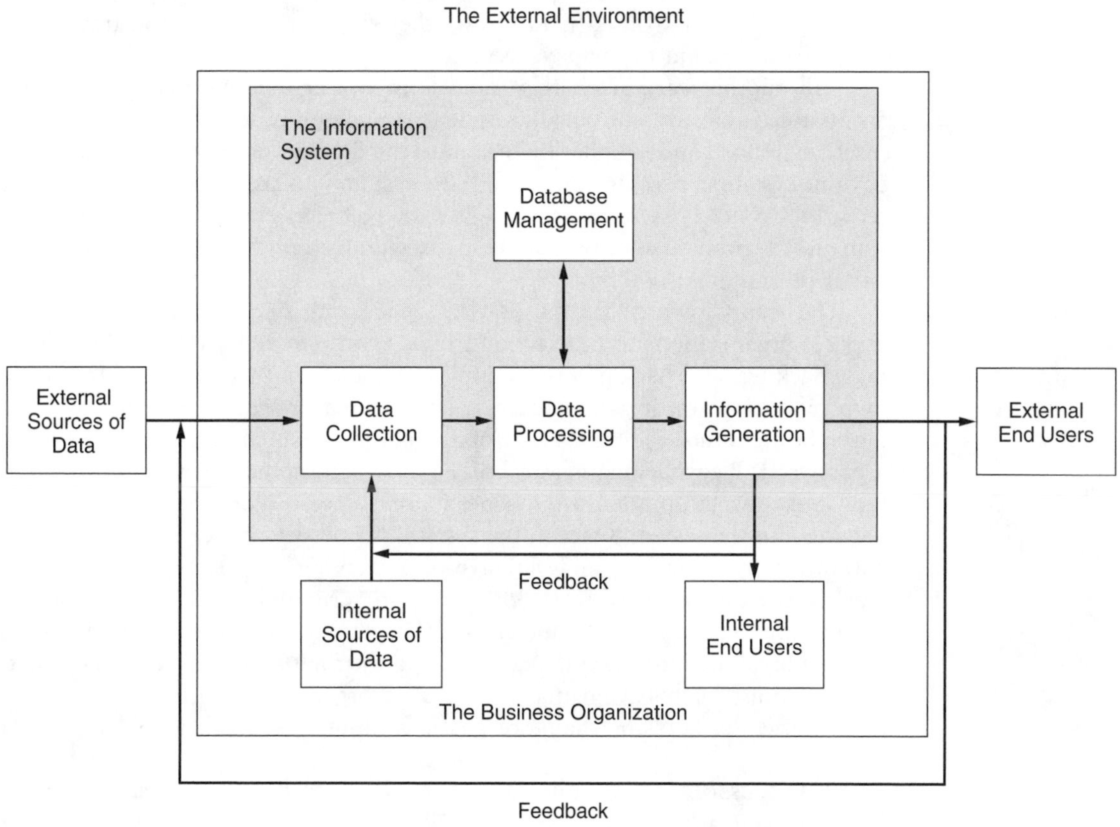

Two rules govern the design of data collection procedures: relevance and efficiency. The information system should capture only relevant data. A fundamental task of the system designer is to determine what is and what is not relevant. He or she does so by analyzing the user's needs. Only data that ultimately contribute to information are relevant. The data-collection stage should be designed to filter irrelevant facts from the system.

Efficient data-collection procedures are designed to collect data only once. These data can then be made available to multiple users. Capturing the same data more than once leads to data redundancy and inconstancy. Information systems have limited collection, processing, and data storage capacity. Data redundancy overloads facilities and reduces the overall efficiency of the system. Inconsistency among data elements can result in inappropriate actions and bad decisions.

The simplest way to perpetrate a computer fraud is at the data collection or data entry stage. This is the computer equivalent of the transaction fraud discussed previously. Frauds of this type require little or no computer skills. The perpetrator need only understand how the system works to enter data that it will process. The fraudulent act involves falsifying data as it enters the system. This can be to delete, alter, or add a transaction. For example, to commit a payroll fraud, the perpetrator may insert a fraudulent payroll transaction along with other legitimate transactions. Unless the insertion is detected by internal controls, the system will generate an additional paycheck for the perpetrator. A variation on this type of fraud is to change the Hours Worked field in an otherwise legitimate payroll transaction to increase the amount of the paycheck.

Still another variant on this fraud is to disburse cash in payment of a false account payable. By entering fraudulent supporting documents (purchase order, receiving report, and supplier invoice) into the data-collection stage of the accounts payable system, a perpetrator can fool the system into creating an accounts payable record for a nonexistent purchase. Once the record is created, the system will presume it is legitimate and, on the due date, will disperse funds to the perpetrator in payment of a bogus liability.

The trend toward distributed data processing and networking increasingly exposes organizations to transaction frauds from remote locations. Masquerading, piggybacking, and hacking are examples of such fraud techniques. **Masquerading** involves a perpetrator gaining access to the system from a remote site by pretending to be an authorized user. This usually requires first gaining authorized access to a password. **Piggybacking** is a technique in which the perpetrator at a remote site taps into the telecommunications lines and latches onto an authorized user who is logging into the system. Once in the system, the perpetrator can masquerade as the authorized user. Hacking may involve piggybacking or masquerading techniques. **Hackers** are distinguished from other computer criminals because their motives are not usually to defraud for financial gain. They are motivated primarily by the challenge of breaking into the system rather than the theft of assets. Nevertheless, hackers have caused extensive damage and loss to organizations. Many believe that the line between hackers and the more classic computer criminals is thin.

Data Processing. Once collected, data usually require processing to produce information. Tasks in the data processing stage range from simple to complex. Examples include mathematical algorithms (such as linear programming models) used for production scheduling applications, statistical techniques for sales forecasting, and posting and summarizing procedures used for accounting applications.

Data processing frauds fall into two classes: program fraud and operations fraud. **Program fraud** includes the following techniques: (1) creating illegal programs that can access data files to alter, delete, or insert values into accounting records; (2) destroying or corrupting a program's logic using a computer virus; or (3) altering program logic to cause the application to process data incorrectly. For example, the program a bank uses to calculate interest on its customers' accounts will produce rounding errors. This happens because the precision of the interest calculation is greater than the reporting precision. Therefore, interest figures that are calculated to a fraction of one cent must be rounded to whole numbers for reporting purposes. A complex routine in the interest-calculation program keeps track of the rounding errors so that the total interest charge to the bank equals the sum of the individual credits. This involves temporarily holding the fractional amounts left over from each calculation in an internal memory accumulator. When the amount in the accumulator totals one cent (plus or minus), the penny is added to the customer's account that is being processed. In other words, one cent is added to (or deleted from) customer accounts randomly. A type of program fraud called the *salami fraud* involves modifying the rounding logic of the program so it no longer adds the one cent randomly.

Instead, the modified program always adds the plus cent to the perpetrator's account but still adds the minus cent randomly. This can divert a considerable amount of cash to the perpetrator, but the accounting records stay in balance to conceal the crime.

Operations fraud is the misuse or theft of the firm's computer resources. This often involves using the computer to conduct personal business. For example, a programmer may use the firm's computer time to write software that he sells commercially. A CPA in the controller's office may use the company's computer to prepare tax returns and financial statements for her private clients. Similarly, a corporate lawyer with a private practice on the side may use the firm's computer to search for court cases and decisions in commercial databases. The cost of accessing the database is charged to the organization and hidden among other legitimate charges.

Database Management. The organization's database is its physical repository for financial and nonfinancial data. Database management involves three fundamental tasks: storage, retrieval, and deletion. The *storage* task assigns keys to new records and stores them in their proper location in the database. *Retrieval* is the task of locating and extracting an existing record from the database for processing. After processing is complete, the storage task restores the updated record to its place in the database. *Deletion* is the task of permanently removing obsolete or redundant records from the database.

Database management fraud includes altering, deleting, corrupting, destroying, or stealing an organization's data. Because access to database files is an essential element of this fraud, it is usually associated with transaction or program fraud. The most common technique is to access the database from a remote site and browse the files for useful information that can be copied and sold to competitors. Disgruntled employees have been known to destroy company data files simply to harm the organization. One method is to insert a destructive routine called a *logic bomb* into a program. At a specified time, or when certain conditions are met, the logic bomb erases the data files that the program accesses. For example, a disgruntled programmer who was contemplating leaving an organization inserted a logic bomb into the payroll system. Weeks later, when the system detected that the programmer's name had been removed from the payroll file, the logic bomb was activated and erased the payroll file.

Information Generation. Information generation is the process of compiling, arranging, formatting, and presenting information to users. Information can be an operational document such as a sales order, a structured report, or a message on a computer screen. Regardless of physical form, useful information has the following characteristics: **relevance**, **timeliness**, **accuracy**, **completeness**, and **summarization**.

- *Relevance.* The contents of a report or document must serve a purpose. This could be to support a manager's decision or a clerk's task. We have established that only data relevant to a user's action have information content. Therefore, the information system should present only relevant data in its reports. Reports containing irrelevancies waste resources and may be counterproductive to the user. Irrelevancies detract attention from the true message of the report and may result in incorrect decisions or actions.
- *Timeliness.* The age of information is a critical factor in determining its usefulness. Information must be no older than the time period of the action it supports. For example, if a manager makes decisions daily to purchase inventory

from a supplier based upon an inventory status report, then the information in the report should be no more than a day old.

- *Accuracy.* Information must be free from material errors. However, materiality is a difficult concept to quantify. It has no absolute value; it is a problem-specific concept. This means that in some cases, information must be perfectly accurate. In other instances, the level of accuracy may be lower. Material error exists when the amount of inaccuracy in information causes the user to make poor decisions or to fail to make necessary decisions. We sometimes must sacrifice absolute accuracy to obtain timely information. Often perfect information is not available within the decision time frame of the user. Therefore, in providing information, system designers seek a balance between information that is as accurate as possible, yet timely enough to be useful.
- *Completeness.* No piece of information essential to a decision or task should be missing. For example, a report should provide all necessary calculations and present its message clearly and unambiguously.
- *Summarization.* Information should be aggregated in accordance with a user's needs. Lower-level managers tend to need information that is highly detailed. As information flows upward through the organization to top management, it becomes more summarized. Later in this chapter, we shall look more closely at the effects that organizational structure and managerial level have on information reporting.

A common form of fraud at the information generation stage is to steal, misdirect, or misuse computer output. One simple but effective technique called **scavenging** involves searching through the trash cans of the computer center for discarded output. A perpetrator can often obtain useful information from the carbon sheets removed from multipart reports or from paper reports that were rejected during processing. Sometimes output reports are misaligned on the paper or slightly garbled during printing. When this happens, the output must be reprinted and the original output is often thrown in the trash.

Another form of fraud called **eavesdropping** involves listening to output transmissions over telecommunications lines. Technologies are readily available that enable perpetrators to intercept messages being sent over unprotected telephone lines and microwave channels. Most experts agree that it is practically impossible to prevent a determined perpetrator from accessing data communication channels. Data encryption can, however, render useless any data captured through eavesdropping.

Auditor's Responsibility for Detecting Fraud

The passage of the Sarbanes-Oxley Act of 2002 (S-OX) has had a tremendous impact on public accounting and on the external auditor's responsibilities for fraud detection during a financial audit. The current authoritative guidelines on fraud detection are presented in **SAS No. 99, *Consideration of Fraud in a Financial Statement Audit.*** SAS No. 99 pertains to the following areas of a financial audit:

1. Description and characteristics of fraud
2. Professional skepticism

3. Engagement personnel discussion
4. Obtaining audit evidence and information
5. Identifying risks
6. Assessing the identified risks
7. Responding to the assessment
8. Evaluating audit evidence and information
9. Communicating possible fraud
10. Documenting consideration of fraud

This list demonstrates how the external auditor must now think about fraud during every phase of the audit processes. The objective of SAS 99 is to seamlessly blend the auditor's consideration of fraud into the audit process until its completion. In addition SAS 99 requires the auditor to perform new steps such as a brainstorming during audit planning as to the potential risk from fraud schemes. The auditor is required to assess the risk of material misstatement of the financial statements due to fraud and should factor the **risk assessment** into the design of audit procedures. The assessment should include risk factors that relate to both **fraudulent financial reporting** and the **misappropriation of assets.**

Fraudulent Financial Reporting

Risk factors that relate to fraudulent financial reporting are grouped according to the following classifications:

- *Management's characteristics and influence over the control environment.* These factors relate to the tone-at-the-top regarding internal control, management style, situational pressures, and the financial reporting process.
- *Industry conditions.* This includes the economic and regulatory environment in which the entity operates. For example, a company in a declining industry or with key customers experiencing business failures is at greater risk to fraud than one whose industry base is stable.
- *Operating characteristics and financial stability.* This pertains to the nature of the entity and the complexity of its transactions. For example, an organization involved with related-party transactions with organizations that are not audited may be at risk to fraud.

In the case of financial fraud (management fraud), external auditors should look for the following kinds of common schemes:

- Improper revenue recognition
- Improper treatment of sales
- Improper asset valuation
- Improper deferral of costs and expenses
- Improper recording of liabilities
- Inadequate disclosures

Misappropriation of Assets

Two risk factors are related to misappropriation of assets:

1. *Susceptibility of assets to misappropriation.* The susceptibility of an asset pertains to its nature and the degree to which it is subject to theft. Liquid assets such as cash and bearer bonds are more susceptible to misappropriation than nonliquid assets such as steel girders and physical plant equipment.

2. *Controls.* This class of risk factors involves the inadequacy or lack of controls designed to prevent or detect misappropriation of assets. For example, a database management system that does not adequately restrict access to accounting records increases the risk of asset misappropriation.

Examples of common schemes related to employee theft (asset misappropriation) include the following:

- Personal purchases
- Ghost employees
- Fictitious expenses
- Altered payee
- Pass-through vendors
- Theft of cash (or inventory)
- Lapping

Auditor's Response to Risk Assessment

The auditor's judgments about the risk of material misstatements due to fraud may affect the audit in the following ways:

- *Engagement staffing and extent of supervision.* The knowledge, skill, and ability of personnel assigned to the engagement should be commensurate with the assessment of the level of risk of the engagement.
- *Professional skepticism.* Exercising professional skepticism involves maintaining an attitude that includes a questioning mind and critical assessment of audit evidence.
- *Nature, timing, and extent of procedures performed.* Fraud risk factors that have control implications may limit the auditor's ability to assess control risk below the maximum and thus reduce substantive testing.

Response to Detected Misstatements Due to Fraud

To some degree, the risk of material misstatement due to fraud always exists. The auditor's response is thus influenced by the degree of assessed risk. In some cases, the auditor may determine that currently planned audit procedures are sufficient to respond to the risk factors. In other cases, the auditor may decide to extend the audit and modify planned procedures. In rare instances, the auditor may conclude that procedures cannot be sufficiently modified to address the risk, in which case the auditor should consider withdrawing from the engagement and communicating the reasons for withdrawal to the audit committee.

When the auditor has determined that fraud exists but has had no material effect on the financial statements, the auditor should

- Refer the matter to an appropriate level of management at least one level above those involved.
- Be satisfied that implications for other aspects of the audit have been adequately considered.

When the fraud has had a material effect on the financial statements or the auditor is unable to evaluate its degree of materiality, the auditor should

- Consider the implications for other aspects of the audit.
- Discuss the matter with senior management and with a board of director's audit committee.

- Attempt to determine whether the fraud is material.
- Suggest that the client consult with legal counsel, if appropriate.

Documentation Requirements

The auditor should document in the working papers the criteria used for assessing the fraud risk factors. Where risk factors are identified, the documentation should include (1) those risk factors identified and (2) the auditor's response to them.

Fraud Detection Techniques

Because of the need to falsify accounting records, many fraud schemes leave a trail in the underlying accounting data that the forensic auditor can follow if he or she knows what to look for. For businesses with a large volume of transactions, however, finding the telltale trail using manual procedures may be impossible. Computer-based data extraction and analysis tools such as ACL are thus essential.

To find the trail in the masses of data, the auditor first develops a "fraud profile" that identifies the data characteristics that one would expect to find in a specific type of fraud scheme.[4] This identification requires an understanding of the enterprise's processes and internal controls (and their weaknesses). Once the fraud profile is developed, ACL can be used to manipulate the organization's data to search for transactions that fit the profile. In this section, we examine the operational and data characteristics of three common fraud schemes. The ACL features used for fraud detection are outlined in Chapters 9 and 10 and explained in detail in the ACL workbook that accompanies this text. The following discussion presumes that the reader is familiar with that material.

Payments to Fictitious Vendors

The purchasing function is particularly vulnerable to fraud, and for many organizations represents a significant area of risk. A common fraud scheme involves making a payment to a fictitious company. A preliminary step in this scheme requires the perpetrator to create a phony vendor organization and establish it in the victim organization's records as a legitimate supplier. The embezzler then submits invoices from the fake vendor, which are processed by the accounts payable system of the victim company. Depending on the organizational structure and internal controls in place, this type of fraud may require collusion between two or more individuals. For example, the purchasing agent prepares a purchase order for items from the fake vendor and the receiving clerk prepares a fictitious receiving report for the items. Accounts payable receives these documents, which appear to be legitimate, and matches them to the phony invoice when it arrives. An accounts payable is recorded and payment is subsequently made. In smaller organizations, a single individual with the authority to authorize payments can hatch a simpler version of the scheme. The fraud profile describing the false-vendor scheme and the audit procedures are described next.

4 D. Johnson, "Finding the Needle in the Haystack," *ACL Services Ltd. (internal publication)* (Vancouver BC, Canada, 1997).

Sequential Invoice Numbers

Since the victim organization is the only recipient of the invoices, the supporting invoices "issued" by the phony vendor may actually be in something close to an unbroken numerical sequence. The audit procedure is to use ACL to *sort* the records of the invoice file by invoice number and vendor number. This will highlight records that possess series characteristics, which can then be retrieved for further review.

Vendors with P.O. Boxes

Most legitimate suppliers have a complete business address. Since fake suppliers have no physical facilities, the perpetrator of the fraud will sometimes rent a P.O. box to receive payments by mail. Although it is also possible for a legitimate vendor to use a P.O. box, these suppliers are candidates for further review. The audit procedure is this: Using ACL's expression builder, create a *filter* to select vendor records from the invoice file that use P.O. box addresses. From this list, verify the legitimacy of the vendor.

Vendors with Employee Addresses

Rather than rent a P.O. box, the perpetrator may use his or her home address on the invoice. Although it is also possible that an employee's home-based business is a legitimate supplier, this is not likely and should be investigated. The audit procedure is to use ACL to *join* the employee file and the invoice file using the address fields as the common key for both files. Only records that match should be passed to the resulting combined file. These records can then be reviewed further.

Multiple Companies with the Same Address

To divert attention away from excessive purchases made from the same vendor, a perpetrator may create several phony suppliers that share the same mailing address. As an audit safeguard, use ACL's *Duplicates* command to generate a listing of mailing addresses that are common to two or more vendors.

Invoice Amounts Slightly below the Review Threshold

Many organizations control disbursements by establishing a materiality threshold. A management review and signature is required for all checks that exceed the threshold. Those that fall below the limit are not reviewed. Knowing this, the perpetrator may falsify payments that fall just under the threshold to maximize his or her benefit from the fraud. The audit procedure for this situation is to use ACL's expression builder to *create* a value range around the control threshold. To highlight suspicious activity that warrants further investigation, sort payments records that fall within this range by vendor.

PAYROLL FRAUD

The two common forms of **payroll fraud** are overpayment of employees and payments to nonexistent employees. The first scheme typically involves inflating the number of hours worked and/or issuing duplicate payroll checks. The second approach involves entering fictitious employees into the payroll system. A supervisor, who then receives the resulting payroll checks, usually perpetrates this type of fraud. A variation on this scheme is to keep a terminated employee on the payroll. Suggested audit procedures for detecting these frauds are described next.

Test for Excessive Hours Worked

Use ACL's *Expression Builder* to select payroll records that reflect excessive hours worked. The determination of what is excessive will depend on the nature of organization and its policies. If moderate overtime is fairly common, then filtering records with hours worked of greater than 50 hours may uncover instances of fraud. Using this filter to review employee records over time may disclose a pattern of abuse.

Test for Duplicate Payments

Use ACL's *Duplicates* function to search payroll records for employees with the following characteristics:

- Same employee number, same name, same address, etc. (duplicate payments)
- Same name with different mailing addresses
- Same name with different checking accounts
- Same name with different social security numbers
- Same mailing address with different employee names

Some duplicate records detected in the search will be due to natural phenomena (i.e., unrelated individuals who happen to have the same name). The results, however, provide the auditor with a basis for further review.

Tests for Nonexistent Employees

Use ACL's *Join* feature to link the payroll and employee files using Employee Number as the common attribute. The resulting joined file should contain only those records from the payroll file that do not match valid employee records. These records need to be reviewed with management.

Lapping Accounts Receivable

Lapping was described earlier in the chapter as the theft of a customer's check received in payment on his account. The perpetrator then covers the theft in the following period by applying cash received from a second customer to the account of the first. The simplicity of this fraud technique is key to its success because it presents a very obscure fraud profile. The only evidence of fraud in the underlying data is in the timing difference between when payment is received and when it is recorded. Depending on how the organization structures its accounts receivable, this may be difficult to detect. The problem is illustrated by comparing two common methods of managing accounts receivable.

The Balance Forward Method

The **balance forward method** is used extensively for consumer accounts. Total sales to customers for the period are itemized and billed at the period end. Customers are required to pay only a minimum amount off the balance. The rest of the balance, plus interest, is carried forward to the next period.

Lapping is difficult to detect in this type of system. For example, assume the perpetrator embezzles a customer payment of $500. This amount would not be posted to the customer's account in the current period and the balance carried forward to the next period would be overstated by $500. In the following period, cash taken from another customer would be used to cover this amount. Since balances carried forward are commonplace, an overstated amount does not draw attention internally. The customer, however, may complain that the payment was not recorded. If the embezzler himself deals with the complaint, he could explain that the payment was received too late to be reflected on the current statement but would show up in the next period.

The Open Invoice Method

The **open invoice method** is often used to manage trade accounts receivable (sales to other business organizations). Each invoice is recorded as a separate item in the invoice file. Checks received from customers are usually in payment of individual invoices. Since good credit relations between customer and supplier are critical, payments tend to be on time and in full. Partial payments resulting in balances carried forward are the exception rather than the norm.

To illustrate lapping in this situation, assume that Customer A remits a check for $1,523.61 in payment of an open invoice for the same amount. The perpetrator pockets the check, but does not close the invoice. Therefore, the invoice balance is carried forward. In the next period, Customer B remits a check for $2,636.88 in full payment of an open invoice. The embezzler applies $1,523.61 of this payment to Customer A's open invoice, thus closing it. The remainder ($1,113.27) is applied to Customer B's invoice, which remains open. The balance of $1,523.61 is carried forward into the next period. This carry-forward characteristic provides the forensic auditor with a basis for constructing a fraud profile. To illustrate, refer to invoice record structure in Table 12-2.

The Invoice Amount field in Table 12-2 is the accounts receivable amount due. The Due Date field is calculated at the time of the sale, and the Closed Date field is entered when the payment is received. The Remittance Amount field reflects the amount of payment received from the customer.

The audit procedure is as follows: Lapping is a fraud that must to be actively continued by the perpetrator. The fraud profile is thus best observed over time. If the organization follows proper backup procedures, the invoice file will be copied frequently throughout the period, thus producing several archived versions of the file. Collectively, these files reflect the invoice amounts carried forward from month to month for the period under review. If the auditor suspects lapping, he or she may employ the following ACL tests:

TABLE 12-2 Sales Invoice File

Invoice Number	Customer Number	Invoice Amount	Sales Date	Due Date	Closed Date	Remittance Amount
77885	23671	2,636.88	02/12/04	02/25/04	03/28/04	1,113.27

- Use ACL's *expression builder* to select items from each file version whose Remittance Amount field is greater than zero and less than the Invoice Amount field. These sets of records may contain legitimate items that are being disputed by the customers. For example, damaged goods, overcharges, and refused deliveries may result in customers making only partial payments. The auditor will need to sift through these legitimate issues to identify lapping.
- *Merge* the resulting carry-forward files into a single file reflecting activity for the entire period.
- Create a *calculated field* of the amount carried forward (Invoice Amount – Remittance Amount).
- Use the *duplicates* command to search the file for calculated carry-forward amounts that are the same. Following the example just illustrated, a carry-forward pattern of $1,523.61 will emerge.

Summary

In this chapter, we examined fraud schemes and the auditor's responsibility for fraud detection. The chapter began with a review of three general categories of fraud schemes: financial misrepresentation (management fraud), corruption, and asset misappropriation (employee fraud). Management fraud typically involves the material misstatement of financial data to attain additional compensation or promotion or to escape the penalty for poor performance. Managers that perpetrate fraud often do so by overriding the internal control structure. Corruption involves using one's position to defraud another person or entity. Employee frauds are generally designed to direct cash or other assets directly to the employee's personal benefit. Typically, the employee circumvents the company's internal control structure for personal gain. However, if a company has an effective system of internal control, defalcations or embezzlements can usually be prevented or detected. The section examined several well-documented fraud schemes used in both manual and computer-based systems. The second section of the chapter presented an overview of SAS No. 99, which defines the external auditor's responsibilities for the detection of fraud during a financial audit. In addition, several risk-assessment factors related to management fraud and asset misappropriation were presented. The chapter concluded with a review of fraud detection techniques. Three common forms of fraud were examined: false payments to vendors, payroll fraud, and lapping. Audit procedures employing ACL technology were described.

Key Terms

accuracy
balance forward method
bribery
charges to expense accounts
completeness
computer fraud
conflict of interest
corruption
data collection
database management fraud
eavesdropping
economic extortion

fraudulent financial reporting
hackers
illegal gratuity
lapping
masquerading
misappropriation of assets
open invoice method
operations fraud
payroll fraud
piggybacking
program fraud
relevance
risk assessment
SAS No. 99, Consideration of Fraud in a Financial Statement Audit
scavenging
summarization
timeliness
transaction fraud

Review Questions

1. What is financial statement fraud?
2. Why is financial statement fraud particularly appalling?
3. What is corruption?
4. Define bribery.
5. What is illegal gratuity fraud?
6. Explain conflict of interest.
7. What is economic extortion?
8. Explain charges to expense account fraud.
9. What is lapping?
10. What is collusion?
11. What is transaction fraud.
12. What is masquerading?
13. What is piggybacking?
14. What is a hacker?
15. Define program fraud.
16. Describe the key elements of database management fraud.
17. What are the five characteristics of information?
18. What is scavenging?
19. What is eavesdropping?
20. What document contains the current authoritative guideline on fraud detection?

Discussion Questions

1. Most accounting firms allow their employees to marry within the accounting firm; however, they do not allow an employee to remain working for them if he or she marries an employee of one of their auditing clients. Why do you think this policy exists?
2. Discuss whether a firm with fewer employees than there are incompatible tasks should rely more heavily on general authority than specific authority.
3. An organization's internal audit department is usually considered to be an effective control mechanism for evaluating the organization's internal control structure. The Birch Company's internal auditing function reports directly to the controller. Comment on the effectiveness of this organizational structure.
4. The proper segregation of functions is an effective internal control procedure. Comment on the exposure (if any) caused by combining the tasks of paycheck preparation and distribution to employees.
5. Give two examples of employee fraud and explain how the thefts might occur.
6. Discuss the fraud schemes of bribery, illegal gratuities, and economic extortion. Explain how they are similar and how they differ.
7. Explain at least three forms of computer fraud.
8. A profile of fraud perpetrators prepared by the Association of Certified Fraud Examiners revealed that adult males with advanced degrees commit a disproportionate amount of fraud. Explain these findings.

9. Explain why collusion between employees and management in the commission of a fraud is difficult to both prevent and detect.
10. Since all fraud involves some form of financial misstatement, how is *Fraudulent Statement* fraud different?
11. Explain how the balance forward and the open invoice methods of maintaining accounts receivable differ.

MULTIPLE-CHOICE QUESTIONS

1. Management can expect various benefits to follow from implementing a system of strong internal control. Which of the following benefits is least likely to occur?
   a. reduced cost of an external audit
   b. preventing employee collusion to commit fraud
   c. availability of reliable data for decision-making purposes
   d. some assurance of compliance with the Foreign Corrupt Practices Act of 1977
   e. some assurance that important documents and records are protected
2. Which of the following situations is not a segregation of duties violation?
   a. The treasurer has the authority to sign checks but gives the signature block to the assistant treasurer to run the check-signing machine.
   b. The warehouse clerk, who has the custodial responsibility over inventory in the warehouse, selects the vendor and authorizes purchases when inventories are low.
   c. The sales manager has the responsibility to approve credit and the authority to write off accounts.
   d. The department time clerk is given the undistributed payroll checks to mail to absent employees.
   e. The accounting clerk who shares the recordkeeping responsibility for the accounts receivable subsidiary ledger performs the monthly reconciliation of the subsidiary ledger and the control account.
3. What does the underlying assumption of reasonable assurance regarding implementation of internal control mean?
   a. Auditor's are reasonably assured that fraud has not occurred in the period.
   b. Auditor's are reasonably assured that employee carelessness can weaken an internal control structure.
   c. Implementation of the control procedure should not have a significant adverse effect on efficiency or profitability.
   d. Management assertions about control effectiveness should provide auditors with reasonable assurance.
   e. A control applies reasonably well to all forms of computer technology.
4. To conceal the theft of cash receipts from customers in payment of their accounts, which of the following journal entries should the bookkeeper make?

	DR	CR
a.	Miscellaneous Expense	Cash
b.	Petty Cash	Cash
c.	Cash	Accounts Receivable
d.	Sales Returns	Accounts Receivable
e.	None of the above	

5. Which of the following controls would best prevent the lapping of accounts receivable?
   a. Segregate duties so that the clerk responsible for recording in the accounts receivable subsidiary ledger has no access to the general ledger.
   b. Request that customers review their monthly statements and report any unrecorded cash payments.
   c. Require customers to send payments directly to the company's bank.
   d. Request that customers make the check payable to the company.

6. Providing timely information about transactions in sufficient detail to permit proper classification and financial reporting is an example of
   a. the control environment.
   b. risk assessment.
   c. information and communication.
   d. monitoring.
7. What fraud scheme is similar to the "borrowing from Peter to pay Paul" scheme?
   a. expense account fraud
   b. kiting
   c. lapping
   d. transaction fraud
8. Which of the following best describes lapping?
   a. applying cash receipts to a different customer's account in an attempt to conceal previous thefts of funds
   b. inflating bank balances by transferring money among different bank accounts
   c. expensing an asset that has been stolen
   d. creating a false transaction
9. Operations fraud includes
   a. altering program logic to cause the application to process data incorrectly.
   b. misusing the firm's computer resources.
   c. destroying or corrupting a program's logic using a computer virus.
   d. creating illegal programs that can access data files to alter, delete, or insert values.

PROBLEMS

1. Fraud Scheme

A purchasing agent for a home improvement center is also part owner in a wholesale lumber company. The agent has sole discretion in selecting vendors for the lumber sold through the center. The agent directs a disproportionate number of purchase orders to his company, which charges above-market prices for its products. The agent's financial interest in the supplier is unknown to his employer.

Required:

What type of fraud is this, and what controls can be implemented to prevent or detect the fraud?

2. Fraud Scheme

A procurement agent for a large metropolitan building authority threatens to blacklist a building contractor if he does not make a financial payment to the agent. If the contractor does not cooperate, the contractor will be denied future work. Faced with a threat of economic loss, the contractor makes the payment.

Required:

What type of fraud is this, and what controls can be implemented to prevent or detect the fraud?

3. Mailroom Fraud and Internal Control

Sarat Sethi, a professional criminal, took a job as a mailroom clerk for a large department store called "Benson & Abernathy and Company." The mailroom was an extremely hectic work environment consisting of 45 clerks and one supervisor. The clerks were responsible for handling promotional mailings, catalogs, interoffice mail, as well as receiving and distributing a wide range of outside correspondence to various internal departments. One of Sethi's jobs was to open cash receipts envelopes from customers making payments on their credit-card balances. He separated the remittance advices (the bills) and the checks into two piles. He then sent remittance advices to the Accounts Receivable department, where the customer accounts were updated to reflect the payment. He sent the checks to the Cash Receipts department, where they were recorded in the cash journal and then deposited into the bank. Batch totals of cash received and accounts receivable updated were reconciled each night to ensure that everything was accounted for. Nevertheless, over a one-month period Sethi managed to steal $100,000 in customer payments and then left the state without warning.

The fraud occurred as follows: Because the name of the company was rather long, some people had adopted the habit of making out checks simply to "Benson." Sethi had a false ID prepared in the name of John Benson. Whenever he came across a check made out to "Benson," he would steal it along with the remittance advice. Sometimes people would even leave the payee section on the check blank. These checks he also stole. He would then modify the checks to make them payable to "J. Benson" and cash them. Since the accounts receivable department received no remittance advice, the end-of-day reconciliation with cash received disclosed no discrepancies.

Required:

a. This seems like a foolproof scheme. Why did Sethi limit himself to only one month's activity before leaving town?
b. What controls could Benson & Abernathy implement to prevent this from happening again?

4. CMA 1288 3-23 Segregation of Duties

Explain why each of the following combinations of tasks should, or should not, be separated to achieve adequate internal control.

a. Approval of bad debt write-offs and the reconciliation of the accounts receivable subsidiary ledger and the general ledger control account
b. Distribution of payroll checks to employees and approval of employee time cards
c. Posting of amounts from both the cash receipts and the cash disbursements journals to the general ledger
d. Writing checks to vendors and posting to the cash account
e. Recording cash receipts in the journal and preparing the bank reconciliation

5. Expense Account Fraud

While auditing the financial statements of Petty Corporation, the certified public accounting firm of Trueblue and Smith discovered that its client's legal expense account was abnormally high. Further investigation of the records indicated the following:

- Since the beginning of the year, several disbursements totaling $15,000 had been made to the law firm of Swindle, Fox, and Kreip.
- Swindle, Fox, and Kreip were not Petty Corporation's attorneys.
- A review of the canceled checks showed that they had been written and approved by Mary Boghas, the cash disbursements clerk.
- Boghas's other duties included performing the end-of-month bank reconciliation.
- Subsequent investigation revealed that Swindle, Fox, and Kreip are representing Mary Boghas in an unrelated embezzlement case in which she is the defendant. The checks had been written in payment of her personal legal fees.

Required:

a. What control procedures could Petty Corporation have employed to prevent this unauthorized use of cash? Classify each control procedure in accordance with the SAS 78 framework (authorization, segregation of functions, supervision, and so on).
b. Comment on the ethical issues in this case.

6. Tollbooth Fraud

Collectors at Tollbooths A and B (see figure) have colluded to perpetrate a fraud. Each day, Tollbooth Collector B provides A with a number of toll tickets pre-stamped from Tollbooth B. The price of the toll from Point B to Point A is 35 cents. The fraud works as follows:

Drivers entering the turnpike at distant points south of B will pay tolls up to $5. When these drivers leave the turnpike at Point A, they pay the full amount of the toll printed on their tickets.

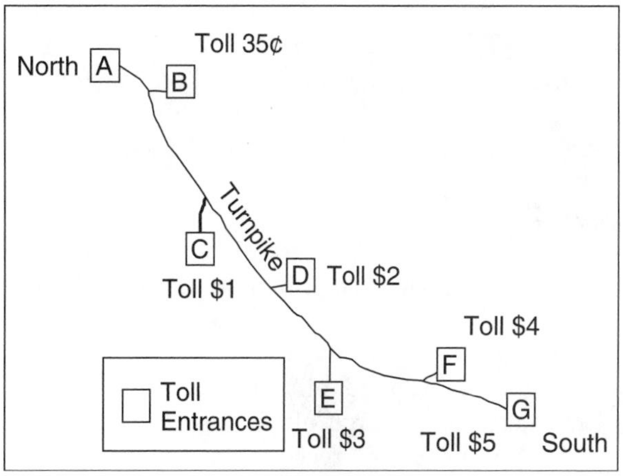

However, the tollbooth collector replaces the tickets collected from the drivers with the 35-cent tickets provided by B, thus making it appear that the drivers entered the turnpike at Point B. The difference between the 35-cent tickets submitted as a record of the cash receipts and the actual amounts paid by the drivers is pocketed by Tollbooth Collector A and shared with B at the end of the day. Using this technique, Collectors A and B have stolen over $20,000 in unrecorded tolls this year.

Required:

What control procedures could be implemented to prevent or detect this fraud? Classify the control procedures in accordance with SAS 78.

7. Financial Aid Fraud

Harold Jones, the financial aid officer at a small university, manages all aspects of the financial aid program for needy students. Jones receives requests for aid from students, determines whether the students meet the aid criteria, authorizes aid payments, notifies the applicants that their request has been either approved or denied, writes the financial aid checks on the account he controls, and requires that the students come to his office to receive the checks in person. For years, Jones has used his position of authority to perpetrate the following fraud:

Jones encourages students who clearly will not qualify to apply for financial aid. Although the students do not expect aid, they apply on the off chance that it will be awarded. Jones modifies the financial information in the students' applications so that it falls within the established guidelines for aid. He then approves aid and writes aid checks payable to the students. The students, however, are informed that aid was denied. Since the students expect no aid, the checks in Jones's office are never collected. Jones forges the students' signatures and cashes the checks.

Required:

Identify the internal control procedures (classified per SAS 78) that could prevent or detect this fraud.

8. Evaluation of Controls

Gaurav Mirchandaniis is the Warehouse Manager for a large office supply wholesaler. Mr. Mirchandaniis receives two copies of the customer sales order from the Sales Department. He picks the goods from the shelves and sends them and one copy of the sales order to the shipping department. He then files the second copy in a temporary file. At the end of the day, Mr. Mirchandaniis retrieves the sales orders from the temporary file and updates the Inventory subsidiary ledger from a terminal in his office. At that time he identifies items that have fallen to low levels, selects a supplier, and prepares three copies of a purchase order. One copy is sent to the supplier, one goes to the Account Payable clerk, and one is filed in the warehouse. When the goods arrive from the supplier, Mr. Mirchandaniis reviews the attached packing slip, counts and inspects the goods, places them on the shelves, and updates the inventory ledger to reflect the receipt. He then prepares a receiving report and sends it to the Accounts Payable department.

Required:

a. Prepare a systems flowchart of the procedures just described.
b. Identify any control problems in the system.
c. What sort of frauds are possible in this system?

9. Evaluation of Controls

Matt Demko is the loading dock supervisor for a dry cement packaging company. His work crew is composed of unskilled workers who load large transport trucks with bags of cement, gravel, and sand. The work is hard and the employee turnover rate is high. Employees record their attendance on separate timecards. Demko authorizes payroll payments each week by signing the timecards and submitting them to the payroll department. The paychecks are then prepared by payroll and distributed to Demko, who distributes them to his work crew.

Required:

a. Prepare a systems flowchart of the procedures described above.
b. Identify any control problems in the system.
c. What sort of frauds are possible in this system?

INTERNAL CONTROL CASES

1. Bern Fly Rod Company

Bern Fly Rod Company is a small manufacturer of high-quality graphite fly-fishing rods. It sells its products to fly-fishing shops throughout the United States and Canada. Bern began as a small company with four salespeople, all family members of the owner. Due to the high popularity and recent growth in fly-fishing, Bern now employs a sales force of 16, and for the first time employs nonfamily members. The salespeople travel around the country giving fly-casting demos of their new models. Once the sales orders are generated, inventory availability is determined and, if necessary, the salesperson sends the order directly to the manufacturing department for immediate production. Sales staff compensation is tied directly to their sales figures. Bern's financial statements for the December year-end reflect unprecedented sales, 35 percent higher than last year. Further, sales for December account for 40 percent of all sales. Last year, December sales accounted for only 20 percent of all sales.

Required:

Analyze the above situation and assess any potential internal control issues and exposures. Discuss some preventive measures this firm may wish to implement.

2. Breezy Company

(This case was prepared by Elizabeth Morris, Lehigh University)

Breezy Company of Bethlehem, Pennsylvania, is a small wholesale distributor of heating and cooling fans. The company deals with retailing firms that buy small-to-medium quantities of fans. The president, Chuck Breezy, was very pleased with the marked increase in sales over the past couple of years. Recently, however, the accountant informed Chuck that although net income has increased, the percentage of uncollectibles has tripled. Due to the small size of the business, Chuck fears he may not be able to sustain these increased losses in the future. He asked his accountant to analyze the situation.

Background

In 1998, the sales manager, John Breezy, moved to Alaska, and Chuck hired a young college graduate to take over the position. The company had always been a family business and, therefore, measurements of individual performance had never been a large consideration. The sales levels had been relatively constant because John had been content to sell to certain customers with whom he had been dealing for years. Chuck was leery about hiring outside of the family for this position. To try to keep sales levels up, he established a reward incentive based on net sales. The new sales manager, Bob Sellmore, was eager to set his career in motion and decided he would attempt to increase the sales levels. To do this, he recruited new customers while keeping the old clientele. After one year, Bob had proved himself to Chuck, who decided to introduce an advertising program to further increase sales. This brought in orders from a number of new customers, many of whom Breezy had never done business with before. The influx of orders excited Chuck so much that he instructed Jane Breezy, the finance manager, to raise the initial credit level for new customers. This induced some customers to purchase more.

Existing System

The accountant wrote up a comparative income statement to show changes in revenues and expenses over the last three years, shown in Exhibit A. Currently, Bob is receiving a commission of 2 percent of net sales. Breezy Company uses credit terms of net 30 days. At the end of previous years, bad debt expense amounted to approximately 2 percent of net sales.

As the finance manager, Jane performs credit checks. In previous years, Jane had been familiar with most clients and approved credit on the basis of past behavior. When dealing with new customers, Jane usually approved a low credit amount and increased it after the customer exhibited reliability. With the large increase in sales, Chuck felt that the current policy was restricting a further rise in sales levels. He decided to increase credit limits to eliminate this restriction. This policy, combined with the new advertising program, should attract many new customers.

EXHIBIT A
BREEZY COMPANY
COMPARATIVE INCOME STATEMENT
FOR YEARS 1999, 2000, 2001

	1999	2000	2001
Revenues			
Net Sales	350,000	500,000	600,000
Other Revenue	60,000	60,000	62,000
Total Revenue	410,000	560,000	662,000
Expenses			
Cost of Goods Sold	140,00	200,000	240,000
Bad Debt Expense	7,000	20,000	36,000
Salaries Expense	200,000	210,000	225,000
Selling Expense	5,000	15,000	20,000
Advertising Expense	0	0	10,000
Other Expenses	20,000	30,000	35,000
Total Expenses	372,000	475,000	566,000
Net Income	30,000	85,000	96,000

Future

The new level of sales impresses Chuck and he wishes to expand, but he also wants to keep uncollectibles to a minimum. He believes the amount of uncollectibles should remain relatively constant as a percentage of sales. Chuck is thinking of expanding his production line, but wants to see uncollectibles drop and sales stabilize before he proceeds with this plan.

Required:

Analyze the weaknesses in internal control and suggest improvements.

3. Whodunit?

(This case was prepared by Karen Collins, Lehigh University)

The following facts relate to an actual embezzlement case.

Someone stole more than $40,000 from a small company in less than two months. Your job is to study the following facts, try to figure out who was responsible for the theft and how it was perpetrated, and (most important) suggest ways to prevent something like this from happening again.

Facts

Location of company: a small town on the eastern shore of Maryland. Type of company: crabmeat processor, selling crabmeat to restaurants located in Maryland. Characters in the story (names are made up):

- John Smith, president and stockholder (husband of Susan).
- Susan Smith, vice president and stockholder (wife of John).
- Tommy Smith, shipping manager (son of John and Susan).
- Debbie Jones, office worker. She began working part-time for the company six months before the theft. (At that time, she was a high school senior and was allowed to work afternoons through a school internship program.) Upon graduation from high school (several weeks before the theft was discovered), she began working full time. Although she is not a member of the family, the Smiths have been close friends with Debbie's parents for more than 10 years.

Accounting Records

All accounting records are maintained on a microcomputer. The software being used consists of the following modules:

a. A general ledger system, which keeps track of all balances in the general ledger accounts and produces a trial balance at the end of each month.
b. A purchases program, which keeps track of purchases and maintains detailed records of accounts payable.
c. An accounts receivable program, which keeps track of sales and collections on account and maintains individual detailed balances of accounts receivable.
d. A payroll program.

The modules are not integrated (that is, data are not transferred automatically between modules). At the end of the accounting period, summary information generated by the purchases, accounts receivable, and payroll programs must be entered into the general ledger program to update the accounts affected by these programs.

Performance of Key Functions by Individual(s)

John, president
Susan, vice president
Tommy, son and shipping manager
Debbie, office worker

	Individual(s) Performing Task	
	Most of the Time	**Sometimes**
1. Receiving order from customers	John	All others
2. Overseeing production of crabmeat	John or Tommy	—
3. Handling shipping	Tommy	John
4. Billing customers (entering sales into accounts receivable program)	Debbie	Susan
5. Opening mail	John	All others
6. Preparing bank deposit tickets and making bank deposits	Susan or Debbie	All others
7. Recording receipt of cash and checks (entering collections of accounts receivable into accounts receivable program)	Debbie	Susan
8. Preparing checks (payroll checks and payments of accounts payable)	Susan or Debbie	—
9. Signing checks	John	—
10. Preparing bank reconciliations	John	—
11. Preparing daily sales reports showing sales by type of product	Susan	—
12. Summarizing daily sales reports to obtain monthly sales report by type of product	Susan or Debbie	—
13. Running summaries of AR program, AP program, and payroll program at month end and inputting summaries into GL program	Susan or Debbie	—
14. Analyzing trial balance at month end and analyzing open balances in accounts receivable and accounts payable	Susan	—

Sales

The crabmeat processing industry in this particular town was unusual in that selling prices for crabmeat were set at the beginning of the year and remained unchanged for the entire year. The company's customers, all restaurants located within 100 miles of the plant, ordered the same quantity of crabmeat each week. Because prices for the crabmeat remained the same all year and the quantity ordered was always the same, the weekly invoice to each customer was always for the same dollar amount.

Manual sales invoices were produced when orders were taken, although these manual invoices were not prenumbered. One copy of the manual invoice was attached to the order shipped to the customer. The other copy was used to enter the sales information into the computer.

When the customer received the order, the customer would send a check to the company for the amount of the invoice. Monthly bills were not sent to customers unless the customer was behind in payments (that is, did not make a payment for the invoiced amount each week).

Note: The industry was unique in another way: many of the companies paid their workers with cash each week (rather than by check). It was, therefore, not unusual for companies to request large sums of cash from the local banks.

When Trouble Was Spotted

Shortly after the May 30 trial balance was run, Susan began analyzing the balances in the various accounts. The balance in the cash account agreed with the cash balance she obtained from a reconciliation of the company's bank account.

However, the balance in the accounts receivable control account in the general ledger did not agree with the total of the accounts receivable subsidiary ledger (which shows a detail of the balances owed by each customer). The difference was not very large, but the balances should be in 100 percent agreement.

At this point, Susan asked me if I would help her locate the problem. In reviewing the computerized accounts receivable subsidiary ledger, I noticed the following:

a. The summary totals from this report were not the totals that were entered into the general ledger program at month end. Different amounts had been entered. No one could explain why this had happened.
b. Some sheets in the computer listing had been ripped apart at the bottom. (In other words, the listing of the individual accounts receivable balances was not a continuous list but had been split at several points.)
c. When an adding machine tape of the individual account balances was run, the individual balances did not add up to the total at the bottom of the report.

Susan concluded that the accounts receivable program was not running properly. My recommendation was that an effort be made to find out why the accounts receivable control account and the summary totals per the accounts receivable subsidiary ledger were not in agreement and why we were finding problems with the accounts receivable listing. Since the accounts receivable subsidiary and accounts receivable control account in the general ledger had been in agreement at the end of April, the effort should begin with the April ending balances for each customer by manually updating all of the accounts. The manually adjusted May 30 balances should then be compared with the computer-generated balances and any differences investigated.

After doing this, Susan and John found several differences. The largest difference was the following:

CUSTOMER ACCOUNT PER
MANUAL RECONSTRUCTION

		Dr.	Cr.
Sale #1	5,000	Pmt. #1	5,000
Sale #2	5,000	Pmt. #2	5,000
Sale #3	5,000	Pmt. #3	5,000
Sale #4	5,000	—	—
Ending Balance	5,000		

CUSTOMER ACCOUNT PER
MANUAL RECONSTRUCTION

	Dr.	Cr.	
Sale #1	5,000	Pmt. #1	5,000
Sale #3	5,000	Pmt. #2	5,000
Sale #3	5,000	Pmt. #3	5,000
Ending Balance	0		

Although they found the manual sales invoice for Sale #2, Susan and John concluded (based on the computer records) that Sale #2 did not take place. I was not sure, so I recommended that they call this customer and ask him the following:

a. Did he receive this order?
b. Did he receive an invoice for it?
c. Did he pay for the order?
d. If so, did he have a copy of his canceled check?

Although John felt that this would be a waste of time, he called the customer. He received an affirmative answer to all of his questions. In addition, he found that the customer's check was stamped on the back not with the normally used "for deposit only" stamp of the company but with an address stamp giving only the company's name and city. When questioned, Debbie said that she sometimes used this stamp.

Right after this question, Debbie, who was sitting nearby at the computer, called Susan to the computer and showed her the customer's account. She said that the payment for $5,000 was in fact recorded in the customer's account. I came over to the computer and looked at the account. The payments were listed like this:

Amount	Date of Payment
$5,000	May 3
$5,000	May 17
$5,000	May 23
$5,000	May 10

I questioned the order of the payments—why was a check supposedly received on May 10 entered in the computer after checks received on May 17 and 23? About 30 seconds later, the computer malfunctioned and the accounts receivable file was lost. Every effort to retrieve the file gave the message "file not found."

About five minutes later, Debbie presented Susan with a copy of a bank deposit ticket dated May 10 with several checks listed on it, including the check that the customer said had been sent to the company. The deposit ticket, however, was not stamped by the bank (which would have verified that the deposit had been received by the bank) and did not add up to the total at the bottom of the ticket (it was off by 20 cents).

At this point, being very suspicious, I gathered all documents I could and left the company to work on the problem at home, away from any potential suspects. I received a call from Susan about four hours later saying that she felt much better. She and Debbie had gone to Radio Shack (the maker of their computer program) and Radio Shack had confirmed Susan's conclusion that the computer program was malfunctioning. She and Debbie were planning to work all weekend reentering transactions into the computer. She said that everything looked fine and not to waste my time working on the problem.

I felt differently. How do you feel?

Required:

a. If you were asked to help this company, could you conclude from the evidence presented that an embezzlement took place? What would you do next?
b. Who do you think was the embezzler?
c. How was the embezzlement accomplished?
d. What improvements would you recommend in internal control to prevent this from happening again? In answering this question, try to identify at least one suggestion from each of the six classes of internal control activities discussed in this chapter (under the section "Control Activities"): transaction authorization, segregation of duties, supervision, accounting records, access control, and independent verification.
e. Would the fact that the records were maintained on a microcomputer aid in this embezzlement scheme?

ACL Cases

1. False Vendor Fraud

You are the auditor of a large company. You suspect that employees may have established themselves as false vendors. A copy of the Vendor and Empmast (employee master) files are located in the ACL Workbook document on the CD that accompanies this textbook. Perform the necessary audit tests to produce a list of employees that may be guilty of this fraud scheme.

The following Assignments are located in the **ACL Tutorial** folder on the CD accompanying this text:

2. Fraud Tutorial 1

Required:

Complete this tutorial. The assignment involves performing five tests for detecting payroll fraud.

3. Fraud Tutorial 2

Required:

Complete this tutorial. The assignment involves performing six tests for detecting purchasing fraud including employee theft and fictitious vendors.

4. Fraud Tutorial 3

Required:

Complete this tutorial. The assignment pertains to the identification of unusual trends in marketing salaries.

5. Bradmark Comprehensive Case

Required:

Access the Bradmark folder on the CD accompanying this text. The Bradmark case is a Word file located in a subfolder named CASE. The data used to solve the case are located in the DATA subfolder. Your instructor will advise you as to which questions to answer.

GLOSSARY

The chapter in which the term is first defined is set in parentheses following the definition.

A

Access controls: Controls that ensure that only authorized personnel have access to the firm's assets. (1)

Access method: The technique used to locate records and to navigate through the database. (3)

Access tests: Tests that ensure that the application prevents authorized users from unauthorized access to data. (7)

Accounting records: The documents, journals, and ledgers used in transaction cycles. (1)

Accuracy: the need for information to be free from errors. (12)

Accuracy tests: Tests that ensure that the system processes only data values that conform to specified tolerances. (7)

American National Standards Institute (ANSI): The most popular EDI standard in the United States. (5)

Amplitude: Strength of transmission signal. (5)

Association of Certified Fraud Examiners (ACFE): A company that conducts studies to estimate losses from fraud and abuse. (11)

Assurance services: Professional services that are designed to improve the quality of information, both financial and nonfinancial, used by decision makers. (1)

Asynchronous: Transmission method in which there is no continuous synchronization between the sending and receiving devices. (5)

Attendance file: File created by the time-keeping department upon receipt of approved time cards. (10)

Attributes: Equivalents to adjectives in the English language that serve to describe the objects. (3)

Audit objectives: Audit goals derived from management assertions that lead to the development of audit procedures. (1)

Audit opinion: Opinion of auditor regarding the presentation of financial statements. (1)

Audit planning: Stage at which the auditor identifies the financially significant applications and attempts to understand the controls over the primary transactions that are processed by these applications. (1)

Audit procedure: Tasks performed by auditors to gather evidence that supports or refutes management assertions. (1)

Audit risk: Probability that the auditor will render unqualified opinions on financial statements that are, in fact, materially misstated. (1)

Audit trail: Accounting records that trace transactions from their source documents to the financial statements. (2)

Auditing: Form of independent attestation performed by an expert who expresses an opinion about the fairness of a company's financial statements. (1)

Authenticity tests: Tests verifying that an individual, a programmed procedure, or a message attempting to access a system is authentic. (7)

B

Backbone systems: Basic system structure on which to build. (4)

Balance forward method: A method in which total sales to customers for the period are itemized and billed at the period end. (12)

Base case system evaluation (BCSE): Variant of the test data technique, in which comprehensive test data are used. (7)

Batch control totals: Record that accompanies the sales order file through all of the data processing runs. (9)

Batch controls: Effective method of managing high volumes of transaction data through a system. (7)

Big bang approach: An attempt to switch operations from the old legacy systems to the new system in a single event that implements the ERP across the entire company. (6)

Bill of lading: Formal contract between the seller and the shipping company that transports the goods to the customer. (9)

Biometric devices: Devices that measure various personal characteristics, such as fingerprints, voice prints, retina prints, or signature characteristics. (3)

Bolt-on software: A company's use of a third party vendor to perform a specialized function. (6)

Bribery: The influence of an official in the performance of his or her lawful duties. (12)

Bus topology: Nodes in the topology that are connected to a common cable. (5)

C

Call-back device: Hardware component that asks the caller to enter a password and then breaks the connection to perform a security check. (5)

Carrier sensing: Random access technique that detects collisions when they occur. (5)

Charges to expense accounts: The act of charging an asset to an expense account and reducing equity by the same amount. (12)

Check digit: Method for detecting data coding errors. A control digit is added to the code when it is originally designed to allow the integrity of the code to be established during subsequent processing. (7)

Client-server model: A form of network topology in which a user's computer or terminal (the client) accesses the ERP programs and data via a host computer (the server). (6)

Client-server topology: Topology involving the distribution of data processing between the user's application—the client—and the server. (5)

Closed database architecture: Database management system used to provide minimal technological advantage over flat-file systems. (6)

Compilers: Language translation modules of the operation system. (2)

Completeness tests: Tests identifying missing data within a single record and entire records missing from a batch. (7)

Completeness: the idea that no piece of information essential to a decision or task should be missing. (12)

Computer fraud: The use of a computer to commit fraud. (12)

Conceptual design: The production of several alternative designs for the new system. (4)

Conflict of interest: When an employee acts on behalf of a third party during the discharge of his or her duties or has self-interest in the activity being performed. (12)

Consolidation: The aggregation or roll-up of data. (6)

Control activities: Policies and procedures used to ensure that appropriate actions are taken to deal with the organization's risks. (1)

Control environment: The foundation of internal control. (1)

Control risk: Likelihood that the control structure is flawed because controls are either absent or inadequate to prevent or detect errors in the account. (1)

Core applications: Operations that support the day-to-day activities of the business. (6)

Corrective controls: Actions taken to reverse the effects of errors detected in the previous step. (1)

Corruption: The act of an official or fiduciary person who unlawfully and wrongfully uses his station or character to procure some benefit for himself or for another person, contrary to duty and the rights of others. (12)

Customer open order file: File containing a copy of the sales order. (9)

Customer order: Document that indicates the type and quantity of merchandise being requested. (9)

Cycle billing: Method of spreading the billing process out over the month. (9)

D

Data definition language (DDL): Programming language used to define the database to the database management system. (3)

Data dictionary: Description of every data element in the database. (3)

Data encryption: Technique that uses an algorithm to scramble selected data, making it unreadable to an intruder browsing the database. (3)

Data encryption standard (DES): Approach that uses a single key known to both the sender and the receiver of the message. (5)

Data manipulation language (DML): Language used to insert special database commands into application programs written in conventional languages. (3)

Data mart: Data warehouse organized for a single department or function. (6)

Data normalization: Process that promotes effective database design. (7)

Data structures: Techniques for physically arranging records in the database. (3)

Data warehouse: A relational or multidimensional database that supports online analytical processing (OLAP). (6)

Database administrator: The individual responsible for managing the database resource. (2)

Database authorization table: Table containing rules that limit the actions a user can take. (3)

Database lockout: Software control that prevents multiple simultaneous access to data. (3)

Database management fraud: The act(s) of altering, deleting, corrupting, destroying, or stealing an organization's data. (12)

Database management system (DBMS): Software system that controls access to the data resource. (3)

Deletion anomaly: The unintentional deletion of data from a table. (7)

Detailed design: Design of screen outputs, reports, and operational documents; entity relationship diagrams; normal form designs for database tables; updated data dictionary; designs for all screen inputs and source documents; context diagrams for overall system; low-level data flow diagrams; and structure diagrams for program modules. (4)

Detection risk: Risk that auditors are willing to take that errors not detected or prevented by the control structure will also not be detected by the auditor. (1)

Detective controls: Devices, techniques, and procedures designed to identify and expose undesirable events that elude preventive controls. (1)

Disaster recovery plan (DRP): Comprehensive statement of all actions to be taken before, during, and after a disaster, along with documented, tested procedures that will ensure the continuity of operations. (2)

Disk locks: Devices that prevent unauthorized individuals from accessing the floppy disk drive of a computer. (2)

Documentation: Written description of how the system works. (4)

Drill-down: The disaggregation of data to reveal underlying details that explain certain phenomena. (6)

E

Eavesdropping: listening to output transmissions over telecommunication lines. (12)

Echo check: Technique that involves the receiver of the message returning the message to the sender. (5)

Economic extortion: The use (or threat) of force (including economic sanctions) by an individual or an organization to obtain something of value. (12)

Electronic data interchange (EDI): The intercompany exchange of computer-processible business information in standard format. (5)

Embedded audit module (EAM): Technique in which one or more specially programmed modules embedded in a host application select and record predetermined types of transactions for subsequent analysis. (7)

Employee file: A file used with the attendance file to create an online payroll register. (10)

Employee fraud: Fraud by nonmanagement employees. (11)

Employee fraud: Performance fraud by nonmanagement employees generally designed to directly convert cash or other assets to the employee's personal benefit. (11)

Empty shell: Arrangement that involves two or more user organizations that buy or lease a building and remodel it into a computer site, but without the computer and peripheral equipment. (2)

Encryption: Technique that uses a computer program to transform a standard message being transmitted into a coded (ciphertext) form. (5)

End users: Users for whom the system is built. (4)

Enterprise resource planning (ERP): A generalized system that incorporates the best business practices in use. (6)

Entity: A resource, event, or agent. (3)

Error file: Transaction file that lists any detected errors. (7)

Ethics: The principles of conduct that individuals use in making choices and guiding their behavior in situations that involve the concepts of right and wrong. (11)

Exposure: Absence or weakness of a control. (1)

F

False misrepresentation: The condition to a fraudulent act that a false statement or a nondisclosure. (11)

Firewall: Software and hardware that provide a focal point for security by channeling all network connections through a control gateway. (5)

Fraud: a false representation of a material fact made by one party to another party with the intent to deceive and induce the other party to justifiably rely on the fact that to his or her detriment. (11)

Fraud triangle: The combination of situational pressures, opportunities, and personal characteristics that can lead to the act of fraud. (11)

Fraudulent financial reporting: Fraud commonly committed by persons at the management level. (12)

Frequency: Number of cycles or oscillations occurring per second. (5)

Front end processors (FEP): A special purpose computer that manages the flow of data between the host computer and the communication's network. (5)

Full duplex: Transmission method that allows signals to be sent and received simultaneously. (5)

G

Generalized audit software (GAS): Software that allows auditors to access electronically coded data files and perform various operations on their contents. (7)

Grandparent-parent-child (GPC): Backup technique used in sequential batch systems. (3)

H

Hacking: The act of breaking into a computer system. (12)

Hash total: Control technique that uses nonfinancial data to keep track of the records in a batch. (7)

Hashing structure: Structure employing an algorithm that converts the primary key of a record directly into a storage address. (8)

Hierarchical data model: A database model that represents data in a hierarchical structure and permits only a single parent record for each child. (3)

Hierarchical topology: Topology where a host computer is connected to several levels of subordinate smaller computers in a master-slave relationship. (5)

I

Illegal gratuity: The act of "rewarding" an official for taking a particular course of action. (12)

Indexed random file: Randomly organized file that is accessed via an index. (8)

Indexed sequential access method (ISAM): Sequential structure used for large table files that can be accessed by an index. (8)

Indexed sequential file: Sequential file structure that is accessed via an index. (8)

Indexed structure: A class of file structure that use indexes for its primary access method. (8)

Inference controls: Controls that prevent users from inferring specific data values through normal query features. (3)

Inherent risk: Risk that is associated with the unique characteristics of the business or industry of the client. (1)

Injury or loss: The condition to a fraudulent act that the deception must have caused injury or loss to the victim of the fraud. (11)

Insertion anomaly: The unintentional insertion of data into a table. (8)

Integrated test facility (ITF): Automated technique that enables the auditor to test an application's logic and controls during its normal operation. (7)

Intent: The condition to a fraudulent act that the intent to deceive or the knowledge that one's statement is false. (11)

Internal control system: Policies a firm employs to safeguard the firm's assets, ensure accurate and reliable accounting records and information, promote efficiency, and measure compliance with established policies. (1)

Internal view: The physical arrangement of records in the database. (3)

Interpreters: Language translation modules of the operating system that convert one line of logic at a time. (2)

Invented list: A cross reference created from multiple indexes. (8)

J

Justice: The idea that the benefits of the decision should be distributed fairly to those who share the risks. (11)

Justifiable reliance: The condition to a fraudulent act that the misrepresentation must have been a substantial factor on which the injured party relied. (11)

L

Lapping: Use of customer checks, received in payment of their accounts, to conceal cash previously stolen by an employee. (12)

Local area networks: Network generally confined to a close geographical area. (5)

Logic bomb: Destructive program, such as a virus, that is triggered by some predetermined event. (2)

Logical key pointer: A pointer containing the primary key of the related record. (8)

M

Management assertions: Explicit or implicit statements made by management within the financial statements pertaining to the financial health of the organization. (1)

Management fraud: Performance fraud that often uses deceptive practices to inflate earnings or to forestall the recognition of either insolvency or a decline in earnings. (10, 11)

Masquerading: A perpetrator gaining access to the system from a remote site by pretending to be an authorized user. (12)

Material fact: The condition to a fraudulent act that is a substantial factor in inducing someone to act. (11)

Misappropriation of assets: Fraud commonly committed by employees. (12)

Modem: Hardware device that performs the modular-demodulator task. (5)

Modulation: Process of converting from digital to wave form. (5)

Monitoring: The process by which the quality of internal control design and operation can be assessed. (1)

Multiplexer: Device that permits the simultaneous transmission of multiple signals while maintaining a separation between each of them. (5)

Mutual aid pact: Agreement between two or more organizations (with comparable computer facilities) to aid each other with their data processing needs in the event of a disaster. (2)

N

Navigational model: Model that possesses explicit links or paths among data elements. (3)

Network model: Variation of the hierarchical model. (3)

Network protocols: Rules and standards governing the degree of hardware and software that permit users of networks manufactured by different vendors to communicate and share data. (5)

Network topology: Physical arrangement of the components. (5)

New systems development: Process that involves five steps: identifying the problem, understanding what needs to be done, considering alternative solutions, selecting the best solution, and implementing the solution. (4)

O

Object-oriented design: Building information systems from reusable standard components or modules. (4)

Objects: Equivalent to nouns in the English language. (4)

Online analytical processing (OLAP): A branch of ERP that includes decision support, modeling, information retrieval, ad hoc reporting/analysis, and what-if analysis. (6)

Online transaction processing (OLTP): Processes consisting of large numbers of relatively simple transactions. (6)

Open invoice method: A method in which each invoice is recorded as a separate item in the invoice file. (12)

Operations fraud: The misuse or theft of a firm's computer resources. (12)

Opportunities: A force within an individual's personality and external environment that can lead to the act of fraud. (11)

Ownership: The personal information a person owns. (11)

P

Packing slip: Document that travels with the goods to the customer to describe the contents of the order. (9)

Para computer ethics: Taking a real interest in computer ethics cases and acquiring some level of skill and knowledge in the field. (11)

Parallel simulation: Technique that requires the auditor to write a program that simulates key features of processes of the application under review. (7)

Parity check: Technique that incorporates an extra bit into the structure of a bit string when it is created or transmitted. (5)

Partitioned database approach: Database approach that splits the central database into segments or partitions that are distributed to their primary users. (3)

Password: Secret code entered by the user to gain access to the data files. (2)

Payroll fraud: The overpayment of employees and payments to nonexistent employees. (12)

Payroll imprest account: An account into which a single check for the entire amount of the payroll is deposited. (10)

Performance fraud: Deceptive practices to inflate earnings or to forestall the recognition of either insolvency or a decline in earnings. (11)

Personal characteristics: A force within a person that can lead to the act of fraud. (11)

Phased-in approach: The ERP systems are installed independently in each business unit over a period of time. (6)

Piggybacking: The action in which a perpetrator taps into the telecommunications line from a remote source and latches onto an authorized user who is logging onto the system. (12)

Pointer structure: A structure in which the address (pointer) of one record is stored in the field on a related record. (8)

Polling: Popular technique for establishing communication sessions in WANs. (5)

Pop computer ethics: The exposure to stories and reports found in the popular media regarding the good or bad ramifications of computer technology. (11)

Preventive controls: Passive techniques designed to reduce the frequency of occurrence of undesirable events. (1)

Privacy: A matter of restricted access to persons or information about persons. (11)

Private branch exchange (PBX): Method used for switching data and voice communications locally with a firm. (5)

Program fraud: A form of data processing fraud that involves creating illegal programs to alter accounting records, destroying a program's logic using a virus, or altering the program logic to cause the application to process the data incorrectly. (12)

Project planning: Allocation of resources to individual applications within the framework of the strategic plan. (4)

Project schedule: Document that formally presents management's commitment to the project. (4)

Proportionality: The idea that the benefit from a decision must outweigh the risks. (11)

Protocols: Rules and standards governing the design of hardware and software that permit network users to communicate and share data. (5)

Public Company Accounting Oversight Board (PCAOB): A company created by the Sarbarnes-Oxley Act to set auditing, quality control, and ethics standards, to inspect registered accounting firms, to conduct investigations, and to take disciplinary actions. (11)

Public key encryption: Technique that uses two keys: one for encoding the message, the other for decoding it. (5)

R

Recovery operations center (ROC): Arrangement involving two or more user organizations that buy or lease a building and remodel it into a completely equipped computer site. (2)

Redundancy tests: Tests that determine that an application processes each record only once. (7)

Reengineering: The identification and elimination of non-value-added tasks by replacing traditional procedures with those that are innovative and different. (9)

Relevance: the need for the contents of a report or document to serve a purpose. (12)

Replicated databases: Database approach in which the central database is replicated at each IPU site. (3)

Request-response technique: Technique in which a control message from the sender and a response from the sender are sent at periodic synchronized intervals. (5)

Reusable password: A network password that can be used more than one time. (2)

Ring topology: Topology that eliminates the central site. All nodes in this configuration are of equal status. (5)

Risk assessment: Risk factors included in the design of an audit report. (12)

Risk assessment: The identification, analysis, and management of risks relevant to financial reporting. (1)

Rounding error tests: Tests that verify the correctness of rounding procedures. (7)

Run-to-run controls: Controls that use batch figures to monitor the batch as it moves from one programmed procedure to another. (7)

S

Salami frauds: Fraud in which each victim is unaware of being defrauded. (7)

Sales order: Source document that captures such vital information as the name and address of the customer making the purchase; the customer's account number; the name, number, and description of product; quantities and unit price of items sold; and other financial information. (9)

SAS No. 99: Consideration of Fraud in a Financial Statement Audit: the current guidelines on fraud detection. (12)

Scalabilty: The system's ability to grow smoothly and economically as user requirements increase. (6)

Scavenging: Searching through the trash cans of the computer center for discarded output. (12)

Schema (conceptual view): Description of the entire database. (3)

Segregation of duties: Separation of employee duties to minimize incompatible functions. (1)

Sequential structure: A data structure in which all records in the file lie in contiguous storage spaces in a specified sequence arranged by their primary key. (8)

Servers: Special-purpose computers that manage common resources, such as programs, data, and printers of the LAN. (5)

Shipping notice: Document that informs the billing department that the customer's order has been filled and shipped. (9)

Simplex: Transmission method allowing transmission in one direction only. (5)

Situational pressures: A force within an individual's personality and external environment that can lead to the act of fraud. (11)

Slicing and dicing: The process that enables the user to examine data from different viewpoints. (6)

Stakeholders: Entities either inside or outside an organization that have direct or indirect interest in the firm. (4)

Steering committee: An organizational committee consisting of senior-level management responsible for systems planning. (4)

Stock release (picking ticket): Document that identifies which items of inventory must be located and picked from the warehouse shelves. (9)

Structured design: Disciplined way of designing systems from the top down. (4)

Subschema (user view): User view of the database. (3)

Substantive tests: Tests that determine whether database contents fairly reflect the organization's transactions. (1)

Summarization: The idea that information should be aggregated in accordance with a user's needs. (12)

Supervision: A control activity involving the critical oversight of employees. (1)

Supplier's (vendor's) invoice: The bill sent from the seller to the buyer showing unit costs, taxes, freight, and other charges. (10)

Supply chain management (SCM): The convergence between ERP and bolt-on software to move goods from raw material stage to the consumer. (6)

Synchronous: Transmission method that uses a separate timing signal to keep the receiving end's device in constant synchronization. (5)

System survey: Determination of what elements, if any, of the current system should be preserved as part of the new system. (4)

Systems analysis: Two-step process that involves a survey of the current system and then an analysis of the user's needs. (4)

Systems development life cycle (SDLC): Formal process consisting of two major phases: new systems development and maintenance. (4)

Systems planning: Linking of individual system projects or applications to the strategic objectives of the firm. (4)

T

Test data method: Technique used to establish application integrity by processing specially prepared sets of input data through production applications that are under review. (7)

Tests of controls: Tests that establish whether internal controls are functioning properly. (1)

Theoretical computer ethics: Applying the theories of philosophy, sociology, and psychology to computer science with the goal of bringing some new understanding to the field. (11)

Timeliness: The idea that information must be no older than the time period of the action it supports. (12)

Token passing: Transmission of a special signal (token) around the network from node to node in a specific sequence. (5)

Tracing: Test data technique that performs an electronic walkthrough of the application's internal logic. (7)

Transaction authorization: Procedure to ensure that employees process only valid transactions within the scope of their authority. (1)

Transaction fraud: Deleting, altering, or adding false transactions to divert assets to the perpetrator. (12)

Transcription errors: Type of error that can corrupt a data code and cause processing errors. (7)

Transfer Control Protocol/Internet Protocol (TCP/IP): The basic protocol that permits communication between Internet nodes. (5)

Transposition errors: Error that occurs when digits are transposed. (7)

Trojan horse: Program that attaches to another legitimate program but does not replicate itself like a virus. (2)

Turnkey systems: Completely finished and tested systems that are ready for implementation. (4)

U

Update anomaly: The unintentional updating of data in a table, resulting from data redundancy. (8)

User views: The set of data that a particular user needs to achieve his or her assigned tasks. (3)

V

Valid vendor file: A file containing vendor mailing information. (10)

Validation controls: Controls intended to detect errors in transaction data before the data are processed. (7)

Value-added banks (VAB): Banks that can accept electronic disbursements and remittance advices from its clients in any format. (5)

Value-added network (VAN): Network that provides service by managing the distribution of the messages between trading partners. (5)

Vendor-supported systems: Custom systems that organizations purchase from commercial vendors. (4)

Virtual table: A table derived from the base tables that is a partial representation of the actual physical base tables. (8)

Virus: Program that attaches itself to a legitimate program to penetrate the operating system. (2)

W

Walkthrough: Analysis of system design to ensure the design is free from conceptual errors that could become programmed into the final system. (4)

Wide area network: Network that exceeds the geographic limitations of a local area network. (5)

Worm: Software program that "burrows" into the computer's memory and replicates itself into areas of idle memory. (2)

INDEX

E

F

G

H

I

J

K

L

M

Q

R

T